THE LIFE OF
SAMUEL JOHNSON

THE LIFE OF

SAMUEL

JOHNSON

by James Boswell

ABRIDGED, WITH AN INTRODUCTION, BY

BERGEN EVANS

PROFESSOR OF ENGLISH, NORTHWESTERN UNIVERSITY

THE MODERN LIBRARY · NEW YORK

Library of Congress Catalog Card Number: 52-5875

The text followed in this abridgment is that edited by George Birkbeck Hill, revised and enlarged by L. F. Powell, in six volumes, published by the Oxford University Press from 1934 to 1950. A few changes in punctuation have been made to meet the exigencies of abridgment.

The Powell-Hill *Johnson* is one of the monuments of scholarship, probably *the* great edition of any English classic. The reader who wishes to read the entire *Life of Johnson* is, of course, referred to this edition. We are grateful to the Oxford University Press for their gracious permission to use the Powell-Hill text in this abridgment.

Random House IS THE PUBLISHER OF *The Modern Library*

BENNETT A. CERF · DONALD S. KLOPFER · ROBERT K. HAAS

Manufactured in the United States of America

By H. Wolff

INTRODUCTION

THREE YEARS after Samuel Johnson trudged up to London there was born in Edinburgh, in 1740, the man who was to bring him greater fame than he could have dared to hope for.

James Boswell came of a well-to-do Scotch family. His father and his grandfather were distinguished lawyers and James himself was destined for the bar from the beginnings of his education. Fathers rarely consulted their sons on such matters in those days and his father, Alexander Boswell of Auchinleck, one of the Scotch Law Lords, a peevish, opinionated and crusty man, would have been the last person in the world to have consulted his son. And in all fairness to him, it must be admitted that James might have been the last person in the world to consult, for his tastes seemed to run directly contrary to any respectable occupation. All he wanted to do was to get drunk, play with the girls and enjoy the company of actors and other low people—writers, philosophers, distinguished murderers, and the like.

In 1760 he visited London and found town life so much to his liking that only the strongest measures were able to get him back home and once there he began to force his company on every available celebrity and to dabble in literature. He kept a journal, he published an "Ode to Tragedy" (which he dedicated to himself) and "The Cub at Newmarket," a poem in the Preface to which he boasted that he had been laughed at by the Duke of York.

Edinburgh soon palled upon so lively a spirit and he decided to become a soldier but abandoned this ambition when his father, in desperation, agreed to allow him to study Civil Law on the continent.

Accordingly, in November, 1762, he set out for the continent by way of London where he was resolved—among other things —to become acquainted with Mr. Samuel Johnson, the great dictator of letters.

This was an astonishing ambition for a young rake of twenty-two, but in a few months—on the sixteenth of May, to be exact, in the back shop of Tom Davies, the bookseller—it was realized. He finally met the Moralist—and was so severely snubbed, in his efforts to be ingratiating, that, as he himself confesses, had not his ardor been uncommonly persevering he would have abandoned forever all hope of knowing Johnson better.

But Boswell was not to be deterred merely by a rough reception. As he left the shop, Tom Davies comforted him with the amazing assurance that Johnson really liked him and so a week later he mustered resolution enough to call upon Johnson in his chambers and had the honor of being pressed to stay. He stayed. He came again and yet again, until, on the twenty-fifth of June, Johnson interrupted a flow of naive self-revelation to cry impulsively, "Give me your hand; I have taken a liking to you."

And so began one of the world's most famous friendships, a friendship that for all its superficial incongruities had a solid basis. Johnson's vigor and Boswell's sedateness bridged the gap of their years. They were both "clubbable" men, religious men and Tories. Both loved conversation and both had the leisure, the breadth of interest and the wit and humanity that talk requires. And underneath all else there was a deep reciprocal affection: Boswell found in Johnson the father he could not find in Lord Auchinleck, and Johnson found in Boswell the son that fate had denied him.

After some months in London, Boswell proceeded to the continent to study law. Johnson accompanied him to Harwich where he dispersed a great deal of sound advice and refuted Bishop Berkeley by kicking a stone. Boswell, gazing back from the deck of the ship, observed Johnson on the pier "rolling his majestick frame in his usual manner."

Boswell studied law for a while at Leyden but managed to find time for considerable extracurricular drinking and wooing. He journeyed to France, where he forced himself upon Voltaire and Rousseau. In Italy he became friendly with the notorious John Wilkes and then crossed over to Corsica which was at that time in revolt against Genoa. He wanted to meet

General Paoli, the Corsican chieftain and, after taking some risks, managed to do so. Paoli (who must have been in his way as great a simpleton as his visitor) at first mistook Boswell for a spy because of his habit of writing everything down in a notebook, but an understanding was eventually reached and the two men became friends. On his return to England Boswell published an *Account of Corsica*. The book was a success and Boswell was so excited by it that Johnson was compelled to order him to "empty his head of Corsica."

Soon after this Boswell married his cousin, Margaret Montgomery, and settled down to the practice of law in Edinburgh. Visits to London were necessarily few and brief, but in 1773 he managed to persuade Johnson to tour the Highlands of Scotland and the Hebrides with him. It was an extraordinary undertaking. The Hebrides are wild and stormy islands, off the west coast of Scotland, difficult, and often dangerous, of access. Their fare was coarse and their accommodations often bad. Johnson's forthrightness and the highlanders' touchy pride frequently created tense situations, and Johnson himself had irritable and explosive moments. But Boswell's "gaiety of conversation and civility of manners," as Johnson later generously acknowledged, brought them safely through and made the expedition, on the whole, a pleasant one.

On their return to the lowlands Boswell was able at last to exhibit Johnson to his father and his wife. Neither was favorably impressed. His son's enthusiasm for this uncouth and overbearing "auld dominie" merely confirmed Lord Auchinleck's opinion that "Jamie's gane clean gyte." Mrs. Boswell referred to Johnson as a "bear" and objected to his habit of holding lighted candles upside down, over the parlor rug, to make them burn brighter.

Johnson published an account of the journey after their return. It seems harmless to the modern reader but it gave offense at the time because he said that he had seen very few trees in Scotland.

Boswell had kept a journal during the tour, a journal chiefly of Johnson's conversations. He did not publish it until after Johnson's death and when he did its indiscretions earned him a challenge to a duel and its excellences earned him three edi tions in one year. It is not quite as good as the *Life of Johnson* but it remains an invaluable supplement to the greater work. He showed parts of his journal to Johnson himself and profited by his suggestions and corrections.

In 1775 Boswell began to keep terms for the English bar. This required him to be in London for long periods at a time, a fact that may have had more to do with the change than the expectation of professional advancement. At any rate, it permitted him to see much more of Johnson and of the town life that he so passionately loved.

In 1782 his father died, leaving him what with prudent management would have been a fair estate. But Boswell, though he was a good landlord, was not a prudent manager and was always in difficulties. In 1784 Johnson died and two years later Boswell moved to London. Three years after that his wife died, leaving him with five children. She had been a good mother and despite her husband's drunkenness and infidelities a devoted wife and after her death he sank into sad excesses.

In 1791 the first edition of the *Life of Johnson* appeared and was recognized at once for the supremely great book that it is. Boswell was preparing a third edition when he died in 1795.

*   *   *

The reader of Boswell's *Life of Johnson,* like those who knew its author in life, finds that he cannot respect Boswell but at the same time cannot help liking him. A fool of sorts he unquestionably was. He has an irrepressible frankness. "I have a strange kind of feeling," he wrote in his diary, "as if I wished nothing to be secret that concerns myself." And, indeed, he does make some shocking revelations. Thus, without any apparent awareness of the ordinary response to such a suggestion, he tells us that he was amazed to find upon his return from the Hebrides that although Johnson had left a secret diary at their house during their absence Mrs. Boswell had not only not had it copied out but had not even looked into it!

Yet his manner of relating such things wins us over; he shares his own preposterousness with us, and not in a self-belittling way, either. He just knew absurdity wher*ever* he saw it.

On the positive side, Boswell was an epicure of experience. He loved to wring the fullest possible sensation from the moment and he was hungry to know all of life. Keats seems the most unlikely of English writers to compare to Boswell, yet few people would have sympathized more than Boswell with Keats's famous desire to identify himself with a bird pecking at the gravel. He wrote to his friend Temple that he could be a rock on the face of a mountain were it possible for him to be conscious of it and to "brave the elements by glorious insensibility."

That "glorious" is wonderfully revealing. Boswell plainly wanted an extra sensation—the literary sensation, one might call it—of objectivizing his experience. It wasn't enough to be; he had to *know* that he *was* being. And it was this that led him into little ceremonies to mark moments, little rapturous asides to remind himself that he, James Boswell, was doing thus and so at this very moment. It was his lust for experience that led him to seek out unusual people and it was his desire to be conscious of experiencing that led him to set it all down in writing. It made the moment more real and dramatic—and it offered riches of recollection for the long, dreary hours at Edinburgh and Auchinleck.

He had an unabashed admiration for great men and an unerring perception of true greatness. And it must always be emphasized that he sought no material advantages from his friendships. In fact, they undoubtedly did his fortunes harm. He could have had a lucrative practice and a sound estate had he cared to stay at home and cultivate those whom the world esteemed as great, instead of running after the learned and the literary, who were of even less social consequence then than now.

In his own day and throughout the nineteenth century he was accused of being a toady, but since it takes two to make a successful sycophant the charge founders in its own implications. For if Boswell was servile, then Johnson, Reynolds, Goldsmith, Hume, Voltaire, Rousseau, Garrick and Burke were men who delighted in servility. Indeed, the only man of con

sequence with whom Boswell did *not* get on was the psycho-
pathic bully, Lord Lonsdale, a man who insisted on servility
from all who attended him.

*   *   *

Writing excitedly about his book just before it came off the
press, Boswell said: "I will venture to say that he [Johnson]
will be seen in this work more completely than any man who
has ever yet lived."

That was no empty boast, and after more than a hundred
and sixty years it still holds good. Thanks to Boswell, Samuel
Johnson is better known to educated English-speaking people
today than anyone except their immediate friends. His plan
was so simple that its revolutionary nature may be easily overlooked: he proposed to make Johnson show himself; he would
not only describe the man and relate the events of his life, but
he would interleave with this his letters and his conversations
and show him to us under a hundred varied circumstances.

And that is what he does. [There are the direct descriptions
of Johnson that we know so well—his gigantic, unwieldy body,
his slovenly clothes, his squinting eyes, scrofulous scars, cramps
and convulsions, his loud voice with its Staffordshire burr, his
habit of whistling to himself, of reciting snatches of poems or
prayers under his breath, of rolling heavily to and fro when
preparing a rebuttal and of blowing away the demolished fragments of his opponent's argument with a violent exhalation.
We are shown his stern piety, his impetuous temper, his benevolence, his sentimentality, his heavy dogmatism, his light wit,
his orgies of merriment, his "grave and aweful" deportment,
his indolence and (though here, we now know, Boswell only
touched the surface) [his terrifying melancholia]

At first glance the *Life* may seem pedestrian, a mere statement of the biographical facts in their chronological order, arranged prosaically under each year, with Johnson's age for that
year baldly stated. But this is deceptive. Once Boswell has advanced his narrative to the point where he came to know Johnson, where, that is, his own powers of observation could be
brought into play, we begin to get a wealth of *characteristic*
detail—Johnson paring his fingernails to the quick and then

scraping his knuckles with the penknife until they bled; John-son hurling his lemonade out of the window because a waiter had put a lump of sugar in it with dirty fingers; Johnson touch-ing every rail of a fence as he went along and going back to touch one that he had missed; Johnson beaming with pleasure at a young hussy in the Highlands who, on a dare, sat on his lap; Johnson "smiling with a soft humorous satisfaction" as he pushed a dead cat over a waterfall.

"A Flemish portrait," Boswell called it, and like a good Dutch picture, it isn't all flattering. We often see Johnson in-tolerant and rude—dismissing Lady Diana Beauclerk angrily from the conversation: "The woman's a whore; let's hear no more on't"—and insulting Sir Joshua Reynolds: "Sir, you're drunk; I will not talk with you."

Boswell had the power of dramatizing trifles, of re-creating for us, that is, those incidents which usually seem trifling in the telling but which serve, in the experiencing, to make every man's existence interesting to himself. Most civilized lives *are* measured out with coffee spoons, but almost everyone seems to find the measuring an engrossing pastime, though few are able to convey the fascination of the uneventful. Jane Austen could and James Boswell could.

A minor instance will suffice. One evening, in a fashionable gathering at Mrs. Garrick's, Johnson said of a certain woman, who though absurd in some things was basically intelligent, that she had "a bottom of good sense."

The word *bottom* [says Boswell] thus introduced, was so ludicrous when contrasted with his gravity, that most of us could not for-bear tittering and laughing; though I recollect that the Bishop of Killaloe kept his countenance with perfect steadiness, while Miss Hannah More slyly hid her face behind a lady's back who sat on the same settee with her. His pride could not bear that any expression of his should excite ridicule, when he did not intend it; he therefore resolved to assume and exercise despotick power, glanced sternly around, and called out in a strong tone, "Where's the merriment?" Then collecting himself, and looking aweful, to make us feel how he could impose restraint, and as it were search-ing his mind for a still more ludicrous word, he slowly pronounced, "I say the *woman* was *fundamentally* sensible;" as if he had said, hear this now, and laugh if you dare. We all sat composed as at a funeral.

Now all that has been said is that some prudish people tittered at a homely word and that Johnson, annoyed at their prudery, had substituted another word for it and rebuked them —and triumphed over them—by substituting a word really much more indecent but one which, because it was a Latin derivative, was acceptable to their ignorant finickiness.

Yet it is a good anecdote, dramatic and interesting because it is well told. There is a good selection of relevant detail—a whole character is illuminated in Miss Hannah More's "slyly" hiding her face; no wonder that her protégé, Macaulay, had it in for Boswell!

The common reader may protest, of course, that nothing much was actually done, that, after all, Boswell merely reported what happened. But it is not as easy as that. Sir John Hawkins and Arthur Murphy, who were competent writers, and Mrs. Thrale, who was a talented writer, and Fanny Burney, who was a writer of genius, have all left anecdotes of Johnson. But they failed, in varying degrees, where Boswell succeeded. Boswell's anecdotes have an authenticity that carries immediate conviction; theirs do not.

No, Boswell was doing a great deal more than just reporting. In the first place, the mere collection of his materials was a tremendous accomplishment. The *Life of Johnson* is one of the chief sources for our knowledge of eighteenth-century England. It is unparalleled in its accuracy. Boswell himself said:

The labour and anxious attention with which I have collected and arranged the materials of which these volumes are composed, will hardly be conceived by those who read them with careless facility. The stretch of mind and prompt assiduity by which so many conversations were preserved, I myself, at some distance of time, contemplate with wonder. . . . Were I to detail the books which I have consulted, and the inquiries which I have found it necessary to make by various channels, I should probably be thought ridiculously ostentatious. Let me only observe, as a specimen of my trouble, that I have sometimes been obliged to run half over London, in order to fix a date correctly; which, when I had accomplished, I well knew would obtain me no praise, though a failure would have been to my discredit.

Half a dozen generations of readers have failed to find much to Boswell's discredit, in the matter of accuracy; he who would impugn anything which Boswell states as a fact must bring a solid mass of evidence with him if he expects to gain credence among scholars.

That Boswell had so much to record (it has been estimated that he and Johnson were actually in each other's company only two hundred and seventy days in the twenty-one years of their acquaintance) is as much due to the agility of his mind as to the compendiousness of Johnson's. Boswell must be the only biographer who deliberately manipulated the life of his subject in order to furnish materials for a better biography. For that is exactly what he did when he persuaded Johnson to visit the Hebrides and—still more astonishing—arranged for him to dine with Jack Wilkes. He took Johnson out of his way to meet Lord Monboddo, though he knew well that the two men disliked each other. In the Highlands, happening to come downstairs before Johnson, he persuaded their hostess to offer Johnson a cold sheep's head for breakfast, knowing quite well that it would be rejected with disgust. "I was entertained," he noted in his journal, "to see their ludicrous cross purposes."

He dinged questions at Johnson all the time. "Sir," he suddenly asked, "if you were shut up in a castle and a new-born child with you, what would you do?" "Pray, Sir, have you ever been accustomed to wear a nightcap?" "What do you do with orange peel when you have eaten the pulp?" "Pray, Sir, do you know anything of the trade of a butcher?" Johnson came shouting in exasperation to Mrs. Thrale once because Boswell had asked him if he knew why an apple is round and a pear pointed.

These absurd excesses of his method make Boswell seem a greater fool than he really was. Johnson *had* to be prodded. Though probably the greatest talker of whom we have any record, he was not a *talkative* man. Tom Tyers, who knew him well, said that he was like a ghost: he never spoke until he was spoken to. He often sat silent for long periods of time, sometimes for the entire evening. He did not like to be drawn out, either; and would often turn with irritable fury on those who were trying to get him started. Fanny Burney has left us a very amusing account of a dreadful evening when Johnson refused to talk at all because he suspected he was on exhibition.

But Boswell could get him to talk. He reaped a wonderful harvest of notes by being able to do it, but he was often mauled in the attempt. "Sir," bellowed Johnson, "you have but two topicks, yourself and me. I am heartily sick of both." And when Boswell asked him, after a long nagging on the subject, if a man might not be permitted to drink if drink made him forget something disagreeable, Johnson growled, "Why yes, Sir, if he sat next to you."

There are scores of such attacks scattered through the *Life*, many more than the ordinary reader would suspect; for whenever "a gentleman present" or "one of the company" gets a stinging rebuke, there is a strong probability that it was Boswell himself—Boswell, who appreciated and obviously admired the justice or wit of the attack but who, even in retrospect, could not face the humiliation of acknowledging himself as its victim. He was not indifferent to these blows; they hurt him terribly, and again and again he resolved that he wouldn't go on with it. But he couldn't stay away. His sincere love for Johnson and his sincere delight in wit and good conversation always drew him back. Fortunately for us.

There are limitations to Boswell's portrait. We do not see much of the wintry spring of Johnson's youthful discontent. We see him, as Boswell saw him, in the long autumn afternoon of his life, when fame and the pension and the care of the Thrales had softened a little the fierce edge of his early bitterness. We probably see Johnson a little too much irritated by Boswell—a fact which may have done much to create the popular impression of him as a blustering bully. Boswell knew that he showed too much of "Grave Sam, Great Sam, Solemn Sam and Learned Sam." He knew that Mrs. Thrale and Fanny Burney had notes that would show more of "Gay Sam, Agreeable Sam [and] Pleasant Sam," but these ladies were competitors and kept their collections for their own books.

Boswell's gravest fault is an excess of reverence. To him Johnson was always the "literary colossus," the "Rambler," the "aweful and majestick Philosopher." In fact, after they had been at ease together one evening, he was disturbed and wrote in his journal: "I feel a sort of regret that I was so easy. I missed that awful reverence with which I used to contemplate Mr. Samuel Johnson, in the complex magnitude of his literary, moral and religious character." "I have a wonderful superstitious love of mystery," he added candidly.

But neither his awe nor his love of mystery stopped him from being honest. Many of Johnson's friends begged him to soften the harsh outlines of his portrait and to omit certain incidents and details. But Johnson had told him that if a man professed to write a life, and not just a panegyric, he must tell the whole truth and Boswell had sufficient faith in humanity to believe that the whole truth would always have a dignity that no partial truth could attain to.

And his book justifies his faith. It tells us a great deal about Johnson that most ordinary friends would have suppressed, but the candor of these confessions enlists our credence and we are willing to accept the man's virtues, too—a willingness which no eulogy could extort from us. And certainly Johnson does not suffer from Boswell's method. No one has ever read *The Life of Johnson* without feeling that he has been in the company of a very great man. Actually, he has been in the company of two.

SELECTED BIBLIOGRAPHY

Balderston, Katherine C. (ed.), *Thraliana*, 2 vols., Oxford, 1942.

Conley, C. H. (ed.), *The Reader's Johnson*, New York, 1940.

Hill, George Birkbeck (ed.), *Boswell's Life of Johnson*, revised and enlarged by L. F. Powell, 6 vols., Oxford, 1934-50.

Kingsmill, Hugh (ed.), *Johnson Without Boswell*, New York, 1941.

———, *Samuel Johnson*, New York, 1934.

Krutch, Joseph Wood, *Samuel Johnson*, New York, 1944.

Pearson, Hesketh, and Kingsmill, Hugh, *Skye High*, London, 1937.

Piozzi, Hesther Lynch, *Anecdotes of Samuel Johnson*, ed. S. C. Roberts, Cambridge, 1925.

Pottle, Frederick A. (ed.), *Boswell's London Journal*, 1762-1763, New York, 1951.

——— and Bennett, C. H. (eds.), *Boswell's Journal of a Tour to the Hebrides*, New York, 1936.

Raleigh, Walter, *Six Essays on Johnson*, Oxford, 1910.

Roberts, S. C., *Dr. Johnson*, New York, 1935.

Smith-Dampier, J. L., *Who's Who in Boswell*, Oxford, 1935.

Tinker, Chauncey B., *Young Boswell*, Boston, 1922.

——— (ed.), *Letters of James Boswell*, 2 vols., Oxford, 1924.

Turberville, A. S. (ed.), *Johnson's England*, 2 vols., Oxford, 1933.

Vulliamy, C. E., *James Boswell*, New York, 1933.

Watkins, W. B. C., "Samuel Johnson," in *Perilous Balance*, Princeton, 1939.

Wilson, Mona (ed.), *Johnson's Prose and Poetry*, Cambridge, Mass., 1951.

THE

LIFE

OF

SAMUEL JOHNSON, LL.D.

COMPREHENDING

AN ACCOUNT OF HIS STUDIES
AND NUMEROUS WORKS,

IN CHRONOLOGICAL ORDER;

A SERIES OF HIS EPISTOLARY CORRESPONDENCE

AND CONVERSATIONS WITH MANY EMINENT PERSONS;

AND

VARIOUS ORIGINAL PIECES OF HIS COMPOSITION,
NEVER BEFORE PUBLISHED:

THE WHOLE EXHIBITING A VIEW OF LITERATURE AND
LITERARY MEN IN GREAT-BRITAIN, FOR NEAR
HALF A CENTURY, DURING WHICH HE
FLOURISHED.

———*Quò fit ut* OMNIS
Votiva pateat veluti descripta tabella
VITA SENIS.——   HORAT.

DEDICATION

TO

SIR JOSHUA REYNOLDS.

My Dear Sir,

Every liberal motive that can actuate an Authour in the dedication of his labours, concurs in directing me to you, as the person to whom the following Work should be inscribed.

If there be a pleasure in celebrating the distinguished merit of a contemporary, mixed with a certain degree of vanity not altogether inexcusable, in appearing fully sensible of it, where can I find one, in complimenting whom I can with more general approbation gratify those feelings? Your excellence, not only in the Art over which you have long presided with unrivalled fame, but also in Philosophy and elegant Literature, is well known to the present, and will continue to be the admiration of future ages. Your equal and placid temper, your variety of conversation, your true politeness, by which you are so amiable in private society, and that enlarged hospitality which has long made your house a common centre of union for the great, the accomplished, the learned, and the ingenious; all these qualities I can, in perfect confidence of not being accused of flattery, ascribe to you.

If a man may indulge an honest pride, in having it known to the world, that he has been thought worthy of particular attention by a person of the first eminence in the age in which he lived, whose company has been universally courted, I am justified in availing myself of the usual privilege of a Dedication, when I mention that there has been a long and uninterrupted friendship between us.

If gratitude should be acknowledged for favours received, I have this opportunity, my dear Sir, most sincerely to thank you for the many happy hours which I owe to your kindness,—for the cordiality with which you have at all times been pleased to welcome me,—for the number of valuable acquaintances to whom you have introduced me,—for the *noctes cœnæque Deûm,* which I have enjoyed under your roof.

If a work should be inscribed to one who is master of the subject of it, and whose approbation, therefore, must ensure it credit and success, the Life of Dr. Johnson is, with the greatest propriety, dedicated to Sir Joshua Reynolds, who was the intimate and beloved friend of that great man; the friend, whom he declared to be 'the most invulnerable man he knew; whom, if he should quarrel with him, he should find the most difficulty how to abuse.' You, my dear Sir, studied him, and knew him well: you venerated and admired him. Yet, luminous as he was upon the whole, you perceived all the shades which mingled in the grand composition; all the little peculiarities and slight blemishes which marked the literary Colossus. Your very warm commendation of the specimen which I gave in my 'Journal of a Tour to the Hebrides,' of my being able to preserve his conversation in an authentick and lively manner, which opinion the Publick has confirmed, was the best encouragement for me to persevere in my purpose of producing the whole of my stores.

In one respect, this Work will, in some passages, be different from the former. In my 'Tour,' I was almost unboundedly open in my communications; and from my eagerness to display the wonderful fertility and readiness of Johnson's wit, freely shewed to the world its dexterity, even when I was myself the object of it. I trusted that I should be liberally understood, as knowing very well what I was about, and by no means as simply unconscious of the pointed effects of the satire. I own, indeed, that I was arrogant enough to suppose that the tenour of the rest of the book would sufficiently guard me against such a strange imputation. But it seems I judged too well of the world; for, though I could scarcely believe it, I have been undoubtedly informed, that many persons, especially in distant quarters, not penetrating enough into Johnson's character, so as to understand his mode of treating his friends, have arraigned my judgement, instead of seeing that I was sensible of all that they could observe.

It is related of the great Dr. Clarke, that when in one of his leisure hours he was unbending himself with a few friends in the most playful and frolicksome manner, he observed Beau Nash approaching; upon which he suddenly stopped:—'My boys, (said he,) let us be grave: here comes a fool.' The world, my friend, I have found to be a great fool, as to that particular, on which it has become necessary to speak very plainly. I have, therefore, in this Work been more reserved; and though I tell nothing but the truth, I have still kept in my mind that the whole truth is not always to be exposed. This, however, I have managed so as to occasion no diminution of the pleasure which my book should afford; though malignity may sometimes be disappointed of its gratifications.

      I am,

           My dear Sir,

                Your much obliged friend,

                    And faithful humble servant,

                        JAMES BOSWELL.

London,
April 20, 1791.

ADVERTISEMENT

FIRST EDITION.

I AT last deliver to the world a Work which I have long promised, and of which, I am afraid, too high expectations have been raised. The delay of its publication must be imputed, in a considerable degree, to the extraordinary zeal which has been shewn by distinguished persons in all quarters to supply me with additional information concerning its illustrious subject; resembling in this the grateful tribes of ancient nations, of which every individual was eager to throw a stone upon the grave of a departed Hero, and thus to share in the pious office of erecting an honourable monument to his memory.

The labour and anxious attention with which I have collected and arranged the materials of which these volumes are composed, will hardly be conceived by those who read them with careless facility. The stretch of mind and prompt assiduity by which so many conversations were preserved, I myself, at some distance of time, contemplate with wonder; and I must be allowed to suggest, that the nature of the work, in other respects, as it consists of innumerable detached particulars, all which, even the most minute, I have spared no pains to ascertain with a scrupulous authenticity, has occasioned a degree of trouble far beyond that of any other species of composition. Were I to detail the books which I have consulted, and the inquiries which I have found it necessary to make by various channels, I should probably be thought ridiculously ostentatious. Let me only observe, as a specimen of my trouble, that I have sometimes been obliged to run half over London, in order to fix a date correctly; which, when I had accomplished, I well knew would obtain me no praise, though a failure would *have been to my discredit. And after all, perhaps, hard as it may be, I shall not be surprized if omissions or mistakes be pointed out with invidious severity. I have also been extremely careful as to the exactness of my quotations; holding that there is a respect due to the Publick which should oblige every Authour to attend to this, and never to presume to introduce them with,—'I think I have read;'—or,—'If I remember right;'—when the originals may be examined.*

I beg leave to express my warmest thanks to those who have been pleased to favour me with communications and advice in the conduct of my Work. But I cannot sufficiently acknowledge my obligations to my friend Mr. Malone, who was so good as to allow me to read to him almost the whole of my manuscript, and made such remarks as were greatly for the advantage of the Work; though it is but fair to him to mention, that upon many occasions I differed from him, and followed my own judgement. I regret exceedingly that I was deprived of the benefit of his revision, when not more than one half of the book had passed through the press; but after having completed his very laborious and admirable edition of Shakspeare, for which he generously would accept of no other reward but that fame which he has so deservedly obtained, he fulfilled his promise of a long-wished-for visit to his relations in Ireland; from whence his safe return finibus Atticis is desired by his friends here, with all the classical ardour of Sic te Diva potens Cypri; for there is no man in whom more elegant and worthy qualities are united; and whose society, therefore, is more valued by those who know him.

It is painful to me to think, that while I was carrying on this Work, several of those to whom it would have been most interesting have died. Such melancholy disappointments we know to be incident to humanity; but we do not feel them the less. Let me particularly lament the Reverend Thomas Warton, and the Reverend Dr. Adams. Mr. Warton, amidst his variety of genius and learning, was an excellent Biographer. His contributions to my Collection are highly estimable; and as he had a true relish of my 'Tour of the Hebrides,' I trust I should now have been gratified with a larger share of his kind approbation. Dr. Adams, eminent as the Head of a College, as a writer, and as a most amiable man, had known Johnson from his early years, and was his friend through life. What reason I had to hope for the countenance of that venerable Gentleman to this Work, will appear from what he wrote to me upon a former occasion from Oxford, November 17, 1785: —'Dear Sir, I hazard this letter, not knowing where it will find you, to thank you for your very agreeable "Tour," which I found here on my return from the country, and in which you have depicted our friend so perfectly to my fancy, in every attitude, every scene and situation, that I have thought myself in the company, and of the party almost throughout. It has given very general satisfaction; and those who have found most fault with a passage here and there, have agreed that they could not help going through, and being entertained with the whole. I wish, indeed, some few gross expressions had been softened, and a few of our hero's foibles had been a little more shaded; but it is useful to see the weaknesses incident to great minds; and you have given us Dr. Johnson's authority that in history all ought to be told.'

Such a sanction to my faculty of giving a just representation of Dr. Johnson I could not conceal. Nor will I suppress my satisfaction in the consciousness, that by recording so considerable a portion of the wisdom and wit of 'the brightest ornament of the eighteenth century,' *I have largely provided for the instruction and entertainment of mankind.*

London, April 20, 1791.

ADVERTISEMENT

SECOND EDITION.

THAT I was anxious for the success of a Work which had employed much of my time and labour, I do not wish to conceal: but whatever doubts I at any time entertained, have been entirely removed by the very favourable reception with which it has been honoured. That reception has excited my best exertions to render my Book more perfect; and in this endeavour I have had the assistance not only of some of my particular friends, but of many other learned and ingenious men, by which I have been enabled to rectify some mistakes, and to enrich the Work with many valuable additions. These I have ordered to be printed separately in quarto, for the accommodation of the purchasers of the first edition. May I be permitted to say that the typography of both editions does honour to the press of Mr. Henry Baldwin, now Master of the Worshipful Company of Stationers, whom I have long known as a worthy man and an obliging friend.

In the strangely mixed scenes of human existence, our feelings are often at once pleasing and painful. Of this truth, the progress of the present Work furnishes a striking instance. It was highly gratifying to me that my friend, Sir Joshua Reynolds, to whom it is inscribed, lived to peruse it, and to give the strongest testimony to its fidelity; but before a second edition, which he contributed to improve, could be finished, the world has been deprived of that most valuable man; a loss of which the regret will be deep, and lasting, and extensive, proportionate to the felicity which he diffused through a wide circle of admirers and friends.

In reflecting that the illustrious subject of this Work, by being more extensively and intimately known, however elevated

*before, has risen in the veneration and love of mankind, I feel
a satisfaction beyond what fame can afford. We cannot, indeed,
too much or too often admire his wonderful powers of mind,
when we consider that the principal store of wit and wisdom
which this Work contains, was not a particular selection from
his general conversation, but was merely his occasional talk at
such times as I had the good fortune to be in his company;
and, without doubt, if his discourse at other periods had been
collected with the same attention, the whole tenor of what he
uttered would have been found equally excellent.*

*His strong, clear, and animated enforcement of religion,
morality, loyalty, and subordination, while it delights and improves the wise and the good, will, I trust, prove an effectual
antidote to that detestable sophistry which has been lately imported from France, under the false name of Philosophy, and
with a malignant industry has been employed against the
peace, good order, and happiness of society, in our free and
prosperous country; but thanks be to GOD, without producing
the pernicious effects which were hoped for by its propagators.*

*It seems to me, in my moments of self-complacency, that
this extensive biographical work, however inferior in its nature,
may in one respect be assimilated to the ODYSSEY. Amidst a
thousand entertaining and instructive episodes the HERO is
never long out of sight; for they are all in some degree connected with him; and HE, in the whole course of the History,
is exhibited by the Authour for the best advantage of his readers.*

> —Quid virtus et quid sapientia possit,
> Utile proposuit nobis exemplar Ulyssen.

*Should there be any cold-blooded and morose mortals who
really dislike this Book, I will give them a story to apply. When
the great* Duke of Marlborough, *accompanied by Lord Cadogan, was one day reconnoitering the army in Flanders, a heavy
rain came on, and they both called for their cloaks. Lord Cadogan's servant, a good humoured alert lad, brought his Lordship's in a minute. The Duke's servant, a lazy sulky dog, was
so sluggish, that his Grace being wet to the skin, reproved him,
and had for answer with a grunt, 'I came as fast as I could,'*

upon which the Duke calmly said, 'Cadogan, I would not for a thousand pounds have that fellow's temper.'

There are some men, I believe, who have, or think they have, a very small share of vanity. Such may speak of their literary fame in a decorous style of diffidence. But I confess, that I am so formed by nature and by habit, that to restrain the effusion of delight, on having obtained such fame, to me would be truly painful. Why then should I suppress it? Why 'out of the abundance of the heart' should I not speak? Let me then mention with a warm, but no insolent exultation, that I have been regaled with spontaneous praise of my work by many and various persons eminent for their rank, learning, talents and accomplishments; much of which praise I have under their hands to be reposited in my archives at Auchinleck. An honourable and reverend friend speaking of the favourable reception of my volumes, even in the circles of fashion and elegance, said to me, 'you have made them all talk Johnson,'—Yes, I may add, I have Johnsonised the land; and I trust they will not only talk, but think, Johnson.

To enumerate those to whom I have been thus indebted, would be tediously ostentatious. I cannot however but name one whose praise is truly valuable, not only on account of his knowledge and abilities, but on account of the magnificent, yet dangerous embassy, in which he is now employed, which makes every thing that relates to him peculiarly interesting. Lord Macartney favoured me with his own copy of my book, with a number of notes, of which I have availed myself. On the first leaf I found in his Lordship's hand-writing, an inscription of such high commendation, that even I, vain as I am, cannot prevail on myself to publish it.

[*July* 1, 1793.]

THE LIFE OF
SAMUEL JOHNSON, LL.D.

To WRITE the Life of him who excelled all mankind in writing the lives of others, and who, whether we consider his extraordinary endowments, or his various works, has been equalled by few in any age, is an arduous, and may be reckoned in me a presumptuous task.

Had Dr. Johnson written his own life, in conformity with the opinion which he has given, that every man's life may be best written by himself; had he employed in the preservation of his own history, that clearness of narration and elegance of language in which he has embalmed so many eminent persons, the world would probably have had the most perfect example of biography that was ever exhibited. But although he at different times, in a desultory manner, committed to writing many particulars of the progress of his mind and fortunes, he never had persevering diligence enough to form them into a regular composition. Of these memorials a few have been preserved; but the greater part was consigned by him to the flames, a few days before his death.

As I had the honour and happiness of enjoying his friendship for upwards of twenty years; as I had the scheme of writing his life constantly in view; as he was well apprised of this circumstance, and from time to time obligingly satisfied my inquiries, by communicating to me the incidents of his early years; as I acquired a facility in recollecting, and was very assiduous in recording, his conversation, of which the extraordinary vigour and vivacity constituted one of the first features of his character; and as I have spared no pains in obtaining materials concerning him, from every quarter where I could discover that they were to be found, and have been favoured with the most liberal communications by his friends; I flatter myself that few biographers have entered upon such a work as this, with more advantages; independent of literary abilities, in which I am not vain enough to compare myself with some great names who have gone before me in this kind of writing.

Had his other friends been as diligent and ardent as I was, he might have been almost entirely preserved. As it is, I will venture to say that he will be seen in this work more completely than any man who has ever yet lived.

What I consider as the peculiar value of the following work, is, the quantity that it contains of Johnson's conversation; which is universally acknowledged to have been eminently instructive and entertaining; and of which the specimens that I have given upon a former occasion, have been received with so much approbation, that I have good grounds for supposing that the world will not be indifferent to more ample communications of a similar nature.

Of one thing I am certain, that considering how highly the small portion which we have of the table-talk and other anecdotes of our celebrated writers is valued, and how earnestly it is regretted that we have not more, I am justified in preserving rather too many of Johnson's sayings, than too few; especially as from the diversity of dispositions it cannot be known with certainty beforehand, whether what may seem trifling to some, and perhaps to the collector himself, may not be most agreeable to many; and the greater number that an authour can please in any degree, the more pleasure does there arise to a benevolent mind.

To those who are weak enough to think this a degrading task, and the time and labour which have been devoted to it misemployed, I shall content myself with opposing the authority of the greatest man of any age, *Julius Cæsar*, of whom Bacon observes, that 'in his book of Apothegms which he collected, we see that he esteemed it more honour to make himself but a pair of tables, to take the wise and pithy words of others, than to have every word of his own to be made an apothegm or an oracle.'

Having said thus much by way of introduction, I commit the following pages to the candour of the Publick.

Samuel Johnson was born at Lichfield, in Staffordshire, on the 18th of September, N.S. 1709; and his initiation into the

Christian church was not delayed; for his baptism is recorded,
in the register of St. Mary's parish in that city, to have been
performed on the day of his birth: His father is there stiled
Gentleman, a circumstance of which an ignorant panegyrist
has praised him for not being proud; when the truth is, that
the appellation of Gentleman, though now lost in the indiscriminate assumption of *Esquire,* was commonly taken by those
who could not boast of gentility. His father was Michael Johnson, a native of Derbyshire, of obscure extraction, who settled
in Lichfield as a bookseller and stationer. His mother was Sarah
Ford, descended of an ancient race of substantial yeomanry in
Warwickshire. They were well advanced in years when they
married, and never had more than two children, both sons;
Samuel, their first born, who lived to be the illustrious character whose various excellence I am to endeavour to record, and
Nathanael, who died in his twenty-fifth year.

Mr. Michael Johnson was a man of a large and robust body,
and of a strong and active mind; yet, as in the most solid rocks
veins of unsound substance are often discovered, there was in
him a mixture of that disease, the nature of which eludes the
most minute enquiry, though the effects are well known to be
a weariness of life, an unconcern about those things which agitate the greater part of mankind, and a general sensation of
gloomy wretchedness. From him then his son inherited, with
some other qualities, 'a vile melancholy,' which in his too
strong expression of any disturbance of the mind, 'made him
mad all his life, at least not sober.' Michael was, however,
forced by the narrowness of his circumstances to be very diligent in business, not only in his shop, but by occasionally re-
sorting to several towns in the neighbourhood, some of which
were at a considerable distance from Lichfield. At that time
booksellers' shops in the provincial towns of England were very
rare, so that there was not one even in Birmingham, in which
town old Mr. Johnson used to open a shop every market-day.
He was a pretty good Latin scholar, and a citizen so creditable
as to be made one of the magistrates of Lichfield; and, being a
man of good sense, and skill in his trade, he acquired a reasonable share of wealth, of which however he afterwards lost the
greatest part, by engaging unsuccessfully in a manufacture of

parchment. He was a zealous high-churchman and royalist, and retained his attachment to the unfortunate house of Stuart, though he reconciled himself, by casuistical arguments of expediency and necessity, to take the oaths imposed by the prevailing power.

Johnson's mother was a woman of distinguished understanding. I asked his old school-fellow, Mr. Hector, surgeon, of Birmingham, if she was not vain of her son. He said, 'she had too much good sense to be vain, but she knew her son's value.' Her piety was not inferiour to her understanding; and to her must be ascribed those early impressions of religion upon the mind of her son, from which the world afterwards derived so much benefit. He told me, that he remembered distinctly having had the first notice of Heaven, 'a place to which good people went,' and Hell, 'a place to which bad people went,' communicated to him by her, when a little child in bed with her; and that it might be the better fixed in his memory, she sent him to repeat it to Thomas Jackson, their man-servant; he not being in the way, this was not done; but there was no occasion for any artificial aid for its preservation.

Nor can I omit a little instance of that jealous independence of spirit, and impetuosity of temper, which never forsook him. The fact was acknowledged to me by himself, upon the authority of his mother. One day, when the servant who used to be sent to school to conduct him home, had not come in time, he set out by himself, though he was then so near-sighted, that he was obliged to stoop down on his hands and knees to take a view of the kennel before he ventured to step over it. His schoolmistress, afraid that he might miss his way, or fall into the kennel, or be run over by a cart, followed him at some distance. He happened to turn about and perceive her. Feeling her careful attention as an insult to his manliness, he ran back to her in a rage, and beat her, as well as his strength would permit.

Of the power of his memory, for which he was all his life eminent to a degree almost incredible, the following early instance was told me in his presence at Lichfield, in 1776, by his step-daughter, Mrs. Lucy Porter, as related to her by his mother. When he was a child in petticoats, and had learnt to read, Mrs. Johnson one morning put the common prayer-book into his hands, pointed to the collect for the day, and said, 'Sam, you must get this by heart.' She went up stairs, leaving him to study it: But by the time she had reached the second floor, she heard him following her. 'What's the matter?' said she. 'I can say it,' he replied; and repeated it distinctly, though he could not have read it over more than twice.

But there has been another story of his infant precocity generally circulated, and generally believed, the truth of which I am to refute upon his own authority. It is told, that, when a child of three years old, he chanced to tread upon a duckling, the eleventh of a brood, and killed it; upon which, it is said, he dictated to his mother the following epitaph:

'Here lies good master duck,
    Whom Samuel Johnson trod on;
If it had liv'd, it had been *good luck*,
    For then we'd had an *odd one*.'

There is surely internal evidence that this little composition combines in it, what no child of three years old could produce, without an extension of its faculties by immediate inspiration; yet Mrs. Lucy Porter, Dr. Johnson's step-daughter, positively maintained to me, in his presence, that there could be no doubt of the truth of this anecdote, for she had heard it from his mother. So difficult is it to obtain an authentick relation of facts, and such authority may there be for errour; for he assured me, that his father made the verses, and wished to pass them for his child's. He added, 'my father was a foolish old man; that is to say, foolish in talking of his children.'

Young Johnson had the misfortune to be much afflicted with the scrophula, or king's evil, which disfigured a countenance naturally well formed, and hurt his visual nerves so much, that he did not see at all with one of his eyes, though its appearance was little different from that of the other. There is amongst his prayers, one inscribed 'When my eye was restored to its use,' which ascertains a defect that many of his friends knew he had, though I never perceived it. It has been said, that he contracted this grievous malady from his nurse. His mother yielding to the superstitious notion, which, it is wonderful to think, prevailed so long in this country, as to the virtue of the regal touch; a notion, which our kings encouraged, and to which a man of such inquiry and such judgement as Carte could give credit; carried him to London, where he was actually touched by Queen Anne. Mrs. Johnson indeed, as Mr. Hector informed me, acted by the advice of the celebrated Sir John Floyer, then a physician in Lichfield. Johnson used to talk of this very frankly; and Mrs. Piozzi has preserved his very picturesque description of the scene, as it remained upon his fancy. Being asked if he could remember Queen Anne, 'He had (he said) a confused, but somehow a sort of solemn recollection of a lady in diamonds, and a long black hood.' This touch, however, was without any effect. I ventured to say to him, in allusion to the political principles in which he was educated, and of which he ever retained some odour, that 'his mother had not carried him far enough; she should have taken him to ROME.'

He was first taught to read English by Dame Oliver, a widow, who kept a school for young children in Lichfield. He told me she could read the black letter, and asked him to borrow for her, from his father, a bible in that character. When he was going to Oxford, she came to take leave of him, brought him, in the simplicity of her kindness, a present of gingerbread, and said he was the best scholar she had ever had. He delighted in mentioning this early compliment: adding, with a smile, that 'this was as high a proof of his merit as he could conceive.' His next instructor in English was a master, whom, when he spoke of him to me, he familiarly called Tom Brown, who, said he, 'published a spelling-book, and dedicated it to the UNIVERSE; but, I fear, no copy of it can now be had.'

He began to learn Latin with Mr. Hawkins, usher, or undermaster of Lichfield school, 'a man (said he) very skilful in his little way.' With him he continued two years, and then rose to be under the care of Mr. Hunter, the head-master, who, according to his account, 'was very severe, and wrong-headedly severe. He used (said he) to beat us unmercifully; and he did not distinguish between ignorance and negligence; for he would beat a boy equally for not knowing a thing, as for neglecting to know it. He would ask a boy a question; and if he did not answer it, he would beat him, without considering whether he had an opportunity of knowing how to answer it. For instance, he would call up a boy and ask him Latin for a candlestick, which the boy could not expect to be asked. Now, Sir, if a boy could answer every question, there would be no need of a master to teach him.'

It is, however, but justice to the memory of Mr. Hunter to mention, that though he might err in being too severe, the school of Lichfield was very respectable in his time. [Indeed Johnson was very sensible how much he owed to Mr. Hunter.] Mr. Langton one day asked him how he had acquired so accurate a knowledge of Latin, in which, I believe, he was exceeded by no man of his time; he said, 'My master whipt me very well. Without that, Sir, I should have done nothing.' He told Mr. Langton, that while Hunter was flogging his boys unmercifully, he used to say, 'And this I do to save you from the gallows.' Johnson, upon all occasions, expressed his approbation of enforcing instruction by means of the rod. 'I would rather (said he) have the rod to be the general terrour to all, to make them learn, than tell a child, if you do thus, or thus, you will be more esteemed than your brothers or sisters. The rod produces an effect which terminates in itself. A child is afraid of being whipped, and gets his task, and there's an end on't; whereas, by exciting emulation and comparisons of superiority, you lay the foundation of lasting mischief; you make brothers and sisters hate each other.'

That superiority over his fellows, which he maintained with so much dignity in his march through life, was not assumed from vanity and ostentation, but was the natural and constant effect of those extraordinary powers of mind, of which he could not but be conscious by comparison; the intellectual difference, which in other cases of comparison of characters is often a matter of undecided contest, being as clear in his case as the superiority of stature in some men above others. Johnson did not strut or stand on tip-toe: He only did not stoop. From his earliest years, his superiority was perceived and acknowledged. His schoolfellow, Mr. Hector, has obligingly furnished me with many particulars of his boyish days: and assured me that he never knew him corrected at school, but for talking and diverting other boys from their business. His favourites used to receive very liberal assistance from him; and such was the submission and deference with which he was treated, such the desire to obtain his regard, that three of the boys, of whom Mr. Hector was sometimes one, used to come in the morning as his humble attendants, and carry him to school. One in the middle stooped, while he sat upon his back, and one on each side supported him; and thus he was borne triumphant.

He never joined with the other boys in their ordinary diversions: his only amusement was in winter, when he took a pleasure in being drawn upon the ice by a boy barefooted, who pulled him along by a garter fixed round him; no very easy operation, as his size was remarkably large(His defective sight, indeed, prevented him from enjoying the common sports;] and he once pleasantly remarked to me, 'how wonderfully well he had contrived to be idle without them.'

1725: ÆTAT. 16.]—After having resided for some time at the house of his uncle, Cornelius Ford, Johnson was, at the age of fifteen, removed to the school of Stourbridge, in Worcestershire, of which Mr. Wentworth was then master. This step was taken by the advice of his cousin, the Reverend Mr. Ford, a man in whom both talents and good dispositions were disgraced by licentiousness, but who was a very able judge of what was right. At this school he did not receive so much benefit as was expected. It has been said, that he acted in the capacity of an assistant to Mr. Wentworth, in teaching the younger boys. 'Mr. Wentworth (he told me) was a very able man, but an idle man, and to me very severe; but I cannot blame him much.'

He thus discriminated, to Dr. Percy, Bishop of Dromore, his progress at his two grammar-schools. 'At one, I learnt much in the school, but little from the master; in the other, I learnt much from the master, but little in the school.'

The Bishop also informs me, that 'Dr. Johnson's father, before he was received at Stourbridge, applied to have him admitted as a scholar and assistant to the Reverend Samuel Lea, M.A. head master of Newport school, in Shropshire; (a very diligent good teacher, at that time in high reputation, under whom Mr. Hollis is said, in the Memoirs of his Life, to have been also educated). This application to Mr. Lea was not successful; but Johnson had afterwards the gratification to hear that the old gentleman, who lived to a very advanced age, mentioned it as one of the most memorable events of his life, that "he was *very near* having that great man for his scholar".

The two years which he spent at home, after his return from Stourbridge, he passed in what he thought idleness, and was scolded by his father for his want of steady application. He had no settled plan of life, nor looked forward at all, but merely lived from day to day. Yet he read a great deal in a desultory manner, without any scheme of study, as chance threw books in his way, and inclination directed him through them. He used to mention one curious instance of his casual reading, when but a boy. Having imagined that his brother had hid some apples behind a large folio upon an upper shelf in his father's shop, he climbed up to search for them. There were no apples; but the large folio proved to be Petrarch, whom he had seen mentioned, in some preface, as one of the restorers of learning. His curiosity having been thus excited, he sat down with avidity, and read a great part of the book. What he read during these two years, he told me, was not works of mere amusement, 'not voyages and travels, but all literature, Sir, all ancient writers, all manly: though but little Greek, only some of Anacreon and Hesiod; but in this irregular manner (added he) I had looked into a great many books, which were not commonly known at the Universities, where they seldom read any books but what are put into their hands by their tutors; so that when I came to Oxford, Dr. Adams, now master of Pembroke College, told me, I was the best qualified for the University that he had ever known come there.'

That a man in Mr. Michael Johnson's circumstances should think of sending his son to the expensive University of Oxford, at his own charge, seems very improbable. The subject was too delicate to question Johnson upon: But I have been assured by Dr. Taylor, that the scheme never would have taken place, had not a gentleman of Shropshire, one of his schoolfellows, spontaneously undertaken to support him at Oxford, in the character of his companion; though, in fact, he never received any assistance whatever from that gentleman.

He, however, went to Oxford, and was entered a Commoner of Pembroke College, on the 31st of October, 1728, being then in his nineteenth year.

The Reverend Dr. Adams, who afterwards presided over Pembroke College with universal esteem, told me he was present, and gave me some account of what passed on the night of Johnson's arrival at Oxford. On that evening, his father, who had anxiously accompanied him, found means to have him introduced to Mr. Jorden, who was to be his tutor. His father seemed very full of the merits of his son, and told the company he was a good scholar, and a poet, and wrote Latin verses. His figure and manner appeared strange to them; but he behaved modestly, and sat silent, till upon something which occurred in the course of conversation, he suddenly struck in and quoted Macrobius; and thus he gave the first impression of that more extensive reading in which he had indulged himself.

His tutor, Mr. Jorden, fellow of Pembroke, was not, it seems, a man of such abilities as we should conceive requisite for the instructor of Samuel Johnson, who gave me the following account of him. 'He was a very worthy man, but a heavy man, and I did not profit much by his instructions. Indeed, I did not attend him much. The first day after I came to college, I waited upon him, and then staid away four. On the sixth, Mr. Jorden asked me why I had not attended. I answered, I had been sliding in Christ-Church meadow. And this I said with as much *nonchalance* as I am now talking to you. I had no notion that I was wrong or irreverent to my tutor.' *Boswell.* 'That, Sir, was great fortitude of mind.' *Johnson.* 'No, Sir; stark insensibility.' He had a love and respect for Jorden, not for his literature, but for his worth. 'Whenever (said he) a young man becomes Jorden's pupil, he becomes his son.'

The 'morbid melancholy,' which was lurking in his constitution, and to which we may ascribe those particularities, and that aversion to regular life, which, at a very early period, marked his character, gathered such strength in his twentieth year, as to afflict him in a dreadful manner. While he was at

Lichfield, in the college vacation of the year 1729, he felt himself overwhelmed with an horrible hypochondria, with perpetual irritation, fretfulness, and impatience; and with a dejection, gloom, and despair, which made existence misery. From
this dismal malady he never afterwards was perfectly relieved;
and all his labours, and all his enjoyments, were but temporary
interruptions of its baleful influence. He told Mr. Paradise
that he was sometimes so languid and inefficient, that he could
not distinguish the hour upon the town-clock.

Johnson, upon the first violent attack of this disorder, strove
to overcome it by forcible exertions. He frequently walked to
Birmingham and back again, and tried many other expedients,
but all in vain. His expression concerning it to me was, 'I did
not then know how to manage it.' His distress became so intolerable, that he applied to Dr. Swinfen, physician in Lichfield, his godfather, and put into his hands a state of his case,
written in Latin. Dr. Swinfen was so much struck with the extraordinary acuteness, research, and eloquence of this paper,
that in his zeal for his godson he shewed it to several people.
His daughter, Mrs. Desmoulins, who was many years humanely supported in Dr. Johnson's house in London, told me,
that upon his discovering that Dr. Swinfen had communicated his case, he was so much offended, that he was never
afterwards fully reconciled to him.

The history of his mind as to religion is an important article.
I have mentioned the early impressions made upon his tender
imagination by his mother, who continued her pious care with
assiduity, but, in his opinion, not with judgement. 'Sunday
(said he) was a heavy day to me when I was a boy. My mother
confined me on that day, and made me read "The Whole
Duty of Man," from a great part of which I could derive no
instruction. When, for instance, I had read the chapter on
theft, which from my infancy I had been taught was wrong, I
was no more convinced that theft was wrong than before; so
there was no accession of knowledge.'

He communicated to me the following particulars upon the
subject of his religious progress. 'I fell into an inattention to
religion, or an indifference about it, in my ninth year. The
church at Lichfield, in which we had a seat, wanted repara-

tion, so I was to go and find a seat in other churches; and having bad eyes, and being awkward about this, I used to go and read in the fields on Sunday. This habit continued till my fourteenth year; and still I find a great reluctance to go to church. I then became a sort of lax *talker* against religion, for I did not much *think* against it; and this lasted till I went to Oxford, where it would not be *suffered*. When at Oxford, I took up "Law's Serious Call to a Holy Life," expecting to find it a dull book, (as such books generally are,) and perhaps to laugh at it. But I found Law quite an overmatch for me; and this was the first occasion of my thinking in earnest of religion, after I became capable of rational inquiry.' From this time forward, religion was the predominant object of his thoughts; though, with the just sentiments of a conscientious christian, he lamented that his practice of its duties fell far short of what it ought to be.

How seriously Johnson was impressed with a sense of religion, even in the vigour of his youth, appears from the following passage in his minutes kept by way of diary: 'Sept. 7, 1736. I have this day entered upon my 28th year. Mayest thou, O GOD, enable me, for *Jesus Christ's* sake, to spend this in such a manner, that I may receive comfort from it at the hour of death, and in the day of judgement! Amen.'

The particular course of his reading while at Oxford, and during the time of vacation which he passed at home, cannot be traced. Enough has been said of his irregular mode of study. He told me, that from his earliest years he loved to read poetry, but hardly ever read any poem to an end; that he read Shakspeare at a period so early, that the speech of the Ghost in Hamlet terrified him when he was alone; that Horace's Odes were the compositions in which he took most delight, and it was long before he liked his Epistles and Satires. He told me what he read *solidly* at Oxford was Greek; not the Grecian historians, but Homer and Euripides, and now and then a little Epigram; that the study of which he was most fond was Metaphysicks, but he had not read much, even in that way. I always thought that he did himself injustice in his account of what he had read, and that he must have been speaking with reference to the vast portion of study which is possible, and to which a few scholars in the whole history of literature have attained. Dr. Adam Smith, than whom few were better judges on this subject, once observed to me that 'Johnson knew more books than any man alive.'

No man had a more ardent love of literature, or a higher respect for it, than Johnson. His apartment in Pembroke College was that upon the second floor, over the gateway. The enthusiasts of learning will ever contemplate it with veneration. One day, while he was sitting in it quite alone, Dr. Panting, then master of the College, whom he called 'a fine Jacobite fellow,' overheard him uttering this soliloquy in his strong emphatick voice: 'Well, I have a mind to see what is done in other places of learning. I'll go and visit the Universities abroad. I'll go to France and Italy. I'll go to Padua.—And I'll mind my business. For an *Athenian* blockhead is the worst of all blockheads.'

Dr. Adams told me that Johnson, while he was at Pembroke College, 'was caressed and loved by all about him, was a gay and frolicksome fellow, and passed there the happiest part of his life.' But this is a striking proof of the fallacy of appearances, and how little any of us know of the real internal state even of those whom we see most frequently; for the truth is, that he was then depressed by poverty, and irritated by disease. When I mentioned to him this account as given me by Dr. Adams, he said, 'Ah, Sir, I was mad and violent. It was bitterness which they mistook for frolick. I was miserably poor, and I thought to fight my way by my literature and my wit; so I disregarded all power and all authority.'

The Bishop of Dromore observes in a letter to me,

'I have heard from some of his contemporaries that he was generally seen lounging at the College gate, with a circle of young students round him, whom he was entertaining with wit, and keeping from their studies, if not spiriting them up to rebellion against the College discipline, which in his maturer years he so much extolled.'

I do not find that he formed any close intimacies with his fellow-collegians. But Dr. Adams told me, that he contracted a love and regard for Pembroke College, which he retained to the last. A short time before his death he sent to that College a present of all his works, to be deposited in their library. Being himself a poet, Johnson was peculiarly happy in mentioning how many of the sons of Pembroke were poets; adding, with a smile of sportive triumph, 'Sir, we are a nest of singing birds.'

He was not, however, blind to what he thought the defects of his own College; and I have, from the information of Dr. Taylor, a very strong instance of that rigid honesty which he ever inflexibly preserved. Taylor had obtained his father's consent to be entered of Pembroke, that he might be with his schoolfellow Johnson, with whom, though some years older than himself, he was very intimate. This would have been a great comfort to Johnson. But he fairly told Taylor that he could not, in conscience, suffer him to enter where he knew he could not have an able tutor. He then made inquiry all round the University, and having found that Mr. Bateman, of Christ-Church, was the tutor of highest reputation, Taylor was entered of that College. Mr. Bateman's lectures were so excellent, that Johnson used to come and get them at second-hand from Taylor, till his poverty being so extreme, that his shoes were worn out, and his feet appeared through them, he saw that this humiliating circumstance was perceived by the Christ-Church-men, and he came no more. He was too proud to accept of money, and somebody having set a pair of new shoes at his door, he threw them away with indignation. How must we feel when we read such an anecdote of Samuel Johnson!

The *res angusta domi*[1] prevented him from having the advantage of a complete academical education. The friend to whom he had trusted for support had deceived him. His debts in College, though not great, were increasing; and his scanty remittances from Lichfield, which had all along been made with great difficulty, could be supplied no longer, his father having fallen into a state of insolvency. Compelled, therefore, by irresistible necessity, he left the College in autumn, 1731, without a degree, having been a member of it little more than three years.

And now (I had almost said *poor*) Samuel Johnson returned

[1] The narrowness of his domestic affairs, i.e., his poverty. The phrase is from Juvenal's third satire.

to his native city, destitute, and not knowing how he should gain even a decent livelihood. His father's misfortunes in trade rendered him unable to support his son; and for some time there appeared no means by which he could maintain himself. In the December of this year his father died.

In the forlorn state of his circumstances, he accepted of an offer to be employed as usher in the school of Market-Bosworth, in Leicestershire. This employment was very irksome to him in every respect, and he complained grievously of it in his letters to his friend Mr. Hector, who was now settled as a surgeon at Birmingham. The letters are lost; but Mr. Hector recollects his writing 'that the poet had described the dull sameness of his existence in these words, *"Vitam continet una dies"* (one day contains the whole of my life); that it was unvaried as the note of the cuckow; and that he did not know whether it was more disagreeable for him to teach, or the boys to learn, the grammar rules.' His general aversion to this painful drudgery was greatly enhanced by a disagreement between him and Sir Wolstan Dixey, the patron of the school, in whose house, I have been told, he officiated as a kind of domestick chaplain, so far, at least, as to say grace at table, but was treated with what he represented as intolerable harshness; and, after suffering for a few months such complicated misery, he relinquished a situation which all his life afterwards he recollected with the strongest aversion, and even a degree of horrour.

Being now again totally unoccupied, he was invited by Mr. Hector to pass some time with him at Birmingham, as his guest, at the house of Mr. Warren, with whom Mr. Hector lodged and boarded.

He continued to live as Mr. Hector's guest for about six months, and then hired lodgings in another part of the town, finding himself as well situated at Birmingham as he supposed he could be any where, while he had no settled plan of life, and very scanty means of subsistence. He made some valuable acquaintances there, amongst whom were Mr. Porter, a mercer, whose widow he afterwards married, and Mr. Taylor, who by his ingenuity in mechanical inventions, and his success in trade, acquired an immense fortune. But the comfort of being

near Mr. Hector, his old schoolfellow and intimate friend, was
Johnson's chief inducement to continue here.

In what manner he employed his pen at this period, or
whether he derived from it any pecuniary advantage, I have
not been able to ascertain. He probably got a little money from
Mr. Warren; and we are certain, that he executed here one
piece of literary labour, of which Mr. Hector has favoured me
with a minute account. Having mentioned that he had read
at Pembroke College a Voyage to Abyssinia, by Lobo, a Portu-
guese Jesuit, and that he thought an abridgement and translation of it from the French into English might be an useful and
profitable publication, Mr. Warren and Mr. Hector joined in
urging him to undertake it. He accordingly agreed; and the
book not being to be found in Birmingham, he borrowed it of
Pembroke College. A part of the work being very soon done,
one Osborn, who was Mr. Warren's printer, was set to work
with what was ready, and Johnson engaged to supply the press
with copy as it should be wanted; but his constitutional indolence soon prevailed, and the work was at a stand. Mr. Hector, who knew that a motive of humanity would be the most
prevailing argument with his friend, went to Johnson, and
represented to him, that the printer could have no other employment till this undertaking was finished, and that the poor
man and his family were suffering. Johnson upon this exerted
the powers of his mind, though his body was relaxed. He lay in
bed with the book, which was a quarto, before him, and dictated while Hector wrote. Mr. Hector carried the sheets to the
press, and corrected almost all the proof sheets, very few of
which were even seen by Johnson. In this manner, with the aid
of Mr. Hector's active friendship, the book was completed,
and was published in 1735, with *London* upon the title-page,
though it was in reality printed at Birmingham, a device too
common with provincial publishers. For this work he had from
Mr. Warren only the sum of five guineas.

Johnson returned to Lichfield early in 1734, and in August
that year he made an attempt to procure some little subsistence
by his pen; for he published proposals for printing by subscription the Latin Poems of Politian.

It appears that his brother Nathanael had taken up his father's trade; for it is mentioned that 'subscriptions are taken in by the Editor, or N. Johnson, bookseller, of Lichfield.' Notwithstanding the merit of Johnson, and the cheap price at which this book was offered, there were not subscribers enough to insure a sufficient sale; so the work never appeared, and, probably, never was executed.

We find him again this year at Birmingham, and there is preserved the following letter from him to Mr. Edward Cave, the original compiler and editor of the Gentleman's Magazine:

TO MR. CAVE.

'Nov. 25, 1734.

'SIR,
    'As YOU appear no less sensible than your readers of the defects of your poetical article, you will not be displeased, if, in order to the improvement of it, I communicate to you the sentiments of a person, who will undertake, on reasonable terms, sometimes to fill a column.

'His opinion is, that the publick would not give you a bad reception, if, beside the current wit of the month, which a critical examination would generally reduce to a narrow compass, you admitted not only poems, inscriptions, &c. never printed before, which he will sometimes supply you with; but likewise short literary dissertations in Latin or English, critical remarks on authours ancient or modern, forgotten poems that deserve revival, or loose pieces, like Floyer's, worth preserving. By this method, your literary article, for so it might be called, will, he thinks, be better recommended to the publick, than by low jests, aukward buffoonery, or the dull scurrilities of either party.

'If such a correspondence will be agreeable to you, be pleased to inform me in two posts, what the conditions are on which you shall expect it. Your late offer gives me no reason to distrust your generosity. If you engage in any literary projects besides this paper, I have other designs to impart, if I could be secure from having others reap the advantage of what I should hint.

'Your letter by being directed to S. *Smith,* to be left at the Castle in Birmingham, Warwickshire, will reach

'Your humble servant.'

Mr. Cave has put a note on this letter, 'Answered Dec. 2.' But whether any thing was done in consequence of it we are not informed.

⌈Johnson had, from his early youth, been sensible to the influence of female charms.⌉ When at Stourbridge school, he was much enamoured of Olivia Lloyd, a young quaker, to whom he wrote a copy of verses, which I have not been able to recover.

His juvenile attachments to the fair sex were, however, very transient; and it is certain, that he formed no criminal connection whatsoever. Mr. Hector, who lived with him in his younger days in the utmost intimacy and social freedom, has assured me, that even at that ardent season his conduct was strictly virtuous in that respect; and that though he loved to exhilarate himself with wine, he never knew him intoxicated but once.

In a man whom religious education has secured from licentious indulgences, the passion of love, when once it has seized him, is exceedingly strong; being unimpaired by dissipation, and totally concentrated in one object. This was experienced by Johnson, when he became the fervent admirer of Mrs. Porter, after her first husband's death. Miss Porter told me, that when he was first introduced to her mother, his appearance was very forbidding: he was then lean and lank, so that his immense structure of bones was hideously striking to the eye, and the scars of the scrophula were deeply visible. He also wore his hair, which was straight and stiff, and separated behind; and he often had, seemingly, convulsive starts and odd gesticulations, which tended to excite at once surprize and ridicule. Mrs. Porter was so much engaged by his conversation that she overlooked all these external disadvantages, and said to her daughter, 'this is the most sensible man that I ever saw in my life.'

Though Mrs. Porter was double the age of Johnson, and her person and manner, as described to me by the late Mr. Garrick, were by no means pleasing to others, she must have had a superiority of understanding and talents, as she certainly inspired him with a more than ordinary passion; and she having signified her willingness to accept of his hand, he went to Lichfield to ask his mother's consent to the marriage, which he could not but be conscious was a very imprudent scheme, both on account of their disparity of years, and her want of fortune.

But Mrs. Johnson knew too well the ardour of her son's temper, and was too tender a parent to oppose his inclinations.

I know not for what reason the marriage ceremony was not performed at Birmingham; but a resolution was taken that it should be at Derby, for which place the bride and bridegroom set out on horseback, I suppose in very good humour. But though Mr. Topham Beauclerk used archly to mention Johnson's having told him, with much gravity, 'Sir, it was a love-marriage upon both sides,' I have had from my illustrious friend the following curious account of their journey to church upon the nuptial morn. 'Sir, she had read the old romances, and had got into her head the fantastical notion that a woman of spirit should use her lover like a dog. So, Sir, at first she told me that I rode too fast, and she could not keep up with me; and, when I rode a little slower, she passed me, and complained that I lagged behind. I was not to be made the slave of caprice; and I resolved to begin as I meant to end. I therefore pushed on briskly, till I was fairly out of her sight. The road lay between two hedges, so I was sure she could not miss it; and I contrived that she should soon come up with me. When she did, I observed her to be in tears.'

This, it must be allowed, was a singular beginning of connubial felicity; but there is no doubt that Johnson, though he thus shewed a manly firmness, proved a most affectionate and indulgent husband to the last moment of Mrs. Johnson's life: and in his 'Prayers and Meditations' we find very remarkable evidence that his regard and fondness for her never ceased, even after her death.

He now set up a private academy, for which purpose he hired a large house, well situated near his native city. In the Gentleman's Magazine for 1736, there is the following advertisement:

'At Edial, near Lichfield, in Staffordshire, young gentlemen are boarded and taught the Latin and Greek languages, by *Samuel Johnson*.'

But the only pupils that were put under his care were the celebrated David Garrick and his brother George, and a Mr. Offely, a young gentleman of good fortune, who died early.

Johnson was not more satisfied with his situation as the master of an academy, than with that of the usher of a school; we need not wonder, therefore, that he did not keep his academy above a year and a half. From Mr. Garrick's account he did not appear to have been profoundly reverenced by his pupils. His oddities of manner, and uncouth gesticulations, could not but be the subject of merriment to them; and, in particular, the young rogues used to listen at the door of his bed-chamber, and peep through the key-hole, that they might turn into ridicule his tumultuous and aukward fondness for Mrs. Johnson, whom he used to name by the familiar appellation of *Tetty* or *Tetsey,* which, like *Betty* or *Betsey,* is provincially used as a contraction for *Elisabeth,* her christian name, but which to us seems ludicrous, when applied to a woman of her age and appearance. Mr. Garrick described her to me as very fat, with a bosom of more than ordinary protuberance, with swelled cheeks, of a florid red, produced by thick painting, and increased by the liberal use of cordials; flaring and fantastick in her dress, and affected both in her speech and her general behaviour. I have seen Garrick exhibit her, by his exquisite talent for mimickry, so as to excite the heartiest bursts of laughter; but he, probably, as is the case in all such representations, considerably aggravated the picture.

While Johnson kept his academy, there can be no doubt that he was insensibly furnishing his mind with various knowledge; but I have not discovered that he wrote any thing except a great part of his tragedy of *Irene.* Mr. Peter Garrick, the elder brother of David, told me that he remembered Johnson's borrowing the Turkish History of him, in order to form his play from it.

Johnson now thought of trying his fortune in London, the great field of genius and exertion, where talents of every kind have the fullest scope, and the highest encouragement. It is a memorable circumstance that his pupil David Garrick went thither at the same time, with intention to complete his education, and follow the profession of the law, from which he was soon diverted by his decided preference for the stage.

They were recommended to Mr. Colson, an eminent mathe-

matician and master of an academy, by the following letter
from Mr. Walmsley:

'To the Reverend Mr. Colson.

'Lichfield, March 2, 1737.

'Dear Sir,

'I had the favour of yours, and am extremely obliged to you;
but I cannot say I had a greater affection for you upon it than I
had before, being long since so much endeared to you, as well by
an early friendship, as by your many excellent and valuable qualifications; and, had I a son of my own, it would be my ambition,
instead of sending him to the University, to dispose of him as this
young gentleman is.

'He, and another neighbour of mine, one Mr. Samuel Johnson,
set out this morning for London together. Davy Garrick is to be
with you early the next week, and Mr. Johnson to try his fate with
a tragedy, and to see to get himself employed in some translation,
either from the Latin or the French. Johnson is a very good
scholar and poet, and I have great hopes will turn out a fine
tragedy-writer. If it should any way lie in your way, doubt not but
you would be ready to recommend and assist your countryman.

'G. Walmsley.'

He had a little money when he came to town, and he knew
how he could live in the cheapest manner. His first lodgings
were at the house of Mr. Norris, a staymaker, in Exeter-street,
adjoining Catharine-street, in the Strand. 'I dined (said he)
very well for eight-pence, with very good company, at the Pine
Apple in New-street, just by. Several of them had travelled.
They expected to meet every day; but did not know one another's names. It used to cost the rest a shilling, for they drank
wine; but I had a cut of meat for six-pence, and bread for a
penny, and gave the waiter a penny; so that I was quite well
served, nay, better than the rest, for they gave the waiter nothing.'

He at this time, I believe, abstained entirely from fermented
liquors: a practice to which he rigidly conformed for many
years together, at different periods of his life.

His *Ofellus* in the *Art of living in London,* I have heard
him relate, was an Irish painter, whom he knew at Birming-

ham, and who had practised his own precepts of œconomy for several years in the British capital. He assured Johnson, who, I suppose, was then meditating to try his fortune in London, but was apprehensive of the expence, 'that thirty pounds a year was enough to enable a man to live there without being contemptible. He allowed ten pounds for clothes and linen. He said a man might live in a garret at eighteen-pence a week; few people would inquire where he lodged; and if they did, it was easy to say, "Sir, I am to be found at such a place." By spending three-pence in a coffee-house, he might be for some hours every day in very good company; he might dine for six-pence, breakfast on bread and milk for a penny, and do without supper. On *clean-shirt-day* he went abroad, and paid visits.' I have heard him more than once talk of this frugal friend, whom he recollected with esteem and kindness, and did not like to have any one smile at the recital. 'This man (said he, gravely) was a very sensible man, who perfectly understood common affairs: a man of a great deal of knowledge of the world, fresh from life, not strained through books.'

Amidst this cold obscurity, there was one brilliant circumstance to cheer him; he was well acquainted with Mr. Henry Hervey, one of the branches of the noble family of that name, who had been quartered at Lichfield as an officer of the army, and had at this time a house in London, where Johnson was frequently entertained, and had an opportunity of meeting genteel company. Not very long before his death, he mentioned this, among other particulars of his life, which he was kindly communicating to me; and he described this early friend, 'Harry Hervey,' thus: 'He was a vicious man, but very kind to me. If you call a dog *Hervey*, I shall love him.'

In the course of the summer he returned to Lichfield, where he had left Mrs. Johnson, and there he at last finished his tragedy, which was not executed with his rapidity of composition upon other occasions, but was slowly and painfully elaborated.

Johnson's residence at Lichfield, on his return to it at this time, was only for three months; and as he had as yet seen but a small part of the wonders of the Metropolis, he had little to tell his townsmen. He related to me the following minute anecdote of this period: 'In the last age, when my mother lived in London, there were two sets of people, those who gave the wall, and those who took it; the peaceable and the quarrelsome. When I returned to Lichfield, after having been in London, my mother asked me, whether I was one of those who gave the wall, or those who took it. *Now* it is fixed that every man keeps to the right; or, if one is taking the wall, another yields it; and it is never a dispute.'

He now removed to London with Mrs. Johnson; but her daughter, who had lived with them at Edial, was left with her relations in the country. His lodgings were for some time in Woodstock-street, near Hanover-square, and afterwards in Castle-street, near Cavendish-square.

His tragedy being by this time, as he thought, completely finished and fit for the stage, he was very desirous that it should be brought forward. Mr. Peter Garrick told me, that Johnson and he went together to the Fountain tavern, and read it over, and that he afterwards solicited Mr. Fleetwood, the patentee of Drury-lane theatre, to have it acted at his house; but Mr. Fleetwood would not accept it, probably because it was not patronized by some man of high rank; and it was not acted till 1749, when his friend David Garrick was manager of that theatre.

The Gentleman's Magazine, begun and carried on by Mr. Edward Cave, under the name of *Sylvanus Urban,* had attracted the notice and esteem of Johnson, in an eminent degree, before he came to London as an adventurer in literature. He told me, that when he first saw St. John's Gate, the place where that deservedly popular miscellany was originally printed, he 'beheld it with reverence.'

It appears that he was now enlisted by Mr. Cave as a regular coadjutor in his magazine, by which he probably obtained a tolerable livelihood. At what time, or by what means, he had acquired a competent knowledge both of French and Italian I do not know; but he was so well skilled in them, as to be sufficiently qualified for a translator. That part of his labour which consisted in emendation and improvement of the productions of other contributors, like that employed in levelling ground, can be perceived only by those who had an opportunity of comparing the original with the altered copy. What we certainly know to have been done by him in this way, was the Debates in both houses of Parliament, under the name of 'The Senate of Lilliput,' sometimes with feigned denominations of the several speakers, sometimes with denominations formed of the letters of their real names, in the manner of what is called anagram, so that they might easily be decyphered. Parliament then kept the press in a kind of mysterious awe, which made it necessary to have recourse to such devices.

This important article of the Gentleman's Magazine was, for several years, executed by Mr. William Guthrie, a man who deserves to be respectably recorded in the literary annals of this country. The debates in Parliament, which were brought home and digested by Guthrie, whose memory, though surpassed by others who have since followed him in the same department, was yet very quick and tenacious, were sent by Cave to Johnson for his revision; and, after some time, when Guthrie had attained to greater variety of employment, and the speeches were more and more enriched by the accession of Johnson's genius, it was resolved that he should do the whole himself, from the scanty notes furnished by persons employed to attend in both houses of Parliament. Sometimes, however, as he himself told me, he had nothing more communicated to him than the names of the several speakers, and the part which they had taken in the debate.

Johnson's 'London' was published in May, 1738; and it is remarkable, that it came out on the same morning with Pope's satire, entitled '1738.' The Reverend Dr. Douglas, now Bishop of Salisbury, to whom I am indebted for some obliging communications, was then a student at Oxford, and remembers well the effect which 'London' produced. Every body was delighted with it; and there being no name to it, the first buz of the literary circles was 'here is an unknown poet, greater even than Pope.' And it is recorded in the Gentleman's Magazine of that year, that it 'got to the second edition in the course of a week.'

One of the warmest patrons of this poem on its first appearance was General *Oglethorpe*, whose 'strong benevolence of soul' was unabated during the course of a very long life.

Pope, who then filled the poetical throne without a rival,

it may reasonably be presumed, must have been particularly
struck by the sudden appearance of such a poet; and, to his
credit, let it be remembered, that his feelings and conduct on
the occasion were candid and liberal. He requested Mr. Richardson, son of the painter, to endeavour to find out who this
new authour was. Mr. Richardson, after some inquiry, having
informed him that he had discovered only that his name was
Johnson, and that he was some obscure man, Pope said, 'He
will soon be *déterré*.' We shall presently see, from a note written by Pope, that he was himself afterwards more successful
in his inquiries than his friend.

Though thus elevated into fame, and conscious of uncommon powers, he had not that bustling confidence, or, I may
rather say, that animated ambition, which one might have supposed would have urged him to endeavour at rising in life. But
such was his inflexible dignity of character, that he could not
stoop to court the great; without which, hardly any man has
made his way to high station. He could not expect to produce
many such works as his *London*, and he felt the hardship of
writing for bread; he was, therefore, willing to resume the office of a schoolmaster, so as to have a sure, though moderate
income for his life; and an offer being made to him of the mas-
tership of a school, provided he could obtain the degree of
Master of Arts, Dr. Adams was applied to, by a common friend,
to know whether that could be granted him as a favour from
the University of Oxford. But though he had made such a figure in the literary world, it was then thought too great a favour
to be asked.

Pope, without any knowledge of him but from his 'London,'
recommended him to Earl Gower, who endeavoured to procure
for him a degree from Dublin, by the following letter to a
friend of Dean Swift:

'SIR,

'MR. SAMUEL JOHNSON (authour of *London*, a satire, and
some other poetical pieces) is a native of this country, and much
respected by some worthy gentlemen in his neighbourhood, who
are trustees of a charity school now vacant; the certain salary is
sixty pounds a year, of which they are desirous to make him master; but, unfortunately, he is not capable of receiving their bounty,

which *would make him happy for life,* by not being a *Master of Arts;* which, by the statutes of this school, the master of it must be.

'Now these gentlemen do me the honour to think that I have interest enough in you, to prevail upon you to write to Dean Swift, to persuade the University of Dublin to send a diploma to me, constituting this poor man Master of Arts in their University. They highly extol the man's learning and probity; and will not be persuaded, that the University will make any difficulty of conferring such a favour upon a stranger, if he is recommended by the Dean. They say he is not afraid of the strictest examination, though he is of so long a journey; and will venture it, if the Dean thinks it necessary; choosing rather to die upon the road, *than be starved to death in translating for booksellers;* which has been his only subsistence for some time past.

'I fear there is more difficulty in this affair, than those goodnatured gentlemen apprehend; especially as their election cannot be delayed longer than the 11th of next month. If you see this matter in the same light that it appears to me, I hope you will burn this, and pardon me for giving you so much trouble about an impracticable thing; but, if you think there is a probability of obtaining the favour asked, I am sure your humanity, and propensity to relieve merit in distress, will incline you to serve the poor man, without my adding any more to the trouble I have already given you, than assuring you that I am, with great truth, Sir,

'Your faithful humble servant,
'GOWER.
'Trentham, Aug. 1, 1739.'

It was, perhaps, no small disappointment to Johnson that this respectable application had not the desired effect; yet how much reason has there been, both for himself and his country, to rejoice that it did not succeed, as he might probably have wasted in obscurity those hours in which he afterwards produced his incomparable works.

About this time he made one other effort to emancipate himself from the drudgery of authorship. He applied to Dr. Adams, to consult Dr. Smalbroke of the Commons, whether a person might be permitted to practice as an advocate there, without a doctor's degree in Civil Law. 'I am (said he) a total stranger to these studies; but whatever is a profession, and maintains numbers, must be within the reach of common abilities, and some degree of industry.' But here, also, the want of a degree was an insurmountable bar.

He was, therefore, under the necessity of persevering in that course, into which he had been forced; and we find, that his proposal from Greenwich to Mr. Cave, for a translation of Father Paul Sarpi's History, was accepted.

Some sheets of this translation were printed off, but the design was dropt; for it happened, oddly enough, that another person of the name of Samuel Johnson, Librarian of St. Martin's in the Fields, and Curate of that parish, engaged in the same undertaking, and was patronised by the Clergy, particularly by Dr. Pearce, afterwards Bishop of Rochester. Several light skirmishes passed between the rival translators, in the newspapers of the day; and the consequence was, that they destroyed each other, for neither of them went on with the work.

I have in my possession, by the favour of Mr. John Nichols, a paper in Johnson's hand-writing, entitled 'Account between Mr. Edward Cave and Sam. Johnson, in relation to a version of Father Paul, &c. begun August the 2d, 1738;' by which it appears, that from that day to the 21st of April, 1739, Johnson received for this work £49 7s, in sums of one, two, three, and sometimes four guineas at a time, most frequently two. And it is curious to observe the minute and scrupulous accuracy with which Johnson has pasted upon it a slip of paper, which he has entitled 'Small Account,' and which contains one article, 'Sept. 9th, Mr. Cave laid down 2s. 6d.' There is subjoined to this account, a list of some subscribers to the work, partly in Johnson's hand-writing, partly in that of another person; and there follows a leaf or two on which are written a number of characters which have the appearance of a short hand, which, perhaps, Johnson was then trying to learn.

In 1739, beside the assistance which he gave to the Parliamentary Debates, his writings in the Gentleman's Magazine were, 'The Life of Boerhaave,' in which it is to be observed, that he discovers that love of chymistry which never forsook him; 'An Appeal to the publick in behalf of the Editor;' 'An Address to the Reader;' 'An Epigram both in Greek and Latin to Eliza,' and also English verses to her; and 'A Greek Epigram to Dr. Birch.' His separate publications were, 'A Complete Vindication of the Licensers of the Stage, from the malicious and scandalous Aspersions of Mr. Brooke, Authour of Gustavus Vasa,' being an ironical Attack upon them for their Suppression of that Tragedy; and, 'Marmor Norfolciense; or an Essay on an ancient prophetical Inscription in monkish Rhyme, lately discovered near Lynne in Norfolk, by *Probus Britannicus.*' In this performance, he, in a feigned inscription, supposed to have been found in Norfolk, the county of Sir Robert Walpole, then the obnoxious prime minister of this country, inveighs against the Brunswick succession, and the measures of government consequent upon it. To this supposed prophecy he added a Commentary, making each expression apply to the times, with warm Anti-Hanoverian zeal.

This anonymous pamphlet, I believe, did not make so much noise as was expected, and, therefore, had not a very extensive circulation. Sir John Hawkins relates, that 'warrants were issued, and messengers employed to apprehend the authour; who, though he had forborne to subscribe his name to the pamphlet, the vigilance of those in pursuit of him had discovered;' and we are informed, that he lay concealed in Lambeth-marsh till the scent after him grew cold. This, however, is altogether without foundation; for Mr. Steele, one of the Secretaries of the Treasury, who, amidst a variety of important business, politely obliged me with his attention to my inquiry, informs me, that 'he directed every possible search to be made in the records of the Treasury and Secretary of State's Office, but could find no trace whatever of any warrant having been issued to apprehend the authour of this pamphlet.'

As Mr. Pope's note concerning Johnson, alluded to in a former page, refers both to his 'London,' and his 'Marmor Norfolciense,' I have deferred inserting it till now. I have transcribed it with minute exactness, that the peculiar mode of writing, and imperfect spelling of that celebrated poet, may be exhibited to the curious in literature. It justifies Swift's epithet of 'paper-sparing Pope,' for it is written on a slip no larger than a common message-card, and was sent to Mr. Richardson, along with the Imitation of Juvenal.

'This is imitated by one Johnson who put in for a Publick
School in Shropshire, but was Disappointed. He has an Infirmity
of the convulsive kind, that attacks him sometimes, so as to make
Him a sad Spectacle. Mr. P. from the Merit of This Work which
was all the knowledge he had of Him endeavour'd to serve Him
without his own application; & wrote to my L^d gore, but he did not
succeed. Mr. Johnson published afterw^ds. another Poem in Latin
with Notes the whole very Humerous call'd the Norfolk Prophecy.'

'P.'

Johnson had been told of this note; and Sir Joshua Reynolds informed him of the compliment which it contained, but,
from delicacy, avoided shewing him the paper itself. When Sir
Joshua observed to Johnson that he seemed very desirous to
see Pope's note, he answered, 'Who would not be proud to have
such a man as Pope so solicitous in inquiring about him?'

The infirmity to which Mr. Pope alludes, appeared to me
also, as I have elsewhere observed, to be of the convulsive kind,
and of the nature of that distemper called St. Vitus's dance;
and in this opinion I am confirmed by the description which
Sydenham gives of that disease. 'This disorder is a kind of convulsion. It manifests itself by halting or unsteadiness of one of
the legs, which the patient draws after him like an ideot. If
the hand of the same side be applied to the breast, or any other
part of the body, he cannot keep it a moment in the same posture, but it will be drawn into a different one by a convulsion, notwithstanding all his efforts to the contrary.' Sir Joshua
Reynolds, however, was of a different opinion, and favoured
me with the following paper.

'Those motions or tricks of Dr. Johnson are improperly called
convulsions. He could sit motionless, when he was told so to do, as
well as any other man; my opinion is, that it proceeded from a
habit which he had indulged himself in, of accompanying his
thoughts with certain untoward actions, and those actions always
appeared to me as if they were meant to reprobate some part of his
past conduct. Whenever he was not engaged in conversation, such
thoughts were sure to rush into his mind; and, for this reason, any
company, any employment whatever, he preferred to being alone.
The great business of his life (he said) was to escape from himself;
this disposition he considered as the disease of his mind, which
nothing cured but company.

'One instance of his absence and particularity, as it is character-istick of the man, may be worth relating. When he and I took a journey together into the West, we visited the late Mr. Banks, of Dorsetshire; the conversation turning upon pictures, which Johnson could not well see, he retired to a corner of the room, stretching out his right leg as far as he could reach before him, then bringing up his left leg, and stretching his right still further on. The old gentle-man observing him, went up to him, and in a very courteous man-ner assured him, that though it was not a new house, the flooring was perfectly safe. The Doctor started from his reverie, like a per-son waked out of his sleep, but spoke not a word.'

While we are on this subject, my readers may not be dis-pleased with another anecdote, communicated to me by the same friend, from the relation of Mr. Hogarth.

Johnson used to be a pretty frequent visiter at the house of Mr. Richardson, authour of Clarissa, and other novels of ex-tensive reputation. Mr. Hogarth came one day to see Richard-son, soon after the execution of Dr. Cameron, for having taken arms for the house of Stuart in 1745-6; and being a warm par-tisan of George the Second, he observed to Richardson, that certainly there must have been some very unfavourable cir-cumstances lately discovered in this particular case, which had induced the King to approve of an execution for rebellion so long after the time when it was committed, as this had the ap-pearance of putting a man to death in cold blood, and was very unlike his Majesty's usual clemency. While he was talking, he perceived a person standing at a window in the room, shaking his head, and rolling himself about in a strange ridiculous man-ner. He concluded that he was an ideot, whom his relations had put under the care of Mr. Richardson, as a very good man. To his great surprize, however, this figure stalked forwards to where he and Mr. Richardson were sitting, and all at once took up the argument, and burst out into an invective against George the Second, as one, who, upon all occasions, was un-relenting and barbarous; mentioning many instances, particu-larly, that when an officer of high rank had been acquitted by a Court Martial, George the Second had, with his own hand, struck his name off the list. In short, he displayed such a power of eloquence, that Hogarth looked at him with astonishment,

an I actually imagined that this ideot had been at the moment
inspired. Neither Hogarth nor Johnson were made known to
each other at this interview.

1740: ÆTAT. 31.]—In 1740 he wrote for the Gentleman's
Magazine the 'Preface,' 'Life of Sir Francis Drake,' and the
first parts of those of 'Admiral Blake,' and of 'Philip Baretier,'
both which he finished the following year. He also wrote an
'Essay on Epitaphs,' and an 'Epitaph on Philips, a Musician,'
which was afterwards published with some other pieces of his,
in Mrs. Williams's Miscellanies. This Epitaph is so exquisitely
beautiful, that I remember even Lord Kames, strangely prejudiced as he was against Dr. Johnson, was compelled to allow
it very high praise. It has been ascribed to Mr. Garrick, from
its appearing at first with the signature G; but I have heard
Mr. Garrick declare, that it was written by Dr. Johnson, and
give the following account of the manner in which it was composed. Johnson and he were sitting together; when, amongst
other things, Garrick repeated an Epitaph upon this Philips by
a Dr. Wilkes, in these words:

> 'Exalted soul! whose harmony could please
> The love-sick virgin, and the gouty ease;
> Could jarring discord, like Amphion, move
> To beauteous order and harmonious love;
> Rest here in peace, till angels bid thee rise,
> And meet thy blessed Saviour in the skies.'

Johnson shook his head at these common-place funereal
lines, and said to Garrick, 'I think, Davy, I can make a better.'
Then, stirring about his tea for a little while, in a state of meditation, he almost extempore produced the following verses:

> 'Philips, whose touch harmonious could remove
> The pangs of guilty power or hapless love;
> Rest here, distress'd by poverty no more,
> Here find that calm thou gav'st so oft before;
> Sleep, undisturb'd, within this peaceful shrine,
> Till angels wake thee with a note like thine!'

He this year, and the two following, wrote the Parliamentary Debates. He told me himself, that he was the sole com-
poser of them for those three years only. He was not, however,

precisely exact in his statement, which he mentioned from hasty recollection; for it is sufficiently evident, that his composition of them began November 19, 1740, and ended February 23, 1742-3.

It appears from some of Cave's letters to Dr. Birch, that Cave had better assistance for that branch of his Magazine, than has been generally supposed; and that he was indefatigable in getting it made as perfect as he could.

Johnson told me, that as soon as he found that the speeches were thought genuine, he determined that he would write no more of them; for 'he would not be accessary to the propagation of falsehood.' And such was the tenderness of his conscience, that a short time before his death he expressed a regret for his having been the authour of fictions, which had passed for realities.

He nevertheless agreed with me in thinking, that the debates which he had framed were to be valued as orations upon questions of publick importance. They have accordingly been collected in volumes, properly arranged, and recommended to the notice of parliamentary speakers by a preface, written by no inferior hand. I must, however, observe, that although there is in those debates a wonderful store of political information, and very powerful eloquence, I cannot agree that they exhibit the manner of each particular speaker, as Sir John Hawkins seems to think. But, indeed, what opinion can we have of his judgement, and taste in publick speaking, who presumes to give, as the characteristicks of two celebrated orators, 'the deepmouthed rancour of Pulteney, and the yelping pertinacity of Pitt.'

1742: ÆTAT. 33.]—In 1742 he wrote for the Gentleman's Magazine the 'Proposals for printing Bibliotheca Harleiana, or a Catalogue of the Library of the Earl of Oxford.' His account of that celebrated collection of books, in which he displays the importance to literature, of what the French call a *catalogue raisonné*, when the subjects of it are extensive and various, and it is executed with ability, cannot fail to impress all his readers with admiration of his philological attainments. It was afterwards prefixed to the first volume of the Catalogue, in which the Latin accounts of books were written by him. He was employed in this business by Mr. Thomas Osborne the bookseller, who purchased the library for 13,000*l*., a sum, which Mr. Oldys says, in one of his manuscripts, was not more than the binding of the books had cost; yet, as Dr. Johnson assured me, the slowness of the sale was such, that there was not much gained by it. It has been confidently related, with many embellishments, that Johnson one day knocked Osborne down in his shop, with a folio, and put his foot upon his neck. The simple truth I had from Johnson himself. 'Sir, he was impertinent to me, and I beat him. But it was not in his shop: it was in my own chamber.'

I have no doubt that he wrote the little abridgement entitled 'Foreign History,' in the Magazine for December. To prove it, I shall quote the Introduction. 'As this is that season of the year in which Nature may be said to command a suspension of hostilities, and which seems intended, by putting a short stop to violence and slaughter, to afford time for malice to relent, and animosity to subside; we can scarce expect any other accounts than of plans, negociations and treaties, of proposals for peace, and preparations for war.' As also this passage: 'Let those who despise the capacity of the Swiss, tell us by what wonderful policy, or by what happy conciliation of interests, it is brought to pass, that in a body made up of different communities and different religions, there should be no civil commotions, though the people are so warlike, that to nominate and raise an army is the same.'

1743: ÆTAT. 34.]—Johnson had now an opportunity of obliging his schoolfellow Dr. James, of whom he once observed, 'no man brings more mind to his profession.' James published this year his 'Medicinal Dictionary,' in three volumes folio. Johnson, as I understood from him, had written, or assisted in writing, the proposals for this work; and being very fond of the study of physick, in which James was his master, he furnished some of the articles. He, however, certainly wrote for it the Dedication to Dr. Mead, which is conceived with great address, to conciliate the patronage of that very eminent man.

It has been circulated, I know not with what authenticity, that Johnson considered Dr. Birch as a dull writer, and said of him, 'Tom Birch is as brisk as a bee in conversation; but no

sooner does he take a pen in his hand, than it becomes a tor-
pedo to him, and benumbs all his faculties.' That the literature
of this country is much indebted to Birch's activity and diligence must certainly be acknowledged. We have seen that
Johnson honoured him with a Greek Epigram; and his correspondence with him, during many years, proves that he had
no mean opinion of him.

His circumstances were at this time much embarrassed; yet
his affection for his mother was so warm, and so liberal, that
he took upon himself a debt of hers, which, though small in
itself, was then considerable to him. This appears from the following letter which he wrote to Mr. Levett, of Lichfield, the
original of which lies now before me.

'To Mr. Levett; in Lichfield.

                                          'December 1, 1743.
'Sir,
    'I am extremely sorry that we have encroached so much upon
your forbearance with respect to the interest, which a great perplexity of affairs hindered me from thinking of with that attention
that I ought, and which I am not immediately able to remit to you,
but will pay it (I think twelve pounds,) in two months. I look
upon this, and on the future interest of that mortgage, as my own
debt; and beg that you will be pleased to give me directions how to
pay it, and not mention it to my dear mother. If it be necessary to
pay this in less time, I believe I can do it; but I take two months for
certainty, and beg an answer whether you can allow me so much
time. I think myself very much obliged to your forbearance, and
shall esteem it a great happiness to be able to serve you. I have
great opportunities of dispersing any thing that you may think it
proper to make publick. I will give a note for the money, payable
at the time mentioned, to any one here that you shall appoint. I
am, Sir,

                        'Your most obedient
                        'And most humble servant,
                                          'Sam. Johnson.
                    'At Mr. Osborne's, bookseller, in Gray's Inn.'

1744: ÆTAT. 35.]—It does not appear that he wrote any
thing in 1744 for the Gentleman's Magazine, but the Preface.
But he produced one work this year, fully sufficient to main-

tain the high reputation which he had acquired. This was
'The Life of Richard Savage;' a man, of whom it is difficult
to speak impartially, without wondering that he was for some
time the intimate companion of Johnscn; for his character was
marked by profligacy, insolence, and ingratitude: yet, as he
undoubtedly had a warm and vigorous, though unregulated
mind, had seen life in all its varieties, and been much in the
company of the statesmen and wits of his time, he could communicate to Johnson an abundant supply of such materials as
his philosophical curiosity most eagerly desired; and as Savage's misfortunes and misconduct had reduced him to the lowest state of wretchedness as a writer for bread, his visits to St.
John's Gate naturally brought Johnson and him together.

It is melancholy to reflect, that Johnson and Savage were
sometimes in such extreme indigence, that they could not pay
for a lodging; so that they have wandered together whole
nights in the streets. Yet in these almost incredible scenes of
distress, we may suppose that Savage mentioned many of the
anecdotes with which Johnson afterwards enriched the life
of his unhappy companion, and those of other Poets.

He told Sir Joshua Reynolds, that one night in particular,
when Savage and he walked round St. James's-square for want
of a lodging, they were not at all depressed by their situation;
but in high spirits and brimful of patriotism, traversed the
square for several hours, inveighed against the minister, and
'resolved they would *stand by their country.*'

That Johnson was anxious that an authentick and favourable account of his extraordinary friend should first get possession of the publick attention, is evident from a letter which he
wrote in the Gentleman's Magazine for August of the year preceding its publication.

'MR. URBAN,
    'As your collections show how often you have owed the orna-
ments of your poetical pages to the correspondence of the unfortunate and ingenious Mr. Savage, I doubt not but you have so
much regard to his memory as to encourage any design that may
have a tendency to the preservation of it from insults or calumnies;
and therefore, with some degree of assurance, intreat you to inform
the publick, that his life will speed:ly be published by a person who

was favoured with his confidence, and received from himself an account of most of the transactions which he proposes to mention, to the time of his retirement to Swansea in Wales.

'From that period, to his death in the prison of Bristol, the account will be continued from materials still less liable to objection; his own letters, and those of his friends, some of which will be inserted in the work, and abstracts of others subjoined in the margin.

'It may be reasonably imagined, that others may have the same design; but as it is not credible that they can obtain the same materials, it must be expected they will supply from invention the want of intelligence; and that under the title of "The Life of Savage," they will publish only a novel, filled with romantick adventures, and imaginary amours. You may therefore, perhaps, gratify the lovers of truth and wit, by giving me leave to inform them in your Magazine, that my account will be published in 8vo. by Mr. Roberts, in Warwick-lane.'

[No signature.]

In February, 1744, it accordingly came forth from the shop of Roberts, between whom and Johnson I have not traced any connection, except the casual one of this publication. In Johnson's 'Life of Savage,' a very useful lesson is inculcated, to guard men of warm passions from a too free indulgence of them; and the various incidents are related in so clear and animated a manner, and illuminated throughout with so much philosophy, that it is one of the most interesting narratives in the English language. Sir Joshua Reynolds told me, that upon his return from Italy he met with it in Devonshire, knowing nothing of its authour, and began to read it while he was standing with his arm leaning against a chimney-piece. It seized his attention so strongly, that, not being able to lay down the book till he had finished it, when he attempted to move, he found his arm totally benumbed. The rapidity with which this work was composed, is a wonderful circumstance. Johnson has been heard to say, 'I wrote forty-eight of the printed octavo pages of the Life of Savage at a sitting; but then I sat up all night.'

It is remarkable, that in this biographical disquisition there appears a very strong symptom of Johnson's prejudice against players; a prejudice, which may be attributed to the following causes: first, the imperfection of his organs, which were so defective that he was not susceptible of the fine impressions which theatrical excellence produces upon the generality of mankind; secondly, the cold rejection of his tragedy; and, lastly, the brilliant success of Garrick, who had been his pupil, who had come to London at the same time with him, not in a much more prosperous state than himself, and whose talents he undoubtedly rated low, compared with his own. His being outstripped by his pupil in the race of immediate fame, as well as of fortune, probably made him feel some indignation, as thinking that whatever might be Garrick's merits in his art, the reward was too great when compared with what the most successful efforts of literary labour could attain. At all periods of his life Johnson used to talk contemptuously of players; but in this work he speaks of them with peculiar acrimony; for which, perhaps, there was formerly too much reason from the licentious and dissolute manners of those engaged in that profession.

His schoolfellow and friend, Dr. Taylor, told me a pleasant anecdote of Johnson's triumphing over his pupil David Garrick. When that great actor had played some little time at Goodman's-fields, Johnson and Taylor went to see him perform, and afterwards passed the evening at a tavern with him and old Giffard. Johnson, who was ever depreciating stage-players, after censuring some mistakes in emphasis which Garrick had committed in the course of that night's acting, said, 'the players, Sir, have got a kind of rant, with which they run on, without any regard either to accent or emphasis.' Both Garrick and Giffard were offended at this sarcasm, and endeavoured to refute it; upon which Johnson rejoined, 'Well now, I'll give you something to speak, with which you are little acquainted, and then we shall see how just my observation is That shall be the criterion. Let me hear you repeat the ninth Commandment, "Thou shalt not bear false witness against thy neighbour."' Both tried at it, said Dr. Taylor, and both mistook the emphasis, which should be upon *not* and *false witness*. Johnson put them right, and enjoyed his victory with great glee.

Johnson's partiality for Savage made him entertain no doubt of his story, however extraordinary and improbable. It never occurred to him to question his being the son of the Countess of Macclesfield, of whose unrelenting barbarity he so loudly complained, and the particulars of which are related in so strong and affecting a manner in Johnson's life of him. Johnson was certainly well warranted in publishing his narrative, however offensive it might be to the lady and her relations, because her alledged unnatural and cruel conduct to her son, and shameful avowal of guilt, were stated in a life of Savage now lying before me, which came out so early as 1727, and no attempt had been made to confute it, or to punish the authour or printer as a libeller: but, for the honour of human nature, we should be glad to find the shocking tale not true; and, from a respectable gentleman connected with the lady's family, I have received such information and remarks, as joined to my own inquiries, will, I think, render it at least somewhat doubtful, especially when we consider that it must have originated from the person himself who went by the name of Richard Savage.[1]

If the maxim *falsum in uno, falsum in omnibus,* were to be received without qualification, the credit of Savage's narrative, as conveyed to us, would be annihilated; for it contains some assertions which, beyond a question, are not true.

In 1745 he published a pamphlet entitled 'Miscellaneous Observations on the Tragedy of Macbeth, with Remarks on Sir T. H.'s (Sir Thomas Hanmer's) Edition of Shakspeare.' To which he affixed proposals for a new edition of that poet.

As we do not trace any thing else published by him during the course of this year, we may conjecture that he was occupied entirely with that work. But the little encouragement which was given by the publick to his anonymous proposals for the execution of a task which Warburton was known to have undertaken, probably damped his ardour.

1746: ÆTAT. 37.]—In 1746 it is probable that he was still employed upon his Shakspeare, which perhaps he laid aside for a time, upon account of the high expectations which were

[1] Richard Savage (1697?-1743) claimed to be the illegitimate son of Richard Savage, fourth Earl Rivers, and insisted that he was deprived of an inheritance and otherwise persecuted by his mother, the Countess of Macclesfield. No very widespread credence was ever given to his claims, which are now generally believed to have been false.

formed of Warburton's edition of that great poet. It is some-what curious, that his literary career appears to have been al-most totally suspended in the years 1745 and 1746, those years which were marked by a civil war in Great-Britain, when a rash attempt was made to restore the House of Stuart to the throne. That he had a tenderness for that unfortunate House, is well known; and some may fancifully imagine, that a sympathetick anxiety impeded the exertion of his intellectual powers: but I am inclined to think, that he was, during this time, sketching the outlines of his great philological work.

1747: ÆTAT. 38.]—In 1747 it is supposed that the Gentle-man's Magazine for May was enriched by him with five short poetical pieces, distinguished by three asterisks.

This year his old pupil and friend, David Garrick, hav-ing become joint patentee and manager of Drury-lane theatre, Johnson honoured his opening of it with a Prologue, which for just and manly dramatick criticism, on the whole range of the English stage, as well as for poetical excellence, is unri-valled.

But the year 1747 is distinguished as the epoch, when John-son's arduous and important work, his *Dictionary of the Eng-lish Language,* was announced to the world, by the publication of its Plan or *Prospectus.*

How long this immense undertaking had been the object of his contemplation, I do not know. I once asked him by what means he had attained to that astonishing knowledge of our language, by which he was enabled to realise a design of such extent, and accumulated difficulty. He told me, that 'it was not the effect of particular study; but that it had grown up in his mind insensibly.' I have been informed by Mr. James Dodsley, that several years before this period, when Johnson was one day sitting in his brother Robert's shop, he heard his brother suggest to him, that a Dictionary of the English Language would be a work that would be well received by the publick; that Johnson seemed at first to catch at the proposition, but, after a pause, said, in his abrupt decisive manner, 'I believe I shall not undertake it.' That he, however, had bestowed much thought upon the subject, before he published his 'Plan,' is evident from the enlarged, clear, and accurate views which it exhibits; and we find him mentioning in that tract, that many of the writers whose testimonies were to be produced as authorities, were selected by Pope; which proves that he had been furnished, probably by Mr. Robert Dodsley, with whatever hints that eminent poet had contributed towards a great literary project, that had been the subject of important consideration in a former reign.

The booksellers who contracted with Johnson, single and unaided, for the execution of a work, which in other countries has not been effected but by the co-operating exertions of many, were Mr. Robert Dodsley, Mr. Charles Hitch, Mr. Andrew Millar, the two Messieurs Longman, and the two Messieurs Knapton. The price stipulated was fifteen hundred and seventy-five pounds.

The 'Plan' was addressed to Philip Dormer, Earl of Chesterfield, then one of his Majesty's Principal Secretaries of State; a nobleman who was very ambitious of literary distinction, and who, upon being informed of the design, had expressed himself in terms very favourable to its success. There is, perhaps, in every thing of any consequence, a secret history which it would be amusing to know, could we have it authentically communicated. Johnson told me, 'Sir, the way in which the Plan of my Dictionary came to be inscribed to Lord Chesterfield, was this: I had neglected to write it by the time appointed. Dodsley suggested a desire to have it addressed to Lord Chesterfield. I laid hold of this as a pretext for delay, that it might be better done, and let Dodsley have his desire. I said to my friend, Dr. Bathurst, "Now if any good comes of my addressing to Lord Chesterfield, it will be ascribed to deep policy, when, in fact, it was only a casual excuse for laziness."'

It is worthy of observation, that the 'Plan' has not only the substantial merit of comprehension, perspicuity, and precision, but that the language of it is unexceptionably excellent; it being altogether free from that inflation of style, and those uncommon but apt and energetick words, which in some of his writings have been censured, with more petulance than justice; and never was there a more dignified strain of compliment, than that in which he courts the attention of one who, he had been persuaded to believe, would be a respectable patron.

'With regard to questions of purity or propriety, (says he) I was once in doubt whether I should not attribute to myself too much in attempting to decide them, and whether my province was to extend beyond the proposition of the question, and the display of the suffrages on each side; but I have been since determined by your Lordship's opinion, to interpose my own judgement, and shall therefore endeavour to support what appears to me most consonant to grammar and reason. And I may hope, my Lord, that since you, whose authority in our language is so generally acknowledged, have commissioned me to declare my own opinion, I shall be considered as exercising a kind of vicarious jurisdiction, and that the power which might have been denied to my own claim, will be readily allowed me as the delegate of your Lordship.'

This passage proves, that Johnson's addressing his 'Plan' to Lord Chesterfield was not merely in consequence of the result of a report by means of Dodsley, that the Earl favoured the design; but that there had been a particular communication with his Lordship concerning it. Dr. Taylor told me, that Johnson sent his 'Plan' to him in manuscript, for his perusal; and that when it was lying upon his table, Mr. William Whitehead happened to pay him a visit, and being shewn it, was highly pleased with such parts of it as he had time to read, and begged to take it home with him, which he was allowed to do; that from him it got into the hands of a noble Lord, who carried it to Lord Chesterfield. When Taylor observed this might be an advantage, Johnson replied, 'No, Sir; it would have come out with more bloom, if it had not been seen before by any body.'

That he was fully aware of the arduous nature of the undertaking, he acknowledges; and shews himself perfectly sensible of it in the conclusion of his 'Plan;' but he had a noble consciousness of his own abilities, which enabled him to go on with undaunted spirit.

Dr. Adams found him one day busy at his Dictionary, when the following dialogue ensued. '*Adams.* This is a great work, Sir. How are you to get all the etymologies? *Johnson.* Why, Sir, here is a shelf with Junius, and Skinner, and others; and there is a Welch gentleman who has published a collection of Welch proverbs, who will help me with the Welch. *Adams.* But, Sir, how can you do this in three years? *Johnson.* Sir, I have no doubt that I can do it in three years. *Adams.* But the

French Academy, which consists of forty members, took forty years to compile their Dictionary. *Johnson.* Sir, thus it is. This is the proportion. Let me see; forty times forty is sixteen hundred. As three to sixteen hundred, so is the proportion of an Englishman to a Frenchman.' With so much ease and pleasantry could he talk of that prodigious labour which he had undertaken to execute.

While the Dictionary was going forward, Johnson lived part of the time in Holborn, part in Gough-square, Fleet-street; and he had an upper room fitted up like a counting-house for the purpose, in which he gave to the copyists their several tasks. The words, partly taken from other dictionaries, and partly supplied by himself, having been first written down with spaces left between them, he delivered in writing their etymologies, definitions, and various significations. The authorities were copied from the books themselves, in which he had marked the passages with a black-lead pencil, the traces of which could easily be effaced. It is remarkable, that he was so attentive in the choice of the passages in which words were authorised, that one may read page after page of his Dictionary with improvement and pleasure; and it should not pass unobserved, that he has quoted no authour whose writings had a tendency to hurt sound religion and morality.

The necessary expence of preparing a work of such magnitude for the press, must have been a considerable deduction from the price stipulated to be paid for the copy-right. I understand that nothing was allowed by the booksellers on that account; and I remember his telling me, that a large portion of it having, by mistake, been written upon both sides of the paper, so as to be inconvenient for the compositor, it cost him twenty pounds to have it transcribed upon one side only.

He is now to be considered as 'tugging at his oar,' as engaged in a steady continued course of occupation, sufficient to employ all his time for some years; and which was the best preventive of that constitutional melancholy which was ever lurking about him, ready to trouble his quiet. But his enlarged and lively mind could not be satisfied without more diversity of employment, and the pleasure of animated relaxation. He therefore not only exerted his talents in occasional composition

very different from Lexicography, but formed a club in Ivy-
lane, Paternoster-row, with a view to enjoy literary discussion,
and amuse his evening hours. The members associated with
him in this little society were his beloved friend Dr. Richard Bathurst, Mr. Hawkesworth, afterwards well known by his
writings, Mr. John Hawkins, an attorney, and a few others of
different professions.

1749: ÆTAT. 40.]—In January, 1749, he published 'The
Vanity of Human Wishes, being the Tenth Satire of Juvenal
imitated.' Mrs. Johnson, for the sake of country air, had lodgings at Hampstead, to which he resorted occasionally, and
there the greatest part, if not the whole, of this Imitation was
written. The fervid rapidity with which it was produced, is
scarcely credible. I have heard him say, that he composed seventy lines of it in one day, without putting one of them upon
paper till they were finished[1].

The profits of a single poem, however excellent, appear to
have been very small in the last reign, compared with what
a publication of the same size has since been known to yield.
I have mentioned, upon Johnson's own authority, that for his
London he had only ten guineas; and now, after his fame was
established, he got for his 'Vanity of Human Wishes' but five
guineas more, as is proved by an authentick document in my
possession.

His 'Vanity of Human Wishes' has less of common life, but
more of a philosophick dignity than his 'London.' More readers, therefore, will be delighted with the pointed spirit of
'London,' than with the profound reflection of 'The Vanity
of Human Wishes.' Garrick, for instance, observed in his
sprightly manner, with more vivacity than regard to just discrimination, as is usual with wits, 'When Johnson lived much
with the Herveys, and saw a good deal of what was passing in
life, he wrote his "London," which is lively and easy. When
he became more retired, he gave us his "Vanity of Human
Wishes," which is as hard as Greek. Had he gone on to imitate
another satire, it would have been as hard as Hebrew.'

Garrick being now vested with theatrical power by being

[1] Johnson wrote most of his compositions this way. Perhaps it was
due to his poor eyesight.

manager of Drury-lane theatre, he kindly and generously made use of it to bring out Johnson's tragedy, which had been long kept back for want of encouragement. But in this benevolent purpose he met with no small difficulty from the temper of Johnson, which could not brook that a drama which he had formed with much study, should be revised and altered at the pleasure of an actor. Johnson was at first very obstinate. 'Sir, (said he) the fellow wants me to make Mahomet run mad, that he may have an opportunity of tossing his hands and kicking his heels.' He was, however, at last, with difficulty, prevailed on to comply with Garrick's wishes, so as to allow of some changes; but still there were not enough.

Dr. Adams was present the first night of the representation of *Irene,* and gave me the following account: 'Before the curtain drew up, there were catcalls whistling, which alarmed Johnson's friends. The Prologue, which was written by himself in a manly strain, soothed the audience, and the play went off tolerably, till it came to the conclusion, when Mrs. Pritchard, the heroine of the piece, was to be strangled upon the stage, and was to speak two lines with the bow-string round her neck. The audience cried out *"Murder! Murder!"* She several times attempted to speak; but in vain. At last she was obliged to go off the stage alive.' This passage was afterwards struck out, and she was carried off to be put to death behind the scenes, as the play now has it.

Notwithstanding all the support of such performers as Garrick, Barry, Mrs. Cibber, Mrs. Pritchard, and every advantage of dress and decoration, the tragedy of Irene did not please the publick. Mr. Garrick's zeal carried it through for nine nights, so that the authour had his three nights' profits; and from a receipt signed by him, now in the hands of Mr. James Dodsley, it appears that his friend Mr. Robert Dodsley gave him one hundred pounds for the copy, with his usual reservation of the right of one edition.

Johnson was wise enough to be convinced that he had not the talents necessary to write successfully for the stage, and never made another attempt in that species of composition. And let it be remembered, as an admonition to the *genus irri-*

tabile[1] of dramatick writers, that this great man, instead of peevishly complaining of the bad taste of the town, submitted to its decision without a murmur. He had, indeed, upon all occasions, a great deference for the general opinion: 'A man (said he) who writes a book, thinks himself wiser or wittier than the rest of mankind; he supposes that he can instruct or amuse them, and the publick to whom he appeals, must, after all, be the judges of his pretensions.'

On occasion of his play being brought upon the stage, Johnson had a fancy that as a dramatick authour his dress should be more gay than what he ordinarily wore; he therefore appeared behind the scenes, and even in one of the side boxes, in a scarlet waistcoat, with rich gold lace, and a gold-laced hat. He humourously observed to Mr. Langton, 'that when in that dress he could not treat people with the same ease as when in his usual plain clothes.' His necessary attendance while his play was in rehearsal, and during its performance, brought him acquainted with many of the performers of both sexes, which produced a more favourable opinion of their profession than he had harshly expressed in his Life of Savage. With some of them he kept up an acquaintance as long as he and they lived, and was ever ready to shew them acts of kindness. He for a considerable time used to frequent the *Green Room,* and seemed to take delight in dissipating his gloom, by mixing in the sprightly chit-chat of the motley circle then to be found there. Mr. David Hume related to me from Mr. Garrick, that Johnson at last denied himself this amusement, from considerations of rigid virtue; saying, 'I'll come no more behind your scenes, David; for the silk stockings and white bosoms of your actresses excite my amorous propensities.'

1750: ÆTAT. 41.]—[In 1750 he came forth in the character for which he was eminently qualified, a majestick teacher of moral and religious wisdom] The vehicle which he chose was that of a periodical paper, which he knew had been, upon former occasions, employed with great success. Johnson was, I think, not very happy in the choice of his title, 'The Rambler.' He gave Sir Joshua Reynolds the following account of its get-

---

[1] The irritable race. The phrase is from Horace.

ting this name: 'What *must* be done, Sir, *will* be done. When
I was to begin publishing that paper, I was at a loss how to
name it. I sat down at night upon my bedside, and resolved
that I would not go to sleep till I had fixed its title. The Rambler seemed the best that occurred, and I took it.'

The first paper of the Rambler was published on Tuesday
the 20th of March, 1750; and its authour was enabled to continue it, without interruption, every Tuesday and Friday, till
Saturday the 17th of March, 1752, on which day it closed.
This is a strong confirmation of the truth of a remark of his,
which I have had occasion to quote elsewhere, that 'a man may
write at any time, if he will set himself doggedly to it;' for, notwithstanding his constitutional indolence, his depression of
spirits, and his labour in carrying on his Dictionary, he answered the stated calls of the press twice a week from the stores
of his mind, during all that time; having received no assistance,
except four billets in No. 10, by Miss Mulso, now Mrs. Cha-
pone; No. 30, by Mrs. Catharine Talbot; No. 97, by Mr. Samuel Richardson, whom he describes in an introductory note as
'An author who has enlarged the knowledge of human nature,
and taught the passions to move at the command of virtue;' and
Numbers 44 and 100, by Mrs. Elizabeth Carter.

Posterity will be astonished when they are told, upon the
authority of Johnson himself, that many of these discourses,
which we should suppose had been laboured with all the slow
attention of literary leisure, were written in haste as the moment pressed, without even being read over by him before they
were printed. Sir Joshua Reynolds once asked him by what
means he had attained his extraordinary accuracy and flow of
language. He told him, that he had early laid it down as a fixed
rule to do his best on every occasion, and in every company; to
impart whatever he knew in the most forcible language he
could put it in; and that by constant practice, and never suffering any careless expressions to escape him, or attempting to
deliver his thoughts without arranging them in the clearest
manner, it became habitual to him.

As the Rambler was entirely the work of one man, there was,
of course, such a uniformity in its texture, as very much to exclude the charm of variety; and the grave and often solemn

cast of thinking, which distinguished it from other periodical papers, made it, for some time, not generally liked. So slowly did this excellent work, of which twelve editions have now issued from the press, gain upon the world at large, that even in the closing number the authour says, 'I have never been much a favourite of the publick.' Yet, very soon after its commencement, there were who felt and acknowledged its uncommon excellence. Verses in its praise appeared in the newspapers; and the editor of the Gentleman's Magazine mentions, in October, his having received several letters to the same purpose from the learned.

Johnson told me, with an amiable fondness, a little pleasing circumstance relative to this work. Mrs. Johnson, in whose judgement and taste he had great confidence, said to him, after a few numbers of the Rambler had come out, 'I thought very well of you before; but I did not imagine you could have written any thing equal to this.'

The Rambler has increased in fame as in age. Soon after its first folio edition was concluded, it was published in six duodecimo volumes; and its authour lived to see ten numerous editions of it in London, beside those of Ireland and Scotland.

[I profess myself to have ever entertained a profound veneration for the astonishing force and vivacity of mind, which the Rambler exhibits.] That Johnson had penetration enough to see, and seeing would not disguise the general misery of man in this state of being, may have given rise to the superficial notion of his being too stern a philosopher. But men of reflection will be sensible that he has given a true representation of human existence, and that he has, at the same time, with a generous benevolence, displayed every consolation which our state affords us; not only those arising from the hopes of futurity, but such as may be attained in the immediate progress through life. He has not depressed the soul to despondency and indifference. He has every where inculcated study, labour, and exertion. Nay, he has shewn, in a very odious light, a man whose practice is to go about darkening the views of others, by perpetual complaints of evil, and awakening those considerations of danger and distress, which are, for the most part, lulled into a quiet oblivion. This he has done very strongly in his character of Suspirius, from which Goldsmith took that of Croaker, in his comedy of 'The Good-natured Man,' as Johnson told me he acknowledged to him, and which is, indeed, very obvious.

I will venture to say, that in no writings whatever can be found *more bark and steel for the mind,* if I may use the expression; more that can brace and invigorate every manly and noble sentiment. I never read the following sentence without feeling my frame thrill: 'I think there is some reason for questioning whether the body and mind are not so proportioned, that the one can bear all which can be inflicted on the other; whether virtue cannot stand its ground as long as life, and whether a soul well principled will not be sooner separated than subdued.'

Though instruction be the predominant purpose of the Rambler, yet it is enlivened with a considerable portion of amusement. Nothing can be more erroneous than the notion which some persons have entertained, that Johnson was then a retired authour, ignorant of the world; and, of consequence, that he wrote only from his imagination when he described characters and manners. He said to me, that before he wrote that work, he had been 'running about the world,' as he expressed it, more than almost any body. Some of the characters are believed to have been actually drawn from the life, particularly that of Prospero from Garrick, who never entirely forgave its pointed satire.

The style of this work has been censured by some shallow criticks as involved and turgid, and abounding with antiquated and hard words. So ill-founded is the first part of this objection, that I will challenge all who may honour this book with a perusal, to point out any English writer whose language conveys his meaning with equal force and perspicuity. It must, indeed, be allowed, that the structure of his sentences is expanded, and often has somewhat of the inversion of Latin; and that he delighted to express familiar thoughts in philosophical language; being in this the reverse of Socrates, who, it was said, reduced philosophy to the simplicity of common life. But let us attend to what he himself says in his concluding paper: 'When common words were less pleasing to the ear, or less dis-

tinct in their signification, I have familiarised the terms of philosophy, by applying them to popular ideas.' And, as to the
second part of this objection, upon a late careful revision of the
work, I can with confidence say, that it is amazing how few of
those words, for which it has been unjustly characterised, are
actually to be found in it; I am sure, not the proportion of one
to each paper. This idle charge has been echoed from one bab-
bler to another, who have confounded Johnson's Essays with
Johnson's Dictionary; and because he thought it right in a
Lexicon of our language to collect many words which had
fallen into disuse, but were supported by great authorities, it
has been imagined that all of these have been interwoven into
his own compositions.

Sir Thomas Browne, whose life Johnson wrote, was remarkably fond of Anglo-Latin diction; and to his example we are
to ascribe Johnson's sometimes indulging himself in this kind
of phraseology. Johnson's comprehension of mind was the
mould for his language. Had his conceptions been narrower,
his expression would have been easier. His sentences have a
dignified march; and, it is certain, that his example has given
a general elevation to the language of his country, for many
of our best writers have approached very near to him; and,
from the influence which he has had upon our composition,
scarcely any thing is written now that is not better expressed
than was usual before he appeared to lead the national taste.

Johnson's language, however, must be allowed to be too
masculine for the delicate gentleness of female writing. His
ladies, therefore, seem strangely formal, even to ridicule; and
are well denominated by the names which he has given them,
as Misella, Zozima, Properantia, Rhodoclia.

It has of late been the fashion to compare the style of Addison and Johnson, and to depreciate, I think very unjustly, the
style of Addison as nerveless and feeble, because it has not the
strength and energy of that of Johnson. Their prose may be
balanced like the poetry of Dryden and Pope. Both are excellent, though in different ways. Addison writes with the ease
of a gentleman. His readers fancy that a wise and accomplished
companion is talking to them; so that he insinuates his sentiments and taste into their minds by an imperceptible influence.

Johnson writes like a teacher. He dictates to his readers as if from an academical chair. They attend with awe and admiration; and his precepts are impressed upon them by his commanding eloquence. Addison's style, like a light wine, pleases every body from the first. Johnson's, like a liquor of more body, seems too strong at first, but, by degrees, is highly relished; and such is the melody of his periods, so much do they captivate the ear, and seize upon the attention, that there is scarcely any writer, however inconsiderable, who does not aim, in some degree, at the same species of excellence. But let us not ungratefully undervalue that beautiful style, which has pleasingly conveyed to us much instruction and entertainment. Though comparatively weak, when opposed to Johnson's Herculean vigour, let us not call it positively feeble. Let us remember the character of his style, as given by Johnson himself: 'What he attempted, he performed; he is *never feeble*, and he did not wish to be energetick; he is never rapid, and he never stagnates. His sentences have neither studied amplitude, nor affected brevity: his periods, though not diligently rounded, are voluble and easy. Whoever wishes to attain an English style, familiar but not coarse, and elegant but not ostentatious, must give his days and nights to the volumes of Addison.'

His just abhorrence of Milton's political notions was ever strong. But this did not prevent his warm admiration of Milton's great poetical merit, to which he has done illustrious justice, beyond all who have written upon the subject. And this year he not only wrote a Prologue, which was spoken by Mr. Garrick before the acting of Comus at Drury-lane theatre, for the benefit of Milton's grand-daughter, but took a very zealous interest in the success of the charity.

1751: ÆTAT. 42.]—Though Johnson's circumstances were at this time far from being easy, his humane and charitable disposition was constantly exerting itself. Mrs. Anna Williams, daughter of a very ingenious Welsh physician, and a woman of more than ordinary talents and literature, having come to London in hopes of being cured of a cataract in both her eyes, which afterwards ended in total blindness, was kindly received as a constant visitor at his house while Mrs. Johnson lived; and after her death having come under his roof in order to have

an operation upon her eyes performed with more comfort to
her than in lodgings, she had an apartment from him during
the rest of her life, at all times when he had a house.

1752: ÆTAT. 43.]—In 1752 he was almost entirely occupied
with his Dictionary. The last paper of his Rambler was published March 2, this year; after which, there was a cessation
for some time of any exertion of his talents as an essayist.

That there should be a suspension of his literary labours
during a part of the year 1752, will not seem strange, when it
is considered that soon after closing his Rambler, he suffered
a loss which, there can be no doubt, affected him with the
deepest distress. For on the 17th of March, O.S. his wife died.
Why Sir John Hawkins should unwarrantably take upon him
even to *suppose* that Johnson's fondness for her was *dissem-
bled* (meaning simulated or assumed,) and to assert, that if
it was not the case, 'it was a lesson he had learned by rote,' I
cannot conceive; unless it proceeded from a want of similar
feelings in his own breast. To argue from her being much older
than Johnson, or any other circumstances, that he could not
really love her, is absurd; for love is not a subject of reasoning,
but of feeling, and therefore there are no common principles
upon which one can persuade another concerning it. Every
man feels for himself, and knows how he is affected by particular qualities in the person he admires, the impressions of which
are too minute and delicate to be substantiated in language.

That his love for his wife was of the most ardent kind, and,
during the long period of fifty years, was unimpaired by the
lapse of time, is evident from various passages in the series of
his Prayers and Meditations, published by the Reverend Mr.
Strahan, as well as from other memorials, two of which I select, as strongly marking the tenderness and sensibility of his
mind.

'March 28, 1753. I kept this day as the anniversary of my Tetty's
death, with prayer and tears in the morning. In the evening I prayed
for her conditionally, if it were lawful.'

'April 23, 1753. I know not whether I do not too much indulge
the vain longings of affection; but I hope they intenerate my heart,
and that when I die like my Tetty, this affection will be acknowledged in a happy interview, and that in the mean time I am incited

by it to piety. I will, however, not deviate too much from common and received methods of devotion.'

I have been told by Mrs. Desmoulins, who, before her marriage, lived for some time with Mrs. Johnson at Hampstead, that she indulged herself in country air and nice living, at an unsuitable expence, while her husband was drudging in the smoke of London, and that she by no means treated him with that complacency which is the most engaging quality in a wife. But all this is perfectly compatible with his fondness for her, especially when it is remembered that he had a high opinion of her understanding, and that the impression which her beauty, real or imaginary, had originally made upon his fancy, being continued by habit, had not been effaced, though she herself was doubtless much altered for the worse. The dreadful shock of separation took place in the night; and he immediately dispatched a letter to his friend, the Reverend Dr. Taylor, which, as Taylor told me, expressed grief in the strongest manner he had ever read; so that it is much to be regretted it has not been preserved. The letter was brought to Dr. Taylor, at his house in the Cloysters, Westminster, about three in the morning; and as it signified an earnest desire to see him, he got up, and went to Johnson as soon as he was dressed, and found him in tears and in extreme agitation. After being a little while together, Johnson requested him to join with him in prayer. He then prayed extempore, as did Dr. Taylor; and thus, by means of that piety which was ever his primary object, his troubled mind was, in some degree, soothed and composed.

That his sufferings upon the death of his wife were severe, beyond what are commonly endured, I have no doubt, from the information of many who were then about him, to none of whom I give more credit than to Mr. Francis Barber, his faithful negro servant, who came into his family about a fortnight after the dismal event. These sufferings were aggravated by the melancholy inherent in his constitution; and although he probably was not oftener in the wrong than she was, in the little disagreements which sometimes troubled his married state, during which, he owned to me, that the gloomy irritability of his existence was more painful to him than ever, he might very naturally, after her death, be tenderly disposed to

charge himself with slight omissions and offences, the sense
of which would give him much uneasiness. Accordingly we
find, about a year after her decease, that he thus addressed the
Supreme Being: 'O *Lord,* who givest the grace of repentance
and hearest the prayers of the penitent, grant that by true contrition I may obtain forgiveness of all the sins committed, and
of all duties neglected in my union with the wife whom thou
hast taken from me; for the neglect of joint devotion, patient
exhortation, and mild instruction.' The kindness of his heart,
notwithstanding the impetuosity of his temper, is well known
to his friends; and I cannot trace the smallest foundation for
the following dark and uncharitable assertion by Sir John
Hawkins: 'The apparition of his departed wife was altogether
of the terrifick kind, and hardly afforded him a hope that she
was in a state of happiness.' That he, in conformity with the
opinion of many of the most able, learned, and pious Christians in all ages, supposed that there was a middle state after
death, previous to the time at which departed souls are finally
received to eternal felicity, appears, I think, unquestionably
from his devotions: 'And, O *Lord,* so far as it may be lawful
in me, I commend to thy fatherly goodness *the soul of my departed wife;* beseeching thee to *grant* her whatever is best in
her *present state,* and *finally to receive her to eternal happiness.*' But this state has not been looked upon with horrour,
but only as less gracious.

From Mr. Francis Barber I have had the following authentick and artless account of the situation in which he found
him recently after his wife's death:

He was in great affliction. Mrs. Williams was then living in his
house, which was in Gough-square. He was busy with the Dictionary. Mr. Shiels, and some others of the gentlemen who had formerly written for him, used to come about him. He had then little
for himself, but frequently sent money to Mr. Shiels when in
distress. The friends who visited him at that time, were chiefly
Dr. Bathurst, and Mr. Diamond, an apothecary in Cork-street,
Burlington-gardens, with whom he and Mrs. Williams generally
dined every Sunday. There was a talk of his going to Iceland with
him, which would probably have happened had he lived. There
were also Mr. Cave, Dr. Hawkesworth, Mr. Ryland, merchant on

Tower-hill, Mrs. Masters, the poetess, who lived with Mr. Cave, Mrs. Carter, and sometimes Mrs. Macaulay; also Mrs. Gardiner, wife of a tallow-chandler on Snow-hill, not in the learned way, but a worthy good woman; Mr. (now Sir Joshua) Reynolds; Mr. Millar, Mr. Dodsley, Mr. Bouquet, Mr. Payne of Paternoster-row, booksellers; Mr. Strahan the printer; the Earl of Orrery, Lord Southwell, Mr. Garrick.

Many are, no doubt, omitted in this catalogue of his friends, and, in particular, his humble friend Mr. Robert Levet, an obscure practiser in physick amongst the lower people, his fees being sometimes very small sums, sometimes whatever provisions his patients could afford him; but of such extensive practice in that way, that Mrs. Williams has told me, his walk was from Houndsditch to Marybone. It appears from Johnson's diary, that their acquaintance commenced about the year 1746; and such was Johnson's predilection for him, and fanciful estimation of his moderate abilities, that I have heard him say he should not be satisfied, though attended by all the College of Physicians, unless he had Mr. Levet with him. Ever since I was acquainted with Dr. Johnson, and many years before, as I have been assured by those who knew him earlier, Mr. Levet had an apartment in his house, or his chambers, and waited upon him every morning, through the whole course of his late and tedious breakfast. He was of a strange grotesque appearance, stiff and formal in his manner, and seldom said a word while any company was present.

The circle of his friends, indeed, at this time was extensive and various, far beyond what has been generally imagined. To trace his acquaintance with each particular person, if it could be done, would be a task, of which the labour would not be repaid by the advantage. But exceptions are to be made; one of which must be a friend so eminent as Sir Joshua Reynolds, and with whom he maintained an uninterrupted intimacy to the last hour of his life. When Johnson lived in Castle-street, Cavendish-square, he used frequently to visit two ladies, who lived opposite to him, Miss Cotterells, daughters of Admiral Cotterell. Reynolds used also to visit there, and thus they met. Mr. Reynolds, as I have observed above, had, from the first reading of his Life of Savage, conceived a very high admiration of

Johnson's powers of writing. His conversation no less delighted him; and he cultivated his acquaintance with the laudable zeal of one who was ambitious of general improvement. Sir Joshua, indeed, was lucky enough at their very first meeting to make a remark, which was so much above the common-place style of conversation, that Johnson at once perceived that Reynolds had the habit of thinking for himself. The ladies were regretting the death of a friend, to whom they owed great obligations; upon which Reynolds observed, 'You have, however, the comfort of being relieved from a burthen of gratitude.' They were shocked a little at this alleviating suggestion, as too selfish; but Johnson defended it in his clear and forcible manner, and was much pleased with the *mind,* the fair view of human nature, which it exhibited, like some of the reflections of Rochefaucault. The consequence was, that he went home with Reynolds, and supped with him.

Sir Joshua told me a pleasant characteristical anecdote of Johnson about the time of their first acquaintance. When they were one evening together at the Miss Cotterells', the then Duchess of Argyle and another lady of high rank came in. Johnson thinking that the Miss Cotterells were too much engrossed by them, and that he and his friend were neglected, as low company of whom they were somewhat ashamed, grew angry; and resolving to shock their supposed pride, by making their great visiters imagine that his friend and he were low indeed, he addressed himself in a loud tone to Mr. Reynolds, saying, 'How much do you think you and I could get in a week, if we were to *work as hard* as we could?'—as if they had been common mechanicks.

His acquaintance with Bennet Langton, Esq. of Langton in Lincolnshire, another much valued friend, commenced soon after the conclusion of his Rambler; which that gentleman, then a youth, had read with so much admiration, that he came to London chiefly with the view of endeavouring to be introduced to its authour. By a fortunate chance he happened to take lodgings in a house where Mr. Levet frequently visited; and having mentioned his wish to his landlady, she introduced him to Mr. Levet, who readily obtained Johnson's permission to bring Mr. Langton to him; as, indeed, Johnson, during the whole course of his life, had no shyness, real or affected, but was easy of access to all who were properly recommended, and even wished to see numbers at his *levee*, as his morning circle of company might, with strict propriety, be called. Mr. Langton was exceedingly surprized when the sage first appeared. He had not received the smallest intimation of his figure, dress, or manner. From perusing his writings, he fancied he should see a decent, well-drest, in short, a remarkably decorous philosopher. Instead of which, down from his bed-chamber, about noon, came, as newly risen, a huge uncouth figure, with a little dark wig which scarcely covered his head, and his clothes hanging loose about him. But his conversation was so rich, so animated, and so forcible, and his religious and political notions so congenial with those in which Mr. Langton had been educated, that he conceived for him that veneration and attachment which he ever preserved. Johnson was not the less ready to love Mr. Langton, for his being of a very ancient family; for I have heard him say, with pleasure, 'Langton, Sir, has a grant of free warren from Henry the Second; and Cardinal Stephen Langton, in King John's reign, was of this family.'

Mr. Langton afterwards went to pursue his studies at Trinity College, Oxford, where he formed an acquaintance with his fellow student, Mr. Topham Beauclerk; who, though their opinions and modes of life were so different, that it seemed utterly improbable that they should at all agree, had so ardent a love of literature, so acute an understanding, such elegance of manners, and so well discerned the excellent qualities of Mr. Langton, a gentleman eminent not only for worth and learning, but for an inexhaustible fund of entertaining conversation, that they became intimate friends.

Johnson, soon after this acquaintance began, passed a considerable time at Oxford. He at first thought it strange that Langton should associate so much with one who had the character of being loose, both in his principles and practice; but, by degrees, he himself was fascinated. Mr. Beauclerk's being of the St. Alban's family, and having, in some particulars, a resemblance to Charles the Second, contributed, in Johnson's imagination, to throw a lustre upon his other qualities; and, in a short time, the moral, pious Johnson, and the gay, dissipated

Beauclerk, were companions. 'What a coalition! (said Garrick, when he heard of this;) I shall have my old friend to bail out of the Round-house.' But I can bear testimony that it was a very agreeable association. Beauclerk was too polite, and valued learning and wit too much, to offend Johnson by sallies of infidelity or licentiousness; and Johnson delighted in the good qualities of Beauclerk, and hoped to correct the evil. Innumerable were the scenes in which Johnson was amused by these young men. Beauclerk could take more liberty with him, than any body with whom I ever saw him; but, on the other hand, Beauclerk was not spared by his respectable companion, when reproof was proper. Beauclerk had such a propensity to satire, that at one time Johnson said to him, 'You never open your mouth but with intention to give pain; and you have often given me pain, not from the power of what you said, but from seeing your intention.' At another time applying to him, with a slight alteration, a line of Pope, he said,

'Thy love of folly, and thy scorn of fools—

Every thing thou dost shews the one, and every thing thou say'st the other.' At another time he said to him, 'Thy body is all vice, and thy mind all virtue.' Beauclerk not seeming to relish the compliment, Johnson said, 'Nay, Sir, Alexander the Great, marching in triumph into Babylon, could not have desired to have had more said to him.'

Johnson was some time with Beauclerk at his house at Windsor, where he was entertained with experiments in natural philosophy. One Sunday, when the weather was very fine, Beauclerk enticed him, insensibly, to saunter about all the morning. They went into a church-yard, in the time of divine service, and Johnson laid himself down at his ease upon one of the tomb-stones. 'Now, Sir, (said Beauclerk) you are like Hogarth's Idle Apprentice.' When Johnson got his pension, Beauclerk said to him, in the humorous phrase of Falstaff, 'I hope you'll now purge and live cleanly like a gentleman.'

One night when Beauclerk and Langton had supped at a tavern in London, and sat till about three in the morning, it came into their heads to go and knock up Johnson, and see if they could prevail on him to join them in a ramble. They rapped violently at the door of his chambers in the Temple, till at last he appeared in his shirt, with his little black wig on the top of his head, instead of a nightcap, and a poker in his hand, imagining, probably, that some ruffians were coming to attack him. When he discovered who they were, and was told their errand, he smiled, and with great good humour agreed to their proposal: 'What, is it you, you dogs! I'll have a frisk with you.' He was soon drest, and they sallied forth together into Covent-Garden, where the green-grocers and fruiterers were beginning to arrange their hampers, just come in from the country. Johnson made some attempts to help them; but the honest gardeners stared so at his figure and manner, and odd interference, that he soon saw his services were not relished. They then repaired to one of the neighbouring taverns, and made a bowl of that liquor called *Bishop,* which Johnson had always liked; while in joyous contempt of sleep, from which he had been roused, he repeated the festive lines,

> 'Short, O short then be thy reign,
> And give us to the world again!'

They did not stay long, but walked down to the Thames, took a boat, and rowed to Billingsgate. Beauclerk and Johnson were so well pleased with their amusement, that they resolved to persevere in dissipation for the rest of the day: but Langton deserted them, being engaged to breakfast with some young Ladies. Johnson scolded him for 'leaving his social friends, to go and sit with a set of wretched *un-idea'd* girls.' Garrick being told of this ramble, said to him smartly, 'I heard of your frolick t'other night. You'll be in the Chronicle.' Upon which Johnson afterwards observed, '*He* durst not do such a thing. His *wife* would not *let* him!'

1753: ÆTAT. 44.]—He now relieved the drudgery of his Dictionary, and the melancholy of his grief, by taking an active part in the composition of 'The Adventurer,' in which he began to write April 10, marking his essays with the signature T, by which most of his papers in that collection are distinguished.

Johnson's papers in the Adventurer are very similar to those of the Rambler; but being rather more varied in their subjects, and being mixed with essays by other writers, upon topicks more generally attractive than even the most elegant ethical discourses, the sale of the work, at first, was more extensive. Without meaning, however, to depreciate the Adventurer, I must observe that as the value of the Rambler came, in the progress of time, to be better known, it grew upon the publick estimation, and that its sale has far exceeded that of any other periodical papers since the reign of Queen Anne.

In one of the books of his diary I find the following entry:

'Apr. 3, 1753. I began the second vol. of my Dictionary, room being left in the first for Preface, Grammar, and History, none of them yet begun.

'O GOD, who hast hitherto supported me, enable me to proceed in this labour, and in the whole task of my present state; that when I shall render up, at the last day, an account of the talent committed to me, I may receive pardon, for the sake of JESUS CHRIST. Amen.'

1754: ÆTAT. 45.]—In 1754 I can trace nothing published by him, except his numbers of the Adventurer, and 'The Life of Edward Cave,' in the Gentleman's Magazine for February. Cave was certainly a man of estimable qualities, and was eminently diligent and successful in his own business, which, doubtless, entitled him to respect. But he was peculiarly fortunate in being recorded by Johnson, who, of the narrow life of a printer and publisher, without any digressions or adventitious circumstances, has made an interesting and agreeable narrative.

The Dictionary, we may believe, afforded Johnson full occupation this year. As it approached to its conclusion, he probably worked with redoubled vigour, as seamen increase their exertion and alacrity when they have a near prospect of their haven.

Lord Chesterfield, to whom Johnson had paid the high compliment of addressing to his Lordship the Plan of his Dictionary, had behaved to him in such a manner as to excite his contempt and indignation. The world has been for many years amused with a story confidently told, and as confidently repeated with additional circumstances, that a sudden disgust

was taken by Johnson upon occasion of his having been one
day kept long in waiting in his Lordship's antechamber, for
which the reason assigned was, that he had company with him;
and that at last, when the door opened, out walked Colley Cibber; and that Johnson was so violently provoked when he
found for whom he had been so long excluded, that he went
away in a passion, and never would return. It may seem strange
even to entertain a doubt concerning a story so long and so
widely current, and thus implicitly adopted, if not sanctioned,
by the authority which I have mentioned; but Johnson himself
assured me, that there was not the least foundation for it. He
told me, that there never was any particular incident which
produced a quarrel between Lord Chesterfield and him; but
that his Lordship's continued neglect was the reason why he
resolved to have no connection with him. When the Dictionary was upon the eve of publication, Lord Chesterfield, who,
it is said, had flattered himself with expectations that Johnson
would dedicate the work to him, attempted, in a courtly manner, to sooth, and insinuate himself with the Sage, conscious,
as it should seem, of the cold indifference with which he had
treated its learned authour; and further attempted to conciliate
him, by writing two papers in 'The World,' in recommendation of the work; and it must be confessed, that they contain
some studied compliments, so finely turned, that if there had
been no previous offence, it is probable that Johnson would
have been highly delighted. Praise, in general, was pleasing
to him; but by praise from a man of rank and elegant accomplishments, he was peculiarly gratified.

His Lordship says,

'I think the publick in general, and the republick of letters in
particular, are greatly obliged to Mr. Johnson, for having undertaken, and executed, so great and desirable a work. Perfection is
not to be expected from man; but if we are to judge by the various
works of Johnson already published, we have good reason to believe, that he will bring this as near to perfection as any one man
could do. The Plan of it, which he published some years ago, seems
to me to be a proof of it. Nothing can be more rationally imagined,
or more accurately and elegantly expressed. I therefore recommend

the previous perusal of it to all those who intend to buy the Dictionary, and who, I suppose, are all those who can afford it.'

*   *   *   *   *   *   *

'It must be owned, that our language is, at present, in a state of anarchy, and hitherto, perhaps, it may not have been the worse for it. During our free and open trade, many words and expressions have been imported, adopted, and naturalized from other languages, which have greatly enriched our own. Let it still preserve what real strength and beauty it may have borrowed from others; but let it not, like the Tarpeian maid,[1] be overwhelmed and crushed by unnecessary ornaments. The time for discrimination seems to be now come. Toleration, adoption, and naturalization have run their lengths. Good order and authority are now necessary. But where shall we find them, and, at the same time, the obedience due to them? We must have recourse to the old Roman expedient in times of confusion, and chuse a dictator. Upon this principle, I give my vote for Mr. Johnson to fill that great and arduous post. And I hereby declare, that I make a total surrender of all my rights and privileges in the English language, as a free-born British subject, to the said Mr. Johnson, during the term of his dictatorship. Nay more, I will not only obey him, like an old Roman, as my dictator, but, like a modern Roman, I will implicitly believe in him as my Pope, and hold him to be infallible while in the chair, but no longer. More than this he cannot well require; for, I presume, that obedience can never be expected, when there is neither terrour to enforce, nor interest to invite it.'

*   *   *   *   *   *   *

This courtly device failed of its effect. Johnson, who thought that 'all was false and hollow,' despised the honeyed words, and was even indignant that Lord Chesterfield should, for a moment, imagine, that he could be the dupe of such an artifice. His expression to me concerning Lord Chesterfield, upon this occasion, was, 'Sir, after making great professions, he had, for many years, taken no notice of me; but when my Dictionary

[1] Tarpeia, daughter of Spurius Tarpeius, governor of the citadel on the Capitoline Hill, traitorously opened the gates to the Sabines for the "ornaments on their arms." The soldiers crushed her to death with their shields, saying that these were the ornaments they had promised her. Traitors were afterwards put to death in Rome by being hurled from a rock that crowned this hill.

was coming out, he fell a scribbling in "The World" about it. Upon which, I wrote him a letter expressed in civil terms, but such as might shew him that I did not mind what he said or wrote, and that I had done with him.'

This is that celebrated letter of which so much has been said, and about which curiosity has been so long excited, without being gratified. I for many years solicited Johnson to favour me with a copy of it, that so excellent a composition might not be lost to posterity. He delayed from time to time to give it me; till at last in 1781, when we were on a visit at Mr. Dilly's, at Southill in Bedfordshire, he was pleased to dictate it to me from memory. He afterwards found among his papers a copy of it, which he had dictated to Mr. Baretti, with its title and corrections, in his own hand-writing. This he gave to Mr. Langton; adding, that if it were to come into print, he wished it to be from that copy. By Mr. Langton's kindness, I am enabled to enrich my work with a perfect transcript of what the world has so eagerly desired to see.

'To the Right Honourable the Earl of Chesterfield

'February 7, 1755.

'My Lord,

'I have been lately informed, by the proprietor of the World, that two papers, in which my Dictionary is recommended to the publick, were written by your Lordship. To be so distinguished, is an honour, which, being very little accustomed to favours from the great, I know not well how to receive, or in what terms to acknowledge.

'When, upon some slight encouragement, I first visited your Lordship, I was overpowered, like the rest of mankind, by the enchantment of your address; and could not forbear to wish that I might boast myself *Le vainqueur du vainqueur de la terre*[1];—that I might obtain that regard for which I saw the world contending; but I found my attendance so little encouraged, that neither pride nor modesty would suffer me to continue it. When I had once addressed your Lordship in publick, I had exhausted all the art of pleasing which a retired and uncourtly scholar can possess. I had done all that I could, and no man is well pleased to have his all neglected, be it ever so little.

[1] The conqueror of the conqueror of the earth. Johnson has slightly modified a phrase from Boileau's *l'Art poétique*.

'Seven years, my Lord, have now past, since I waited in your outward rooms, or was repulsed from your door; during which time I have been pushing on my work through difficulties, of which it is useless to complain, and have brought it, at last, to the verge of publication, without one act of assistance, one word of encouragement, or one smile of favour. Such treatment I did not expect, for I never had a Patron before.

'The shepherd in Virgil grew at last acquainted with Love, and found him a native of the rocks.

'Is not a Patron, my Lord, one who looks with unconcern on a man struggling for life in the water, and, when he has reached ground, encumbers him with help? The notice which you have been pleased to take of my labours, had it been early, had been kind; but it has been delayed till I am indifferent, and cannot enjoy it; till I am solitary, and cannot impart it; till I am known, and do not want it. I hope it is no very cynical asperity not to confess obligations where no benefit has been received, or to be unwilling that the Publick should consider me as owing that to a Patron, which Providence has enabled me to do for myself.

'Having carried on my work thus far with so little obligation to any favourer of learning, I shall not be disappointed though I should conclude it, if less be possible, with less; for I have been long wakened from that dream of hope, in which I once boasted myself with so much exultation,

                                'My Lord,
                        'Your Lordship's most humble,
                                'Most obedient servant,
                                        'SAM. JOHNSON.'

'While this was the talk of the town, (says Dr. Adams, in a letter to me) I happened to visit Dr. Warburton, who finding that I was acquainted with Johnson, desired me earnestly to carry his compliments to him, and to tell him, that he honoured him for his manly behaviour in rejecting these condescensions of Lord Chesterfield, and for resenting the treatment he had received from him, with a proper spirit. Johnson was visibly pleased with this compliment, for he had always a high opinion of Warburton.—Indeed, the force of mind which appeared in this letter, was congenial with that which Warburton himself amply possessed.'

There is a curious minute circumstance which struck me, in comparing the various editions of Johnson's imitations of

Juvenal. In the tenth Satire, one of the couplets upon the vanity of wishes even for literary distinction stood thus:

> 'Yet think what ills the scholar's life assail,
> Toil, envy, want, the *garret*, and the jail.'

But after experiencing the uneasiness which Lord Chesterfield's fallacious patronage made him feel, he dismissed the word *garret* from the sad group, and in all the subsequent editions the line stands

> 'Toil, envy, want, the *Patron*, and the jail.'

That Lord Chesterfield must have been mortified by the lofty contempt, and polite, yet keen satire with which Johnson exhibited him to himself in this letter, it is impossible to doubt. He, however, with that glossy duplicity which was his constant study, affected to be quite unconcerned. Dr. Adams mentioned to Mr. Robert Dodsley that he was sorry Johnson had written his letter to Lord Chesterfield. Dodsley, with the true feelings of trade, said 'he was very sorry too; for that he had a property in the Dictionary, to which his Lordship's patronage might have been of consequence.' He then told Dr. Adams, that Lord Chesterfield had shewn him the letter. 'I should have imagined (replied Dr. Adams) that Lord Chesterfield would have concealed it.' 'Poh! (said Dodsley) do you think a letter from Johnson could hurt Lord Chesterfield? Not at all, Sir. It lay upon his table, where any body might see it. He read it to me; said, "this man has great powers," pointed out the severest passages, and observed how well they were expressed.' This air of indifference, which imposed upon the worthy Dodsley, was certainly nothing but a specimen of that dissimulation which Lord Chesterfield inculcated as one of the most essential lessons for the conduct of life. His Lordship endeavoured to justify himself to Dodsley from the charges brought against him by Johnson; but we may judge of the flimsiness of his defence, from his having excused his neglect of Johnson, by saying that 'he had heard he had changed his lodgings, and did not know where he lived;' as if there could have been the smallest difficulty to inform himself of that circumstance, by inquiring in the literary circle with which his

Lordship was well acquainted, and was, indeed, himself one
of its ornaments.

Dr. Adams expostulated with Johnson, and suggested, that
his not being admitted when he called on him, was, probably,
not to be imputed to Lord Chesterfield; for his Lordship had
declared to Dodsley, that 'he would have turned off the best
servant he ever had, if he had known that he denied him to a
man who would have been always more than welcome;' and,
in confirmation of this, he insisted on Lord Chesterfield's general affability and easiness of access, especially to literary men.
'Sir, (said Johnson) that is not Lord Chesterfield; he is the
proudest man this day existing.' 'No, (said Dr. Adams) there
is one person, at least, as proud; I think, by your own account,
you are the prouder man of the two.' 'But mine (replied Johnson, instantly) was *defensive* pride.' This, as Dr. Adams well
observed, was one of those happy turns for which he was so
remarkably ready.

Johnson having now explicitly avowed his opinion of Lord
Chesterfield, did not refrain from expressing himself concerning that nobleman with pointed freedom: 'This man (said
he) I thought had been a Lord among wits; but, I find, he is
only a wit among Lords!' And when his Letters to his natural
son were published, he observed, that 'they teach the morals of
a whore, and the manners of a dancing master.'

The character of a 'respectable Hottentot,' in Lord Chesterfield's letters, has been generally understood to be meant for
Johnson, and I have no doubt that it was. But I remember
when the *Literary Property* of those letters was contested in
the Court of Session in Scotland, and Mr. Henry Dundas, one
of the counsel for the proprietors, read this character as an exhibition of Johnson, Sir David Dalrymple, Lord Hailes, one of
the Judges, maintained, with some warmth, that it was not intended as a portrait of Johnson, but of a late noble Lord, distinguished for abstruse science. I have heard Johnson himself
talk of the character, and say that it was meant for George Lord
Lyttelton, in which I could by no means agree; for his Lordship had nothing of that violence which is a conspicuous fea-
ture in the composition. Finding that my illustrious friend
could bear to have it supposed that it might be meant for him,

I said, laughingly, that there was one trait which unquestionably did not belong to him; 'he throws his meat any where but down his throat.' 'Sir, (said he) Lord Chesterfield never saw me eat in his life.'

On the 6th of March came out Lord Bolingbroke's works, published by Mr. David Mallet. The wild and pernicious ravings, under the name of 'Philosophy,' which were thus ushered into the world, gave great offence to all well-principled men. Johnson, hearing of their tendency, which nobody disputed, was roused with a just indignation, and pronounced this memorable sentence upon the noble authour and his editor. 'Sir, he was a scoundrel, and a coward: a scoundrel, for charging a blunderbuss against religion and morality; a coward, because he had not resolution to fire it off himself, but left half a crown to a beggarly Scotchman, to draw the trigger after his death!'

Johnson this year found an interval of leisure to make an excursion to Oxford, for the purpose of consulting the libraries there. Of his conversation while at Oxford at this time, Mr. Warton preserved and communicated to me the following memorial, which, though not written with all the care and attention which that learned and elegant writer bestowed on those compositions which he intended for the publick eye, is so happily expressed in an easy style, that I should injure it by any alteration:

'When Johnson came to Oxford in 1754, the long vacation was beginning, and most people were leaving the place. This was the first time of his being there, after quitting the University. The next morning after his arrival, he wished to see his old College, *Pembroke*. I went with him. He was highly pleased to find all the College-servants which he had left there still remaining, particularly a very old butler; and expressed great satisfaction at being recognised by them, and conversed with them familiarly. He waited on the master, Dr. Radcliffe, who received him very coldly. Johnson at least expected, that the master would order a copy of his Dictionary, now near publication: but the master did not choose to talk on the subject, never asked Johnson to dine, nor even to visit him, while he stayed at Oxford. After we had left the Lodgings, Johnson said to me, "*There* lives a man, who lives by the revenues of literature, and will not move a finger to support it. If I come to live at Oxford, I shall take up my abode at Trinity." We then

called on the Reverend Mr. Meeke, one of the fellows, and of
Johnson's standing. Here was a most cordial greeting on both sides.
On leaving him, Johnson said, "I used to think Meeke had excellent
parts, when we were boys together at the College: but, alas!

'Lost in a convent's solitary gloom!'

I remember, at the classical lecture in the Hall, I could not bear
Meeke's superiority, and I tried to sit as far from him as I could,
that I might not hear him construe."

'He much regretted that his *first* tutor was dead; for whom he
seemed to retain the greatest regard. He said, "I once had been a
whole morning sliding in Christ-Church Meadow, and missed his
lecture in logick. After dinner, he sent for me to his room. I expected a sharp rebuke for my idleness, and went with a beating
heart. When we were seated, he told me he had sent for me to drink
a glass of wine with him, and to tell me, he was *not* angry with
me for missing his lecture. This was, in fact, a most severe reprimand. Some more of the boys were then sent for, and we spent
a very pleasant afternoon."

'In the course of this visit (1754,) Johnson and I walked, three
or four times, to Ellsfield, a village beautifully situated about three
miles from Oxford, to see Mr. Wise, Radclivian librarian, with
whom Johnson was much pleased. In an evening, we frequently
took long walks from Oxford into the country, returning to supper.
Once, in our way home, we viewed the ruins of the abbies of
Oseney and Rewley, near Oxford. After at least half an hour's
silence, Johnson said, "I viewed them with indignation!" We had
then a long conversation on Gothick buildings; and in talking of the
form of old halls, he said, "In these halls, the fire place was an-
ciently always in the middle of the room, till the Whigs removed
it on one side."—About this time there had been an execution of
two or three criminals at Oxford on a Monday. Soon afterwards,
one day at dinner, I was saying that Mr. Swinton the chaplain of
the gaol, and also a frequent preacher before the University, a
learned man, but often thoughtless and absent, preached the con-
demnation-sermon on repentance, before the convicts, on the preceding day, Sunday; and that in the close he told his audience, that
he should give them the remainder of what he had to say on the
subject, the next Lord's Day. Upon which, one of our company, a
Doctor of Divinity, and a plain matter-of-fact man, by way of offer-
ing an apology for Mr. Swinton, gravely remarked, that he had
probably preached the same sermon before the University: "Yes,

Sir, (says Johnson) but the University were not to be hanged the next morning."

'I forgot to observe before, that when he left Mr. Meeke, (as I have told above) he added, "About the same time of life, Meeke was left behind at Oxford to feed on a Fellowship, and I went to London to get my living: now, Sir, see the difference of our literary characters!"'

The degree of Master of Arts, which, it has been observed, could not be obtained for him at an early period of his life, was now considered as an honour of considerable importance, in order to grace the title-page of his Dictionary; and his character in the literary world being by this time deservedly high, his friends thought that, if proper exertions were made, the University of Oxford would pay him the compliment.

1755: ÆTAT. 46.]—In 1755 we behold him to great advantage; his degree of Master of Arts conferred upon him, his Dictionary published, his correspondence animated, his benevolence exercised.

As the Publick will doubtless be pleased to see the whole progress of this well-earned academical honour, I shall insert the Chancellor of Oxford's letter to the University.

'To the Reverend Dr. HUDDESFORD, Vice-Chancellor *of the* University *of* Oxford; *to be communicated to the Heads of Houses, and proposed in Convocation.*

'MR. VICE-CHANCELLOR, AND GENTLEMEN,

'MR. SAMUEL JOHNSON, who was formerly of Pembroke College, having very eminently distinguished himself by the publication of a series of essays, excellently calculated to form the manners of the people, and in which the cause of religion and morality is every where maintained by the strongest powers of argument and language; and who shortly intends to publish a Dictionary of the English Tongue, formed on a new plan, and executed with the greatest labour and judgement; I persuade myself that I shall act agreeably to the sentiments of the whole University, in desiring that it may be proposed in convocation to confer on him the degree of Master of Arts by diploma, to which I readily give my consent; and am,

'Mr. Vice-Chancellor, and Gentlemen,
'Your affectionate friend and servant,
'ARRAN.'

'Grosvenor-street, Feb. 4, 1755.'

Mr. Charles Burney, who has since distinguished himself so much in the science of Musick, and obtained a Doctor's degree from the University of Oxford, had been driven from the capital by bad health, and was now residing at Lynne Regis, in Norfolk. He had been so much delighted with Johnson's Rambler, and the Plan of his Dictionary, that when the great work was announced in the news-papers as nearly finished, he wrote to Dr. Johnson, begging to be informed when and in what manner his Dictionary would be published; intreating, if it should be by subscription, or he should have any books at his own disposal, to be favoured with six copies for himself and friends.

In answer to this application, Dr. Johnson wrote the following letter, of which (to use Dr. Burney's own words) 'if it be remembered that it was written to an obscure young man, who at this time had not much distinguished himself even in his own profession, but whose name could never have reached the authour of THE RAMBLER, the politeness and urbanity may be opposed to some of the stories which have been lately circulated of Dr. Johnson's natural rudeness and ferocity.'

'TO MR. BURNEY, IN LYNNE REGIS, NORFOLK.
'SIR,
'IF YOU imagine that by delaying my answer I intended to shew any neglect of the notice with which you have favoured me, you will neither think justly of yourself nor of me. Your civilities were offered with too much elegance not to engage attention; and I have too much pleasure in pleasing men like you, not to feel very sensibly the distinction which you have bestowed upon me.

'Few consequences of my endeavours to please or to benefit mankind have delighted me more than your friendship thus voluntarily offered, which now I have it I hope to keep, because I hope to continue to deserve it.

'I have no Dictionaries to dispose of for myself, but shall be glad to have you direct your friends to Mr. Dodsley, because it was by his recommendation that I was employed in the work.

'When you have leisure to think again upon me, let me be favoured with another letter; and another yet, when you have looked into my Dictionary. If you find faults, I shall endeavour to mend them; if you find none, I shall think you blinded by kind partiality: but to have made you partial in his favour, will very much gratify the ambition of, Sir,

> 'Your most obliged
> 'And most humble servant,
> 'SAM. JOHNSON.'

'Gough-square, Fleet-street,
    'April 8, 1755.'

Mr. Andrew Millar, bookseller in the Strand, took the principal charge of conducting the publication of Johnson's Dictionary; and as the patience of the proprietors was repeatedly tried and almost exhausted, by their expecting that the work would be completed within the time which Johnson had sanguinely supposed, the learned authour was often goaded to dispatch, more especially as he had received all the copy-money, by different drafts, a considerable time before he had finished his task. When the messenger who carried the last sheet to Millar returned, Johnson asked him, 'Well, what did he say?'—'Sir, (answered the messenger) he said, thank GOD I have done with him.' 'I am glad (replied Johnson, with a smile,) that he thanks GOD for any thing.' It is remarkable, that those with whom Johnson chiefly contracted for his literary labours were Scotchmen, Mr. Millar and Mr. Strahan. Millar, though himself no great judge of literature, had good sense enough to have for his friends very able men to give him their opinion and advice in the purchase of copy-right; the consequence of which was his acquiring a very large fortune, with great liberality. Johnson said of him, 'I respect Millar, Sir; he has raised the price of literature.'

The Dictionary, with a Grammar and History of the English Language, being now at length published, in two volumes folio, the world contemplated with wonder so stupendous a work atchieved by one man, while other countries had thought such undertakings fit only for whole academies. Vast as his powers were, I cannot but think that his imagination deceived him, when he supposed that by constant application he might have performed the task in three years. Let the Preface be attentively perused, in which is given, in a clear, strong, and glowing style, a comprehensive, yet particular view of what he had done; and it will be evident, that the time he employed upon it was comparatively short. I am unwilling to swell my book with long quotations from what is in every body's hands; and I believe there are few prose compositions in the English language that are read with more delight, or are more impressed upon the memory, than that preliminary discourse. One of its excellencies has always struck me with peculiar admiration; I mean the perspicuity with which he has expressed abstract scientifick notions. As an instance of this, I shall quote the following sentence: 'When the radical idea branches out into parallel ramifications, how can a consecutive series be formed of senses in their own nature collateral?' We have here an example of what has been often said, and I believe with justice, that there is for every thought a certain nice adaptation of words which none other could equal, and which, when a man has been so fortunate as to hit, he has attained, in that particular case, to the perfection of language.

Well might he say, that 'the English Dictionary was written with little assistance of the learned;' for he told me, that the only aid which he received was a paper containing twenty etymologies, sent to him by a person then unknown, who he was afterwards informed was Dr. Pearce, Bishop of Rochester. The etymologies, though they exhibit learning and judgement, are not, I think, entitled to the first praise amongst the various parts of this immense work. The definitions have always appeared to me such astonishing proofs of acuteness of intellect and precision of language, as indicate a genius of the highest rank. This it is which marks the superiour excellence of Johnson's Dictionary over others equally or even more voluminous, and must have made it a work of much greater mental labour than mere Lexicons, or *Word-Books,* as the Dutch call them.

A few of his definitions must be admitted to be erroneous. Thus, *Windward* and *Leeward,* though directly of opposite meaning, are defined identically the same way; as to which inconsiderable specks it is enough to observe, that his Preface announces that he was aware there might be many such in so immense a work; nor was he at all disconcerted when an instance was pointed out to him. A lady once asked him how he came to define *Pastern* the *knee* of a horse: instead of making an elaborate defence, as she expected, he at once answered,

'Ignorance, Madam, pure ignorance.' His definition of *Net-work*[1] has been often quoted with sportive malignity, as obscuring a thing in itself very plain. But to these frivolous censures no other answer is necessary than that with which we are furnished by his own Preface.

'To explain, requires the use of terms less abstruse than that which is to be explained, and such terms cannot always be found. For as nothing can be proved but by supposing something intuitively known, and evident without proof, so nothing can be defined but by the use of words too plain to admit of definition. Sometimes easier words are changed into harder; as, *burial,* into *sepulture* or *interment; dry,* into *desiccative; dryness,* into *siccity* or *aridity; fit,* into *paroxysm;* for, the *easiest* word, whatever it be, can never be translated into one more easy.'

His introducing his own opinions, and even prejudices, under general definitions of words, while at the same time the original meaning of the words is not explained, as his *Tory, Whig, Pension, Oats, Excise,* and a few more, cannot be fully defended, and must be placed to the account of capricious and humourous indulgence. Talking to me upon this subject when we were at Ashbourne in 1777, he mentioned a still stronger instance of the predominance of his private feelings in the composition of this work, than any now to be found in it. 'You know, Sir, Lord Gower forsook the old Jacobite interest. When I came to the word *Renegado,* after telling that it meant "one who deserts to the enemy, a revolter," I added, *Sometimes we say a* Gower. Thus it went to the press; but the printer had more wit than I, and struck it out.'

Let it, however, be remembered, that this indulgence does not display itself only in sarcasm towards others, but sometimes in playful allusion to the notions commonly entertained of his own laborious task. Thus: '*Grub-street,* the name of a street in London, much inhabited by writers of small histories, *dictionaries,* and temporary poems; whence any mean produc-

[1] Johnson defined *Network* as "Any thing reticulated or decussated, at equal distances, with interstices between the intersections." At first glance this does seem, indeed, to be obscuring the obvious; but as a *definition* it is still superior to anything given in any other dictionary of the English language.

tion is called *Grub-street.'*—'*Lexicographer,* a writer of dictionaries, a *harmless drudge.'*

At the time when he was concluding his very eloquent Preface, Johnson's mind appears to have been in such a state of
depression, that we cannot contemplate without wonder the
vigorous and splendid thoughts which so highly distinguish
that performance. 'I (says he) may surely be contented without the praise of perfection, which if I could obtain in this
gloom of solitude, what would it avail me? I have protracted
my work till most of those whom I wished to please have sunk
into the grave; and success and miscarriage are empty sounds.
I therefore dismiss it with frigid tranquillity, having little to
fear or hope from censure or from praise.'

It must undoubtedly seem strange, that the conclusion of
his Preface should be expressed in terms so desponding, when
it is considered that the authour was then only in his forty-
sixth year. But we must ascribe its gloom to that miserable dejection of spirits to which he was constitutionally subject, and
which was aggravated by the death of his wife two years before. I have heard it ingeniously observed by a lady of rank and
elegance, that 'his melancholy was then at its meridian.' It
pleased *God* to grant him almost thirty years of life after this
time; and once, when he was in a placid frame of mind, he
was obliged to own to me that he had enjoyed happier days,
and had had many more friends, since that gloomy hour than
before.

It is a sad saying, that 'most of those whom he wished to
please had sunk into the grave;' and his case at forty-five was
singularly unhappy, unless the circle of his friends was very
narrow. I have often thought, that as longevity is generally
desired, and, I believe, generally expected, it would be wise to
be continually adding to the number of our friends, that the
loss of some may be supplied by others. Friendship, 'the wine
of life,' should, like a well-stocked cellar, be thus continually
renewed; and it is consolatory to think, that although we can
seldom add what will equal the generous *first-growths* of our
youth, yet friendship becomes insensibly old in much less time
than is commonly imagined, and not many years are required
to make it very mellow and pleasant.

The proposition which I have now endeavoured to illustrate was, at a subsequent period of his life, the opinion of Johnson himself. He said to Sir Joshua Reynolds, 'If a man does not make new acquaintance as he advances through life, he will soon find himself left alone. A man, Sir, should keep his friendship *in constant repair.*'

Johnson this year gave at once a proof of his benevolence, quickness of apprehension, and admirable art of composition, in the assistance which he gave to Mr. Zachariah Williams, father of the blind lady whom he had humanely received under his roof. Mr. Williams had followed the profession of physick in Wales; but having a very strong propensity to the study of natural philosophy, had made many ingenious advances towards a discovery of the longitude, and repaired to London in hopes of obtaining the great parliamentary reward. He failed of success; but Johnson having made himself master of his principles and experiments, wrote for him a pamphlet, published in quarto, with the following title: 'An Account of an Attempt to ascertain the Longitude at Sea, by an exact Theory of the Variation of the Magnetical Needle; with a Table of the Variations at the most remarkable Cities in Europe, from the year 1660 to 1860.'

1756: ÆTAT. 47.]—In 1756 Johnson found that the great fame of his Dictionary had not set him above the necessity of 'making provision for the day that was passing over him.'

He had spent, during the progress of the work, the money for which he had contracted to write his Dictionary. We have seen that the reward of his labour was only fifteen hundred and seventy-five pounds; and when the expence of amanuenses and paper, and other articles are deducted, his clear profit was very inconsiderable. I once said to him, 'I am sorry, Sir, you did not get more for your Dictionary.' His answer was, 'I am sorry too. But it was very well. The booksellers are generous liberal-minded men.' He, upon all occasions, did ample justice to their character in this respect. He considered them as the patrons of literature; and, indeed, although they have eventually been considerable gainers by his Dictionary, it is to them that we owe its having been undertaken and carried through at the risk of great expence, for they were not absolutely sure of being indemnified.

On the first day of this year we find from his private devotions, that he had then recovered from sickness; and in February that his eye was restored to its use. The pious gratitude with which he acknowledges mercies upon every occasion is very edifying; as is the humble submission which he breathes, when it is the will of his heavenly Father to try him with afflictions.

His works this year were, an abstract or epitome, in octavo, of his folio Dictionary, and a few essays in a monthly publication, entitled, 'The Universal Visiter.' Christopher Smart, with whose unhappy vacillation of mind he sincerely sympathised, was one of the stated undertakers of this miscellany; and it was to assist him that Johnson sometimes employed his pen. He engaged also to superintend and contribute largely to another monthly publication, entitled 'The Literary Magazine, or Universal Review;' the first number of which came out in May this year. What were his emoluments from this undertaking, and what other writers were employed in it, I have not discovered. He continued to write in it, with intermissions, till the fifteenth number; and I think that he never gave better proofs of the force, acuteness, and vivacity of his mind, than in this miscellany, whether we consider his original essays, or his reviews of the works of others.

His original essays are, 'An Introduction to the Political State of Great Britain;' 'Remarks on the Militia Bill;' 'Observations on his Britannick Majesty's Treaties with the Empress of Russia and the Landgrave of Hesse Cassel;' 'Observations on the Present State of Affairs;' and, 'Memoirs of Frederick III. King of Prussia.' In all these he displays extensive political knowledge and sagacity, expressed with uncommon energy and perspicuity, without any of those words which he sometimes took a pleasure in adopting, in imitation of Sir Thomas Browne; of whose 'Christian Morals' he this year gave an edition, with his 'Life' prefixed to it, which is one of Johnson's best biographical performances. In one instance only in these essays has he indulged his *Brownism*. Dr. Robertson, the his-

torian, mentioned it to me, as having at once convinced him
that Johnson was the author of the 'Memoirs of the King of
Prussia.' Speaking of the pride which the old King, the father
of his hero, took in being master of the tallest regiment in
Europe, he says, 'To review this *towering* regiment was his
daily pleasure, and to perpetuate it was so much his care, that
when he met a tall woman he immediately commanded one of
his *Titanian* retinue to marry her, that they might *propagate
procerity.*' For this Anglo-Latian word *procerity*, Johnson had,
however, the authority of Addison.

It is worthy of remark, in justice to Johnson's political character, which has been misrepresented as abjectly submissive to
power, that his 'Observations on the present State of Affairs'
glow with as animated a spirit of constitutional liberty as can
be found any where. Thus he begins:

'The time is now come, in which every Englishman expects to
be informed of the national affairs, and in which he has a right to
have that expectation gratified. For whatever may be urged by
ministers, or those whom vanity or interest make the followers of
ministers, concerning the necessity of confidence in our governours,
and the presumption of prying with profane eyes into the recesses
of policy, it is evident that this reverence can be claimed only by
counsels yet unexecuted, and projects suspended in deliberation.
But when a design has ended in miscarriage or success, when every
eye and every ear is witness to general discontent, or general satisfaction, it is then a proper time to disentangle confusion and illustrate obscurity; to shew by what causes every event was produced,
and in what effects it is likely to terminate; to lay down with distinct particularity what rumour always huddles in general exclama-
tion, or perplexes by indigested narratives; to shew whence
happiness or calamity is derived, and whence it may be expected;
and honestly to lay before the people what inquiry can gather of
the past, and conjecture can estimate of the future.'

Here we have it assumed as an incontrovertible principle,
that in this country the people are the superintendants of the
conduct and measures of those by whom government is administered; of the beneficial effect of which the present reign afforded an illustrious example, when addresses from all parts
of the kingdom controuled an audacious attempt to introduce
a new power subversive of the crown.

Some of his reviews in this Magazine are very short accounts of the pieces noticed but many of them are examples of elaborate criticism, in the most masterly style. In his review of the 'Memoirs of the Court of Augustus,' he has the resolution to think and speak from his own mind, regardless of the cant transmitted from age to age, in praise of the ancient Romans. Thus,

'I know not why any one but a school-boy in his declamation should whine over the Common-wealth of Rome, which grew great only by the misery of the rest of mankind. The Romans, like others, as soon as they grew rich, grew corrupt; and in their corruption sold the lives and freedoms of themselves, and of one another.'

His defence of tea against Mr. Jonas Hanway's violent attack upon that elegant and popular beverage, shews how very well a man of genius can write upon the slightest subject, when he writes, as the Italians say, *con amore:* I suppose no person ever enjoyed with more relish the infusion of that fragrant leaf than Johnson. The quantities which he drank of it at all hours were so great, that his nerves must have been uncommonly strong, not to have been extremely relaxed by such an intemperate use of it. He assured me, that he never felt the least inconvenience from it; which is a proof that the fault of his constitution was rather a too great tension of fibres, than the contrary. Mr. Hanway wrote an angry answer to Johnson's review of his Essay on Tea, and Johnson, after a full and deliberate pause, made a reply to it; the only instance, I believe, in the whole course of his life, when he condescended to oppose any thing that was written against him. But, indeed, the good Mr. Hanway laid himself so open to ridicule, that Johnson's animadversions upon his attack were chiefly to make sport.

He this year resumed his scheme of giving an edition of Shakspeare with notes. He issued Proposals of considerable length, in which he shewed that he perfectly well knew what a variety of research such an undertaking required; but his indolence prevented him from pursuing it with that diligence which alone can collect those scattered facts that genius, however acute, penetrating, and luminous, cannot discover by its own force. It is remarkable, that at this time his fancied activity was for the moment so vigorous, that he promised his work should be published before Christmas, 1757. Yet nine years elapsed before it saw the light. His throes in bringing it forth had been severe and remittent; and at last we may almost conclude that the Cæsarian operation was performed by the knife of Churchill, whose upbraiding satire, I dare say, made Johnson's friends urge him to dispatch.

> 'He for subscribers bates his hook,
> And takes your cash; but where's the book?
> No matter where; wise fear, you know,
> Forbids the robbing of a foe;
> But what, to serve our private ends,
> Forbids the cheating of our friends?'

About this period he was offered a living of considerable value in Lincolnshire, if he were inclined to enter into holy orders. It was a rectory in the gift of Mr. Langton, the father of his much valued friend. But he did not accept of it; partly I believe from a conscientious motive, being persuaded that his temper and habits rendered him unfit for that assiduous and familiar instruction of the vulgar and ignorant, which he held to be an essential duty in a clergyman; and partly because his love of a London life was so strong, that he would have thought himself an exile in any other place, particularly if residing in the country.

1757: ÆTAT. 48.]—In 1757 it does not appear that he published any thing, except some of those articles in the Literary Magazine, which have been mentioned.

In 1758 we find him, it should seem, in as easy and pleasant a state of existence, as constitutional unhappiness ever permitted him to enjoy.

On the fifteenth of April he began a new periodical paper, entitled 'The Idler,' which came out every Saturday in a weekly news-paper, called 'The Universal Chronicle, or Weekly Gazette,' published by Newbery. These essays were continued till April 5, 1760. Of one hundred and three, their total number, twelve were contributed by his friends.

The *Idler* is evidently the work of the same mind which pro-

duced the *Rambler,* but has less body and more spirit. It has
more variety of real life, and greater facility of language. He
describes the miseries of idleness, with the lively sensations of
one who has felt them; and in his private memorandums while
engaged in it, we find 'This year I hope to learn diligence.'
Many of these excellent essays were written as hastily as an
ordinary letter. Mr. Langton remembers Johnson, when on a
visit at Oxford, asking him one evening how long it was till
the post went out; and on being told about half an hour, he
exclaimed, 'then we shall do very well.' He upon this instantly
sat down and finished an Idler, which it was necessary should
be in London the next day. Mr. Langton having signified a
wish to read it, 'Sir, (said he) you shall not do more than I
have done myself.' He then folded it up, and sent it off.

'To BENNET LANGTON, ESQ. AT LANGTON, NEAR SPILSBY,
LINCOLNSHIRE.

'DEAR SIR,
    'I SHOULD be sorry to think that what engrosses the attention
of my friend, should have no part of mine. Your mind is now full
of the fate of Dury[1]; but his fate is past, and nothing remains but
to try what reflection will suggest to mitigate the terrours of a
violent death, which is more formidable at the first glance, than on
a nearer and more steady view. A violent death is never very painful; the only danger is lest it should be unprovided. But if a man
can be supposed to make no provision for death in war, what can
be the state that would have awakened him to the care of futurity?
when would that man have prepared himself to die, who went to
seek death without preparation? What then can be the reason why
we lament more him that dies of a wound, than him that dies of a
fever? A man that languishes with disease, ends his life with more
pain, but with less virtue; he leaves no example to his friends, nor
bequeaths any honour to his descendants. The only reason why we
lament a soldier's death, is, that we think he might have lived
longer; yet this cause of grief is common to many other kinds of
death which are not so passionately bewailed. The truth is, that
every death is violent which is the effect of accident; every death,
which is not gradually brought on by the miseries of age, or when
life is extinguished for any other reason than that it is burnt out.

[1] Major General Alexander Dury, Langton's uncle, who had just
been killed in battle.

He that dies before sixty, of a cold or consumption, dies, in reality, by a violent death; yet his death is borne with patience only because the cause of his untimely end is silent and invisible. Let us endeavour to see things as they are, and then enquire whether we ought to complain. Whether to see life as it is, will give us much consolation, I know not; but the consolation which is drawn from truth, if any there be, is solid and durable; that which may be derived from errour, must be, like its original, fallacious and fugitive. I am, dear, dear Sir, your most humble servant,

'SAM JOHNSON.'

'Sept. 21, 1758.'

1759: ÆTAT. 50.]—In 1759, in the month of January, his mother died at the great age of ninety, an event which deeply affected him; not that 'his mind had acquired no firmness by the contemplation of mortality,' but that his reverential affection for her was not abated by years, as indeed he retained all his tender feelings even to the latest period of his life. I have been told that he regretted much his not having gone to visit his mother for several years, previous to her death. But he was constantly engaged in literary labours which confined him to London; and though he had not the comfort of seeing his aged parent, he contributed liberally to her support.

Soon after this event, he wrote his *'Rasselas, Prince of Abyssinia.'* The late Mr. Strahan the printer told me, that Johnson wrote it, that with the profits he might defray the expence of his mother's funeral, and pay some little debts which she had left. He told Sir Joshua Reynolds that he composed it in the evenings of one week, sent it to the press in portions as it was written, and had never since read it over. Mr. Strahan, Mr. Johnston, and Mr. Dodsley purchased it for a hundred pounds, but afterwards paid him twenty-five pounds more, when it came to a second edition.

Considering the large sums which have been received for compilations, and works requiring not much more genius than compilations, we cannot but wonder at the very low price which he was content to receive for this admirable performance; which, though he had written nothing else, would have rendered his name immortal in the world of literature. None of his writings has been so extensively diffused over Europe;

for it has been translated into most, if not all, of the modern languages. This Tale, with all the charms of oriental imagery, and all the force and beauty of which the English language is capable, leads us through the most important scenes of human life, and shews us that this stage of our being is full of 'vanity and vexation of spirit.' Voltaire's *Candide,* written to refute the system of Optimism, which it has accomplished with brilliant success, is wonderfully similar in its plan and conduct to Johnson's *Rasselas;* insomuch, that I have heard Johnson say, that if they had not been published so closely one after the other that there was not time for imitation, it would have been in vain to deny that the scheme of that which came latest was taken from the other. Though the proposition illustrated by both these works was the same, namely, that in our present state there is more evil than good, the intention of the writers was very different. Voltaire, I am afraid, meant only by wanton profaneness to obtain a sportive victory over religion, and to discredit the belief of a superintending Providence: Johnson meant, by shewing the unsatisfactory nature of things temporal, to direct the hopes of man to things eternal.

Notwithstanding my high admiration of Rasselas, I will not maintain that the 'morbid melancholy' in Johnson's constitution may not, perhaps, have made life appear to him more insipid and unhappy than it generally is; for I am sure that he had less enjoyment from it than I have. Yet, whatever additional shade his own particular sensations may have thrown on his representation of life, attentive observation and close inquiry have convinced me, that there is too much of reality in the gloomy picture.

He now refreshed himself by an excursion to Oxford, of which the following short characteristical notice, in his own words, is preserved:

* * * is now making tea for me. I have been in my gown ever since I came here. It was at my first coming quite new and handsome. I have swum thrice, which I had disused for many years. I have proposed to Vansittart, climbing over the wall, but he has refused me. And I have clapped my hands till they are sore, at Dr King's speech.'

His negro servant, Francis Barber, having left him, and been some time at sea, not pressed as has been supposed, but with his own consent, it appears from a letter to John Wilkes, Esq. from Dr. Smollet, that his master kindly interested himself in procuring his release from a state of life of which Johnson always expressed the utmost abhorrence. He said, 'No man will be a sailor who has contrivance enough to get himself into a jail; for being in a ship is being in a jail, with the chance of being drowned.' And at another time, 'A man in a jail has more room, better food, and commonly better company.' The letter was as follows:

'Chelsea, March 16, 1759.

'DEAR SIR,

'I AM again your petitioner, in behalf of that great *Cham* of literature, Samuel Johnson. His black servant, whose name is Francis Barber, has been pressed on board the Stag Frigate, Captain Angel, and our lexicographer is in great distress. He says the boy is a sickly lad, of a delicate frame, and particularly subject to a malady in his throat, which renders him very unfit for his Majesty's service. You know what matter of animosity the said Johnson has against you; and I dare say you desire no other opportunity of resenting it than that of laying him under an obligation. He was humble enough to desire my assistance on this occasion, though he and I were never cater-cousins; and I gave him to understand that I would make application to my friend Mr. Wilkes, who, perhaps, by his interest with Dr. Hay and Mr. Elliot, might be able to procure the discharge of his lacquey. It would be superfluous to say more on the subject, which I leave to your own consideration; but I cannot let slip this opportunity of declaring that I am, with the most inviolable esteem and attachment, dear Sir,

'Your affectionate obliged humble servant,

'T. SMOLLET.'

Mr. Wilkes, who upon all occasions has acted, as a private gentleman, with most polite liberality, applied to his friend Sir George Hay, then one of the Lords Commissioners of the Admiralty; and Francis Barber was discharged, as he has told me, without any wish of his own. He found his old master in Chambers in the Inner Temple, and returned to his service.

1760: ÆTAT. 51.]—In 1760 he wrote 'An Address of the Painters to George III. on his Accession to the Throne of these Kingdoms,' which no monarch ever ascended with more sincere congratulations from his people. Two generations of foreign princes had prepared their minds to rejoice in having again a King, who gloried in being 'born a Briton.'

Johnson was now either very idle, or very busy with his Shakspeare; for I can find no other publick composition by him except an Introduction to the proceedings of the Committee for cloathing the French Prisoners; one of the many proofs that he was ever awake to the calls of humanity; and an account which he gave in the Gentleman's Magazine of Mr. Tytler's acute and able vindication of Mary Queen of Scots.

This year Mr. Murphy, having thought himself ill-treated by the Reverend Dr. Francklin, who was one of the writers of 'The Critical Review,' published an indignant vindication in 'A Poetical Epistle to Samuel Johnson, A.M.' in which he compliments Johnson in a just and elegant manner.

I take this opportunity to relate the manner in which an acquaintance first commenced between Dr. Johnson and Mr. Murphy. During the publication of 'The Gray's-Inn Journal,' a periodical paper which was successfully carried on by Mr. Murphy alone, when a very young man, he happened to be in the country with Mr. Foote; and having mentioned that he was obliged to go to London in order to get ready for the press one of the numbers of that Journal, Foote said to him, 'You need not go on that account. Here is a French magazine, in which you will find a very pretty oriental tale; translate that, and send it to your printer.' Mr. Murphy having read the tale, was highly pleased with it, and followed Foote's advice. When he returned to town, this tale was pointed out to him in 'The Rambler,' from whence it had been translated into the French magazine. Mr. Murphy then waited upon Johnson, to explain this curious incident. His talents, literature, and gentleman-like manners, were soon perceived by Johnson, and a friendship was formed which was never broken.

1761: ÆTAT. 52.]—In 1761 Johnson appears to have done little. He was still, no doubt, proceeding in his edition of Shakspeare; but what advances he made in it cannot be ascertained. He certainly was at this time not active; for in his scrupulous examination of himself on Easter eve, he laments, in his too rigorous mode of censuring his own conduct, that his life, since the communion of the preceding Easter, had been 'dissipated and useless.' He, however, contributed this year the Preface to 'Rolt's Dictionary of Trade and Commerce,' in which he displays such a clear and comprehensive knowledge of the subject, as might lead the reader to think that its authour had devoted all his life to it. I asked him, whether he knew much of Rolt, and of his work. 'Sir, (said he) I never saw the man, and never read the book. The booksellers wanted a Preface to a Dictionary of Trade and Commerce. I knew very well what such a Dictionary should be, and I wrote a Preface accordingly.' Rolt, who wrote a great deal for the booksellers, was, as Johnson told me, a singular character. Though not in the least acquainted with him, he used to say, 'I am just come from Sam. Johnson.' This was a sufficient specimen of his vanity and impudence. But he gave a more eminent proof of it in our sister kingdom, as Dr. Johnson informed me. When Akenside's 'Pleasures of the Imagination' first came out, he did not put his name to the poem. Rolt went over to Dublin, published an edition of it, and put his own name to it. Upon the fame of this he lived for several months, being entertained at the best tables as 'the ingenious Mr. Rolt.' His conversation, indeed, did not discover much of the fire of a poet; but it was recollected, that both Addison and Thomson were equally dull till excited by wine. Akenside having been informed of this imposition, vindicated his right by publishing the poem with its real authour's name.

Johnson had now for some years admitted Mr. Baretti to his intimacy; nor did their friendship cease upon their being separated by Baretti's revisiting his native country.

1762: ÆTAT. 53.]—In 1762 he wrote for the Reverend Dr. Kennedy, Rector of Bradley in Derbyshire in a strain of very courtly elegance, a Dedication to the King of that gentleman's work, entitled, 'A complete System of Astronomical Chronology, unfolding the Scriptures.'

He this year wrote also the Dedication to the Earl of Middlesex of Mrs. Lennox's 'Female Quixote,' and the Preface to the 'Catalogue of the Artists' Exhibition.'

A lady having at this time solicited him to obtain the Archbishop of Canterbury's patronage to have her son sent to the University, one of those solicitations which are too frequent, where people, anxious for a particular object, do not consider propriety, or the opportunity, which the persons whom they solicit have to assist them, he wrote to her the following answer; with a copy of which I am favoured by the Reverend Dr. Farmer, Master of Emanuel College, Cambridge.

'MADAM,

'I HOPE you will believe that my delay in answering your letter could proceed only from my unwillingness to destroy any hope that you had formed. Hope is itself a species of happiness, and, perhaps, the chief happiness which this world affords: but, like all other pleasures immoderately enjoyed, the excesses of hope must be expiated by pain; and expectations improperly indulged, must end in disappointment. If it be asked, what is the improper expectation which it is dangerous to indulge, experience will quickly answer, that it is such expectation as is dictated not by reason, but by desire; expectation raised, not by the common occurrences of life, but by the wants of the expectant; an expectation that requires the common course of things to be changed, and the general rules of action to be broken.

'When you made your request to me, you should have considered, Madam, what you were asking. You ask me to solicit a great man, to whom I never spoke, for a young person whom I had never seen, upon a supposition which I had no means of knowing to be true. There is no reason why, amongst all the great, I should chuse to supplicate the Archbishop, nor why, among all the possible objects of his bounty, the Archbishop should chuse your son. I know, Madam, how unwillingly conviction is admitted, when interest opposes it; but surely, Madam, you must allow, that there is no reason why that should be done by me, which every other man may do with equal reason, and which, indeed, no man can do properly, without some very particular relation both to the Archbishop and to you. If I could help you in this exigence by any proper means, it would give me pleasure; but this proposal is so very remote from all usual methods, that I cannot comply with it, but at the risk of such answer and suspicions as I believe you do not wish me to undergo.

'I have seen your son this morning; he seems a pretty youth,

and will, perhaps, find some better friend than I can procure him;
but, though he should at last miss the University, he may still be
wise, useful, and happy. I am, Madam,

'Your most humble servant,

SAM. JOHNSON.

'June 8, 1762.'

The accession of George the Third to the throne of these
kingdoms, opened a new and brighter prospect to men of literary merit, who had been honoured with no mark of royal favour in the preceding reign. His present Majesty's education
in this country, as well as his taste and beneficence, prompted
him to be the patron of science and the arts; and early this year
Johnson, having been represented to him as a very learned
and good man, without any certain provision, his Majesty was
pleased to grant him a pension of three hundred pounds a year.
The Earl of Bute, who was then Prime Minister, had the honour to announce this instance of his Sovereign's bounty, concerning which many and various stories, all equally erroneous,
have been propagated; maliciously representing it as a political
bribe to Johnson, to desert his avowed principles, and become
the tool of a government which he held to be founded in usur-
pation. I have taken care to have it in my power to refute them
from the most authentick information. Lord Bute told me, that
Mr. Wedderburne, now Lord Loughborough, was the person
who first mentioned this subject to him. Lord Loughborough
told me, that the pension was granted to Johnson solely as the
reward of his literary merit, without any stipulation whatever,
or even tacit understanding that he should write for administration. His Lordship added, that he was confident the political tracts which Johnson afterwards did write, as they were
entirely consonant with his own opinions, would have been
written by him, though no pension had been granted to him.

Mr. Thomas Sheridan and Mr. Murphy, who then lived a
good deal both with him and Mr. Wedderburne, told me, that
they previously talked with Johnson upon this matter, and that
it was perfectly understood by all parties that the pension was
merely honorary. Sir Joshua Reynolds told me, that Johnson
called on him after his Majesty's intention had been notified
to him, and said he wished to consult his friends as to the pro-

priety of his accepting this mark of the royal favour, after the definitions which he had given in his Dictionary of *pension* and *pensioners*. He said he would not have Sir Joshua's answer till next day, when he would call again, and desired he might think of it. Sir Joshua answered that he was clear to give his opinion then, that there could be no objection to his receiving from the King a reward for literary merit; and that certainly the definitions in his Dictionary were not applicable to him. Johnson, it should seem, was satisfied, for he did not call again till he had accepted the pension, and had waited on Lord Bute to thank him. He then told Sir Joshua that Lord Bute said to him expressly, 'It is not given you for any thing you are to do, but for what you have done.' His Lordship, he said, behaved in the handsomest manner. He repeated the words twice, that he might be sure Johnson heard them, and thus set his mind perfectly at ease.

Mr. Murphy and the late Mr. Sheridan severally contended for the distinction of having been the first who mentioned to Mr. Wedderburne that Johnson ought to have a pension. When I spoke of this to Lord Loughborough, wishing to know if he recollected the prime mover in the business, he said, 'All his friends assisted:' and when I told him that Mr. Sheridan strenuously asserted his claim to it, his Lordship said, 'He rang the bell.' And it is but just to add, that Mr. Sheridan told me, that when he communicated to Dr. Johnson that a pension was to be granted him, he replied, in a fervour of gratitude, 'The English language does not afford me terms adequate to my feelings on this occasion. I must have recourse to the French. I am *pénétré* with his Majesty's goodness.' When I repeated this to Dr. Johnson, he did not contradict it.

His definitions of *pension* and *pensioner*, partly founded on the satirical verses of Pope, which he quotes, may be generally true; and yet every body must allow, that there may be, and have been, instances of pensions given and received upon liberal and honourable terms. Thus, then, it is clear, that there was nothing inconsistent or humiliating in Johnson's accepting of a pension so unconditionally and so honourably offered to him.

But I shall not detain my readers longer by any words of my

own, on a subject on which I am happily enabled, by the favour of the Earl of Bute, to present them with what Johnson himself wrote; his lordship having been pleased to communicate to me a copy of the following letter to his late father, which does great honour both to the writer, and to the noble person to whom it is addressed:

'To THE RIGHT HONOURABLE THE EARL OF BUTE.

'MY LORD,

'WHEN the bills were yesterday delivered to me by Mr. Wedderburne, I was informed by him of the future favours which his Majesty has, by your Lordship's recommendation, been induced to intend for me.

'Bounty always receives part of its value from the manner in which it is bestowed; your Lordship's kindness includes every circumstance that can gratify delicacy, or enforce obligation. You have conferred your favours on a man who has neither alliance nor interest, who has not merited them by services, nor courted them by officiousness; you have spared him the shame of solicitation, and the anxiety of suspense.

'What has been thus elegantly given, will, I hope, not be reproachfully enjoyed; I shall endeavour to give your Lordship the only recompense which generosity desires,—the gratification of finding that your benefits are not improperly bestowed. I am, my Lord,

'Your Lordship's most obliged,

'Most obedient, and most humble servant,

'SAM. JOHNSON.'

'July 20, 1762.'

This year his friend Sir Joshua Reynolds paid a visit of some weeks to his native county, Devonshire, in which he was accompanied by Johnson, who was much pleased with this jaunt, and declared he had derived from it a great accession of new ideas. He was entertained at the seats of several noblemen and gentlemen in the west of England; but the greatest part of the time was passed at Plymouth, where the magnificence of the navy, the ship-building and all its circumstances, afforded him a grand subject of contemplation. The Commissioner of the Dock-yard paid him the compliment of ordering the yacht to convey him and his friend to the Eddystone, to which they accordingly sailed. But the weather was so tempestuous that they could not land.

Sir Joshua Reynolds, to whom I was obliged for my information concerning this excursion, mentions a very characteristical anecdote of Johnson while at Plymouth. Having observed that in consequence of the Dock-yard a new town had arisen about two miles off as a rival to the old; and knowing from his sagacity, and just observation of human nature, that it is certain if a man hates at all, he will hate his next neighbour; he concluded that this new and rising town could not but excite the envy and jealousy of the old, in which conjecture he was very soon confirmed; he therefore set himself resolutely on the side of the old town, the *established* town, in which his lot was cast, considering it as a kind of duty to *stand by* it. He accordingly entered warmly into its interests, and upon every occasion talked of the *dockers,* as the inhabitants of the new town were called, as upstarts and aliens. Plymouth is very plentifully supplied with water by a river brought into it from a great distance, which is so abundant that it runs to waste in the town. The Dock, or New-town, being totally destitute of water, petitioned Plymouth that a small portion of the conduit might be permitted to go to them, and this was now under consideration. Johnson, affecting to entertain the passions of the place, was violent in opposition; and half-laughing at himself for his pretended zeal, where he had no concern, exclaimed, 'No, no! I am against the *dockers;* I am a Plymouth-man. Rogues! let them die of thirst. They shall not have a drop!'

Lord Macartney obligingly favoured me with a copy of the following letter, in his own hand-writing, from the original, which was found, by the present Earl of Bute, among his father's papers.

'To the Right Honourable the Earl of Bute.

'My Lord,

'That generosity, by which I was recommended to the favour of his Majesty, will not be offended at a solicitation necessary to make that favour permanent and effectual.

'The pension appointed to be paid me at Michaelmas I have not received, and know not where or from whom I am to ask it. I beg, therefore, that your Lordship will be pleased to supply Mr. Wedderburne with such directions as may be necessary, which, I

believe, his friendship will make him think it no trouble to co: ᷄
to me.

'To interrupt your Lordship, at a time like this, with such petty
difficulties, is improper and unseasonable; but your knowledge of
the world has long since taught you, that every man's affairs, how·-
ever little, are important to himself. Every man hopes that he sha᷄
escape neglect; and, with reason, may every man, whose vices do
not preclude his claim, expect favour from that beneficence which
has been extended to,

'My Lord,

'Your Lordship's

'Most obliged

'And

'Most humble servant,

'SAM. JOHNSON.'

'Temple Lane,
    'Nov. 3, 1762.'

1763: ÆTAT. 54.]—This is to me a memorable year; for in
it I had the happiness to obtain the acquaintance of that extraordinary man whose memoirs I am now writing; an acquaintance which I shall ever esteem as one of the most fortunate
circumstances in my life. Though then but two-and-twenty,
I had for several years read his works with delight and instruction, and had the highest reverence for their authour, which
had grown up in my fancy into a kind of mysterious veneration, by figuring to myself a state of solemn elevated abstraction, in which I supposed him to live in the immense
metropolis of London. Mr. Gentleman, a native of Ireland,
who passed some years in Scotland as a player, and as an instructor in the English language, a man whose talents and
worth were depressed by misfortunes, had given me a representation of the figure and manner of *Dictionary Johnson!* as
he was then generally called; and during my first visit to London, which was for three months in 1760, Mr. Derrick the
poet, who was Gentleman's friend and countryman, flattered
me with hopes that he would introduce me to Johnson, an
honour of which I was very ambitious. But he never found
an opportunity; which made me doubt that he had promised
to do what was not in his power; till Johnson some years after-

wards told me, 'Derrick, Sir, might very well have introduced you. I had a kindness for Derrick, and am sorry he is dead.'

In the summer of 1761 Mr. Thomas Sheridan was at Edinburgh, and delivered lectures upon the English Language and Publick Speaking to large and respectable audiences. I was often in his company, and heard him frequently expatiate upon Johnson's extraordinary knowledge, talents, and virtues, repeat his pointed sayings, describe his particularities, and boast of his being his guest sometimes till two or three in the morning. At his house I hoped to have many opportunities of seeing the sage, as Mr. Sheridan obligingly assured me I should not be disappointed.

When I returned to London in the end of 1762, to my surprise and regret I found an irreconcileable difference had taken place between Johnson and Sheridan. A pension of two hundred pounds a year had been given to Sheridan. Johnson, who, as has been already mentioned, thought slightingly of Sheridan's art, upon hearing that he was also pensioned, exclaimed, 'What! have they given *him* a pension? Then it is time for me to give up mine.'

Johnson complained that a man who disliked him repeated his sarcasm to Mr. Sheridan, without telling him what followed, which was, that after a pause he added, 'However, I am glad that Mr. Sheridan has a pension, for he is a very good man.' Sheridan could never forgive this hasty contemptuous expression. It rankled in his mind; and though I informed him of all that Johnson said, and that he would be very glad to meet him amicably, he positively declined repeated offers which I made, and once went off abruptly from a house where he and I were engaged to dine, because he was told that Dr. Johnson was to be there.

This rupture with Sheridan deprived Johnson of one of his most agreeable resources for amusement in his lonely evenings; for Sheridan's well-informed, animated, and bustling mind never suffered conversation to stagnate; and Mrs. Sheridan was a most agreeable companion to an intellectual man. She was sensible, ingenious, unassuming, yet communicative.

Mr. Thomas Davies the actor, who then kept a bookseller's

shop in Russel-street, Covent-garden, told me that Johnson was very much his friend, and came frequently to his house, where he more than once invited me to meet him; but by some unlucky accident or other he was prevented from coming to us.

Mr. Thomas Davies was a man of good understanding and talents, with the advantage of a liberal education. Though somewhat pompous, he was an entertaining companion; and his literary performances have no inconsiderable share of merit. He was a friendly and very hospitable man. Both he and his wife, (who has been celebrated for her beauty,) though upon the stage for many years, maintained an uniform decency of character; and Johnson esteemed them, and lived in as easy an intimacy with them as with any family which he used to visit. Mr. Davies recollected several of Johnson's remarkable sayings, and was one of the best of the many imitators of his voice and manner, while relating them. He increased my impatience more and more to see the extraordinary man whose works I highly valued, and whose conversation was reported to be so peculiarly excellent.

At last, on Monday the 16th of May, when I was sitting in Mr. Davies's back-parlour, after having drunk tea with him and Mrs. Davies, Johnson unexpectedly came into the shop; and Mr. Davies having perceived him through the glass-door in the room in which we were sitting, advancing towards us,—he announced his aweful approach to me, somewhat in the manner of an actor in the part of Horatio, when he addresses Hamlet on the appearance of his father's ghost, 'Look, my Lord, it comes.' I found that I had a very perfect idea of Johnson's figure, from the portrait of him painted by Sir Joshua Reynolds soon after he had published his Dictionary, in the attitude of sitting in his easy chair in deep meditation, which was the first picture his friend did for him, which Sir Joshua very kindly presented to me. Mr. Davies mentioned my name, and respectfully introduced me to him. I was much agitated; and recollecting his prejudice against the Scotch, of which I had heard much, I said to Davies, 'Don't tell where I come from.'—'From Scotland,' cried Davies, roguishly. 'Mr. Johnson, (said I) I do indeed come from Scotland, but I cannot help

it.' I am willing to flatter myself that I meant this as light pleasantry to sooth and conciliate him, and not as an humiliating
abasement at the expence of my country. But however that
might be, this speech was somewhat unlucky; for with that
quickness of wit for which he was so remarkable, he seized the
expression 'come from Scotland,' which I used in the sense of
being of that country; and, as if I had said that I had come
away from it, or left it, retorted, 'That, Sir, I find, is what a
very great many of your countrymen cannot help.' This stroke
stunned me a good deal; and when we had sat down, I felt myself not a little embarrassed, and apprehensive of what might
come next. He then addressed himself to Davies: 'What do
you think of Garrick? He has refused me an order for the play
for Miss Williams, because he knows the house will be full,
and that an order would be worth three shillings.' Eager to
take any opening to get into conversation with him, I ventured
to say, 'O, Sir, I cannot think Mr. Garrick would grudge such
a trifle to you.' 'Sir, (said he, with a stern look,) I have known
David Garrick longer than you have done: and I know no
right you have to talk to me on the subject.' Perhaps I deserved
this check; for it was rather presumptuous in me, an entire
stranger, to express any doubt of the justice of his animadversion upon his old acquaintance and pupil. I now felt myself
much mortified, and began to think that the hope which I had
long indulged of obtaining his acquaintance was blasted. And,
in truth, had not my ardour been uncommonly strong, and
my resolution uncommonly persevering, so rough a reception
might have deterred me for ever from making any further attempts. Fortunately, however, I remained upon the field not
wholly discomfited; and was soon rewarded by hearing some of
his conversation, of which I preserved the following short minute, without marking the questions and observations by which
it was produced.

'People (he remarked) may be taken in once, who imagine
that an authour is greater in private life than other men.
Uncommon parts require uncommon opportunities for their
exertion.

'In barbarous society, superiority of parts is of real consequence. Great strength or great wisdom is of much value to

an individual. But in more polished times there are people to do every thing for money; and then there are a number of other superiorities, such as those of birth and fortune, and rank, that dissipate men's attention, and leave no extraordinary share of respect for personal and intellectual superiority. This is wisely ordered by Providence, to preserve some equality among mankind.'

'Sir, this book ("The Elements of Criticism," which he had taken up,) is a pretty essay, and deserves to be held in some estimation, though much of it is chimerical.'

Speaking of one who with more than ordinary boldness attacked publick measures and the royal family, he said,

'I think he is safe from the law, but he is an abusive scoundrel; and instead of applying to my Lord Chief Justice to punish him, I would send half a dozen footmen and have him well ducked.'

'The notion of liberty amuses the people of England, and helps to keep off the *tædium vitæ*. When a butcher tells you that *his heart bleeds for his country*, he has, in fact, no uneasy feeling.'

'Sheridan will not succeed at Bath with his oratory. Ridicule has gone down before him, and, I doubt, Derrick is his enemy.'

'Derrick may do very well, as long as he can outrun his character; but the moment his character gets up with him, it is all over.'

It is, however, but just to record, that some years afterwards, when I reminded him of this sarcasm, he said, 'Well, but Derrick has now got a character that he need not run away from.'

I was highly pleased with the extraordinary vigour of his conversation, and regretted that I was drawn away from it by an engagement at another place. I had, for a part of the evening, been left alone with him, and had ventured to make an observation now and then, which he received very civilly; so that I was satisfied that though there was a roughness in his manner, there was no ill-nature in his disposition. Davies followed me to the door, and when I complained to him a little of the hard blows which the great man had given me, he kindly took upon him to console i   by saying, 'Don't be uneasy. I can see he likes you very well.'

A few days afterwards I called on Davies, and asked him if
he thought I might take the liberty of waiting on Mr. Johnson
at his Chambers in the Temple. He said I certainly might, and
that Mr. Johnson would take it as a compliment. So upon
Tuesday the 24th of May, after having been enlivened by the
witty sallies of Messieurs Thornton, Wilkes, Churchill and
Lloyd, with whom I had passed the morning, I boldly repaired
to Johnson. His Chambers were on the first floor of No. 1,
Inner-Temple-lane, and I entered them with an impression
given me by the Reverend Dr. Blair, of Edinburgh, who had
been introduced to him not long before, and described his having 'found the Giant in his den;' an expression, which, when
I came to be pretty well acquainted with Johnson, I repeated
to him, and he was diverted at this picturesque account of
himself.

He received me very courteously; but, it must be confessed,
that his apartment, and furniture, and morning dress, were
sufficiently uncouth. His brown suit of cloaths looked very
rusty; he had on a little old shrivelled unpowdered wig, which
was too small for his head; his shirt-neck and knees of his
breeches were loose; his black worsted stockings ill drawn up;
and he had a pair of unbuckled shoes by way of slippers. But
all these slovenly particularities were forgotten the moment
that he began to talk. Some gentlemen, whom I do not recollect, were sitting with him; and when they went away, I also
rose; but he said to me, 'Nay, don't go.'—'Sir, (said I,) I am
afraid that I intrude upon you. It is benevolent to allow me to
sit and hear you.' He seemed pleased with this compliment,
which I sincerely paid him, and answered, 'Sir, I am obliged
to any man who visits me.'—I have preserved the following
short minute of what passed this day.

'Madness frequently discovers itself merely by unnecessary
deviation from the usual modes of the world. My poor friend
Smart shewed the disturbance of his mind, by falling upon
his knees, and saying his prayers in the street, or in any other
unusual place. Now although, rationally speaking, it is greater
madness not to pray at all, than to pray as Smart did, I am
afraid there are so many who do not pray, that their understanding is not called in question.'

Concerning this unfortunate poet, Christopher Smart, who was confined in a mad-house, he had, at another time, the following conversation with Dr. Burney.—*Burney.* 'How does poor Smart do, Sir; is he likely to recover?' *Johnson.* 'It seems as if his mind had ceased to struggle with the disease; for he grows fat upon it.' *Burney.* 'Perhaps, Sir, that may be from want of exercise.' *Johnson.* 'No, Sir; he has partly as much exercise as he used to have, for he digs in the garden. Indeed, before his confinement, he used for exercise to walk to the alehouse; but he was *carried* back again. I did not think he ought to be shut up. His infirmities were not noxious to society. He insisted on people praying with him; and I'd as lief pray with Kit Smart as any one else. Another charge was, that he did not love clean linen; and I have no passion for it.'

When I rose a second time he again pressed me to stay, which I did.

He told me, that he generally went abroad at four in the afternoon, and seldom came home till two in the morning. I took the liberty to ask if he did not think it wrong to live thus, and not make more use of his great talents. He owned it was a bad habit. On reviewing, at the distance of many years, my journal of this period, I wonder how, at my first visit, I ventured to talk to him so freely, and that he bore it with so much indulgence.

Before we parted, he was so good as to promise to favour me with his company one evening at my lodgings; and, as I took my leave, shook me cordially by the hand. It is almost needless to add, that I felt no little elation at having now so happily established an acquaintance of which I had been so long ambitious.

My readers will, I trust, excuse me for being thus minutely circumstantial, when it is considered that the acquaintance of Dr. Johnson was to me a most valuable acquisition, and laid the foundation of whatever instruction and entertainment they may receive from my collections concerning the great subject of the work which they are now perusing.

I did not visit him again till Monday, June 13, at which time I recollect no part of his conversation, except that when I told him I had been to see Johnson ride upon three horses,

he said, 'Such a man, Sir, should be encouraged; for his performances shew the extent of the human powers in one instance, and thus tend to raise our opinion of the faculties of
man. He shews what may be attained by persevering application; so that every man may hope, that by giving as much application, although perhaps he may never ride three horses at
a time, or dance upon a wire, yet he may be equally expert in
whatever profession he has chosen to pursue.'

He again shook me by the hand at parting, and asked me
why I did not come oftener to him. Trusting that I was now
in his good graces, I answered, that he had not given me much
encouragement, and reminded him of the check I had received
from him at our first interview. 'Poh, poh! (said he, with a
complacent smile,) never mind these things. Come to me as
often as you can. I shall be glad to see you.'

I had learnt that his place of frequent resort was the Mitre
tavern in Fleet-street, where he loved to sit up late, and I
begged I might be allowed to pass an evening with him there
soon, which he promised I should. A few days afterwards I
met him near Temple-bar, about one o'clock in the morning,
and asked if he would then go to the Mitre. 'Sir, (said he) it
is too late; they won't let us in. But I'll go with you another
night with all my heart.'

A revolution of some importance in my plan of life had just
taken place; for instead of procuring a commission in the foot-
guards, which was my own inclination, I had, in compliance
with my father's wishes, agreed to study the law, and was soon
to set out for Utrecht, to hear the lectures of an excellent Civil-
ian in that University, and then to proceed on my travels.
Though very desirous of obtaining Dr. Johnson's advice and
instructions on the mode of pursuing my studies, I was at this
time so occupied, shall I call it? or so dissipated, by the amusements of London, that our next meeting was not till Saturday,
June 25, when happening to dine at Clifton's eating-house, in
Butcher-row, I was surprized to perceive Johnson come in and
take his seat at another table. The mode of dining, or rather
being fed, at such houses in London, is well known to many
to be particularly unsocial, as there is no Ordinary, or united
company, but each person has his own mess, and is under no

obligation to hold any intercourse with any one. A liberal and full-minded man, however, who loves to talk, will break through this churlish and unsocial restraint. Johnson and an Irish gentleman got into a dispute concerning the cause of some part of mankind being black. 'Why, Sir, (said Johnson,) it has been accounted for in three ways: either by supposing that they are the posterity of Ham, who was cursed; or that GOD at first created two kinds of men, one black and another white; or that by the heat of the sun the skin is scorched, and so acquires a sooty hue. This matter has been much canvassed among naturalists, but has never been brought to any certain issue.' What the Irishman said is totally obliterated from my mind; but I remember that he became very warm and intemperate in his expressions; upon which Johnson rose, and quietly walked away. When he had retired, his antagonist took his revenge, as he thought, by saying, 'He has a most ungainly figure, and an affectation of pomposity, unworthy of a man of genius.'

Johnson had not observed that I was in the room. I followed him, however, and he agreed to meet me in the evening at the Mitre. I called on him, and we went thither at nine. We had a good supper, and port wine, of which he then sometimes drank a bottle. The orthodox high-church sound of the *Mitre*,—the figure and manner of the celebrated *Samuel Johnson*,—the extraordinary power and precision of his conversation, and the pride arising from finding myself admitted as his companion, produced a variety of sensations, and a pleasing elevation of mind beyond what I had ever before experienced. I find in my journal the following minute of our conversation, which, though it will give but a very faint notion of what passed, is, in some degree, a valuable record; and it will be curious in this view, as shewing how habitual to his mind were some opinions which appear in his works.

'Sir, I do not think Gray a first-rate poet. He has not a bold imagination, nor much command of words. The obscurity in which he has involved himself will not persuade us that he is sublime. His Elegy in a Church-yard has a happy selection of images, but I don't like what are called his great things. His Ode which begins

> "Ruin seize thee, ruthless King,
>   Confusion on thy banners wait!"

has been celebrated for its abruptness, and plunging into the subject all at once. But such arts as these have no merit, unless when they are original. We admire them only once; and this abruptness has nothing new in it. We have had it often before. Nay, we have it in the old song of Johnny Armstrong:

> "Is there ever a man in all Scotland
>   From the highest estate to the lowest degree, &c."

And then, Sir,

> "Yes, there is a man in Westmoreland,
>   And Johnny Armstrong they do him call."

There, now, you plunge at once into the subject. You have no previous narration to lead you to it.—The two next lines in that Ode are, I think, very good:

> "Though fann'd by conquest's crimson wing,
>   They mock the air with idle state."'

Finding him in a placid humour, and wishing to avail myself of the opportunity which I fortunately had of consulting a sage, to hear whose wisdom, I conceived in the ardour of youthful imagination, that men filled with a noble enthusiasm for intellectual improvement would gladly have resorted from distant lands;—I opened my mind to him ingenuously, and gave him a little sketch of my life, to which he was pleased to listen with great attention.

I acknowledged, that though educated very strictly in the principles of religion, I had for some time been misled into a certain degree of infidelity; but that I was come now to a better way of thinking, and was fully satisfied of the truth of the Christian revelation, though I was not clear as to every point considered to be orthodox. Being at all times a curious examiner of the human mind, and pleased with an undisguised display of what had passed in it, he called to me with warmth, 'Give me your hand; I have taken a liking to you.' He then began to descant upon the force of testimony, and the little we could know of final causes; so that the objections of, why was it so? or why was it not so? ought not to disturb us: adding, that he himself had at one period been guilty of a temporary neglect of religion, but that it was not the result of argument, but mere absence of thought.

We talked of belief in ghosts. He said, 'Sir, I make a distinction between what a man may experience by the mere strength of his imagination, and what imagination cannot possibly produce. Thus, suppose I should think that I saw a form, and heard a voice cry "Johnson, you are a very wicked fellow, and unless you repent you will certainly be punished;" my own unworthiness is so deeply impressed upon my mind, that I might *imagine* I thus saw and heard, and therefore I should not believe that an external communication had been made to me. But if a form should appear, and a voice should tell me that a particular man had died at a particular place, and a particular hour, a fact which I had no apprehension of, nor any means of knowing, and this fact, with all its circumstances, should afterwards be unquestionably proved, I should, in that case, be persuaded that I had supernatural intelligence imparted to me.'

Here it is proper, once for all, to give a true and fair statement of Johnson's way of thinking upon the question, whether departed spirits are ever permitted to appear in this world, or in any way to operate upon human life. He has been ignorantly misrepresented as weakly credulous upon that subject; and, therefore, though I feel an inclination to disdain and treat with silent contempt so foolish a notion concerning my illustrious friend, yet as I find it has gained ground, it is necessary to refute it. The real fact then is, that Johnson had a very philosophical mind, and such a rational respect for testimony, as to make him submit his understanding to what was authentically proved, though he could not comprehend why it was so. Being thus disposed, he was willing to inquire into the truth of any relation of supernatural agency, a general belief of which has prevailed in all nations and ages. But so far was he from being the dupe of implicit faith, that he examined the matter with a jealous attention, and no man was more ready to refute its falsehood when he had discovered it. Churchill, in his poem entitled 'The Ghost,' availed himself of the absurd credulity imputed to Johnson, and drew a caricature of him under the name of 'Pomposo,' representing him as one of the believers of the story of a Ghost in Cock-lane, which, in the year 1762, had gained very general credit in London. Many of my readers, I am convinced, are to this hour under an impression that Johnson was thus foolishly deceived. It will therefore surprise them a good deal when they are informed upon undoubted authority, that Johnson was one of those by whom the imposture was detected. The story had become so popular, that he thought it should be investigated; and in this research he was assisted by the Reverend Dr. Douglas, now Bishop of Salisbury, the great detecter of impostures; who informs me, that after the gentlemen who went and examined into the evidence were satisfied of its falsity, Johnson wrote in their presence an account of it, which was published in the newspapers and Gentleman's Magazine, and undeceived the world.

Our conversation proceeded. 'Sir, (said he) I am a friend to subordination, as most conducive to the happiness of society. There is a reciprocal pleasure in governing and being governed.'

'Dr. Goldsmith is one of the first men we now have as an authour, and he is a very worthy man too. He has been loose in his principles, but he is coming right.'

I mentioned Mallet's tragedy of 'Elvira,' which had been acted the preceding winter at Drury-lane, and that the Honourable Andrew Erskine, Mr. Dempster, and myself, had joined in writing a pamphlet, entitled 'Critical Strictures' against it. That the mildness of Dempster's disposition had, however, relented; and he had candidly said, 'We have hardly a right to abuse this tragedy; for bad as it is, how vain should either of us be to write one not near so good.' *Johnson.* 'Why no, Sir; this is not just reasoning. You *may* abuse a tragedy, though you cannot write one. You may scold a carpenter who has made you a bad table, though you cannot make a table. It is not your trade to make tables.'

I complained to him that I had not yet acquired much knowledge, and asked his advice as to my studies. He said, 'Don't talk of study now. I will give you a plan; but it will require some time to consider of it.' 'It is very good in you (I replied,) to allow me to be with you thus. Had it been foretold to me some years ago that I should pass an evening with the authour of the *Rambler,* how should I have exulted!' What I then expressed, was sincerely from the heart. He was satisfied that it was, and cordially answered, 'Sir, I am glad we have met. I hope we shall pass many evenings and mornings too, together.' We finished a couple of bottles of port, and sat till between one and two in the morning.

As Dr. Oliver Goldsmith will frequently appear in this narrative, I shall endeavour to make my readers in some degree acquainted with his singular character. He was a native of Ireland, and a contemporary with Mr. Burke, at Trinity College, Dublin, but did not then give much promise of future celebrity. He, however, observed to Mr. Malone, that 'though he made no great figure in mathematicks, which was a study in much repute there, he could turn an Ode of Horace into English better then any of them.' He afterwards studied physick at Edinburgh, and upon the Continent; and I have been informed, was enabled to pursue his travels on foot, partly by demanding at Universities to enter the lists as a disputant, by which, according to the custom of many of them, he was entitled to the premium of a crown, when luckily for him his challenge was not accepted; so that, as I once observed to Dr. Johnson, he *disputed* his passage through Europe. He then came to England, and was employed successively in the capacities of an usher to an academy, a corrector of the press, a reviewer, and a writer for a news-paper. He had sagacity enough to cultivate assiduously the acquaintance of Johnson, and his faculties were gradually enlarged by the contemplation of such a model. To me and many others it appeared that he studiously copied the manner of Johnson, though, indeed, upon a smaller scale.

His mind resembled a fertile, but thin soil. There was a quick, but not a strong vegetation, of whatever chanced to be thrown upon it. No deep root could be struck. The oak of the forest did not grow there; but the elegant shrubbery and the fragrant parterre appeared in gay succession. It has been generally circulated and believed that he was a mere fool in conversation; but, in truth, this has been greatly exaggerated. He had, no doubt, a more than common share of that hurry of ideas which we often find in his countrymen, and which sometimes produces a laughable confusion in expressing them. His person was short, his countenance coarse and vulgar, his deportment that of a scholar aukwardly affecting the easy gentleman. Those who were in any way distinguished, excited envy in him to so ridiculous an excess, that the instances of it are hardly credible. When accompanying two beautiful young ladies with their mother on a tour in France, he was seriously angry that more attention was paid to them than to him; and once at the exhibition of the *Fantoccini* in London, when those who sat next him observed with what dexterity a puppet was made to toss a pike, he could not bear that it should have such praise, and exclaimed with some warmth, 'Pshaw! I can do it better myself.'

He boasted to me at this time of the power of his pen in commanding money, which I believe was true in a certain degree, though in the instance he gave he was by no means correct. He told me that he had sold a novel for four hundred pounds. This was his 'Vicar of Wakefield.' But Johnson informed me, that he had made the bargain for Goldsmith, and the price was sixty pounds. 'And, Sir, (said he,) a sufficient price too, when it was sold; for then the fame of Goldsmith had not been elevated, as it afterwards was, by his "Traveller"; and the bookseller had such faint hopes of profit by his bargain, that he kept the manuscript by him a long time, and did not publish it till after the "Traveller" had appeared. Then, to be sure, it was accidentally worth more money.'

Mrs. Piozzi and Sir John Hawkins have strangely mis-stated the history of Goldsmith's situation and Johnson's friendly interference, when this novel was sold. I shall give it authentically from Johnson's own exact narration: 'I received one morning a message from poor Goldsmith that he was in great distress, and, as it was not in his power to come to me, begging that I would come to him as soon as possible. I sent him a guinea, and promised to come to him directly. I accordingly went as soon as I was drest, and found that his landlady had arrested him for his rent, at which he was in a violent passion. I perceived that he had already changed my guinea, and had got a bottle of Madeira and a glass before him. I put the cork into the bottle, desired he would be calm, and began to talk to him of the means by which he might be extricated. He then told me that he had a novel ready for the press, which he produced to me. I looked into it, and saw its merit; told the landlady I should soon return, and having gone to a bookseller, sold it for sixty pounds. I brought Goldsmith the money, and he discharged his rent, not without rating his landlady in a high tone for having used him so ill.'

My next meeting with Johnson was on Friday the 1st of July, when he and I and Dr. Goldsmith supped together at the Mitre. I was before this time pretty well acquainted with Goldsmith, who was one of the brightest ornaments of the Johnsonian school. Goldsmith's respectful attachment to Johnson was then at its height; for his own literary reputation had not yet distinguished him so much as to excite a vain desire of competition with his great Master. He had increased my admiration of the goodness of Johnson's heart, by incidental remarks in the course of conversation, such as, when I mentioned Mr. Levet, whom he entertained under his roof, 'He is poor and honest, which is recommendation enough to Johnson;' and when I wondered that he was very kind to a man of whom I had heard a very bad character, 'He is now become miserable, and that insures the protection of Johnson.'

Dr. John Campbell, the celebrated political and biographical writer, being mentioned, Johnson said, 'Campbell is not always rigidly careful of truth in his conversation; but I do not believe there is any thing of this carelessness in his books. Campbell is a good man, a pious man. I am afraid he has not been in the inside of a church for many years; but he never passes a church without pulling off his hat. This shews that he has good principles. I used to go pretty often to Campbell's on a Sunday evening, till I began to consider that the shoals of Scotchmen who flocked about him might probably say, when any thing of mine was well done, "Ay, ay, he has learnt this of *Cawmell!*" '

He talked very contemptuously of Churchill's poetry, observing, that 'it had a temporary currency, only from its audacity of abuse, and being filled with living names, and that it would sink into oblivion. However, I will acknowledge that I have a better opinion of him now, than I once had; for he has shewn more fertility than I expected. To be sure, he is a tree that cannot produce good fruit: he only bears crabs. But, Sir, a tree that produces a great many crabs is better than a tree which produces only a few.'

Let me here apologize for the imperfect manner in which I am obliged to exhibit Johnson's conversation at this period. In the early part of my acquaintance with him, I was so wrapt in admiration of his extraordinary colloquial talents, and so little acustomed to his peculiar mode of expression, that I found it extremely difficult to recollect and record his conversation with its genuine vigour and vivacity. In progress of time, when my mind was, as it were, *strongly impregnated with the Johnsonian æther,* I could, with much more facility and exactness, carry in my memory and commit to paper the exuberant variety of his wisdom and wit.

At this time *Miss* Williams, as she was then called, though she did not reside with him in the Temple under his roof, but had lodgings in Bolt-court, Fleet-street, had so much of his attention, that he every night drank tea with her before he went home, however late it might be, and she always sat up for him. This, it may be fairly conjectured, was not alone a proof of his regard for *her,* but of his own unwillingness to go into solitude, before that unseasonable hour at which he had habituated himself to expect the oblivion of repose. Dr. Goldsmith, being a privileged man, went with him this night, strutting away, and calling to me with an air of superiority, like that of an esoterick over an exoterick disciple of a sage of antiquity, 'I go to Miss Williams.' I confess, I then envied him this mighty privilege, of which he seemed so proud; but it was not long before I obtained the same mark of distinction.

On Tuesday the 5th of July, I again visited Johnson. Talking of London, he observed, 'Sir, if you wish to have a just notion of the magnitude of this city, you must not be satisfied with seeing its great streets and squares, but must survey the innumerable little lanes and courts. It is not in the showy evolutions of buildings, but in the multiplicity of human habitations which are crouded together, that the wonderful immensity of London consists.'

On Wednesday, July 6, he was engaged to sup with me at my lodgings in Downing-street, Westminster. But on the preceding night my landlord having behaved very rudely to me and some company who were with me, I had resolved not to remain another night in his house. I was exceedingly uneasy at the aukward appearance I supposed I should make to Johnson and the other gentlemen whom I had invited, not being able to receive them at home, and being obliged to order supper at the Mitre. I went to Johnson in the morning, and talked of it as of a serious distress. He laughed, and said, 'Consider, Sir, how insignificant this will appear a twelvemonth hence.' —Were this consideration to be applied to most of the little vexatious incidents of life, by which our quiet is too often disturbed, it would prevent many painful sensations. I have tried it frequently, with good effect. 'There is nothing (continued he) in this mighty misfortune; nay, we shall be better at the Mitre.'

I had as my guests this evening at the Mitre tavern, Dr. Johnson, Dr. Goldsmith, Mr. Thomas Davies, Mr. Eccles, an Irish gentleman, for whose agreeable company I was obliged to Mr. Davies, and the Reverend Mr. John Ogilvie, who was desirous of being in company with my illustrious friend, while I, in my turn, was proud to have the honour of shewing one of my countrymen upon what easy terms Johnson permitted me to live with him.

Mr. Ogilvie was unlucky enough to choose for the topick of his conversation the praises of his native country. He began with saying, that there was very rich land round Edinburgh. Goldsmith, who had studied physick there, contradicted this, very untruly, with a sneering laugh. Disconcerted a little by this, Mr. Ogilvie then took new ground, where, I suppose, he thought himself perfectly safe; for he observed, that Scotland had a great many noble wild prospects. *Johnson*. 'I believe, Sir, you have a great many. Norway, too, has noble wild prospects; and Lapland is remarkable for prodigious noble wild prospects. But, Sir, let me tell you, the noblest prospect which

a Scotchman ever sees, is the high road that leads him to England!'

On Saturday, July 9, I found Johnson surrounded with a
numerous levee, but have not preserved any part of his conversation. On the 14th we had another evening by ourselves at
the Mitre.

To such a degree of unrestrained frankness had he now accustomed me, that in the course of this evening I talked of the
numerous reflections which had been thrown out against him
on account of his having accepted a pension from his present
Majesty. 'Why, Sir, (said he, with a hearty laugh,) it is a
mighty foolish noise that they make. I have accepted of a pension as a reward which has been thought due to my literary
merit; and now that I have this pension, I am the same man in
every respect that I have ever been; I retain the same principles. It is true, that I cannot now curse (smiling) the House
of Hanover; nor would it be decent for me to drink King
James's health in the wine that King George gives me money
to pay for. But, Sir, I think that the pleasure of cursing the
House of Hanover, and drinking King James's health, are amply overbalanced by three hundred pounds a year.'

There was here, most certainly, an affectation of more Jaco-
bitism than he really had; for I have heard him declare, that
if holding up his right hand would have secured victory at
Culloden to Prince Charles's army, he was not sure he would
have held it up; so little confidence had he in the right claimed
by the house of Stuart, and so fearful was he of the consequences of another revolution on the throne of Great-Britain;
and Mr. Topham Beauclerk assured me, he had heard him say
this before he had his pension. He no doubt had an early attachment to the House of Stuart; but his zeal had cooled as
his reason strengthened. Indeed I heard him once say, that
'after the death of a violent Whig, with whom he used to contend with great eagerness, he felt his Toryism much abated.'

He recommended to me to keep a journal of my life, full
and unreserved. He said it would be a very good exercise, and
would yield me great satisfaction when the particulars were
faded from my remembrance. I was uncommonly fortunate in
having had a previous coincidence of opinion with him upon

this subject, for I had kept such a journal for some time; and it was no small pleasure to me to have this to tell him, and to receive his approbation. He counselled me to keep it private, and said I might surely have a friend who would burn it in case of my death. From this habit I have been enabled to give the world so many anecdotes, which would otherwise have been lost to posterity. I mentioned that I was afraid I put into my journal too many little incidents. *Johnson.* 'There is nothing, Sir, too little for so little a creature as man. It is by studying little things that we attain the great art of having as little misery and as much happiness as possible.'

On Tuesday, July 18, I found tall Sir Thomas Robinson sitting with Johnson. Sir Thomas said, that the King of Prussia valued himself upon three things;—upon being a hero, a musician, and an authour. *Johnson.* 'Pretty well, Sir, for one man. As to his being an authour, I have not looked at his poetry; but his prose is poor stuff. He writes just as you might suppose Voltaire's footboy to do, who has been his amanuensis. He has such parts as the valet might have, and about as much of the colouring of the style as might be got by transcribing his works.' When I was at Ferney, I repeated this to Voltaire, in order to reconcile him somewhat to Johnson, whom he, in affecting the English mode of expression, had previously characterised as 'a superstitious dog;' but after hearing such a criticism on Frederick the Great, with whom he was then on bad terms, he exclaimed, 'An honest fellow!'

Mr. Levet this day shewed me Dr. Johnson's library, which was contained in two garrets over his Chambers, where Lintot, son of the celebrated bookseller of that name, had formerly his warehouse. I found a number of good books, but very dusty and in great confusion. The floor was strewed with manuscript leaves, in Johnson's own hand-writing, which I beheld with a degree of veneration, supposing they perhaps might contain portions of the Rambler, or of Rasselas. I observed an apparatus for chymical experiments, of which Johnson was all his life very fond. The place seemed to be very favourable for retirement and meditation. Johnson told me, that he went up thither without mentioning it to his servant, when he wanted to study, secure from interruption; for he would not allow his

servant to say he was not at home when he really was. 'A servant's strict regard for truth, (said he) must be weakened by
such a practice. A philosopher may know that it is merely a
form of denial; but few servants are such nice distinguishers.
If I accustom a servant to tell a lie for *me,* have I not reason to
apprehend that he will tell many lies for *himself?*' I am, however, satisfied that every servant, of any degree of intelligence,
understands saying his master is not at home, not at all as the
affirmation of a fact, but as customary words, intimating that
his master wishes not to be seen; so that there can be no bad
effect from it.

Mr. Dempster having endeavoured to maintain that intrin-
sick merit *ought* to make the only distinction amongst mankind. *Johnson.* 'Why, Sir, mankind have found that this
cannot be. How shall we determine the proportion of intrin-
sick merit? Were that to be the only distinction amongst mankind, we should soon quarrel about the degrees of it. Were all
distinctions abolished, the strongest would not long acquiesce,
but would endeavour to obtain a superiority by their bodily
strength. But, Sir, as subordination is very necessary for society,
and contentions for superiority very dangerous, mankind, that
is to say, all civilised nations, have settled it upon a plain invariable principle. A man is born to hereditary rank; or his
being appointed to certain offices, gives him a certain rank.
Subordination tends greatly to human happiness. Were we all
upon an equality, we should have no other enjoyment than
mere animal pleasure.'

Next morning I found him alone, and have preserved the following fragments of his conversation. 'Hume, and other scep-
tical innovators, are vain men, and will gratify themselves at
any expence. Truth will not afford sufficient food to their vanity; so they have betaken themselves to errour. Truth, Sir, is a
cow that will yield such people no more milk, and so they are
gone to milk the bull. If I could have allowed myself to gratify
my vanity at the expence of truth, what fame might I have
acquired. Every thing which Hume has advanced against
Christianity had passed through my mind long before he wrote.
Always remember this, that after a system is well settled upon
positive evidence, a few partial objections ought not to shake

it. The human mind is so limited, that it cannot take in all the parts of a subject, so that there may be objections raised against any thing. There are objections against a *plenum,* and objections against a *vacuum;* yet one of them must certainly be true.'

At night, Mr. Johnson and I supped in a private room at the Turk's Head coffee-house, in the Strand. 'I encourage this house (said he); for the mistress of it is a good civil woman, and has not much business.'

'Sir, I love the acquaintance of young people; because, in the first place, I don't like to think myself growing old. In the next place, young acquaintances must last longest, if they do last; and then, Sir, young men have more virtue than old men; they have more generous sentiments in every respect. I love the young dogs of this age: they have more wit and humour and knowledge of life than we had; but then the dogs are not so good scholars. Sir, in my early years I read very hard. It is a sad reflection, but a true one, that I knew almost as much at eighteen as I do now. My judgement, to be sure, was not so good; but, I had all the facts. I remember very well, when I was at Oxford, an old gentleman said to me, "Young man, ply your book diligently now, and acquire a stock of knowledge; for when years come upon you, you will find that poring upon books will be but an irksome task." '

He again insisted on the duty of maintaining subordination of rank. 'Sir, I would no more deprive a nobleman of his respect, than of his money. I consider myself as acting a part in the great system of society, and I do to others as I would have them to do to me. I would behave to a nobleman as I should expect he would behave to me, were I a nobleman and he Sam. Johnson. Sir, there is one Mrs. Macaulay in this town, a great republican. One day when I was at her house, I put on a very grave countenance, and said to her, "Madam, I am now become a convert to your way of thinking. I am convinced that all mankind are upon an equal footing; and to give you an unquestionable proof, Madam, that I am in earnest, here is a very sensible, civil, well-behaved fellow-citizen, your footman; I desire that he may be allowed to sit down and dine with us." I thus, Sir, shewed her the absurdity of the levelling doctrine. She has never liked me since.'

I spoke of Sir James Macdonald as a young man of most distinguished merit, who united the highest reputation at Eton and Oxford, with the patriarchal spirit of a great Highland Chieftain. I mentioned that Sir James had said to me, that he had never seen Mr. Johnson, but he had a great respect for him, though at the same time it was mixed with some degree of terrour. *Johnson.* 'Sir, if he were to be acquainted with me, it might lessen both.'

The mention of this gentleman led us to talk of the Western Islands of Scotland, to visit which he expressed a wish that then appeared to me a very romantick fancy, which I little thought would be afterwards realized. He said, he would go to the Hebrides with me, when I returned from my travels, unless some very good companion should offer when I was absent, which he did not think probable; adding, 'There are few people to whom I take so much to as you.'—I cannot too often remind my readers, that although such instances of his kindness are doubtless very flattering to me, yet I hope my recording them will be ascribed to a better motive than to vanity; for they afford unquestionable evidence of his tenderness and complacency, which some, while they were forced to acknowledge his great powers, have been so strenuous to deny.

He maintained that a boy at school was the happiest of human beings. I supported a different opinion, from which I have never yet varied, that a man is happier; and I enlarged upon the anxiety and sufferings which are endured at school. *Johnson.* 'Ah! Sir, a boy's being flogged is not so severe as a man's having the hiss of the world against him. Men have a solicitude about fame; and the greater share they have of it, the more afraid they are of losing it.'

We talked of the education of children; and I asked him what he thought was best to teach them first. *Johnson.* 'Sir, it is no matter what you teach them first, any more than what leg you shall put into your breeches first. Sir, you may stand disputing which is best to put in first, but in the mean time your breech is bare. Sir, while you are considering which of two things you should teach your child first, another boy has learnt them both.'

On Thursday, July 28, we again supped in private at the

Turk's Head coffee-house. *Johnson*. 'Swift has a higher reputation than he deserves. His excellence is strong sense; for his humour, though very well, is not remarkably good. I doubt whether the "Tale of a Tub" be his; for he never owned it, and it is much above his usual manner.'

I again begged his advice as to my method of study at Utrecht. 'Come, (said he) let us make a day of it. Let us go down to Greenwich and dine, and talk of it there.' The following Saturday was fixed for this excursion.

As we walked along the Strand to-night, arm in arm, a woman of the town accosted us, in the usual enticing manner. 'No, no, my girl, (said Johnson) it won't do.' He, however, did not treat her with harshness, and we talked of the wretched life of such women; and agreed, that much more misery than happiness, upon the whole, is produced by illicit commerce between the sexes.

On Saturday, July 30, Dr. Johnson and I took a sculler at the Temple-stairs, and set out for Greenwich. I asked him if he really thought a knowledge of the Greek and Latin languages an essential requisite to a good education. *Johnson*. 'Most certainly, Sir; for those who know them have a very great advantage over those who do not. Nay, Sir, it is wonderful what a difference learning makes upon people even in the common intercourse of life, which does not appear to be much connected with it.' 'And yet, (said I) people go through the world very well, and carry on the business of life to good advantage, without learning.' *Johnson*. 'Why, Sir, that may be true in cases where learning cannot possibly be of any use; for instance, this boy rows us as well without learning, as if he could sing the song of Orpheus to the Argonauts, who were the first sailors.' He then called to the boy, 'What would you give, my lad, to know about the Argonauts?' 'Sir, (said the boy,) I would give what I have.' Johnson was much pleased with his answer, and we gave him a double fare.

We landed at the Old Swan, and walked to Billingsgate, where we took oars, and moved smoothly along the silver Thames. It was a very fine day. We were entertained with the immense number and variety of ships that were lying at anchor, and with the beautiful country on each side of the river

I talked of preaching, and of the great success which those called Methodists have. *Johnson.* 'Sir, it is owing to their expressing themselves in a plain and familiar manner, which is the only way to do good to the common people. To insist against drunkenness as a crime, because it debases Reason, the noblest faculty of man, would be of no service to the common people: but to tell them that they may die in a fit of drunkenness, and shew them how dreadful that would be, cannot fail to make a deep impression.'

Afterwards he entered upon the business of the day, which was to give me his advice as to a course of study. And here I am to mention with much regret, that my record of what he said is miserably scanty. I recollect with admiration an animating blaze of eloquence, which rouzed every intellectual power in me to the highest pitch, but must have dazzled me so much, that my memory could not preserve the substance of his discourse; for the note which I find of it is no more than this:— 'He ran over the grand scale of human knowledge; advised me to select some particular branch to excel in, but to acquire a little of every kind.'

We walked in the evening in Greenwich Park. He asked me, I suppose, by way of trying my disposition, 'Is not this very fine?' Having no exquisite relish of the beauties of Nature, and being more delighted with 'the busy hum of men,' I answered, 'Yes, Sir; but not equal to Fleet-street.' *Johnson.* 'You are right, Sir.'

We staid so long at Greenwich, that our sail up the river, in our return to London, was by no means so pleasant as in the morning; for the night air was so cold that it made me shiver. I was the more sensible of it from having sat up all the night before, recollecting and writing in my journal what I thought worthy of preservation; an exertion, which, during the first part of my acquaintance with Johnson, I frequently made. I remember having sat up four nights in one week, without being much incommoded in the day time.

Johnson, whose robust frame was not in the least affected by the cold, scolded me, as if my shivering had been a paltry effeminacy, saying, 'Why do you shiver?' Sir William Scott, of the Commons, told me, that when he complained of a head-ach in the post-chaise, as they were travelling together to Scotland, Johnson treated him in the same manner: 'At your age, Sir, I had no head-ach.'

We concluded the day at the Turk's Head coffee-house very socially. He was pleased to listen to a particular account which I gave him of my family, and of its hereditary estate, as to the extent and population of which he asked questions, and made calculations; recommending, at the same time, a liberal kindness to the tenantry, as people over whom the proprietor was placed by Providence. He took delight in hearing my description of the romantick seat of my ancestors. 'I must be there, Sir, (said he) and we will live in the old castle; and if there is not a room in it remaining, we will build one.' I was highly flattered, but could scarcely indulge a hope that Auchinleck would indeed be honoured by his presence, and celebrated by a description, as it afterwards was, in his 'Journey to the Western Islands.'

After we had again talked of my setting out for Holland, he said 'I must see thee out of England: I will accompany you to Harwich.' I could not find words to express what I felt upon this unexpected and very great mark of his affectionate regard.

Next day, Sunday, July 31, I told him I had been that morning at a meeting of the people called Quakers, where I had heard a woman preach. *Johnson.* 'Sir, a woman's preaching is like a dog's walking on his hinder legs. It is not done well; but you are surprized to find it done at all.'

On Tuesday, August 2, (the day of my departure from London having been fixed for the 5th,) Dr. Johnson did me the honour to pass a part of the morning with me at my Chambers. He said, that 'he always felt an inclination to do nothing.' I observed, that it was strange to think that the most indolent man in Britain had written the most laborious work, *The English Dictionary.*

I had now made good my title to be a privileged man, and was carried by him in the evening to drink tea with Miss Williams, whom, though under the misfortune of having lost her sight, I found to be agreeable in conversation; for she had a variety of literature, and expressed herself well; but her peculiar value was the intimacy in which she had long lived with Johnson, by which she was well acquainted with his habits, and knew how to lead him on to talk.

On Wednesday, August 3, we had our last social evening at the Turk's Head coffee-house, before my setting out for foreign parts. I had the misfortune, before we parted, to irritate him unintentionally. I mentioned to him how common it was in the world to tell absurd stories of him, and to ascribe to him very strange sayings. *Johnson.* 'What do they make me say, Sir?' *Boswell.* 'Why, Sir, as an instance very strange indeed, (laughing heartily as I spoke,) David Hume told me, you said that you would stand before a battery of cannon, to restore the Convocation to its full powers.'—Little did I apprehend that he had actually said this: but I was soon convinced of my errour; for, with a determined look, he thundered out 'And would I not, Sir? Shall the Presbyterian *Kirk* of Scotland have its General Assembly, and the Church of England be denied its Convocation?' He was walking up and down the room while I told him the anecdote; but when he uttered this explosion of high-church zeal, he had come close to my chair, and his eyes flashed with indignation. I bowed to the storm, and diverted the force of it, by leading him to expatiate on the influence which religion derived from maintaining the church with great external respectability.

On Friday, August 5, we set out early in the morning in the Harwich stage coach. A fat elderly gentlewoman, and a young Dutchman, seemed the most inclined among us to conversation. At the inn where we dined, the gentlewoman said that she had done her best to educate her children; and, particularly, that she had never suffered them to be a moment idle. *Johnson.* 'I wish, Madam, you would educate me too; for I have been an idle fellow all my life.' 'I am sure, Sir, (said she) you have not been idle.' *Johnson.* 'Nay, Madam, it is very true; and that gentleman there (pointing to me,) has been idle. He was idle at Edinburgh. His father sent him to Glasgow, where he continued to be idle. He then came to London, where he has been very idle; and now he is going to Utrecht, where he will be as idle as ever.' I asked him privately how he could expose me so. *Johnson.* 'Poh, poh! (said he) they knew nothing about you, and will think of it no more.' In the afternoon the gentlewoman talked violently against the Roman Catholicks, and of the horrours of the Inquisition. To the utter astonishment of all the passengers but myself, who knew that he could talk upon any side of a question, he defended the Inquisition, and maintained, that 'false doctrine should be checked on its first appearance; that the civil power should unite with the church in punishing those who dared to attack the established religion, and that such only were punished by the Inquisition.' Though by no means niggardly, his attention to what was generally right was so minute, that having observed at one of the stages that I ostentatiously gave a shilling to the coachman, when the custom was for each passenger to give only sixpence, he took me aside and scolded me, saying that what I had done would make the coachman dissatisfied with all the rest of the passengers, who gave him no more than his due.

At supper this night he talked of good eating with uncommon satisfaction. 'Some people (said he,) have a foolish way of not minding, or pretending not to mind, what they eat. For my part, I mind my belly very studiously, and very carefully; for I look upon it, that he who does not mind his belly will hardly mind any thing else.' I never knew any man who relished good eating more than he did. When at table, he was totally absorbed in the business of the moment; his looks seemed rivetted to his plate; nor would he, unless when in very high company, say one word, or even pay the least attention to what was said by others, till he had satisfied his appetite, which was so fierce, and indulged with such intenseness, that while in the act of eating, the veins of his forehead swelled, and generally a strong perspiration was visible. But it must be owned, that Johnson, though he could be rigidly *abstemious,* was not a *temperate* man either in eating or drinking. He could refrain, but he could not use moderately. He told me, that he had fasted two days without inconvenience, and that he had never been hungry but once. They who beheld with wonder how much he eat upon all occasions when his dinner was to his taste, could not easily conceive what he must have meant by hunger; and not only was he remarkable for the extraordinary quantity which he eat, but he was, or affected to be, a man of very nice discernment in the science of cookery. He used to descant critically on the dishes which had been at table where he had dined or supped, and to recollect very minutely what he had liked. When invited to dine, even with an intimate friend, he was not pleased if something better than a plain dinner was not prepared for him. I have heard him say on such an occasion, 'This was a good dinner enough, to be sure; but it was not a dinner to *ask* a man to.'

Next day we got to Harwich to dinner; and my passage in the packet-boat to Helvoetsluys being secured, and my baggage put on board, we dined at our inn by ourselves. I happened to say it would be terrible if he should not find a speedy opportunity of returning to London, and be confined to so dull a place. *Johnson.* 'Don't, Sir, accustom yourself to use big words for little matters. It would *not* be *terrible*, though I *were* to be detained some time here.' The practice of using words of disproportionate magnitude, is, no doubt, too frequent every where; but, I think, most remarkable among the French, of which, all who have travelled in France must have been struck with innumerable instances.

We went and looked at the church, and having gone into it and walked up to the altar, Johnson, whose piety was constant and fervent, sent me to my knees, saying, 'Now that you are going to leave your native country, recommend yourself to the protection of your *Creator* and *Redeemer*.'

After we came out of the church, we stood talking for some time together of Bishop Berkeley's ingenious sophistry to prove the non-existence of matter, and that every thing in the universe is merely ideal. I observed, that though we are satisfied his doctrine is not true, it is impossible to refute it. I never shall forget the alacrity with which Johnson answered, striking his foot with mighty force against a large stone, till he rebounded from it, 'I refute it *thus*.'

My revered friend walked down with me to the beach, where we embraced and parted with tenderness, and engaged to correspond by letters. I said, 'I hope, Sir, you will not forget me in my absence.' *Johnson.* 'Nay, Sir, it is more likely you should forget me, than that I should forget you.' As the vessel put out to sea, I kept my eyes upon him for a considerable time, while he remained rolling his majestick frame in his usual manner: and at last I perceived him walk back into the town, and he disappeared.

1764: ÆTAT. 55.]—Early in 1764 Johnson paid a visit to the Langton family, at their seat of Langton, in Lincolnshire, where he passed some time, much to his satisfaction. His friend Bennet Langton, it will not be doubted, did every thing in his power to make the place agreeable to so illustrious a guest; and the elder Mr. Langton and his lady, being fully capable of understanding his value, were not wanting in attention. He, however, told me, that old Mr. Langton, though a man of considerable learning, had so little allowance to make for his occasional 'laxity of talk,' that because in the course of discussion he sometimes mentioned what might be said in favour of the peculiar tenets of the Romish church, he went to his grave believing him to be of that communion.

Soon after his return to London, which was in February, was founded that *Club* which existed long without a name, but at Mr. Garrick's funeral became distinguished by the title of *The Literary Club*. Sir Joshua Reynolds had the merit of being the first proposer of it, to which Johnson acceded, and the original members were, Sir Joshua Reynolds, Dr. Johnson, Mr. Edmund Burke, Dr. Nugent, Mr. Beauclerk, Mr. Langton, Dr. Goldsmith, Mr. Chamier, and Sir John Hawkins. They met at the Turk's Head, in Gerrard-street, Soho, one evening in every week, at seven, and generally continued their conversation till a pretty late hour.

Sir John Hawkins represents himself as a *'seceder'* from this society, and assigns as the reason of his *'withdrawing'* himself from it, that its late hours were inconsistent with his domestick arrangements. In this he is not accurate; for the fact was, that he one evening attacked Mr. Burke, in so rude a manner, that all the company testified their displeasure; and at their next meeting his reception was such, that he never came again.

He is equally inaccurate with respect to Mr. Garrick, of whom he says, 'he trusted that the least intimation of a desire to come among us, would procure him a ready admission; but in this he was mistaken. Johnson consulted me upon it; and when I could find no objection to receiving him, exclaimed,— "He will disturb us by his buffoonery;"—and afterwards so managed matters, that he was never formally proposed, and, by consequence, never admitted.'

In justice both to Mr. Garrick and Dr. Johnson, I think it necessary to rectify this mis-statement. The truth is, that not very long after the institution of our club, Sir Joshua Reynolds was speaking of it to Garrick. 'I like it much, (said he,) I think I shall be of you.' When Sir Joshua mentioned this to Dr. Johnson, he was much displeased with the actor's conceit. '*He'll be of us,* (said Johnson) how does he know we will *permit* him? The first Duke in England has no right to hold such language.' However, when Garrick was regularly proposed some time afterwards, Johnson, though he had taken a momentary offence at his arrogance, warmly and kindly supported him, and he was accordingly elected, was a most agreeable member, and continued to attend our meetings to the time of his death.

In this year, except what he may have done in revising Shakspeare, we do not find that he laboured much in literature. The ease and independence to which he had at last attained by royal munificence, increased his natural indolence. In his 'Meditations' he thus accuses himself:

'GOOD FRIDAY, April 20, 1764. I have made no reformation; I have lived totally useless, more sensual in thought, and more addicted to wine and meat.'

And next morning he thus feelingly complains:

'My indolence, since my last reception of the sacrament, has sunk into grosser sluggishness, and my dissipation spread into wilder negligence. My thoughts have been clouded with sensuality; and, except that from the beginning of this year I have, in some measure, forborne excess of strong drink, my appetites have predominated over my reason. A kind of strange oblivion has overspread me, so that I know not what has become of the last year; and perceive that incidents and intelligence pass over me, without leaving any impression.'

He then solemnly says,

'This is not the life to which heaven is promised;'

and he earnestly resolves on amendment.

It was his custom to observe certain days with a pious abstraction; viz. New-year's-day, the day of his wife's death, Good Friday, Easter-day, and his own birth-day. He this year says, 'I have now spent fifty-five years in resolving; having, from the earliest time almost that I can remember, been forming schemes of a better life. I have done nothing. The need of doing, there-'ore, is pressing, since the time of doing is short. O GOD, grant me to resolve aright, and to keep my resolutions, for JESUS CHRIST's sake. Amen.'

About this time he was afflicted with a very severe return of the hypochondriack disorder, which was ever lurking about him. He was so ill, as, notwithstanding his remarkable love of company, to be entirely averse to society, the most fatal symptom of that malady. Dr. Adams told me, that, as an old friend, he was admitted to visit him, and that he found him in a deplorable state, sighing, groaning, talking to himself, and restlessly walking from room to room. He then used this emphatical expression of the misery which he felt: 'I would consent to have a limb amputated to recover my spirits.'

Talking to himself was, indeed, one of his singularities ever since I knew him. I was certain that he was frequently uttering pious ejaculations; for fragments of the Lord's Prayer have been distinctly overheard. His friend Mr. Thomas Davies, of whom Churchill says,

'That Davies hath a very pretty wife:'

when Dr. Johnson muttered 'lead us not into temptation,' used with waggish and gallant humour to whisper Mrs. Davies, 'You, my dear, are the cause of this.'

He had another particularity, of which none of his friends ever ventured to ask an explanation. It appeared to me some superstitious habit, which he had contracted early, and from which he had never called upon his reason to disentangle him. This was his anxious care to go out or in at a door or passage, by a certain number of steps from a certain point, or at least so as that either his right or his left foot, (I am not certain which,) should constantly make the first actual movement when he came close to the door or passage. Thus I conjecture: for I have, upon innumerable occasions, observed him suddenly stop, and then seem to count his steps with a deep ear-

nestness; and when he had neglected or gone wrong in this
sort of magical movement, I have seen him go back again, put
himself in a proper posture to begin the ceremony, and, having
gone through it, break from his abstraction, walk briskly on,
and join his companion.

That the most minute singularities which belonged to him,
and made very observable parts of his appearance and manner,
may not be omitted, it is requisite to mention, that while talking or even musing as he sat in his chair, he commonly held
his head to one side towards his right shoulder, and shook it
in a tremulous manner, moving his body backwards and forwards, and rubbing his left knee in the same direction, with
the palm of his hand. In the intervals of articulating he made
various sounds with his mouth, sometimes as if ruminating, or
what is called chewing the cud, sometimes giving a half whistle, sometimes making his tongue play backwards from the
roof of his mouth, as if clucking like a hen, and sometimes
protruding it against his upper gums in front, as if pronouncing quickly under his breath, *too, too, too:* all this accompanied
sometimes with a thoughtful look, but more frequently with a
smile. Generally when he had concluded a period, in the
course of a dispute, by which time he was a good deal exhausted by violence and vociferation, he used to blow out his
breath like a Whale. This I suppose was a relief to his lungs;
and seemed in him to be a contemptuous mode of expression,
as if he had made the arguments of his opponent fly like chaff
before the wind.

1765: ÆTAT. 56.]—Early in the year 1765 he paid a short
visit to the University of Cambridge, with his friend Mr. Beauclerk.

Trinity College, Dublin, at this time surprised Johnson with
a spontaneous compliment of the highest academical honours,
by creating him Doctor of Laws.

This unsolicited mark of distinction, conferred on so great
a literary character, did much honour to the judgement and
liberal spirit of that learned body. Johnson acknowledged the
favour in a letter to Dr. Leland, one of their number; but I
have not been able to obtain a copy of it.

This year was distinguished by his being introduced into

the family of Mr. Thrale, one of the most eminent brewers in England, and Member of Parliament for the borough of Southwark. Mr. Thrale had married Miss Hesther Lynch Salusbury, of good Welch extraction, a lady of lively talents, improved by education. That Johnson's introduction into Mr. Thrale's family, which contributed so much to the happiness of his life, was owing to her desire for his conversation, is very probable and a general supposition: but it is not the truth. Mr. Murphy, who was intimate with Mr. Thrale, having spoken very highly of Dr. Johnson, he was requested to make them acquainted. This being mentioned to Johnson, he accepted of an invitation to dinner at Thrale's, and was so much pleased with his reception, both by Mr. and Mrs. Thrale, and they so much pleased with him, that his invitations to their house were more and more frequent, till at last he became one of the family, and an apartment was appropriated to him, both in their house in Southwark, and in their villa at Streatham.

As this family will frequently be mentioned in the course of the following pages, and as a false notion has prevailed that Mr. Thrale was inferiour, and in some degree insignificant, compared with Mrs. Thrale, it may be proper to give a true state of the case from the authority of Johnson himself, in his own words.

'I know no man, (said he,) who is more master of his wife and family than Thrale. If he but holds up a finger, he is obeyed. It is a great mistake to suppose that she is above him in literary attainments. She is more flippant; but he has ten times her learning: he is a regular scholar; but her learning is that of a school-boy in one of the lower forms.' My readers may naturally wish for some representation of the figures of this couple. Mr. Thrale was tall, well proportioned, and stately. As for *Madam*, or *my Mistress*, by which epithets Johnson used to mention Mrs. Thrale, she was short, plump, and brisk. She has herself given us a lively view of the idea which Johnson had of her person, on her appearing before him in a dark-coloured gown: 'You little creatures should never wear those sort of clothes, however; they are unsuitable in every way. What! have not all insects gay colours?'

Nothing could be more fortunate for Johnson than this connection. He had at Mr. Thrale's all the comforts and even luxuries of life; his melancholy was diverted, and his irregular habits lessened by association with an agreeable and well-ordered family. He was treated with the utmost respect, and even affection. The vivacity of Mrs. Thrale's literary talk roused him to cheerfulness and exertion, even when they were alone. But this was not often the case; for he found here a constant succession of what gave him the highest enjoyment: the society of the learned, the witty, and the eminent in every way, who were assembled in numerous companies, called forth his wonderful powers, and gratified him with admiration, to which no man could be insensible.

In the October of this year he at length gave to the world his edition of Shakspeare, which, if it had no other merit but that of producing his Preface, in which the excellencies and defects of that immortal bard are displayed with a masterly hand, the nation would have had no reason to complain. A blind indiscriminate admiration of Shakspeare had exposed the British nation to the ridicule of foreigners. Johnson, by candidly admitting the faults of his poet, had the more credit in bestowing on him deserved and indisputable praise.

IN 1764 and 1765 it should seem that Dr. Johnson was so busily employed with his edition of Shakspeare, as to have had little leisure for any other literary exertion, or, indeed, even for private correspondence. He did not favour me with a single letter for more than two years, for which it will appear that he afterwards apologised.

1766: ÆTAT. 57.]—I returned to London in February, and found Dr. Johnson in a good house in Johnson's-court, Fleet-street, in which he had accommodated Miss Williams with an apartment on the ground floor, while Mr. Levett occupied his post in the garret: his faithful Francis was still attending upon him. He received me with much kindness. The fragments of our first conversation, which I have preserved, are these: I told him that Voltaire, in a conversation with me, had distinguished Pope and Dryden thus:—'Pope drives a handsome chariot, with a couple of neat trim nags; Dryden a coach, and six stately horses.' *Johnson.* 'Why, Sir, the truth is, they both drive coaches and six; but Dryden's horses are either galloping or stumbling:

Pope's go at a steady even trot.' He sa.. of Goldsmith's 'Traveller', which had been published in my absence, 'There has not
been so fine a poem since Pope's time.'

And here it is proper to settle, with authentick precision,
what has long floated in publick report, as to Johnson's being
himself the authour of a considerable part of that poem. Much,
no doubt, both of the sentiments and expression, were derived
from conversation with him; and it was certainly submitted to
his friendly revision: but in the year 1783, he, at my request,
marked with a pencil the lines which he had furnished, which
are only line 420th,

> 'To stop too fearful, and too faint to go;'

and the concluding ten lines, except the last couplet but one,
which I distinguish by the Italick character:

> 'How small of all that human hearts endure,
> That part which kings or laws can cause or cure.
> Still to ourselves in every place consign'd,
> Our own felicity we make or find;
> With secret course, which no loud storms annoy,
> Glides the smooth current of domestick joy.
> *The lifted axe, the agonizing wheel,*
> *Luke's iron crown, and Damien's bed of steel,*
> To men remote from power, but rarely known,
> Leave reason, faith, and conscience, all our own.'

He added, 'These are all of which I can be sure.' They bear a
small proportion to the whole, which consists of four hundred
and thirty-eight verses.

Dr. Johnson at the same time favoured me by marking the
lines which he furnished to Goldsmith's 'Deserted Village,'
which are only the last four:

> 'That trade's proud empire hastes to swift decay,
> As ocean sweeps the labour'd mole away:
> While self-dependent power can time defy,
> As rocks resist the billows and the sky.'

Talking of education, 'People have now a-days, (said he,)
got a strange opinion that every thing should be taught by
lectures. Now, I cannot see that lectures can do so much good

as reading the books from which the lectures are taken. I know nothing that can be best taught by lectures, except where experiments are to be shewn. You may teach chymistry by lectures.—You might teach making of shoes by lectures!'

At night I supped with him at the Mitre tavern, that we might renew our social intimacy at the original place of meeting. But there was now a considerable difference in his way of living. Having had an illness, in which he was advised to leave off wine, he had, from that period, continued to abstain from it, and drank only water, or lemonade.

I told him that a foreign friend of his, whom I had met with abroad, was so wretchedly perverted to infidelity, that he treated the hopes of immortality with brutal levity; and said, 'As man dies like a dog, let him lie like a dog.' *Johnson.* 'If he dies like a dog, *let* him lie like a dog.' I added, that this man said to me, 'I hate mankind, for I think myself one of the best of them, and I know how bad I am.' *Johnson.* 'Sir, he must be very singular in his opinion, if he thinks himself one of the best of men; for none of his friends think him so.'—He said, no honest man could be a Deist; for no man could be so after a fair examination of the proofs of Christianity.' I named Hume. *Johnson.* 'No, Sir; Hume owned to a clergyman in the bishoprick of Durham, that he had never read the New Testament with attention.' I mentioned Hume's notion, that all who are happy are equally happy; a little miss with a new gown at a dancing-school ball, a general at the head of a victorious army, and an orator, after having made an eloquent speech in a great assembly. *Johnson.* 'Sir, that all who are happy, are equally happy, is not true. A peasant and a philosopher may be equally *satisfied,* but not equally *happy.* Happiness consists in the multiplicity of agreeable consciousness. A peasant has not capacity for having equal happiness with a philosopher.' I remember this very question very happily illustrated in opposition to Hume, by the Reverend Mr. Robert Brown, at Utrecht. 'A small drinking-glass and a large one, (said he,) may be equally full; but the large one holds more than the small.'

I talked of the mode adopted by some to rise in the world, by courting great men, and asked him whether he had ever submitted to it. *Johnson.* 'Why, Sir, I never was near enough to great men to court them. You may be prudently attached to great men, and yet independent. You are not to do what you think wrong; and, Sir, you are to calculate, and not pay too dear for what you get. You must not give a shilling's worth of court for six-pence worth of good. But if you can get a shilling's worth of good for six-pence worth of court, you are a fool if you do not pay court.'

I introduced the subject of second sight, and other mysterious manifestations; the fulfilment of which, I suggested, might happen by chance. *Johnson.* 'Yes, Sir; but they have happened so often, that mankind have agreed to think them not fortuitous.'

Our next meeting at the Mitre was on Saturday the 15th of February, when I presented to him my old and most intimate friend, the Reverend Mr. Temple, then of Cambridge. I having mentioned that I had passed some time with Rousseau in his wild retreat, and having quoted some remark made by Mr. Wilkes, with whom I had spent many pleasant hours in Italy, Johnson said, (sarcastically,) 'It seems, Sir, you have kept very good company abroad, Rousseau and Wilkes!' Thinking it enough to defend one at a time, I said nothing as to my gay friend, but answered with a smile, 'My dear Sir, you don't call Rousseau bad company. Do you really think *him* a bad man?' *Johnson.* 'Sir, if you are talking jestingly of this, I don't talk with you. If you mean to be serious, I think him one of the worst of men; a rascal, who ought to be hunted out of society, as he has been. Three or four nations have expelled him; and it is a shame that he is protected in this country.' *Boswell.* 'I don't deny, Sir, but that his novel may, perhaps, do harm; but I cannot think his intention was bad.' *Johnson.* 'Sir, that will not do. We cannot prove any man's intention to be bad. You may shoot a man through the head, and say you intended to miss him; but the Judge will order you to be hanged. An alledged want of intention, when evil is committed, will not be allowed in a court of justice. Rousseau, Sir, is a very bad man. I would sooner sign a sentence for his transportation, than that of any felon who has gone from the Old Bailey these many years. Yes, I should like to have him work in the plantations.' *Boswell.* 'Sir, do you think him as bad a man as Voltaire?'

Johnson. 'Why, Sir, it is difficult to settle the proportion of iniquity between them.'

On his favourite subject of subordination, Johnson said, 'So far is it from being true that men are naturally equal, that no two people can be half an hour together, but one shall acquire an evident superiority over the other.'

I mentioned the advice given us by philosophers, to console ourselves, when distressed or embarrassed, by thinking of those who are in a worse situation than ourselves. This, I observed, could not apply to all, for there must be some who have nobody worse than they are. *Johnson.* 'Why, to be sure, Sir, there are; but they don't know it. There is no being so poor and so contemptible, who does not think there is somebody still poorer, and still more contemptible.'

Another evening Dr. Goldsmith and I called on him, with the hope of prevailing on him to sup with us at the Mitre. We found him indisposed, and resolved not to go abroad. 'Come then, (said Goldsmith,) we will not go to the Mitre to-night, since we cannot have the big man with us.' Johnson then called for a bottle of port, of which Goldsmith and I partook, while our friend, now a water-drinker, sat by us. *Goldsmith.* 'I think, Mr. Johnson, you don't go near the theatres now. You give yourself no more concern about a new play, than if you had never had any thing to do with the stage.' *Johnson.* 'Why, Sir, our tastes greatly alter. The lad does not care for the child's rattle, and the old man does not care for the young man's whore.' *Goldsmith.* 'Nay, Sir; but your Muse was not a whore.' *Johnson.* 'Sir, I do not think she was. But as we advance in the journey of life, we drop some of the things which have pleased us; whether it be that we are fatigued and don't choose to carry so many things any farther, or that we find other things which we like better.' *Boswell.* 'But, Sir, why don't you give us something in some other way?' *Goldsmith.* 'Ay, Sir, we have a claim upon you.' *Johnson.* 'No, Sir, I am not obliged to do any more. No man is obliged to do as much as he can do. A man is to have part of his life to himself. If a soldier has fought a good many campaigns, he is not to be blamed if he retires to ease and tranquillity. A physician, who has practised long in a great city, may be excused if he retires to a small town, and takes less practice. Now, Sir, the good I can do by my conversation bears the same proportion to the good I can do by my writings, that the practice of a physician, retired to a small town, does to his practice in a great city.' *Boswell*. 'But I wonder, Sir, you have not more pleasure in writing than in not writing.' *Johnson*. 'Sir, you *may* wonder.'

He talked of making verses, and observed, 'The great difficulty is to know when you have made good ones. When composing, I have generally had them in my mind, perhaps fifty at a time, walking up and down in my room; and then I have written them down, and often, from laziness, have written only half lines. I have written a hundred lines in a day. I remember I wrote a hundred lines of "The Vanity of Human Wishes" in a day. Doctor, (turning to Goldsmith,) I am not quite idle; I made one line t'other day; but I made no more.' *Goldsmith*. 'Let us hear it; we'll put a bad one to it.' *Johnson*. 'No, Sir; I have forgot it.'

Such specimens of the easy and playful conversation of the great Dr. Samuel Johnson are, I think, to be prized; as exhibiting the little varieties of a mind so enlarged and so powerful when objects of consequence required its exertions, and as giving us a minute knowledge of his character and modes of thinking.

After I had been some time in Scotland, I mentioned to him in a letter that 'On my first return to my native country, after some years of absence, I was told of a vast number of my acquaintance who were all gone to the land of forgetfulness, and I found myself like a man stalking over a field of battle, who every moment perceives some one lying dead.' I complained of irresolution, and mentioned my having made a vow as a security for good conduct. I wrote to him again, without being able to move his indolence; nor did I hear from him till he had received a copy of my inaugural Exercise, or Thesis in Civil Law, which I published at my admission as an Advocate, as is the custom in Scotland. He then wrote to me as follows:

'To JAMES BOSWELL, ESQ.

'DEAR SIR,

'THE reception of your Thesis put me in mind of my debt to you.

'Your resolution to obey your father I sincerely approve; but do not accustom yourself to enchain your volatility by vows: they will sometime leave a thorn in your mind, which you will, perhaps, never be able to extract or eject. Take this warning, it is of great importance.

'The study of the law is what you very justly term it, copious and generous; and in adding your name to its professors, you have done exactly what I always wished, when I wished you best. I hope that you will continue to pursue it vigorously and constantly. You gain, at least, what is no small advantage, security from those troublesome and wearisome discontents, which are always obtruding themselves upon a mind vacant, unemployed, and undetermined.

'You ought to think it no small inducement to diligence and perseverance, that they will please your father. We all live upon the hope of pleasing somebody; and the pleasure of pleasing ought to be greatest, and at last always will be greatest, when our endeavours are exerted in consequence of our duty.

'Life is not long, and too much of it must not pass in idle deliberation how it shall be spent; deliberation, which those who begin it by prudence, and continue it with subtilty, must, after long expence of thought, conclude by chance. To prefer one future mode of life to another, upon just reasons, requires faculties which it has not pleased our Creator to give us.

'If, therefore, the profession you have chosen has some unexpected inconveniencies, console yourself by reflecting that no profession is without them; and that all the importunities and perplexities of business are softness and luxury, compared with the incessant cravings of vacancy, and the unsatisfactory expedients of idleness.

'As to your History of Corsica, you have no materials which others have not, or may not have. You have, somehow or other, warmed your imagination. I wish there were some cure, like the lover's leap, for all heads of which some single idea has obtained an unreasonable and irregular possession. Mind your own affairs, and leave the Corsicans to theirs. I am, dear Sir,

'Your most humble servant,
'SAM. JOHNSON.'

'London, Aug. 21, 1766.'

It appears from Johnson's diary, that he was this year at Mr. Thrale's, from before Midsummer till after Michaelmas, and that he afterwards passed a month at Oxford. He had then contracted a great intimacy with Mr. Chambers of that University, afterwards Sir Robert Chambers, one of the Judges in India.

He published nothing this year in his own name; but the noble dedication to the King, of Gwyn's 'London and West-minster Improved,' was written by him; and he furnished the Preface, and several of the pieces, which compose a volume of Miscellanies by Mrs. Anna Williams, the blind lady who had an asylum in his house. There is in this collection a poem 'On the Death of Stephen Grey, the Electrician;'[1] which, on reading it, appeared to me to be undoubtedly Johnson's. I asked Mrs. Williams whether it was not his. 'Sir, (said she, with some warmth,) I wrote that poem before I had the honour of Dr. Johnson's acquaintance.' I, however, was so much impressed with my first notion, that I mentioned it to Johnson, repeating, at the same time, what Mrs. Williams had said. His answer was, 'It is true, Sir, that she wrote it before she was acquainted with me; but she has not told you that I wrote it all over again, except two lines.'

He wrote this year a letter, not intended for publication, which has, perhaps, as strong marks of his sentiment and style, as any of his compositions. The original is in my possession. It is addressed to the late Mr. William Drummond, bookseller in Edinburgh, a gentleman of good family, but small estate, who took arms for the house of Stuart in 1745; and during his concealment in London till the act of general pardon came out, obtained the acquaintance of Dr. Johnson, who justly esteemed him as a very worthy man. It seems, some of the members of the society in Scotland for propagating Christian knowledge, had opposed the scheme of translating the holy scriptures into the Erse or Gaelick language, from political considerations of the disadvantage of keeping up the distinction between the Highlanders and the other inhabitants of North-Britain. Dr. Johnson being informed of this, I suppose by Mr. Drummond, wrote with a generous indignation as follows:

'To Mr. William Drummond.

'Sir,

'I DID not expect to hear that it could be, in an assembly con-vened for the propagation of Christian knowledge, a question

---

[1] i.e., one versed in the science of electricity.

whether any nation uninstructed in religion should receive instruction; or whether that instruction should be imparted to them by a translation of the holy books into their own language. If obedience to the will of GOD be necessary to happiness, and knowledge of his will be necessary to obedience, I know not how he that withholds this knowledge, or delays it, can be said to love his neighbour as himself. He that voluntarily continues ignorance, is guilty of all the crimes which ignorance produces; as to him that should extinguish the tapers of a light-house, might justly be imputed the calamities of shipwrecks. Christianity is the highest perfection of humanity; and as no man is good but as he wishes the good of others, no man can be good in the highest degree, who wishes not to others the largest measures of the greatest good. To omit for a year, or for a day, the most efficacious method of advancing Christianity, in compliance with any purposes that terminate on this side of the grave, is a crime of which I know not that the world has yet had an example, except in the practice of the planters of America, a race of mortals whom, I suppose, no other man wishes to resemble.

'The Papists have, indeed, denied to the laity the use of the bible; but this prohibition, in few places now very rigorously enforced, is defended by arguments, which have for their foundation the care of souls. To obscure, upon motives merely political, the light of revelation, is a practice reserved for the reformed; and, surely, the blackest midnight of popery is meridian sunshine to such a reformation. I am not very willing that any language should be totally extinguished. The similitude and derivation of languages afford the most indubitable proof of the traduction of nations, and the genealogy of mankind. They add often physical certainty to historical evidence; and often supply the only evidence of ancient migrations, and of the revolutions of ages which left no written monuments behind them.

'Every man's opinions, at least his desires, are a little influenced by his favourite studies. My zeal for languages may seem, perhaps, rather over-heated, even to those by whom I desire to be well-esteemed. To those who have nothing in their thoughts but trade or policy, present power, or present money, I should not think it necessary to defend my opinions; but with men of letters I would not unwillingly compound, by wishing the continuance of every language, however narrow in its extent, or however incommodious for common purposes, till it is reposited in some version of a known book, that it may be always hereafter examined and compared with other languages, and then permitting its disuse. For this purpose, the translation of the bible is most to be desired. It is not certain that the same method will not preserve the Highland language, for the purposes of learning, and abolish it from daily use. When the Highlanders read the Bible, they will naturally wish to have its obscurities cleared, and to know the history, collateral or append-ant. Knowledge always desires increase: it is like fire, which must first be kindled by some external agent, but which will afterwards propagate itself. When they once desire to learn, they will naturally have recourse to the nearest language by which that desire can be gratified; and one will tell another that if he would attain knowl-edge, he must learn English.

'This speculation may, perhaps, be thought more subtle than the grossness of real life will easily admit. Let it, however, be remem-bered, that the efficacy of ignorance has been long tried, and has not produced the consequence expected. Let knowledge, therefore, take its turn; and let the patrons of privation stand awhile aside, and admit the operation of positive principles.

'You will be pleased, Sir, to assure the worthy man who is em-ployed in the new translation, that he has my wishes for his success; and if here or at Oxford I can be of any use, that I shall think it more than honour to promote his undertaking.

'I am sorry that I delayed so long to write.

'I am, Sir,

'Your most humble servant,

'SAM. JOHNSON.'

'Johnson's-court, Fleet-street,
      Aug. 13, 1766.'

The opponents of this pious scheme being made ashamed of their conduct, the benevolent undertaking was allowed to go on.

1767: ÆTAT. 58.]—In February, 1767, there happened one of the most remarkable incidents of Johnson's life, which gratified his monarchical enthusiasm, and which he loved to relate with all its circumstances, when requested by his friends. This was his being honoured by a private conversation with his Majesty, in the library at the Queen's house. He had frequently visited those splendid rooms and noble collection of books, which he used to say was more numerous and curious than he supposed any person could have made in the time which the King had employed. Mr. Barnard, the librarian, took care that he should have every accommodation that could contribute to his ease and convenience, while indulging his literary taste in that place; so that he had here a very agreeable resource at leisure hours.

His Majesty having been informed of his occasional visits, was pleased to signify a desire that he should be told when Dr. Johnson came next to the library. Accordingly, the next time that Johnson did come, as soon as he was fairly engaged with a book, on which, while he sat by the fire, he seemed quite intent, Mr. Barnard stole round to the apartment where the King was, and, in obedience to his Majesty's commands, mentioned that Dr. Johnson was then in the library. His Majesty said he was at leisure, and would go to him; upon which Mr. Barnard took one of the candles that stood on the King's table, and lighted his Majesty through a suite of rooms, till they came to a private door into the library, of which his Majesty had the key. Being entered, Mr. Barnard stepped forward hastily to Dr. Johnson, who was still in a profound study, and whispered him, 'Sir, here is the King.' Johnson started up, and stood still. His Majesty approached him, and at once was courteously easy.

His Majesty began by observing, that he understood he came sometimes to the library; and then mentioning his having heard that the Doctor had been lately at Oxford, asked him if he was not fond of going thither. To which Johnson answered, that he was indeed fond of going to Oxford sometimes, but was likewise glad to come back again. The King then asked him what they were doing at Oxford. Johnson answered, he could not much commend their diligence, but that in some respects they were mended, for they had put their press under better regulations, and were at that time printing Polybius. He was then asked whether there were better libraries at Oxford or Cambridge. He answered, he believed the Bodleian was larger than any they had at Cambridge; at the same time adding, 'I hope, whether we have more books or not than they have at Cambridge, we shall make as good use of them as they do.' Being asked whether All-Souls or Christ-Church library was the largest, he answered, 'All-Souls library is the largest we have, except the Bodleian.' 'Aye, (said the King,) that is the publick library.'

His Majesty enquired if he was then writing any thing. He answered, he was not, for he had pretty well told the world what he knew, and must now read to acquire more knowledge. The King, as it should seem with a view to urge him to rely on his own stores as an original writer, and to continue his labours, then said, 'I do not think you borrow much from any body.' Johnson said, he thought he had already done his part as a writer. 'I should have thought so too, (said the King,) if you had not written so well.'—Johnson observed to me, upon this, that 'No man could have paid a handsomer compliment; and it was fit for a King to pay. It was decisive.' When asked by another friend, at Sir Joshua Reynolds's, whether he made any reply to this high compliment, he answered, 'No, Sir. When the King had said it, it was to be so. It was not for me to bandy civilities with my Sovereign.' Perhaps no man who had spent his whole life in courts could have shewn a more nice and dignified sense of true politeness, than Johnson did in this instance.

The King then talked of literary journals, mentioned particularly the *Journal des Savans*, and asked Johnson if it was well done. Johnson said, it was formerly very well done, and gave some account of the persons who began it, and carried it on for some years; enlarging, at the same time, on the nature and use of such works. The King asked him if it was well done now. Johnson answered, he had no reason to think that it was. The King then asked him if there were any other literary journals published in this kingdom, except the Monthly and Critical Reviews; and on being answered there were no other, his Majesty asked which of them was the best: Johnson answered, that the Monthly Review was done with most care, the Critical upon the best principles; adding that the authours of the Monthly Review were enemies to the Church. This the King said he was sorry to hear.

His Majesty expressed a desire to have the literary biography of this country ably executed, and proposed to Dr. Johnson to undertake it. Johnson signified his readiness to comply with his Majesty's wishes.

During the whole of this interview, Johnson talked to his

Majesty with profound respect, but still in his firm manly manner, with a sonorous voice, and never in that subdued tone
which is commonly used at the levee and in the drawing-room.
After the King withdrew, Johnson shewed himself highly
pleased with his Majesty's conversation and gracious behaviour. He said to Mr. Barnard, 'Sir, they may talk of the King
as they will; but he is the finest gentleman I have ever seen.'
And he afterwards observed to Mr. Langton, 'Sir, his manners
are those of as fine a gentleman as we may suppose Lewis the
Fourteenth or Charles the Second.'

At Sir Joshua Reynolds's, where a circle of Johnson's friends
was collected round him to hear his account of this memorable
conversation, Dr. Joseph Warton, in his frank and lively manner, was very active in pressing him to mention the particulars.
'Come now, Sir, this is an interesting matter; do favour us with
it.' Johnson, with great good humour, complied.

He told them, 'I found his Majesty wished I should talk,
and I made it my business to talk. I find it does a man good
to be talked to by his Sovereign. In the first place, a man cannot be in a passion—.' Here some question interrupted him,
which is to be regretted, as he certainly would have pointed
out and illustrated many circumstances of advantage, from being in a situation, where the powers of the mind are at once
excited to vigorous exertion, and tempered by reverential awe.

During all the time in which Dr. Johnson was employed in
relating to the circle at Sir Joshua Reynolds's the particulars of
what passed between the King and him, Dr. Goldsmith remained unmoved upon a sopha at some distance, affecting not
to join in the least in the eager curiosity of the company. He
assigned as a reason for his gloom and seeming inattention,
that he apprehended Johnson had relinquished his purpose of
furnishing him with a Prologue to his play, with the hopes of
which he had been flattered; but it was strongly suspected that
he was fretting with chagrin and envy at the singular honour
Dr. Johnson had lately enjoyed. At length, the frankness and
simplicity of his natural character prevailed. He sprung from
the sopha, advanced to Johnson, and in a kind of flutter, from
imagining himself in the situation which he had just been

hearing described, exclaimed, 'Well, you acquitted yourself in this conversation better than I should have done; for I should have bowed and stammered through the whole of it.'

1768: ÆTAT. 59.]—In the spring of this year, having published my 'Account of Corsica, with the Journal of a Tour to that Island', I returned to London, very desirous to see Dr. Johnson, and hear him upon the subject. I found he was at Oxford, with his friend Mr. Chambers, who was now Vinerian Professor, and lived in New Inn Hall. Having been told by somebody that he was offended at my having put into my book an extract of his letter to me at Paris, I was impatient to be with him, and therefore followed him to Oxford, where I was entertained by Mr. Chambers, with a civility which I shall ever gratefully remember. I found that Dr. Johnson had sent a letter to me to Scotland, and that I had nothing to complain of but his being more indifferent to my anxiety than I wished him to be. Instead of giving, with the circumstances of time and place, such fragments of his conversation as I preserved during this visit to Oxford, I shall throw them together in continuation.

I asked him whether, as a moralist, he did not think that the practice of the law, in some degree, hurt the nice feeling of honesty. *Johnson.* 'Why no, Sir, if you act properly. You are not to deceive your clients with false representations of your opinion: you are not to tell lies to a judge.' *Boswell.* 'But what do you think of supporting a cause which you know to be bad?' *Johnson.* 'Sir, you do not know it to be good or bad till the Judge determines it. I have said that you are to state facts fairly; so that your thinking, or what you call knowing, a cause to be bad, must be from reasoning, must be from your supposing your arguments to be weak and inconclusive. But, Sir, that is not enough. An argument which does not convince yourself, may convince the Judge to whom you urge it: and if it does convince him, why, then, Sir, you are wrong, and he is right. It is his business to judge; and you are not to be confident in your own opinion that a cause is bad, but to say all you can for your client, and then hear the Judge's opinion.' *Boswell.* 'But, Sir, does not affecting a warmth when you have no warmth, and appearing to be clearly of one opinion when you are in reality of another opinion, does not such dissimula-

tion impair one's honesty? Is there not some danger that a lawyer may put on the same mask in common life, in the intercourse with his friends?' *Johnson.* 'Why no, Sir. Every body
knows you are paid for affecting warmth for your client; and
it is, therefore, properly no dissimulation: the moment you
come from the bar you resume your usual behaviour. Sir, a
man will no more carry the artifice of the bar into the common
intercourse of society, than a man who is paid for tumbling
upon his hands will continue to tumble upon his hands when
he should walk on his feet.'

Talking of some of the modern plays, he praised Goldsmith's
'Good-natured Man;' said, it was the best comedy that had appeared since 'The Provoked Husband,' and that there had not
been of late any such character exhibited on the stage as that
of Croaker. I observed it was the Suspirius of his Rambler. He
said, Goldsmith had owned he had borrowed it from thence.
'Sir, (continued he,) there is all the difference in the world
between characters of nature and characters of manners; and
there is the difference between the characters of Fielding and
those of Richardson. Characters of manners are very entertaining; but they are to be understood, by a more superficial observer, than characters of nature, where a man must dive into
the recesses of the human heart.'

It always appeared to me that he estimated the compositions
of Richardson too highly, and that he had an unreasonable
prejudice against Fielding. In comparing those two writers,
he used this expression; 'that there was as great a difference
between them as between a man who knew how a watch was
made, and a man who could tell the hour by looking on the
dial-plate.' This was a short and figurative state of his distinction between drawing characters of nature and characters only
of manners. But I cannot help being of opinion, that the neat
watches of Fielding are as well constructed as the large clocks
of Richardson, and that his dial-plates are brighter.

He renewed his promise of coming to Scotland, and going
with me to the Hebrides, but said he would now content himself with seeing one or two of the most curious of them. He
said, 'Macaulay, who writes the account of St. Kilda, set out
with a prejudice against prejudices, and wanted to be a smart

modern thinker; and yet he affirms for a truth, that when a
ship arrives there all the inhabitants are seized with a cold.'

Dr. John Campbell, the celebrated writer, took a great deal
of pains to ascertain this fact, and attempted to account for it
on physical principles, from the effect of effluvia from human
bodies. Johnson, at another time, praised Macaulay for his
'magnanimity,' in asserting this wonderful story, because it
was well attested. A Lady of Norfolk, by a letter to my friend
Dr. Burney, has favoured me with the following solution:
'Now for the explication of this seeming mystery, which is so
very obvious as, for that reason, to have escaped the penetration of Dr. Johnson and his friend, as well as that of the authour. Reading the book with my ingenious friend, the late
Reverend Mr. Christian of Docking—after ruminating a little,
"The cause, (says he,) is a natural one. The situation of St.
Kilda renders a North-East Wind indispensably necessary before a stranger can land. The wind, not the stranger, occasions
an epidemic cold." If I am not mistaken, Mr. Macaulay is dead;
if living, this solution might please him, as I hope it will Mr.
Boswell, in return for the many agreeable hours his works have
afforded us.'

He said he had lately been a long while at Lichfield, but
had grown very weary before he left it. *Boswell.* 'I wonder at
that, Sir; it is your native place.' *Johnson.* 'Why, so is Scotland
your native place.'

His prejudice against Scotland appeared remarkably strong
at this time. When I talked of our advancement in literature,
'Sir, (said he,) you have learnt a little from us, and you think
yourselves very great men. Hume would never have written
History, had not Voltaire written it before him. He is an echo
of Voltaire.' *Boswell.* 'But, Sir, we have Lord Kames.' *Johnson.*
'You *have* Lord Kames. Keep him; ha, ha, ha! We don't envy
you him. Do you ever see Dr. Robertson?' *Boswell.* 'Yes, Sir.'
Johnson. 'Does the dog talk of me?' *Boswell.* 'Indeed, Sir, he
does, and loves you.' Thinking that I now had him in a corner, and being solicitous for the literary fame of my country,
I pressed him for his opinion on the merit of Dr. Robertson's
History of Scotland. But, to my surprize, he escaped.—'Sir, I
love Robertson, and I won't talk of his book.'

An essay, written by Mr. Deane, a divine of the Church of
England, maintaining the future life of brutes, by an explica
tion of certain parts of the scriptures, was mentioned, and the
doctrine insisted on by a gentleman who seemed fond of curious speculation. Johnson, who did not like to hear of any thing
concerning a future state which was not authorised by the
regular canons of orthodoxy, discouraged this talk; and being
offended at its continuation, he watched an opportunity to
give the gentleman a blow of reprehension. So, when the
poor speculatist, with a serious metaphysical pensive face, ad
dressed him, 'But really, Sir, when we see a very sensible dog
we don't know what to think of him.' Johnson, rolling with
joy at the thought which beamed in his eye, turned quickly
round, and replied, 'True, Sir: and when we see a very foolish
fellow, we don't know what to think of *him.*' He then rose up
strided to the fire, and stood for some time laughing and exult
ing.

I told him that I had several times, when in Italy, seen the
experiment of placing a scorpion within a circle of burning
coals; that it ran round and round in extreme pain; and finding no way to escape, retired to the centre, and like a true
Stoick philosopher, darted its sting into its head, and thus at
once freed itself from its woes. '*This must end 'em.*' I said, this
was a curious fact, as it shewed deliberate suicide in a reptile.
Johnson would not admit the fact. He said, Maupertuis was
of opinion that it does not kill itself, but dies of the heat; that
it gets to the centre of the circle, as the coolest place; that its
turning its tail in upon its head is merely a convulsion, and
that it does not sting itself. He said he would be satisfied if
the great anatomist Morgagni, after dissecting a scorpion on
which the experiment had been tried, should certify that its
sting had penetrated into its head.

He seemed pleased to talk of natural philosophy. 'That
woodcocks, (said he,) fly over to the northern countries, is
proved, because they have been observed at sea. Swallows certainly sleep all the winter. A number of them conglobulate
together, by flying round and round, and then all in a heap
throw themselves under water, and lye in the bed of a river.'
He told us, one of his first essays was a Latin poem upon the

glow-worm. I am sorry I did not ask where it was to be found.

He talked of the heinousness of the crime of adultery, by which the peace of families was destroyed. He said, 'Confusion of progeny constitutes the essence of the crime; and therefore a woman who breaks her marriage vows is much more criminal than a man who does it. A man, to be sure, is criminal in the sight of GOD: but he does not do his wife a very material injury, if he does not insult her; if, for instance, from mere wantonness of appetite, he steals privately to her chambermaid. Sir, a wife ought not greatly to resent this. I would not receive home a daughter who had run away from her husband on that account. A wife should study to reclaim her husband by more attention to please him. Sir, a man will not, once in a hundred instances, leave his wife and go to a harlot, if his wife has not been negligent of pleasing.'

I asked him if it was not hard that one deviation from chastity should so absolutely ruin a young woman. *Johnson.* 'Why no, Sir; it is the great principle which she is taught. When she has given up that principle, she has given up every notion of female honour and virtue, which are all included in chastity.'

A gentleman talked to him of a lady whom he greatly admired and wished to marry, but was afraid of her superiority of talents. 'Sir, (said he,) you need not be afraid; marry her. Before a year goes about, you'll find that reason much weaker, and that wit not so bright.' Yet the gentleman may be justified in his apprehension by one of Dr. Johnson's admirable sentences in his life of Waller: 'He doubtless praised many whom he would have been afraid to marry; and, perhaps, married one whom he would have been ashamed to praise. Many qualities contribute to domestick happiness, upon which poetry has no colours to bestow; and many airs and sallies may delight imagination, which he who flatters them never can approve.'

At this time I observed upon the dial-plate of his watch a short Greek inscription, taken from the New Testament, being the first words of our *Saviour's* solemn admonition to the improvement of that time which is allowed us to prepare for eternity: 'the night cometh, when no man can work.' He some time afterwards laid aside this dial-plate; and when I asked him the reason, he said, 'It might do very well upon a clock which a man keeps in his closet; but to have it upon his watch which he carries about with him, and which is often looked at by others, might be censured as ostentatious.'

Upon his arrival in London in May, he surprized me one morning with a visit at my lodgings in Half-Moon-street. As he had objected to a part of one of his letters being published, I thought it right to take this opportunity of asking him explicitly whether it would be improper to publish his letters after his death. His answer was, 'Nay, Sir, when I am dead, you may do as you will.'

He talked in his usual style with a rough contempt of popular liberty. 'They make a rout about *universal* liberty, without considering that all that is to be valued, or indeed can be enjoyed by individuals, is *private* liberty. Political liberty is good only so far as it produces private liberty. Now, Sir, there is the liberty of the press, which you know is a constant topick. Suppose you and I and two hundred more were restrained from printing our thoughts; what then? What proportion would that restraint upon us bear to the private happiness of the nation?'

His sincere regard for Francis Barber, his faithful negro servant, made him so desirous of his further improvement, that he now placed him at a school at Bishop Stortford, in Hertfordshire. This humane attention does Johnson's heart much honour.

'To Mr. Francis Barber.

'Dear Francis,

'I have been very much out of order. I am glad to hear that you are well, and design to come soon to see you. I would have you stay at Mrs. Clapp's for the present, till I can determine what we shall do. Be a good boy.

'My compliments to Mrs. Clapp and to Mr. Fowler. I am,

'Yours affectionately,

'Sam. Johnson.'

'May 28, 1768.'

Soon afterwards, he supped at the Crown and Anchor tavern, in the Strand, with a company whom I collected to meet him. They were Dr. Percy, now Bishop of Dromore, Dr. Douglas, now Bishop of Salisbury, Mr. Langton, Dr. Robertson the Historian, Dr. Hugh Blair, and Mr. Thomas Davies, who wished much to be introduced to these eminent Scotch literati; but on the present occasion he had very little opportunity of hearing them talk, for with an excess of prudence, for which Johnson afterwards found fault with them, they hardly opened their lips, and that only to say something which they were certain would not expose them to the sword of Goliath; such was their anxiety for their fame when in the presence of Johnson. He was this evening in remarkable vigour of mind, and eager to exert himself in conversation, which he did with great readiness and fluency; but I am sorry to find that I have preserved but a small part of what passed.

He was vehement against old Dr. Mounsey, of Chelsea College, as 'a fellow who swore and talked bawdy.' 'I have been often in his company, (said Dr. Percy,) and never heard him swear or talk bawdy.' Mr. Davies, who sat next to Dr. Percy, having after this had some conversation aside with him, made a discovery which, in his zeal to pay court to Dr. Johnson, he eagerly proclaimed aloud from the foot of the table: 'O, Sir, I have found out a very good reason why Dr. Percy never heard Mounsey swear or talk bawdy; for he tells me, he never saw him but at the Duke of Northumberland's table.' 'And so, Sir, (said Johnson loudly, to Dr. Percy,) you would shield this man from the charge of swearing and talking bawdy, because he did not do so at the Duke of Northumberland's table. Sir, you might as well tell us that you had seen him hold up his hand at the Old Bailey, and he neither swore nor talked bawdy; or that you had seen him in the cart at Tyburn, and he neither swore nor talked bawdy. And is it thus, Sir, that you presume to controvert what I have related?' Dr. Johnson's animadversion was uttered in such a manner, that Dr. Percy seemed to be displeased, and soon afterwards left the company, of which Johnson did not at that time take any notice.

Swift having been mentioned, Johnson, as usual, treated him with little respect as an authour. Some of us endeavoured to support the Dean of St. Patrick's by various arguments. One in particular praised his 'Conduct of the Allies.' *Johnson.* 'Sir,

his "Conduct of the Allies" is a performance of very little ability.' 'Surely, Sir, (said Dr. Douglas,) you must allow it has
strong facts.' *Johnson.* 'Why yes, Sir; but what is that to the
merit of the composition? In the Sessions-paper of the Old
Bailey there are strong facts. Housebreaking is a strong fact;
robbery is a strong fact; and murder is a *mighty* strong fact:
but is great praise due to the historian of those strong facts?
No, Sir. Swift has told what he had to tell distinctly enough,
but that is all. He had to count ten, and he has counted it
right.'—Then recollecting that Mr. Davies, by acting as an
informer, had been the occasion of his talking somewhat too
harshly to his friend Dr. Percy, for which, probably, when
the first ebullition was over, he felt some compunction, he
took an opportunity to give him a hit; so added, with a preparatory laugh, 'Why, Sir, Tom Davies might have written
"the Conduct of the Allies".' Poor Tom being thus suddenly
dragged into ludicrous notice in presence of the Scottish Doctors, to whom he was ambitious of appearing to advantage, was
grievously mortified.

When I called upon Dr. Johnson next morning, I found
him highly satisfied with his colloquial prowess the preceding
evening. 'Well, (said he,) we had good talk.' *Boswell.* 'Yes,
Sir; you tossed and gored several persons.'

The late Alexander, Earl of Eglintoune, who loved wit more
than wine, and men of genius more than sycophants, had a
great admiration of Johnson; but from the remarkable elegance
of his own manners, was, perhaps, too delicately sensible of
the roughness which sometimes appeared in Johnson's behaviour. One evening about this time, when his Lordship did me
the honour to sup at my lodgings with Dr. Robertson and several other men of literary distinction, he regretted that Johnson had not been educated with more refinement, and lived
more in polished society. 'No, no, my Lord, (said Signor
Baretti,) do with him what you would, he would always have
been a bear.' 'True, (answered the Earl, with a smile,) but he
would have been a *dancing* bear.'

To obviate all the reflections which have gone round the
world to Johnson's prejudice, by applying to him the epithet
of a *bear,* let me impress upon my readers a just and happy say-

ing of my friend Goldsmith, who knew him well: 'Johnson, to be sure, has a roughness in his manner; but no man alive has a more tender heart. *He has nothing of the bear but his skin.*'

1769: ÆTAT. 60.]—In 1769, so far as I can discover, the publick was favoured with nothing of Johnson's composition, either for himself or any of his friends. His 'Meditations' too strongly prove that he suffered much both in body and mind.

His Majesty having the preceding year instituted the Royal Academy of Arts in London, Johnson had now the honour of being appointed Professor in Ancient Literature.

I came to London in the autumn, and having informed him that I was going to be married in a few months, I wished to have as much of his conversation as I could before engaging in a state of life which would probably keep me more in Scotland, and prevent my seeing him so often as when I was a single man; but I found he was at Brighthelmstone with Mr. and Mrs. Thrale. I was very sorry that I had not his company with me at the Jubilee,[1] in honour of Shakspeare, at Stratford-upon-Avon, the great poet's native town. Johnson's connection both with Shakspeare and Garrick founded a double claim to his presence; and it would have been highly gratifying to Mr. Garrick. Upon this occasion I particularly lamented that he had not that warmth of friendship for his brilliant pupil, which we may suppose would have had a benignant effect on both. When almost every man of eminence in the literary world was happy to partake in this festival of genius, the absence of Johnson could not but be wondered at and regretted. The only trace of him there, was in the whimsical advertisement of a haberdasher, who sold *Shaksperian ribbands* of various dyes;

[1] A pageant under Garrick's supervision and direction. It was not a success. The proceedings were rhetorical and designed, the wits charged, more to exalt Garrick than Shakespeare. A vast company gathered but the lodgings were wretched and the prices charged were exorbitant. It rained persistently and the Avon overflowed its banks. Boswell distinguished himself by appearing in the dress of "an armed Corsican Chief" (which included a red waistcoat), carrying "by way of staff" a vine-stalk carved at the top "with a bird, emblematic of the sweet Bard of Avon." Johnson wisely absented himself from this felicity.

and, by way of illustrating their appropriation to the bard, introduced a line from the celebrated Prologue at the opening of Drury-lane theatre:

'Each change of *many-colour'd* life he drew.'

From Brighthelmstone Dr. Johnson wrote me the following letter, which they who may think that I ought to have suppressed, must have less ardent feelings than I have always avowed.

'To JAMES BOSWELL, ESQ.

'DEAR SIR,

'WHY do you charge me with unkindness? I have omitted nothing that could do you good, or give you pleasure, unless it be that I have forborne to tell you my opinion of your "Account of Corsica." I believe my opinion, if you think well of my judgement, might have given you pleasure; but when it is considered how much vanity is excited by praise, I am not sure that it would have done you good. Your History is like other histories, but your Journal is in a very high degree curious and delightful. There is between the history and the journal that difference which there will always be found between notions borrowed from without, and notions generated within. Your history was copied from books; your journal rose out of your own experience and observation. You express images which operated strongly upon yourself, and you have impressed them with great force upon your readers. I know not whether I could name any narrative by which curiosity is better excited, or better gratified.

'I am glad that you are going to be married; and as I wish you well in things of less importance, wish you well with proportionate ardour in this crisis of your life. What I can contribute to your happiness, I should be very unwilling to with-hold; for I have always loved and valued you, and shall love you and value you still more, as you become more regular and useful: effects which a happy marriage will hardly fail to produce.

'I do not find that I am likely to come back very soon from this place. I shall, perhaps, stay a fortnight longer; and a fortnight is a long time to a lover absent from his mistress. Would a fortnight ever have an end?

'I am, dear Sir,
'Your most affectionate humble servant,
'SAM. JOHNSON.'

'Brighthelmstone,
Sept. 9, 1769.'

After his return to town, we met frequently, and I contin·ued the practice of making notes of his conversation, though not with so much assiduity as I wish I had done. At this time, indeed, I had a sufficient excuse for not being able to appropriate so much time to my journal; for General Paoli, after Corsica had been overpowered by the monarchy of France, was now no longer at the head of his brave countrymen, but having with difficulty escaped from his native island, had sought an asylum in Great-Britain; and it was my duty, as well as my pleasure, to attend much upon him. Such particulars of Johnson's conversation at this period as I have committed to writing, I shall here introduce, without any strict attention to methodical arrangement. Sometimes short notes of different days shall be blended together, and sometimes a day may seem important enough to be separately distinguished.

On the 30th of September we dined together at the Mitre. I attempted to argue for the superior happiness of the savage life, upon the usual fanciful topicks. *Johnson.* 'Sir, there can be nothing more false. The savages have no bodily advantages beyond those of civilised men. They have not better health; and as to care or mental uneasiness, they are not above it, but below it, like bears. No, Sir; you are not to talk such paradox: let me have no more on't. It cannot entertain, far less can it instruct. Lord Monboddo, one of your Scotch Judges, talked a great deal of such nonsense. I suffered *him;* but I will not suffer *you.'*—*Boswell.* 'But, Sir, does not Rousseau talk such nonsense?' *Johnson.* 'True, Sir; but Rousseau *knows* he is talking nonsense, and laughs at the world for staring at him.' *Boswell.* 'How so, Sir?' *Johnson.* 'Why, Sir, a man who talks nonsense so well, must know that he is talking nonsense. But I am *afraid,* (chuckling and laughing,) Monboddo[1] does *not* know that he is talking nonsense.' *Boswell.* 'Is it wrong then, Sir, to affect singularity, in order to make people stare?' *Johnson.* 'Yes,

[1] James Burnett (1714-1799), who assumed the title of Lord Monboddo in 1767 when he was made one of the Scotch Law Lords. He was the butt of the wits in his own day because he maintained in his writings that men and apes were related. He believed that the orangoutan was a class of the human species. He was eccentric in his personal behavior and a little credulous, but his ideas would not seem as absurd in the twentieth century as they did in the eighteenth.

if you do it by propagating errour: and, indeed, it is wrong in any way. There is in human nature a general inclination to make people stare; and every wise man has himself to cure of it, and does cure himself. If you wish to make people stare by doing better than others, why, make them stare till they stare their eyes out. But consider how easy it is to make people stare, by being absurd. I may do it by going into a drawing-room without my shoes. You remember the gentleman in "The Spectator," who had a commission of lunacy taken out against him for his extreme singularity, such as never wearing a wig, but a night-cap. Now, Sir, abstractedly, the night-cap was best; but, relatively, the advantage was overbalanced by his making the boys run after him.'

When I censured a gentleman of my acquaintance for marrying a second time, as it shewed a disregard of his first wife, he said, 'Not at all, Sir. On the contrary, were he not to marry again, it might be concluded that his first wife had given him a disgust to marriage; but by taking a second wife he pays the highest compliment to the first, by shewing that she made him so happy as a married man, that he wishes to be so a second time.' So ingenious a turn did he give to this delicate question. And yet, on another occasion, he owned that he once had almost asked a promise of Mrs. Johnson that she would not marry again, but had checked himself. Indeed, I cannot help thinking, that in his case the request would have been unreasonable; for if Mrs. Johnson forgot, or thought it no injury to the memory of her first love,—the husband of her youth and the father of her children,—to make a second marriage, why should she be precluded from a third, should she be so inclined? In Johnson's persevering fond appropriation of his *Tetty*, even after her decease, he seems totally to have overlooked the prior claim of the honest Birmingham trader. I presume that her having been married before had, at times, given him some uneasiness; for I remember his observing upon the marriage of one of our common friends, 'He has done a very foolish thing, Sir; he has married a widow, when he might have had a maid.'

We drank tea with Mrs. Williams. I had last year the pleasure of seeing Mrs. Thrale at Dr. Johnson's one morning, and had conversation enough with her to admire her talents, and to shew her that I was as Johnsonian as herself. Dr. Johnson had probably been kind enough to speak well of me, for this evening he delivered me a very polite card from Mr. Thrale and her, inviting me to Streatham.

On the 6th of October I complied with this obliging invitation, and found, at an elegant villa, six miles from town, every circumstance that can make society pleasing. Johnson, though quite at home, was yet looked up to with an awe, tempered by affection, and seemed to be equally the care of his host and hostess. I rejoiced at seeing him so happy.

He played off his wit against Scotland with a good humoured pleasantry, which gave me, though no bigot to national prejudices, an opportunity for a little contest with him. I having said that England was obliged to us for gardeners, almost all their good gardeners being Scotchmen;—*Johnson.* 'Why, Sir, that is because gardening is much more necessary amongst you than with us, which makes so many of your people learn it. It is *all* gardening with you. Things which grow wild here, must be cultivated with great care in Scotland. Pray now, (throwing himself back in his chair, and laughing.) are you ever able to bring the *sloe* to perfection?'

Mrs. Thrale praised Garrick's talent for light gay poetry; and, as a specimen, repeated his song in 'Florizel and Perdita,' and dwelt with peculiar pleasure on this line:

'I'd smile with the simple, and feed with the poor.'

Johnson. 'Nay, my dear Lady, this will never do. Poor David! Smile with the simple! What folly is that! And who would feed with the poor that can help it? No, no; let me smile with the wise, and feed with the rich.' I repeated this sally to Garrick, and wondered to find his sensibility as a writer not a little irritated by it.

On the evening of October 10, I presented Dr. Johnson to General Paoli. I had greatly wished that two men, for whom I had the highest esteem, should meet. They met with a manly ease, mutually conscious of their own abilities, and of the abilities of each other. The General spoke Italian, and Dr. Johnson English, and understood one another very well, with a little

aid of interpretation from me, in which I compared myself to
an isthmus which joins two great continents.

Dr. Johnson went home with me, and drank tea till late in
the night. He said, 'General Paoli had the loftiest port of any
man he had ever seen.' He denied that military men were always the best bred men. 'Perfect good breeding, he observed,
consists in having no particular mark of any profession, but a
general elegance of manners; whereas, in a military man, you
can commonly distinguish the *brand* of a soldier.'

Dr. Johnson shunned to-night any discussion of the perplexed question of fate and free will, which I attempted to agitate: 'Sir, (said he,) we *know* our will is free, and *there's* an
end on't.'

He honoured me with his company at dinner on the 16th
of October, at my lodgings in Old Bond-street, with Sir Joshua
Reynolds, Mr. Garrick, Dr. Goldsmith, Mr. Murphy, Mr.
Bickerstaff, and Mr. Thomas Davies. Garrick played round
him with a fond vivacity, taking hold of the breasts of his coat,
and, looking up in his face with a lively archness, compli-
mented him on the good health which he seemed then to enjoy; while the sage, shaking his head, beheld him with a gentle
complacency. One of the company not being come at the
appointed hour, I proposed, as usual upon such occasions, to
order dinner to be served; adding, 'Ought six people to be kept
waiting for one?' 'Why, yes, (answered Johnson, with a delicate humanity,) if the one will suffer more by your sitting
down, than the six will do by waiting.' Goldsmith, to divert
the tedious minutes, strutted about, bragging of his dress, and
I believe was seriously vain of it, for his mind was wonderfully
prone to such impressions. 'Come, come, (said Garrick,) talk
no more of that. You are, perhaps, the worst—eh, eh!'—Goldsmith was eagerly attempting to interrupt him, when Garrick
went on, laughing ironically, 'Nay, you will always *look* like
a gentleman; but I am talking of being well or ill *drest*.' 'Well,
let me tell you, (said Goldsmith,) when my tailor brought
home my bloom-coloured coat, he said, "Sir, I have a favour to
beg of you. When any body asks you who made your clothes,
be pleased to mention John Filby, at the Harrow, in Water-
lane."' *Johnson.* 'Why, Sir, that was because he knew the

strange colour would attract crouds to gaze at it, and thus they might hear of him, and see how well he could make a coat even of so absurd a colour.'

After dinner our conversation first turned upon Pope. Johnson said, his characters of men were admirably drawn, those of women not so well. He repeated to us, in his forcible melodious manner, the concluding lines of the Dunciad. While he was talking loudly in praise of those lines, one of the company ventured to say, 'Too fine for such a poem:—a poem on what?' *Johnson,* (with a disdainful look,) 'Why, on *dunces.* It was worth while being a dunce then. Ah, Sir, hadst *thou* lived in those days! It is not worth while being a dunce now, when there are no wits.' Bickerstaff observed, as a peculiar circumstance, that Pope's fame was higher when he was alive than it was then. Johnson said, his Pastorals were poor things, though the versification was fine. He observed, that in Dryden's poetry there were passages drawn from a profundity which Pope could never reach.

Mrs. Montagu, a lady distinguished for having written an Essay on Shakspeare, being mentioned;—*Reynolds.* 'I think that essay does her honour.' *Johnson.* 'Yes, Sir; it does *her* honour, but it would do nobody else honour. I have, indeed, not read it all. But when I take up the end of a web, and find it packthread, I do not expect, by looking further, to find embroidery. Sir, I will venture to say, there is not one sentence of true criticism in her book.' *Garrick.* 'But, Sir, surely it shews how much Voltaire has mistaken Shakspeare, which nobody else has done.' *Johnson.* 'Sir, nobody else has thought it worth while. And what merit is there in that? You may as well praise a schoolmaster for whipping a boy who has construed ill. No, Sir, there is no real criticism in it: none shewing the beauty of thought, as formed on the workings of the human heart.'

One day at Sir Joshua's table, when it was related that Mrs. Montagu, in an excess of compliment to the authour of a modern tragedy, had exclaimed, 'I tremble for Shakspeare;' Johnson said, 'When Shakspeare has got——[1] for his rival, and Mrs. Montagu for his defender, he is in a poor state indeed.'

On Thursday, October 19, I passed the evening with him

[1] probably Robert Jephson (1736-1803), a minor playwright.

at his house. He advised me to complete a Dictionary of words peculiar to Scotland, of which I shewed him a specimen. 'Sir, (said he,) Ray has made a collection of north-country words. By collecting those of your country, you will do a useful thing towards the history of the language.' He bade me also go on with collections which I was making upon the antiquities of Scotland. 'Make a large book; a folio.' *Boswell*. 'But of what use will it be, Sir?' *Johnson*. 'Never mind the use; do it.'

I complained that he had not mentioned Garrick in his Preface to Shakspeare; and asked him if he did not admire him. *Johnson*. 'Yes, as "a poor player, who frets and struts his hour upon the stage;"—as a shadow.' *Boswell*. 'But has he not brought Shakspeare into notice?' *Johnson*. 'Sir, to allow that, would be to lampoon the age. Many of Shakspeare's plays are the worse for being acted: Macbeth, for instance.' *Boswell*. 'What, Sir, is nothing gained by decoration and action? Indeed, I do wish that you had mentioned Garrick.' *Johnson*. 'My dear Sir, had I mentioned him, I must have mentioned many more: Mrs. Pritchard, Mrs. Cibber,—nay, and Mr. Cibber too; he too altered Shakspeare.'

I mentioned to him that I had seen the execution of several convicts at Tyburn, two days before, and that none of them seemed to be under any concern. *Johnson*. 'Most of them, Sir, have never thought at all.' *Boswell*. 'But is not the fear of death natural to man?' *Johnson*. 'So much so, Sir, that the whole of life is but keeping away the thoughts of it.' He then, in a low and earnest tone, talked of his meditating upon the aweful hour of his own dissolution, and in what manner he should conduct himself upon that occasion: 'I know not (said he,) whether I should wish to have a friend by me, or have it all between GOD and myself.'

Talking of our feeling for the distresses of others;—*Johnson*. 'Why, Sir, there is much noise made about it, but it is greatly exaggerated. No, Sir, we have a certain degree of feeling to prompt us to do good: more than that, Providence does not intend. It would be misery to no purpose.' *Boswell*. 'But suppose now, Sir, that one of your intimate friends were apprehended for an offence for which he might be hanged.' *Johnson*. 'I should do what I could to bail him, and give him any other assistance; but if he were once fairly hanged, I should not suffer.' *Boswell*. 'Would you eat your dinner that day, Sir?' *Johnson*. 'Yes, Sir; and eat it as if he were eating it with me. Why, there's Baretti, who is to be tried for his life to-morrow, friends have risen up for him on every side; yet if he should be hanged, none of them will eat a slice of plum-pudding the less. Sir, that sympathetick feeling goes a very little way in depressing the mind.'

I told him that I had dined lately at Foote's, who shewed me a letter which he had received from Tom Davies, telling him that he had not been able to sleep from the concern which he felt on account of '*This sad affair of Baretti*,' begging of him to try if he could suggest any thing that might be of service; and, at the same time, recommending to him an industrious young man who kept a pickle-shop. *Johnson*. 'Ay, Sir, here you have a specimen of human sympathy; a friend hanged, and a cucumber pickled. We know not whether Baretti or the pickle-man has kept Davies from sleep; nor does he know himself. And as to his not sleeping, Sir; Tom Davies is a very great man; Tom has been upon the stage, and knows how to do those things: I have not been upon the stage, and cannot do those things.' *Boswell*. 'I have often blamed myself, Sir, for not feeling for others as sensibly as many say they do.' *Johnson*. 'Sir, don't be duped by them any more. You will find these very feeling people are not very ready to do you good. They *pay* you by *feeling*.'

He again talked of the passage in Congreve with high commendation, and said, 'Shakspeare never has six lines together without a fault. Perhaps you may find seven: but this does not refute my general assertion. If I come to an orchard, and say there's no fruit here, and then comes a poring man, who finds two apples and three pears, and tells me, "Sir, you are mistaken, I have found both apples and pears," I should laugh at him: what would that be to the purpose?'

Next day, October 20, he appeared, for the only time I suppose in his life, as a witness in a Court of Justice, being called to give evidence to the character of Mr. Baretti, who having stabbed a man in the street, was arraigned at the Old Bailey

for murder[1]. Never did such a constellation of genius en-
lighten the aweful Sessions-House, emphatically called *Justice
Hall*; Mr. Burke, Mr. Garrick, Mr. Beauclerk, and Dr. Johnson: and undoubtedly their favourable testimony had due
weight with the Court and Jury. Johnson gave his evidence
in a slow, deliberate, and distinct manner, which was uncommonly impressive. It is well known that Mr. Baretti was acquitted.

We went home to his house to tea. Mrs. Williams made
it with sufficient dexterity, notwithstanding her blindness,
though her manner of satisfying herself that the cups were
full enough appeared to me a little aukward; for I fancied she
put her finger down a certain way, till she felt the tea touch
it. In my first elation at being allowed the privilege of attending Dr. Johnson at his late visits to this lady, I willingly drank
cup after cup, as if it had been the Heliconian spring. But as
the charm of novelty went off, I grew more fastidious; and besides, I discovered that she was of a peevish temper.

There was a pretty large circle this evening. Dr. Johnson
was in very good humour, lively, and ready to talk upon all
subjects. Mr. Fergusson, the self-taught philosopher, told him
of a new-invented machine which went without horses: a man
who sat in it turned a handle, which worked a spring that
drove it forward. 'Then, Sir, (said Johnson,) what is gained
is, the man has his choice whether he will move himself alone,
or himself and the machine too.' Dominicetti being mentioned,
he would not allow him any merit. 'There is nothing in all this
boasted system. No, Sir; medicated baths can be no better than
warm water: their only effect can be that of tepid moisture.'
One of the company took the other side, maintaining that medicines of various sorts, and some too of most powerful effect,
are introduced into the human frame by the medium of the
pores; and, therefore, when warm water is impregnated with

---

[1] Giuseppe Baretti (1719-1789), a learned but timorous man, had
been assaulted by three bullies in the street. He ran and they pursued
him until turning—possibly through an excess of fear—he stabbed
one of them with a pocket knife. The man died and Baretti was
charged with murder. He was, as Boswell states, acquitted.

salutiferous substances, it may produce great effects as a bath. This appeared to me very satisfactory. Johnson did not answer it; but talking for victory, and determined to be master of the field, he had recourse to the device which Goldsmith imputed to him in the witty words of one of Cibber's comedies: 'There is no arguing with Johnson; for when his pistol misses fire, he knocks you down with the butt end of it.' He turned to the gentleman, 'Well, Sir, go to Dominicetti, and get thyself fumigated; but be sure that the steam be directed to thy *head*, for *that* is the *peccant part*.' This produced a triumphant roar of laughter from the motley assembly of philosophers, printers, and dependents, male and female.

I know not how so whimsical a thought came into my mind, but I asked, 'If, Sir, you were shut up in a castle, and a newborn child with you, what would you do?' *Johnson*. 'Why, Sir, I should not much like my company.' *Boswell*. 'But would you take the trouble of rearing it?' He seemed, as may well be supposed, unwilling to pursue the subject: but upon my persevering in my question, replied, 'Why yes, Sir, I would; but I must have all conveniencies. If I had no garden, I would make a shed on the roof, and take it there for fresh air. I should feed it, and wash it much, and with warm water to please it, not with cold water to give it pain.' *Boswell*. 'But, Sir, does not heat relax?' *Johnson*. 'Sir, you are not to imagine the water is to be very hot. I would not *coddle* the child. No, Sir, the hardy method of treating children does no good. I'll take you five children from London, who shall cuff five Highland children. Sir, a man bred in London will carry a burthen, or run, or wrestle, as well as a man brought up in the hardiest manner in the country.' *Boswell*. 'Good living, I suppose, makes the Londoners strong.' *Johnson*. 'Why, Sir, I don't know that it does. Our chairmen from Ireland, who are as strong men as any, have been brought up upon potatoes. Quantity makes up for quality.' *Boswell*. 'Would you teach this child that I have furnished you with, any thing?' *Johnson*. 'No, I should not be apt to teach it.' *Boswell*. 'Would not you have a pleasure in teaching it?' *Johnson*. 'No, Sir, I should *not* have a pleasure in teaching it.' *Boswell*. 'Have you not a pleasure in teaching men? —*There* I have you. You have the same pleasure in teaching men, that I should have in teaching children.' *Johnson.* 'Why, something about that.'

Boswell. 'Do you think, Sir, that what is called natural affection is born with us? It seems to me to be the effect of habit, or of gratitude for kindness. No child has it for a parent whom it has not seen.' *Johnson.* 'Why, Sir, I think there is an instinctive natural affection in parents towards their children.'

Russia being mentioned as likely to become a great empire, by the rapid increase of population:—*Johnson.* 'Why, Sir, I see no prospect of their propagating more. They can have no more children than they can get. I know of no way to make them breed more than they do. It is not from reason and prudence that people marry, but from inclination. A man is poor; he thinks, "I cannot be worse, and so I'll e'en take Peggy."' *Boswell.* 'But have not nations been more populous at one period than another?' *Johnson.* 'Yes, Sir; but that has been owing to the people being less thinned at one period than another, whether by emigrations, war, or pestilence, not by their being more or less prolifick. Births at all times bear the same proportion to the same number of people.' *Boswell.* 'But, to consider the state of our own country;—does not throwing a number of farms into one hand hurt population?' *Johnson.* 'Why no, Sir; the same quantity of food being produced, will be consumed by the same number of mouths, though the people may be disposed of in different ways. We see, if corn be dear, and butchers' meat cheap, the farmers all apply themselves to the raising of corn, till it becomes plentiful and cheap, and then butchers' meat becomes dear; so that an equality is always preserved. No, Sir, let fanciful men do as they will, depend upon it, it is difficult to disturb the system of life.' *Boswell.* 'But, Sir, is it not a very bad thing for landlords to oppress their tenants, by raising their rents?' *Johnson.* 'Very bad. But, Sir, it never can have any general influence; it may distress some individuals. For, consider this: landlords cannot do without tenants. Now tenants will not give more for land, than land is worth. If they can make more of their money by keeping a shop, or any other way, they'll do it, and so oblige landlords to let land come back to a reasonable rent, in order that they may get tenants. Land, in England, is an article of commerce. A tenant who pays his landlord his rent, thinks himself no more obliged to him than you think yourself obliged to a man in whose shop you buy a piece of goods. He knows the landlord does not let him have his land for less than he can get from others, in the same manner as the shopkeeper sells his goods. No shopkeeper sells a yard of ribband for six-pence when seven-pence is the current price.' *Boswell.* 'But, Sir, is it not better that tenants should be dependent on landlords?' *Johnson.* 'Why, Sir, as there are many more tenants than landlords, perhaps, strictly speaking, we should wish not. But if you please you may let your lands cheap, and so get the value, part in money and part in homage. I should agree with you in that.' *Boswell.* 'So, Sir, you laugh at schemes of political improvement.' *Johnson.* 'Why, Sir, most schemes of political improvement are very laughable things.'

He said, 'Mankind have a strong attachment to the habitations to which they have been accustomed. You see the inhabitants of Norway do not with one consent quit it, and go to some part of America, where there is a mild climate, and where they may have the same produce from land, with the tenth part of the labour. No, Sir; their affection for their old dwellings, and the terrour of a general change, keep them at home. Thus, we see many of the finest spots in the world thinly inhabited, and many rugged spots well inhabited.'

When we were alone, I introduced the subject of death, and endeavoured to maintain that the fear of it might be got over. I told him that David Hume said to me, he was no more uneasy to think he should *not be* after this life, than that he *had not been* before he began to exist. *Johnson.* 'Sir, if he really thinks so, his perceptions are disturbed; he is mad; if he does not think so, he lies. He may tell you, he holds his finger in the flame of a candle, without feeling pain; would you believe him? When he dies, he at least gives up all he has.' *Boswell.* 'Foote, Sir, told me, that when he was very ill he was not afraid to die.' *Johnson.* 'It is not true, Sir. Hold a pistol to Foote's breast, or to Hume's breast, and threaten to kill them, and you'll see how they behave.' *Boswell.* 'But may we not fortify our minds for the approach of death?'—Here I am sensible I was in the wrong, to bring before his view what he ever looked upon with horrour; for although when in a celestial frame, in his 'Vanity of human Wishes,' he has supposed death to be 'kind Nature's signal for retreat,' from this state of being to 'a happier seat,' his thoughts upon this aweful change were in general full of dismal apprehensions. His mind resembled the vast amphitheatre, the Colisæum at Rome. In the centre stood his judgement, which, like a mighty gladiator, combated those apprehensions that, like the wild beasts of the *Arena*, were all around in cells, ready to be let out upon him. After a conflict, he drove them back into their dens; but not killing them, they were still assailing him. To my question, whether we might not fortify our minds for the approach of death, he answered, in a passion, 'No, Sir, let it alone. It matters not how a man dies, but how he lives. The act of dying is not of importance, it lasts so short a time.' He added, (with an earnest look,) 'A man knows it must be so, and submits. It will do him no good to whine.'

I attempted to continue the conversation. He was so provoked, that he said, 'Give us no more of this;' and was thrown into such a state of agitation, that he expressed himself in a way that alarmed and distressed me; shewed an impatience that I should leave him, and when I was going away, called to me sternly, 'Don't let us meet to-morrow.'

I went home exceedingly uneasy. All the harsh observations which I had ever heard made upon his character, crowded into my mind; and I seemed to myself like the man who had put his head into the lion's mouth a great many times with perfect safety, but at last had it bit off.

Next morning I sent him a note, stating, that I might have been in the wrong, but it was not intentionally; he was therefore, I could not help thinking, too severe upon me. That notwithstanding our agreement not to meet that day, I would call on him in my way to the city, and stay five minutes by my watch. 'You are, (said I,) in my mind, since last night, surrounded with cloud and storm. Let me have a glimpse of sunshine, and go about my affairs in serenity and chearfulness.'

Upon entering his study, I was glad that he was not alone, which would have made our meeting more aukward. There were with him, Mr. Steevens and Mr. Tyers, both of whom I now saw for the first time. My note had, on his own reflection, softened him, for he received me very complacently; so that I unexpectedly found myself at ease, and joined in the conversation.

I whispered him, 'Well, Sir, you are now in good humour.' *Johnson.* 'Yes, Sir.' I was going to leave him, and had got as far as the staircase. He stopped me, and smiling, said, 'Get you gone *in;*' a curious mode of inviting me to stay, which I accordingly did for some time longer.

This little incidental quarrel and reconciliation, which, perhaps, I may be thought to have detailed too minutely, must be esteemed as one of many proofs which his friends had, that though he might be charged with *bad humour* at times, he was always a *good-natured* man; and I have heard Sir Joshua Reynolds, a nice and delicate observer of manners, particularly remark, that when upon any occasion Johnson had been rough to any person in company, he took the first opportunity of reconciliation, by drinking to him, or addressing his discourse to him; but if he found his dignified indirect overtures sullenly neglected, he was quite indifferent, and considered himself as having done all that he ought to do, and the other as now in the wrong.

1770: ÆTAT. 61.]—During this year there was a total cessation of all correspondence between Dr. Johnson and me, without any coldness on either side, but merely from procrastination, continued from day to day; and as I was not in London, I had no opportunity of enjoying his company and recording his conversation. To supply this blank, I shall present my readers with some *Collectanea*, obligingly furnished to me by the Rev. Dr. Maxwell, of Falkland, in Ireland, some time assistant preacher at the Temple, and for many years the social friend of Johnson, who spoke of him with a very kind regard.

'In politicks he was deemed a Tory, but certainly was not so in the obnoxious or party sense of the term; for while he asserted the legal and salutary prerogatives of the crown, he no less respected the constitutional liberties of the people. Whiggism, at the time of the Revolution, he said, was accompanied with certain principles; but latterly, as a mere party distinction under Walpole and the

Pelhams, was no better than the politicks of stock-jobbers, and the religion of infidels.

'He detested the idea of governing by parliamentary corruption, and asserted most strenuously, that a prince steadily and conspicuously pursuing the interests of his people, could not fail of parliamentary concurrence. A prince of ability, he contended, might and should be the directing soul and spirit of his own administration; in short, his own minister, and not the mere head of a party: and then, and not till then, would the royal dignity be sincerely respected.

'Johnson seemed to think, that a certain degree of crown influence over the Houses of Parliament, (not meaning a corrupt and shameful dependence,) was very salutary, nay, even necessary, in our mixed government. "For, (said he,) if the members were under no crown influence, and disqualified from receiving any gratification from Court, and resembled, as they possibly might, Pym and Haslerig, and other stubborn and sturdy members of the long Parliament, the wheels of government would be totally obstructed. Such men would oppose, merely to shew their power, from envy, jealousy, and perversity of disposition; and not gaining themselves, would hate and oppose all who did: not loving the person of the prince, and conceiving they owed him little gratitude, from the mere spirit of insolence and contradiction, they would oppose and thwart him upon all occasions."

'The inseparable imperfection annexed to all human governments, consisted, he said, in not being able to create a sufficient fund of virtue and principle to carry the laws into due and effectual execution. Wisdom might plan, but virtue alone could execute. And where could sufficient virtue be found? A variety of delegated, and often discretionary, powers must be entrusted somewhere; which, if not governed by integrity and conscience, would necessarily be abused, till at last the constable would sell his for a shilling.

'But let us view him in some instances of more familiar life.

'His general mode of life, during my acquaintance, seemed to be pretty uniform. About twelve o'clock I commonly visited him, and frequently found him in bed, or declaiming over his tea, which he drank very plentifully. He generally had a levee of morning visitors, chiefly men of letters; Hawkesworth, Goldsmith, Murphy, Langton, Steevens, Beauclerk, &c. &c. and sometimes learned ladies, particularly I remember a French lady of wit and fashion doing him the honour of a visit. He seemed to me to be considered as a kind of publick oracle, whom every body thought they had a right to visit and consult; and doubtless they were well rewarded. I never could discover how he found time for his compositions. He declaimed all the morning, then went to dinner at a tavern, where he commonly staid late, and then drank his tea at some friend's house, over which he loitered a great while, but seldom took supper. I fancy he must have read and wrote chiefly in the night, for I can scarcely recollect that he ever refused going with me to a tavern, and he often went to Ranelagh[1], which he deemed a place of innocent recreation.

'He frequently gave all the silver in his pocket to the poor, who watched him, between his house and the tavern where he dined. He walked the streets at all hours, and said he was never robbed, for the rogues knew he had little money, nor had the appearance of having much.

'Though the most accessible and communicative man alive, yet when he suspected he was invited to be exhibited, he constantly spurned the invitation.

'Two young women from Staffordshire visited him when I was present, to consult him on the subject of Methodism, to which they were inclined. "Come, (said he,) you pretty fools, dine with Maxwell and me at the Mitre, and we will talk over that subject;" which they did, and after dinner he took one of them upon his knee, and fondled her for half an hour together.

'Upon a visit to me at a country lodging near Twickenham, he asked what sort of society I had there. I told him, but indifferent; as they chiefly consisted of opulent traders, retired from business. He said, he never much liked that class of people; "For, Sir, (said he,) they have lost the civility of tradesmen, without acquiring the manners of gentlemen."

'Johnson was much attached to London: he observed, that a man stored his mind better there, than any where else; and that in remote situations a man's body might be feasted, but his mind was starved, and his faculties apt to degenerate, from want of exercise and competition. No place, (he said,) cured a man's vanity or arrogance so well as London; for as no man was either great or good *per se*, but as compared with others not so good or great, he was

[1] This was a public pleasure garden, in Chelsea, established on the estate of the earl of Ranelagh (d.1711). A building called the Rotunda was erected for concerts and the gardens were the favorite resort of fashionable society. It was a great place for promenading, for seeing and being seen. Its shades and alleys favored intrigues and it came to have something of a bad reputation.

sure to find in the metropolis many his equals, and some his superiours. He observed, that a man in London was in less danger of falling in love indiscreetly, than any where else; for there the difficulty of deciding between the conflicting pretensions of a vast variety of objects, kept him safe. He told me, that he had frequently been offered country preferment, if he would consent to take orders; but he could not leave the improved society of the capital, or consent to exchange the exhilarating joys and splendid decorations of publick life, for the obscurity, insipidity, and uniformity of remote situations.

'He loved, he said, the old black letter books; they were rich in matter, though their style was inelegant; wonderfully so, considering how conversant the writers were with the best models of antiquity.

'Burton's "Anatomy of Melancholy," he said, was the only book that ever took him out of bed two hours sooner than he wished to rise.

'He frequently exhorted me to set about writing a History of Ireland, and archly remarked, there had been some good Irish writers, and that one Irishman might at least aspire to be equal to another. He had great compassion for the miseries and distresses of the Irish nation, particularly the Papists; and severely reprobated the barbarous debilitating policy of the British government, which, he said, was the most detestable mode of persecution. To a gentleman, who hinted such policy might be necessary to support the authority of the English government, he replied by saying, "Let the authority of the English government perish, rather than be maintained by iniquity. Better would it be to restrain the turbulence of the natives by the authority of the sword, and to make them amenable to law and justice by an effectual and vigorous police, than to grind them to powder by all manner of disabilities and incapacities. Better (said he,) to hang or drown people at once, than by an unrelenting persecution to beggar and starve them."

'Dr. Johnson was often accused of prejudices, nay, antipathy, with regard to the natives of Scotland. Surely, so illiberal a prejudice never entered his mind: and it is well known, many natives of that respectable country possessed a large share in his esteem; nor were any of them ever excluded from his good offices, as far as opportunity permitted. True it is, he considered the Scotch, nationally, as a crafty, designing people, eagerly attentive to their own interest, and too apt to overlook the claims and pretentions of other people.

'Being solicited to compose a funeral sermon for the daughter of a tradesman, he naturally enquired into the character of the deceased; and being told she was remarkable for her humility and condescension to inferiours, he observed, that those were very laudable qualities, but it might not be so easy to discover who the lady's inferiours were.

'When exasperated by contradiction, he was apt to treat his opponents with too much acrimony: as, "Sir, you don't see your way through that question:"—"Sir, you talk the language of ignorance." On my observing to him that a certain gentleman had remained silent the whole evening, in the midst of a very brilliant and learned society, "Sir, (said he,) the conversation overflowed, and drowned him."

'He much commended "Law's Serious Call,"[1] which he said was the finest piece of hortatory theology in any language. "Law, (said he,) fell latterly into the reveries of Jacob Behmen[2], whom Law alledged to have been somewhat in the same state with St. Paul, and to have seen *unutterable things*[3]. Were it even so, (said Johnson,) Jacob would have resembled St. Paul still more, by not attempting to utter them."

'He was much affected by the death of his mother, and wrote to me to come and assist him to compose his mind, which indeed I found extremely agitated.

'He used frequently to observe, that there was more to be endured than enjoyed, in the general condition of human life; and frequently quoted those lines of Dryden:

"Strange cozenage! none would live past years again,
    Yet all hope pleasure from what still remain."

For his part, he said, he never passed that week in his life which he would wish to repeat, were an angel to make the proposal to him.

'Speaking of the *inward light*, to which some methodists pretended, he said, it was a principle utterly incompatible with social or civil security. "If a man (said he,) pretends to a principle of action of which I can know nothing, nay, not so much as that he has it, but only that he pretends to it; how can I tell what that person may be prompted to do? When a person professes to be

---

[1] William Law (1686-1761), whose *A Serious Call to a Devout and Holy Life* was first published in 1728.
[2] Jacob Behmen, or Boehme (1575-1624), was a German mystical writer.
[3] *"unutterable things"* is from II Corinthians.

governed by a written ascertained law, I can then know where to find him."

'Being asked by a young nobleman, what was become of the gallantry and military spirit of the old English nobility, he replied, "Why, my Lord, I'll tell you what is become of it; it is gone into the city to look for a fortune."

'Much enquiry having been made concerning a gentleman, who had quitted a company where Johnson was, and no information being obtained; at last Johnson observed, that "he did not care to speak ill of any man behind his back, but he believed the gentleman was an *attorney*."

'A gentleman who had been very unhappy in marriage, married immediately after his wife died: Johnson said, it was the triumph of hope over experience.

'He observed, that a man of sense and education should meet a suitable companion in a wife. It was a miserable thing when the conversation could only be such as, whether the mutton should be boiled or roasted, and probably a dispute about that.

'He did not approve of late marriages, observing, that more was lost in point of time, than compensated for by any possible advantages. Even ill assorted marriages were preferable to cheerless celibacy.

'He said few people had intellectual resources sufficient to forego the pleasures of wine. They could not otherwise contrive how to fill the interval between dinner and supper.

'One evening at Mrs. Montagu's, where a splendid company was assembled, consisting of the most eminent literary characters, I thought he seemed highly pleased with the respect and attention that were shewn him, and asked him on our return home if he was not highly *gratified* by his visit: "No, Sir, (said he) not highly *gratified*; yet I do not recollect to have passed many evenings *with fewer objections*."

'He said, "the poor in England were better provided for, than in any other country of the same extent: he did not mean little Cantons, or petty Republicks. Where a great proportion of the people (said he,) are suffered to languish in helpless misery, that country must be ill policed, and wretchedly governed: a decent provision for the poor, is the true test of civilization.—Gentlemen of education, he observed, were pretty much the same in all countries; the condition of the lower orders, the poor especially, was the true mark of national discrimination."

'Speaking of economy, he remarked, it was hardly worth while to save anxiously twenty pounds a year. If a man could save to that degree, so as to enable him to assume a different rank in society, then indeed, it might answer some purpose.

'Talking of the Irish clergy, he said, Swift was a man of great parts, and the instrument of much good to his country.—Berkeley was a profound scholar, as well as a man of fine imagination; but Usher, he said, was the great luminary of the Irish church; and a greater, he added, no church could boast of; at least in modern times.

'We dined *tête à tête* at the Mitre, as I was preparing to return to Ireland, after an absence of many years. I regretted much leaving London, where I had formed many agreeable connexions: "Sir, (said he,) I don't wonder at it; no man, fond of letters, leaves London without regret. But remember, Sir, you have seen and enjoyed a great deal;—you have seen life in its highest decorations, and the world has nothing new to exhibit.—No man is so well qualified to leave publick life as he who has long tried it and known it well. We are always hankering after untried situations, and imagining greater felicity from them than they can afford. No, Sir, knowledge and virtue may be acquired in all countries, and your local consequence will make you some amends for the intellectual gratifications you relinquish." '

1771: ÆTAT. 62.]—In 1771 he published another political pamphlet, entitled 'Thoughts on the late Transactions respecting Falkland's Islands,' in which, upon materials furnished to him by ministry, and upon general topicks expanded in his richest style, he successfully endeavoured to persuade the nation that it was wise and laudable to suffer the question of right to remain undecided, rather than involve our country in another war. It has been suggested by some, with what truth I shall not take upon me to decide, that he rated the consequence of those islands to Great-Britain too low. But however this may be, every humane mind must surely applaud the earnestness with which he averted the calamity of war; a calamity so dreadful, that it is astonishing how civilised, nay, Christian nations, can deliberately continue to renew it. His description of its miseries in this pamphlet, is one of the finest pieces of eloquence in the English language. Upon this occasion, too, we find Johnson lashing the party in opposition with unbounded severity, and making the fullest use of what he ever reckoned a most effectual argumentative instrument,—

contempt. His character of their very able mysterious champion, *Junius,* is executed with all the force of his genius, and finished with the highest care. He seems to have exulted in sallying forth to single combat against the boasted and formidable hero, who bade defiance to 'principalities and powers, and the rulers of this world.'

Mr. Strahan, the printer, who had been long in intimacy with Johnson, in the course of his literary labours, who was at once his friendly agent in receiving his pension for him, and his banker in supplying him with money when he wanted it; who was himself now a Member of Parliament, and who loved much to be employed in political negociation; thought he should do eminent service, both to government and Johnson, if he could be the means of his getting a seat in the House of Commons. With this view, he wrote a letter to one of the Secretaries of the Treasury, of which he gave me a copy in his own hand-writing.

This recommendation, we know, was not effectual; but how, or for what reason, can only be conjectured. It is not to be believed that Mr. Strahan would have applied, unless Johnson had approved of it. I never heard him mention the subject; but at a later period of his life, when Sir Joshua Reynolds told him that Mr. Edmund Burke had said, that if he had come early into parliament, he certainly would have been the greatest speaker that ever was there, Johnson exclaimed, 'I should like to try my hand now.'

It has been much agitated among his friends and others, whether he would have been a powerful speaker in Parliament, had he been brought in when advanced in life. I am inclined to think, that his extensive knowledge, his quickness and force of mind, his vivacity and richness of expression, his wit and humour, and above all his poignancy of sarcasm, would have had great effect in a popular assembly; and that the magnitude of his figure, and striking peculiarity of his manner, would have aided the effect. But I remember it was observed by Mr. Flood, that Johnson, having been long used to sententious brevity and the short flights of conversation, might have failed in that continued and expanded kind of argument, which is requisite in stating complicated matters in publick speaking; and as a proof of this he mentioned the supposed speeches in Parliament written by him for the magazine, none of which, in his opinion, were at all like real debates. The opinion of one who was himself so eminent an orator, must be allowed to have great weight. It was confirmed by Sir William Scott, who mentioned that Johnson had told him, that he had several times tried to speak in the Society of Arts and Sciences, but 'had found he could not get on.' From Mr. William Gerrard Hamilton I have heard, that Johnson, when observing to him that it was prudent for a man who had not been accustomed to speak in publick, to begin his speech in as simple a manner as possible, acknowledged that he rose in that society to deliver a speech which he had prepared; 'but (said he,) all my flowers of oratory forsook me.' I however cannot help wishing, that he *had* 'tried his hand' in Parliament; and I wonder that ministry did not make the experiment.

I at length renewed a correspondence which had been too long discontinued:

'To Dr. Johnson.

'Edinburgh, April 18, 1771.

'My Dear Sir,
'I can now fully understand those intervals of silence in your correspondence with me, which have often given me anxiety and uneasiness; for although I am conscious that my veneration and love for Mr. Johnson have never in the least abated, yet I have deferred for almost a year and a half to write to him.'

In the subsequent part of this letter, I gave him an account of my comfortable life as a married man, and a lawyer in practice at the Scotch bar; invited him to Scotland, and promised to attend him to the Highlands, and Hebrides.

'To James Boswell, Esq.

'Dear Sir,
'If you are now able to comprehend that I might neglect to write without diminution of affection, you have taught me, likewise, how that neglect may be uneasily felt without resentment. I wished for your letter a long time, and when it came, it amply recompensed the delay. I never was so much pleased as now with your account of yourself; and sincerely hope, that between publick

business, improving studies, and domestick pleasures, neither melancholy nor caprice will find any place for entrance. Whatever philosophy may determine of material nature, it is certainly true of intellectual nature, that it *abhors a vacuum*: our minds cannot be empty; and evil will break in upon them, if they are not preoccupied by good. My dear Sir, mind your studies, mind your business, make your lady happy, and be a good Christian.

'If we perform our duty, we shall be safe and steady, whether we climb the Highlands, or are tost among the Hebrides; and I hope the time will come when we may try our powers both with cliffs and water. I am this day going into Staffordshire and Derbyshire for six weeks.

> 'I am, dear Sir,
> > 'Your most affectionate
> > > 'And most humble servant,
> > > > 'SAM. JOHNSON.'

'London, June 20, 1771.'

'To DR. JOHNSON.

'Edinburgh, March 3, 1772.

'MY DEAR SIR,

'IT IS hard that I cannot prevail on you to write to me oftener. But I am convinced that it is in vain to expect from you a private correspondence with any regularity. I must, therefore, look upon you as a fountain of wisdom, from whence few rills are communicated to a distance, and which must be approached at its source, to partake fully of its virtues.

'I am coming to London soon, and am to appear in an appeal from the Court of Session in the House of Lords. A schoolmaster in Scotland was, by a court of inferiour jurisdiction, deprived of his office, for being somewhat severe in the chastisement of his scholars. The Court of Session, considering it to be dangerous to the interest of learning and education, to lessen the dignity of teachers, and make them afraid of too indulgent parents, instigated by the complaints of their children, restored him. His enemies have appealed to the House of Lords, though the salary is only twenty pounds a year. I was Counsel for him here. I hope there will be little fear of a reversal; but I must beg to have your aid in my plan of supporting the decree. It is a general question, and not a point of particular law.

> 'I am, &c.
> > 'JAMES BOSWELL.'

'To JAMES BOSWELL, ESQ.

'DEAR SIR,

'THAT you are coming so soon to town I am very glad; and still more glad that you are coming as an advocate. I think nothing more likely to make your life pass happily away, than that consciousness of your own value, which eminence in your profession will certainly confer. If I can give you any collateral help, I hope you do not suspect that it will be wanting. My kindness for you has neither the merit of singular virtue, nor the reproach of singular prejudice. Whether to love you be right or wrong, I have many on my side: Mrs. Thrale loves you, and Mrs. Williams loves you, and what would have inclined me to love you, if I had been neutral before, you are a great favourite of Dr. Beattie.

'Of Dr. Beattie I should have thought much, but that his lady puts him out of my head: she is a very lovely woman.

'The ejection which you come hither to oppose, appears very cruel, unreasonable and oppressive. I should think there could not be much doubt of your success.

'How comes it that you tell me nothing of your lady? I hope to see her some time, and till then shall be glad to hear of her.

'I am, dear Sir, &c.

'SAM. JOHNSON.'

'March 15, 1772.'

On the 21st of March, I was happy to find myself again in my friend's study, and was glad to see my old acquaintance, Mr. Francis Barber, who was now returned home. Dr. Johnson received me with a hearty welcome; saying, 'I am glad you are come, and glad you are come upon such an errand:' (alluding to the cause of the schoolmaster.) *Boswell.* 'I hope, Sir, he will be in no danger. It is a very delicate matter to interfere between a master and his scholars: nor do I see how you can fix the degree of severity that a master may use.' *Johnson.* 'Why, Sir, till you can fix the degree of obstinacy and negligence of the scholars, you cannot fix the degree of severity of the master. Severity must be continued until obstinacy be subdued, and negligence be cured.' He mentioned the severity of Hunter, his own master. 'Sir, (said I,) Hunter is a Scotch name: so it should seem this schoolmaster who beat you so severely was a Scotchman. I can now account for your prejudice against the Scotch.' *Johnson*. 'Sir, he was not Scotch; and abating his brutality, he was a very good master.'

He was engaged to dine abroad, and asked me to return to him in the evening, at nine, which I accordingly did.

We drank tea with Mrs. Williams, who told us a story of second sight, which happened in Wales where she was born.— He listened to it very attentively, and said he should be glad to have some instances of that faculty well authenticated. His elevated wish for more and more evidence for spirit, in opposition to the groveling belief of materialism, led him to a love of such mysterious disquisitions. He again justly observed, that we could have no certainty of the truth of supernatural appearances, unless something was told us which we could not know by ordinary means, or something done which could not be done but by supernatural power; that Pharaoh in reason and justice required such evidence from Moses; nay, that our Saviour said, 'If I had not done among them the works which none other man did, they had not had sin.' He had said in the morning, that 'Macaulay's History of St. Kilda,' was very well written, except some foppery about liberty and slavery. I mentioned to him that Macaulay told me, he was advised to leave out of his book the wonderful story that upon the approach of a stranger all the inhabitants catch cold; but that it had been so well authenticated, he determined to retain it. *Johnson*, 'Sir, to leave things out of a book, merely because people tell you they will not be believed, is meanness. Macaulay acted with more magnanimity.'

We talked of the Roman Catholick religion, and how little difference there was in essential matters between ours and it. *Johnson*. 'True, Sir; all denominations of Christians have really little difference in point of doctrine, though they may differ widely in external forms. There is a prodigious difference between the external form of one of your Presbyterian churches in Scotland, and a church in Italy; yet the doctrine taught is essentially the same.'

In the morning we had talked of old families, and the respect due to them. *Johnson*. 'Sir, you have a right to that kind of respect, and are arguing for yourself. I am for supporting the principle, and am disinterested in doing it, as I have no such right.' *Boswell.* 'Why, Sir, it is one more incitement to a man to do well.' *Johnson.* 'Yes, Sir, and it is a matter of opinion, very necessary to keep society together. What is it but opinion, by which we have a respect for authority, that prevents us, who are the rabble, from rising up and pulling down you who are gentlemen from your places, and saying "We will be gentlemen in our turn"? Now, Sir, that respect for authority is much more easily granted to a man whose father has had it, than to an upstart, and so Society is more easily supported.' *Boswell.* 'Perhaps, Sir, it might be done by the respect belonging to office, as among the Romans, where the dress, the *toga,* inspired reverence.' *Johnson.* 'Why, Sir, we know very little about the Romans. But, surely, it is much easier to respect a man who has always had respect, than to respect a man who we know was last year no better than ourselves, and will be no better next year. In republicks there is not a respect for authority, but a fear of power.' *Boswell.* 'At present, Sir, I think riches seem to gain most respect.' *Johnson.* 'No, Sir, riches do not gain hearty respect; they only procure external attention. A very rich man, from low beginnings, may buy his election in a borough; but, a man of family will be preferred. People will prefer a man for whose father their fathers have voted, though they should get no more money, or even less. That shows that the respect for family is not merely fanciful, but has an actual operation. If gentlemen of family would allow the rich upstarts to spend their money profusely, which they are ready enough to do, and not vie with them in expence, the upstarts would soon be at an end, and the gentlemen would remain: but if the gentlemen will vie in expence with the upstarts, which is very foolish, they must be ruined.'

On Monday, March 23, I found him busy, preparing a fourth edition of his folio Dictionary. Mr. Peyton, one of his original amanuenses, was writing for him. I put him in mind of a meaning of the word *side,* which he had omitted, viz. relationship; as father's side, mother's side. He inserted it. I asked him if *humiliating* was a good word. He said, he had seen it frequently used, but he did not know it to be legitimate English. He would not admit *civilization,* but only *civility.* With great deference to him, I thought *civilization*, from *to civilize*, better in the sense opposed to *barbarity*, than *civility*; as it is better to have a distinct word for each sense, than one word with two senses, which *civility* is, in his way of using it.

He seemed also to be intent on some sort of chymical operation. I was entertained by observing how he contrived to send Mr. Peyton on an errand, without seeming to degrade him. 'Mr. Peyton,—Mr. Peyton, will you be so good as to take a walk to Temple-Bar? You will there see a chymist's shop; at which you will be pleased to buy for me an ounce of oil of vitriol; not spirit of vitriol, but oil of vitriol. It will cost three half-pence.'

On Saturday, March 27, I introduced to him Sir Alexander Macdonald, with whom he had expressed a wish to be acquainted. He received him very courteously.

Sir Alexander observed, that the Chancellors in England are chosen from views much inferiour to the office, being chosen from temporary political views. *Johnson*. 'Why, Sir, in such a government as ours, no man is appointed to an office because he is the fittest for it, nor hardly in any other government; because there are so many connections and dependencies to be studied. A despotick prince may choose a man to an office, merely because he is the fittest for it. The King of Prussia may do it.' *Sir A.* 'I have been correcting several Scotch accents in my friend Boswell. I doubt, Sir, if any Scotchman ever attains to a perfect English pronunciation.' *Johnson*. 'Why, Sir, few of them do, because they do not persevere after acquiring a certain degree of it. But, Sir, there can be no doubt that they may attain to a perfect English pronunciation, if they will. We find how near they come to it; and certainly, a man who conquers nineteen parts of the Scottish accent, may conquer the twentieth. But, Sir, when a man has got the better of nine tenths, he grows weary, he relaxes his diligence, he finds he has corrected his accent so far as not to be disagreeable, and he no longer desires his friends to tell him when he is wrong; nor does he choose to be told. Sir, when people watch me narrowly, and I do not watch myself, they will find me out to be of a particular county[1]. So most Scotchmen may be found out. But, Sir, little

---

[1] Johnson had a Staffordshire accent. Boswell was much concerned about his own Scotch accent and labored to eradicate it.

aberrations are of no disadvantage. I never catched Mallet in a Scotch accent; and yet Mallet, I suppose, was past five-and-twenty before he came to London.'

Upon another occasion I talked to him on this subject, having myself taken some pains to improve my pronunciation. Johnson said to me, 'Sir, your pronunciation is not offensive.' With this concession I was pretty well satisfied; and let me give my countrymen of North-Britain an advice not to aim at absolute perfection in this respect; not to speak *High English*, as we are apt to call what is far removed from the *Scotch*, but which is by no means *good English*, and makes 'the fools who use it,' truly ridiculous. Good English is plain, easy, and smooth in the mouth of an unaffected English Gentleman. A studied and factitious pronunciation, which requires perpetual attention, and imposes perpetual constraint, is exceedingly disgusting. A small intermixture of provincial peculiarities may, perhaps, have an agreeable effect, as the notes of different birds concur in the harmony of the grove, and please more than if they were all exactly alike.

Boswell. 'It may be of use, Sir, to have a Dictionary to ascertain the pronunciation.' *Johnson.* 'Why, Sir, my Dictionary shows you the accents of words, if you can but remember them.' *Boswell.* 'But, Sir, we want marks to ascertain the pronunciation of the vowels. Sheridan, I believe, has finished such a work.' *Johnson.* 'Why, Sir, consider how much easier it is to learn a language by the ear, than by any marks. Sheridan's Dictionary may do very well; but you cannot always carry it about with you: and, when you want the word, you have not the Dictionary. It is like a man who has a sword that will not draw. It is an admirable sword, to be sure: but while your enemy is cutting your throat, you are unable to use it. Besides, Sir, what entitles Sheridan to fix the pronunciation of English? He has, in the first place, the disadvantage of being an Irishman: and if he says he will fix it after the example of the best company, why they differ among themselves. I remember an instance: when I published the Plan for my Dictionary, Lord Chesterfield told me that the word *great* should be pronounced so as to rhyme to *state*; and Sir William Yonge sent me word that it should be pronounced so as to rhyme to *seat*, and that none but

an Irishman would pronounce it *grait*. Now here were two men
of the highest rank, the one, the best speaker in the House of
Lords, the other, the best speaker in the House of Commons,
differing entirely.'

I again visited him at night. Finding him in a very good humour, I ventured to lead him to the subject of our situation in
a future state, having much curiosity to know his notions on
that point. *Johnson.* 'Why, Sir, the happiness of an unembodied spirit will consist in a consciousness of the favour of
GOD, in the contemplation of truth, and in the possession of
felicitating ideas.' *Boswell.* 'But, Sir, is there any harm in our
forming to ourselves conjectures as to the particulars of our
happiness, though the scripture has said but very little on the
subject? "We know not what we shall be." ' *Johnson.* 'Sir, there
is no harm. What philosophy suggests to us on this topick is
probable: what scripture tells us is certain. Dr. Henry More
has carried it as far as philosophy can. You may buy both his
theological and philosophical works in two volumes folio, for
about eight shillings.' *Boswell.* 'One of the most pleasing
thoughts is, that we shall see our friends again.' *Johnson.* 'Yes,
Sir; but you must consider, that when we are become purely
rational, many of our friendships will be cut off. Many friendships are formed by a community of sensual pleasures: all these
will be cut off. We form many friendships with bad men, because they have agreeable qualities, and they can be useful to
us; but, after death, they can no longer be of use to us. We
form many friendships by mistake, imagining people to be
different from what they really are. After death, we shall see
every one in a true light. Then, Sir, they talk of our meeting
our relations: but then all relationship is dissolved; and we
shall have no regard for one person more than another, but for
their real value. However, we shall either have the satisfaction
of meeting our friends, or be satisfied without meeting them.'
Boswell. 'As to our employment in a future state, the sacred
writings say little. The Revelation, however, of St. John gives
us many ideas, and particularly mentions musick.' *Johnson.*
'Why, Sir, ideas must be given you by means of something
which you know: and as to musick, there are some philosophers
and divines who have maintained that we shall not be spirit-

ualized to such a degree, but that something of matter, very much refined, will remain. In that case, musick may make a part of our future felicity.'

Boswell. 'I do not know whether there are any well-attested stories of the appearance of ghosts. You know there is a famous story of the appearance of Mrs. Veal, prefixed to "Drelincourt on Death".' *Johnson.* 'I believe, Sir, that is given up. I believe the woman declared upon her death-bed that it was a lie.' *Boswell.* 'This objection is made against the truth of ghosts appearing: that if they are in a state of happiness, it would be a punishment to them to return to this world; and if they are in a state of misery, it would be giving them a respite.' *Johnson.* 'Why, Sir, as the happiness or misery of unembodied spirits does not depend upon place, but is intellectual, we cannot say that they are less happy or less miserable by appearing upon earth.'

On Tuesday, March 31, he and I dined at General Paoli's. A question was started, whether the state of marriage was natural to man. *Johnson.* 'Sir, it is so far from being natural for a man and woman to live in a state of marriage, that we find all the motives which they have for remaining in that connection, and the restraints which civilized society imposes to prevent separation, are hardly sufficient to keep them together.' The General said, that in a state of nature a man and woman uniting together would form a strong and constant affection, by the mutual pleasure each would receive; and that the same causes of dissention would not arise between them, as occur between husband and wife in a civilized state. *Johnson.* 'Sir, they would have dissentions enough, though of another kind. One would choose to go a hunting in this wood, the other in that; one would choose to go a fishing in this lake, the other in that; or, perhaps, one would choose to go a hunting, when the other would choose to go a fishing; and so they would part. Besides, Sir, a savage man and a savage woman meet by chance; and when the man sees another woman that pleases him better, he will leave the first.'

We then fell into a disquisition whether there is any beauty independent of utility. The General maintained there was not.

Dr. Johnson maintained that there was; and he instanced a coffee-cup which he held in his hand, the painting of which was of no real use, as the cup would hold the coffee equally well if plain; yet the painting was beautiful.

Dr. Johnson went home with me to my lodgings in Conduit-street and drank tea, previous to our going to the Pantheon,[1] which neither of us had seen before.

He said, 'Goldsmith's Life of Parnell is poor; not that it is poorly written, but that he had poor materials; for nobody can write the life of a man, but those who have eat and drunk and lived in social intercourse with him.'

I said, that if it was not troublesome and presuming too much, I would request him to tell me all the little circumstances of his life; what schools he attended, when he came to Oxford, when he came to London, &c. &c. He did not disapprove of my curiosity as to these particulars; but said, 'They'll come out by degrees as we talk together.'

We talked of the proper use of riches. *Johnson.* 'If I were a man of a great estate, I would drive all the rascals whom I did not like out of the county at an election.'

I asked him how far he thought wealth should be employed in hospitality. *Johnson.* 'You are to consider that ancient hospitality, of which we hear so much, was in an uncommercial country, when men being idle, were glad to be entertained at rich men's tables. But in a commercial country, a busy country, time becomes precious, and therefore hospitality is not so much valued. No doubt there is still room for a certain degree of it; and a man has a satisfaction in seeing his friends eating and drinking around him. But promiscuous hospitality is not the way to gain real influence. You must help some people at table before others; you must ask some people how they like their wine oftener than others. You therefore offend more people than you please.' *Boswell.* 'May not a man, Sir, employ his riches to advantage in educating young men of merit?' *John-*

[1] The Pantheon, a palatial structure in Oxford Street, was designed to be a winter Ranelagh, a place for assemblies, concerts and balls. Its magnificence was much admired and, of course, condemned by some.

son. 'Yes, Sir, if they fall in your way; but if it is understood that you patronize young men of merit, you will be harassed with solicitations.

'Were I a rich man, I would propagate all kinds of trees that will grow in the open air. A green-house is childish. I would introduce foreign animals into the country; for instance, the rein-deer.'

We then walked to the Pantheon. The first view of it did not strike us so much as Ranelagh. However, as Johnson observed, we saw the Pantheon in time of mourning, when there was a dull uniformity; whereas we had seen Ranelagh when the view was enlivened with a gay profusion of colours. I said there was not half a guinea's worth of pleasure in seeing this place. *Johnson.* 'But, Sir, there is half a guinea's worth of inferiority to other people in not having seen it.' *Boswell.* 'I doubt, Sir, whether there are many happy people here.' *Johnson.* 'Yes, Sir, there are many happy people here. There are many people here who are watching hundreds, and who think hundreds are watching them.'

Happening to meet Sir Adam Fergusson, I presented him to Dr. Johnson. Sir Adam expressed some apprehension that the Pantheon would encourage luxury. 'Sir, (said Johnson,) I am a great friend to publick amusements; for they keep people from vice. You now (addressing himself to me,) would have been with a wench, had you not been here.—O! I forgot you were married.'

Sir Adam suggested, that luxury corrupts a people, and destroys the spirit of liberty. *Johnson.* 'Sir, that is all visionary. I would not give half a guinea to live under one form of government rather than another. It is of no moment to the happiness of an individual. Sir, the danger of the abuse of power is nothing to a private man. What Frenchman is prevented from passing his life as he pleases?' *Sir Adam.* 'But, Sir, in the British constitution it is surely of importance to keep up a spirit in the people, so as to preserve a balance against the crown.' *Johnson.* 'Sir, I perceive you are a vile Whig.—Why all this childish jealousy of the power of the crown? The crown has not power enough. When I say that all governments are alike, I consider that in no government power can be abused long. Mankind will not bear it. If a sovereign oppresses his people to a great degree, they will rise and cut off his head. There is a remedy in human nature against tyranny, that will keep us safe under every form of government. Had not the people of France thought themselves honoured as sharing in the brilliant actions of Lewis XIV, they would not have endured him; and we may say the same of the King of Prussia's people.' Sir Adam introduced the ancient Greeks and Romans. *Johnson.* 'Sir, the mass of both of them were barbarians. The mass of every people must be barbarous where there is no printing, and consequently knowledge is not generally diffused. Knowledge is diffused among our people by the news-papers.' Sir Adam mentioned the orators, poets, and artists of Greece. *Johnson.* 'Sir, I am talking of the mass of the people. We see even what the boasted Athenians were. The little effect which Demosthenes's orations had upon them, shews that they were barbarians.'

On Sunday, April 5, after attending divine service at St. Paul's church, I found him alone. Of a schoolmaster of his acquaintance, a native of Scotland, he said, 'He has a great deal of good about him; but he is also very defective in some respects. His inner part is good, but his outer part is mighty aukward. You in Scotland do not attain that nice critical skill in languages, which we get in our schools in England. I would not put a boy to him, whom I intended for a man of learning. But for the sons of citizens, who are to learn a little, get good morals, and then go to trade, he may do very well.'

I mentioned a cause in which I had appeared as counsel at the bar of the General Assembly of the Church of Scotland, where a *Probationer,* (as one licensed to preach, but not yet ordained, is called,) was opposed in his application to be inducted, because it was alledged that he had been guilty of fornication five years before. *Johnson.* 'Why, Sir, if he has repented, it is not a sufficient objection. A man who is good enough to go to heaven, is good enough to be a clergyman.' This was a humane and liberal sentiment. But the character of a clergyman is more sacred than that of an ordinary Christian. I told him, that by the rules of the Church of Scotland, in their 'Book of Discipline,' if a *scandal,* as it is called, is not prosecuted for five years, it cannot afterwards be proceeded upon,

'unless it be *of a heinous nature,* or again become flagrant;' and
that hence a question arose, whether fornication was a sin of a
heinous nature; and that I had maintained, that it did not deserve that epithet, in as much as it was not one of those sins
which argue very great depravity of heart: in short, was not,
in the general acceptation of mankind, a heinous sin. *Johnson.*
'No, Sir, it is not a heinous sin. A heinous sin is that for which
a man is punished with death or banishment.' *Boswell.* 'But,
Sir, after I had argued that it was not a heinous sin, an old
clergyman rose up, and repeating the text of scripture denounc-
ing judgement against whoremongers, asked, whether, considering this, there could be any doubt of fornication being a
heinous sin.' *Johnson.* 'Why, Sir, observe the word *whoremonger.* Every sin, if persisted in, will become heinous.
Whoremonger is a dealer in whores, as ironmonger is a dealer
in iron. But as you don't call a man an ironmonger for buying
and selling a pen-knife; so you don't call a man a whoremonger
for getting one wench with child.'

On Monday, April 6, I dined with him at Sir Alexander
Macdonald's, where was a young officer in the regimentals of
the Scots Royal, who talked with a vivacity, fluency, and precision so uncommon, that he attracted particular attention. He
proved to be the Honourable Thomas Erskine, youngest
brother to the Earl of Buchan, who has since risen into such
brilliant reputation at the bar in Westminster-hall.

Fielding being mentioned, Johnson exclaimed, 'he was a
blockhead;' and upon my expressing my astonishment at so
strange an assertion, he said, 'What I mean by his being a
blockhead is that he was a barren rascal.' *Boswell.* 'Will you
not allow, Sir, that he draws very natural pictures of human
life?' *Johnson.* 'Why, Sir, it is of very low life. Richardson used
to say, that had he not known who Fielding was, he should
have believed he was an ostler. Sir, there is more knowledge of
the heart in one letter of Richardson's, than in all "Tom Jones".
I, indeed, never read "Joseph Andrews".' *Erskine.* 'Surely, Sir,
Richardson is very tedious.' *Johnson.* 'Why, Sir, if you were to
read Richardson for the story, your impatience would be so
much fretted that you would hang yourself. But you must read

him for the sentiment, and consider the story as only giving occasion to the sentiment.'

We talked of gaming, and animadverted on it with severity. *Johnson.* 'Nay, gentlemen, let us not aggravate the matter. It is not roguery to play with a man who is ignorant of the game, while you are master of it, and so win his money; for he thinks he can play better than you, as you think you can play better than he; and the superiour skill carries it.' *Erskine.* 'He is a fool, but you are not a rogue.' *Johnson.* 'That's much about the truth, Sir. It must be considered, that a man who only does what every one of the society to which he belongs would do, is not a dishonest man. In the republick of Sparta, it was agreed, that stealing was not dishonourable, if not discovered. I do not commend a society where there is an agreement that what would not otherwise be fair, shall be fair; but I maintain, that an individual of any society, who practises what is allowed, is not a dishonest man.' *Boswell.* 'So then, Sir, you do not think ill of a man who wins perhaps forty thousand pounds in a winter?' *Johnson.* 'Sir, I do not call a gamester a dishonest man; but I call him an unsocial man, an unprofitable man. Gaming is a mode of transferring property without producing any intermediate good. Trade gives employment to numbers, and so produces intermediate good.'

I talked of the little attachment which subsisted between near relations in London. 'Sir, (said Johnson,) in a country so commercial as ours, where every man can do for himself, there is not so much occasion for that attachment. No man is thought the worse of here, whose brother was hanged. In uncommercial countries, many of the branches of a family must depend on the stock; so, in order to make the head of the family take care of them, they are represented as connected with his reputation, that, self-love being interested, he may exert himself to promote their interest. You have first large circles, or clans; as commerce increases, the connection is confined to families. By degrees, that too goes off, as having become unnecessary, and there being few opportunities of intercourse. One brother is a merchant in the city, and another is an officer in the guards. How little intercourse can these two have!'

I argued warmly for the old feudal system. Sir Alexander opposed it, and talked of the pleasure of seeing all men free and independent. *Johnson.* 'I agree with Mr. Boswell that there must be a high satisfaction in being a feudal Lord; but we are to consider, that we ought not to wish to have a number of men unhappy for the satisfaction of one.'—I maintained that numbers, namely, the vassals or followers, were not unhappy; for that there was a reciprocal satisfaction between the Lord and them: he being kind in his authority over them; they being respectful and faithful to him.

On Thursday, April 9, I called on him to beg he would go and dine with me at the Mitre tavern. He had resolved not to dine at all this day, I know not for what reason; and I was so unwilling to be deprived of his company, that I was content to submit to suffer a want, which was at first somewhat painful, but he soon made me forget it; and a man is always pleased with himself when he finds his intellectual inclinations predominate.

He observed, that to reason too philosophically on the nature of prayer, was very unprofitable.

Talking of ghosts, he said, he knew one friend, who was an honest man and a sensible man, who told him he had seen a ghost, old Mr. Edward Cave, the printer at St. John's Gate. He said, Mr. Cave did not like to talk of it, and seemed to be in great horrour whenever it was mentioned. *Boswell.* 'Pray, Sir, what did he say was the appearance?' *Johnson.* 'Why, Sir, something of a shadowy being.'

I mentioned witches, and asked him what they properly meant. *Johnson.* 'Why, Sir, they properly mean those who make use of the aid of evil spirits.' *Boswell.* 'There is no doubt, Sir, a general report and belief of their having existed.' *Johnson.* 'Sir, you have not only the general report and belief, but you have many voluntary solemn confessions.' He did not affirm any thing positively upon a subject which it is the fashion of the times to laugh at as a matter of absurd credulity. He only seemed willing, as a candid enquirer after truth, however strange and inexplicable, to shew that he understood what might be urged for it.

On Friday, April 10, I dined with him at General Ogle-thorpe's, where we found Dr. Goldsmith.

Armorial bearings having been mentioned, Johnson said, they were as ancient as the siege of Thebes, which he proved by a passage in one of the tragedies of Euripides.

I started the question whether duelling was consistent with moral duty. The brave old General fired at this, and said, with a lofty air, 'Undoubtedly a man has a right to defend his honour.' *Goldsmith,* (turning to me.) 'I ask you first, Sir, what would you do if you were affronted?' I answered I should think it necessary to fight. 'Why then, (replied Goldsmith,) that solves the question.' *Johnson.* 'No, Sir, it does not solve the question. It does not follow that what a man would do is there-fore right.' I said, I wished to have it settled, whether duelling was contrary to the laws of Christianity. Johnson immediately entered on the subject, and treated it in a masterly manner; and so far as I have been able to recollect, his thoughts were these: 'Sir, as men become in a high degree refined, various causes of offence arise; which are considered to be of such im-portance, that life must be staked to atone for them, though in reality they are not so. A body that has received a very fine polish may be easily hurt. Before men arrive at this artificial refinement, if one tells his neighbour he lies, his neighbour tells him he lies; if one gives his neighbour a blow, his neigh-bour gives him a blow: but in a state of highly polished soci-ety, an affront is held to be a serious injury. It must, therefore, be resented, or rather a duel must be fought upon it; as men have agreed to banish from their society one who puts up with an affront without fighting a duel. Now, Sir, it is never unlaw-ful to fight in self-defence. He, then, who fights a duel, does not fight from passion against his antagonist, but out of self-defence; to avert the stigma of the world, and to prevent him-self from being driven out of society. I could wish there was not that superfluity of refinement; but while such notions pre-vail, no doubt a man may lawfully fight a duel.'

Let it be remembered, that this justification is applicable only to the person who *receives* an affront. All mankind must condemn the aggressor.

The General told us, that when he was a very young man, I think only fifteen, serving under Prince Eugene of Savoy, he was sitting in a company at table with a Prince of Wirtemberg. The Prince took up a glass of wine, and, by a fillip, made some of it fly in Oglethorpe's face. Here was a nice dilemma. To have challenged him instantly, might have fixed a quarrelsome character upon the young soldier: to have taken no notice of it might have been considered as cowardice. Oglethorpe, therefore, keeping his eye upon the Prince, and smiling all the time, as if he took what his Highness had done in jest, said 'Mon Prince,—' (I forget the French words he used, the purport however was,) 'That's a good joke; but we do it much better in England;' and threw a whole glass of wine in the Prince's face.

Dr. Johnson said, 'Pray, General, give us an account of the siege of Belgrade.' Upon which the General, pouring a little wine upon the table, described every thing with a wet finger: 'Here we were, here were the Turks,' &c. &c. Johnson listened with the closest attention.

A question was started, how far people who disagree in any capital point can live in friendship together. Johnson said they might. Goldsmith said they could not, as they had not the same likings and the same aversions. *Johnson.* 'Why, Sir, you must shun the subject as to which you disagree. For instance, I can live very well with Burke: I love his knowledge, his genius, his diffusion, and affluence of conversation; but I would not talk to him of the Rockingham party.' *Goldsmith.* 'But, Sir, when people live together who have something as to which they disagree, and which they want to shun, they will be in the situation mentioned in the story of Bluebeard: "You may look into all the chambers but one." But we should have the greatest inclination to look into that chamber, to talk of that subject.' *Johnson.* (with a loud voice.) 'Sir, I am not saying that *you* could live in friendship with a man from whom you differ as to some point: I am only saying that *I* could do it.'

Goldsmith told us, that he was now busy in writing a natural history, and, that he might have full leisure for it, he had taken lodgings, at a farmer's house, near to the six mile-stone, on the Edgeware-road, and had carried down his books in two returned post-chaises. Mr. Mickle and I, went to visit him at this place a few days afterwards. He was not at home; but having a curiosity to see his apartment, we went in and found curious scraps of descriptions of animals, scrawled upon the walls with a black lead pencil.

The subject of ghosts being introduced, Johnson repeated what he had told me of a friend of his, an honest man and a man of sense, having asserted to him, that he had seen an apparition. Goldsmith told us, he was assured by his brother, the Reverend Mr. Goldsmith, that he also had seen one. General Oglethorpe told us, that Prendergast, an officer in the Duke of Marlborough's army, had mentioned to many of his friends, that he should die on a particular day. That upon that day a battle took place with the French; that after it was over, and Prendergast was still alive, his brother officers, while they were yet in the field, jestingly asked him, where was his prophecy now. Prendergast gravely answered. 'I shall die, notwithstanding what you see.' Soon afterwards, there came a shot from a French battery, to which the orders for a cessation of arms had not yet reached, and he was killed upon the spot. Colonel Cecil, who took possession of his effects, found in his pocketbook the following solemn entry:

[Here the date.] 'Dreamt—or —— Sir John Friend meets me:' (here the very day on which he was killed was mentioned.) Prendergast had been connected with Sir John Friend, who was executed for high treason. General Oglethorpe said, he was in company with Colonel Cecil when Pope came and enquired into the truth of this story, which made a great noise at the time, and was then confirmed by the Colonel.

On Saturday, April 11, he appointed me to come to him in the evening, when he should be at leisure to give me some assistance for the defence of Hastie, the schoolmaster of Campbelltown, for whom I was to appear in the House of Lords. When I came, I found him unwilling to exert himself. I pressed him to write down his thoughts upon the subject. He said, 'There's no occasion for my writing. I'll talk to you.' He was, however, at last prevailed on to dictate to me, while I wrote as follows:

'The charge is, that he has used immoderate and cruel correction. Correction, in itself, is not cruel; children, being not reasonable, can be governed only by fear. To impress this fear, is therefore one of the first duties of those who have the care of children. It is the duty of a parent; and has never been thought inconsistent with parental tenderness. It is the duty of a master, who is in his highest exaltation when he is *loco parentis.* Yet, as good things become evil by excess, correction, by being immoderate, may become cruel. But when is correction immoderate? When it is more frequent or more severe than is required *ad monendum et docendum,* for reformation and instruction. No severity is cruel which obstinacy makes necessary; for the greatest cruelty would be to desist, and leave the scholar too careless for instruction, and too much hardened for reproof. Locke, in his treatise of Education, mentions a mother, with applause, who whipped an infant eight times before she had subdued it; for had she stopped at the seventh act of correction, her daughter, says he, would have been ruined. The degrees of obstinacy in young minds are very different; as different must be the degrees of persevering severity. A stubborn scholar must be corrected till he is subdued. The discipline of a school is military. There must be either unbounded licence or absolute authority. The master, who punishes, not only consults the future happiness of him who is the immediate subject of correction; but he propagates obedience through the whole school; and establishes regularity by exemplary justice. The victorious obstinacy of a single boy would make his future endeavours of reformation or instruction totally ineffectual. Obstinacy, therefore, must never be victorious. Yet, it is well known, that there sometimes occurs a sullen and hardy resolution, that laughs at all common punishment, and bids defiance to all common degrees of pain. Correction must be proportioned to occasions. The flexible will be reformed by gentle discipline, and the refractory must be subdued by harsher methods. The degrees of scholastick, as of military punishment, no stated rules can ascertain. It must be enforced till it overpowers temptation; till stubbornness becomes flexible, and perverseness regular. Custom and reason have, indeed, set some bounds to scholastick penalties. The schoolmaster inflicts no capital punishments; nor enforces his edicts by either death or mutilation. The civil law has wisely determined, that a master who strikes at a scholar's eye shall be considered as criminal. But punishments, however severe, that produce no lasting evil, may be just and reasonable, because they may be necessary. Such have been the punishments used by the respondent. No scholar has gone from him either blind or lame, or with any of his limbs or powers injured or impaired. They were irregular, and he punished them: they were obstinate, and he enforced his punishment. But, however provoked, he never exceeded the limits of moderation, for he inflicted nothing beyond present pain; and how much of that was required, no man is so little able to determine as those who have determined against him;—the parents of the offenders.—It has been said, that he used unprecedented and improper instruments of correction. Of this accusation the meaning is not very easy to be found. No instrument of correction is more proper than another, but as it is better adapted to produce present pain without lasting mischief. Whatever were his instruments, no lasting mischief has ensued; and therefore, however unusual, in hands so cautious they were proper.—It has been objected, that the respondent admits the charge of cruelty, by producing no evidence to confute it. Let it be considered, that his scholars are either dispersed at large in the world, or continue to inhabit the place in which they were bred. Those who are dispersed cannot be found; those who remain are the sons of his persecutors, and are not likely to support a man to whom their fathers are enemies. If it be supposed that the enmity of their fathers proves the justice of the charge, it must be considered how often experience shews us, that men who are angry on one ground will accuse on another; with how little kindness, in a town of low trade, a man who lives by learning is regarded; and how implicitly, where the inhabitants are not very rich, a rich man is hearkened to and followed. In a place like Campbelltown, it is easy for one of the principal inhabitants to make a party. It is easy for that party to heat themselves with imaginary grievances. It is easy for them to oppress a man poorer than themselves; and natural to assert the dignity of riches, by persisting in oppression. The argument which attempts to prove the impropriety of restoring him to his school, by alledging that he has lost the confidence of the people, is not the subject of juridical consideration; for he is to suffer, if he must suffer, not for their judgement, but for his own actions. It may be convenient for them to have another master; but it is a convenience of their own making. It would be likewise convenient for him to find another school; but this convenience he cannot obtain.—The question is not what is now convenient, but what is generally right. If the people of Campbelltown be distressed by the restoration of the respondent, they are distressed only by their own fault; by turbulent passions and unreasonable desires; by tyranny, which law has defeated, and by malice, which virtue has surmounted.'

'This, Sir, (said he,) you are to turn in your mind, and make the best use of it you can in your speech.'

On Tuesday, April 14, the decree of the Court of Session in the schoolmaster's cause was reversed in the House of Lords, after a very eloquent speech by Lord Mansfield, who shewed himself an adept in school discipline, but I thought was too rigorous towards my client. On the evening of the next day I supped with Dr. Johnson, at the Crown and Anchor tavern, in the Strand, in company with Mr. Langton and his brother-in-law, Lord Binning. I repeated a sentence of Lord Mansfield's speech, of which, by the aid of Mr. Longlands, the solicitor on the other side, who obligingly allowed me to compare his note with my own, I have a full copy: 'My Lords, severity is not the way to govern either boys or men.' 'Nay, (said Johnson,) it is the way to *govern* them. I know not whether it be the way to *mend* them.'

I talked of the recent expulsion of six students from the University of Oxford, who were methodists,[1] and would not desist from publickly praying and exhorting. *Johnson.* 'Sir, that expulsion was extremely just and proper. What have they to do at an University who are not willing to be taught, but will presume to teach? Where is religion to be learnt but at an University? Sir, they were examined, and found to be mighty ignorant fellows.' *Boswell.* 'But, was it not hard, Sir, to expel them, for I am told they were good beings?' *Johnson.* 'Sir, I believe they might be good beings; but they were not fit to be in the University of Oxford. A cow is a very good animal in the field; but we turn her out of a garden.' Lord Elibank used to repeat this as an illustration uncommonly happy.

Mr. Langton told us he was about to establish a school upon his estate, but it had been suggested to him, that it might have a tendency to make the people less industrious. *Johnson.* 'No, Sir. While learning to read and write is a distinction, the few who have that distinction may be the less inclined to work; but when every body learns to read and write, it is no longer a distinction. A man who has a laced waistcoat is too fine a man to work; but if every body had laced waistcoats, we should have people working in laced waistcoats. There are no people what-

[1] These six young men were expelled from St. Edmund Hall in 1768. Their "ignorance" was given as the nominal reason.

ever more industrious, none who work more, than our manu-
facturers; yet they have all learnt to read and write. Sir, you
must not neglect doing a thing immediately good, from fear of
remote evil;—from fear of its being abused. A man who has
candles may sit up too late, which he would not do if he had
not candles; but nobody will deny that the art of making candles, by which light is continued to us beyond the time that the
sun gives us light, is a valuable art, and ought to be preserved.'
Boswell. 'But, Sir, would it not be better to follow Nature; and
go to bed and rise just as Nature gives us light or with-holds
it?' *Johnson.* 'No, Sir; for then we should have no kind of
equality in the partition of our time between sleeping and waking. It would be very different in different seasons and in different places. In some of the northern parts of Scotland how
little light is there in the depth of winter!'

While I remained in London this spring, I was with him at
several other times, both by himself and in company. I dined
with him one day at the Crown and Anchor tavern, in the
Strand, with Lord Elibank, Mr. Langton, and Dr. Vansittart
of Oxford. Without specifying each particular day, I have preserved the following memorable things.

I regretted the reflection in his Preface to Shakspeare against
Garrick, to whom we cannot but apply the following passage:
'I collated such copies as I could procure, and wished for more,
but have not found the collectors of these rarities very communicative.' I told him, that Garrick had complained to me of
it, and had vindicated himself by assuring me, that Johnson
was made welcome to the full use of his collection, and that he
left the key of it with a servant, with orders to have a fire and
every convenience for him. I found Johnson's notion was, that
Garrick wanted to be courted for them, and that, on the contrary, Garrick should have courted him, and sent him the plays
of his own accord. But, indeed, considering the slovenly and
careless manner in which books were treated by Johnson, it
could not be expected that scarce and valuable editions should
have been lent to him.

A gentleman having to some of the usual arguments for
drinking added this: 'You know, Sir, drinking drives away

care, and makes us forget whatever is disagreeable. Would not you allow a man to drink for that reason?' *Johnson.* 'Yes, Sir, if he sat next *you.*'

When one of his friends endeavoured to maintain that a country gentleman might contrive to ραss his life very agreeably, 'Sir (said he,) you cannot give me an instance of any man who is permitted to lay out his own time, contriving not to have tedious hours.' This observation, however, is equally applicable to gentlemen who live in cities, and are of no profession.

A learned gentleman who in the course of conversation wished to inform us of this simple fact, that the Counsel upon the circuit at Shrewsbury were much bitten by fleas, took I suppose, seven or eight minutes in relating it circumstantially. He in a plenitude of phrase told us, that large bales of woollen cloth were lodged in the town-hall;—that by reason of this, fleas nestled there in prodigious numbers;—that the lodgings of the Counsel were near to the town-hall;—and that those little animals moved from place to place with wonderful agility. Johnson sat in great impatience till the gentleman had finished his tedious narrative, and then burst out (playfully however,) 'It is a pity, Sir, that you have not seen a lion; for a flea has taken you such a time, that a lion must have served you a twelvemonth.'

1773: ÆTAT. 64.]—In 1773 his only publication was an edition of his folio Dictionary, with additions and corrections; nor did he, so far as is known, furnish any productions of his fertile pen to any of his numerous friends or dependants, except the Preface to his old amanuensis Macbean's 'Dictionary of ancient Geography.' His Shakspeare, indeed, which had been received with high approbation by the publick, and gone through several editions, was this year re-published by George Steevens, Esq. a gentleman not only deeply skilled in ancient learning, and of very extensive reading in English literature, especially the early writers, but at the same time of acute discernment and elegant taste.

'To James Boswell, Esq.

'Dear Sir,

'I have read your kind letter much more than the elegant Pindar which it accompanied. I am always glad to find myself not

forgotten; and to be forgotten by you would give me great uneasiness. My northern friends have never been unkind to me: I have
from you, dear Sir, testimonies of affection, which I have not often
been able to excite; and Dr. Beattie rates the testimony which I
was desirous of paying to his merit, much higher than I should
have thought it reasonable to expect.

'I have heard of your masquerade. What says your synod to such
innovations? I am not studiously scrupulous, nor do I think a masquerade either evil in itself, or very likely to be the occasion of evil;
yet as the world thinks it a very licentious relaxation of manners, I
would not have been one of the *first* masquers in a country where
no masquerade had ever been before.

'A new edition of my great Dictionary is printed, from a copy
which I was persuaded to revise; but having made no preparation,
I was able to do very little. Some superfluities I have expunged, and
some faults I have corrected, and here and there have scattered a
remark; but the main fabrick of the work remains as it was. I had
looked very little into it since I wrote it, and, I think, I found it
full as often better, as worse, than I expected.

'Baretti and Davies have had a furious quarrel; a quarrel, I
think, irreconcileable. Dr. Goldsmith has a new comedy, which is
expected in the spring. No name is yet given it. The chief diversion arises from a stratagem by which a lover is made to mistake his
future father-in-law's house for an inn. This, you see, borders upon
farce. The dialogue is quick and gay, and the incidents are so prepared as not to seem improbable.

'My health seems in general to improve; but I have been troubled
for many weeks with a vexatious catarrh, which is sometimes sufficiently distressful. I have not found any great effects from bleeding and physick; and am afraid, that I must expect help from
brighter days and softer air.

'Write to me now and then; and whenever any good befalls you,
make haste to let me know it, for no one will rejoice at it more
than, dear Sir,

> 'Your most humble servant,
> 'SAM. JOHNSON.'

'London, Feb. 24, 1773.'

'You continue to stand very high in the favour of Mrs. Thrale.'

On Saturday, April 3, the day after my arrival in London
this year, I went to his house late in the evening, and sat with
Mrs. Williams till he came home. I found in the London

Chronicle, Dr. Goldsmith's apology to the publick for beating
Evans, a bookseller, on account of a paragraph in a news-paper
published by him, which Goldsmith thought impertinent to
him and to a lady of his acquaintance. The apology was written
so much in Dr. Johnson's manner, that both Mrs. Williams and
I supposed it to be his; but when he came home, he soon undeceived us. When he said to Mrs. Williams, 'Well, Dr. Goldsmith's *manifesto* has got into your paper;' I asked him if Dr.
Goldsmith had written it, with an air that made him see I suspected it was his, though subscribed by Goldsmith. *Johnson*.
'Sir, Dr. Goldsmith would no more have asked me to write
such a thing as that for him, than he would have asked me to
feed him with a spoon, or to do any thing else that denoted his
imbecility. I as much believe that he wrote it, as if I had seen
him do it. Sir, had he shewn it to any one friend, he would not
have been allowed to publish it. He has, indeed, done it very
well; but it is a foolish thing well done. I suppose he has been
so much elated with the success of his new comedy, that he
has thought every thing that concerned him must be of importance to the publick.' *Boswell*. 'I fancy, Sir, this is the first
time that he has been engaged in such an adventure.' *Johnson*.
'Why, Sir, I believe it is the first time he has *beat*; he may have
been beaten before. This, Sir, is a new plume to him.'

At Mr. Thrale's, in the evening, he repeated his usual para-
doxical declamation against action in publick speaking. 'Action can have no effect upon reasonable minds. It may augment
noise, but it never can enforce argument. If you speak to a dog,
you use action; you hold up your hand thus, because he is a
brute; and in proportion as men are removed from brutes, action will have the less influence upon them.' *Mrs. Thrale*.
'What then, Sir, becomes of Demosthenes's saying? "Action,
action, action!"' *Johnson*. 'Demosthenes, Madam, spoke to an
assembly of brutes; to a barbarous people.'

Lord Chesterfield being mentioned, Johnson remarked, that
almost all of that celebrated nobleman's witty sayings were
puns. He, however, allowed the merit of good wit to his Lordship's saying of Lord Tyrawley and himself, when both very
old and infirm: 'Tyrawley and I have been dead these two
years; but we don't choose to have it known.

The conversation having turned on modern imitations of ancient ballads, and some one having praised their simplicity, he treated them with that ridicule which he always displayed when this subject was mentioned.

On Thursday, April 8, I sat a good part of the evening with him, but he was very silent. Though he was not disposed to talk, he was unwilling that I should leave him; and when I looked at my watch, and told him it was twelve o'clock, he cried, 'What's that to you and me?' and ordered Frank to tell Mrs. Williams that we were coming to drink tea with her, which we did. It was settled that we should go to church to- gether next day.

On the 9th of April, being Good Friday, I breakfasted with him on tea and cross-buns; *Doctor* Levet, as Frank called him, making the tea. He carried me with him to the church of St. Clement Danes, where he had his seat; and his behaviour was, as I had imaged to myself, solemnly devout. I never shall forget the tremulous earnestness with which he pronounced the awe- ful petition in the Litany: 'In the hour of death, and at the day of judgement, good LORD deliver us.'

We went to church both in the morning and evening. In the interval between the two services we did not dine; but he read in the Greek New Testament, and I turned over several of his books.

I told him that Goldsmith had said to me a few days before, 'As I take my shoes from the shoemaker, and my coat from the taylor, so I take my religion from the priest.' I regretted this loose way of talking. *Johnson.* 'Sir, he knows nothing; he has made up his mind about nothing.'

To my great surprize he asked me to dine with him on Easter-day. I never supposed that he had a dinner at his house; for I had not then heard of any one of his friends having been entertained at his table. He told me, 'I generally have a meat pye on Sunday: it is baked at a publick oven, which is very properly allowed, because one man can attend it; and thus the advantage is obtained of not keeping servants from church to dress dinners.'

April 11, being Easter-Sunday, after having attended Divine Service at St. Paul's, I repaired to Dr. Johnson's. I had gratified my curiosity much in dining with *Jean Jacques Rousseau*, while he lived in the wilds of Neufchatel: I had as great a curiosity to dine with *Dr. Samuel Johnson*, in the dusky recess of a court in Fleet-street. I supposed we should scarcely have knives and forks, and only some strange, uncouth, ill-drest dish: but I found every thing in very good order. We had no other company but Mrs. Williams and a young woman whom I did not know. As a dinner here was considered as a singular phænomenon, and as I was frequently interrogated on the subject, my readers may perhaps be desirous to know our bill of fare. Foote, I remember, in allusion to Francis, the *negro*, was willing to suppose that our repast was *black broth*. But the fact was, that we had a very good soup, a boiled leg of lamb and spinach, a veal pye, and a rice pudding.

Goldsmith, he said, had great merit. *Boswell.* 'But, Sir, he is much indebted to you for his getting so high in the publick estimation.' *Johnson.* 'Why, Sir, he has, perhaps, got *sooner* to it by his intimacy with me.' Goldsmith, though his vanity often excited him to occasional competition, had a very high regard for Johnson, which he at this time expressed in the strongest manner in the Dedication of his comedy, entitled, 'She stoops to conquer.'

I put a question to him upon a fact in common life, which he could not answer, nor have I found any one else who could. What is the reason that women servants, though obliged to be at the expense of purchasing their own clothes, have much lower wages than men servants, to whom a great proportion of that article is furnished, and when in fact our female house servants work much harder than the male?

He told me, that he had twelve or fourteen times attempted to keep a journal of his life, but never could persevere. He advised me to do it. 'The great thing to be recorded, (said he), is the state of your own mind; and you should write down every thing that you remember, for you cannot judge at first what is good or bad; and write immediately while the impression is fresh, for it will not be the same a week afterwards.'

I again solicited him to communicate to me the particulars of his early life. He said, 'You shall have them all for two-pence. I hope you shall know a great deal more of me before you write my Life.' He mentioned to me this day many circumstances, which I wrote down when I went home, and have interwoven in the former part of this narrative.

On Tuesday, April 13, he and Dr. Goldsmith and I dined at General Oglethorpe's. Goldsmith expatiated on the common topick, that the race of our people was degenerated, and that this was owing to luxury. *Johnson.* 'Sir, in the first place, I doubt the fact. I believe there are as many tall men in England now, as ever there were. But, secondly, supposing the stature of our people to be diminished, that is not owing to luxury; for, Sir, consider to how very small a proportion of our people luxury can reach. Our soldiery, surely, are not luxurious, who live on six-pence a day; and the same remark will apply to almost all the other classes. Luxury, so far as it reaches the poor, will do good to the race of people; it will strengthen and multiply them. Sir, no nation was ever hurt by luxury; for, as I said before, it can reach but to a very few. I admit that the great increase of commerce and manufactures hurts the military spirit of a people; because it produces a competition for something else than martial honours,—a competition for riches. It also hurts the bodies of the people; for you will observe, there is no man who works at any particular trade, but you may know him from his appearance to do so. One part or other of his body being more used than the rest, he is in some degree deformed: but, Sir, that is not luxury. A tailor sits cross-legged; but that is not luxury. *Goldsmith.* 'Come, you're just going to the same place by another road.' *Johnson.* 'Nay, Sir, I say that is not *luxury.* Let us take a walk from Charing-cross to White-chapel, through, I suppose, the greatest series of shops in the world; what is there in any of these shops, (if you except gin-shops,) that can do any human being any harm?' *Goldsmith.* 'Well, Sir, I'll accept your challenge. The very next shop to Northumberland-house is a pickle-shop.' *Johnson.* 'Well, Sir: do we not know that a maid can in one afternoon make pickles sufficient to serve a whole family for a year? nay, that five pickle-shops can serve all the kingdom? Besides, Sir, there is no harm done to any body by the making of pickles, or the eating of pickles.'

We drank tea with the ladies; and Goldsmith sung Tony

Lumpkin's song in his comedy, 'She stoops to conquer,' and a very pretty one, to an Irish tune, which he had designed for Miss Hardcastle; but as Mrs. Bulkeley, who played the part, could not sing, it was left out. He afterwards wrote it down for me, by which means it was preserved, and now appears amongst his poems. Dr. Johnson, in his way home, stopped at my lodgings in Piccadilly, and sat with me, drinking tea a second time, till a late hour.

I told him that Mrs. Macaulay said, she wondered how he could reconcile his political principles with his moral; his notions of inequality and subordination with wishing well to the happiness of all mankind, who might live so agreeably, had they all their portions of land, and none to domineer over another. *Johnson.* 'Why, Sir, I reconcile my principles very well, because mankind are happier in a state of inequality and subordination. Were they to be in this pretty state of equality, they would soon degenerate into brutes;—they would become Monboddo's nation;—their tails would grow. Sir, all would be losers, were all to work for all:—they would have no intellectual improvement. All intellectual improvement arises from leisure: all leisure arises from one working for another.'

On Thursday, April 15, I dined with him and Dr. Goldsmith at General Paoli's. We found here Signor Martinelli, of Florence, authour of a History of England in Italian, printed at London.

I spoke of Allan Ramsay's 'Gentle Shepherd,' in the Scottish dialect, as the best pastoral that had ever been written; not only abounding with beautiful rural imagery, and just and pleasing sentiments, but being a real picture of manners; and I offered to teach Dr. Johnson to understand it. 'No, Sir, (said he,) I won't learn it. You shall retain your superiority by my not knowing it.'

An animated debate took place whether Martinelli should continue his History of England to the present day. *Goldsmith.* 'To be sure he should.' *Johnson.* 'No, Sir; he would give great offence. He would have to tell of almost all the living great what they do not wish told.' *Goldsmith.* 'It may, perhaps, be necessary for a native to be more cautious; but a foreigner who comes among us without prejudice, may be considered as holding the place of a Judge, and may speak his mind freely.' *Johnson.* 'Sir, a foreigner, when he sends a work from the press, ought to be on his guard against catching the errour and mistaken enthusiasm of the people among whom he happens to be.' *Goldsmith.* 'Sir, he wants only to sell his history, and to tell truth; one an honest, the other a laudable motive.' *Johnson.* 'Sir, they are both laudable motives. It is laudable in a man to wish to live by his labours; but he should write so as he may *live* by them, not so as he may be knocked on the head. I would advise him to be at Calais before he publishes his history of the present age.' *Goldsmith.* 'There are people who tell a hundred political lies every day, and are not hurt by it. Surely, then, one may tell truth with safety.' *Johnson.* 'Why, Sir, in the first place, he who tells a hundred lies has disarmed the force of his lies. But besides; a man had rather have a hundred lies told of him, than one truth which he does not wish should be told.' *Goldsmith.* 'For my part, I'd tell truth, and shame the devil.' *Johnson.* 'Yes, Sir; but the devil will be angry. I wish to shame the devil as much you do, but I should choose to be out of the reach of his claws.' *Goldsmith.* 'His claws can do you no harm, when you have the shield of truth.'

It having been observed that there was little hospitality in London; *Johnson.* 'Nay, Sir, any man who has a name, or who has the power of pleasing, will be very generally invited in London. The man, Sterne, I have been told, has had engagements for three months.' *Goldsmith.* 'And a very dull fellow.' *Johnson.* 'Why no, Sir.'

An eminent publick character being mentioned;—*Johnson.* I remember being present when he shewed himself to be so corrupted, or at least something so different from what I think right, as to maintain, that a member of parliament should go along with his party right or wrong. Now, Sir, this is so remote from native virtue, from scholastick virtue, that a good man must have undergone a great change before he can reconcile himself to such a doctrine. It is maintaining that you may lie to the publick; for you lie when you call that right which you think wrong, or the reverse. A friend of ours, who is too much an echo of that gentleman, observed, that a man who does not stick uniformly to a party, is only waiting to be bought. Why then, said I, he is only waiting to be what that gentleman is already.'

We talked of the King's coming to see Goldsmith's new play. —'I wish he would,' said Goldsmith; adding, however, with an affected indifference, 'Not that it would do me the least good.' *Johnson.* 'Well then, Sir, let us say it would do *him* good, (laughing). No, Sir, this affectation will not pass;—it is mighty idle. In such a state as ours, who would not wish to please the Chief Magistrate?' *Goldsmith.* 'I *do* wish to please him. I remember a line in Dryden,

"And every poet is the monarch's friend."

It ought to be reversed.'

A person was mentioned, who it was said could take down in short hand the speeches in parliament with perfect exactness. *Johnson.* 'Sir, it is impossible. I remember one Angel, who came to me to write for him a Preface or Dedication to a book upon short hand, and he professed to write as fast as a man could speak. In order to try him, I took down a book, and read while he wrote; and I favoured him, for I read more deliberately than usual. I had proceeded but a very little way, when he begged I would desist, for he could not follow me.'

On Monday, April 19, he called on me with Mrs. Williams, in Mr. Strahan's coach, and carried me out to dine with Mr. Elphinston, at his academy at Kensington. A printer having acquired a fortune sufficient to keep his coach, was a good topick for the credit of literature. Mrs. Williams said, that another printer, Mr. Hamilton, had not waited so long as Mr. Strahan, but had kept his coach several years sooner. *Johnson.* 'He was in the right. Life is short. The sooner that a man begins to enjoy his wealth the better.'

Mr. Elphinston talked of a new book that was much admired, and asked Dr. Johnson if he had read it. *Johnson.* 'I have looked into it.' 'What (said Elphinston,) have you not read it through?' Johnson, offended at being thus pressed, and so obliged to own his cursory mode of reading, answered tartly, 'No, Sir; do *you* read books *through*?'

He this day again defended duelling, and put his argument

upon what I have ever thought the most solid basis; that if publick war be allowed to be consistent with morality, private war
must be equally so. Indeed we may observe what strained arguments are used, to reconcile war with the Christian religion.
But, in my opinion, it is exceedingly clear that duelling, having
better reasons for its barbarous violence, is more justifiable than
war, in which thousands go forth without any cause of personal quarrel, and massacre each other.

On Wednesday, April 21, I dined with him at Mr. Thrale's.
A gentleman attacked Garrick for being vain. *Johnson.* 'No
wonder, Sir, that he is vain, a man who is perpetually flattered
in every mode that can be conceived. So many bellows have
blown the fire, that one wonders he is not by this time become
a cinder.' *Boswell.* 'And such bellows too. Lord Mansfield with
his cheeks like to burst: Lord Chatham like an æolus. I have
read such notes from them to him, as were enough to turn his
head.' *Johnson.* 'True. When he whom every body else flatters, flatters me, I then am truly happy.' *Mrs. Thrale.* 'The
sentiment is in Congreve, I think.' *Johnson.* 'Yes, Madam, in
"The Way of the World:"

> "If there's delight in love, 'tis when I see
> That heart which others bleed for, bleed for me.' '

The modes of living in different countries, and the various
views with which men travel in quest of new scenes, having
been talked of, a learned gentleman who holds a considerable
office in the law, expatiated on the happiness of a savage life;
and mentioned an instance of an officer who had actually
lived for some time in the wilds of America, of whom, when in
that state, he quoted this reflection with an air of admiration,
as if it had been deeply philosophical: 'Here am I, free and
unrestrained, amidst the rude magnificence of Nature, with
this Indian woman by my side, and this gun, with which I can
procure food when I want it: what more can be desired for human happiness?' It did not require much sagacity to foresee
that such a sentiment would not be permitted to pass without
due animadversion. *Johnson.* 'Do not allow yourself, Sir, to be
imposed upon by such gross absurdity. It is sad stuff; it is brut-

ish. If a bull could speak, he might as well exclaim,—Here am
I with this cow and this grass; what being can enjoy greater
felicity?'

We talked of the melancholy end of a gentleman who had
destroyed himself. *Johnson.* 'It was owing to imaginary difficulties in his affairs, which, had he talked with any friend,
would soon have vanished.' *Boswell.* 'Do you think, Sir, that
all who commit suicide are mad?' *Johnson.* 'Sir, they are often
not universally disordered in their intellects, but one passion
presses so upon them, that they yield to it, and commit suicide,
as a passionate man will stab another.' He added, 'I have often
thought, that after a man has taken the resolution to kill himself, it is not courage in him to do any thing, however desperate, because he has nothing to fear.' *Goldsmith.* 'I don't see
that.' *Johnson.* 'Nay but, my dear Sir, why should not you see
what every one else sees?' *Goldsmith.* 'It is for fear of something
that he has resolved to kill himself; and will not that timid disposition restrain him?' *Johnson.* 'It does not signify that the
fear of something made him resolve; it is upon the state of his
mind, after the resolution is taken, that I argue. Suppose a
man, either from fear, or pride, or conscience, or whatever motive, has resolved to kill himself; when once the resolution is
taken, he has nothing to fear. He may then go and take the
King of Prussia by the nose, at the head of his army. He cannot fear the rack, who is resolved to kill himself. When Eustace
Budgel was walking down to the Thames, determined to drown
himself, he might, if he pleased, without any apprehension of
danger, have turned aside, and first set fire to St. James's pal-
ace.'

On Tuesday, April 27, Mr. Beauclerk and I called on him in
the morning. As we walked up Johnson's-court, I said, 'I have
a veneration for this court;' and was glad to find that Beauclerk
had the same reverential enthusiasm. We found him alone. We
talked of Mr. Andrew Stuart's elegant and plausible Letters to
Lord Mansfield: a copy of which had been sent by the authour
to Dr. Johnson. *Johnson.* 'They have not answered the end.
They have not been talked of; I have never heard of them. This
is owing to their not being sold. People seldom read a book
which is given to them. The way to spread a work is to sell it

at a low price. No man will send to buy a thing that costs even sixpence, without an intention to read it.'

He said, 'Goldsmith should not be for ever attempting to shine in conversation: he has not temper for it, he is so much mortified when he fails. Sir, a game of jokes is composed partly of skill, partly of chance. A man may be beat at times by one who has not the tenth part of his wit. Now Goldsmith's putting himself against another, is like a man laying a hundred to one who cannot spare the hundred. It is not worth a man's while. A man should not lay a hundred to one, unless he can easily spare it, though he has a hundred chances for him: he can get but a guinea, and he may lose a hundred. Goldsmith is in this state. When he contends, if he gets the better, it is a very little addition to a man of his literary reputation: if he does not get the better, he is miserably vexed.'

Johnson's own superlative power of wit set him above any risk of such uneasiness. Garrick had remarked to me of him, a few days before, 'Rabelais and all other wits are nothing compared with him. You may be diverted by them; but Johnson gives you a forcible hug, and shakes laughter out of you, whether you will or no.'

Goldsmith, however, was often very fortunate in his witty contests, even when he entered the lists with Johnson himself. Sir Joshua Reynolds was in company with them one day, when Goldsmith said, that he thought he could write a good fable, mentioned the simplicity which that kind of composition requires, and observed, that in most fables the animals introduced seldom talk in character. 'For instance, (said he,) the fable of the little fishes, who saw birds fly over their heads, and envying them, petitioned Jupiter to be changed into birds. The skill (continued he,) consists in making them talk like little fishes.' While he indulged himself in this fanciful reverie, he observed Johnson shaking his sides, and laughing. Upon which he smartly proceeded, 'Why, Dr. Johnson, this is not so easy as you seem to think; for if you were to make little fishes talk, they would talk like *whales*.'

On Thursday, April 29, I dined with him at General Oglethorpe's, where were Sir Joshua Reynolds, Mr. Langton, Dr. Goldsmith, and Mr. Thrale. I was very desirous to get Dr.

Johnson absolutely fixed in his resolution to go with me to the Hebrides this year; and I told him that I had received a letter from Dr. Robertson the historian, upon the subject, with which he was much pleased; and now talked in such a manner of his long-intended tour, that I was satisfied he meant to fulfil his engagement.

The custom of eating dogs at Otaheite being mentioned, Goldsmith observed, that this was also a custom in China; that a dog-butcher is as common there as any other butcher; and that when he walks abroad all the dogs fall on him. *Johnson.* 'That is not owing to his killing dogs, Sir. I remember a butcher at Lichfield, whom a dog that was in the house where I lived, always attacked. It is the smell of carnage which provokes this, let the animals he has killed be what they may.' *Goldsmith.* 'Yes, there is a general abhorrence in animals at the signs of massacre. If you put a tub full of blood into a stable, the horses are like to go mad.' *Johnson.* 'I doubt that.' *Goldsmith.* 'Nay, Sir, it is a fact well authenticated.' *Thrale.* 'You had better prove it before you put it into your book on natural history. You may do it in my stable if you will.' *Johnson.* 'Nay, Sir, I would not have him prove it. If he is content to take his information from others, he may get through his book with little trouble, and without much endangering his reputation. But if he makes experiments for so comprehensive a book as his, there would be no end to them; his erroneous assertions would then fall upon himself; and he might be blamed for not having made experiments as to every particular.'

Dr. Goldsmith's new play, 'She stoops to conquer,' being mentioned; *Johnson.* 'I know of no comedy for many years that has so much exhilarated an audience, that has answered so much the great end of comedy—making an audience merry.'

Goldsmith having said, that Garrick's compliment to the Queen, which he introduced into the play of 'The Chances', which he had altered and revised this year, was mean and gross flattery;—*Johnson.* 'Why, Sir, I would not *write*, I would not give solemnly under my hand, a character beyond what I thought really true; but a speech on the stage, let it flatter ever so extravagantly, is formular. It has always been formular to flatter Kings and Queens; so much so, that even in our church-

service we have "our most religious King," used indiscriminately, whoever is King. Nay, they even flatter themselves;—
"we have been graciously pleased to grant."—No modern flattery, however, is so gross as that of the Augustan age, where
the Emperour was deified. And as to meanness, (rising into
warmth,) how is it mean in a player,—a showman,—a fellow
who exhibits himself for a shilling, to flatter his Queen? The
attempt, indeed, was dangerous; for if it had missed, what became of Garrick, and what became of the Queen? As Sir William Temple says of a great General, it is necessary not only
that his designs should be formed in a masterly manner, but
that they should be attended with success. Sir, it is right, at
a time when the Royal Family is not generally liked, to let it
be seen that the people like at least one of them.' *Sir Joshua
Reynolds.* 'I do not perceive why the profession of a player
should be despised; for the great and ultimate end of all the
employments of mankind is to produce amusement. Garrick
produces more amusement than any body.' *Boswell.* 'You say,
Dr. Johnson, that Garrick exhibits himself for a shilling. In
this respect he is only on a footing with a lawyer who exhibits
himself for his fee, and even will maintain any nonsense or
absurdity, if the case requires it. Garrick refuses a play or a part
which he does not like; a lawyer never refuses.' *Johnson.* 'Why,
Sir, what does this prove? only that a lawyer is worse. Boswell
is now like Jack in "The Tale of a Tub," who, when he is puzzled by an argument, hangs himself. He thinks I shall cut him
down, but I'll let him hang,' (laughing vociferously.) *Sir
Joshua Reynolds.* 'Mr. Boswell thinks that the profession of a
lawyer being unquestionably honourable, if he can show the
profession of a player to be more honourable, he proves his
argument.'

On Friday, April 30, I dined with him at Mr. Beauclerk's,
where were Lord Charlemont, Sir Joshua Reynolds, and some
more members of the *Literary Club,* whom he had obligingly
invited to meet me, as I was this evening to be balloted for as
candidate for admission into that distinguished society. Johnson had done me the honour to propose me, and Beauclerk was
very zealous for me.

Goldsmith being mentioned; *Johnson.* 'It is amazing how

little Goldsmith knows. He seldom comes where he is not more ignorant than any one else.' *Sir Joshua Reynolds*. 'Yet there is no man whose company is more liked.' *Johnson*. 'To be sure, Sir. When people find a man of the most distinguished abilities as a writer, their inferiour while he is with them, it must be highly gratifying to them. What Goldsmith comically says of himself is very true,—he always gets the better when he argues alone; meaning, that he is master of a subject in his study, and can write well upon it; but when he comes into company, grows confused, and unable to talk. Take him as a poet, his "Traveller" is a very fine performance; ay, and so is his "Deserted Village," were it not sometimes too much the echo of his "Traveller." Whether, indeed, we take him as a poet,—as a comick writer,—or as an historian, he stands in the first class.'

Johnson praised John Bunyan highly. 'His "Pilgrim's Progress" has great merit, both for invention, imagination, and the conduct of the story; and it has had the best evidence of its merit, the general and continued approbation of mankind. Few books, I believe, have had a more extensive sale. It is remarkable, that it begins very much like the poem of Dante; yet there was no translation of Dante when Bunyan wrote. There is reason to think that he had read Spenser.'

The gentlemen went away to their club, and I was left at Beauclerk's till the fate of my election should be announced to me. I sat in a state of anxiety which even the charming conversation of Lady Di Beauclerk could not entirely dissipate. In a short time I received the agreeable intelligence that I was chosen. I hastened to the place of meeting, and was introduced to such a society as can seldom be found.[1] Mr. Edmund Burke, whom I then saw for the first time, and whose splendid talents had long made me ardently wish for his acquaintance; Dr. Nugent, Mr. Garrick, Dr. Goldsmith, Mr. (afterwards Sir William) Jones, and the company with whom I had dined. Upon my entrance, Johnson placed himself behind a chair,

[1] For once Boswell is almost guilty of an understatement. Burke, Sheridan, Reynolds, Garrick, Johnson, Goldsmith, Boswell himself and (the following year) Gibbon—neither before nor since has any other club boasted of such a galaxy.

on which he leaned as on a desk or pulpit, and with humorous
formality gave me a *Charge,* pointing out the conduct expected
from me as a good member of this club. Goldsmith produced
some very absurd verses which had been publickly recited to
an audience for money.

Much pleasant conversation passed, which Johnson relished
with great good humour. But his conversation alone, or what
led to it, or was interwoven with it, is the business of this work.

On Saturday, May 1, we dined by ourselves at our old ren-
dezvous, the Mitre tavern. He was placid, but not much disposed to talk. He observed that 'The Irish mix better with the
English than the Scotch do; their language is nearer to English; as a proof of which, they succeed very well as players,
which Scotchmen do not. Then, Sir, they have not that extreme nationality which we find in the Scotch. I will do you,
Boswell, the justice to say, that you are the most *unscottified*
of your countrymen. You are almost the only instance of a
Scotchman that I have known, who did not at every other sentence bring in some other Scotchman.'

On Friday, May 7, I breakfasted with him at Mr. Thrale's
in the Borough. While we were alone, I endeavoured as well
as I could to apologise for a lady who had been divorced from
her husband by act of Parliament. I said, that he had used her
very ill, had behaved brutally to her, and that she could not
continue to live with him without having her delicacy contami-
nated; that all affection for him was thus destroyed; that the
essence of conjugal union being gone, there remained only a
cold form, a mere civil obligation; that she was in the prime
of life, with qualities to produce happiness; that these ought
not to be lost; and, that the gentleman on whose account she
was divorced had gained her heart while thus unhappily situated. Seduced, perhaps, by the charms of the lady in question,
I thus attempted to palliate what I was sensible could not be
justified; for, when I had finished my harangue, my venerable
friend gave me a proper check: 'My dear Sir, never accustom
your mind to mingle virtue and vice. The woman's a whore,
and there's an end on't.'

He described the father of one of his friends thus· 'Sir, he was so exuberant a talker at publick meetings, that the gentlemen of his county were afraid of him. No business could be done for his declamation.'

He did not give me full credit when I mentioned that I had carried on a short conversation by signs with some Esquimaux, who were then in London, particularly with one of them who was a priest. He thought I could not make them understand me. No man was more incredulous as to particular facts, which were at all extraordinary; and therefore no man was more scrupulously inquisitive, in order to discover the truth.

I dined with him this day at the house of my friends, Messieurs Edward and Charles Dilly, booksellers in the Poultry: there were present, their elder brother Mr. Dilly of Bedfordshire, Dr. Goldsmith, Mr. Langton, Mr. Claxton, Reverend Dr. Mayo a dissenting minister, the Reverend Mr. Toplady, and my friend the Reverend Mr. Temple.

Hawkesworth's compilation of the voyages to the South Sea being mentioned;—*Johnson.* 'Sir, if you talk of it as a subject of commerce, it will be gainful; if as a book that is to increase human knowledge, I believe there will not be much of that. Hawkesworth can tell only what the voyagers have told him; and they have found very little, only one new animal, I think.' *Boswell.* 'But many insects, Sir.' *Johnson.* 'Why, Sir, as to insects, Ray reckons of British insects twenty thousand species. They might have staid at home and discovered enough in that way.'

Boswell. 'I am well assured that the people of Otaheite who have the bread tree, the fruit of which serves them for bread, laughed heartily when they were informed of the tedious process necessary with us to have bread;—plowing, sowing, harrowing, reaping, threshing, grinding, baking.' *Johnson.* 'Why, Sir, all ignorant savages will laugh when they are told of the advantages of civilized life. Were you to tell men who live without houses, how we pile brick upon brick, and rafter upon rafter, and that after a house is raised to a certain height, a man tumbles off a scaffold, and breaks his neck, he would laugh heartily at our folly in building; but it does not follow that men are better without houses. No, Sir, (holding up a slice of a good loaf,) this is better than the bread tree.'

I introduced the subject of toleration. *Johnson.* 'Every society has a right to preserve publick peace and order, and therefore has a good right to prohibit the propagation of opinions
which have a dangerous tendency. To say the *magistrate* has
this right, is using an inadequate word: it is the *society* for
which the magistrate is agent. He may be morally or theologi-
cally wrong in restraining the propagation of opinions which
he thinks dangerous, but he is politically right.' *Mayo.* 'I am
of opinion, Sir, that every man is entitled to liberty of conscience in religion; and that the magistrate cannot restrain that
right.' *Johnson.* 'Sir, I agree with you. Every man has a right
to liberty of conscience, and with that the magistrate cannot
interfere. People confound liberty of thinking with liberty of
talking; nay, with liberty of preaching. Every man has a physical right to think as he pleases; for it cannot be discovered how
he thinks. He has not a moral right; for he ought to inform
himself, and think justly. But, Sir, no member of a society has
a right to *teach* any doctrine contrary to what that society holds
to be true. The magistrate, I say, may be wrong in what he
thinks: but, while he thinks himself right, he may, and ought
to enforce what he thinks.' *Mayo.* 'Then, Sir, we are to remain
always in errour, and truth never can prevail; and the magistrate was right in persecuting the first Christians.' *Johnson.*
'Sir, the only method by which religious truth can be established is by martyrdom. The magistrate has a right to enforce
what he thinks; and he who is conscious of the truth has a
right to suffer. I am afraid there is no other way of ascertaining
the truth, but by persecution on the one hand and enduring
it on the other.' *Goldsmith.* 'But how is a man to act, Sir?
Though firmly convinced of the truth of his doctrine, may he
not think it wrong to expose himself to persecution? Has he
a right to do so? Is it not, as it were, committing voluntary
suicide?' *Johnson.* 'Sir, as to voluntary suicide, as you call it,
there are twenty thousand men in an army who will go without scruple to be shot at, and mount a breach for five-pence a
day.' *Goldsmith.* 'But have they a moral right to do this?' *Johnson.* 'Nay, Sir, if you will not take the universal opinion of
mankind, I have nothing to say. If mankind cannot defend
their own way of thinking, I cannot defend it. Sir, if a man is

in doubt whether it would be better for him to expose himself to martyrdom or not, he should not do it. He must be convinced that he has a delegation from heaven.' *Goldsmith*. 'I would consider whether there is the greater chance of good or evil upon the whole. If I see a man who has fallen into a well, I would wish to help him out; but if there is a greater probability that he shall pull me in, than that I shall pull him out, I would not attempt it. So were I to go to Turkey, I might wish to convert the Grand Signor to the Christian faith; but when I considered that I should probably be put to death without effectuating my purpose in any degree, I should keep myself quiet.' *Johnson*. 'Sir, you must consider that we have perfect and imperfect obligations. Perfect obligations, which are generally not to do something, are clear and positive; as, "thou shalt not kill." But charity, for instance, is not definable by limits. It is a duty to give to the poor; but no man can say how much another should give to the poor, or when a man has given too little to save his soul. In the same manner, it is a duty to instruct the ignorant, and of consequence to convert infidels to Christianity; but no man in the common course of things is obliged to carry this to such a degree as to incur the danger of martyrdom, as no man is obliged to strip himself to the shirt in order to give charity. I have said, that a man must be persuaded that he has a particular delegation from heaven.' *Goldsmith*. 'How is this to be known? Our first reformers, who were burnt for not believing bread and wine to be CHRIST'—*Johnson*. (interrupting him,) 'Sir, they were not burnt for not believing bread and wine to be CHRIST, but for insulting those who did believe it. And, Sir, when the first reformers began, they did not intend to be martyred: as many of them ran away as could.' *Mayo*. 'But, Sir, is it not very hard that I should not be allowed to teach my children what I really believe to be the truth?' *Johnson*, 'Why, Sir, you might contrive to teach your children *extrà scandalum*; but, Sir, the magistrate, if he knows it, has a right to restrain you. Suppose you teach your children to be thieves?' *Mayo*. 'This is making a joke of the subject.' *Johnson*. 'Nay, Sir, take it thus:—that you teach them the community of goods; for which there are as many plausible arguments as for most erroneous doctrines. You teach them

that all things at first were in common, and that no man had
a right to any thing but as he laid his hands upon it; and that
this still is, or ought to be, the rule amongst mankind. Here,
Sir, you sap a great principle in society,—property. And don't
you think the magistrate would have a right to prevent you?
Or, suppose you should teach your children the notions of the
Adamites, and they should run naked into the streets, would
not the magistrate have a right to flog 'em into their doublets?'
Mayo. 'I think the magistrate has no right to interfere till there
is some overt act.' *Boswell.* 'So, Sir, though he sees an enemy
to the state charging a blunderbuss, he is not to interfere till
it is fired off?' *Mayo.* 'He must be sure of its direction against
the state.' *Johnson.* 'The magistrate is to judge of that.—He
has no right to restrain your thinking, because the evil centers
in yourself. If a man were sitting at this table, and chopping
off his fingers, the magistrate, as guardian of the community,
has no authority to restrain him, however he might do it from
kindness as a parent.—Though, indeed, upon more consideration, I think he may; as it is probable, that he who is chopping
off his own fingers, may soon proceed to chop off those of other
people. If I think it right to steal Mr. Dilly's plate, I am a bad
man; but he can say nothing to me. If I make an open declaration that I think so, he will keep me out of his house. If I put
forth my hand, I shall be sent to Newgate. This is the gradation of thinking, preaching, and acting: if a man thinks erroneously, he may keep his thoughts to himself, and nobody will
trouble him; if he preaches erroneous doctrine, society may
expel him; if he acts in consequence of it, the law takes place,
and he is hanged.' *Mayo.* 'But, Sir, ought not Christians to
have liberty of conscience?' *Johnson.* 'I have already told you
so, Sir. You are coming back to where you were.' *Boswell.* 'Dr.
Mayo is always taking a return post-chaise, and going the stage
over again. He has it at half price.' *Johnson.* 'Dr. Mayo, like
other champions for unlimited toleration, has got a set of
words. Sir, it is no matter, politically, whether the magistrate
be right or wrong. Suppose a club were to be formed, to drink
confusion to King George the Third, and a happy restoration
to Charles the Third; this would be very bad with respect to
the State; but every member of that club must either conform

to its rules, or be turned out of it. Old Baxter, I remember, maintains, that the magistrate should "tolerate all things that are tolerable." This is no good definition of toleration upon any principle; but it shews that he thought some things were not tolerable.' *Toplady*. 'Sir, you have untwisted this difficult subject with great dexterity.'

During this argument, Goldsmith sat in restless agitation, from a wish to get in and *shine*. Finding himself excluded, he had taken his hat to go away, but remained for some time with it in his hand, like a gamester, who at the close of a long night, lingers for a little while, to see if he can have a favourable opening to finish with success. Once when he was beginning to speak, he found himself overpowered by the loud voice of Johnson, who was at the opposite end of the table, and did not perceive Goldsmith's attempt. Thus disappointed of his wish to obtain the attention of the company, Goldsmith in a passion threw down his hat, looking angrily at Johnson, and exclaiming in a bitter tone, '*Take it.*' When Toplady was going to speak, Johnson uttered some sound, which led Goldsmith to think that he was beginning again, and taking the words from Toplady. Upon which, he seized this opportunity of venting his own envy and spleen, under the pretext of supporting another person: 'Sir, (said he to Johnson,) the gentleman has heard you patiently for an hour; pray allow us now to hear him.' *Johnson.* (sternly,) 'Sir, I was not interrupting the gentleman. I was only giving him a signal of my attention. Sir, you are impertinent.' Goldsmith made no reply, but continued in the company for some time.

A gentleman present ventured to ask Dr. Johnson if there was not a material difference as to toleration of opinions which lead to action, and opinions merely speculative; for instance, would it be wrong in the magistrate to tolerate those who preach against the doctrine of the TRINITY? Johnson was highly offended, and said, 'I wonder, Sir, how a gentleman of your piety can introduce this subject in a mixed company.' He told me afterwards, that the impropriety was, that perhaps some of the company might have talked on the subject in such terms as would have shocked him; or he might have been forced to appear in their eyes a narrow-minded man. The gen-

tleman, with submissive deference, said, he had only hinted
at the question from a desire to hear Dr. Johnson's opinion
upon it. *Johnson.* 'Why then, Sir, I think that permitting men
to preach any opinion contrary to the doctrine of the established church, tends, in a certain degree, to lessen the authority of the church, and, consequently, to lessen the influence of
religion.' 'It may be considered, (said the gentleman,) whether
it would not be politick to tolerate in such a case.' *Johnson.*
'Sir, we have been talking of *right:* this is another question.
I think it is *not* politick to tolerate in such a case.'

Boswell. 'Pray, Mr. Dilly, how does Dr. Leland's "History
of Ireland" sell?' *Johnson.* (bursting forth with a generous indignation,) 'The Irish are in a most unnatural state; for we
see there the minority prevailing over the majority. There is
no instance, even in the ten persecutions, of such severity as
that which the Protestants of Ireland have exercised against
the Catholicks. Did we tell them we have conquered them,
it would be above board: to punish them by confiscation and
other penalties, as rebels, was monstrous injustice. King William was not their lawful sovereign: he had not been acknowledged by the Parliament of Ireland, when they appeared in
arms against him.'

I here suggested something favourable of the Roman Catholicks. *Toplady.* 'Does not their invocation of saints suppose
omnipresence in the saints?' *Johnson.* 'No, Sir; it supposes only
pluri-presence; and when spirits are divested of matter, it seems
probable that they should see with more extent than when in
an embodied state. There is, therefore, no approach to an
invasion of any of the divine attributes, in the invocation of
saints. But I think it is will-worship, and presumption. I see
no command for it, and therefore think it is safer not to practise it.'

He and Mr. Langton and I went together to *the Club,*
where we found Mr. Burke, Mr. Garrick, and some other
members, and amongst them our friend Goldsmith, who sat
silently brooding over Johnson's reprimand to him after dinner. Johnson perceived this, and said aside to some of us, 'I'll
make Goldsmith forgive me;' and then called to him in a loud
voice, 'Dr. Goldsmith,—something passed to-day where you

and I dined; I ask your pardon.' Goldsmith answered placidly, 'It must be much from you, Sir, that I take ill.' And so at once the difference was over, and they were on as easy terms as ever, and Goldsmith rattled away as usual.

In our way to the club to-night, when I regretted that Goldsmith would, upon every occasion, endeavour to shine, by which he often exposed himself, Mr. Langton observed, that he was not like Addison, who was content with the fame of his writings, and did not aim also at excellency in conversation, for which he found himself unfit; and that he said to a lady, who complained of his having talked little in company, 'Madam, I have but nine-pence in ready money, but I can draw for a thousand pounds.' I observed, that Goldsmith had a great deal of gold in his cabinet, but, not content with that, was always taking out his purse. *Johnson.* 'Yes, Sir, and that so often an empty purse!'

Goldsmith's incessant desire of being conspicuous in company, was the occasion of his sometimes appearing to such disadvantage as one should hardly have supposed possible in a man of his genius. When his literary reputation had risen deservedly high, and his society was much courted, he became very jealous of the extraordinary attention which was every where paid to Johnson. One evening, in a circle of wits, he found fault with me for talking of Johnson as entitled to the honour of unquestionable superiority. 'Sir, (said he,) you are for making a monarchy of what should be a republick.'

He was still more mortified, when talking in a company with fluent vivacity, and, as he flattered himself, to the admiration of all who were present: a German who sat next him, and perceived Johnson rolling himself, as if about to speak, suddenly stopped him, saying, 'Stay, stay,—Toctor Shonson is going to say something.' This was, no doubt, very provoking, especially to one so irritable as Goldsmith, who frequently mentioned it with strong expressions of indignation.

It may also be observed, that Goldsmith was sometimes content to be treated with an easy familiarity, but, upon occasions, would be consequential and important. An instance of this occurred in a small particular. Johnson had a way of contracting the names of his friends; as, Beauclerk, Beau; Boswell,

Bozzy; Langton, Lanky; Murphy, Mur; Sheridan, Sherry. I
remember one day, when Tom Davies was telling that Dr.
Johnson said, 'We are all in labour for a name to *Goldy's* play,'
Goldsmith seemed displeased that such a liberty should be
taken with his name, and said, 'I have often desired him not
to call me *Goldy.*' Tom was remarkably attentive to the most
minute circumstance about Johnson. I recollect his telling me
once, on my arrival in London, 'Sir, our great friend has made
an improvement on his appellation of old Mr. Sheridan. He
calls him now *Sherry derry.*'

On Monday, May 9, as I was to set out on my return to
Scotland next morning, I was desirous to see as much of Dr.
Johnson as I could. But I first called on Goldsmith to take
leave of him. The jealousy and envy which, though possessed
of many most amiable qualities, he frankly avowed, broke out
violently at this interview. Upon another occasion, when Goldsmith confessed himself to be of an envious disposition, I contended with Johnson that we ought not to be angry with him,
he was so candid in owning it. 'Nay, Sir, (said Johnson,) we
must be angry that a man has such a superabundance of an
odious quality, that he cannot keep it within his own breast,
but it boils over.' In my opinion, however, Goldsmith had not
more of it than other people have, but only talked of it freely.

He now seemed very angry that Johnson was going to be
a traveller; said, 'he would be a dead weight for me to carry,
and that I should never be able to lug him along through the
Highlands and Hebrides.' Nor would he patiently allow me
to enlarge upon Johnson's wonderful abilities; but exclaimed,
'Is he like Burke, who winds into a subject like a serpent?'
'But, (said I,) Johnson is the Hercules who strangled serpents
in his cradle.'

I dined with Dr. Johnson at General Paoli's. He was obliged,
by indisposition, to leave the company early; he appointed me,
however, to meet him in the evening at Mr. (now Sir Robert) Chambers's in the Temple, where he accordingly came,
though he continued to be very ill. Chambers, as is common
on such occasions, prescribed various remedies to him. *Johnson.* (fretted by pain,) 'Pr'ythee don't teaze me. Stay till I am
well, and then you shall tell me how to cure myself.' He grew

better, and talked with a noble enthusiasm of keeping up the representation of respectable families. His zeal on this subject was a circumstance in his character exceedingly remarkable, when it is considered that he himself had no pretensions to blood. I heard him once say, 'I have great merit in being zealous for subordination and the honours of birth; for I can hardly tell who was my grandfather.' He maintained the dignity and propriety of male succession, in opposition to the opinion of one of our friends, who had that day employed Mr. Chambers to draw his will, devising his estate to his three sisters, in preference to a remote heir male. Johnson called them 'three *dowdies,*' and said, with as high a spirit as the boldest Baron in the most perfect days of the feudal system, 'An ancient estate should always go to males. It is mighty foolish to let a stranger have it because he marries your daughter, and takes your name. As for an estate newly acquired by trade, you may give it, if you will, to the dog *Towser,* and let him keep his *own* name.'

I have known him at times exceedingly diverted at what seemed to others a very small sport. He now laughed immoderately, without any reason that we could perceive, at our friend's making his will; called him the *testator,* and added, 'I dare say, he thinks he has done a mighty thing. He won't stay till he gets home to his seat in the country, to produce this wonderful deed: he'll call up the landlord of the first inn on the road; and, after a suitable preface upon mortality and the uncertainty of life, will tell him that he should not delay making his will; and here, Sir, will he say, is my will, which I have just made, with the assistance of one of the ablest lawyers in the kingdom; and he will read it to him (laughing all the time). He believes he has made this will; but he did not make it: you, Chambers, made it for him. I trust you have had more conscience than to make him say, "being of sound understanding;" ha, ha, ha! I hope he has left me a legacy. I'd have his will turned into verse, like a ballad.'

In this playful manner did he run on, exulting in his own pleasantry, which certainly was not such as might be expected from the authour of 'The Rambler,' but which is here preserved, that my readers may be acquainted even with the slightest occasional characticks of so eminent a man.

Mr. Chambers did not by any means relish this jocularity and seemed impatient till he got rid of us. Johnson could not stop his merriment, but continued it all the way till we got without the Temple-gate. He then burst into such a fit of laughter, that he appeared to be almost in a convulsion; and, in order to support himself, laid hold of one of the posts at the side of the foot pavement, and sent forth peals so loud, that in the silence of the night his voice seemed to resound from Temple-bar to Fleet-ditch.

This most ludicrous exhibition of the aweful, melancholy, and venerable Johnson, happened well to counteract the feelings of sadness which I used to experience when parting with him for a considerable time. I accompanied him to his door, where he gave me his blessing.

In a letter from Edinburgh, dated the 29th of May, I pressed him to persevere in his resolution to make this year the projected visit to the Hebrides, of which he and I had talked for many years, and which I was confident would afford us much entertainment.

'To James Boswell, Esq.
'Dear Sir,

'When your letter came to me, I was so darkened by an inflammation in my eye, that I could not for some time read it. I can now write without trouble, and can read large prints. My eye is gradually growing stronger; and I hope will be able to take some delight in the survey of a Caledonian loch.

'Chambers is going a Judge, with six thousand a year, to Bengal. He and I shall come down together as far as Newcastle, and thence I shall easily get to Edinburgh. Let me know the exact time when your Courts intermit. I must conform a little to Chambers's occasions, and he must conform a little to mine. The time which you shall fix, must be the common point to which we will come as near as we can. Except this eye, I am very well.

'I hope your dear lady and her dear baby are both well. I shall see them too when I come; and I have that opinion of your choice, as to suspect that when I have seen Mrs. Boswell, I shall be less willing to go away. I am, dear Sir,

'Your affectionate humble servant,
'Sam. Johnson.'

'Johnson's-court, Fleet-street,
    July 5, 1773.'

His stay in Scotland was from the 18th of August, on which day he arrived, till the 22d of November, when he set out on his return to London; and I believe ninety-four days were never passed by any man in a more vigorous exertion.

He came by the way of Berwick upon Tweed to Edinburgh, where he remained a few days, and then went by St. Andrew's, Aberdeen, Inverness, and Fort Augustus, to the Hebrides, to visit which was the principal object he had in view. He visited the isles of Sky, Rasay, Col, Mull, Inchkenneth, and Icolmkill. He travelled through Argyleshire by Inverary, and from thence by Lochlomond and Dunbarton to Glasgow, then by Loudon to Auchinleck in Ayrshire, the seat of my family, and then by Hamilton, back to Edinburgh, where he again spent some time. He thus saw the four Universities of Scotland, its three principal cities, and as much of the Highland and insular life as was sufficient for his philosophical contemplation. I had the pleasure of accompanying him during the whole of this journey. He was respectfully entertained by the great, the learned, and the elegant, wherever he went; nor was he less delighted with the hospitality which he experienced in humbler life.

His various adventures, and the force and vivacity of his mind, as exercised during this peregrination, upon innumerable topicks, have been faithfully, and to the best of my abilities, displayed in my 'Journal of a Tour to the Hebrides,' to which, as the publick has been pleased to honour it by a very extensive circulation, I beg leave to refer, as to a separate and remarkable portion of his life, which may be there seen in detail, and which exhibits as striking a view of his powers in conversation, as his works do of his excellence in writing.

During his stay at Edinburgh, after his return from the Hebrides, he was at great pains to obtain information concerning Scotland; and it will appear from his subsequent letters, that he was not less solicitous for intelligence on this subject after his return to London.

'To James Boswell, Esq.

'Dear Sir,

'I came home last night, without any incommodity, danger, or weariness, and am ready to begin a new journey. I shall go to Oxford on Monday. I know Mrs. Boswell wished me well to go; her wishes have not been disappointed. Mrs. Williams has received Sir A's letter.

'Make my compliments to all those to whom my compliments may be welcome.

'Let the box be sent as soon as it can, and let me know when to expect it.

'Enquire, if you can, the order of the Clans: Macdonald is first, Maclean second; further I cannot go. Quicken Dr. Webster.[1]

'I am, Sir,

'Yours affectionately,

'SAM. JOHNSON.'

'Nov. 27, 1773.'

His humane forgiving disposition was put to a pretty strong test on his return to London, by a liberty which Mr. Thomas Davies had taken with him in his absence, which was, to publish two volumes, entitled, 'Miscellaneous and fugitive Pieces,' which he advertised in the news-papers, 'By the Authour of the Rambler.' In this collection, several of Dr. Johnson's acknowledged writings, several of his anonymous performances, and some which he had written for others, were inserted; but there were also some in which he had no concern whatever. He was at first very angry, as he had good reason to be. But, upon consideration of his poor friend's narrow circumstances, and that he had only a little profit in view, and meant no harm, he soon relented, and continued his kindness to him as formerly.

1774: ÆTAT. 65.]—He was now seriously engaged in writing an account of our travels in the Hebrides, in consequence of which I had the pleasure of a more frequent correspondence with him.

'To JAMES BOSWELL, ESQ.

'DEAR SIR,

'MY OPERATIONS have been hindered by a cough; at least I flatter myself, that if the cough had not come, I should have been further advanced. But I have had no intelligence from Dr. W——, [Webster,] nor from the Excise-office, nor from you. No account of the little borough. Nothing of the Erse language. I have yet heard nothing of my box.

[1] Dr. Alexander Webster, a minister at Edinburgh, who had promised to send Johnson certain information concerning the Western Islands.

'You must make haste and gather me all you can, and do it quickly, or I will and shall do without it.

'Make my compliments to Mrs. Boswell, and tell her that I do not love her the less for wishing me away. I gave her trouble enough, and shall be glad, in recompence, to give her any pleasure.

'I would send some porter into the Hebrides, if I knew which way it could be got to my kind friends there. Enquire, and let me know.

'Make my compliments to all the Doctors of Edinburgh, and to all my friends, from one end of Scotland to the other.

'Write to me, and send me what intelligence you can: and if any thing is too bulky for the post, let me have it by the carrier. I do not like trusting winds and waves.

'I am, dear Sir,

'Your most, &c.

'Sam. Johnson.'

'Jan. 29, 1774.'

To the Same.

'Dear Sir,

'In a day or two after I had written the last discontented letter, I received my box, which was very welcome. But still I must entreat you to hasten Dr. Webster, and continue to pick up what you can that may be useful.

'Mr. Oglethorpe was with me this morning. You know his errand. He was not unwelcome.

'Tell Mrs. Boswell that my good intentions towards her still continue. I should be glad to do any thing that would either benefit or please her.

'Chambers is not yet gone, but so hurried, or so negligent, or so proud, that I rarely see him. I have, indeed, for some weeks past, been very ill of a cold and cough, and have been at Mrs. Thrale's, that I might be taken care of. I am much better but I am yet tender, and easily disordered. How happy it was that neither of us were ill in the Hebrides.

'I will write to you as any thing occurs, and do you send me something about my Scottish friends. I have very great kindness for them. Let me know likewise how fees come in, and when we are to see you.

'I am, Sir,

'Yours affectionately,

'Sam. Johnson.'

'London, Feb. 7, 1774.'

On the 5th of March I wrote to him, requesting his counsel whether I should this spring come to London. I stated to him on the one hand some pecuniary embarrassments, which, together with my wife's situation at that time, made me hesitate; and, on the other, the pleasure and improvement which my annual visit to the metropolis always afforded me; and particularly mentioned a peculiar satisfaction which I experienced in celebrating the festival of Easter in St. Paul's cathedral; that to my fancy it appeared like going up to Jerusalem at the feast of the Passover; and that the strong devotion which I felt on that occasion diffused its influence on my mind through the rest of the year.

'To James Boswell, Esq.

[*Not dated, but written about
the 15th of March.*]

'Dear Sir,

'I am ashamed to think that since I received your letter I have passed so many days without answering it.

'I think there is no great difficulty in resolving your doubts. The reasons for which you are inclined to visit London, are, I think, not of sufficient strength to answer the objections. That you should delight to come once a year to the fountain of intelligence and pleasure, is very natural; but both information and pleasure must be regulated by propriety. Pleasure, which cannot be obtained but by unseasonable or unsuitable expence, must always end in pain; and pleasure, which must be enjoyed at the expence of another's pain, can never be such as a worthy mind can fully delight in.

'I need not tell you what regard you owe to Mrs. Boswell's entreaties; or how much you ought to study the happiness of her who studies yours with so much diligence, and of whose kindness you enjoy such good effects. Life cannot subsist in society but by reciprocal concessions. She permitted you to ramble last year, you must permit her now to keep you at home.

'Your last reason is so serious, that I am unwilling to oppose it. Yet you must remember, that your image of worshipping once a year in a certain place, in imitation of the Jews, is but a comparison; if the annual resort to Jerusalem was a duty to the Jews, it was a duty because it was commanded; and you have no such command, therefore no such duty. It may be dangerous to receive too readily, and indulge too fondly, opinions, from which, perhaps, no pious mind is wholly disengaged, of local sanctity and local devotion. You know what strange effects they have produced over a great part of the Christian world. I am now writing, and you, when you read this, are reading under the Eye of Omnipresence.

'Thus I have answered your letter, and have not answered it negligently. I love you too well to be careless when you are serious.

'I think I shall be very diligent next week about our travels, which I have too long neglected.

'I am, dear Sir,

'Your most, &c.

'SAM. JOHNSON.'

'Compliments to Madam and Miss.'

'To JAMES BOSWELL, ESQ.

'Streatham, June 21, 1774.

'DEAR SIR,

'YESTERDAY I put the first sheets of the "Journey to the Hebrides" to the press. I have endeavoured to do you some justice in the first paragraph. It will be one volume in octavo, not thick.

'It will be proper to make some presents in Scotland. You shall tell me to whom I shall give; and I have stipulated twenty-five for you to give in your own name. Some will take the present better from me, others better from you. In this, you who are to live in the place ought to direct. Consider it. Whatever you can get for my purpose, send me; and make my compliments to your lady and both the young ones.

'I am, Sir, your, &c.

'SAM. JOHNSON.'

'To JAMES BOSWELL, ESQ.

'DEAR SIR,

'I WISH you could have looked over my book before the printer, but it could not easily be. I suspect some mistakes; but as I deal, perhaps, more in notions than in facts, the matter is not great, and the second edition will be mended, if any such there be. The press will go on slowly for a time, because I am going into Wales to-morrow.

'Of poor dear Dr. Goldsmith there is little to be told, more than the papers have made publick. He died of a fever, made, I am afraid, more violent by uneasiness of mind. His debts began to be heavy, and all his resources were exhausted. Sir Joshua is of opinion that he owed not less than two thousand pounds. Was ever poet so trusted before?

'Of your second daughter you certainly gave the account your-self, though you have forgotten it. While Mrs. Boswell is well, never doubt of a boy. Mrs. Thrale brought, I think, five girls running, but while I was with you she had a boy.

'I am obliged to you for all your pamphlets, and of the last I hope to make some use. I made some of the former.

'I am, dear Sir,

'Your most affectionate servant,

SAM. JOHNSON.'

'July 4, 1774.'

'My compliments to all the three ladies.'

1775: ÆTAT. 66.]—The first effort of his pen in 1775, was, 'Proposals for publishing the Works of Mrs. Charlotte Len-nox,' in three volumes quarto. In his diary, January 2, I find this entry: 'Wrote Charlotte's Proposals.' But, indeed, the in-ternal evidence would have been quite sufficient.

'To JAMES BOSWELL, ESQ.

'DEAR SIR,

'I LONG to hear how you like the book; it is, I think, much liked here. But Macpherson[1] is very furious; can you give me any more intelligence about him, or his Fingal? Do what you can, and do it quickly. Is Lord Hailes on our side?

'Pray let me know what I owed you when I left you, that I may send it to you.

'I am going to write about the Americans. If you have picked up any hints among your lawyers, who are great masters of the law of nations, or if your own mind suggests any thing, let me know. But mum, it is a secret.

'Poor Beauclerk is so ill, that his life is thought to be in danger. Lady Di nurses him with very great assiduity.

'Reynolds has taken too much to strong liquor, and seems to delight in his new character.

[1] James Macpherson (1736-1796), who professed to have discovered an ancient Gaelic epic in the Highlands of Scotland and the Western Islands. While on his tour with Boswell, Johnson had made particular inquiries regarding the existence of such a poem or even of manuscripts in the Gaelic of Scotland. He found nothing and in his account of the tour had branded Macpherson as an impostor. Subsequent scholarship has tended to support Johnson, though it is believed that Macpherson may have had a few genuine scraps, orally transmitted, as the basis for his epic.

'This is all the news that I have; but as you love verses, I will send you a few which I made upon Inchkenneth; but remember the condition, that you shall not show them, except to Lord Hailes, whom I love better than any man whom I know so little. If he asks you to transcribe them for him, you may do it, but I think he must promise not to let them be copied again, nor to show them as mine.

'Make my compliments to dear Mrs. Boswell, and to Miss Veronica.

'I am, dear Sir,
'Yours most faithfully,
'SAM. JOHNSON.'

'Jan. 21, 1775.'

'MR. BOSWELL TO DR. JOHNSON.

'Edinburgh, Jan. 27, 1775.

'I am ashamed to say that I have read little and thought little on the subject of America. I will be much obliged to you, if you will direct me where I shall find the best information of what is to be said on both sides. It is a subject vast in its present extent and future consequences. The imperfect hints which now float in my mind, tend rather to the formation of an opinion that our government has been precipitant and severe in the resolutions taken against the Bostonians. Well do you know that I have no kindness for that race. But nations, or bodies of men, should, as well as individuals, have a fair trial, and not be condemned on character alone. Have we not express contracts with our colonies, which afford a more certain foundation of judgement, than general political speculations on the mutual rights of States and their provinces or colonies? Pray let me know immediately what to read, and I shall diligently endeavour to gather for you any thing that I can find. Is Burke's speech on American taxation published by himself? Is it authentick? I remember to have heard you say, that you had never considered East-Indian affairs; though, surely, they are of much importance to Great-Britain. Under the recollection of this, I shelter myself from the reproach of ignorance about the Americans. If you write upon the subject, I shall certainly understand it. But, since you seem to expect that I should know something of it, without your instruction, and that my own mind should suggest something, I trust you will put me in the way.

'As to Macpherson, I am anxious to have from yourself a full and pointed account of what has passed between you and him. It is confidently told here, that before your book came out he sent to you, to let you know that he understood you meant to deny the authenticity of Ossian's poems; that the originals were in his possession; that you might have inspection of them, and might take the evidence of people skilled in the Erse language; and that he hoped, after this fair offer, you would not be so uncandid as to assert that he had refused reasonable proof. That you paid no regard to his message, but published your strong attack upon him; that then he wrote a letter to you, in such terms as he thought suited to one who had not acted as a man of veracity. You may believe it gives me pain to hear your conduct represented as unfavourable, while I can only deny what is said, on the ground that your character refutes it, without having any information to oppose. Let me, I beg it of you, be furnished with a sufficient answer to any calumny upon this occasion.

'To James Boswell, Esq.

'My dear Boswell,

'I am surprised that, knowing as you do the disposition of your countrymen to tell lies in favour of each other, you can be at all affected by any reports that circulate among them. Macpherson never in his life offered me the sight of any original or of any evidence of any kind; but thought only of intimidating me by noise and threats, till my last answer,—that I would not be deterred from detecting what I thought a cheat, by the menaces of a ruffian,—put an end to our correspondence.

'The state of the question is this. He, and Dr. Blair, whom I consider as deceived, say, that he copied the poem from old manuscripts. His copies, if he had them, and I believe him to have none, are nothing. Where are the manuscripts? They can be shown if they exist, but they were never shown.

'But whatever he has, he never offered to show. If old manuscripts should now be mentioned, I should, unless there were more evidence than can be easily had, suppose them another proof of Scotch conspiracy in national falsehood.

'Do not censure the expression; you know it to be true.

'I am now engaged, but in a little time I hope to do all you would have. My compliments to Madam and Veronica.

'I am, Sir,
'Your most humble servant,
'Sam. Johnson.'

'February 7, 1775.'

What words were used by Mr. Macpherson in his letter to the venerable Sage, I have never heard; but they are generally said to have been of a nature very different from the language of literary contest. Dr. Johnson's answer appeared in the newspapers of the day, and has since been frequently re-published; but not with perfect accuracy. I give it as dictated to me by himself, written down in his presence, and authenticated by a note in his own hand-writing, '*This, I think, is a true copy.*'

'MR. JAMES MACPHERSON,

'I RECEIVED your foolish and impudent letter. Any violence offered me I shall do my best to repel; and what I cannot do for myself, the law shall do for me. I hope I shall never be deterred from detecting what I think a cheat, by the menaces of a ruffian.

'What would you have me retract? I thought your book an imposture; I think it an imposture still. For this opinion I have given my reasons to the publick, which I here dare you to refute. Your rage I defy. Your abilities, since your Homer are not so formidable; and what I hear of your morals inclines me to pay regard not to what you shall say, but to what you shall prove. You may print this if you will.

'SAM JOHNSON.'

Mr. Macpherson little knew the character of Dr. Johnson, if he supposed that he could be easily intimidated; for no man was ever more remarkable for personal courage. He had, indeed, an aweful dread of death, or rather, 'of something after death;' and what rational man, who seriously thinks of quitting all that he has ever known, and going into a new and unknown state of being, can be without that dread? But his fear was from reflection; his courage natural. His fear, in that one instance, was the result of philosophical and religious consideration. He feared death, but he feared nothing else, not even what might occasion death. Many instances of his resolution may be mentioned. One day, at Mr. Beauclerk's house in the country, when two large dogs were fighting, he went up to them, and beat them till they separated; and at another time, when told of the danger there was that a gun might burst if charged with many balls, he put in six or seven, and fired it off against a wall. Mr. Langton told me, that when they were swimming together near Oxford, he cautioned Dr. Johnson against a pool, which was reckoned particularly dangerous; upon which Johnson directly swam into it. He told me himself that one night he was attacked in the street by four men, to whom he would not yield, but kept them all at bay, till the watch came up, and carried both him and them to the round-house. In the play-house at Lichfield, as Mr. Garrick informed me, Johnson having for a moment quitted a chair which was placed for him between the side-scenes, a gentleman took possession of it, and when Johnson on his return civilly demanded his seat, rudely refused to give it up; upon which Johnson laid hold of it, and tossed him and the chair into the pit. Foote, who so successfully revived the old comedy, by exhibiting living characters, had resolved to imitate Johnson on the stage, expecting great profits from his ridicule of so celebrated a man. Johnson being informed of his intention, and being at dinner at Mr. Thomas Davies's the bookseller, from whom I had the story, he asked Mr. Davies 'what was the common price of an oak stick;' and being answered six-pence, 'Why then, Sir, (said he,) give me leave to send your servant to purchase me a shilling one. I'll have a double quantity; for I am told Foote means to *take me off*, as he calls it, and I am determined the fellow shall not do it with impunity.' Davies took care to acquaint Foote of this, which effectually checked the wantonness of the mimick. Mr. Macpherson's menaces made Johnson provide himself with the same implement of defence; and had he been attacked, I have no doubt that, old as he was, he would have made his corporal prowess be felt as much as his intellectual.

His 'Journey to the Western Islands of Scotland' is a most valuable performance. It abounds in extensive philosophical views of society, and in ingenious sentiments and lively description. A considerable part of it, indeed, consists of speculations, which many years before he saw the wild regions which we visited together, probably had employed his attention, though the actual sight of those scenes undoubtedly quickened and augmented them. Mr. Orme, the very able historian, agreed with me in this opinion, which he thus strongly expressed:—'There are in that book thoughts, which, by long revolution in the great mind of Johnson, have been formed and polished like pebbles rolled in the ocean!'

That he was to some degree of excess a *true-born Englishman*, so as to have ever entertained an undue prejudice against both the country and the people of Scotland, must be allowed. But it was a prejudice of the head, and not of the heart. He had no ill will to the Scotch; for, if he had been conscious of that, he would never have thrown himself into the bosom of their country, and trusted to the protection of its remote inhabitants with a fearless confidence. His remark upon the nakedness of the country, from its being denuded of trees[1], was made after having travelled two hundred miles along the eastern coast, where certainly trees are not to be found near the road; and he said it was 'a map of the road' which he gave. His disbelief of the authenticity of the poems ascribed to Ossian, a Highland bard, was confirmed in the course of his journey, by a very strict examination of the evidence offered for it; and although their authenticity was made too much a national point by the Scotch, there were many respectable persons in that country, who did not concur in this; so that his judgement upon the question ought not to be decried, even by those who differ from him. As to myself, I can only say, upon a subject now become very uninteresting, that when the fragments of Highland poetry first came out, I was much pleased with their wild peculiarity, and was one of those who subscribed to enable their editor, Mr. Macpherson, then a young man, to make a search in the Highlands and Hebrides for a long poem in the Erse language, which was reported to be preserved somewhere in those regions. But when there came forth an Epick Poem in six books, with all the common circumstances of former compositions of that nature; and when, upon an attentive examination of it, there was found a perpetual recurrence of the same images which appear in the fragments; and when no ancient manuscript, to authenticate the work, was deposited in any publick library, though that was insisted on as a reasonable proof, *who* could forbear to doubt?

Johnson's grateful acknowledgements of kindnesses received in the course of this tour, completely refute the brutal reflections which have been thrown out against him, as if he had made an ungrateful return; and his delicacy in sparing in his

---

[1] Nothing in Johnson's account of his journey gave more violent offense to the Scotch than his statement that the country he traversed was practically treeless. It was practically treeless.

book those who we find from his letters to Mrs. Thrale, were just objects of censure, is much to be admired. His private letters to Mrs. Thrale, written during the course of his journey, which therefore may be supposed to convey his genuine feelings at the time, abound in such benignant sentiments towards the people who showed him civilities, that no man whose temper is not very harsh and sour, can retain a doubt of the goodness of his heart.

It is painful to recollect with what rancour he was assailed by numbers of shallow irritable North Britons, on account of his supposed injurious treatment of their country and countrymen, in his 'Journey.' Johnson treated Scotland no worse than he did even his best friends, whose characters he used to give as they appeared to him, both in light and shade. Some people, who had not exercised their minds sufficiently, condemned him for censuring his friends. But Sir Joshua Reynolds, whose philosophical penetration and justness of thinking were not less known to those who lived with him, than his genius in his art is admired by the world, explained his conduct thus: 'He was fond of discrimination, which he could not show without pointing out the bad as well as the good in every character; and as his friends were those whose characters he knew best, they afforded him the best opportunity for showing the acuteness of his judgement.'

He expressed to his friend Mr. Windham of Norfolk, his wonder at the extreme jealousy of the Scotch, and their resentment at having their country described by him as it really was; when, to say that it was a country as good as England, would have been a gross falsehood. 'None of us, (said he,) would be offended if a foreigner who has travelled here should say, that vines and olives don't grow in England.' And as to his prejudice against the Scotch, which I always ascribed to that nationality which he observed in *them,* he said to the same gentleman, 'When I find a Scotchman, to whom an Englishman is as a Scotchman, that Scotchman shall be as an Englishman to me.'

My much-valued friend Dr. Barnard, now Bishop of Killaloe, having once expressed to him an apprehension, that if he should visit Ireland he might treat the people of that country more unfavourably than he had done the Scotch, he answered, with strong pointed double-edged wit, 'Sir, you have no reason to be afraid of me. The Irish are not in a conspiracy to cheat the world by false representations of the merits of their countrymen. No, Sir; the Irish are a *fair people;*—they never speak well of one another.'

Johnson told me an instance of Scottish nationality, which made a very unfavourable impression upon his mind. A Scotchman, of some consideration in London, solicited him to recommend, by the weight of his learned authority, to be master of an English school, a person of whom he who recommended him confessed he knew no more but that he was his countryman. Johnson was shocked at this unconscientious conduct.

All the miserable cavillings against his 'Journey,' in newspapers, magazines, and other fugitive publications, I can speak from certain knowledge, only furnished him with sport. At last there came out a scurrilous volume, larger than Johnson's own, filled with malignant abuse. The effect which it had upon Johnson was, to produce this pleasant observation to Mr. Seward, to whom he lent the book: 'This fellow must be a blockhead. They don't know how to go about their abuse. Who will read a five shilling book against me? No, Sir, if they had wit, they should have kept pelting me with pamphlets.'

On Tuesday, March 21, I arrived in London; and on repairing to Dr. Johnson's before dinner, found him in his study, sitting with Mr. Peter Garrick, the elder brother of David, strongly resembling him in countenance and voice, but of more sedate and placid manners. Johnson informed me, that 'though Mr. Beauclerk was in great pain, it was hoped he was not in danger, and that he now wished to consult Dr. Heberden to try the effect of a *new understanding.*' Both at this interview, and in the evening at Mr. Thrale's, where he and Mr. Peter Garrick and I met again, he was vehement on the subject of the Ossian controversy; observing, 'We do not know that there are any ancient Erse manuscripts; and we have no other reason to disbelieve that there are men with three heads, but that we do not know that there are any such men.' He also was outrageous, upon his supposition that my countrymen 'loved Scotland better than truth,' saying, 'All of them,—nay not all, –but *droves* of them, would come up, and attest any thing for the honour of Scotland.' He also persevered in his wild allegation, that he questioned if there was a tree between Edinburgh and the English border older than himself. I assured him he was mistaken, and suggested that the proper punishment would be that he should receive a stripe at every tree above a hundred years old, that was found within that space. He laughed, and said, 'I believe I might submit to it for a *baubee!*'

The doubts which, in my correspondence with him, I had ventured to state as to the justice and wisdom of the conduct of Great-Britain towards the American colonies, while I at the same time requested that he would enable me to inform myself upon that momentous subject, he had altogether disregarded; and had recently published a pamphlet, entitled, 'Taxation no Tyranny; an Answer to the Resolutions and Address of the American Congress.'

He had long before indulged most unfavourable sentiments of our fellow-subjects in America. For, as early as 1769, I was told by Dr. John Campbell, that he had said of them, 'Sir, they are a race of convicts, and ought to be thankful for any thing we allow them short of hanging.'

Of this performance I avoided to talk with him; for I had now formed a clear and settled opinion, that the people of America were well warranted to resist a claim that their fellow-subjects in the mother-country should have the entire command of their fortunes, by taxing them without their own consent; and the extreme violence which it breathed, appeared to me so unsuitable to the mildness of a Christian philosopher, and so directly opposite to the principles of peace which he had so beautifully recommended in his pamphlet respecting Falkland's Islands, that I was sorry to see him appear in so unfavourable a light. Besides, I could not perceive in it that ability of argument, or that felicity of expression, for which he was, upon other occasions, so eminent. Positive assertion, sarcastical severity, and extravagant ridicule, which he himself reprobated as a test of truth, were united in this rhapsody.

That this pamphlet was written at the desire of those who were then in power, I have no doubt; and, indeed, he owned to me, that it had been revised and curtailed by some of them.

His pamphlets in support of the measures of administration were published on his own account, and he afterwards collected them into a volume, with the title of 'Political Tracts, by the Authour of the Rambler.'

These pamphlets drew upon him numerous attacks. Against the common weapons of literary warfare he was hardened; but there were two instances of animadversion which I communicated to him, and from what I could judge, both from his silence and his looks, appeared to me to impress him much.

One was, 'A Letter to Dr. Samuel Johnson, occasioned by his late political Publications.' It appeared previous to his 'Taxation no Tyranny,' and was written by Dr. Joseph Towers. It concluded thus:

'I would, however, wish you to remember, should you again address the publick under the character of a political writer, that luxuriance of imagination or energy of language will ill compensate for the want of candour, of justice, and of truth. And I shall only add, that should I hereafter be disposed to read, as I heretofore have done, the most excellent of all your performances, "The Rambler," the pleasure which I have been accustomed to find in it will be much diminished by the reflection that the writer of so moral, so elegant, and so valuable a work, was capable of prostituting his talents in such productions as "The False Alarm," the "Thoughts on the Transactions respecting Falkland's Islands," and "The Patriot."'

I am willing to do justice to the merit of Dr. Towers, of whom I will say, that although I abhor his Whiggish democratical notions and propensities, (for I will not call them principles,) I esteem him as an ingenious, knowing, and very convivial man.

The other instance was a paragraph of a letter to me, from my old and most intimate friend, the Reverend Mr. Temple. The words were,

'How can your great, I will not say your *pious,* but your *moral* friend, support the barbarous measures of administration, which they have not the face to ask even their infidel pensioner Hume to defend.'

However confident of the rectitude of his own mind, Johnson may have felt sincere uneasiness that his conduct should be erroneously imputed to unworthy motives, by good men; and that the influence of his valuable writings should on that account be in any degree obstructed or lessened.

He complained to a Right Honourable friend of distinguished talents and very elegant manners, with whom he maintained a long intimacy, and whose generosity towards him will afterwards appear, that his pension having been given to him as a literary character, he had been applied to by administration to write political pamphlets; and he was even so much irritated, that he declared his resolution to resign his pension. His friend shewed him the impropriety of such a measure, and he afterwards expressed his gratitude, and said he had received good advice.

On Friday, March 24, I met him at the *Literary Club*, where were Mr. Beauclerk, Mr. Langton, Mr. Colman, Dr. Percy, Mr. Vesey, Sir Charles Bunbury, Dr. George Fordyce, Mr. Steevens, and Mr. Charles Fox. Before he came in, we talked of his 'Journey to the Western Islands,' and of his coming away, 'willing to believe the second sight,' which seemed to excite some ridicule. I was then so impressed with the truth of many of the stories of it which I had been told, that I avowed my conviction, saying, 'He is only *willing* to believe: I *do* believe. The evidence is enough for me, though not for his great mind. What will not fill a quart bottle will fill a pint bottle. I am filled with belief.' 'Are you? (said Colman,) then cork it up.'

Johnson was in high spirits this evening at the club, and talked with great animation and success. He attacked Swift, as he used to do upon all occasions. 'The "Tale of a Tub" is so much superiour to his other writings, that one can hardly believe he was the authour of it. There is in it such a vigour of mind, such a swarm of thoughts, so much of nature, and art, and life.' I wondered to hear him say of 'Gulliver's Travels,' 'When once you have thought of big men and little men, it is very easy to do all the rest.' I endeavoured to make a stand for Swift, and tried to rouse those who were much more able to defend him; but in vain. Johnson at last, of his own accord, allowed very great merit to the inventory of articles found in the pockets of the Man Mountain, particularly the description of his watch, which it was conjectured was his GOD, as he consulted it upon all occasions.

From Swift, there was an easy transition to Mr. Thomas Sheridan.—*Johnson*. 'Sheridan is a wonderful admirer of the tragedy of Douglas, and presented its authour with a gold medal. Some years ago, at a coffee-house in Oxford, I called to him, "Mr. Sheridan, Mr. Sheridan, how came you to give a gold medal to Home, for writing that foolish play?" This, you see, was wanton and insolent; but I *meant* to be wanton and insolent. A medal has no value but as a stamp of merit. And was Sheridan to assume to himself the right of giving that stamp? If Sheridan was magnificent enough to bestow a gold medal as an honorary reward of dramatick excellence, he should have requested one of the Universities to choose the person on whom it should be conferred. Sheridan had no right to give a stamp of merit: it was counterfeiting Apollo's coin.'

On Monday, March 27, I breakfasted with him at Mr. Strahan's. He told us, that he was engaged to go that evening to Mrs. Abington's benefit. 'She was visiting some ladies whom I was visiting, and begged that I would come to her benefit. I told her I could not hear: but she insisted so much on my coming, that it would have been brutal to have refused her.' This was a speech quite characteristical. He loved to bring forward his having been in the gay circles of life; and he was, perhaps, a little vain of the solicitations of this elegant and fashionable actress.

Mr. Strahan talked of launching into the great ocean of London, in order to have a chance for rising into eminence; and, observing that many men were kept back from trying their fortunes there, because they were born to a competency, said, 'Small certainties are the bane of men of talents;' which Johnson confirmed. Mr. Strahan put Johnson in mind of a remark which he had made to him; 'There are few ways in which a man can be more innocently employed than in getting money.' 'The more one thinks of this, (said Strahan,) the juster it will appear.'

Mr. Strahan had taken a poor boy from the country as an apprentice, upon Johnson's recommendation. Johnson having enquired after him, said, 'Mr. Strahan, let me have five guineas on account, and I'll give this boy one. Nay, if a man recommends a boy, and does nothing for him, it is sad work. Call him down.'

I followed him into the court-yard, behind Mr. Strahan's house; and there I had a proof of what I had heard him profess, that he talked alike to all. 'Some people (said he), tell you that they let themselves down to the capacity of their hearers. I never do that. I speak uniformly, in as intelligible a manner as I can.'

'Well, my boy, how do you go on?'—'Pretty well, Sir; but they are afraid I an't strong enough for some parts of the business.' *Johnson.* 'Why I shall be sorry for it; for when you consider with how little mental power and corporeal labour a printer can get a guinea a week, it is a very desirable occupation for you. Do you hear,—take all the pains you can; and if this does not do, we must think of some other way of life for you. There's a guinea.'

Here was one of the many, many instances of his active benevolence. At the same time, the slow and sonorous solemnity with which, while he bent himself down, he addressed a little thick short-legged boy, contrasted with the boy's aukwardness and awe, could not but excite some ludicrous emotions.

I met him at Drury-lane play-house in the evening. Sir Joshua Reynolds, at Mrs. Abington's request, had promised to bring a body of wits to her benefit; and having secured forty places in the front boxes, had done me the honour to put me in the group. Johnson sat on the seat directly behind me; and as he could neither see nor hear at such a distance from the stage, he was wrapped up in grave abstraction, and seemed quite a cloud, amidst all the sunshine of glitter and gaiety. I wondered at his patience in sitting out a play of five acts, and a farce of two. He said very little; but after the prologue had been spoken, which he could hear pretty well from the more slow and distinct utterance, he talked of prologue-writing, and observed, 'Dryden has written prologues superiour to any that David Garrick has written; but David Garrick has written more good prologues than Dryden has done. It is wonderful that he has been able to write such a variety of them.'

At Mr. Beauclerk's, where I supped, was Mr. Garrick, whom

I made happy with Johnson's praise of his prologues; and I suppose, in gratitude to him, he took up one of his favourite topicks, the nationality of the Scotch, which he maintained in his pleasant manner, with the aid of a little poetical fiction. 'Come, come, don't deny it: they are really national. Why, now, the Adams are as liberal-minded men as any in the world: but, I don't know how it is, all their workmen are Scotch. You are, to be sure, wonderfully free from that nationality: but so it happens, that you employ the only Scotch shoe-black in London.' He imitated the manner of his old master with ludicrous exaggeration, looking down downwards all the time, and absolutely touching the ground with a kind of contorted gesticulation.

Garrick, however, when he pleased, could imitate Johnson very exactly; for that great actor, with his distinguished powers of expression which were so universally admired, possessed also an admirable talent of mimickry. He was always jealous that Johnson spoke lightly of him. I recollect his exhibiting him to me one day, as if saying, 'Davy has some convivial pleasantry about him, but 'tis a futile fellow;' which he uttered perfectly with the tone and air of Johnson.

I cannot too frequently request of my readers, while they peruse my account of Johnson's conversation, to endeavour to keep in mind his deliberate and strong utterance. His mode of speaking was indeed very impressive; and I wish it could be preserved as musick is written, according to the very ingenious method of Mr. Steele, who has shown how the recitation of Mr. Garrick, and other eminent speakers, might be transmitted to posterity *in score*.

Next day I dined with Johnson at Mr. Thrale's. He attacked Gray, calling him 'a dull fellow.' *Boswell.* 'I understand he was reserved, and might appear dull in company; but surely he was not dull in poetry.' *Johnson.* 'Sir, he was dull in company, dull in his closet, dull every where. He was dull in a new way, and that made many people think him GREAT. He was a mechanical poet.'

A young lady who had married a man much her inferiour in rank being mentioned, a question arose how a woman's relations should behave to her in such a situation. While I

contended that she ought to be treated with an inflexible steadiness of displeasure, Mrs. Thrale was all for mildness and forgiveness, and, according to the vulgar phrase, 'making the best
of a bad bargain.' *Johnson.* 'Madam, we must distinguish.
Were I a man of rank, I would not let a daughter starve who
had made a mean marriage; but having voluntarily degraded
herself from the station which she was originally entitled to
hold, I would support her only in that which she herself had
chosen; and would not put her on a level with my other daughters. You are to consider, Madam, that it is our duty to maintain the subordination of civilized society; and when there is
a gross and shameful deviation from rank, it should be punished so as to deter others from the same perversion.'

On Friday, March 31, I supped with him and some friends
at a tavern. One of the company attempted, with too much
forwardness, to rally him on his late appearance at the theatre;
but had reason to repent of his temerity. 'Why, Sir, did you
go to Mrs. Abington's benefit? Did you see?' *Johnson.* 'No,
Sir.' 'Did you hear?' *Johnson.* 'No, Sir.' 'Why then, Sir, did
you go?' *Johnson.* 'Because, Sir, she is a favourite of the publick; and when the publick cares the thousandth part for you
that it does for her, I will go to your benefit too.'

Next morning I won a small bet from Lady Diana Beauclerk,
by asking him as to one of his particularities, which her Lady-
ship laid I durst not do. It seems he had been frequently observed at the Club to put into his pocket the Seville oranges,
after he had squeezed the juice of them into the drink which
he made for himself. Beauclerk and Garrick talked of it to me,
and seemed to think that he had a strange unwillingness to be
discovered. We could not divine what he did with them; and
this was the bold question to be put. I saw on his table the
spoils of the preceding night, some fresh peels nicely scraped
and cut into pieces. 'O, Sir, (said I,) I now partly see what
you do with the squeezed oranges which you put into your
pocket at the Club.' *Johnson.* 'I have a great love for them.'
Boswell. 'And pray, Sir, what do you do with them? You scrape
them, it seems, very neatly, and what next?' *Johnson.* 'I let
them dry, Sir.' *Boswell.* 'And what next?' *Johnson.* 'Nay, Sir,
you shall know their fate no further.' *Boswell.* 'Then the world

must be left in the dark. It must be said (assuming a mock solemnity,) he scraped them, and let them dry, but what he did with them next, he never could be prevailed upon to tell.' *Johnson.* 'Nay, Sir, you should say it more emphatically:—he could not be prevailed upon, even by his dearest friends, to tell.'

He had this morning received his Diploma as Doctor of Laws from the University of Oxford. He did not vaunt of his new dignity, but I understood he was highly pleased with it.

I visited him by appointment in the evening, and we drank tea with Mrs. Williams. He told me that he had been in the company of a gentleman whose extraordinary travels had been much the subject of conversation. But I found that he had not listened to him with that full confidence, without which there is little satisfaction in the society of travellers. I was curious to hear what opinion so able a judge as Johnson had formed of his abilities, and I asked if he was not a man of sense. *Johnson.* 'Why, Sir, he is not a distinct relater; and I should say, he is neither abounding nor deficient in sense. I did not perceive any superiority of understanding.' *Boswell.* 'But will you not allow him a nobleness of resolution, in penetrating into distant regions?' *Johnson.* 'That, Sir, is not to the present purpose: we are talking of his sense. A fighting cock has a nobleness of resolution.'

Next day, Sunday, April 2, I dined with him at Mr. Hoole's. We talked of Pope. *Johnson.* 'He wrote his "Dunciad" for fame. That was his primary motive. Had it not been for that, the dunces might have railed against him till they were weary, without his troubling himself about them. He delighted to vex them, no doubt; but he had more delight in seeing how well he could vex them.'

I talked of the chearfulness of Fleet-street, owing to the constant quick succession of people which we perceive passing through it. *Johnson.* 'Why, Sir, Fleet-street has a very animated appearance; but I think the full tide of human existence is at Charing-cross.'

He made the common remark on the unhappiness which men who have led a busy life experience, when they retire in expectation of enjoying themselves at ease, and that they generally languish for want of their habitual occupation, and wish to return to it. He mentioned as strong an instance of this as can well be imagined. 'An eminent tallow-chandler in London, who had acquired a considerable fortune, gave up the trade in favour of his foreman, and went to live at a country-house near town. He soon grew weary, and paid frequent visits to his old shop, where he desired they might let him know their *melting-days,* and he would come and assist them; which he accordingly did. Here, Sir, was a man, to whom the most disgusting circumstance in the business to which he had been used, was a relief from idleness.'

We talked of publick speaking.—*Johnson.* 'We must not estimate a man's powers by his being able or not able to deliver his sentiments in publick. For my own part, I think it is more disgraceful never to try to speak, than to try it and fail; as it is more disgraceful not to fight, than to fight and be beaten.' This argument appeared to me fallacious; for if a man has not spoken, it may be said that he would have done very well if he had tried; whereas, if he has tried and failed, there is nothing to be said for him. 'Why then, (I asked,) is it thought disgraceful for a man not to fight, and not disgraceful not to speak in publick?' *Johnson.* 'Because there may be other reasons for a man's not speaking in publick than want of resolution: he may have nothing to say, (laughing.) Whereas, Sir, you know courage is reckoned the greatest of all virtues; because, unless a man has that virtue, he has no security for preserving any other.'

He observed, that 'the statutes against bribery were intended to prevent upstarts with money from getting into Parliament;' adding, that 'if he were a gentleman of landed property, he would turn out all his tenants who did not vote for the candidate whom he supported.' *Langton.* 'Would not that, Sir, be checking the freedom of election?' *Johnson.* 'Sir, the law does not mean that the privilege of voting should be independent of old family interest; of the permanent property of the country.'

On Thursday, April 6, I dined with him at Mr. Thomas Davies's, with Mr. Hicky, the painter, and my old acquaintance Mr. Moody, the player.

Dr. Johnson, as usual, spoke contemptuously of Colley Cibber. 'It is wonderful that a man, who for forty years had lived with the great and the witty, should have acquired so ill the talents of conversation: and he had but half to furnish; for one half of what he said was oaths.' He, however, allowed considerable merit to some of his comedies, and said there was no reason to believe that 'The Careless Husband' was not written by himself. Davies said, he was the first dramatick writer who introduced genteel ladies upon the stage. Johnson refuted this observation by instancing several such characters in comedies before his time. *Davies.* (trying to defend himself from a charge of ignorance,) 'I mean genteel moral characters.' 'I think (said Hicky,) gentility and morality are inseparable.' *Boswell.* 'By no means, Sir. The genteelest characters are often the most immoral. Does not Lord Chesterfield give precepts for uniting wickedness and the graces? A man, indeed, is not genteel when he gets drunk; but most vices may be committed very genteelly: a man may debauch his friend's wife genteelly: he may cheat at cards genteelly.' *Hicky.* 'I do not think *that* is genteel.' *Johnson.* 'You are meaning two different things. One means exteriour grace; the other honour. It is certain that a man may be very immoral with exteriour grace. Tom Hervey, who died t'other day, though a vicious man, was one of the genteelest men that ever lived.' Tom Davies instanced Charles the Second. *Johnson,* (taking fire at any attack upon that Prince, for whom he had an extraordinary partiality,) 'Charles the Second was licentious in his practice; but he always had a reverence for what was good.'

I mentioned that Dr. Thomas Campbell had come from Ireland to London, principally to see Dr. Johnson. He seemed angry at this observation. *Davies.* 'Why, you know, Sir, there came a man from Spain to see Livy; and Corelli came to England to see Purcell, and, when he heard he was dead, went directly back again to Italy.' *Johnson.* 'I should not have wished to be dead to disappoint Campbell, had he been so foolish as you represent him; but I should have wished to have been a hundred miles off.' This was apparently perverse; and I do believe it was not his real way of thinking: he could not but like

a man who came so far to see him. He laughed with some complacency, when I told him Campbell's odd expression to me
concerning him: 'That having seen such a man, was a thing
to talk of a century hence,'—as if he could live so long.

We got into an argument whether the Judges who went to
India might with propriety engage in trade. Johnson warmly
maintained that they might. 'For why (he urged) should not
Judges get riches, as well as those who deserve them less?' I
said, they should have sufficient salaries, and have nothing to
take off their attention from the affairs of the publick. *Johnson.*
'No Judge, Sir, can give his whole attention to his office; and it
is very proper that he should employ what time he has to himself, for his own advantage, in the most profitable manner.'
'Then, Sir, (said Davies, who enlivened the dispute by making
it somewhat dramatick,) he may become an insurer; and when
he is going to the bench, he may be stopped,—"Your Lordship
cannot go yet: here is a bunch of invoices: several ships are
about to sail."' *Johnson.* 'Sir, you may as well say a Judge
should not have a house; for they may come and tell him, "Your
Lordship's house is on fire;" and so, instead of minding the
business of his Court, he is to be occupied in getting the en-
gine with the greatest speed. There is no end of this. Every
Judge who has land, trades to a certain extent in corn or in cattle; and in the land itself, undoubtedly. His steward acts for
him, and so do clerks for a great merchant. A Judge may be a
farmer; but he is not to geld his own pigs. A Judge may play a
little at cards for his amusement; but he is not to play at mar-
bles, or at chuck-farthing in the Piazza. No, Sir; there is no profession to which a man gives a very great proportion of his
time. It is wonderful, when a calculation is made, how little
the mind is actually employed in the discharge of any profession. No man would be a Judge, upon the condition of being
obliged to be totally a Judge. The best employed lawyer has
his mind at work but for a small proportion of his time: a great
deal of his occupation is merely mechanical.—I once wrote for
a magazine: I made a calculation, that if I should write but a
page a day, at the same rate, I should, in ten years, write nine
volumes in folio, of an ordinary size and print.' *Boswell.* 'Such

as Carte's History?' *Johnson.* 'Yes, Sir. When a man writes from his own mind, he writes very rapidly. The greatest part of a writer's time is spent in reading, in order to write: a man will turn over half a library to make one book.'

While the dispute went on, Moody once tried to say something upon our side. Tom Davies clapped him on the back, to encourage him. Beauclerk, to whom I mentioned this circumstance; said, 'that he could not conceive a more humiliating situation than to be clapped on the back by Tom Davies.'

We spoke of Rolt, to whose Dictionary of Commerce, Dr. Johnson wrote the Preface. *Johnson.* 'Old Gardner the bookseller employed Rolt and Smart to write a monthly miscellany, called "The Universal Visitor." There was a formal written contract, which Allen the printer saw. Gardner thought as you do of the Judge. They were bound to write nothing else; they were to have, I think, a third of the profits of this sixpenny pamphlet; and the contract was for ninety-nine years. I wrote for some months in "The Universal Visitor," for poor Smart, while he was mad, not then knowing the terms on which he was engaged to write, and thinking I was doing him good. I hoped his wits would soon return to him. Mine returned to me, and I wrote in "The Universal Visitor" no longer.'

Friday, April 7, I dined with him at a tavern, with a numerous company. *Johnson.* 'I have been reading "Twiss's Travels in Spain," which are just come out. They are as good as the first book of travels that you will take up. I have not, indeed, cut the leaves yet; but I have read in them where the pages are open, and I do not suppose that what is in the pages which are closed is worse than what is in the open pages.'

Ossian being mentioned;—*Johnson.* 'Supposing the Irish and Erse languages to be the same, which I do not believe, yet as there is no reason to suppose that the inhabitants of the Highlands and Hebrides ever wrote their native language, it is not to be credited that a long poem was preserved among them. If we had no evidence of the art of writing being practised in one of the counties of England, we should not believe that a long poem was preserved *there,* though in the neighbouring counties, where the same language was spoken, the inhabitants

could write.' *Beauclerk.* 'The ballad of Lilliburlero[1] was once
in the mouths of all the people of this country, and is said to
have had a great effect in bringing about the Revolution. Yet
I question whether any body can repeat it now; which shews
how improbable it is that much poetry should be preserved by
tradition.'

One of the company suggested an internal objection to the
antiquity of the poetry said to be Ossian's, that we do not find
the wolf in it, which must have been the case had it been of
that age.

The mention of the wolf had led Johnson to think of other
wild beasts; and while Sir Joshua Reynolds and Mr. Langton
were carrying on a dialogue about something which engaged
them earnestly, he, in the midst of it, broke out, 'Pennant tells
of Bears—' [what he added, I have forgotten.] They went on,
which he being dull of hearing, did not perceive, or, if he did,
was not willing to break off his talk; so he continued to vo-
ciferate his remarks, and *Bear* ('like a word in a catch', as Beauclerk said,) was repeatedly heard at intervals, which coming
from him who, by those who did not know him, had been so
often assimilated to that ferocious animal, while we who were
sitting round could hardly stifle laughter, produced a very
ludicrous effect. Silence having ensued, he proceeded: 'We are
told, that the black bear is innocent; but I should not like to
trust myself with him.' Mr. Gibbon muttered, in a low tone of
voice, 'I should not like to trust myself with *you*.' This piece of
sarcastick pleasantry was a prudent resolution, if applied to a
competition of abilities.

Patriotism having become one of our topicks, Johnson suddenly uttered, in a strong determined tone, an apophthegm, at
which many will start: 'Patriotism is the last refuge of a scoundrel.' But let it be considered, that he did not mean a real and
generous love of our country, but that pretended patriotism
which so many, in all ages and countries, have made a cloak
for self-interest.

---

[1] A song with doggerel verses and a lilting air, intensely popular during the English revolution of 1688. It at once reflected and exacerbated
popular discontent over James II. The title of the song is from the mean-
ingless refrain, *Lilliburlero bullen a la.*

Mrs. Pritchard being mentioned, he said, 'Her playing was quite mechanical. It is wonderful how little mind she had. Sir, she had never read the tragedy of Macbeth all through. She no more thought of the play out of which her part was taken, than a shoemaker thinks of the skin, out of which the piece of leather, of which he is making a pair of shoes, is cut.'

On Saturday, May 8, I dined with him at Mr. Thrale's, where we met the Irish Dr. Campbell. Johnson had supped the night before at Mrs. Abington's, with some fashionable people whom he named; and he seemed much pleased with having made one in so elegant a circle. Nor did he omit to pique his *mistress* a little with jealousy of her housewifery; for he said, (with a smile,) 'Mrs. Abington's jelly, my dear Lady, was better than yours.'

Mrs. Thrale, who frequently practised a coarse mode of flattery, by repeating his *bon mots* in his hearing, told us that he had said, a certain celebrated actor was just fit to stand at the door of an auction-room with a long pole, and cry 'Pray gentlemen, walk in;' and that a certain authour, upon hearing this, had said, that another still more celebrated actor was fit for nothing better than that, and would pick your pocket after you came out. *Johnson.* 'Nay, my dear lady, there is no wit in what our friend added; there is only abuse. You may as well say of any man that he will pick a pocket. Besides, the man who is stationed at the door does not pick people's pockets; that is done within, by the auctioneer.'

Mrs. Thrale told us, that Tom Davies repeated, in a very bald manner, the story of Dr. Johnson's first repartee to me, which I have related exactly. He made me say, 'I *was born* in Scotland,' instead of 'I *come from* Scotland;' so that Johnson's saying, 'That, Sir, is what a great many of your countrymen cannot help,' had no point, or even meaning: and that upon this being mentioned to Mr. Fitzherbert, he observed, 'It is not every man that can *carry* a *bon mot.*'

On Monday, April 10, I dined with him at General Oglethorpe's, with Mr. Langton and the Irish Dr. Campbell, whom the General had obligingly given me leave to bring with me. This learned gentleman was thus gratified with a very high intellectual feast, by not only being in company with Dr. Johnson, but with General Oglethorpe, who had been so long a celebrated name both at home and abroad.

I must, again and again, intreat of my readers not to suppose that my imperfect record of conversation contains the whole of what was said by Johnson, or other eminent persons who lived with him. What I have preserved, however, has the value of the most perfect authenticity.

He this day enlarged upon Pope's melancholy remark,

'Man never *is*, but always *to be* blest.'

He asserted, that *the present* was never a happy state to any human being; but that, as every part of life, of which we are conscious, was at some point of time a period yet to come, in which felicity was expected, there was some happiness produced by hope. Being pressed upon this subject, and asked if he really was of opinion, that though, in general, happiness was very rare in human life, a man was not sometimes happy in the moment that was present, he answered, 'Never, but when he is drunk.'

No more of his conversation for some days appears in my journal, except that when a gentleman told him he had bought a suit of laces for his lady, he said, 'Well, Sir, you have done a good thing and a wise thing.' 'I have done a good thing, (said the gentleman,) but I do not know that I have done a wise thing.' *Johnson.* 'Yes, Sir; no money is better spent than what is laid out for domestick satisfaction. A man is pleased that his wife is drest as well as other people; and a wife is pleased that she is drest.'

On Friday, April 14, being Good-Friday, I repaired to him in the morning, according to my usual custom on that day, and breakfasted with him. I observed that he fasted so very strictly, that he did not even taste bread, and took no milk with his tea; I suppose because it is a kind of animal food.

As we walked to St. Clement's church, and saw several shops open upon this most solemn fast-day of the Christian world, I remarked, that one disadvantage arising from the immensity of London, was, that nobody was heeded by his neighbour; there was no fear of censure for not observing Good-Friday, as it ought to be kept, and as it is kept in country-towns. He said, it was, upon the whole, very well observed even in London. He, however, owned, that London was too large; but added, 'It is nonsense to say the head is too big for the body. It would be as much too big, though the body were ever so large; that is to say, though the country were ever so extensive. It has no similarity to a head connected with a body.'

Dr. Wetherell, Master of University College, Oxford, accompanied us home from church; and after he was gone, there came two other gentlemen, one of whom uttered the commonplace complaints, that by the increase of taxes, labour would be dear, other nations would undersell us, and our commerce would be ruined. *Johnson,* (smiling). 'Never fear, Sir. Our commerce is in a very good state; and suppose we had no commerce at all, we could live very well on the produce of our own country.' I cannot omit to mention, that I never knew any man who was less disposed to be querulous than Johnson. Whether the subject was his own situation, or the state of the publick, or the state of human nature in general, though he saw the evils, his mind was turned to resolution, and never to whining or complaint.

We went again to St. Clement's in the afternoon. He had found fault with the preacher in the morning for not choosing a text adapted to the day. The preacher in the afternoon had chosen one extremely proper: 'It is finished.'

After the evening service, he said, 'Come, you shall go home with me, and sit just an hour.' But he was better than his word; for after we had drunk tea with Mrs. Williams, he asked me to go up to his study with him, where we sat a long while together in a serene undisturbed frame of mind, sometimes in silence, and sometimes conversing, as we felt ourselves inclined, or more properly speaking, as *he* was inclined; for during all the course of my long intimacy with him, my respectful attention never abated, and my wish to hear him was such, that I constantly watched every dawning of communication from that great and illuminated mind.

He observed, 'All knowledge is of itself of some value. There is nothing so minute or inconsiderable, that I would not rather know it than not. In the same manner, all power, of whatever sort, is of itself desirable. A man would not submit to learn to hem a ruffle, of his wife, or his wife's maid; but if a mere wish could attain it, he would rather wish to be able to hem a ruffle.'

He again advised me to keep a journal fully and minutely, but not to mention such trifles as, that meat was too much or too little done, or that the weather was fair or rainy. He had, till very near his death, a contempt for the notion that the weather affects the human frame.

I told him that our friend Goldsmith had said to me, that he had come too late into the world, for that Pope and other poets had taken up the places in the Temple of Fame; so that as but a few at any period can possess poetical reputation, a man of genius can now hardly acquire it. *Johnson.* 'That is one of the most sensible things I have ever heard of Goldsmith. It is difficult to get literary fame, and it is every day growing more difficult. Ah, Sir, that should make a man think of securing happiness in another world, which all who try sincerely for it may attain. In comparison of that, how little are all other things! The belief of immortality is impressed upon all men, and all men act under an impression of it, however they may talk, and though, perhaps, they may be scarcely sensible of it.' I said, it appeared to me that some people had not the least notion of immortality; and I mentioned a distinguished gentleman of our acquaintance. *Johnson.* 'Sir, if it were not for the notion of immortality, he would cut a throat to fill his pockets.' When I quoted this to Beauclerk, who knew much more of the gentleman than we did, he said, in his acid manner, 'He would cut a throat to fill his pockets, if it were not for fear of being hanged.'

Dr. Johnson proceeded: 'Sir, there is a great cry about infidelity; but there are, in reality, very few infidels. I have heard a person, originally a Quaker, but now, I am afraid, a Deist, say, that he did not believe there were, in all England, above two hundred infidels.'

He was pleased to say, 'If you come to settle here, we will have one day in the week on which we will meet by ourselves. That is the happiest conversation where there is no competition, no vanity, but a calm quiet interchange of sentiments.' In his private register this evening is thus marked, 'Boswell sat with me till night; we had some serious talk.' It also appears from the same record, that after I left him he was occupied in religious duties, in 'giving Francis, his servant, some directions for preparation to communicate; in reviewing his life, and re-solving on better conduct.'

On Tuesday, April 18, he and I were engaged to go with Sir Joshua Reynolds to dine with Mr. Cambridge, at his beautiful villa on the banks of the Thames, near Twickenham. Dr. John-son's tardiness was such, that Sir Joshua, who had an ap-pointment at Richmond, early in the day, was obliged to go by himself on horseback, leaving his coach to Johnson and me. Johnson was in such good spirits, that every thing seemed to please him as we drove along.

Our conversation turned on a variety of subjects. He thought portrait-painting an improper employment for a woman. 'Publick practice of any art, (he observed,) and star-ing in men's faces, is very indelicate in a female.' I happened to start a question of propriety, whether, when a man knows that some of his intimate friends are invited to the house of another friend, with whom they are all equally intimate, he may join them without an invitation. *Johnson.* 'No, Sir; he is not to go when he is not invited. They may be invited on purpose to abuse him', (smiling).

As a curious instance how little a man knows, or wishes to know, his own character in the world, or, rather, as a convinc-ing proof that Johnson's roughness was only external, and did not proceed from his heart, I insert the following dialogue. *Johnson.* 'It is wonderful, Sir, how rare a quality good humour is in life. We meet with very few good humoured men.' I men-tioned four of our friends, none of whom he would allow to be good humoured. One was *acid,* another was *muddy,* and to the others he had objections which have escaped me. Then, shak-ing his head and stretching himself at his ease in the coach, and smiling with much complacency, he turned to me and said, 'I look upon *myself* as a good humoured fellow.' I answered, also smiling, 'No, no, Sir; that will *not* do. You are good na-tured, but not good humoured: you are irascible. You have not patience with folly and absurdity. I believe you would par-don them, if there were time to deprecate your vengeance; but punishment follows so quick after sentence, that they cannot escape.'

I had brought with me a great bundle of Scotch magazines and news-papers, in which his 'Journey to the Western Islands' was attacked in every mode; and I read a great part of them to him, knowing they would afford him entertainment. I wish the writers of them had been present: they would have been sufficiently vexed. He defended his remark upon the general insufficiency of education in Scotland; and confirmed to me the authenticity of his witty saying on the learning of the Scotch;—'Their learning is like bread in a besieged town: every man gets a little, but no man gets a full meal.' 'There is (said he,) in Scotland a diffusion of learning, a certain portion of it widely and thinly spread. A merchant there has as much learning as one of their clergy.'

He talked of Isaac Walton's Lives, which was one of his most favourite books. Dr. Donne's Life, he said, was the most perfect of them. He observed, that 'it was wonderful that Walton, who was in a very low situation in life, should have been familiarly received by so many great men, and that at a time when the ranks of society were kept more separate than they are now.' He supposed that Walton had then given up his business as a linen-draper and sempster, and was only an authour; and added, 'that he was a great panegyrist.' *Boswell.* 'No quality will get a man more friends than a disposition to admire the qualities of others. I do not mean flattery, but a sincere admiration.' *Johnson.* 'Nay, Sir, flattery pleases very generally. In the first place, the flatterer may think what he says to be true: but, in the second place, whether he thinks so or not, he certainly thinks those whom he flatters of consequence enough to be flattered.'

No sooner had we made our bow to Mr. Cambridge, in his library, than Johnson ran eagerly to one side of the room, intent on poring over the backs of the books. Sir Joshua observed, (aside,) 'He runs to the books, as I do to the pictures: but I have the advantage. I can see much more of the pictures than he can of the books.' Mr. Cambridge, upon this, politely said, 'Dr. Johnson, I am going, with your pardon, to accuse my self, for I have the same custom which I perceive you have·

But it seems odd that one should have such a desire to look at the backs of books.' Johnson, ever ready for contest, instantly started from his reverie, wheeled about, and answered, 'Sir, the reason is very plain. Knowledge is of two kinds. We know a subject ourselves, or we know where we can find information upon it. When we enquire into any subject, the first thing we have to do is to know what books have treated of it. This leads us to look at catalogues, and at the backs of books in libraries.'

The common remark as to the utility of reading history being made;—*Johnson.* 'We must consider how very little history there is; I mean real authentick history. That certain Kings reigned, and certain battles were fought, we can depend upon as true; but all the colouring, all the philosophy, of history is conjecture.' *Boswell.* 'Then, Sir, you would reduce all history to no better than an almanack, a mere chronological series of remarkable events.' Mr. Gibbon, who must at that time have been employed upon his history, of which he published the first volume in the following year, was present; but did not step forth in defence of that species of writing. He probably did not like to *trust* himself with *Johnson!*

'The Beggar's Opera,' and the common question, whether it was pernicious in its effects, having been introduced;—*Johnson.* 'As to this matter, which has been very much contested, I myself am of opinion, that more influence has been ascribed to "The Beggar's Opera," than it in reality ever had; for I do not believe that any man was ever made a rogue by being present at its representation. At the same time I do not deny that it may have some influence, by making the character of a rogue familiar, and in some degree pleasing.' Then collecting himself, as it were, to give a heavy stroke: 'There is in it such a *labefactation* of all principles, as may be injurious to morality.'

While he pronounced this response, we sat in a comical sort of restraint, smothering a laugh, which we were afraid might burst out. In his Life of Gay, he has been still more decisive as to the inefficiency of 'The Beggar's Opera' in corrupting society. But I have ever thought somewhat differently; for, indeed, not only are the gaiety and heroism of a highwayman very captivating to a youthful imagination, but the arguments for adventurous depredation are so plausible, the allusions so lively, and the contrasts with the ordinary and more painful modes of acquiring property are so artfully displayed, that it requires a cool and strong judgement to resist so imposing an aggregate: yet, I own, I should be very sorry to have 'The Beggar's Opera' suppressed; for there is in it so much of real London life, so much brilliant wit, and such a variety of airs, which, from early association of ideas, engage, soothe, and enliven the mind, that no performance which the theatre exhibits, delights me more.

We talked of a young gentleman's marriage with an eminent singer, and his determination that she should no longer sing in publick, though his father was very earnest she should, because her talents would be liberally rewarded, so as to make her a good fortune. It was questioned whether the young gentleman, who had not a shilling in the world, but was blest with very uncommon talents, was not foolishly delicate, or foolishly proud, and his father truely rational without being mean. Johnson, with all the high spirit of a Roman senator, exclaimed, 'He resolved wisely and nobly to be sure. He is a brave man. Would not a gentleman be disgraced by having his wife singing publickly for hire? No, Sir, there can be no doubt here. I know not if I should not *prepare* myself for a publick singer, as readily as let my wife be one.'

Somebody found fault with writing verses in a dead language, maintaining that they were merely arrangements of so many words, and laughed at the Universities of Oxford and Cambridge, for sending forth collections of them not only in Greek and Latin, but even in Syriack, Arabick, and other more unknown tongues. *Johnson.* 'I would have as many of these as possible; I would have verses in every language that there are the means of acquiring. Nobody imagines that an University is to have at once two hundred poets; but it should be able to show two hundred scholars. Pieresc's death was lamented, I think, in forty languages. And I would have at every coronation, and every death of a King, University-verses, in as many languages as can be acquired. I would have the world to be thus told, "Here is a school where everything may be learnt."'

Having set out next day on a visit to the Earl of Pembroke,

at Wilton, and to my friend, Mr. Temple, at Mamhead, in Devonshire, and not having returned to town till the second of May, I did not see Dr. Johnson for a considerable time, and during the remaining part of my stay in London, kept very imperfect notes of his conversation, which had I according to my usual custom written out at large soon after the time, much might have been preserved, which is now irretrievably lost. I can now only record some particular scenes.

On Monday, May 8, we went together and visited the mansions of Bedlam. I had been informed that he had once been there before with Mr. Wedderburne, (now Lord Loughborough,) Mr. Murphy, and Mr. Foote; and I had heard Foote give a very entertaining account of Johnson's happening to have his attention arrested by a man who was very furious, and who, while beating his straw, supposed it to be William Duke of Cumberland, whom he was punishing for his cruelties in Scotland, in 1746. There was nothing peculiarly remarkable this day; but the general contemplation of insanity was very affecting. I accompanied him home, and dined and drank tea with him.

On Friday, May 12, as he had been so good as to assign me a room in his house, where I might sleep occasionally, when I happened to sit with him to a late hour, I took possession of it this night, found every thing in excellent order, and was attended by honest Francis with a most civil assiduity.

On Saturday, May 13, I breakfasted with him by invitation, accompanied by Mr. Andrew Crosbie, a Scotch Advocate, whom he had seen at Edinburgh, and the Hon. Colonel (now General) Edward Stopford, brother to Lord Courtown, who was desirous of being introduced to him. His tea and rolls and butter, and whole breakfast apparatus were all in such decorum, and his behaviour was so courteous, that Colonel Stopford was quite surprized, and wondered at his having heard so much said of Johnson's slovenliness and roughness. I have preserved nothing of what passed, except that Crosbie pleased him much by talking learnedly of alchymy, as to which Johnson was not a positive unbeliever, but rather delighted in considering what progress had actually been made in the transmutation of metals, what near approaches there had been to the making of gold; and told us that it was affirmed, that a person in the Russian dominions had discovered the secret, but died without revealing it, as imagining it would be prejudicial to society. He added, that it was not impossible but it might in time be generally known.

It being asked whether it was reasonable for a man to be angry at another whom a woman had preferred to him;—*Johnson*. 'I do not see, Sir, that it is reasonable for a man to be angry at another, whom a woman has preferred to him: but angry he is, no doubt; and he is loath to be angry at himself.'

I passed many hours with him on the 17th, of which I find all my memorial is, 'much laughing.' It should seem he had that day been in a humour for jocularity and merriment, and upon such occasions I never knew a man laugh more heartily. We may suppose, that the high relish of a state so different from his habitual gloom, produced more than ordinary exertions of that distinguishing faculty of man, which has puzzled philosophers so much to explain. Johnson's laugh was as remarkable as any circumstance in his manner. It was a kind of good humoured growl. Tom Davies described it drolly enough: 'He laughs like a rhinoceros.'

'TO JAMES BOSWELL, ESQ.

'DEAR SIR,

'I AM now returned from the annual ramble into the middle counties. Having seen nothing I had not seen before, I have nothing to relate. Time has left that part of the island few antiquities; and commerce has left the people no singularities. I was glad to go abroad, and, perhaps, glad to come home; which is, in other words, I was, I am afraid, weary of being at home, and weary of being abroad. Is not this the state of life? But, if we confess this weariness, let us not lament it; for all the wise and all the good say, that we may cure it.

'For the black fumes which rise in your mind, I can prescribe nothing but that you disperse them by honest business or innocent pleasure, and by reading, sometimes easy and sometimes serious. Change of place is useful; and I hope that your residence at Auchinleck will have many good effects.

'Mrs. Thrale was so entertained with your "Journal," that she almost read herself blind. She has a great regard for you.

'Of Mrs. Boswell, though she knows in her heart that she does not love me, I am always glad to hear any good, and hope that she and the little dear ladies will have neither sickness nor any other affliction. But she knows that she does not care what becomes of me, and for that she may be sure that I think her very much to blame.

'Never, my dear Sir, do you take it into your head to think that I do not love you; you may settle yourself in full confidence both of my love and my esteem; I love you as a kind man, I value you as a worthy man, and hope in time to reverence you as a man of exemplary piety. I hold you as Hamlet has it, "in my heart of heart," and therefore, it is little to say, that I am, Sir,

'Your affectionate humble servant,
' SAM. JOHNSON.'

'London, August 7, 1775.'

To THE SAME.

'MY DEAR SIR,

'I NOW write to you, lest in some of your freaks and humours you should fancy yourself neglected. Such fancies I must entreat you never to admit, at least never to indulge; for my regard for you is so radicated and fixed, that it is become part of my mind, and cannot be effaced but by some cause uncommonly violent; therefore, whether I write or not, set your thoughts at rest. I now write to tell you that I shall not very soon write again, for I am to set out to-morrow on another journey.

'Your friends are all well at Streatham, and in Leicester-fields. Make my compliments to Mrs. Boswell, if she is in good humour with me.

'I am, Sir, &c.
' SAM. JOHNSON.'

'September 14, 1775.'

What he mentions in such light terms as, 'I am to set out to-morrow on another journey,' I soon afterwards discovered was no less than a tour to France with Mr. and Mrs. Thrale. This was the only time in his life that he went upon the Continent.

'To MR. ROBERT LEVET.

'Sept. 18, 1775.
Calais.

'DEAR SIR,

'WE ARE here in France, after a very pleasing passage of no more than six hours. I know not when I shall write again, and therefore I write now, though you cannot suppose that I have much to say. You have seen France yourself. From this place we are going to Rouen, and from Rouen to Paris, where Mr. Thrale designs to stay about five or six weeks. We have a regular recommendation to the English resident, so we shall not be taken for vagabonds. We think to go one way and return another, and see as much as we can. I will try to speak a little French; I tried hitherto but little, but I spoke sometimes. If I heard better, I suppose I should learn faster. I am, Sir,

'Your humble servant,
'SAM. JOHNSON.'

TO THE SAME.

'Paris, Oct. 22, 1775.
'DEAR SIR,
'WE ARE still here, commonly very busy in looking about us. We have been to-day at Versailles. You have seen it, and I shall not describe it. We came yesterday from Fontainbleau, where the Court is now. We went to see the King and Queen at dinner, and the Queen was so impressed by Miss[1], that she sent one of the Gentlemen to enquire who she was. I find all true that you have ever told me of Paris. Mr. Thrale is very liberal, and keeps us two coaches, and a very fine table; but I think our cookery very bad. Mrs. Thrale got into a convent of English nuns, and I talked with her through the grate, and I am very kindly used by the English Benedictine friars. But upon the whole I cannot make much acquaintance here; and though the churches, palaces, and some private houses are very magnificent, there is no very great pleasure after having seen many, in seeing more; at least the pleasure, whatever it be, must some time have an end, and we are beginning to think when we shall come home. Mr. Thrale calculates that as we left Streatham on the fifteenth of September, we shall see it again about the fifteenth of November.

'I think I had not been on this side of the sea five days before I found a sensible improvement in my health. I ran a race in the rain this day, and beat Baretti. Baretti is a fine fellow, and speaks French, I think, quite as well as English.

'Make my compliments to Mrs. Williams; and give my love to Francis; and tell my friends that I am not lost.

'I am, dear Sir,
'Your affectionate humble, &c.
'SAM. JOHNSON.'

[1] Miss Thrale. The queen was Marie Antoinette.

'To Dr. Samuel Johnson.

'Edinburgh, Oct. 24, 1775.

'My Dear Sir,

'If I had not been informed that you were at Paris, you should have had a letter from me by the earliest opportunity, announcing the birth of my Son, on the 9th instant; I have named him Alexander, after my father. I now write, as I suppose your fellow traveller, Mr. Thrale, will return to London this week, to attend his duty in Parliament, and that you will not stay behind him.

'Shall we have "*A Journey to Paris*" from you in the winter? You will, I hope, at any rate be kind enough to give me some account of your French travels very soon, for I am very impatient. What a different scene have you viewed this autumn, from that which you viewed in autumn 1773! I ever am, my dear Sir,

'Your much obliged and

'Affectionate humble servant,

'James Boswell.'

'To James Boswell, Esq.

'Dear Sir,

'I am glad that the young Laird is born, and an end, as I hope, put to the only difference that you can ever have with Mrs. Boswell. I know that she does not love me; but I intend to persist in wishing her well till I get the better of her.

'Paris is, indeed, a place very different from the Hebrides, but it is to a hasty traveller not so fertile of novelty, nor affords so many opportunities of remark. I cannot pretend to tell the publick any thing of a place better known to many of my readers than to myself. We can talk of it when we meet.

'I have been remarkably healthy all the journey, and hope you and your family have known only that trouble and danger which has so happily terminated. Among all the congratulations that you may receive, I hope you believe none more warm or sincere, than those of, dear Sir,

'Your most affectionate,

'Sam. Johnson.'

'November 16, 1775.'

'To Mrs. Lucy Porter, in Lichfield.

'Dear Madam,

'This week I came home from Paris. I have brought you a little box, which I thought pretty; but I know not whether it is properly a snuff-box, or a box for some other use. I will send it, when I can find an opportunity. I have been through the whole journey remarkably well. My fellow-travellers were the same whom you saw at Lichfield, only we took Baretti with us. Paris is not so fine a place as you would expect. The palaces and churches, however, are very splendid and magnificent; and what would please you, there are many very fine pictures; but I do not think their way of life commodious or pleasant.

'Let me know how your health has been all this while. I hope the fine summer has given you strength sufficient to encounter the winter.

'Make my compliments to all my friends; and, if your fingers will let you, write to me, or let your maid write, if it be troublesome to you. I am, dear Madam,

'Your most affectionate humble servant,
'SAM. JOHNSON.'

'Nov. 16, 1775.'

TO THE SAME.

'DEAR MADAM,

'SOME weeks ago I wrote to you, to tell you that I was just come home from a ramble, and hoped that I should have heard from you. I am afraid winter has laid hold on your fingers, and hinders you from writing. However, let somebody write, if you cannot, and tell me how you do, and a little of what has happened at Lichfield among our friends. I hope you are all well.

'When I was in France, I thought myself growing young, but am afraid that cold weather will take part of my new vigour from me. Let us, however, take care of ourselves, and lose no part of our health by negligence.

'Do, my dear love, write to me; and do not let us forget each other. This is the season of good wishes, and I wish you all good.

'I am, dear Madam,
'Yours most affectionately,
'SAM. JOHNSON.'

'December, 1775.'

It is to be regretted, that he did not write an account of his travels in France; for as he is reported to have once said, that 'he could write the Life of a Broomstick,' [1] so, notwithstanding so many former travellers have exhausted almost every subject for remark in that great kingdom, his very accurate observa-

[1] Swift, in 1710, had written an essay entitled "A Meditation upon a Broom-Stick."

tion, and peculiar vigour of thought and illustration, would have produced a valuable work. During his visit to it, which lasted but about two months, he wrote notes or minutes of what he saw. He promised to show me them, but I neglected to put him in mind of it; and the greatest part of them has been lost, or, perhaps, destroyed in a precipitate burning of his papers a few days before his death, which must ever be lamented.

When I met him in London the following year, the account which he gave me of his French tour, was, 'Sir, I have seen all the visibilities of Paris, and around it; but to have formed an acquaintance with the people there, would have required more time than I could stay. I was just beginning to creep into acquaintance by means of Colonel Drumgould, a very high man, Sir, head of *L'Ecole Militaire,* a most complete character, for he had first been a professor of rhetorick, and then became a soldier. And, Sir, I was very kindly treated by the English Benedictines, and have a cell appropriated to me in their convent.'

He observed, 'The great in France live very magnificently, but the rest very miserably. There is no happy middle state as in England. The shops of Paris are mean; the meat in the markets is such as would be sent to a gaol in England: and Mr. Thrale justly observed, that the cookery of the French was forced upon them by necessity; for they could not eat their meat, unless they added some taste to it. The French are an indelicate people; they will spit upon any place. At Madame ⸺'s, a literary lady of rank, the footman took the sugar in his fingers, and threw it into my coffee. I was going to put it aside; but hearing it was made on purpose for me, I e'en tasted Tom's fingers. The same lady would needs make tea *à l'Angloise.* The spout of the tea-pot did not pour freely: she bad the footman blow into it. France is worse than Scotland in every thing but climate. Nature has done more for the French; but they have done less for themselves than the Scotch have done.'

It happened that Foote was at Paris at the same time with Dr. Johnson, and his description of my friend while there, was abundantly ludicrous. He told me, that the French were quite astonished at his figure and manner, and at his dress, which he obstinately continued exactly as in London;—his brown clothes, black stockings, and plain shirt.

While Johnson was in France, he was generally very resolute in speaking Latin. It was a maxim with him that a man should not let himself down, by speaking a language which he speaks imperfectly. Indeed, we must have often observed how infe-riour, how much like a child a man appears, who speaks a broken tongue. When Sir Joshua Reynolds, at one of the din-ners of the Royal Academy, presented him to a Frenchman of great distinction, he would not deign to speak French, but talked Latin, though his Excellency did not understand it, ow-ing, perhaps, to Johnson's English pronunciation: yet upon another occasion he was observed to speak French to a French-man of high rank, who spoke English; and being asked the reason, with some expression of surprise,—he answered, 'be-cause I think my French is as good as his English.'

Here let me not forget a curious anecdote, as related to me by Mr. Beauclerk, which I shall endeavour to exhibit as well as I can in that gentleman's lively manner; and in justice to him it is proper to add, that Dr. Johnson told me I might rely both on the correctness of his memory, and the fidelity of his narrative. 'When Madame de Boufflers was first in England, (said Beauclerk,) she was desirous to see Johnson. I accord-ingly went with her to his chambers in the Temple, where she was entertained with his conversation for some time. When our visit was over, she and I left him, and were got into Inner Temple-lane, when all at once I heard a noise like thunder. This was occasioned by Johnson, who it seems, upon a little recollection, had taken it into his head that he ought to have done the honours of his literary residence to a foreign lady of quality, and eager to show himself a man of gallantry, was hurrying down the stair-case in violent agitation. He overtook us before we reached the Temple-gate, and brushing in be-tween me and Madame de Boufflers, seized her hand, and con-ducted her to her coach. His dress was a rusty brown morning suit, a pair of old shoes by way of slippers, a little shrivelled wig sticking on the top of his head, and the sleeves of his shirt and the knees of his breeches hanging loose. A considerable crowd of people gathered round, and were not a little struck by this singular appearance.'

In the course of this year Dr. Burney informs me, that 'he very frequently met Dr. Johnson at Mr. Thrale's, at Streatham, where they had many long conversations, often sitting up as long as the fire and candles lasted, and much longer than the patience of the servants subsisted.'

A few of Johnson's sayings, which that gentleman recollects, shall here be inserted.

'I never take a nap after dinner but when I have had a bad night, and then the nap takes me.'

'The writer of an epitaph should not be considered as saying nothing but what is strictly true. Allowance must be made for some degree of exaggerated praise. In lapidary inscriptions a man is not upon oath.'

'There is now less flogging in our great schools than formerly, but then less is learned there; so that what the boys get at one end, they lose at the other.'

'I hate by-roads in education. Education is as well known, and has long been as well known, as ever it can be. Endeavouring to make children prematurely wise is useless labour. Suppose they have more knowledge at five or six years old than other children, what use can be made of it? It will be lost before it is wanted, and the waste of so much time and labour of the teacher can never be repaid. Too much is expected from precocity, and too little performed. Miss —— was an instance of early cultivation, but in what did it terminate? In marrying a little Presbyterian parson, who keeps an infant boarding-school, so that all her employment now is,

"To suckle fools, and chronicle small-beer."

She tells the children, "This is a cat, and that is a dog, with four legs and a tail; see there! you are much better than a cat or a dog, for you can speak."'

'After having talked slightingly of musick, he was observed to listen very attentively while Miss Thrale played on the harp-sichord, and with eagerness he called to her, "Why don't you dash away like Burney?" Dr. Burney upon this said to him, "I believe, Sir, we shall make a musician of you at last." Johnson with candid complacency replied, "Sir, I shall be glad to have a new sense given to me." '

'He had come down one morning to the breakfast-room, and been a considerable time by himself before any body appeared. When on a subsequent day, he was twitted by Mrs. Thrale for being very late, which he generally was, he defended himself by alluding to the extraordinary morning, when he had been too early, "Madam, I do not like to come down to *vacuity*." '

'Dr. Burney having remarked that Mr. Garrick was beginning to look old, he said, "Why, Sir, you are not to wonder at that; no man's face has had more wear and tear." '

Not having heard from him for a longer time than I supposed he would be silent, I wrote to him December 18, not in good spirits,

'Sometimes I have been afraid that the cold which has gone over Europe this year like a sort of pestilence has seized you severely: sometimes my imagination, which is upon occasions prolifick of evil, hath figured that you may have somehow taken offence at some part of my conduct.'

'To JAMES BOSWELL, ESQ.
'DEAR SIR,
'NEVER dream of any offence. How should you offend me? I consider your friendship as a possession, which I intend to hold till you take it from me, and to lament if ever by my fault I should lose it. However, when such suspicions find their way into your mind, always give them vent; I shall make haste to disperse them; but hinder their first ingress if you can. Consider such thoughts as morbid.

'You and your lady will now have no more wrangling about feudal inheritance. How does the young Laird of Auchinleck? I suppose Miss Veronica is grown a reader and discourser.

'I have just now got a cough, but it has never yet hindered me from sleeping: I have had quieter nights than are common with me.

'My compliments to Mrs. Boswell, who does not love me; and of all the rest, I need only send them to those that do: and I am afraid it will give you very little trouble to distribute them.

'I am, my dear, dear Sir,
'Your affectionate humble servant,
'SAM. JOHNSON.'
'December 23, 1775.'

1776: ÆTAT. 67.]—In 1776, Johnson wrote, so far as I can discover, nothing for the publick: but that his mind was still ardent, and fraught with generous wishes to attain to still higher degrees of literary excellence, is proved by his private notes of this year, which I shall insert in their proper place.

Having arrived in London late on Friday, the 15th of March, I hastened next morning to wait on Dr. Johnson, at his house; but found he was removed from Johnson's-court, No. 7, to Bolt-court, No. 8, still keeping to his favourite Fleet-street. My reflection at the time upon this change as marked in my Journal, is as follows: 'I felt a foolish regret that he had left a court which bore his name; but it was not foolish to be affected with some tenderness of regard for a place in which I had seen him a great deal, from whence I had often issued a better and a happier man than when I went in, and which had often appeared to my imagination while I trod its pavement, in the solemn darkness of the night, to be sacred to wisdom and piety.' Being informed that he was at Mr. Thrale's, in the Borough, I hastened thither, and found Mrs. Thrale and him at breakfast. I was kindly welcomed. In a moment he was in a full glow of conversation, and I felt myself elevated as if brought into another state of being. Mrs. Thrale and I looked to each other while he talked, and our looks expressed our congenial admiration and affection for him. I shall ever recollect this scene with great pleasure. I exclaimed to her, 'I am quite restored by him, by transfusion of *mind*.' 'There are many (she replied) who admire and respect Mr. Johnson; but you and I *love* him.'

He seemed very happy in the near prospect of going to Italy with Mr. and Mrs. Thrale. 'But, (said he,) before leaving England I am to take a jaunt to Oxford, Birmingham, my native city Lichfield, and my old friend, Dr. Taylor's, at Ashbourn, in Derbyshire. I shall go in a few days, and you, Boswell, shall go with me.' I was ready to accompany him; being willing even to leave London to have the pleasure of his conversation.

I mentioned with much regret the extravagance of the representative of a great family in Scotland, by which there was danger of its being ruined; and as Johnson respected it for its antiquity, he joined with me in thinking it would be happy if his person should die. Mrs. Thrale seemed shocked at this, as eudal barbarity; and said, 'I do not understand this preference of the estate to its owner; of the land to the man who walks upon that land.' *Johnson.* 'Nay, Madam, it is not a preference of the land to its owner; it is the preference of a family to an individual. Here is an establishment in a country, which is of importance for ages, not only to the chief but to his people; an establishment which extends upwards and downwards; that this should be destroyed by one idle fellow is a sad thing.'

He said, 'Entails are good, because it is good to preserve in a country, serieses of men, to whom the people are accustomed to look up as to their leaders. But I am for leaving a quantity of land in commerce, to excite industry, and keep money in the country.'

I mentioned Dr. Adam Smith's book on 'The Wealth of Nations,' which was just published, and that Sir John Pringle had observed to me, that Dr. Smith, who had never been in trade, could not be expected to write well on that subject any more than a lawyer upon physick. *Johnson.* 'He is mistaken, Sir: a man who has never been engaged in trade himself may undoubtedly write well upon trade, and there is nothing which requires more to be illustrated by philosophy than trade does. As to mere wealth, that is to say, money, it is clear that one nation or one individual cannot increase its store but by making another poorer: but trade procures what is more valuable, the reciprocation of the peculiar advantages of different countries. A merchant seldom thinks but of his own particular trade. To write a good book upon it, a man must have extensive views. It is not necessary to have practised, to write well upon a subject.'

We got into a boat to cross over to Black-friars; and as we moved along the Thames, I talked to him of a little volume, which, altogether unknown to him, was advertised to be published in a few days, under the title of '*Johnsoniana*, or *Bon Mots* of Dr. Johnson.' *Johnson.* 'Sir, it is a mighty impudent thing.' *Boswell.* 'Pray, Sir, could you have no redress if you were to prosecute a publisher for bringing out, under your name, what you never said, and ascribing to you dull stupid nonsense, or making you swear profanely, as many ignorant relaters of your *bon mots* do?' *Johnson*. 'No, Sir; there will always be some truth mixed with the falsehood, and how can it be ascertained how much is true and how much is false? Besides, Sir, what damages would a jury give me for having been represented as swearing?' *Boswell*. 'I think, Sir, you should at least disavow such a publication, because the world and posterity might with much plausible foundation say, "Here is a volume which was publickly advertised and came out in Dr. Johnson's own time, and, by his silence, was admitted by him to be genuine."' *Johnson*. 'I shall give myself no trouble about the matter.'

He was, perhaps, above suffering from such spurious publications; but I could not help thinking, that many men would be much injured in their reputation, by having absurd and vicious sayings imputed to them; and that redress ought in such cases to be given.

He said, 'The value of every story depends on its being true. A story is a picture either of an individual or of human nature in general: if it be false, it is a picture of nothing. For instance: suppose a man should tell that Johnson, before setting out for Italy, as he had to cross the Alps, sat down to make himself wings. This many people would believe; but it would be a picture of nothing.'

The importance of strict and scrupulous veracity cannot be too often inculcated. Johnson was known to be so rigidly attentive to it, that even in his common conversation the slightest circumstance was mentioned with exact precision. The knowledge of his having such a principle and habit made his friends have a perfect reliance on the truth of every thing that he told, however it might have been doubted if told by many others. As an instance of this, I may mention an odd incident which he related as having happened to him one night in Fleet-street. 'A gentlewoman (said he) begged I would give her my arm to assist her in crossing the street, which I accordingly did; upon which she offered me a shilling, supposing me to be the watchman. I perceived that she was somewhat in liquor.' This, if told by most people, would have been thought an invention; when told by Johnson, it was believed by his friends as much as if they had seen what passed.

We landed at the Temple-stairs, where we parted.

I found him in the evening in Mrs. Williams's room. We talked of religious orders. He said, 'It is as unreasonable for a man to go into a Carthusian convent for fear of being immoral, as for a man to cut off his hands for fear he should steal. There is, indeed, great resolution in the immediate act of dismembering himself; but when that is once done, he has no longer any merit: for though it is out of his power to steal, yet he may all his life be a thief in his heart. So when a man has once become a Carthusian, he is obliged to continue so, whether he chooses it or not. Their silence, too, is absurd. We read in the Gospel of the apostles being sent to preach, but not to hold their tongues. All severity that does not tend to increase good, or prevent evil, is idle. I said to the Lady Abbess of a convent, "Madam, you are here, not for the love of virtue, but the fear of vice." She said, "She should remember this as long as she lived."' I thought it hard to give her this view of her situation, when she could not help it; and, indeed, I wondered at the whole of what he now said; because, both in his 'Rambler' and 'Idler,' he treats religious austerities with much solemnity of respect.

Finding him still persevering in his abstinence from wine, I ventured to speak to him of it.—*Johnson.* 'Sir, I have no objection to a man's drinking wine, if he can do it in moderation. I found myself apt to go to excess in it, and therefore, after having been for some time without it, on account of illness, I thought it better not to return to it. Every man is to judge for himself, according to the effects which he experiences. One of the fathers tells us, he found fasting made him so peevish that he did not practise it.'

Though he often enlarged upon the evil of intoxication, he was by no means harsh and unforgiving to those who indulged in occasional excess in wine. One of his friends, I well remember, came to sup at a tavern with him and some other gentlemen, and too plainly discovered that he had drunk too much at dinner. When one who loved mischief, thinking to produce a severe censure, asked Johnson, a few days afterwards, 'Well, Sir, what did your friend say to you, as an apology for being in such a situation?' Johnson answered, 'Sir, he said all that a man *should* say: he said he was sorry for it.'

I heard him once give a very judicious practical advice upon this subject: 'A man, who has been drinking wine at all freely should never go into a new company. With those who have partaken of wine with him, he may be pretty well in unison but he will probably be offensive, or appear ridiculous, to other people.'

He allowed very great influence to education. 'I do not deny Sir, but there is some original difference in minds; but it is nothing in comparison of what is formed by education. We may instance the science of *numbers,* which all minds are equally capable of attaining; yet we find a prodigious difference in the powers of different men, in that respect, after they are grown up, because their minds have been more or less exercised in it: and I think the same cause will explain the difference of excellence in other things, gradations admitting always some difference in the first principles.'

I again visited him on Monday. He took occasion to enlarge, as he often did, upon the wretchedness of a sea-life. 'A ship is worse than a gaol. There is, in a gaol, better air, better company, better conveniency of every kind; and a ship has the additional disadvantage of being in danger. When men come to like a sea-life, they are not fit to live on land.'—'Then (said I) it would be cruel in a father to breed his son to the sea.' *Johnson.* 'It would be cruel in a father who thinks as I do. Men go to sea, before they know the unhappiness of that way of life; and when they have come to know it, they cannot escape from it, because it is then too late to choose another profession; as indeed is generally the case with men, when they have once engaged in any particular way of life.'

On Tuesday, March 19, which was fixed for our proposed jaunt, we met in the morning at the Somerset coffee-house in the Strand, where we were taken up by the Oxford coach. He was accompanied by Mr. Gwyn, the architect; and a gentleman of Merton College, whom we did not know, had the fourth seat. We soon got into conversation; for it was very remarkable of Johnson, that the presence of a stranger was no restraint upon his talk. I observed that Garrick, who was about to quit the stage, would soon have an easier life. *Johnson.* 'I doubt that, Sir.' *Boswell.* 'Why, Sir, he will be Atlas with the burthen off his back.' *Johnson.* 'But I know not, Sir, if he will be so steady without his load. However, he should never play any more, but be entirely the gentleman, and not partly the player: he should no longer subject himself to be hissed by a mob, or to be insolently treated by performers, whom he used to rule with a high hand, and who would gladly retaliate.' *Boswell.* 'I think he should play once a year for the benefit of decayed actors, as it has been said he means to do.' *Johnson.* 'Alas, Sir! he will soon be a decayed actor himself.'

Johnson expressed his disapprobation of ornamental architecture, such as magnificent columns supporting a portico, or expensive pilasters supporting merely their own capitals, 'because it consumes labour disproportionate to its utility.' For the same reason he satyrised statuary. 'Painting (said he) consumes labour not disproportionate to its effect; but a fellow will hack half a year at a block of marble to make something in stone that hardly resembles a man. The value of statuary is owing to its difficulty. You would not value the finest head cut upon a carrot.' Here he seemed to me to be strangely deficient in taste; for surely statuary is a noble art of imitation, and preserves a wonderful expression of the varieties of the human frame; and although it must be allowed that the circumstances of difficulty enhance the value of a marble head, we should consider, that if it requires a long time in the performance, it has a proportionate value in durability.

Gwyn was a fine lively rattling fellow. Dr. Johnson kept him in subjection, but with a kindly authority. The spirit of the artist, however, rose against what he thought a Gothick attack, and he made a brisk defence. 'What, Sir, will you allow no value to beauty in architecture or in statuary? Why should we allow it then in writing? Why do you take the trouble to give us so many fine allusions, and bright images, and elegant phrases? You might convey all your instruction without these ornaments.' Johnson smiled with complacency; but said, 'Why, Sir, all these ornaments are useful, because they obtain an easier reception for truth; but a building is not at all more convenient for being decorated with superfluous carved work.'

Gwyn at last was lucky enough to make one reply to Dr. Johnson, which he allowed to be excellent. Johnson censured him for taking down a church which might have stood many years, and building a new one at a different place, for no other reason but that there might be a direct road to a new bridge; and his expression was, 'You are taking a church out of the way, that the people may go in a straight line to the bridge.'— 'No, Sir, (said Gwyn,) I am putting the church *in* the way, that the people may not *go out of the way.*' *Johnson.* (with a hearty loud laugh of approbation,) 'Speak no more. Rest your colloquial fame upon this.'

Upon our arrival at Oxford, Dr. Johnson and I went directly to University College, but were disappointed on finding that one of the fellows, his friend Mr. Scott, who accompanied him from Newcastle to Edinburgh, was gone to the country. We put up at the Angel inn, and passed the evening by ourselves in easy and familiar conversation. Talking of constitutional melancholy, he observed, 'A man so afflicted, Sir, must divert distressing thoughts, and not combat with them.' *Boswell.* 'May not he think them down, Sir?' *Johnson.* 'No, Sir. To attempt to *think them down* is madness. He should have a lamp constantly burning in his bed-chamber during the night, and if wakefully disturbed, take a book, and read, and compose himself to rest. To have the management of the mind is a great art, and it may be attained in a considerable degree by experience and habitual exercise.' *Boswell.* 'Should not he provide amusements for himself? Would it not, for instance, be right for him to take a course of chymistry?' *Johnson.* 'Let him take a course of chymistry, or a course of rope-dancing, or a course of any thing to which he is inclined at the time. Let him contrive to have as many retreats for his mind as he can, as many things to which it can fly from itself. Burton's "Anatomy of Melancholy" is a valuable work. It is, perhaps, overloaded with quotation. But there is great spirit and great power in what Burton says, when he writes from his own mind.'

We went to Pembroke College, and waited on his old friend Dr. Adams, the master of it, whom I found to be a most polite, pleasing, communicative man. Before his advancement to the headship of his college, I had intended to go and visit him at

Shrewsbury, where he was rector of St. Chad's, in order to get from him what particulars he could recollect of Johnson's academical life. He now obligingly gave me part of that authentick information, which, with what I afterwards owed to his kindness, will be found incorporated in its proper place in this work.

Dr. Adams had distinguished himself by an able answer to David Hume's 'Essay on Miracles.' He told me he had once dined in company with Hume in London; that Hume shook hands with him, and said, 'You have treated me much better than I deserve;' and that they exchanged visits. I took the liberty to object to treating an infidel writer with smooth civility. Where there is a controversy concerning a passage in a classick authour, or concerning a question in antiquities, or any other subject in which human happiness is not deeply interested, a man may treat his antagonist with politeness and even respect. But where the controversy is concerning the truth of religion, it is of such vast importance to him who maintains it, to obtain the victory, that the person of an opponent ought not to be spared. If a man firmly believes that religion is an invaluable treasure, he will consider a writer who endeavours to deprive mankind of it as a *robber*; he will look upon him as *odious*, though the Infidel might think himself in the right. A robber who reasons as the gang do in the 'Beggar's Opera,' who call themselves *practical* philosophers, and may have as much sincerity as pernicious *speculative* philosophers, is not the less an object of just indignation. An abandoned profligate may think that it is not wrong to debauch my wife; but shall I, therefore, not detest him? And if I catch him in making an attempt, shall I treat him with politeness? No, I will kick him down stairs, or run him through the body; that is, if I really love my wife, or have a true rational notion of honour. An Infidel then shall not be treated handsomely by a Christian, merely because he endeavours to rob with ingenuity.[1] Johnson coincided with me and said, 'When a man voluntarily engages in an important controversy, he is to do all he can to lessen his antagonist, be-

---

[1] It is a little difficult to reconcile these sentiments with the eagerness, even self-abasement, with which Boswell sought the society of Hume, Voltaire, Rousseau and Wilkes.

cause authority from personal respect has much weight with most people, and often more than reasoning. If my antagonist writes bad language, though that may not be essential to the question, I will attack him for his bad language.' *Adams.* 'You would not jostle a chimney-sweeper.' *Johnson.* 'Yes, Sir, if it were necessary to jostle him *down*.'

Dr. Adams told us, that in some of the Colleges at Oxford, the fellows had excluded the students from social intercourse with them in the common room. *Johnson.* 'They are in the right, Sir, for there can be no real conversation, no fair exertion of mind amongst them, if the young men are by; for a man who has a character does not choose to stake it in their presence.' *Boswell.* 'But, Sir, may there not be very good conversation without a contest for superiority?' *Johnson.* 'No animated conversation, Sir, for it cannot be but one or other will come off superiour. I do not mean that the victor must have the better of the argument, for he may take the weak side; but his superiority of parts and knowledge will necessarily appear: and he to whom he thus shews himself superiour is lessened in the eyes of the young men.'

We walked with Dr. Adams into the master's garden, and into the common room. *Johnson.* (after a reverie of meditation,) 'Ay! Here I used to play at draughts with Phil. Jones and Fludyer. Jones loved beer, and did not get very forward in the church. Fludyer turned out a scoundrel, a Whig, and said he was ashamed of having been bred at Oxford. He had a living at Putney, and got under the eye of some retainers to the court at that time, and so became a violent Whig: but he had been a scoundrel all along, to be sure.' *Boswell.* 'Was he a scoundrel, Sir, in any other way than that of being a political scoundrel? Did he cheat at draughts?' *Johnson.* 'Sir, we never played for *money*.'

He then carried me to visit Dr. Bentham, Canon of Christ-Church, and Divinity Professor, with whose learned and lively conversation we were much pleased. He gave us an invitation to dinner, which Dr. Johnson told me was a high honour. 'Sir, it is a great thing to dine with the Canons at Christ-Church.' We could not accept his invitation, as we were engaged to dine at University College. We had an excellent dinner there, with the Master and Fellows, it being St. Cuthbert's day, which is kept by them as a festival, as he was a saint of Durham, with which this college is much connected.

We then went to Trinity College, where he introduced me to Mr. Thomas Warton, with whom we passed a part of the evening. We talked of biography.—*Johnson*. 'It is rarely well executed. They only who live with a man can write his life with any genuine exactness and discrimination; and few people who have lived with a man know what to remark about him. The chaplain of a late Bishop, whom I was to assist in writing some memoirs of his Lordship, could tell me scarcely any thing.'

I said, Mr. Robert Dodsley's life should be written, as he had been so much connected with the wits of his time, and by his literary merit had raised himself from the station of a footman. Mr. Warton said, he had published a little volume under the title of 'The Muse in Livery.' *Johnson*. 'I doubt whether Dodsley's brother would thank a man who should write his life: yet Dodsley himself was not unwilling that his original low condition should be recollected. When Lord Lyttelton's "Dialogues of the Dead" came out, one of which is between Apicius, an ancient epicure, and Dartineuf, a modern epicure, Dodsley said to me, "I knew Dartineuf well, for I was once his footman."'

Biography led us to speak of Dr. John Campbell, who had written a considerable part of the *'Biographia Britannica.'* Johnson, though he valued him highly, was of opinion that there was not so much in his great work, 'A Political Survey of Great Britain,' as the world had been taught to expect; and had said to me, that he believed Campbell's disappointment, on account of the bad success of that work, had killed him. He this evening observed of it, 'That work was his death.' Mr. Warton, not adverting to his meaning, answered, 'I believe so; from the great attention he bestowed on it.' *Johnson*. 'Nay, Sir, he died of *want* of attention, if he died at all by that book.'

We talked of a work much in vogue at that time, written in a very mellifluous style, but which, under pretext of another subject, contained much artful infidelity.[1] I said it was not fair to attack us thus unexpectedly; he should have warned us of our danger, before we entered his garden of flowery eloquence, by advertising, 'Spring-guns and man-traps set here.' The authour had been an Oxonian, and was remembered there for having 'turned Papist.' I observed, that as he had changed several times—from the Church of England to the Church of Rome,—from the Church of Rome to infidelity,—I did not despair yet of seeing him a methodist preacher. *Johnson.* (laughing.) 'It is said, that his range has been more extensive, and that he has once been Mahometan. However, now that he has published his infidelity, he will probably persist in it.'

Mr. Warton, being engaged, could not sup with us at our inn; we had therefore another evening by ourselves. I asked Johnson, whether a man's being forward in making himself known to eminent people, and seeing as much of life, and getting as much information as he could in every way was not yet lessening himself by his forwardness. *Johnson.* 'No, Sir; a man always makes himself greater as he increases his knowledge.'

I censured some ludicrous fantastick dialogues between two coach-horses, and other such stuff, which Baretti had lately published. He joined with me, and said, 'Nothing odd will do long. "Tristram Shandy" did not last.' I expressed a desire to be acquainted with a lady who had been much talked of, and universally celebrated for extraordinary address and insinuation. *Johnson.* 'Never believe extraordinary characters which you hear of people. Depend upon it, Sir, they are exaggerated. You do not see one man shoot a great deal higher than another.' I mentioned Mr. Burke. *Johnson.* 'Yes; Burke *is* an extraordinary man. His stream of mind is perpetual.' It *is* very pleasing to me to record, that Johnson's high estimation of the talents of this gentleman was uniform from their early acquaintance. Sir Joshua Reynolds informs me, that when Mr. Burke was first elected a member of Parliament, and Sir John Hawkins expressed a wonder at his attaining a seat, Johnson said, 'Now we who know Burke, know, that he will be one of

---

[1] Gibbon's *Decline and Fall of the Roman Empire,* the first volume of which had just appeared.

the first men in this country.' And once, when Johnson was ill, and unable to exert himself as much as usual without fatigue, Mr. Burke having been mentioned, he said, 'That fellow calls forth all my powers. Were I to see Burke now, it would kill me.' So much was he accustomed to consider conversation as a con·test, and such was his notion of Burke as an opponent.

Next morning, Thursday, March 21, we set out in a post-chaise to pursue our ramble. It was a delightful day, and we drove through Blenheim Park. I observed to him, while in the midst of the noble scene around us, 'You and I, Sir, have, I think, seen together the extremes of what can be seen in Britain:—the wild rough island of Mull, and Blenheim Park.'

We dined at an excellent inn at Chapel-house, where he expatiated on the felicity of England in its taverns and inns, and triumphed over the French for not having, in any perfection, the tavern life. 'There is no private house, (said he,) in which people can enjoy themselves so well, as at a capital tavern. Let there be ever so great plenty of good things, ever so much grandeur, ever so much elegance, ever so much desire that every body should be easy; in the nature of things it cannot be: there must always be some degree of care and anxiety. The master of the house is anxious to entertain his guests; the guests are anxious to be agreeable to him: and no man, but a very impudent dog indeed, can as freely command what is in another man's house, as if it were his own. Whereas, at a tavern, there is a general freedom from anxiety. You are sure you are welcome: and the more noise you make, the more trouble you give, the more good things you call for, the welcomer you are. No servants will attend you with the alacrity which waiters do, who are incited by the prospect of an immediate reward in proportion as they please. No, Sir; there is nothing which has yet been contrived by man, by which so much happiness is produced as by a good tavern or inn.'

In the afternoon, as we were driven rapidly along in the post-chaise, he said to me, 'Life has not many things better than this.'

We stopped at Stratford-upon-Avon, and drank tea and coffee; and it pleased me to be with him upon the classick ground of Shakspeare's native place.

I told him, that I heard Dr. Percy was writing the history of the wolf in Great-Britain. *Johnson.* 'The wolf, Sir! why the wolf? Why does he not write of the bear, which we had formerly? Nay, it is said we had the beaver. Or why does he not write of the grey rat, the Hanover rat, as it is called, because it is said to have come into this country about the time that the family of Hanover came? I should like to see *"The History of the Grey Rat, by Thomas Percy, D.D. Chaplain in Ordinary to His Majesty,"* ' (laughing immoderately). *Boswell.* 'I am afraid a court chaplain could not decently write of the grey rat.' *Johnson.* 'Sir, he need not give it the name of the Hanover rat.' Thus could he indulge a luxuriant sportive imagination, when talking of a friend whom he loved and esteemed.

He mentioned to me the singular history of an ingenious acquaintance. 'He had practised physick in various situations with no great emolument. A West-India gentleman, whom he delighted by his conversation, gave him a bond for a handsome annuity during his life, on the condition of his accompanying him to the West-Indies, and living with him there for two years. He accordingly embarked with the gentleman; but upon the voyage fell in love with a young woman who happened to be one of the passengers, and married the wench. From the imprudence of his disposition he quarrelled with the gentleman, and declared he would have no connection with him. So he forfeited the annuity. He settled as a physician in one of the Leeward Islands. A man was sent out to him merely to compound his medicines. This fellow set up as a rival to him in his practice of physick, and got so much the better of him in the opinion of the people of the island, that he carried away all the business; upon which he returned to England, and soon after died.'

On Friday, March 22, having set out early from Henley, where we had lain the preceding night, we arrived at Birmingham about nine o'clock, and, after breakfast, went to call on his old schoolfellow Mr. Hector. A very stupid maid, who opened the door, told us, that 'her master was gone out; he was gone to the country; she could not tell when he would return.' In short, she gave us a miserable reception; and Johnson observed, 'She would have behaved no better to people who wanted him in the way of his profession.' He said to her, 'My name is Johnson; tell him I called. Will you remember the name?' She answered with rustick simplicity, in the Warwickshire pronunciation, 'I don't understand you, Sir.'—'Blockhead, (said he,) I'll write.' I never heard the word *blockhead* applied to a woman before, though I do not see why it should not, when there is evident occasion for it. He, however, made another attempt to make her understand him, and roared loud in her ear, *'Johnson,'* and then she catched the sound.

We next called on Mr. Lloyd, one of the people called Quakers. He too was not at home; but Mrs. Lloyd was, and received us courteously, and asked us to dinner. Johnson said to me, 'After the uncertainty of all human things at Hector's, this invitation came very well.' We walked about the town, and he was pleased to see it increasing.

I talked of legitimation by subsequent marriage, which obtained in the Roman law, and still obtains in the law of Scotland. *Johnson.* 'I think it a bad thing; because the chastity of women being of the utmost importance, as all property depends upon it, they who forfeit it should not have any possibility of being restored to good character; nor should the children, by an illicit connection, attain the full rights of lawful children, by the posteriour consent of the offending parties.'

Mr. Lloyd joined us in the street; and in a little while we met *Friend Hector,* as Mr. Lloyd called him. It gave me pleasure to observe the joy which Johnson and he expressed on seeing each other again. Mr. Lloyd and I left them together, while he obligingly shewed me some of the manufactures of this very curious assemblage of artificers. We all met at dinner at Mr. Lloyd's, where we were entertained with great hospitality. Mr. and Mrs. Lloyd had been married the same year with their Majesties, and, like them, had been blessed with a numerous family of fine children, their numbers being exactly the same. Johnson said, 'Marriage is the best state for man in general; and every man is a worse man, in proportion as he is unfit for the married state.'

Mr. Hector was so good as to accompany me to see the great works of Mr. Bolton, at a place which he has called Soho, about two miles from Birmingham, which the very ingenious proprietor shewed me himself to the best advantage. I wish that Johnson had been with us; for it was a scene which I should have been glad to contemplate by his light. The vastness and the contrivance of some of the machinery would have 'matched his mighty mind.' I shall never forget Mr. Bolton's expression to me: 'I sell here, Sir, what all the world desires to have—*Power*.'

From Mr. Hector I now learnt many particulars of Dr. Johnson's early life, which, with others that he gave me at different times since, have contributed to the formation of this work.

Dr. Johnson said to me in the morning, 'You will see, Sir, at Mr. Hector's, his sister, Mrs. Careless, a clergyman's widow. She was the first woman with whom I was in love. It dropt out of my head imperceptibly; but she and I shall always have a kindness for each other.' He laughed at the notion that a man never can be really in love but once, and considered it as a mere romantick fancy.

On our return from Mr. Bolton's, Mr. Hector took me to his house, where we found Johnson sitting placidly at tea, with his *first love*; who, though now advanced in years, was a genteel woman, very agreeable, and well-bred.

Johnson lamented to Mr. Hector the state of one of their school-fellows, Mr. Charles Congreve, a clergyman, which he thus described: 'He obtained, I believe, considerable preferment in Ireland, but now lives in London, quite as a valetudinarian, afraid to go into any house but his own. He takes a short airing in his post-chaise every day. He has an elderly woman, whom he calls cousin, who lives with him, and jogs his elbow, when his glass has stood too long empty, and encourages him in drinking, in which he is very willing to be encouraged; not that he gets drunk, for he is a very pious man, but he is always muddy. He confesses to one bottle of port every day, and he probably drinks more. He is quite unsocial; his conversation is monosyllabical: and when, at my last visit, I asked him what a clock it was? that signal of my departure had so pleasing an effect on him, that he sprung up to look at his watch, like a greyhound bounding at a hare.'

When he again talked of Mrs. Careless to-night, he seemed to have had his affection revived; for he said, 'If I had married her, it might have been as happy for me.' *Boswell.* 'Pray, Sir, do you not suppose that there are fifty women in the world, with any one of whom a man may be as happy, as with any one woman in particular.' *Johnson.* 'Ay, Sir, fifty thousand.' *Boswell.* 'Then, Sir, you are not of opinion with some who imagine that certain men and certain women are made for each other; and that they cannot be happy if they miss their counterparts.' *Johnson.* 'To be sure not, Sir. I believe marriages would in general be as happy, and often more so, if they were all made by the Lord Chancellor, upon a due consideration of characters and circumstances, without the parties having any choice in the matter.'

I wished to have staid at Birmingham to-night, to have talked more with Mr. Hector; but my friend was impatient to reach his native city: so we drove on that stage in the dark, and were long pensive and silent. When we came within the focus of the Lichfield lamps, 'Now (said he,) we are getting out of a state of death.' We put up at the Three Crowns, not one of the great inns, but a good old fashioned one, which was kept by Mr. Wilkins, and was the very next house to that in which Johnson was born and brought up, and which was still his own property. We had a comfortable supper, and got into high spirits. I felt all my Toryism glow in this old capital of Staffordshire.

Next morning he introduced me to Mrs. Lucy Porter, his step-daughter. She was now an old maid, with much simplicity of manner. She had never been in London. Her brother, a Captain in the navy, had left her a fortune of ten thousand pounds; about a third of which she had laid out in building a stately house, and making a handsome garden, in an elevated situation in Lichfield. Johnson, when here by himself, used to live at her house. She reverenced him, and he had a parental tenderness for her.

We then visited Mr. Peter Garrick, who had that morning received a letter from his brother David, announcing our coming to Lichfield. He was engaged to dinner, but asked us to tea, and to sleep at his house. Johnson, however, would not quit his old acquaintance Wilkins, of the Three Crowns. The family likeness of the Garricks was very striking; and Johnson thought that David's vivacity was not so peculiar to himself as was supposed. 'Sir, (said he,) I don't know but if Peter had cultivated all the arts of gaiety as much as David has done, he might have been as brisk and lively. Depend upon it, Sir, vivacity is much an art, and depends greatly on habit.'

We dined at our inn, and had with us a Mr. Jackson, one of Johnson's schoolfellows, whom he treated with much kindness, though he seemed to be a low man, dull and untaught. He had a coarse grey coat, black waistcoat, greasy leather breeches, and a yellow uncurled wig; and his countenance had the ruddiness which betokens one who is in no haste to 'leave his can.' He drank only ale. He had tried to be a cutler at Birmingham, but had not succeeded; and now he lived poorly at home, and had some scheme of dressing leather in a better manner than common; to his indistinct account of which, Dr. Johnson listened with patient attention, that he might assist him with his advice. Here was an instance of genuine humanity and real kindness in this great man, who has been most unjustly represented as altogether harsh and destitute of tenderness. A thousand such instances might have been recorded in the course of his long life; though, that his temper was warm and hasty, and his manner often rough, cannot be denied.

He expatiated in praise of Lichfield and its inhabitants, who, he said, were 'the most sober, decent people in England, the genteelest in proportion to their wealth, and spoke the purest English.' I doubted as to the last article of this eulogy: for they had several provincial sounds; as, *there,* pronounced like *fear,* instead of like *fair; once* pronounced *woonse,* instead of *wunse,* or *wonse.* Johnson himself never got entirely free of those provincial accents. Garrick sometimes used to take him off, squeezing a lemon into a punch-bowl, with uncouth gesticulations, looking round the company, and calling out, 'Who's for *poonsh?'*

Very little business appeared to be going forward in Lichfield. I found however two strange manufactures for so inland a place, sail-cloth and streamers for ships; and I observed them making some saddle-cloths, and dressing sheepskins: but upon the whole, the busy hand of industry seemed to be quite slackened. 'Surely, Sir, (said I,) you are an idle set of people.' 'Sir, (said Johnson,) we are a city of philosophers: we work with our heads, and make the boobies of Birmingham work for us with their hands.'

When we were by ourselves he told me, 'Forty years ago, Sir, I was in love with an actress here, Mrs. Emmet, who acted Flora, in "Hob in the Well".' What merit this lady had as an actress, or what was her figure, or her manner, I have not been informed: but, if we may believe Mr. Garrick, his old master's taste in theatrical merit was by no means refined. Garrick used to tell, that Johnson said of an actor, who played Sir Harry Wildair at Lichfield, 'There is a courtly vivacity about the fellow;' when in fact, according to Garrick's account, 'he was the most vulgar ruffian that ever went upon *boards.*'

We went and viewed the museum of Mr. Richard Green, apothecary here, who told me he was proud of being a relation of Dr. Johnson's. It was, truely, a wonderful collection, both of antiquities and natural curiosities, and ingenious works of art. He had all the articles accurately arranged, with their names upon labels, printed at his own little press; and on the staircase leading to it was a board, with the names of contributors marked in gold letters. A printed catalogue of the collection was to be had at a bookseller's. Johnson expressed his admiration of the activity and diligence and good fortune of Mr. Green, in getting together, in his situation, so great a variety of things; and Mr. Green told me that Johnson once said to him, 'Sir, I should as soon have thought of building a man of war, as of collecting such a museum.' Mr. Green's obliging alacrity in shewing it was very pleasing.

A physician being mentioned who had lost his practice, because his whimsically changing his religion had made people distrustful of him, I maintained that this was unreasonable, as religion is unconnected with medical skill. *Johnson.* 'Sir, it is not unreasonable; for when people see a man absurd in what they understand, they may conclude the same of him in what they do not understand. If a physician were to take to eating of horse-flesh, nobody would employ him; though one may eat horse-flesh, and be a very skilful physician. If a man were educated in an absurd religion, his continuing to profess it would not hurt him, though his changing to it would.'

On Sunday, March 24, we breakfasted with Mrs. Cobb, a widow lady, who lived in an agreeable sequestered place close by the town, called the Friary, it having been formerly a religious house. She and her niece, Miss Adey, were great admirers of Dr. Johnson; and he behaved to them with a kindness and easy pleasantry, such as we see between old and intimate acquaintance. He accompanied Mrs. Cobb to St. Mary's church, and I went to the cathedral, where I was very much delighted with the musick, finding it to be peculiarly solemn, and accordant with the words of the service.

We dined at Mr. Peter Garrick's, who was in a very lively humour, and verified Johnson's saying, that if he had cultivated gaiety as much as his brother David, he might have equally excelled in it. He was to-day quite a London narrator, telling us a variety of anecdotes with that earnestness and attempt at mimickry which we usually find in the wits of the metropolis. Dr. Johnson went with me to the cathedral in the afternoon. It was grand and pleasing to contemplate this illustrious writer, now full of fame, worshipping in 'the solemn temple' of his native city.

I returned to tea and coffee at Mr. Peter Garrick's, and then found Dr. Johnson at the Reverend Mr. Seward's. His lady was the daughter of Mr. Hunter, Johnson's first schoolmaster. And now, for the first time, I had the pleasure of seeing his celebrated daughter, Miss Anna Seward, to whom I have since been indebted for many civilities, as well as some obliging communications concerning Johnson.

On Monday, March 25, we breakfasted at Mrs. Lucy Porter's. Johnson had sent an express to Dr. Taylor's, acquainting him of our being at Lichfield, and Taylor had returned an answer that his post-chaise should come for us this day. While we sat at breakfast, Dr. Johnson received a letter by the post, which seemed to agitate him very much. When he had read it, he exclaimed, 'One of the most dreadful things that has happened in my time.' The phrase *my time*, like the word *age*, is usually understood to refer to an event of a publick or general nature. I imagined something like an assassination of the King—like a gunpowder plot carried into execution—or like another fire of London. When asked, 'What is it, Sir?' he an-

swered, 'Mr. Thrale has lost his only son!' This was, no doubt,
a very great affliction to Mr. and Mrs. Thrale, which their
friends would consider accordingly; but from the manner in
which the intelligence of it was communicated by Johnson, it
appeared for the moment to be comparatively small. I, however, soon felt a sincere concern, and was curious to observe,
how Dr. Johnson would be affected. He said, 'This is a total
extinction to their family, as much as if they were sold into
captivity.' Upon my mentioning that Mr. Thrale had daughters, who might inherit his wealth;—'Daughters, (said Johnson, warmly,) he'll no more value his daughters than—' I was
going to speak.—'Sir, (said he,) don't you know how you yourself think? Sir, he wishes to propagate his name.' In short, I
saw male succession strong in his mind, even where there was
no name, no family of any long standing. I said, it was lucky
he was not present when this misfortune happened. *Johnson.*
'It is lucky for *me*. People in distress never think that you feel
enough.' *Boswell.* 'And Sir, they will have the hope of seeing
you, which will be a relief in the mean time; and when you
get to them, the pain will be so far abated, that they will be
capable of being consoled by you, which, in the first violence
of it, I believe, would not be the case.' *Johnson.* 'No, Sir; violent pain of mind, like violent pain of body, *must* be severely
felt.' *Boswell.* 'I own, Sir, I have not so much feeling for the
distress of others, as some people have, or pretend to have: but
I know this, that I would do all in my power to relieve them.'
Johnson. 'Sir, it is affectation to pretend to feel the distress of
others, as much as they do themselves. It is equally so, as if one
should pretend to feel as much pain while a friend's leg is cutting off, as he does. No, Sir; you have expressed the rational
and just nature of sympathy. I would have gone to the extremity of the earth to have preserved this boy.'

He was soon quite calm. The letter was from Mr. Thrale's
clerk, and concluded, 'I need not say how much they wish to
see you in London.' He said, 'We shall hasten back from Taylor's.'

After dinner Dr. Johnson wrote a letter to Mrs. Thrale on
the death of her son. I said it would be very distressing to
Thrale, but she would soon forget it, as she had so many things

to think of. Johnson. 'No, Sir, Thrale will forget it first. *She* has many things that she *may* think of. *He* has many things that he *must* think of.' This was a very just remark upon the different effect of those light pursuits which occupy a vacant and easy mind, and those serious engagements which arrest attention, and keep us from brooding over grief.

In the evening we went to the Town-hall, which was converted into a temporary theatre, and saw 'Theodosius,' with 'The Stratford Jubilee.' I was happy to see Dr. Johnson sitting in a conspicuous part of the pit, and receiving affectionate homage from all his acquaintance. We were quite gay and merry. I afterwards mentioned to him that I condemned myself for being so, when poor Mr. and Mrs. Thrale were in such distress. *Johnson.* 'You are wrong, Sir; twenty years hence Mr. and Mrs. Thrale will not suffer much pain from the death of their son. Now, Sir, you are to consider, that distance of place, as well as distance of time, operates upon the human feelings. I would not have you be gay in the presence of the distressed, because it would shock them; but you may be gay at a distance. Pain for the loss of a friend, or of a relation whom we love, is occasioned by the want which we feel. In time the vacuity is filled with something else; or, sometimes the vacuity closes up of itself.'

Here I shall record some fragments of my friend's conversation during this jaunt.

'Marriage, Sir, is much more necessary to a man than to a woman; for he is much less able to supply himself with domestick comforts. You will recollect my saying to some ladies the other day, that I had often wondered why young women should marry, as they have so much more freedom, and so much more attention paid to them while unmarried, than when married. I indeed did not mention the *strong* reason for their marrying—the *mechanical* reason.' *Boswell.* 'Why that *is* a strong one. But does not imagination make it seem much more important than it is in reality? Is it not, to a certain degree, a delusion in us as well as in women?' *Johnson.* 'Why yes, Sir; but it is a delusion that is always beginning again.' *Boswell.* 'I don't know but there is upon the whole more misery than happiness produced by that passion.' *Johnson.* 'I don't think so, Sir.'

'Never speak of a man in his own presence. It is always indelicate, and may be offensive.'

'Questioning is not the mode of conversation among gentlemen. It is assuming a superiority, and it is particularly wrong to question a man concerning himself. There may be parts of his former life which he may not wish to be made known to other persons, or even brought to his own recollection.'

'A man should be careful never to tell tales of himself to his own disadvantage. People may be amused and laugh at the time, but they will be remembered, and brought out against him upon some subsequent occasion.'

I mentioned an acquaintance of mine, a sectary, who was a very religious man, who not only attended regularly on publick worship with those of his communion, but made a particular study of the Scriptures, and even wrote a commentary on some parts of them, yet was known to be very licentious in indulging himself with women; maintaining that men are to be saved by faith alone, and that the Christian religion had not prescribed any fixed rule for the intercourse between the sexes. *Johnson.* 'Sir, there is no trusting to that crazy piety.'

On Tuesday, March 26, there came for us an equipage properly suited to a wealthy well-beneficed clergyman;—Dr. Taylor's large roomy post-chaise, drawn by four stout plump horses, and driven by two steady jolly postillions, which conveyed us to Ashbourne; where I found my friend's schoolfellow living upon an establishment perfectly corresponding with his substantial creditable equipage: his house, garden, pleasure-grounds, table, in short every thing good, and no scantiness appearing. I could not perceive in his character much congeniality of any sort with that of Johnson, who, however, said to me, 'Sir, he has a very strong understanding.' His size, and figure, and countenance, and manner, were that of a hearty English 'Squire, with the parson super-induced: and I took particular notice of his upper servant, Mr. Peters, a decent grave man, in purple clothes, and a large white wig, like the butler or *major domo* of a Bishop.

Dr. Johnson and Dr. Taylor met with great cordiality; and Johnson soon gave him the same sad account of their school-fellow, Congreve, that he had given to Mr. Hector; adding a remark of such moment to the rational conduct of a man in the decline of life, that it deserves to be imprinted upon every mind: 'There is nothing against which an old man should be so much upon his guard as putting himself to nurse.' Innumerable have been the melancholy instances of men once distinguished for firmness, resolution, and spirit, who in their latter days have been governed like children, by interested female artifice.

Dr. Taylor commended a physician who was known to him and Dr. Johnson, and said, 'I fight many battles for him, as many people in the country dislike him.' *Johnson.* But you should consider, Sir, that by every one of your victories he is a loser; for, every man of whom you get the better, will be very angry, and will resolve not to employ him; whereas if people get the better of you in argument about him, they'll think, "We'll send for Dr. ****** nevertheless." ' This was an observation deep and sure in human nature.

Next day we talked of a book in which an eminent judge was arraigned before the bar of the publick, as having pronounced an unjust decision in a great cause. Dr. Johnson maintained that this publication would not give any uneasiness to the Judge. 'For (said he,) either he acted honestly, or he meant to do injustice. If he acted honestly, his own consciousness will protect him; if he meant to do injustice, he will be glad to see the man who attacks him, so much vexed.'

Next day, as Dr. Johnson had acquainted Dr. Taylor of the reason for his returning speedily to London, it was resolved that we should set out after dinner.

Having left Ashbourne in the evening, we stopped to change horses at Derby, and availed ourselves of a moment to enjoy the conversation of my countryman, Dr. Butter, then physician there. We lay this night at Loughborough.

On Thursday, March 28, we pursued our journey. I enjoyed the luxury of our approach to London, that metropolis which we both loved so much, for the high and varied intellectual pleasure which it furnishes. I experienced immediate happiness while whirled along with such a companion, and said to him, 'Sir, you observed one day at General Oglethorpe's, that a man is never happy for the present, but when he is drunk. Will you not add,—or when driving rapidly in a post-chaise?' *Johnson.* 'No, Sir, you are driving rapidly *from* something, or *to* something.'

Talking of melancholy, he said, 'Some men, and very thinking men too, have not those vexing thoughts. Sir Joshua Reynolds is the same all the year round. Beauclerk, except when ill and in pain, is the same. But I believe most men have them in the degree in which they are capable of having them. If I were in the country, and were distressed by that malady, I would force myself to take a book; and every time I did it I should find it the easier. Melancholy, indeed, should be diverted by every means but drinking.'

We stopped at Messieurs Dillys, booksellers in the Poultry; from whence he hurried away, in a hackney coach, to Mr. Thrale's, in the Borough. I called at his house in the evening, having promised to acquaint Mrs. Williams of his safe return; when, to my surprize, I found him sitting with her at tea, and, as I thought, not in a very good humour: for, it seems, when he had got to Mr. Thrale's, he found the coach was at the door waiting to carry Mrs. and Miss Thrale, and Signor Baretti, their Italian master, to Bath. This was not shewing the attention which might have been expected to the 'Guide, Philosopher, and Friend,' the *Imlac* who had hastened from the country to console a distressed mother, who he understood was very anxious for his return. They had, I found, without ceremony, proceeded on their intended journey. I was glad to understand from him that it was still resolved that his tour to Italy with Mr. and Mrs. Thrale should take place, of which he had entertained some doubt, on account of the loss which they had suffered; and his doubts afterwards proved to be well-founded. He observed, indeed very justly, that 'their loss was an additional reason for their going abroad; and if it had not been fixed that he should have been one of the party, he would force them out; but he would not advise them unless his advice was asked, lest they might suspect that he recommended what he wished on his own account.' I was not pleased that his intimacy with

Mr. Thrale's family, though it no doubt contributed much to his comfort and enjoyment, was not without some degree of restraint. Not, as has been grossly suggested, that it was required of him as a task to talk for the entertainment of them and their company; but that he was not quite at his ease; which, however, might partly be owing to his own honest pride—that dignity of mind which is always jealous of appearing too compliant.

On Wednesday, April 3, in the morning I found him very busy putting his books in order, and as they were generally very old ones, clouds of dust were flying around him. He had on a pair of large gloves, such as hedgers use. His present appearance put me in mind of my uncle, Dr. Boswell's description of him, 'A robust genius, born to grapple with whole libraries.'

I gave him an account of a conversation which had passed between me and Captain Cook, the day before, at dinner at Sir John Pringle's; and he was much pleased with the conscientious accuracy of that celebrated circumnavigator, who set me right as to many of the exaggerated accounts given by Dr. Hawkesworth of his Voyages. I told him that while I was with the Captain, I catched the enthusiasm of curiosity and adventure, and felt a strong inclination to go with him on his next voyage. *Johnson.* 'Why, Sir, a man *does* feel so, till he considers how very little he can learn from such voyages.' *Boswell.* 'But one is carried away with the general grand and indistinct notion of *A Voyage round the World.*' *Johnson.* 'Yes, Sir, but a man is to guard himself against taking a thing in general.' I said I was certain that a great part of what we are told by the travellers to the South Sea must be conjecture, because they had not enough of the language of those countries to understand so much as they have related. Objects falling under the observation of the senses might be clearly known; but every thing intellectual, every thing abstract—politicks, morals, and religion, must be darkly guessed. Dr. Johnson was of the same opinion. He upon another occasion, when a friend mentioned to him several extraordinary facts, as communicated to him by the circumnavigators, slily observed, 'Sir, I never before knew how much I was respected by these gentlemen; they told *me* none of these things.'

He had been in company with Omai,[1] a native of one of the South Sea Islands, after he had been some time in this country. He was struck with the elegance of his behaviour, and accounted for it thus: 'Sir, he had passed his time, while in England, only in the best company; so that all that he had acquired of our manners was genteel. As a proof of this, Sir, Lord Mulgrave and he dined one day at Streatham; they sat with their backs to the light fronting me, so that I could not see distinctly; and there was so little of the savage in Omai, that I was afraid to speak to either, lest I should mistake one for the other.'

We agreed to dine to-day at the Mitre-tavern. I mentioned Mr. Solicitor's relation, Lord Charles Hay, with whom I knew Dr. Johnson had been acquainted. *Johnson.* 'I suffered a great loss when he died; he was a mighty pleasing man in conversation, and a reading man. The character of a soldier is high. They who stand forth the foremost in danger, for the community, have the respect of mankind. An officer is much more respected than any other man who has as little money. In a commercial country, money will always purchase respect. But you find, an officer, who has, properly speaking, no money, is every where well received and treated with attention. The character of a soldier always stands him in stead.' The peculiar respect paid to the military character in France was mentioned. *Boswell.* 'I should think that where military men are so numerous, they would be less valued as not being rare.' *Johnson.* 'Nay, Sir, wherever a particular character or profession is high in the estimation of a people, those who are of it will be valued above other men. We value an Englishman highly in this country, and yet Englishmen are not rare in it.'

[1] Omai—his real name was Mai; the prefixed O was due to a misunderstanding—was a young Polynesian brought to London from the Tahitian Islands by Captain Cook in 1774. The charm of his naïveté, the grace of his manners and the dignity of his bearing served to confirm the fashionable belief in the innate nobility of the "savage," and he was taken up enthusiastically by high society. Captain Cook took him back to Tahiti in 1776 where for the remainder of his short life he seems to have been cordially disliked.

Mr. Murray praised the ancient philosophers for the candour and good humour wtih which those of different sects disputed with each other. *Johnson.* 'Sir, they disputed with good humour, because they were not in earnest as to religion. Had the ancients been serious in their belief, we should not have had their Gods exhibited in the manner we find them represented in the Poets. The people would not have suffered it. They disputed with good humour upon their fanciful theories, because they were not interested in the truth of them: when a man has nothing to lose, he may be in good humour with his opponent. Every man who attacks my belief, diminishes in some degree my confidence in it, and therefore makes me uneasy; and I am angry with him who makes me uneasy. Those only who believed in Revelation have been angry at having their faith called in question; because they only had something upon which they could rest as matter of fact.' *Murray.* 'It seems to me that we are not angry at a man for controverting an opinion which we believe and value; we rather pity him.' *Johnson.* 'Why, Sir; to be sure when you wish a man to have that belief which you think is of infinite advantage, you wish well to him; but your primary consideration is your own quiet. If a madman were to come into this room with a stick in his hand, no doubt we should pity the state of his mind; but our primary consideration would be to take care of ourselves. We should knock him down first, and pity him afterwards. No, Sir; every man will dispute with great good humour upon a subject in which he is not interested. I will dispute very calmly upon the probability of another man's son being hanged; but if a man zealously enforces the probability that my own son will be hanged, I shall certainly not be in a very good humour with him.' *Murray.* 'But, Sir, truth will always bear an examination.' *Johnson.* 'Yes, Sir, but it is painful to be forced to defend it. Consider, Sir, how should you like, though conscious of your innocence, to be tried before a jury for a capital crime, once a week.'

I introduced the topick, which is often ignorantly urged, that the Universities of England are too rich; so that learning does not flourish in them as it would do, if those who teach had smaller salaries, and depended on their assiduity for a great part of their income. *Johnson.* 'Sir, the very reverse of this is the truth; the English Universities are not rich enough. Our fellowships are only sufficient to support a man during his studies to fit him for the world, and accordingly in general they are held no longer than till an opportunity offers of getting away. Now and then, perhaps, there is a fellow who grows old in his college; but this is against his will, unless he be a man very indolent indeed. A hundred a year is reckoned a good fellowship, and that is no more than is necessary to keep a man decently as a scholar. We do not allow our fellows to marry, because we consider academical institutions as preparatory to a settlement in the world. It is only by being employed as a tutor, that a fellow can obtain any thing more than a livelihood. To be sure a man, who has enough without teaching, will probably not teach; for we would all be idle if we could. In the same manner, a man who is to get nothing by teaching, will not exert himself. That they are too rich is certainly not true; for they have nothing good enough to keep a man of eminent learning with them for his life. In the foreign Universities a professorship is a high thing. It is as much almost as a man can make by his learning; and therefore we find the most learned men abroad are in the Universities. It is not so with us. Our Universities are impoverished of learning, by the penury of their provisions. I wish there were many places of a thousand a-year at Oxford, to keep first-rate men of learning from quitting the University.' Undoubtedly if this were the case, Literature would have a still greater dignity and splendour at Oxford, and there would be grander living sources of instruction.

On Friday, April 5, being Good Friday, after having attended the morning service at St. Clement's church, I walked home with Johnson.

I stated to him this case:—'Suppose a man has a daughter, who he knows has been seduced, but her misfortune is concealed from the world: should he keep her in his house? Would he not, by doing so, be accessary to imposition? And, perhaps, a worthy, unsuspecting man might come and marry this woman, unless the father inform him of the truth.' *Johnson.* 'Sir, he is accessary to no imposition. His daughter is in his house;

and if a man courts her, he takes his chance. If a friend, or indeed, if any man asks his opinion whether he should marry her, he ought to advise him against it, without telling why, because his real opinion is then required. Or, if he has other daughters who know of her frailty, he ought not to keep her in his house. You are to consider the state of life is this; we are to judge of one another's characters as well as we can; and a man is not bound, in honesty or honour, to tell us the faults of his daughter or of himself. A man who has debauched his friend's daughter is not obliged to say to every body—"Take care of me; don't let me into your houses without suspicion. I once debauched a friend's daughter: I may debauch yours." '

Mr. Thrale called upon him, and appeared to bear the loss of his son with a manly composure. There was no affectation about him; and he talked, as usual, upon indifferent subjects. He seemed to me to hesitate as to the intended Italian tour, on which, I flattered myself, he and Mrs. Thrale and Dr. Johnson were soon to set out; and, therefore, I pressed it as much as I could. I mentioned, that Mr. Beauclerk had said, that Baretti, whom they were to carry with them, would keep them so long in the little towns of his own district, that they would not have time to see Rome. I mentioned this, to put them on their guard. *Johnson.* 'Sir, we do not thank Mr. Beauclerk for supposing that we are to be directed by Baretti. No, Sir; Mr. Thrale is to go, by my advice, to Mr. Jackson, (the all-knowing) and get from him a plan for seeing the most that can be seen in the time that we have to travel. We must, to be sure, see Rome, Naples, Florence, and Venice, and as much more as we can.' (Speaking with a tone of animation.)

He gave us one of the many sketches of character which were treasured in his mind, and which he was wont to produce quite unexpectedly in a very entertaining manner. 'I lately, (said he,) received a letter from the East-Indies, from a gentleman whom I formerly knew very well; he had returned from that country with a handsome fortune, as it was reckoned, before means were found to acquire those immense sums which have been brought from thence of late; he was a scholar, and an agreeable man, and lived very prettily in London, till his wife died. After her death, he took to dissipation and gaming, and lost all he had. One evening he lost a thousand pounds to a gentleman whose name I am sorry I have forgotten. Next morning he sent the gentleman five hundred pounds, with an apology that it was all he had in the world. The gentleman sent the money back to him, declaring he would not accept of it; and adding, that if Mr. —— had occasion for five hundred pounds more, he would lend it to him. He resolved to go out again to the East-Indies, and make his fortune anew. He got a considerable appointment, and I had some intention of accompanying him. Had I thought then as I do now, I should have gone: but, at that time, I had objections to quitting England.'

It was a very remarkable circumstance about Johnson, whom shallow observers have supposed to have been ignorant of the world, that very few men had seen greater variety of characters; and none could observe them better, as was evident from the strong, yet nice portraits which he often drew. The suddenness with which his accounts of some of them started out in conversation, was not less pleasing than surprising. I remember he once observed to me, 'It is wonderful, Sir, what is to be found in London. The most literary conversation that I ever enjoyed, was at the table of Jack Ellis, a money-scrivener behind the Royal Exchange, with whom I at one period used to dine generally once a week.'

Volumes would be required to contain a list of his numerous and various acquaintance, none of whom he ever forgot; and could describe and discriminate them all with precision and vivacity. He associated with persons the most widely different in manners, abilities, rank, and accomplishments. He was at once the companion of the brilliant Colonel Forrester of the guards, who wrote 'The Polite Philosopher' and of the aukward and uncouth Robert Levet; and has dined one day with the beautiful, gay, and fascinating Lady Craven, and the next with good Mrs. Gardiner, the tallow-chandler, on Snow-hill.

A curious incident happened to-day, while Mr. Thrale and I sat with him. Francis announced that a large packet was brought to him from the post-office, said to have come from Lisbon, and it was charged *seven pounds ten shillings*. He would not receive it, supposing it to be some trick, nor did he even look at it. But upon enquiry afterwards he found that it was a real packet for him, from that very friend in the East-Indies of whom he had been speaking; and the ship which carried it having come to Portugal, this packet, with others, had been put into the post-office at Lisbon.

I mentioned a new gaming-club of which Mr. Beauclerk had given me an account, where the members played to a desperate extent. *Johnson.* 'Depend upon it, Sir, this is mere talk. *Who* is ruined by gaming? You will not find six instances in an age. There is a strange rout made about deep play: whereas you have many more people ruined by adventurous trade, and yet we do not hear such an outcry against it.' *Thrale.* 'There may be few people absolutely ruined by deep play; but very many are much hurt in their circumstances by it.' *Johnson.* 'Yes, Sir, and so are very many by other kinds of expence.' I had heard him talk once before in the same manner; and at Oxford he said, 'he wished he had learnt to play at cards.' The truth, however, is, that he loved to display his ingenuity in argument; and therefore would sometimes in conversation maintain opinions which he was sensible were wrong, but in supporting which, his reasoning and wit would be most conspicuous. He would begin thus: 'Why, Sir, as to the good or evil of card-playing—' 'Now, (said Garrick,) he is thinking which side he shall take.' He appeared to have a pleasure in contradiction, especially when any opinion whatever was delivered with an air of confidence; so that there was hardly any topick, if not one of the great truths of Religion and Morality, that he might not have been incited to argue, either for or against it.

We sat together till it was too late for the afternoon service. Thrale said, he had come with intention to go to church with us. We went at seven to evening prayers at St. Clement's church, after having drank coffee; an indulgence, which I understood Johnson yielded to on this occasion, in compliment to Thrale.

On Sunday, April 7, Easter-day, after having been at St. Paul's cathedral, I came to Dr. Johnson, according to my usual custom. It seemed to me, that there was always something peculiarly mild and placid in his manner upon this holy festival, the commemoration of the most joyful event in the history of our world, the resurrection of our LORD and SAVIOUR, who, having triumphed over death and the grave, proclaimed immortality to mankind.

I repeated to him an argument of a lady of my acqauintance, who maintained, that her husband's having been guilty of numberless infidelities, released her from conjugal obligations, because they were reciprocal. *Johnson.* 'This is miserable stuff, Sir. To the contract of marriage, besides the man and wife, there is a third party—Society; and, if it be considered as a vow —God: and, therefore, it cannot be dissolved by their consent alone. Laws are not made for particular cases, but for men in general. A woman may be unhappy with her husband; but she cannot be freed from him without the approbation of the civil and ecclesiastical power. A man may be unhappy, because he is not so rich as another; but he is not to seize upon another's property with his own hand.' *Boswell.* 'But, Sir, this lady does not want that the contract should be dissolved; she only argues that she may indulge herself in gallantries with equal freedom as her husband does, provided she takes care not to introduce a spurious issue into his family. *Johnson.* 'This lady of yours, Sir, I think, is very fit for a brothel.'

Mr. Macbean, authour of the 'Dictionary of ancient Geography,' came in. He mentioned, that he had been forty years absent from Scotland. 'Ah, Boswell! (said Johnson, smiling,) what would you give to be forty years from Scotland?' I said, 'I should not like to be so long absent from the seat of my ancestors.' This gentleman, Mrs. Williams, and Mr. Levett, dined with us.

Mrs. Williams was very peevish; and I wondered at Johnson's patience with her now, as I had often done on similar occasions. The truth is, that his humane consideration of the forlorn and indigent state in which this lady was left by her father, induced him to treat her with the utmost tenderness, and even to be desirous of procuring her amusement, so as sometimes to incommode many of his friends, by carrying her with him to their houses, where, from her manner of eating, in consequence of her blindness, she could not but offend the delicacy of persons of nice sensations.

After coffee, we went to afternoon service in St. Clement's church. Observing some beggars in the street as we walked along, I said to him I supposed there was no civilised country in the world, where the misery of want in the lowest classes of the people was prevented. *Johnson.* 'I believe, Sir, there is not; but it is better that some should be unhappy, than that none should be happy, which would be the case in a general state of equality.'

When the service was ended, I went home with him, and we sat quietly by ourselves. Upon the question whether a man who had been guilty of vicious actions would do well to force himself into solitude and sadness; *Johnson.* 'No, Sir, unless it prevent him from being vicious again. With some people, gloomy penitence is only madness turned upside down. A man may be gloomy, till, in order to be relieved from gloom, he has recourse again to criminal indulgencies.'

On Wednesday, April 10, I dined with him at Mr. Thrale's, where were Mr. Murphy and some other company. Before dinner, Dr. Johnson and I passed some time by ourselves. I was sorry to find it was now resolved that the proposed journey to Italy should not take place this year. He said, 'I am disappointed, to be sure; but it is not a great disappointment.' I wondered to see him bear, with a philosophical calmness, what would have made most people peevish and fretful. I perceived, however, that he had so warmly cherished the hope of enjoying classical scenes, that he could not easily part with the scheme; for he said, 'I shall probably contrive to get to Italy some other way. But I won't mention it to Mr. and Mrs. Thrale, as it might vex them.' I suggested, that going to Italy might have done Mr. and Mrs. Thrale good. *Johnson.* 'I rather believe not, Sir. While grief is fresh, every attempt to divert only irritates. You must wait till grief be *digested,* and then amusement will dissipate the remains of it.'

I said, I disliked the custom which some people had of bringing their children into company, because it in a manner forced us to pay foolish compliments to please their parents. *Johnson.* 'You are right, Sir. We may be excused for not caring much about other people's children, for there are many who care very little about their own children. It may be observed, that men, who from being engaged in business, or from their course of life in whatever way, seldom see their children, do not care much about them. I myself should not have had much fondness for a child of my own.' *Mrs. Thrale.* 'Nay, Sir, how can you talk so?' *Johnson.* 'At least, I never wished to have a child.'

Talking of the Reviews, Johnson said, 'I think them very impartial: I do not know an instance of partiality.' 'The Monthly Reviewers are not Deists; but they are Christians with as little christianity as may be; and are for pulling down all establishments. The Critical Reviewers are for supporting the constitution, both in church and state. The Critical Reviewers, I believe, often review without reading the books through; but lay hold of a topick, and write chiefly from their own minds. The Monthly Reviewers are duller men, and are glad to read the books through.'

Johnson mentioned Dr. Barry's System of Physick. 'He was a man (said he,) who had acquired a high reputation in Dublin, came over to England, and brought his reputation with him, but had not great success. His notion was, that pulsation occasions death by attrition; and that, therefore, the way to preserve life is to retard pulsation. But we know that pulsation is strongest in infants, and that we increase in growth while it operates in its regular course; so it cannot be the cause of destruction.' Soon after this, he said something very flattering to Mrs. Thrale, which I do not recollect; but it concluded with wishing her long life. 'Sir, (said I,) if Dr. Barry's system be true, you have now shortened Mrs. Thrale's life, perhaps, some minutes, by accelerating her pulsation.'

On Thursday, April 11, I dined with him at General Paoli's, in whose house I now resided, and where I had ever afterwards the honour of being entertained with the kindest attention as his constant guest, while I was in London, till I had a house of my own there. I mentioned my having that morning introduced to Mr. Garrick, Count Neni, a Flemish Nobleman of great rank and fortune, to whom Garrick talked of Abel Drugger as *a small part.* Garrick added, with an appearance of grave recollection, 'If I were to begin life again, I think I should not play those low characters.' Upon which I observed, 'Sir, you would be in the wrong; for your great excellence is your variety of playing, your representing so well, characters so very different.' *Johnson*. 'Garrick, Sir, was not in earnest in what he said; for, to be sure, his peculiar excellence is his variety: and, perhaps, there is not any one character which has not been as well acted by somebody else, as he could do it.' *Boswell*. 'Why then, Sir, did he talk so?' *Johnson*. 'Why, Sir, to make you answer as you did.' *Boswell*. 'I don't know, Sir; he seemed to dip deep into his mind for the reflection.' *Johnson*. 'He had not far to dip, Sir: he had said the same thing, probably, twenty times before.'

Of a nobleman raised at a very early period to high office, he said, 'His parts, Sir, are pretty well for a Lord; but would not be distinguished in a man who had nothing else but his parts.'

A journey to Italy was still in his thoughts. He said, 'A man who has not been in Italy, is always conscious of an inferiority, from his not having seen what it is expected a man should see. The grand object of travelling is to see the shores of the Mediterranean. On those shores were the four great Empires of the world; the Assyrian, the Persian, the Grecian, and the Roman. —All our religion, almost all our law, almost all our arts, almost all that sets us above savages, has come to us from the shores of the Mediterranean.' The General observed, that *'The Mediterranean* would be a noble subject for a poem.'

A gentleman maintained that the art of printing had hurt real learning, by disseminating idle writings.—*Johnson*. 'Sir, if it had not been for the art of printing, we should now have no learning at all; for books would have perished faster than they could have been transcribed.' This observation seems not just, considering for how many ages books were preserved by writing alone.

The same gentleman maintained, that a general diffusion of knowledge among a people was a disadvantage; for it made the vulgar rise above their humble sphere. *Johnson*. 'Sir, while knowledge is a distinction, those who are possessed of it will naturally rise above those who are not. Merely to read and write was a distinction at first; but we see when reading and writing have become general, the common people keep their stations.

And so, were higher attainments to become general, the effect would be the same.'

'Goldsmith (he said), referred every thing to vanity; his virtues, and his vices too, were from that motive. He was not a social man. He never exchanged mind with you.'

We spent the evening at Mr. Hoole's. Dr. Johnson said, 'Thomson had a true poetical genius, the power of viewing every thing in a poetical light. His fault is such a cloud of words sometimes, that the sense can hardly peep through. Shiels, who compiled "Cibber's Lives of the Poets," was one day sitting with me. I took down Thomson, and read aloud a large portion of him, and then asked,—Is not this fine? Shiels having expressed the highest admiration. Well, Sir, (said I,) I have omitted every other line.'

On Friday, April 12, I dined with him at our friend Tom Davies's, where we met Mr. Cradock, of Leicestershire, author of 'Zobeide,' a tragedy; and Dr. Harwood, who has written and published various works; particularly a fantastical translation of the New Testament, in modern phrase, and with a Socinian twist.

I introduced Aristotle's doctrine in his 'Art of Poetry,' of 'the purging of the passions,' as the purpose of tragedy. 'But how are the passions to be purged by terrour and pity?' (said I, with an assumed air of ignorance, to incite him to talk, for which it was often necessary to employ some address). *Johnson.* 'Why, Sir, you are to consider what is the meaning of purging in the original sense. It is to expel impurities from the human body. The mind is subject to the same imperfection. The passions are the great movers of human actions; but they are mixed with such impurities, that it is necessary they should be purged or refined by means of terrour and pity. For instance, ambition is a noble passion; but by seeing upon the stage, that a man who is so excessively ambitious as to raise himself by injustice, is punished, we are terrified at the fatal consequences of such a passion. In the same manner a certain degree of resentment is necessary; but if we see that a man carries it too far, we pity the object of it, and are taught to moderate that passion.' My record upon this occasion does great injustice to Johnson's expression, which was so forcible and brilliant, that Mr. Cradock whispered me, 'O that his words were written in a book!'

I observed the great defect of the tragedy of 'Othello' was, that it had not a moral; for that no man could resist the circumstances of suspicion which were artfully suggested to Othello's mind. *Johnson*. 'In the first place, Sir, we learn from Othello this very useful moral, not to make an unequal match; in the second place, we learn not to yield too readily to suspicion. The handkerchief is merely a trick, though a very pretty trick; but there are no other circumstances of reasonable suspicion, except what is related by Iago of Cassio's warm expressions concerning Desdemona in his sleep; and that depended entirely upon the assertion of one man. No, Sir, I think Othello has more moral than almost any play.'

Talking of a penurious gentleman of our acquaintance, Johnson said, 'Sir, he is narrow, not so much from avarice, as from impotence to spend his money. He cannot find in his heart to pour out a bottle of wine; but he would not much care if it should sour.'

Johnson and I supt this evening at the Crown and Anchor tavern, in company with Sir Joshua Reynolds, Mr. Langton, Mr. Nairne, now one of the Scotch Judges, with the title of Lord Dunsinan, and my very worthy friend, Sir William Forbes, of Pitsligo.

We discussed the question whether drinking improved conversation and benevolence. Sir Joshua maintained it did. *Johnson*. 'No, Sir: before dinner men meet with great inequality of understanding; and those who are conscious of their inferiority, have the modesty not to talk. When they have drunk wine, every man feels himself happy, and loses that modesty, and grows impudent and vociferous: but he is not improved; he is only not sensible of his defects.' Sir Joshua said the Doctor was talking of the effects of excess in wine; but that a moderate glass enlivened the mind, by giving a proper circulation to the blood. 'I am (said he,) in very good spirits when I get up in the morning. By dinner-time I am exhausted; wine puts me in the same state as when I got up; and I am sure that moderate drinking makes people talk better.' *Johnson*. 'No, Sir; wine gives not light, gay, ideal hilarity; but tumultuous, noisy, clamorous merriment. I have heard none of those drunken,—nay, drunken is a coarse word,—none of those *vinous* flights.' *Sir Joshua*. 'Because you have sat by, quite sober, and felt an envy of the happiness of those who were drinking.' *Johnson*. 'Perhaps, contempt.—And, Sir, it is not necessary to be drunk one's self, to relish the wit of drunkenness. Wit is wit, by whatever means it is produced; and, if good, will appear so at all times. I admit that the spirits are raised by drinking, as by the common participation of any pleasure: cock-fighting, or bear-baiting, will raise the spirits of a company, as drinking does, though surely they will not improve conversation.' Sir William Forbes said, 'Might not a man warmed with wine be like a bottle of beer, which is made brisker by being set before the fire?'—'Nay, (said Johnson, laughing,) I cannot answer that: that is too much for me.'

I observed, that wine did some people harm, by inflaming, confusing, and irritating their minds; but that the experience of mankind had declared in favour of moderate drinking. *Johnson*. 'Sir, I do not say it is wrong to produce self-complacency by drinking; I only deny that it improves the mind. When I drank wine, I scorned to drink it when in company. I have drunk many a bottle by myself; in the first place, because I had need of it to raise my spirits; in the second place, because I would have nobody to witness its effects upon me.'

He told us, 'almost all his Ramblers were written just as they were wanted for the press; that he sent a certain portion of the copy of an essay, and wrote the remainder, while the former part of it was printing. When it was wanted, and he had fairly sat down to it, he was sure it would be done.'

He said, that for general improvement, a man should read whatever his immediate inclination prompts him to; though, to be sure, if a man has a science to learn, he must regularly and resolutely advance. He added, 'what we read with inclination makes a much stronger impression. If we read without inclination, half the mind is employed in fixing the attention; so there is but one half to be employed on what we read.' He told us, he read Fielding's 'Amelia' through without stopping.

He said, 'If a man begins to read in the middle of a book, and feels an inclination to go on, let him not quit it, to go to the beginning. He may, perhaps, not feel again the inclination.'

We talked of the Reviews, and Dr. Johnson spoke of them as he did at Thrale's. Sir Joshua said, what I have often thought, that he wondered to find so much good writing employed in them, when the authours were to remain unknown, and so could not have the motive of fame. *Johnson.* 'Nay, Sir, those who write in them, write well, in order to be paid well.'

Soon after this day, he went to Bath with Mr. and Mrs. Thrale. I had never seen that beautiful city, and wished to take the opportunity of visiting it, while Johnson was there.

On the 26th of April, I went to Bath; and on my arrival at the Pelican inn, found lying for me an obliging invitation from Mr. and Mrs. Thrale, by whom I was agreeably entertained almost constantly during my stay. They were gone to the rooms; but there was a kind note from Dr. Johnson, that he should sit at home all the evening. I went to him directly, and before Mr. and Mrs. Thrale returned, we had by ourselves some hours of tea-drinking and talk.

I shall group together such of his sayings as I preserved during the few days that I was at Bath.

It having been mentioned, I know not with what truth, that a certain female political writer, whose doctrines he disliked, had of late become very fond of dress, sat hours together at her toilet, and even put on rouge:—*Johnson.* 'She is better employed at her toilet, than using her pen. It is better she should be reddening her own cheeks, than blackening other people's characters.'

A literary lady of large fortune was mentioned, as one who did good to many, but by no means 'by stealth,' and instead of 'blushing to find it fame,' acted evidently from vanity. *Johnson.* 'I have seen no beings who do as much good from benevolence, as she does, from whatever motive. If there are such under the earth, or in the clouds, I wish they would come up, or come down. No, Sir; to act from pure benevolence is not possible for finite beings. Human benevolence is mingled with vanity, interest, or some other motive.'

He would not allow me to praise a lady then at Bath; observ-

ing, 'She does not gain upon me, sir; I think her empty-headed.'
He was, indeed, a stern critick upon characters and manners.
Even Mrs. Thrale did not escape his friendly animadversion
at times. When he and I were one day endeavouring to ascertain, article by article, how one of our friends could possibly
spend as much money in his family as he told us he did, she
interrupted us by a lively extravagant sally, on the expence of
clothing his children, describing it in a very ludicrous and
fanciful manner. Johnson looked a little angry, and said, 'Nay,
Madam, when you are declaiming, declaim; and when you
are calculating, calculate.'

A gentleman expressed a wish to go and live three years at
Otaheité, or New-Zealand, in order to obtain a full acquaintance with people, so totally different from all that we have
ever known, and be satisfied what pure nature can do for man.
Johnson. 'What could you learn, Sir? What can savages tell,
but what they themselves have seen? Of the past, or the invisible, they can tell nothing. The inhabitants of Otaheité and
New-Zealand are not in a state of pure nature; for it is plain
they broke off from some other people. Had they grown out
of the ground, you might have judged of a state of pure nature.
Fanciful people may talk of a mythology being amongst them;
but it must be invention. They have once had religion, which
has been gradually debased. And what account of their religion
can you suppose to be learnt from savages? Only consider, Sir,
our own state: our religion is in a book; we have an order of
men whose duty it is to teach it; we have one day in the week
set apart for it, and this is in general pretty well observed: yet
ask the first ten gross men you meet, and hear what they can
tell of their religion.'

Johnson said of Chatterton, 'This is the most extraordinary
young man that has encountered my knowledge. It is wonderful how the whelp has written such things.'

After Dr. Johnson's return to London, I was several times
with him at his house, where I occasionally slept, in the room
that had been assigned to me. I dined with him at Dr. Taylor's, at General Oglethorpe's, and at General Paoli's. To avoid
a tedious minuteness, I shall group together what I have preserved of his conversation during this period also, without

specifying each scene where it passed, except one, which will be found so remarkable as certainly to deserve a very particular relation.

'There is much talk of the misery which we cause to the brute creation; but they are recompensed by existence. If they were not useful to man, and therefore protected by him, they would not be nearly so numerous.' This argument is to be found in the able and benignant Hutchinson's 'Moral Philosophy.' But the question is, whether the animals who endure such sufferings of various kinds, for the service and entertainment of man, would accept of existence upon the terms on which they have it. Madame Sévigné, who, though she had many enjoyments, felt with delicate sensibility the prevalence of misery, complains of the task of existence having been imposed upon her without her consent.

'Lord Chesterfield's Letters to his son, I think, might be made a very pretty book. Take out the immorality, and it should be put into the hands of every young gentleman. An elegant manner and easiness of behaviour are acquired gradually and imperceptibly. No man can say, "I'll be genteel." There are ten genteel women for one genteel man, because they are more restrained. A man without some degree of restraint is insufferable; but we are all less restrained than women. Were a woman sitting in company to put out her legs before her as most men do, we should be tempted to kick them in.'

No man was a more attentive and nice observer of behaviour in those in whose company he happened to be, than Johnson; or, however strange it may seem to many, had a higher estimation of its refinements. Lord Eliot informs me, that one day when Johnson and he were at dinner at a gentleman's house in London, upon Lord Chesterfield's Letters being mentioned, Johnson surprised the company by this sentence: 'Every man of any education would rather be called a rascal, than accused of deficiency in *the graces*.' Mr. Gibbon, who was present, turned to a lady who knew Johnson well, and lived much with him, and in his quaint manner, tapping his box, addressed her thus: 'Don't you think, Madam, (looking towards Johnson,) that among *all* your acquaintance, you could find *one* exception?' The lady smiled, and seemed to acquiesce.

'Mrs. Williams was angry that Thrale's family did not send regularly to her every time they heard from me while I was in the Hebrides. Little people are apt to be jealous: but they should not be jealous; for they ought to consider, that superiour attention will necessarily be paid to superiour fortune or rank. Two persons may have equal merit, and on that account may have an equal claim to attention; but one of them may have also fortune and rank, and so may have a double claim.'

A gentleman, whom I found sitting with him one morning, said, that in his opinion the character of an infidel was more detestable than that of a man notoriously guilty of an atrocious crime. I differed from him, because we are surer of the odiousness of the one, than of the errour of the other. *Johnson*. 'Sir, I agree with him; for the infidel would be guilty of any crime if he were inclined to it.'

'Many things which are false are transmitted from book to book, and gain credit in the world. One of these is the cry against the evil of luxury. Now the truth is, that luxury produces much good. A man gives half a guinea for a dish of green peas. How much gardening does this occasion? how many labourers must the competition to have such things early in the market, keep in employment? You will hear it said, very gravely, "Why was not the half-guinea, thus spent in luxury, given to the poor? To how many might it have afforded a good meal?" Alas! has it not gone to the *industrious* poor, whom it is better to support than the *idle* poor? You are much surer that you are doing good when you *pay* money to those who work, as the recompence of their labour, than when you *give* money merely in charity. And as to the rout that is made about people who are ruined by extravagance, it is no matter to the nation that some individuals suffer. When so much general productive exertion is the consequence of luxury, the nation does not care though there are debtors in gaol; nay, they would not care though their creditors were there too.'

When I complained of having dined at a splendid table without hearing one sentence of conversation worthy of being remembered, he said, 'Sir, there seldom is any such conversation.' *Boswell*. 'Why then meet at table?' *Johnson*. 'Why to eat and drink together, and to promote kindness; and, Sir, this is better done when there is no solid conversation; for when there is, people differ in opinion, and get into bad humour, or some of the company who are not capable of such conversation, are left out, and feel themselves uneasy. It was for this reason, Sir Robert Walpole said, he always talked bawdy at his table, because in that all could join.'

Being irritated by hearing a gentleman ask Mr. Levett a variety of questions concerning him, when he was sitting by, he broke out, 'Sir, you have but two topicks, yourself and me. I am sick of both.'

I am now to record a very curious incident in Dr. Johnson's Life, which fell under my own observation, and which I am persuaded will, with the liberal-minded, be much to his credit.

My desire of being acquainted with celebrated men of every description, had made me, much about the same time, obtain an introduction to Dr. Samuel Johnson and to John Wilkes, Esq. Two men more different could perhaps not be selected out of all mankind. They had even attacked one another with some asperity in their writings; yet I lived in habits of friendship with both. I could fully relish the excellence of each; for I have ever delighted in that intellectual chymistry, which can separate good qualities from evil in the same person.

Sir John Pringle, 'mine own friend and my Father's friend,' between whom and Dr. Johnson I in vain wished to establish an acquaintance, observed to me once, very ingeniously, 'It is not in friendship as in mathematicks, where two things, each equal to a third, are equal between themselves. You agree with Johnson as a middle quality, and you agree with me as a middle quality; but Johnson and I should not agree.' Sir John was not sufficiently flexible; so I desisted; knowing, indeed, that the repulsion was equally strong on the part of Johnson; who, I know not from what cause, unless his being a Scotchman, had formed a very erroneous opinion of Sir John. But I conceived an irresistible wish, if possible, to bring Dr. Johnson and Mr. Wilkes together. How to manage it, was a nice and difficult matter.

My worthy booksellers and friends, Messieurs Dilly in the Poultry, at whose hospitable and well-covered table I have seen a greater number of literary men, than at any other, ex-

cept that of Sir Joshua Reynolds, had invited me to meet Mr.
Wilkes and some more gentlemen on Wednesday, May 15.
'Pray (said I,) let us have Dr. Johnson.'—'What, with Mr.
Wilkes? not for the world, (said Mr. Edward Dilly:) Dr. Johnson would never forgive me.'—'Come, (said I,) if you'll let
me negociate for you, I will be answerable that all shall go
well.' *Dilly.* 'Nay, if you will take it upon you, I am sure I
shall be very happy to see them both here.'

Notwithstanding the high veneration which I entertained
for Dr. Johnson, I was sensible that he was sometimes a little
actuated by the spirit of contradiction, and by means of that
I hoped I should gain my point. I was persuaded that if I had
come upon him with a direct proposal, 'Sir, will you dine in
company with Jack Wilkes?' he would have flown into a passion, and would probably have answered, 'Dine with Jack
Wilkes, Sir! I'd as soon dine with Jack Ketch.' [1] I therefore,
while we were sitting quietly by ourselves at his house in an
evening, took occasion to open my plan thus:—'Mr. Dilly, Sir,
sends his respectful compliments to you, and would be happy
if you would do him the honour to dine with him on Wednesday next along with me, as I must soon go to Scotland.' *Johnson.* 'Sir, I am obliged to Mr. Dilly. I will wait upon him—'
Boswell. 'Provided, Sir, I suppose, that the company which
he is to have, is agreeable to you.' *Johnson.* 'What do you
mean, Sir? What do you take me for? Do you think I am so
ignorant of the world, as to imagine that I am to prescribe to
a gentleman what company he is to have at his table?' *Boswell.*
'I beg your pardon, Sir, for wishing to prevent you from meeting people whom you might not like. Perhaps he may have
some of what he calls his patriotick friends with him.' *Johnson.*
'Well, Sir, and what then? What care I for his *patriotick
friends*? Poh!' *Boswell.* 'I should not be surprized to find
Jack Wilkes there.' *Johnson.* 'And if Jack Wilkes *should* be
there, what is that to *me*, Sir? My dear friend, let us have no
more of this. I am sorry to be angry with you; but really it is
treating me strangely to talk to me as if I could not meet any
company whatever, occasionally.' *Boswell.* 'Pray forgive me,

[1] Jack Ketch was a seventeenth-century executioner (d.1686) famed
for his brutality. By Johnson's time his name was generic for a hangman.

Sir: I meant well. But you shall meet whoever comes, for me.' Thus I secured him, and told Dilly that he would find him very well pleased to be one of his guests on the day appointed.

Upon the much-expected Wednesday, I called on him about half an hour before dinner, as I often did when we were to dine out together, to see that he was ready in time, and to accompany him. I found him buffeting his books, as upon a former occasion, covered with dust, and making no preparation for going abroad. 'How is this, Sir? (said I.) Don't you recollect that you are to dine at Mr. Dilly's?' *Johnson*. 'Sir, I did not think of going to Dilly's: it went out of my head. I have ordered dinner at home with Mrs. Williams.' *Boswell*. 'But, my dear Sir, you know you were engaged to Mr. Dilly, and I told him so. He will expect you, and will be much disappointed if you don't come.' *Johnson*. 'You must talk to Mrs. Williams about this.'

Here was a sad dilemma. I feared that what I was so confident I had secured would yet be frustrated. He had accustomed himself to shew Mrs. Williams such a degree of humane attention, as frequently imposed some restraint upon him; and I knew that if she should be obstinate, he would not stir. I hastened down stairs to the blind lady's room, and told her I was in great uneasiness, for Dr. Johnson had engaged to me to dine this day at Mr. Dilly's, but that he had told me he had forgotten his engagement, and had ordered dinner at home. 'Yes, Sir, (said she, pretty peevishly,) Dr. Johnson is to dine at home.'—'Madam, (said I,) his respect for you is such, that I know he will not leave you unless you absolutely desire it. But as you have so much of his company, I hope you will be good enough to forego it for a day; as Mr. Dilly is a very worthy man, has frequently had agreeable parties at his house for Dr. Johnson, and will be vexed if the Doctor neglects him to-day. And then, Madam, be pleased to consider my situation; I carried the message, and I assured Mr. Dilly that Dr. Johnson was to come, and no doubt he has made a dinner, and invited a company, and boasted of the honour he expected to have. I shall be quite disgraced if the Doctor is not there.' She gradually softened to my solicitations, which were certainly as earnest as most entreaties to ladies upon any oc-

casion, and was graciously pleased to empower me to tell Dr.
Johnson, 'That all things considered, she thought he should
certainly go.' I flew back to him still in dust, and careless of
what should be the event, 'indifferent in his choice to go or
stay;' but as soon as I had announced to him Mrs. Williams's
consent, he roared, 'Frank, a clean shirt,' and was very soon
drest. When I had him fairly seated in a hackney-coach with
me, I exulted as much as a fortune-hunter who has got an
heiress into a post-chaise with him to set out for Gretna-Green.

When we entered Mr. Dilly's drawing room, he found himself in the midst of a company he did not know. I kept myself
snug and silent, watching how he would conduct himself. I
observed him whispering to Mr. Dilly, 'Who is that gentleman,
Sir?'—'Mr. Arthur Lee.'—*Johnson.* 'Too, too, too,' (under his
breath,) which was one of his habitual mutterings. Mr. Arthur
Lee could not but be very obnoxious to Johnson, for he was
not only a *patriot* but an *American.* He was afterwards minister from the United States at the court of Madrid. 'And who
is the gentleman in lace?'—'Mr. Wilkes, Sir.' This information
confounded him still more; he had some difficulty to restrain
himself, and taking up a book, sat down upon a window-seat
and read, or at least kept his eye upon it intently for some time,
till he composed himself. His feelings, I dare say, were aukward enough. But he no doubt recollected his having rated
me for supposing that he could be at all disconcerted by any
company, and he, therefore, resolutely set himself to behave
quite as an easy man of the world, who could adapt himself
at once to the disposition and manners of those whom he might
chance to meet.

The cheering sound of 'Dinner is upon the table,' dissolved
his reverie, and we *all* sat down without any symptom of ill
humour. Mr. Wilkes placed himself next to Dr. Johnson, and
behaved to him with so much attention and politeness, that
he gained upon him insensibly. No man eat more heartily than
Johnson, or loved better what was nice and delicate. Mr.
Wilkes was very assiduous in helping him to some fine veal.
'Pray give me leave, Sir:—It is better here—A little of the
brown—Some fat, Sir—A little of the stuffing—Some gravy—
Let me have the pleasure of giving you some butter—Allow

me to recommend a squeeze of this orange;—or the lemon, perhaps, may have more zest.'—'Sir, Sir, I am obliged to you, Sir,' cried Johnson, bowing, and turning his head to him with a look for some time of 'surly virtue,' but, in a short while, of complacency.

Foote being mentioned, Johnson said, 'He is not a good mimick.' One of the company added, 'A merry Andrew, a buffoon.' *Johnson.* 'But he has wit too, and is not deficient in ideas, or in fertility and variety of imagery, and not empty of reading; he has knowledge enough to fill up his part. One species of wit he has in an eminent degree, that of escape. You drive him into a corner with both hands; but he's gone, Sir, when you think you have got him—like an animal that jumps over your head. Then he has a great range for his wit; he never lets truth stand between him and a jest, and he is sometimes mighty coarse. Garrick is under many restraints from which Foote is free.' *Wilkes.* 'Garrick's wit is more like Lord Chesterfield's.' *Johnson.* 'The first time I was in company with Foote was at Fitzherbert's. Having no good opinion of the fellow, I was resolved not to be pleased; and it is very difficult to please a man against his will. I went on eating my dinner pretty sullenly, affecting not to mind him. But the dog was so very comical, that I was obliged to lay down my knife and fork, throw myself back upon my chair, and fairly laugh it out. No, Sir, he was irresistible. He upon one occasion experienced, in an extraordinary degree, the efficacy of his powers of entertaining. Amongst the many and various modes which he tried of getting money, he became a partner with a small-beer brewer, and he was to have a share of the profits for procuring customers amongst his numerous acquaintance. Fitzherbert was one who took his small-beer; but it was so bad that the servants resolved not to drink it. They were at some loss how to notify their resolution, being afraid of offending their master, who they knew liked Foote much as a companion. At last they fixed upon a little black boy, who was rather a favourite, to be their deputy, and deliver their remonstrance; and having invested him with the whole authority of the kitchen, he was to inform Mr. Fitzherbert, in all their names, upon a certain day, that they would drink Foote's small-beer no longer. On that day

Foote happened to dine at Fitzherbert's, and this boy served at table; he was so delighted with Foote's stories, and merriment, and grimace, that when he went down stairs, he told them, "This is the finest man I have ever seen. I will not deliver your message. I will drink his small-beer." '

Somebody observed that Garrick could not have done this. *Wilkes.* 'Garrick would have made the small-beer still smaller.' I knew that Johnson would let nobody attack Garrick but himself, as Garrick once said to me, and I had heard him praise his liberality; so to bring out his commendation of his celebrated pupil, I said, loudly, 'I have heard Garrick is liberal.' *Johnson.* 'Yes, Sir, I know that Garrick has given away more money than any man in England that I am acquainted with, and that not from ostentatious views. Garrick was very poor when he began life; so when he came to have money, he probably was very unskilful in giving away, and saved when he should not. But Garrick began to be liberal as soon as he could; and I am of opinion, the reputation of avarice which he has had, has been very lucky for him, and prevented his having many enemies. You despise a man for avarice, but do not hate him. Garrick might have been much better attacked for living with more splendour than is suitable to a player: if they had had the wit to have assaulted him in that quarter, they might have galled him more. But they have kept clamouring about his avarice, which has rescued him from much obloquy and envy.'

Talking of the great difficulty of obtaining authentick information for biography, Johnson told us, 'When I was a young fellow I wanted to write the "Life of Dryden," and in order to get materials, I applied to the only two persons then alive who had seen him; these were old Swinney, and old Cibber. Swinney's information was no more than this, "That at Will's coffee-house Dryden had a particular chair for himself, which was set by the fire in winter, and was then called his winter-chair; and that it was carried out for him to the balcony in summer, and was then called his summer-chair." Cibber could tell no more but "That he remembered him a decent old man, arbiter of critical disputes at Will's." '

Mr. Wilkes remarked, that 'among all the bold flights of

Shakspeare's imagination, the boldest was making Birnam-wood march to Dunsinane; creating a wood where there never was a shrub; a wood in Scotland! ha! ha! ha!' And he also observed, that 'the clannish slavery of the Highlands of Scotland was the single exception to Milton's remark of "The Mountain Nymph, sweet Liberty," being worshipped in all hilly countries.'—'When I was at Inverary (said he,) on a visit to my old friend, Archibald, Duke of Argyle, his dependents congratulated me on being such a favourite of his Grace. I said, "It is then, gentlemen, truely lucky for me; for if I had displeased the Duke, and he had wished it, there is not a Campbell among you but would have been ready to bring John Wilkes's head to him in a charger.'

Mr. Arthur Lee mentioned some Scotch who had taken possession of a barren part of America, and wondered why they should choose it. *Johnson.* 'Why, sir, all barrenness is comparative. The *Scotch* would not know it to be barren.' *Boswell.* 'Come, come, he is flattering the English. You have now been in Scotland, Sir, and say if you did not see meat and drink enough there.' *Johnson.* 'Why yes, Sir; meat and drink enough to give the inhabitants sufficient strength to run away from home.' All these quick and lively sallies were said sportively, quite in jest, and with a smile, which showed that he meant only wit. Upon this topick he and Mr. Wilkes could perfectly assimilate; here was a bond of union between them, and I was conscious that as both of them had visited Caledonia, both were fully satisfied of the strange narrow ignorance of those who imagine that it is a land of famine. But they amused themselves with persevering in the old jokes. When I claimed a superiority for Scotland over England in one respect, that no man can be arrested there for a debt merely because another swears it against him; but there must first be the judgement of a court of law ascertaining its justice; and that a seizure of the person, before judgement is obtained, can take place only, if his creditor should swear that he is about to fly from the country. *Wilkes.* 'That, I should think, may be safely sworn of all the Scotch nation.' *Johnson.* (to Mr. Wilkes) 'You must know, Sir, I lately took my friend Boswell and shewed him genuine civilised life in an English provincial town. I turned him loose at Lichfield, my native city, that he might see for once real civility: for you know he lives among savages in Scotland, and among rakes in London.' *Wilkes.* 'Except when he is with grave, sober, decent people like you and me.' *Johnson.* (smiling) 'And we ashamed of him.'

They were quite frank and easy. Johnson told the story of his asking Mrs. Macaulay to allow her footman to sit down with them, to prove the ridiculousness of the argument for the equality of mankind; and he said to me afterwards, with a nod of satisfaction, 'You saw Mr. Wilkes acquiesced.'

After dinner we had an accession of Mrs. Knowles, the Quaker lady, well known for her various talents, and of Mr. Alderman Lee. Amidst some patriotick groans, somebody (I think the Alderman) said, 'Poor Old England is lost.' *Johnson.* 'Sir, it is not so much to be lamented that Old England is lost, as that the Scotch have found it.'

Mr. Wilkes held a candle to shew a fine print of a beautiful female figure which hung in the room, and pointed out the elegant contour of the bosom with the finger of an arch connoisseur. He afterwards, in a conversation with me, waggishly insisted, that all the time Johnson shewed visible signs of a fervent admiration of the corresponding charms of the fair Quaker.

This record, though by no means so perfect as I could wish, will serve to give a notion of a very curious interview, which was not only pleasing at the time, but had the agreeable and benignant effect of reconciling any animosity, and sweetening any acidity, which in the various bustle of political contest, had been produced in the minds of two men, who though widely different, had so many things in common—classical learning, modern literature, wit, and humour, and ready repartee—that it would have been much to be regretted if they had been for ever at a distance from each other.

Mr. Burke gave me much credit for this successful *negociation;* and pleasantly said, that 'there was nothing to equal it in the whole history of the *Corps Diplomatique.*'

I attended Dr. Johnson home, and had the satisfaction to

hear him tell Mrs. Williams how much he had been pleased
with Mr. Wilkes's company, and what an agreeable day he
had passed.

I talked a good deal to him of the celebrated Margaret Caro-
line Rudd,[1] whom I had visited, induced by the fame of her
talents, address, and irresistible power of fascination. To a lady
who disapproved of my visiting her, he said on a former occasion, 'Nay, Madam, Boswell is in the right; I should have
visited her myself, were it not that they have now a trick of
putting every thing into the news-papers.' This evening he
exclaimed, 'I envy him his acquaintance with Mrs. Rudd.'

I mentioned a scheme which I had of making a tour to the
Isle of Man, and giving a full account of it; and that Mr. Burke
had playfully suggested as a motto,

> 'The proper study of mankind is MAN.'

Johnson. 'Sir, you will get more by the book than the jaunt
will cost you; so you will have your diversion for nothing, and
add to your reputation.'

On the evening of the next day I took leave of him, being
to set out for Scotland. I thanked him with great warmth for
all his kindness. 'Sir, (said he,) you are very welcome. Nobody
repays it with more.'

How very false is the notion which has gone round the world
of the rough, and passionate, and harsh manners of this great
and good man. That he had occasional sallies of heat of
temper, and that he was sometimes, perhaps, too 'easily provoked' by absurdity and folly, and sometimes too desirous of
triumph in colloquial contest, must be allowed. The quickness
both of his perception and sensibility disposed him to sudden
explosions of satire; to which his extraordinary readiness of wit

---

[1] In 1776 Mrs. Rudd had been tried for forgery, together with the
Perreau brothers, Robert and Daniel. She had turned King's evidence
and the Perreaus were hung, protesting their innocence. On the stand
she had been so seductive and eloquent that her acquittal had been
greeted with tumultuous applause. Boswell's seeking her out is an
extreme example of the manner in which he was drawn to the famous.
Dr. Johnson would probably not have approved of Boswell's subsequent
relations with Mrs. Rudd.

was a strong and almost irresistible incitement. I admit that the beadle within him was often so eager to apply the lash, that the Judge had not time to consider the case with sufficient deliberation.

That he was occasionally remarkable for violence of temper may be granted: but let us ascertain the degree, and not let it be supposed that he was in a perpetual rage, and never without a club in his hand, to knock down every one who approached him. On the contrary, the truth is, that by much the greatest part of his time he was civil, obliging, nay, polite in the true sense of the word; so much so, that many gentlemen, who were long acquainted with him, never received, or even heard a strong expression from him.

The following letters concerning an Epitaph which he wrote for the monument of Dr. Goldsmith, in Westminster-Abbey, afford at once a proof of his unaffected modesty, his carelessness as to his own writings, and of the great respect which he entertained for the taste and judgement of the excellent and eminent person to whom they are addressed:

'To Sir Joshua Reynolds.

'Dear Sir,
    'I have been kept away from you, I know not well how, and of these vexatious hindrances I know not when there will be an end. I therefore send you the poor dear Doctor's epitaph. Read it first yourself; and if you then think it right, shew it to the Club. I am, you know, willing to be corrected. If you think any thing much amiss, keep it to yourself, till we come together. I have sent two copies, but prefer the card. The dates must be settled by Dr. Percy.

'I am, Sir,
        'Your most humble servant,
                'Sam. Johnson.'
'May 16, 1776.'

To the Same.

'Sir,
    'Miss Reynolds has a mind to send the Epitaph to Dr. Beattie; I am very willing, but having no copy, cannot immediately recollect it. She tells me you have lost it. Try to recollect and put

down as much as you retain; you perhaps may have kept what I have dropped. It was a sorry trick to lose it; help me if you can. I am, Sir,

> 'Your most humble servant,
> > 'SAM. JOHNSON.'

'June 22, 1776.

'The gout grows better but slowly.'

'DR. JOHNSON TO MRS. BOSWELL.

'MADAM,

'You must not think me uncivil in omitting to answer the letter with which you favoured me some time ago. I imagined it to have been written without Mr. Boswell's knowledge, and therefore supposed the answer to require, what I could not find, a private conveyance.

'The difference with Lord Auchinleck is now over; and since young Alexander has appeared, I hope no more difficulties will arise among you; for I sincerely wish you all happy. Do not teach the young ones to dislike me, as you dislike me yourself; but let me at least have Veronica's kindness, because she is my acquaintance.

'You will now have Mr. Boswell home; it is well that you have him; he has led a wild life. I have taken him to Lichfield, and he has followed Mr. Thrale to Bath. Pray take care of him, and tame him. The only thing in which I have the honour to agree with you is, in loving him; and while we are so much of a mind in a matter of so much importance, our other quarrels will, I hope, produce no great bitterness. I am, Madam,

> 'Your most humble servant,
> > 'SAM. JOHNSON.'

'May 16, 1776.'

As the evidence of what I have mentioned at the beginning of this year, I select from his private register the following passage:

'July 25, 1776. O GOD, who hast ordained that whatever is to be desired should be sought by labour, and who, by thy blessing, bringest honest labour to good effect, look with mercy upon my studies and endeavours. Grant me, O LORD, to design only what is lawful and right; and afford me calmness of mind, and steadiness of purpose, that I may so do thy will in this short life, as to obtain happiness in the world to come, for the sake of JESUS CHRIST our Lord. Amen.'

It appears from a note subjoined, that this was composed when he 'purposed to apply vigorously to study, particularly of the Greek and Italian tongues.'

Such a purpose, so expressed, at the age of sixty-seven, is admirable and encouraging; and it must impress all the thinking part of my readers with a consolatory confidence in habitual devotion, when they see a man of such enlarged intellectual powers as Johnson, thus in the genuine earnestness of secrecy, imploring the aid of that Supreme Being, 'from whom cometh down every good and every perfect gift.'

'To Sir Joshua Reynolds.

'Sir,

'A young man, whose name is Paterson, offers himself this evening to the Academy. He is the son of a man for whom I have long had a kindness, and who is now abroad in distress. I shall be glad that you will be pleased to shew him any little countenance, or pay him any small distinction. How much it is in your power to favour or to forward a young man I do not know; nor do I know how much this candidate deserves favour by his personal merit, or what hopes his proficiency may now give of future eminence. I recommend him as the son of my friend. Your character and station enable you to give a young man great encouragement by very easy means. You have heard of a man who asked no other favour of Sir Robert Walpole, than that he would bow to him at his levee.

'I am, Sir,

'Your most humble servant,

'Sam. Johnson.'

'Aug. 3, 1776.'

I again wrote to Dr. Johnson on the 21st of October, informing him, that my father had, in the most liberal manner, paid a large debt for me, and that I had now the happiness of being upon very good terms with him; to which he returned the following answer.

'To James Boswell, Esq.

'Dear Sir,

'I had great pleasure in hearing that you are at last on good terms with your father. Cultivate his kindness by all honest and manly means. Life is but short; no time can be afforded but for the indulgence of real sorrow, or contests upon questions seriously momentous. Let us not throw away any of our days upon useless resentment, or contend who shall hold out longest in stubborn malignity. It is best not to be angry; and best, in the next place, to be quickly reconciled. May you and your father pass the remainder of your time in reciprocal benevolence!

'I hope my irreconcileable enemy, Mrs. Boswell, is well. Desire her not to transmit her malevolence to the young people. Let me have Alexander, and Veronica, and Euphemia, for my friends.

'Mrs. Williams, whom you may reckon as one of your well-wishers, is in a feeble and languishing state, with little hope of growing better. She went for some part of the autumn into the country, but is little benefited; and Dr. Lawrence confesses that his art is at an end. Death is, however, at a distance; and what more than that can we say of ourselves? I am sorry for her pain, and more sorry for her decay. Mr. Levett is sound, wind and limb.

'I was some weeks this autumn at Brighthelmstone. The place was very dull, and I was not well: the expedition to the Hebrides was the most pleasant journey that I ever made. Such an effort annually would give the world a little diversification.

'Every year, however, we cannot wander, and must therefore endeavour to spend our time at home as well as we can. I believe it is best to throw life into a method, that every hour may bring its employment, and every employment have its hour. Xenophon observes, in his "Treatise of Oeconomy", that if every thing be kept in a certain place, when any thing is worn out or consumed, the vacuity which it leaves will shew what is wanting; so if every part of time has its duty, the hour will call into remembrance its proper engagement.

'I have not practised all this prudence myself, but I have suffered much for want of it; and I would have you, by timely recollection and steady resolution, escape from those evils which have lain heavy upon me. I am, my dearest Boswell,

'Your most humble servant,

'SAM. JOHNSON.'

'Bolt-court, Nov. 16, 1776.'

On the 16th of November I informed him that Mr. Strahan had sent me *twelve* copies of the 'Journey to the Western Islands,' handsomely bound, instead of the *twenty* copies which were stipulated; but which, I supposed, were to be only in sheets; requested to know how they should be distributed: and mentioned that I had another son born to me, who was named David, and was a sickly infant.

'To James Boswell, Esq.

'Dear Sir,

'I have been for some time ill of a cold, which, perhaps, I made an excuse to myself for not writing, when in reality I knew not what to say.

'The books you must at last distribute as you think best, in my name, or your own, as you are inclined, or as you judge most proper. Every body cannot be obliged; but I wish that nobody may be offended. Do the best you can.

'I congratulate you on the increase of your family, and hope that little David is by this time well, and his mamma perfectly recovered. I am much pleased to hear of the re-establishment of kindness between you and your father. Cultivate his paternal tenderness as much as you can. To live at variance at all is uncomfortable; and variance with a father is still more uncomfortable. Besides that, in the whole dispute you have the wrong side; at least you gave the first provocations, and some of them very offensive. Let it now be all over. As you have no reason to think that your new mother has shown you any foul play, treat her with respect, and with some degree of confidence; this will secure your father. When once a discordant family has felt the pleasure of peace, they will not willingly lose it. If Mrs. Boswell would but be friends with me, we might now shut the temple of Janus.

'Mrs. Williams has been much out of order; and though she is something better, is likely, in her physician's opinion, to endure her malady for life, though she may, perhaps, die of some other. Mrs. Thrale is big, and fancies that she carries a boy; if it were very reasonable to wish much about it, I should wish her not to be disappointed. The desire of male heirs is not appendant only to feudal tenures. A son is almost necessary to the continuance of Thrale's fortune; for what can misses do with a brewhouse? Lands are fitter for daughters than trades.

'Baretti went away from Thrale's in some whimsical fit of disgust, or ill-nature, without taking any leave. It is well if he finds in any other place as good an habitation, and as many conveniences. He has got five-and-twenty guineas by translating Sir Joshua's Discourses into Italian, and Mr. Thrale gave him an hundred in the spring; so that he is yet in no difficulties.

1777: ÆTAT. 68.]—In 1777, it appears from his 'Prayers and Meditations,' that Johnson suffered much from a state of mind 'unsettled and perplexed,' and from that constitutional gloom, which, together with his extreme humility and anxiety with regard to his religious state, made him contemplate himself through too dark and unfavourable a medium. It may be said of him, that he 'saw GOD in clouds.' Certain we may be of his injustice to himself in the following lamentable paragraph, which it is painful to think came from the contrite heart of this great man, to whose labours the world is so much indebted:

'When I survey my past life, I discover nothing but a barren waste of time, with some disorders of body, and disturbances of the mind, very near to madness, which I hope He that made me will suffer to extenuate many faults, and excuse many deficiencies.'

But we find his devotions in this year eminently fervent; and we are comforted by observing intervals of quiet, composure, and gladness.

On Easter-day we find the following emphatick prayer:

'Almighty and most merciful Father, who seest all our miseries, and knowest all our necessities, look down upon me, and pity me. Defend me from the violent incursion of evil thoughts, and enable me to form and keep such resolutions as may conduce to the discharge of the duties which thy providence shall appoint me; and so help me, by thy Holy Spirit, that my heart may surely there be fixed, where true joys are to be found, and that I may serve Thee with pure affection and a cheerful mind. Have mercy upon me, O GOD, have mercy upon me; years and infirmities oppress me, terrour and anxiety beset me. Have mercy upon me, my Creator and my Judge. In all perplexities relieve and free me; and so help me by thy Holy Spirit, that I may now so commemorate the death of thy Son our Saviour JESUS CHRIST, as that when this short and painful life shall have an end, I may, for his sake, be received to everlasting happiness. Amen.'

'MR. BOSWELL TO DR. JOHNSON.

'Edinburgh, April 4, 1777.

[After informing him of the death of my little son David, and that I could not come to London this spring:—]

'I think it hard that I should be a whole year without seeing you. May I presume to petition for a meeting with you in the autumn? You have, I believe, seen all the cathedrals in England, except that of Carlisle. If you are to be with Dr. Taylor, at Ashbourne, it would not be a great journey to come thither. We may pass a few most agreeable days there by ourselves, and I will accompany you a good part of the way to the southward again. Pray think of this.'

'To Dr. Samuel Johnson.

'Glasgow, April 24, 1777.

'My dear Sir,

'Our worthy friend Thrale's death having appeared in the news-papers, and been afterwards contradicted, I have been placed in a state of very uneasy uncertainty, from which I hoped to be relieved by you: but my hopes have as yet been vain. How could you omit to write to me on such an occasion? I shall wait with anxiety.

'I am going to Auchinleck to stay a fortnight with my father. It is better not to be there very long at one time. But frequent renewals of attention are agreeable to him.

'Pray tell me about this edition of "The English Poets, with a Preface, biographical and critical, to each Authour, by Samuel Johnson, LL.D." which I see advertised. I am delighted with the prospect of it. Indeed I am happy to feel that I am capable of being so much delighted with literature.

'What do you say of Lord Chesterfield's Memoirs and last Letters?

'My wife has made marmalade of oranges for you. I left her and my daughters and Alexander all well yesterday. I have taught Veronica to speak of you thus;—Dr. John*son*, not John*ston*.

'I remain, my dear Sir,

'Your most affectionate,

'And obliged humble servant,

'James Boswell.'

'To James Boswell, Esq.

'Dear Sir,

'The story of Mr. Thrale's death, as he had neither been sick nor in any other danger, made so little impression upon me, that I never thought about obviating its effects on any body else. It is supposed to have been produced by the English custom of making April fools, that is, of sending one another on some foolish errand on the first of April.

'Tell Mrs. Boswell that I shall taste her marmalade cautiously at first. Beware, says the Italian proverb, of a reconciled enemy. But when I find it does me no harm, I shall then receive it and be thankful for it, as a pledge of firm, and, I hope, of unalterable kindness. She is, after all, a dear, dear lady.

'Please to return Dr. Blair thanks for his sermons. The Scotch write English wonderfully well.

'Your frequent visits to Auchinleck, and your short stay there, are very laudable and very judicious. Your present concord with your father gives me great pleasure; it was all that you seemed to want.

'My health is very bad, and my nights are very unquiet. What can I do to mend them? I have for this summer nothing better in prospect than a journey into Staffordshire and Derbyshire, perhaps with Oxford and Birmingham in my way.

'Make my compliments to Miss Veronica; I must leave it to *her* philosophy to comfort you for the loss of little David. You must remember, that to keep three out of four is more than your share. Mrs. Thrale has but four out of eleven.

'I am engaged to write little Lives, and little Prefaces, to a little edition of the English Poets. I think I have persuaded the booksellers to insert something of Thomson; and if you could give me some information about him, for the life which we have is very scanty, I should be glad. I am, dear Sir,

'Your most affectionate humble servant,

'SAM. JOHNSON.'

'May 3, 1777.'

To those who delight in tracing the progress of works of literature, it will be an entertainment to compare the limited design with the ample execution of that admirable performance, 'The Lives of the English Poets,' which is the richest, most beautiful, and indeed most perfect production of Johnson's pen. His notion of it at this time appears in the preceding letter. He has a memorandum in this year, '29 May, Easter Eve, I treated with booksellers on a bargain, but the time was not long.' The bargain was concerning that undertaking; but his tender conscience seems alarmed lest it should have intruded too much on his devout preparation for the solemnity of the ensuing day. But, indeed, very little time was necessary for Johnson's concluding a treaty with the booksellers; as he had, I believe, less attention to profit from his labours than any man to whom literature has been a profession. I shall here insert from a letter to me from my late worthy friend Mr. Edward Dilly, though of a later date, an account of this plan so happily conceived; since it was the occasion of procuring for ʜs an elegant collection of the best biography and criticism of which our language can boast.

'To JAMES BOSWELL, ESQ.

'Southill, Sept. 26, 1777.

'DEAR SIR,

'You will find by this letter, that I am still in the same calm retreat, from the noise and bustle of London, as when I wrote to you last. I am happy to find you had such an agreeable meeting with your old friend Dr. Johnson; I have no doubt your stock is much increased by the interview; few men, nay I may say, scarcely any man, has got that fund of knowledge and entertainment as Dr. Johnson in conversation. When he opens freely, every one is attentive to what he says, and cannot fail of improvement as well as pleasure.

'The edition of the Poets, now printing, will do honour to the English press; and a concise account of the life of each authour, by Dr. Johnson, will be a very valuable addition, and stamp the reputation of this edition superiour to any thing that is gone before. The first cause that gave rise to this undertaking, I believe, was owing to the little trifling edition of the Poets, printing by the Martins, at Edinburgh, and to be sold by Bell, in London. Upon examining the volumes which were printed, the type was found so extremely small, that many persons could not read them; not only this inconvenience attended it, but the inaccuracy of the press was very conspicuous. These reasons, as well as the idea of an invasion of what we call our Literary Property, induced the London Booksellers to print an elegant and accurate edition of all the English Poets of reputation, from Chaucer to the present time.

'Accordingly a select number of the most respectable booksellers met on the occasion; and, on consulting together, agreed, that all the proprietors of copy-right in the various Poets should be summoned together; and when their opinions were given, to proceed immediately on the business. Accordingly a meeting was held, consisting of about forty of the most respectable booksellers of London, when it was agreed that an elegant and uniform edition of "The English Poets" should be immediately printed, with a concise account of the life of each authour, by Dr. Samuel Johnson; and that three persons should be deputed to wait upon Dr. Johnson, to solicit him to undertake the Lives, *viz.* T. Davies, Strahan, and Cadell. The Doctor very politely undertook it, and seemed exceed-

íngly pleased with the proposal. As to the terms, it was left entirely
to the Doctor to name his own: he mentioned two hundred guineas: it was immediately agreed to; and a farther compliment, I
believe, will be made him. A committee was likewise appointed to
engage the best engravers, *viz.* Bartolozzi, Sherwin, Hall, &c. Likewise another committee for giving directions about the paper, printing, &c. so that the whole will be conducted with spirit, and in the
best manner, with respect to authourship, editorship, engravings,
&c. &c. My brother will give you a list of the Poets we mean to
give, many of which are within the time of the Act of Queen
Anne, which Martin and Bell cannot give, as they have no property in them; the proprietors are almost all the booksellers in
London, of consequence. I am, dear Sir,

'Ever your's,
'EDWARD DILLY.'

I shall afterwards have occasion to consider the extensive
and varied range which Johnson took, when he was once led
upon ground which he trod with a peculiar delight, having
long been intimately acquainted with all the circumstances
of it that could interest and please.

A circumstance which could not fail to be very pleasing to
Johnson occurred this year. The Tragedy of 'Sir Thomas Over-
bury,' written by his early companion in London, Richard
Savage, was brought out with alterations at Drury-lane
theatre. The Prologue to it was written by Mr. Richard Brins-
ley Sheridan; in which, after describing very pathetically the
wretchedness of

'Ill-fated Savage, at whose birth was giv'n
No parent but the Muse, no friend but Heav'n:'

he introduced an elegant compliment to Johnson on his Dictionary, that wonderful performance which cannot be too often
or too highly praised. The concluding lines of this Prologue
were these:

'So pleads the tale that gives to future times
The son's misfortunes and the parent's crimes;
There shall his fame (if own'd to-night) survive,
Fix'd by THE HAND THAT BIDS OUR LANGUAGE LIVE.'

Mr. Sheridan here at once did honour to his taste and to his
liberality of sentiment, by shewing that he was not prejudiced

from the unlucky difference which had taken place between his worthy father and Dr. Johnson. I have already mentioned, that Johnson was very desirous of reconciliation with old Mr. Sheridan. It will, therefore, not seem at all surprizing that he was zealous in acknowledging the brilliant merit of his son. While it had as yet been displayed only in the drama, Johnson proposed him as a member of The Literary Club, observing, that 'He who has written the two best comedies of his age, is surely a considerable man.' And he had, accordingly, the honour to be elected; for an honour it undoubtedly must be allowed to be, when it is considered of whom that society consists, and that a single black ball excludes a candidate.

'MR. BOSWELL TO DR. JOHNSON.

'June 9, 1777.

'MY DEAR SIR,
    'FOR the health of my wife and children I have taken the little country-house at which you visited my uncle, Dr. Boswell, who, having lost his wife, is gone to live with his son. We took possession of our villa about a week ago; we have a garden of three quarters of an acre, well stocked with fruit-trees and flowers, and gooseberries and currants, and pease and beans, and cabbages, &c. &c. and my children are quite happy. I now write to you in a little study, from the window of which I see around me a verdant grove, and beyond it the lofty mountain called Arthur's Seat.
    'Your last letter, in which you desire me to send you some additional information concerning Thomson, reached me very fortunately just as I was going to Lanark, to put my wife's two nephews, the young Campbells, to school there, under the care of Mr. Thomson, the master of it, whose wife is sister to the authour of "The Seasons." She is an old woman; but her memory is very good; and she will with pleasure give me for you every particular that you wish to know, and she can tell. Pray then take the trouble to send me such questions as may lead to biographical materials. As Thomson never returned to Scotland, (which *you* will think very wise,) his sister can speak from her own knowledge only as to the early part of his life. She has some letters from him, which may probably give light as to his more advanced progress, if she will let us see them, which I suppose she will. I believe George Lewis Scott and Dr. Armstrong are now his only surviving companions, while he lived in and about London; and they, I dare say, can tell more of

him than is yet known. My own notion is, that Thomson was a much coarser man than his friends are willing to acknowledge. His "Seasons" are indeed full of elegant and pious sentiments: but a rank soil, nay a dunghill, will produce beautiful flowers.

'You do not take the least notice of my proposal for our meeting at Carlisle. Though I have meritoriously refrained from visiting London this year, I ask you if it would not be wrong that I should be two years without having the benefit of your conversation, when, if you come down as far as Derbyshire, we may meet at the expence of a few days' journeying, and not many pounds. I wish you to see Carlisle, which made me mention that place. But if you have not a desire to complete your tour of the English cathedrals, I will take a larger share of the road between this place and Ashbourne. So tell me *where* you will fix for our passing a few days by ourselves. Now don't cry "foolish fellow," or "idle dog." Chain your humour, and let your kindness play.

'Without doubt you have read what is called "The *Life* of David Hume," written by himself, with the letter from Dr. Adam Smith subjoined to it. Is not this an age of daring effrontery? My friend Mr. Anderson, Professor of Natural Philosophy at Glasgow, at whose house you and I supped, paid me a visit lately; and after we had talked with indignation and contempt of the poisonous productions with which this age is infested, he said there was now an excellent opportunity for Dr. Johnson to step forth. I agreed with him that you might knock Hume's and Smith's heads together, and make vain and ostentatious infidelity exceedingly ridiculous. Would it not be worth your while to crush such noxious weeds in the moral garden?

'You have said nothing to me of Dr. Dodd. I know not how you think on that subject; though the newspapers give us a saying of your's in favour of mercy to him. But I own I am very desirous that the royal prerogative of remission of punishment should be employed to exhibit an illustrious instance of the regard which GOD's VICEGERENT will ever shew to piety and virtue. If for ten righteous men the ALMIGHTY would have spared Sodom, shall not a thousand acts of goodness done by Dr. Dodd counterbalance one crime? Such an instance would do more to encourage goodness, than his execution would do to deter from vice. I am not afraid of any bad consequence to society; for who will persevere for a long course of years in a distinguished discharge of religious duties, with a view to commit a forgery with impunity?

'Pray make my best compliments acceptable to Mr. and Mrs.

Thrale, by assuring them of my hearty joy that the *Master,* as you call him, is alive. I hope I shall often taste his Champagne— *soberly.*

> 'I remain, my dear Sir,
> 'Your most affectionate
> 'And faithful humble servant,
> 'JAMES BOSWELL.'

'TO JAMES BOSWELL, ESQ.

'DEAR SIR,

'POOR Dodd was put to death yesterday, in opposition to the recommendation of the jury—the petition of the city of London— and a subsequent petition signed by three-and-twenty thousand hands. Surely the voice of the publick, when it calls so loudly, and calls only for mercy, ought to be heard.

'The saying that was given me in the papers I never spoke; but I wrote many of his petitions, and some of his letters. He applied to me very often. He was, I am afraid, long flattered with hopes of life; but I had no part in the dreadful delusion; for as soon as the King had signed his sentence, I obtained from Mr. Chamier an account of the disposition of the court towards him, with a declaration that there *was no hope even of a respite.* This letter immediately was laid before Dodd; but he believed those whom he wished to be right, as it is thought, till within three days of his end. He died with pious composure and resolution.

'I hope to meet you somewhere towards the north, but am loath to come quite to Carlisle. Can we not meet at Manchester? But we will settle it in some other letters.

'I suppose Miss Boswell reads her book, and young Alexander takes to his learning. Let me hear about them; for every thing that belongs to you, belongs in a more remote degree, and not, I hope, very remote, to, dear Sir,

> 'Yours affectionately,
> 'SAM. JOHNSON.'

'June 28, 1777.'

Johnson's benevolence to the unfortunate was, I am confident, as steady and active as that of any of those who have been most eminently distinguished for that virtue. Innumerable proofs of it I have no doubt will be for ever concealed from mortal eyes. We may, however, form some judgement of it, from the many and very various instances which have been discovered. One, which happened in the course of this summer, is remarkable from the name and connection of the person who was the object of it. The circumstance to which I allude is ascertained by two letters, one to Mr. Langton, and another to the Reverend Dr. Vyse, rector of Lambeth, son of the respectable clergyman at Lichfield, who was contemporary with Johnson, and in whose father's family Johnson had the happiness of being kindly received in his early years.

'DR. JOHNSON TO BENNET LANGTON, ESQ.

'DEAR SIR,

'I HAVE lately been much disordered by a difficulty of breathing, but am now better. I hope your house is well.

'You know we have been talking lately of St. Cross, at Winchester; I have an old acquaintance whose distress makes him very desirous of an hospital, and I am afraid I have not strength enough to get him into the Chartreux. He is a painter, who never rose higher than to get his immediate living, and from that, at eighty-three, he is disabled by a slight stroke of the palsy, such as does not make him at all helpless on common occasions, though his hand is not steady enough for his art.

'My request is, that you will try to obtain a promise of the next vacancy, from the Bishop of Chester. It is not a great thing to ask, and I hope we shall obtain it. Dr. Warton has promised to favour him with his notice, and I hope he may end his days in peace. I am, Sir,

'Your most humble servant,
'SAM. JOHNSON.'

'June 29, 1777.'

'TO THE REVEREND DR. VYSE, AT LAMBETH.

'SIR,

'I DOUBT not but you will readily forgive me for taking the liberty of requesting your assistance in recommending an old friend to his Grace the Archbishop, as Governour of the Charter-house.

'His name is De Groot; he was born at Gloucester; I have known him many years. He has all the common claims to charity, being old, poor, and infirm, in a great degree. He has likewise another claim, to which no scholar can refuse attention; he is by several descents the nephew of Hugo Grotius; of him, from whom perhaps every man of learning has learnt something. Let it not be said that in any lettered country a nephew of Grotius asked a charity and was refused.

> 'I am, reverend Sir,
>> 'Your most humble servant,
>>> 'SAM. JOHNSON.'

'July 19, 1777.'

'DR. JOHNSON TO MR. EDWARD DILLY.

'SIR,

'To THE collection of English Poets, I have recommended the volume of Dr. Watts to be added; his name has long been held by me in veneration, and I would not willingly be reduced to tell of him only that he was born and died. Yet of his life I know very little, and therefore must pass him in a manner very unworthy of his character, unless some of his friends will favour me with the necessary information; many of them must be known to you; and by your influence, perhaps I may obtain some instruction. My plan does not exact much; but I wish to distinguish Watts, a man who never wrote but for a good purpose. Be pleased to do for me what you can.

> 'I am, Sir,
>> 'Your humble servant,

'Bolt-Court, Fleet-street,   'SAM. JOHNSON.'
     July 7, 1777.'

'To JAMES BOSWELL, ESQ.

'DEAR SIR,

'YOUR notion of the necessity of an yearly interview is very pleasing to both my vanity and tenderness. I shall, perhaps, come to Carlisle another year; but my money has not held out so well as it used to do. I shall go to Ashbourne, and I purpose to make Dr. Taylor invite you. If you live awhile with me at his house, we shall have much time to ourselves, and our stay will be no expence to us or him. I shall leave London the 28th; and after some stay at Oxford and Lichfield, shall probably come to Ashbourne about the end of your Session, but of all this you shall have notice. Be satisfied we will meet somewhere.

'What passed between me and poor Dr. Dodd you shall know more fully when we meet.

'You have done right in taking your uncle's house. Some change in the form of life, gives from time to time a new epocha of exist-ence. In a new place there is something new to be done, and a dif-ferent system of thoughts rises in the mind. I wish I could gather currants in your garden. Now fit up a little study, and have your books ready at hand; do not spare a little money, to make your habitation pleasing to yourself.

'Mrs. Williams is in the country to try if she can improve her health; she is very ill. Matters have come so about that she is in the country with very good accommodation; but age and sickness, and pride, have made her so peevish that I was forced to bribe the maid to stay with her, by a secret stipulation of half a crown a week over her wages.

'Our CLUB ended its session about six weeks ago. We now only meet to dine once a fortnight. Mr. Dunning, the great lawyer, is one of our members. The Thrales are well.

                    'I am, dear Sir,
                              'Your most affectionate, &c.
                                        'SAM. JOHNSON.'
'July 22, 1777.'

                'DR. JOHNSON TO MRS. BOSWELL.
'MADAM,
    'THOUGH I am well enough pleased with the taste of sweet-meats, very little of the pleasure which I received at the arrival of your jar of marmalade arose from eating it. I received it as a token of friendship, as a proof of reconciliation, things much sweeter than sweetmeats, and upon this consideration I return you, dear Madam, my sincerest thanks. By having your kindness I think I have a double security for the continuance of Mr. Boswell's, which it is not to be expected that any man can long keep, when the influence of a lady so highly and so justly valued operates against him. Mr. Boswell will tell you that I was always faithful to your interest, and always endeavoured to exalt you in his estimation. You must now do the same for me. We must all help one another, and you must now consider me, as, dear Madam,

                    'Your most obliged,
                         'And most humble servant,
                                        'SAM. JOHNSON.'
'July 22, 1777.'

                'TO JAMES BOSWELL, ESQ.
'DEAR SIR,
    'I AM this day come to Ashbourne, and have only to tell you, that Dr. Taylor says you shall be welcome to him, and you know how welcome you will be to me. Make haste to let me know when you may be expected.

'Make my compliments to Mrs. Boswell, and tell her, I hope we shall be at variance no more. I am, dear Sir,

'Your most humble servant,

'SAM. JOHNSON.'

'August 30, 1777.'

'To JAMES BOSWELL, ESQ.

'DEAR SIR,

'ON SATURDAY I wrote a very short letter, immediately upon my arrival hither, to shew you that I am not less desirous of the interview than yourself. Life admits not of delays; when pleasure can be had, it is fit to catch it: Every hour takes away part of the things that please us, and perhaps part of our disposition to be pleased. When I came to Lichfield, I found my old friend Harry Jackson dead. It was a loss, and a loss not to be repaired, as he was one of the companions of my childhood. I hope we may long continue to gain friends, but the friends which merit or usefulness can procure us, are not able to supply the place of old acquaintance, with whom the days of youth may be retraced, and those images revived which gave the earliest delight. If you and I live to be much older, we shall take great delight in talking over the Hebridean Journey.

'In the mean time it may not be amiss to contrive some other little adventure, but what it can be I know not; leave it, as Sidney says,

"To virtue, fortune, wine, and woman's breast;"

for I believe Mrs. Boswell must have some part in the consultation.

'One thing you will like. The Doctor, so far as I can judge, is likely to leave us enough to ourselves. He was out to-day before I came down, and, I fancy, will stay out till dinner.

'Before I came away I sent poor Mrs. Williams into the country, very ill of a pituitous defluxion, which wastes her gradually away, and which her physician declares himself unable to stop. I supplied her as far as could be desired, with all conveniences to make her excursion and abode pleasant and useful. But I am afraid she can only linger a short time in a morbid state of weakness and pain.

'The Thrales, little and great, are all well, and purpose to go to Brighthelmstone at Michaelmas. They will invite me to go with them, and perhaps I may go, but hardly think I shall like to stay the whole time; but of futurity we know but little.

'Mrs. Porter is well; but Mrs. Aston, one of the ladies at Stow-

hill, has been struck with a palsy, from which she is not likely ever
to recover. How soon may such a stroke fall upon us!

'Write to me, and let us know when we may expect you.

'I am, dear Sir,

'Your most humble servant,

'SAM. JOHNSON.'

'Ashbourne, Sept. 1, 1777.'

On Sunday evening, September 14, I arrived at Ashbourne,
and drove directly up to Dr. Taylor's door. Dr. Johnson and
he appeared before I had got out of the post-chaise, and welcomed me cordially.

I told them that I had travelled all the preceding night,
and gone to bed at Leek in Staffordshire; and that when I rose
to go to church in the afternoon, I was informed there had
been an earthquake, of which, it seems, the shock had been
felt, in some degree, at Ashbourne. *Johnson.* 'Sir, it will be
much exaggerated in popular talk: for, in the first place, the
common people do not accurately adapt their thoughts to the
objects; nor, secondly, do they accurately adapt their words
to their thoughts: they do not mean to lie; but, taking no pains
to be exact, they give you very false accounts. A great part of
their language is proverbial. If anything rocks at all, they say
it rocks like a cradle; and in this way they go on.'

The subject of grief for the loss of relations and friends being
introduced, I observed that it was strange to consider how soon
it in general wears away. Dr. Taylor mentioned a gentleman
of the neighbourhood as the only instance he had ever known
of a person who had endeavoured to *retain* grief. He told Dr.
Taylor, that after his Lady's death, which affected him deeply,
he *resolved* that the grief, which he cherished with a kind of
sacred fondness, should be lasting; but that he found he could
not keep it long. *Johnson.* 'All grief for what cannot in the
course of nature be helped, soon wears away; in some sooner,
indeed, in some later; but it never continues very long, unless
where there is madness, such as will make a man have pride
so fixed in his mind, as to imagine himself a King; or any
other passion in an unreasonable way: for all unnecessary
grief is unwise, and therefore will not be long retained by a
sound mind. If, indeed, the cause of our grief is occasioned by

our own misconduct, if grief is mingled with remorse of conscience, it should be lasting.' *Boswell*. 'But, Sir, we do not approve of a man who very soon forgets the loss of a wife or a friend.' *Johnson*. 'Sir, we disapprove of him, not because he soon forgets his grief, for the sooner it is forgotten the better, but because we suppose, that if he forgets his wife or his friend soon, he has not had much affection for them.'

I was somewhat disappointed in finding that the edition of the English Poets, for which he was to write Prefaces and Lives, was not an undertaking directed by him: but that he was to furnish a Preface and Life to any poet the booksellers pleased. I asked him if he would do this to any dunce's works, if they should ask him. *Johnson*. 'Yes, Sir; and *say* he was a dunce.' My friend seemed now not much to relish talking of this edition.

After breakfast, Johnson carried me to see the garden belonging to the school of Ashbourne, which is very prettily formed upon a bank, rising gradually behind the house. The Reverend Mr. Langley, the head-master, accompanied us.

We had with us at dinner several of Dr. Taylor's neighbours, good civil gentlemen, who seemed to understand Dr. Johnson very well, and not to consider him in the light that a certain person did, who being struck, or rather stunned by his voice and manner, when he was afterwards asked what he thought of him, answered, 'He's a tremendous companion.'

And here is the proper place to give an account of Johnson's humane and zealous interference in behalf of the Reverend Dr. William Dodd, formerly Prebendary of Brecon, and chaplain in ordinary to his Majesty; celebrated as a very popular preacher, an encourager of charitable institutions, and authour of a variety of works, chiefly theological. Having unhappily contracted expensive habits of living, partly occasioned by licentiousness of manners, he in an evil hour, when pressed by want of money, and dreading an exposure of his circumstances, forged a bond of which he attempted to avail himself to support his credit, flattering himself with hopes that he might be able to repay its amount without being detected. The person, whose name he thus rashly and criminally presumed to falsify, was the Earl of Chesterfield, to whom he had been tutor, and who, he perhaps, in the warmth of his feelings, flattered himself would have generously paid the money in case of an alarm being taken, rather than suffer him to fall a victim to the dreadful consequences of violating the law against forgery, the most dangerous crime in a commercial country; but the unfortunate divine had the mortification to find that he was mistaken. His noble pupil appeared against him, and he was capitally convicted.

Johnson told me that Dr. Dodd was very little acquainted with him, having been but once in his company, many years previous to this period (which was precisely the state of my own acquaintance with Dodd); but in his distress he bethought himself of Johnson's persuasive power of writing, if haply it might avail to obtain for him the Royal Mercy. He did not apply to him directly, but, extraordinary as it may seem, through the late Countess of Harrington, who wrote a letter to Johnson, asking him to employ his pen in favour of Dodd. Mr. Allen, the printer, who was Johnson's landlord and next neighbour in Bolt-court, and for whom he had much kindness, was one of Dodd's friends, of whom, to the credit of humanity be it recorded, that he had many who did not desert him, even after his infringement of the law had reduced him to the state of a man under sentence of death. Mr. Allen told me that he carried Lady Harrington's letter to Johnson, that Johnson read it walking up and down his chamber, and seemed much agitated, after which he said, 'I will do what I can;'—and certainly he did make extraordinary exertions.

He this evening, as he had obligingly promised in one of his letters, put into my hands the whole series of his writings upon this melancholy occasion, and I shall present my readers with the abstract which I made from the collection; in doing which I studied to avoid copying what had appeared in print, and now make part of the edition of 'Johnson's Works,' published by the Booksellers of London, but taking care to mark Johnson's variations in some of the pieces there exhibited.

Dr. Johnson wrote in the first place, Dr. Dodd's 'Speech to the Recorder of London,' at the Old-Bailey, when sentence of death was about to be pronounced upon him.

He wrote also 'The Convict's Address to his unhappy Breth-

ren,' a sermon delivered by Dr. Dodd, in the chapel of Newgate.

The other pieces written by Johnson in the above-mentioned
collection, are two letters, one to the Lord Chancellor Bathurst,
(not Lord North, as is erroneously supposed,) and one to
Lord Mansfield;—A Petition from Dr. Dodd to the King;—
A Petition from Mrs. Dodd to the Queen;—Observations of
some length inserted in the news-papers, on occasion of Earl
Percy's having presented to his Majesty a petition for mercy
to Dodd, signed by twenty thousand people, but all in vain.
He told me that he had also written a petition from the city of
London; 'but (said he, with a significant smile) they *mended*
it.'

The last of these articles which Johnson wrote is 'Dr. Dodd's
last solemn Declaration,' which he left with the sheriff at
the place of execution. My friend marked the variations on a
copy of that piece now in my possession. Dodd inserted, 'I
never knew or attended to the calls of frugality, or the needful
minuteness of painful œconomy;' and in the next sentence he
introduced the words which I distinguish by *Italicks*; 'My life
for some *few unhappy* years past has been *dreadfully erroneous.*' Johnson's expression was *hypocritical*; but his remark
on the margin is 'With this he said he could not charge himself.'

Having thus authentically settled what part of the 'Occasional Papers,' concerning Dr. Dodd's miserable situation,
came from the pen of Johnson, I shall proceed to present my
readers with my record of the unpublished writings relating
to that extraordinary and interesting matter.

I found a letter to Dr. Johnson from Dr. Dodd, May 23,
1777, in which 'The Convict's Address' seems clearly to be
meant:

'I am so penetrated, my ever dear Sir, with a sense of your extreme benevolence towards me, that I cannot find words equal to
the sentiments of my heart.

'You are too conversant in the world to need the slightest hint
from me, of what infinite utility the Speech on the aweful day has
been to me. I experience, every hour, some good effect from it. I
am sure that effects still more salutary and important, must follow

from *your kind and intended favour*. I will labour,—GOD being my helper,—to do justice to it from the pulpit. I am sure, had I your sentiments constantly to deliver from thence, in all their mighty force and power, not a soul could be left unconvinced and unpersuaded.

On Sunday, June 22, he writes, begging Dr. Johnson's assistance in framing a supplicatory letter to his Majesty:

'If his Majesty could be moved of his royal clemency to spare me and my family the horrours and ignominy of a *publick death*, which the *publick* itself is solicitous to wave, and to grant me in some silent distant corner of the globe, to pass the remainder of my days in penitence and prayer, I would bless his clemency and be humbled.'

This letter was brought to Dr. Johnson when in church. He stooped down and read it, and wrote, when he went home, the following letter for Dr. Dodd to the King:

'SIR,

'MAY it not offend your Majesty, that the most miserable of men applies himself to your clemency, as his last hope and his last refuge; that your mercy is most earnestly and humbly implored by a clergyman, whom your Laws and Judges have condemned to the horrour and ignominy of a publick execution.

'I confess the crime, and own the enormity of its consequences, and the danger of its example. Nor have I the confidence to petition for impunity; but humbly hope, that publick security may be established, without the spectacle of a clergyman dragged through the streets, to a death of infamy, amidst the derision of the profligate and profane; and that justice may be satisfied with irrevocable exile, perpetual disgrace, and hopeless penury.

'My life, Sir, has not been useless to mankind. I have benefited many. But my offences against GOD are numberless, and I have had little time for repentance. Preserve me, Sir, by your prerogative of mercy, from the necessity of appearing unprepared at that tribunal, before which Kings and Subjects must stand at last together. Permit me to hide my guilt in some obscure corner of a foreign country, where, if I can ever attain confidence to hope that my prayers will be heard, they shall be poured with all the fervour of gratitude for the life and happiness of your Majesty. I am, Sir,

'Your Majesty's, &c.'

Subjoined to it was written as follows:

'To Dr. Dodd.

'Sir,

'I most seriously enjoin you not to let it be at all known that I have written this letter, and to return the copy to Mr. Allen in a cover to me. I hope I need not tell you, that I wish it success.—But do not indulge hope.—Tell nobody.'

Dr. Johnson never went to see Dr. Dodd. He said to me, 'it would have done *him* more harm, than good to Dodd, who once expressed a desire to see him, but not earnestly.'

Dr. Johnson, on the 20th of June, wrote the following letter:

'To the Right Honourable Charles Jenkinson.

'Sir,

'Since the conviction and condemnation of Dr. Dodd, I have had, by the intervention of a friend, some intercourse with him, and I am sure I shall lose nothing in your opinion by tenderness and commiseration. Whatever be the crime, it is not easy to have any knowledge of the delinquent, without a wish that his life may be spared; at least when no life has been taken away by him. I will, therefore, take the liberty of suggesting some reasons for which I wish this unhappy being to escape the utmost rigour of his sentence.

'He is, so far as I can recollect, the first clergyman of our church who has suffered publick execution for immorality; and I know not whether it would not be more for the interest of religion to bury such an offender in the obscurity of perpetual exile, than to expose him in a cart, and on the gallows, to all who for any reason are enemies to the clergy.

'The supreme power has, in all ages, paid some attention to the voice of the people; and that voice does not least deserve to be heard, when it calls out for mercy. There is now a very general desire that Dodd's life should be spared. More is not wished; and, perhaps, this is not too much to be granted.

'If you, Sir, have any opportunity of enforcing these reasons, you may, perhaps, think them worthy of consideration: but whatever you determine, I most respectfully intreat that you will be pleased to pardon for this intrusion, Sir,

'Your most obedient

'And most humble servant,

'Sam. Johnson.'

All applications for the Royal Mercy having failed, Dr. Dodd prepared himself for death; and, with a warmth of gratitude, wrote to Dr. Johnson as follows:

'June 25, *Midnight.*

'ACCEPT, thou *great* and *good* heart, my earnest and fervent thanks and prayers for all thy benevolent and kind efforts in my behalf.—Oh! Dr. Johnson! as I sought your knowledge at an early hour in life, would to heaven I had cultivated the love and acquaintance of so excellent a man!—I pray GOD most sincerely to bless you with the highest transports—the infelt satisfaction of *humane* and benevolent exertions!—And admitted, as I trust I shall be, to the realms of bliss before you, I shall hail *your* arrival there with transport, and rejoice to acknowledge that you was my Comforter, my Advocate, and my *Friend!* GOD *be ever* with *you!*'

Dr. Johnson lastly wrote to Dr. Dodd this solemn and soothing letter:

'To THE REVEREND DR. DODD.

'DEAR SIR,

'THAT which is appointed to all men is now coming upon you. Outward circumstances, the eyes and the thoughts of men, are below the notice of an immortal being about to stand the trial for eternity, before the Supreme Judge of heaven and earth. Be comforted: your crime, morally or religiously considered, has no very deep dye of turpitude. It corrupted no man's principles; it attacked no man's life. It involved only a temporary and reparable injury. Of this, and of all other sins, you are earnestly to repent; and may GOD, who knoweth our frailty, and desireth not our death accept your repentance, for the sake of his Son JESUS CHRIST our Lord.

'In requital of those well-intended offices which you are pleased so emphatically to acknowledge, let me beg that you make in your devotions one petition for my eternal welfare. I am, dear Sir,

'Your affectionate servant,

'SAM. JOHNSON.'

'June 26, 1777.'

Under the copy of this letter I found written, in Johnson's own hand, 'Next day, June 27, he was executed.'

Johnson gave us this evening, in his happy discriminative manner, a portrait of the late Mr. Fitzherbert, of Derbyshire.

'There was (said he) no sparkle, no brilliancy in Fitzherbert; but I never knew a man who was so generally acceptable. He made every body quite easy, overpowered nobody by the superiority of his talents, made no man think worse of himself by being his rival, seemed always to listen, did not oblige you to hear much from him, and did not oppose what you said. Every body liked him; but he had no friend, as I understand the word, nobody with whom he exchanged intimate thoughts. People were willing to think well of every thing about him. A gentleman was making an affected rant, as many people do, of great feelings about "his dear son," who was at school near London; how anxious he was lest he might be ill, and what he would give to see him. "Can't you (said Fitzherbert,) take a post-chaise and go to him?" This, to be sure, *finished* the affected man, but there was not much in it. However, this was circulated as wit for a whole winter, and I believe part of a summer too; a proof that he was no very witty man. He was an instance of the truth of the observation, that a man will please more upon the whole by negative qualities than by positive; by never offending, than by giving a great deal of delight. In the first place, men hate more steadily than they love; and if I have said something to hurt a man once, I shall not get the better of this by saying many things to please him.'

Tuesday, September 16, Dr. Johnson having mentioned to me the extraordinary size and price of some cattle reared by Dr. Taylor, I rode out with our host, surveyed his farm, and was shown one cow which he had sold for a hundred and twenty guineas, and another for which he had been offered a hundred and thirty. Taylor thus described to me his old school-fellow and friend, Johnson: 'He is a man of a very clear head, great power of words, and a very gay imagination; but there is no disputing with him. He will not hear you, and having a louder voice than you, must roar you down.'

In the evening, the Reverend Mr. Seward, of Lichfield, who was passing through Ashbourne in his way home, drank tea with us. Johnson described him thus:—'Sir, his ambition is to be a fine talker; so he goes to Buxton, and such places, where he may find companies to listen to him. And, Sir, he is a valetudinarian, one of those who are always mending themselves. I do not know a more disagreeable character than a valetudinarian, who thinks he may do any thing that is for his ease, and indulges himself in the grossest freedoms: Sir, he brings himself to the state of a hog in a stye.'

Dr. Taylor's nose happening to bleed, he said, it was because he had omitted to have himself blooded four days after a quarter of a year's interval. Dr. Johnson, who was a great dabbler in physick, disapproved much of periodical bleeding.[1]

I mentioned to Dr. Johnson, that David Hume's persisting in his infidelity, when he was dying, shocked me much. *Johnson.* 'Why should it shock you, Sir? Hume owned he had never read the New Testament with attention. Here then was a man, who had been at no pains to inquire into the truth of religion, and had continually turned his mind the other way. It was not to be expected that the prospect of death would alter his way of thinking, unless GOD should send an angel to set him right.' I said, I had reason to believe that the thought of annihilation gave Hume no pain. *Johnson.* 'It was not so, Sir. He had a vanity in being thought easy. It is more probable that he should assume an appearance of ease, than that so very improbable a thing should be, as a man not afraid of going (as, in spite of his delusive theory, he cannot be sure but he may go,) into an unknown state, and not being uneasy at leaving all he knew. And you are to consider, that upon his own principle of annihilation he had no motive to speak the truth.' The horrour of death which I had always observed in Dr. Johnson, appeared strong to-night. I ventured to tell him, that I had been, for moments in my life, not afraid of death; therefore I could suppose another man in that state of mind for a considerable space of time. He said, 'he never had a moment in which death was not terrible to him.' He added, that it had been observed, that scarce any man dies in publick, but with apparent resolution; from that desire of praise which never quits us. I said, Dr. Dodd seemed to be willing to die, and full of hopes of happiness. 'Sir, (said he,) Dr. Dodd would have given both his hands and both his legs to have lived.'

Dr. Johnson was much pleased with a remark which I told

---

[1] The menstruation of women was thought by many to provide a "natural" sanction for phlebotomy at regular intervals.

him was made to me by General Paoli:—'That it is impossible
not to be afraid of death; and that those who at the time of
dying are not afraid, are not thinking of death, but of applause, or something else, which keeps death out of their sight:
so that all men are equally afraid of death when they see it;
only some have a power of turning their sight away from it better than others.'

On Wednesday, September 17, Dr. Butter, physician at
Derby, drank tea with us; and it was settled that Dr. Johnson
and I should go on Friday and dine with him. Johnson said,
'I'm glad of this.' He seemed weary of the uniformity of life
at Dr. Taylor's.

Talking of biography, I said, in writing a life, a man's peculiarities should be mentioned, because they mark his character.
Johnson. 'Sir, there is no doubt as to peculiarities: the question is, whether a man's vices should be mentioned; for instance, whether it should be mentioned that Addison and
Parnell drank too freely: for people will probably more easily
indulge in drinking from knowing this; so that more ill may
be done by the example, than good by telling the whole truth.'
Here was an instance of his varying from himself in talk; for
when Lord Hailes and he sat one morning calmly conversing
in my house at Edinburgh, I well remember that Dr. Johnson
maintained, that 'If a man is to write *A Panegyrick,* he may
keep vices out of sight; but if he professes to write *A Life,* he
must represent it really as it was:' and when I objected to the
danger of telling that Parnell drank to excess, he said, that
'it would produce an instructive caution to avoid drinking,
when it was seen, that even the learning and genius of Parnell
could be debased by it.' And in the Hebrides he maintained,
as appears from my 'Journal,' that a man's intimate friend should
mention his faults, if he writes his life.

Thursday, September 18. Last night Dr. Johnson had proposed that the crystal lustre, or chandelier, in Dr. Taylor's
large room, should be lighted up some time or other. Taylor
said, it should be lighted up next night. 'That will do very
well, (said I,) for it is Dr. Johnson's birth-day.' When we were
in the Isle of Sky, Johnson had desired me not to mention his
birth-day. He did not seem pleased at this time that I men-

tioned it, and said (somewhat sternly) 'he would *not* have the lustre lighted the next day.'

Some ladies, who had been present yesterday when I mentioned his birth-day, came to dinner to-day, and plagued him unintentionally, by wishing him joy. I know not why he disliked having his birth-day mentioned, unless it were that it reminded him of his approaching nearer to death, of which he had a constant dread.

I mentioned to him a friend of mine who was formerly gloomy from low spirits, and much distressed by the fear of death, but was now uniformly placid, and contemplated his dissolution without any perturbation. 'Sir, (said Johnson,) this is only a disordered imagination taking a different turn.'

He observed, that a gentleman of eminence in literature had got into a bad style of poetry of late. 'He puts (said he) a very common thing in a strange dress till he does not know it himself, and thinks other people do not know it.' *Boswell.* 'That is owing to his being so much versant in old English poetry.' *Johnson.* 'What is that to the purpose, Sir? If I say a man is drunk, and you tell me it is owing to his taking much drink, the matter is not mended. No, Sir, ——— has taken to an odd mode. For example; he'd write thus:

> "Hermit hoar, in solemn cell,
>   Wearing out life's evening gray."

Gray evening is common enough; but *evening gray* he'd think fine.—Stay;—we'll make out the stanza:

> "Hermit hoar, in solemn cell,
>   Wearing out life's evening gray;
>   Smite thy bosom, sage, and tell,
>   What is bliss? and which the way?"'

Boswell. 'But why smite his bosom, Sir?' *Johnson.* 'Why to shew he was in earnest,' (smiling).—He at an after period added the following stanza:

> 'Thus I spoke; and speaking sigh'd;
>   —Scarce repress'd the starting tear;—
> When the smiling sage reply'd—
>   —Come, my lad, and drink some beer.'

Friday, September 19, after breakfast, Dr. Johnson and I set out in Dr. Taylor's chaise to go to Derby. The day was fine, and we resolved to go by Keddlestone, the seat of Lord Scarsdale, that I might see his Lordship's fine house. I was struck with the magnificence of the building; and the extensive park, with the finest verdure, covered with deer, and cattle, and sheep, delighted me. The number of old oaks, of an immense size, filled me with a sort of respectful admiration: for one of them sixty pounds was offered. The excellent smooth gravel roads; the large piece of water formed by his Lordship from some small brooks, with a handsome barge upon it; the venerable Gothick church, now the family chapel, just by the house; in short, the grand group of objects agitated and distended my mind in a most agreeable manner. 'One should think (said I) that the proprietor of all this *must* be happy.'—'Nay, Sir, (said Johnson,) all this excludes but one evil—poverty.'

Our names were sent up, and a well-drest elderly housekeeper, a most distinct articulator, shewed us the house; which I need not describe, as there is an account of it published in 'Adam's Works in Architecture.' Dr. Johnson thought better of it to-day than when he saw it before; for he had lately attacked it violently, saying, 'It would do excellently for a town-hall. The large room with the pillars (said he) would do for the Judges to sit in at the assizes; the circular room for a jury-chamber; and the rooms above for prisoners.' Still he thought the large room ill lighted, and of no use but for dancing in; and the bed-chambers but indifferent rooms; and that the immense sum which it cost was injudiciously laid out. Dr. Taylor had put him in mind of his *appearing* pleased with the house. 'But (said he) that was when Lord Scarsdale was present. Politeness obliges us to appear pleased with a man's works when he is present. No man will be so ill bred as to question you. You may therefore pay compliments without saying what is not true. I should say to Lord Scarsdale of his large room, "My Lord, this is the most *costly* room that I ever saw;" which is true.'

Dr. Manningham, physician in London, who was visiting at Lord Scarsdale's, accompanied us through many of the rooms, and soon afterwards my Lord himself, to whom Dr.

Johnson was known, appeared, and did the honours of the house. We talked of Mr. Langton. Johnson, with a warm vehemence of affectionate regard, exclaimed, 'The earth does not bear a worthier man than Bennet Langton.' We saw a good many fine pictures. There is a printed catalogue of them which the housekeeper put into my hand; I should like to view them at leisure. I was much struck with Daniel interpreting Nebuchadnezzar's dream by Rembrandt. We were shown a pretty large library. In his Lordship's dressing-room lay Johnson's small Dictionary: he shewed it to me, with some eagerness. He observed, also, Goldsmith's 'Animated Nature;' and said, 'Here's our friend! The poor Doctor would have been happy to hear of this.'

In our way, Johnson strongly expressed his love of driving fast in a post-chaise. 'If (said he) I had no duties, and no reference to futurity, I would spend my life in driving briskly in a post-chaise with a pretty woman; but she should be one who could understand me, and would add something to the conversation.'

When we arrived at Derby, Dr. Butter accompanied us to see the manufactory of china there. I admired the ingenuity and delicate art with which a man fashioned clay into a cup, a saucer, or a tea-pot, while a boy turned round a wheel to give the mass rotundity. I thought this as excellent in its species of power, as making good verses in *its* species. Yet I had no respect for this potter. Neither, indeed, has a man of any extent of thinking for a mere verse-maker, in whose numbers, however perfect, there is no poetry, no mind. The china was beautiful, but Dr. Johnson justly observed it was too dear; for that he could have vessels of silver, of the same size, as cheap as what were here made of porcelain.

I felt a pleasure in walking about Derby, such as I always have in walking about any town to which I am not accustomed. There is an immediate sensation of novelty; and one speculates on the way in which life is passed in it, which, although there is a sameness every where upon the whole, is yet minutely diversified. The minute diversities in every thing are wonderful. Talking of shaving the other night at Dr. Taylor's, Dr. Johnson said, 'Sir, of a thousand shavers, two do not shave so much alike as not to be distinguished.' I thought this not possible, till he specified so many of the varieties in shaving;—holding the razor more or less perpendicular;—drawing long or short strokes;—beginning at the upper part of the face, or the under;—at the right side or the left side. Indeed, when one considers what variety of sounds can be uttered by the wind-pipe, in the compass of a very small aperture, we may be convinced how many degrees of difference there may be in the application of a razor.

We dined with Dr. Butter, whose lady is daughter of my cousin Sir John Douglas, whose grandson is now presumptive heir of the noble family of Queensberry. Johnson and he had a great deal of medical conversation. He told us, 'that whatever a man's distemper was, Dr. Nichols would not attend him as a physician, if his mind was not at ease; for he believed that no medicines would have any influence. He once attended a man in trade, upon whom he found none of the medicines he prescribed had any effect; he asked the man's wife privately whether his affairs were not in a bad way? She said no. He continued his attendance some time, still without success. At length the man's wife told him, she had discovered that her husband's affairs *were* in a bad way. When Goldsmith was dying, Dr. Turton said to him, "Your pulse is in greater disorder than it should be, from the degree of fever which you have: is your mind at ease?" Goldsmith answered it was not.'

Dr. Johnson told us at tea, that when some of Dr. Dodd's pious friends were trying to console him by saying that he was going to leave 'a wretched world,' he had honesty enough not to join in the cant:—'No, no, (said he,) it has been a very agreeable world to me.' Johnson added, 'I respect Dodd for thus speaking the truth; for, to be sure, he had for several years enjoyed a life of great voluptuousness.'

He told us, that Dodd's city friends stood by him so, that a thousand pounds were ready to be given to the gaoler, if he would let him escape. He added, that he knew a friend of Dodd's, who walked about Newgate for some time on the evening before the day of his execution, with five hundred pounds in his pocket, ready to be paid to any of the turnkeys who could get him out: but it was too late; for he was watched with much circumspection. He said, Dodd's friends had an image of him made of wax, which was to have been left in his place; and he believed it was carried into the prison.

Johnson disapproved of Dr. Dodd's leaving the world persuaded that 'The Convict's Address to his unhappy Brethren' was of his own writing. 'But, Sir, (said I,) you contributed to the deception; for when Mr. Seward expressed a doubt to you that it was not Dodd's own, because it had a great deal more force of mind in it than any thing known to be his, you answered,—"Why should you think so? Depend upon it, Sir, when a man knows he is to be hanged in a fortnight, it concentrates his mind wonderfully." ' *Johnson.* 'Sir, as Dodd got it from me to pass as his own, while that could do him any good, there was an *implied promise* that I should not own it. To own it, therefore, would have been telling a lie, with the addition of breach of promise, which was worse than simply telling a lie to make it be believed it was Dodd's. Besides, Sir, I did not *directly* tell a lie: I left the matter uncertain. Perhaps I thought that Seward would not believe it the less to be mine for what I said; but I would not put it in his power to say I had owned it.'

I mentioned that Lord Monboddo told me, he awaked every morning at four, and then for his health got up and walked in his room naked, with the window open, which he called taking *an air bath;* after which he went to bed again, and slept two hours more. Johnson, who was always ready to beat down any thing that seemed to be exhibited with disproportionate importance, thus observed: 'I suppose, Sir, there is no more in it than this, he awakes at four, and cannot sleep till he chills himself, and makes the warmth of the bed a grateful sensation.'

I talked of the difficulty of rising in the morning. Dr. Johnson told me, 'that the learned Mrs. Carter, at that period when she was eager in study, did not awake as early as she wished, and she therefore had a contrivance, that, at a certain hour, her chamber-light should burn a string to which a heavy weight was suspended, which then fell with a strong sudden noise: this roused her from sleep, and then she had no difficulty in getting up.' But I said *that* was my difficulty; and wished there could be some medicine invented which would make one rise without pain, which I never did, unless after lying in bed a very long time. Perhaps there may be something in the stores of Nature which could do this. I have thought of a pulley to raise me gradually; but that would give me pain, as it would counteract my internal inclination. As I imagine that the human body may be put, by the operation of other substances, into any state in which it has ever been; and as I have experienced a state in which rising from bed was not disagreeable, but easy, nay, sometimes agreeable; I suppose that this state may be produced, if we knew by what. We can heat the body, we can cool it; we can give it tension or relaxation; and surely it is possible to bring it into a state in which rising from bed will not be a pain.

Johnson observed, that 'a man should take a sufficient quantity of sleep, which Dr. Mead says is between seven and nine hours.' I told him, that Dr. Cullen said to me, that a man should not take more sleep than he can take at once. *Johnson.* 'This rule, Sir, cannot hold in all cases; for many people have their sleep broken by sickness; and surely, Cullen would not have a man to get up, after having slept but an hour. Such a regimen would soon end in a *long sleep.*' Dr. Taylor remarked, I think very justly, that 'a man who does not feel an inclination to sleep at the ordinary time, instead of being stronger than other people, must not be well; for a man in health has all the natural inclinations to eat, drink, and sleep, in a strong degree.'

Johnson advised me to-night not to *refine* in the education of my children. 'Life (said he) will not bear refinement: you must do as other people do.'

As we drove back to Ashbourne, Dr. Johnson recommended to me, as he had often done, to drink water only: 'For (said he) you are then sure not to get drunk; whereas if you drink wine you are never sure.' I said, drinking wine was a pleasure which I was unwilling to give up. 'Why, Sir, (said he,) there is no doubt that not to drink wine is a great deduction from life; but it may be necessary.' He however owned, that in his opinion a free use of wine did not shorten life; and said, he would not give less for the life of a certain Scotch Lord (whom

he named) celebrated for hard drinking, than for that of a
sober man. 'But stay, (said he, with his usual intelligence,
and accuracy of enquiry,) does it take much wine to make him
drunk?' I answered, 'a great deal either of wine or strong punch.'
—'Then (said he) that is the worse.' I presume to illustrate
my friend's observation thus: 'A fortress which soon surrenders
has its walls less shattered, than when a long and obstinate
resistance is made.'

By the time when we returned to Ashbourne, Dr. Taylor
was gone to bed. Johnson and I sat up a long time by ourselves.

I read to him a letter which Lord Monboddo had written
to me, containing some critical remarks upon the style of his
'Journey to the Western Islands of Scotland.' His Lordship
praised the very fine passage upon landing at Icolmkill; but
his own style being exceedingly dry and hard, he disapproved
of the richness of Johnson's language, and of his frequent use
of metaphorical expressions. *Johnson.* 'Why, Sir, this criticism
would be just, if in my style, superfluous words, or words too
big for the thoughts, could be pointed out; but this I do not
believe can be done. For instance; in the passage which Lord
Monboddo admires, "We were now treading that illustrious
region," the word *illustrious,* contributes nothing to the mere
narration; for the fact might be told without it: but it is not,
therefore, superfluous; for it wakes the mind to peculiar attention, where something of more than usual importance is to be
presented. "Illustrious!"—for what? and then the sentence pro-
ceeds to expand the circumstances connected with Iona. And,
Sir, as to metaphorical expression, that is a great excellence in
style, when it is used with propriety, for it gives you two ideas
for one;—conveys the meaning more luminously, and generally with a perception of delight.'

On Saturday, September 20, after breakfast, when Taylor
was gone out to his farm, Dr. Johnson and I had a serious conversation by ourselves on melancholy and madness; which he
was, I always thought, erroneously inclined to confound together. Melancholy, like 'great wit,' may be 'near allied to
madness;' but there is, in my opinion, a distinct separation between them. When he talked of madness, he was to be under-

stood as speaking of those who were in any great degree disturbed, or as it is commonly expressed, 'troubled in mind.' Some of the ancient philosophers held, that all deviations from right reason were madness; and whoever wishes to see the opinions both of ancients and moderns upon this subject, collected and illustrated with variety of curious facts, may read Dr. Arnold's very entertaining work.

Johnson said, 'A madman loves to be with people whom he fears; not as a dog fears the lash; but of whom he stands in awe.' I was struck with the justice of this observation. To be with those of whom a person, whose mind is wavering and dejected, stands in awe, represses and composes an uneasy tumult of spirits, and consoles him with the contemplation of something steady, and at least comparatively great.

He added, 'Madmen are all sensual in the lower stages of the distemper. They are eager for gratifications to sooth their minds and divert their attention from the misery which they suffer: but when they grow very ill, pleasure is too weak for them, and they seek for pain. Employment, Sir, and hardships, prevent melancholy. I suppose in all our army in America there was not one man who went mad.'

We talked of employment being absolutely necessary to preserve the mind from wearying and growing fretful, especially in those who have a tendency to melancholy; and I mentioned to him a saying which somebody had related of an American savage, who, when an European was expatiating on all the advantages of money, put this question: 'Will it purchase *occupation?*' *Johnson*. 'Depend upon it, Sir, this saying is too refined for a savage. And, Sir, money *will* purchase occupation; it will purchase all the conveniencies of life; it will purchase variety of company; it will purchase all sorts of entertainment.'

On Sunday, September 21, we went to the church of Ashbourne, which is one of the largest and most luminous that I have seen in any town of the same size. I felt great satisfaction in considering that I was supported in my fondness for solemn publick worship by the general concurrence and munificence of mankind.

Johnson and Taylor were so different from each other, that I wondered at their preserving such an intimacy. Their having been at school and college together, might, in some degree, account for this; but Sir Joshua Reynolds has furnished me with a stronger reason; for Johnson mentioned to him, that he had been told by Taylor he was to be his heir. I shall not take upon me to animadvert upon this; but certain it is, that Johnson paid great attention to Taylor. He now, however, said to me, 'Sir, I love him; but I do not love him more; my regard for him does not increase. As it is said in the Apocrypha, "his talk is of bullocks:" I do not suppose he is very fond of my company. His habits are by no means sufficiently clerical: this he knows that I see; and no man likes to live under the eye of perpetual disapprobation.'

I have no doubt that a good many sermons were composed for Taylor by Johnson. Johnson was by no means of opinion, that every man of a learned profession should consider it as incumbent upon him, or as necessary to his credit, to appear as an authour. When in the ardour of ambition for literary fame, I regretted to him one day that an eminent Judge had nothing of it, and therefore would leave no perpetual monument of himself to posterity, 'Alas, Sir, (said Johnson,) what a mass of confusion should we have, if every Bishop, and every Judge, every Lawyer, Physician, and Divine, were to write books.'

In the evening, Johnson, being in very good spirits, entertained us with several characteristical portraits. I regret that any of them escaped my retention and diligence. I found, from experience, that to collect my friend's conversation so as to exhibit it with any degree of its original flavour, it was necessary to write it down without delay. To record his sayings after some distance of time, was like preserving or pickling long-kept and faded fruits, or other vegetables, which, when in that state, have little or nothing of their taste when fresh.

On Monday, September 22, when at breakfast, I unguardedly said to Dr. Johnson, 'I wish I saw you and Mrs. Macaulay together.' He grew very angry; and, after a pause, while a cloud gathered on his brow, he burst out, 'No, Sir; you would not see us quarrel, to make you sport. Don't you know that it is very uncivil to *pit* two people against one another?' Then, checking himself, and wishing to be more gentle, he added, 'I do not say you should be hanged or drowned for this; but it *is* very un-

civil.' Dr. Taylor thought him in the wrong, and spoke to him
privately of it; but I afterwards acknowledged to Johnson that
I was to blame, for I candidly owned, that I meant to express a
desire to see a contest between Mrs. Macaulay and him; but
then I knew how the contest would end; so that I was to see
him triumph. *Johnson.* 'Sir, you cannot be sure how a contest
will end; and no man has a right to engage two people in a
dispute by which their passions may be inflamed, and they may
part with bitter resentment against each other. I would sooner
keep company with a man from whom I must guard my pockets, than with a man who contrives to bring me into a dispute
with somebody that he may hear it.'

He found great fault with a gentleman of our acquaintance
for keeping a bad table. 'Sir, (said he,) when a man is invited
to dinner, he is disappointed if he does not get something good.
I advised Mrs. Thrale, who has no card-parties at her house, to
give sweet-meats, and such good things, in an evening, as are
not commonly given, and she would find company enough
come to her; for every body loves to have things which please
the palate put in their way, without trouble or preparation.'
Such was his attention to the *minutiæ* of life and manners.

He thus characterised the Duke of Devonshire, grandfather
of the present representative of that very respectable family:
'He was not a man of superiour abilities, but he was a man
strictly faithful to his word. If, for instance, he had promised
you an acorn, and none had grown that year in his woods, he
would not have contented himself with that excuse; he would
have sent to Denmark for it. So unconditional was he in keeping his word; so high as to the point of honour.' This was a
liberal testimony from the Tory Johnson to the virtue of a great
Whig nobleman.

Mr. Burke's 'Letter to the Sheriffs of Bristol, on the affairs of
America,' being mentioned, Johnson censured the composition
much, and he ridiculed the definition of a free government,
viz. 'For any practical purpose, it is what the people think so.'
—'I will let the King of France govern me on those conditions,
(said he,) for it is to be governed just as I please.' And when
Dr. Taylor talked of a girl being sent to a parish workhouse,
and asked how much she could be obliged to work, 'Why, (said

Johnson,) as much as is reasonable: and what is that? as much as *she thinks* reasonable.'

Dr. Johnson obligingly proposed to carry me to see Islam, a romantick scene, now belonging to a family of the name of Port, but formerly the seat of the Congreves. Johnson described it distinctly and vividly, at which I could not but express to him my wonder; because, though my eyes, as he observed, were better than his, I could not by any means equal him in representing visible objects. I said, the difference between us in this respect was as that between a man who has a bad instrument, but plays well on it, and a man who has a good instrument, on which he can play very imperfectly.

I recollect a very fine amphitheatre, surrounded with hills covered with wood, and walks neatly formed along the side of a rocky steep, on the quarter next the house, with recesses under projections of rock, overshadowed with trees; in one of which recesses, we were told, Congreve wrote his 'Old Bachelor.' We viewed a remarkable natural curiosity at Islam; two rivers bursting near each other from the rock, not from immediate springs, but after having run for many miles under ground. Plott, in his 'History of Staffordshire,' gives an account of this curiosity; but Johnson would not believe it, though we had the attestation of the gardener, who said, he had put in corks, where the river *Manyfold* sinks into the ground, and had catched them in a net, placed before one of the openings where the water bursts out. Indeed, such subterraneous courses of water are found in various parts of our globe.

Talking of Dr. Johnson's unwillingness to believe extraordinary things, I ventured to say, 'Sir, you come near Hume's argument against miracles, "That it is more probable witnesses should lie, or be mistaken, than that they should happen."' *Johnson.* 'Why, Sir, Hume, taking the proposition simply, is right. But the Christian revelation is not proved by the miracles alone, but as connected with prophecies, and with the doctrines in confirmation of which the miracles were wrought.'

He repeated his observation, that the differences among Christians are really of no consequence. 'For instance, (said he,) if a Protestant objects to a Papist, "You worship images:" the Papist can answer, "I do not insist on *your* doing it; you may be a very good Papist without it: I do it only as a help to my devotion." ' I said, the great article of Christianity is the revelation of immortality. Johnson admitted it was.

In the evening, a gentleman-farmer, who was on a visit at Dr. Taylor's, attempted to dispute with Johnson in favour of Mungo Campbell, who shot Alexander, Earl of Eglintoune,[1] upon his having fallen, when retreating from his Lordship, who he believed was about to seize his gun, as he had threatened to do. He said, he should have done just as Campbell did. *Johnson.* 'Whoever would do as Campbell did, deserves to be hanged; not that I could, as a juryman, have found him legally guilty of murder; but I am glad they found means to convict him.' The gentleman-farmer said, 'A poor man has as much honour as a rich man; and Campbell had *that* to defend.' Johnson exclaimed, 'A poor man has no honour.' The English yeoman, not dismayed, proceeded: 'Lord Eglintoune was a damned fool to run on upon Campbell, after being warned that Campbell would shoot him if he did.' Johnson, who could not bear any thing like swearing, angrily replied, 'He was *not* a *damned* fool: he only thought too well of Campbell. He did not believe Campbell would be such a *damned* scoundrel, as to do so *damned* a thing.' His emphasis on *damned,* accompanied with frowning looks, reproved his opponent's want of decorum in *his* presence.

Talking of the danger of being mortified by rejection, when making approaches to the acquaintance of the great, I observed, 'I am, however, generally for trying, "Nothing venture, nothing have." ' *Johnson.* 'Very true, Sir; but I have always been more afraid of failing, than hopeful of success.' And, indeed, though he had all just respect for rank, no man ever less courted the favour of the great.

During this interview at Ashbourne, Johnson seemed to be more uniformly social, cheerful, and alert, than I had almost ever seen him. He was prompt on great occasions and on small.

[1] Lord Eglintoune found Campbell trespassing on his property and demanded his gun. When he advanced to seize the gun, Campbell, an exciseman, warned him that he would shoot, and when he continued did shoot. Campbell was found guilty of murder and hanged himself in prison.

Taylor, who praised every thing of his own to excess, in short, 'whose geese were all swans,' as the proverb says, expatiated on the excellence of his bull-dog, which, he told us, was 'perfectly well shaped.' Johnson, after examining the animal attentively, thus repressed the vain-glory of our host:—'No, Sir, he is *not* well shaped; for there is not the quick transition from the thickness of the fore-part, to the *tenuity*—the thin part—behind, which a bull-dog ought to have.' This *tenuity* was the only *hard word* that I heard him use during this interview, and it will be observed, he instantly put another expression in its place. Taylor said, a small bull-dog was as good as a large one. *Johnson*, 'No, Sir; for, in proportion to his size, he has strength: and your argument would prove, that a good bull-dog may be as small as a mouse.' It was amazing how he entered with perspicuity and keenness upon every thing that occurred in conversation. Most men, whom I know, would no more think of discussing a question about a bull-dog, than of attacking a bull.

One morning after breakfast, when the sun shone bright, we walked out together, and 'pored' for some time with placid indolence upon an artificial water-fall, which Dr. Taylor had made by building a strong dyke of stone across the river behind his garden. It was now somewhat obstructed by branches of trees and other rubbish, which had come down the river, and settled close to it. Johnson, partly from a desire to see it play more freely, and partly from that inclination to activity which will animate, at times, the most inert and sluggish mortal, took a long pole which was lying on the bank, and pushed down several parcels of this wreck with painful assiduity, while I stood quietly by, wondering to behold the sage thus curiously employed, and smiling with an humorous satisfaction each time when he carried his point. He worked till he was quite out of breath; and having found a large dead cat so heavy that he could not move it after several efforts, 'Come,' said he, (throwing down the pole,) *you* shall take it now;' which I accordingly did, and being a fresh man, soon made the cat tumble over the cascade. This may be laughed at as too trifling to record; but it is a small characteristick trait in the Flemish picture which I give of my friend, and in which, therefore, I mark the most minute particulars.

Talking of Rochester's Poems, he said, he had given them to Mr. Steevens to castrate for the edition of the Poets, to which he was to write Prefaces. Dr. Taylor (the only time I ever heard him say any thing witty) observed, that 'if Rochester had been castrated himself, his exceptionable poems would not have been written.' I asked whether Prior's Poems were to be printed entire: Johnson said they were. I mentioned Lord Hailes's censure of Prior in his Preface to a collection of 'Sacred Poems,' where he mentions, 'those impure tales which will be the eternal opprobrium of their ingenious authour.' *Johnson.* 'Sir, Lord Hailes has forgot. There is nothing in Prior that will excite to lewdness. If Lord Hailes thinks there is, he must be more combustible than other people. No, Sir, Prior is a lady's book. No lady is ashamed to have it standing in her library.'

I complained of a wretched changefulness, so that I could not preserve, for any long continuance, the same views of any thing. It was most comfortable to me to experience, in Dr. Johnson's company, a relief from this uneasiness. His steady vigorous mind held firm before me those objects which my own feeble and tremulous imagination frequently presented, in such a wavering state, that my reason could not judge well of them.

He told me, that Bacon was a favourite authour with him; but he had never read his works till he was compiling the English Dictionary, in which, he said, I might see Bacon very often quoted. Mr. Seward recollects his having mentioned, that a Dictionary of the English Language might be compiled from Bacon's writings alone, and that he had once an intention of giving an edition of Bacon, at least of his English works, and writing the Life of that great man. Had he executed this intention, there can be no doubt that he would have done it in a most masterly manner. Mallet's Life of Bacon has no inconsiderable merit as an acute and elegant dissertation relative to its subject; but Mallet's mind was not comprehensive enough to embrace the vast extent of Lord Verulam's genius and research. Dr. Warburton therefore observed, with witty justness, 'that Mallet in his Life of Bacon had forgotten that he was a philosopher; and if he should write the Life of the Duke of Marlborough, which he had undertaken to do, he would probably forget that he was a General.'

On Tuesday, September 23, Johnson was remarkably cordial to me. It being necessary for me to return to Scotland soon, I had fixed on the next day for my setting out, and I felt a tender concern at the thought of parting with him. He had, at this time, frankly communicated to me many particulars, which are inserted in this work in their proper places; and once, when I happened to mention that the expence of my jaunt would come to much more than I had computed, he said, 'Why, Sir, if the expence were to be an inconvenience, you would have reason to regret it: but, if you have had the money to spend, I know not that you could have purchased as much pleasure with it in any other way.'

During this interview at Ashbourne, Johnson and I frequently talked with wonderful pleasure of mere trifles which had occurred in our tour to the Hebrides; for it had left a most agreeable and lasting impression upon his mind.

He found fault with me for using the phrase to *make* money. 'Don't you see (said he) the impropriety of it? To *make* money is to *coin* it: you should say *get* money.' The phrase, however, is, I think, pretty current. But Johnson was at all times jealous of infractions upon the genuine English language, and prompt to repress colloquial barbarisms; such as, *pledging myself*, for *undertaking*; *line*, for *department* or *branch*, as, the *civil line*, the *banking line*. He was particularly indignant against the almost universal use of the word *idea* in the sense of *notion* or *opinion*, when it is clear that *idea* can only signify something of which an image can be formed in the mind. We may have an *idea* or *image* of a mountain, a tree, a building; but we cannot surely have an *idea* or *image* of an *argument* or *proposition*. Yet we hear the sages of the law 'delivering their *ideas* upon the question under consideration;' and the first speakers in parliament 'entirely coinciding in the *idea* which has been ably stated by an honourable member;'—or 'reprobating an *idea* unconstitutional, and fraught with the most dangerous consequences to a great and free country.' Johnson called this 'modern cant.'

I perceived that he pronounced the word *heard,* as if spelt with a double *e, heerd,* instead of sounding it *herd,* as is most usually done. He said, his reason was, that if it were pronounced *herd,* there would be a single exception from the English pronunciation of the syllable *ear,* and he thought it better not to have that exception.

In the evening our gentleman-farmer, and two others, entertained themselves and the company with a great number of tunes on the fiddle. Johnson desired to have 'Let ambition fire thy mind,' played over again, and appeared to give a patient attention to it; though he owned to me that he was very insensible to the power of musick. I told him, that it affected me to such a degree, as often to agitate my nerves painfully, producing in my mind alternate sensations of pathetick dejection, so that I was ready to shed tears; and of daring resolution, so that I was inclined to rush into the thickest part of the battle. 'Sir, (said he,) I should never hear it, if it made me such a fool.'

This evening, while some of the tunes of ordinary composition were played with no great skill, my frame was agitated, and I was conscious of a generous attachment to Dr. Johnson, as my preceptor and friend, mixed with an affectionate regret that he was an old man, whom I should probably lose in a short time. I said to him, 'My dear Sir, we must meet every year, if you don't quarrel with me.' *Johnson.* 'Nay, Sir, you are more likely to quarrel with me, than I with you. My regard for you is greater almost than I have words to express; but I do not choose to be always repeating it; write it down in the first leaf of your pocket-book, and never doubt of it again.'

After supper I accompanied him to his apartment, and at my request he dictated to me an argument in favour of the negro who was then claiming his liberty, in an action in the Court of Session in Scotland. He had always been very zealous against slavery in every form, in which I with all deference thought that he discovered 'a zeal without knowledge.' Upon one occasion, when in company with some very grave men at Oxford, his toast was, 'Here's to the next insurrection of the negroes in the West Indies.' His violent prejudice against our West Indian and American settlers appeared whenever there was an opportunity. Towards the conclusion of his 'Taxation no Tyranny,' he says, 'how is it that we hear the loudest *yelps* for liberty among the drivers of negroes?'

The argument dictated by Dr. Johnson was as follows:

'If we should admit, what perhaps may with more reason be denied, that there are certain relations between man and man which may make slavery necessary and just, yet it can never be proved that he who is now suing for his freedom ever stood in any of those relations. He is certainly subject by no law, but that of violence, to his present master; who pretends no claim to his obedience, but that he bought him from a merchant of slaves, whose right to sell him never was examined. It is said that, according to the constitutions of Jamaica, he was legally enslaved; these constitutions are merely positive; and apparently injurious to the rights of mankind, because whoever is exposed to sale is condemned to slavery without appeal; by whatever fraud or violence he might have been originally brought into the merchant's power. In our own time Princes have been sold, by wretches to whose care they were entrusted, that they might have an European education; but when once they were brought to a market in the plantations, little would avail either their dignity or their wrongs. The laws of Jamaica afford a Negro no redress. His colour is considered as a sufficient testimony against him. It is to be lamented that moral right should ever give way to political convenience. But if temptations of interest are sometimes too strong for human virtue, let us at least retain a virtue where there is no temptation to quit it. In the present case there is apparent right on one side, and no convenience on the other. Inhabitants of this island can neither gain riches nor power by taking away the liberty of any part of the human species. The sum of the argument is this:—No man is by nature the property of another: The defendant is, therefore, by nature free: The rights of nature must be some way forfeited before they can be justly taken away: That the defendant has by any act forfeited the rights of nature we require to be proved; and if no proof of such forfeiture can be given, we doubt not but the justice of the court will declare him free.'

I record Dr. Johnson's argument fairly upon this particular case; where, perhaps, he was in the right. But I beg leave to enter my most solemn protest against his general doctrine with respect to the *Slave Trade*. For I will resolutely say—that his unfavourable notion of it was owing to prejudice, and imperfect or false information. The wild and dangerous attempt which has for some time been persisted in to obtain an act of our Legislature, to abolish so very important and necessary a branch of commercial interest, must have been crushed at once, had not the insignificance of the zealots who vainly took the lead in it, made the vast body of Planters, Merchants, and others, whose immense properties are involved in that trade, reasonably enough suppose that there could be no danger. The encouragement which the attempt has received excites my wonder and indignation; and though some men of superiour abilities have supported it; whether from a love of temporary popularity, when prosperous; or a love of general mischief, when desperate, my opinion is unshaken. To abolish a *status*, which in all ages GOD has sanctioned, and man has continued, would not only be *robbery* to an innumerable class of our fellow-subjects; but it would be extreme cruelty to the African Savages, a portion of whom it saves from massacre, or intolerable bondage in their own country, and introduces into a much happier state of life; especially now when their passage to the West-Indies and their treatment there is humanely regulated. To abolish that trade would be to

'——shut the gates of mercy on mankind.'[1]

When I said now to Johnson, that I was afraid I kept him too late up, 'No, Sir, (said he,) I don't care though I sit all night with you.' This was an animated speech from a man in his sixty-ninth year.

Had I been as attentive not to displease him as I ought to have been, I know not but this vigil might have been fulfilled; but I unluckily entered upon the controversy concerning the right of Great-Britain to tax America, and attempted to argue in favour of our fellow-subjects on the other side of the Atlantick. I insisted that America might be very well governed, and made to yield a sufficient revenue by the means of *influence*, as exemplified in Ireland, while the people might be pleased with the imagination of their participating of the British con-

[1] These were the stock arguments in favor of slavery.

stitution, by having a body of representatives, without whose consent money could not be exacted from them. Johnson could not bear my thus opposing his avowed opinion, which he had exerted himself with an extreme degree of heat to enforce; and the violent agitation into which he was thrown, while answering, or rather reprimanding me, alarmed me so, that I heartily repented of my having unthinkingly introduced the subject. I myself, however, grew warm, and the change was great, from the calm state of philosophical discussion in which we had a little before been pleasingly employed.

We were fatigued by the contest, which was produced by my want of caution; and he was not then in the humour to slide into easy and cheerful talk. It therefore so happened, that we were after an hour or two very willing to separate and go to bed.

On Wednesday, September 24, I went into Dr. Johnson's room before he got up, and finding that the storm of the preceding night was quite laid, I sat down upon his bed-side, and he talked with as much readiness and good-humour as ever. He recommended to me to plant a considerable part of a large moorish farm which I had purchased, and he made several calculations of the expence and profit: for he delighted in exercising his mind on the science of numbers.

I spoke with gratitude of Dr. Taylor's hospitality; and as evidence that it was not on account of his good table alone that Johnson visited him often, I mentioned a little anecdote which had escaped my friend's recollection, and at hearing which repeated, he smiled. One evening, when I was sitting with him, Frank delivered this message: 'Sir, Dr. Taylor sends his compliments to you, and begs you will dine with him to-morrow. He has got a hare.'—'My compliments (said Johnson) and I'll dine with him—hare or rabbit.'

After breakfast I departed, and pursued my journey northwards.

'To JAMES BOSWELL, Esq.

'DEAR SIR,

'I HOPE you found at your return my dear enemy and all her little people quite well, and had no reason to repent of your journey. I think on it with great gratitude.

'I was not well when you left me at the Doctor's, and I grew worse; yet I staid on, and at Lichfield was very ill. Travelling, however, did not make me worse; and when I came to London, I complied with a summons to go to Brighthelmston, where I saw Beauclerk, and staid three days.

'Our *Club* has recommenced last Friday, but I was not there. Langton has another wench.[1] Mrs. Thrale is in hopes of a young brewer. They got by their trade last year a very large sum, and their expences are proportionate.

'Mrs. Williams's health is very bad. And I have had for some time a very difficult and laborious respiration; but I am better by purges, abstinence, and other methods. I am yet, however, much behind-hand in my health and rest.

'My dear friend, let me thank you once more for your visit; you did me great honour, and I hope met with nothing that displeased you. I staid long at Ashbourne, not much pleased, yet aukward at departing. I then went to Lichfield, where I found my friend at Stow-hill very dangerously diseased. Such is life. Let us try to pass it well, whatever it be, for there is surely something beyond it.

'Well, now I hope all is well, write as soon as you can to, dear Sir,

'Your affectionate servant,
'SAM. JOHNSON.'

'London, Nov. 25, 1777.'

1778: ÆTAT. 69.]—On Wednesday, March 18, I arrived in London, and was informed by good Mr. Francis that his master was better, and was gone to Mr. Thrale's at Streatham, to which place I wrote to him, begging to know when he would be in town. He was not expected for some time; but next day having called on Dr. Taylor, in Dean's-yard, Westminster, I found him there, and was told he had come to town for a few hours. He met me with his usual kindness, but instantly returned to the writing of something on which he was employed when I came in, and on which he seemed much intent. Finding him thus engaged, I made my visit very short, and had no more of his conversation, except his expressing a serious regret that a friend of ours was living at too much expence, considering how poor an appearance he made: 'If (said he) a man has splendour from his expence, if he spends his money in pride or in pleasure, he has

---

[1] i.e., another child, a girl.

value: but if he lets others spend it for him, which is most commonly the case, he has no advantage from it.'

On Friday, March 20, I found him at his own house, sitting with Mrs. Williams, and was informed that the room formerly allotted to me was now appropriated to a charitable purpose; Mrs. Desmoulins, and I think her daughter, and a Miss Carmichael, being all lodged in it. Such was his humanity, and such his generosity, that Mrs. Desmoulins herself told me, he allowed her half-a-guinea a week. Let it be remembered, that this was above a twelfth part of his pension.

His liberality, indeed, was at all periods of his life very remarkable. Mr. Howard, of Lichfield, at whose father's house Johnson had in his early years been kindly received, told me, that when he was a boy at the Charter-House, his father wrote to him to go and pay a visit to Mr. Samuel Johnson, which he accordingly did, and found him in an upper room, of poor appearance. Johnson received him with much courteousness, and talked a great deal to him, as to a school-boy, of the course of his education, and other particulars. When he afterwards came to know and understand the high character of this great man, he recollected his condescension with wonder. He added, that when he was going away, Mr. Johnson presented him with half-a-guinea; and this, said Mr. Howard, was at a time when he probably had not another.

We retired from Mrs. Williams to another room. Tom Davies soon after joined us. He had now unfortunately failed in his circumstances, and was much indebted to Dr. Johnson's kindness for obtaining for him many alleviations of his distress. After he went away, Johnson blamed his folly in quitting the stage, by which he and his wife got five hundred pounds a year. I said, I believed it was owing to Churchill's attack upon him,

'He mouths a sentence, as curs mouth a bone.'

Johnson. 'I believe so too, Sir. But what a man is he, who is to be driven from the stage by a line? Another line would have driven him from his shop.'

In my interview with Dr. Johnson this evening, I was quite easy, quite as his companion; upon which I find in my Journal the following reflection: 'So ready is my mind to suggest matter for dissatisfaction, that I felt a sort of regret that I was so easy. I missed that aweful reverence with which I used to contemplate *Mr. Samuel Johnson,* in the complex magnitude of his literary, moral, and religious character. I have a wonderful superstitious love of *mystery.'*

He returned next day to Streatham, to Mr. Thrale's; where, as Mr. Strahan once complained to me, 'he was in a great measure absorbed from the society of his old friends.' I was kept in London by business, and wrote to him on the 27th, that a separation from him for a week, when we were so near, was equal to a separation for a year, when we were at four hundred miles distance. I went to Streatham on Monday, March 30. Before he appeared, Mrs. Thrale made a very characteristical remark:—'I do not know for certain what will please Dr. Johnson: but I know for certain that it will displease him to praise any thing, even what he likes, extravagantly.'

I had before dinner repeated a ridiculous story told me by an old man who had been a passenger with me in the stage-coach to-day. Mrs. Thrale, having taken occasion to allude to it in talking to me, called it 'The story told you by the old *woman.'*—'Now, Madam, (said I,) give me leave to catch you in the fact: it was not an old *woman,* but an old *man,* whom I mentioned as having told me this.' I presumed to take an opportunity, in presence of Johnson, of shewing this lively lady how ready she was, unintentionally, to deviate from exact authenticity of narration.

When we were at tea and coffee, there came in Lord Trimlestown, in whose family was an ancient Irish peerage, but it suffered by taking the generous side in the troubles of the last century. He was a man of pleasing conversation, and was accompanied by a young gentleman, his son.

I mentioned that I had in my possession the Life of Sir Robert Sibbald, the celebrated Scottish antiquary, and founder of the Royal College of Physicians at Edinburgh, in the original manuscript in his own handwriting; and that it was I believed the most natural and candid account of himself that ever was given by any man. As an instance, he tells that the Duke of Perth, then Chancellor of Scotland, pressed him very

much to come over to the Roman Catholick faith: that he resisted all his Grace's arguments for a considerable time, till one
day he felt himself, as it were, instantaneously convinced, and
with tears in his eyes ran into the Duke's arms, and embraced
the ancient religion; that he continued very steady in it for
some time, and accompanied his Grace to London one winter, and lived in his household; that there he found the rigid
fasting prescribed by the church very severe upon him; that
this disposed him to reconsider the controversy, and having
then seen that he was in the wrong, he returned to Protestant-
ism. I talked of some time or other publishing this curious life.
Mrs. Thrale. 'I think you had as well let alone that publication.
To discover such weakness exposes a man when he is gone.'
Johnson. 'Nay, it is an honest picture of human nature. How
often are the primary motives of our greatest actions as small as
Sibbald's, for his re-conversion.' *Mrs. Thrale.* 'But may they not
as well be forgotten?' *Johnson.* 'No, Madam, a man loves to review his own mind. That is the use of a diary, or journal.'
Lord Trimlestown. 'True, Sir. As the ladies love to see themselves in a glass; so a man likes to see himself in his journal.'
Boswell. 'A very pretty allusion.' *Johnson.* 'Yes, indeed.' *Boswell.* 'And as a lady adjusts her dress before a mirror, a man
adjusts his character by looking at his journal.'

Next morning, while we were at breakfast, Johnson gave a
very earnest recommendation of what he himself practised with
the utmost conscientiousness: I mean a strict attention to truth,
even in the most minute particulars. 'Accustom your children
(said he) constantly to this; if a thing happened at one window, and they, when relating it, say that it happened at another, do not let it pass, but instantly check them; you do not
know where deviation from truth will end.' *Boswell.* 'It may
come to the door: and when once an account is at all varied in
one circumstance, it may by degrees be varied so as to be totally
different from what really happened.' Our lively hostess, whose
fancy was impatient of the rein, fidgeted at this, and ventured
to say, 'Nay, this is too much. If Mr. Johnson should forbid me
to drink tea, I would comply, as I should feel the restraint only
twice a day; but little variations in narrative must happen a
thousand times a day, if one is not perpetually watching.' *John-*

son. 'Well, Madam, and you *ought* to be perpetually watching It is more from carelessness about truth than from intentional lying, that there is so much falsehood in the world.'

Talking of ghosts, he said, 'It is wonderful that five thousand years have now elapsed since the creation of the world, and still it is undecided whether or not there has ever been an instance of the spirit of any person appearing after death. All argument is against it; but all belief is for it.'

He said, 'John Wesley's conversation is good, but he is never at leisure. He is always obliged to go at a certain hour. This is very disagreeable to a man who loves to fold his legs and have out his talk, as I do.'

On Friday, April 3, I dined with him in London, in a company where were present several eminent men, whom I shall not name, but distinguish their parts in the conversation by different letters.

E. 'We hear prodigious complaints at present of emigration. I am convinced that emigration makes a country more populous.' J. 'That sounds very much like a paradox.' E. 'Exportation of men, like exportation of all other commodities, makes more be produced.' *Johnson.* 'But there would be more people were there not emigration, provided there were food for more.' E. No; leave a few breeders, and you'll have more people than if there were no emigration.' *Johnson.* 'Nay, Sir, it is plain there will be more people, if there are more breeders. Thirty cows in good pasture will produce more calves than ten cows, provided they have good bulls.' E. 'There are bulls enough in Ireland.' *Johnson.* (smiling,) 'So, Sir, I should think from your argument.' *Boswell.* 'I can understand that emigration may be the cause that more people may be produced in a country; but the country will not therefore be the more populous; for the people issue from it. It can only be said that there is a flow of people. It is an encouragement to have children, to know that they can get a living by emigration.' R. 'Yes, if there were an emigration of children under six years of age. But they don't emigrate till they could earn their livelihood in some way at home.' C. 'It is remarkable that the most unhealthy countries, where there are the most destructive diseases, such as Egypt and Bengal, are the most populous.' *Johnson.* 'Countries which are the most populous have the most destructive diseases. *That* is the true state of the proposition.' C. 'Holland is very unhealthy, yet it is exceedingly populous.' *Johnson.* 'I know not that Holland is unhealthy. But its populousness is owing to an influx of people from all other countries. Disease cannot be the cause of populousness, for it not only carries off a great proportion of the people; but those who are left are weakened and unfit for the purposes of increase.'

Johnson. 'I have been reading Thicknesse's travels, which I think are entertaining.' *Boswell.* 'What, Sir, a good book?' *Johnson.* 'Yes, Sir, to read once; I do not say you are to make a study of it, and digest it; and I believe it to be a true book in his intention. All travellers generally mean to tell truth; though Thicknesse observes, upon Smollet's account of his alarming a whole town in France by firing a blunderbuss, and frightening a French nobleman till he made him tie on his portmanteau, that he would be loth to say Smollet had told two lies in one page; but he had found the only town in France where these things could have happened. Travellers must often be mistaken. In every thing, except where mensuration can be applied, they may honestly differ. There has been, of late, a strange turn in travellers to be displeased.'

E. 'From the experience which I have had,—and I have had a great deal,—I have learnt to think *better* of mankind.' *Johnson.* 'From my experience I have found them worse in commercial dealings, more disposed to cheat, than I had any notion of; but more disposed to do one another good than I had conceived.' J. 'Less just and more beneficent.' *Johnson.* 'And really it is wonderful, considering how much attention is necessary for men to take care of themselves, and ward off immediate evils which press upon them, it is wonderful how much they do for others. As it is said of the greatest liar, that he tells more truth than falsehood; so it may be said of the worst man, that he does more good than evil.' *Boswell.* 'Perhaps from experience men may be found *happier* than we suppose.' *Johnson.* 'No, Sir; the more we enquire, we shall find men the less happy.' P. 'As to thinking better or worse of mankind from experience, some cunning people will not be satisfied unless they have put men to the test, as they think. There is a very good story told of Sir Godfrey Kneller, in his character of a Justice of the peace. A gentleman brought his servant before him, upon an accusation of having stolen some money from him; but it having come out that he had laid it purposely in the servant's way, in order to try his honesty, Sir Godfrey sent the master to prison.' *Johnson.* 'To resist temptation once, is not a sufficient proof of honesty. If a servant, indeed, were to resist the continued temptation of silver lying in a window, as some people let it lye, when he is sure his master does not know how much there is of it, he would give a strong proof of honesty. But this is a proof to which you have no right to put a man. You know, humanly speaking, there is a certain degree of temptation which will overcome any virtue. Now, in so far as you approach temptation to a man, you do him an injury; and, if he is overcome, you share his guilt.' P. 'And, when once over come, it is easier for him to be got the better of again.' *Boswell.* 'Yes, you are his seducer; you have debauched him. I have known a man resolve to put friendship to the test, by asking a friend to lend him money merely with that view, when he did not want it.' *Johnson.* 'That is very wrong, Sir. Your friend may be a narrow man, and yet have many good qualities: narrowness may be his only fault. Now you are trying his general character as a friend, by one particular singly, in which he happens to be defective, when, in truth, his character is composed of many particulars.'

On Saturday, April 4, I drank tea with Johnson at Dr. Taylor's, where he had dined. He was very silent this evening; and read in a variety of books: suddenly throwing down one, and taking up another.

He talked of going to Streatham that night. *Taylor.* 'You'll be robbed if you do: or you must shoot a highwayman. Now I would rather be robbed than do that; I would not shoot a highwayman.' *Johnson.* 'But I would rather shoot him in the instant when he is attempting to rob me, than afterwards swear against him at the Old-Bailey, to take away his life, after he has robbed me. I am surer I am right in the one case than in the other. I may be mistaken as to the man, when I swear: I cannot be mistaken, if I shoot him in the act. Besides, we feel less reluctance to take away a man's life, when we are heated by the injury, than to do it at a distance of time by an oath, after we have cooled.' *Boswell.* 'So, Sir, you would rather act from the motive of private passion, than that of publick advantage.' *Johnson.* 'Nay, Sir, when I shoot the highwayman I act from both.' *Boswell.* 'Very well, very well.—There is no catching him.' *Johnson.* 'At the same time one does not know what to say. For perhaps one may, a year after, hang himself from un-easiness for having shot a man. Few minds are fit to be trusted with so great a thing.' *Boswell.* 'Then, Sir, you would not shoot him?' *Johnson.* 'But I might be vexed afterwards for that too.'

Thrale's carriage not having come for him, as he expected, I accompanied him some part of the way home to his own house.

On Tuesday, April 7, I breakfasted with him at his house. He said, 'nobody was content.' I mentioned to him a respect-able person in Scotland whom he knew. *Boswell.* 'He seems to amuse himself quite well; to have his attention fixed, and his tranquillity preserved by very small matters. I have tried this; but it would not do with me.' *Johnson.* (laughing) 'No, Sir; it must be born with a man to be contented to take up with little things. Women have a great advantage that they may take up with little things, without disgracing themselves: a man cannot, except with fiddling. Had I learnt to fiddle, I should have done nothing else.' *Boswell.* 'Pray, Sir, did you ever play on any musical instrument?' *Johnson.* 'No, Sir. I once bought me a flagelet; but I never made out a tune.' *Boswell.* 'A flagelet, Sir!—so small an instrument? I should have liked to hear you play on the violoncello. *That* should have been *your* instrument.' *Johnson.* 'Sir, I might as well have played on the violoncello as another; but I should have done nothing else. No, Sir; a man would never undertake great things, could he be amused with small. I once tried knotting. Dempster's sister undertook to teach me; but I could not learn it.' He asked me to go down with him and dine at Mr. Thrale's at Streatham, to which I agreed.

He talked to me with serious concern of a certain female friend's 'laxity of narration, and inattention to truth.'—'I am as much vexed (said he) at the ease with which she hears it men-tioned to her, as at the thing itself. I told her, "Madam, you are contented to hear every day said to you, what the highest of mankind have died for, rather than bear."—You know, Sir, the highest of mankind have died rather than bear to be told they had uttered a falsehood. Do talk to her of it: I am weary.'

Boswell. 'Was not Dr. John Campbell a very inaccurate man in his narrative, Sir? He once told me, that he drank thirteen bottles of port at a sitting.' *Johnson.* 'Why, Sir, I do not know that Campbell ever lied with pen and ink; but you could not entirely depend on any thing he told you in conversation, if there was fact mixed with it. However, I loved Campbell: he was a solid orthodox man: he had a reverence for religion. Though defective in practice, he was religious in principle; and he did nothing grossly wrong that I have heard.'

I told him, that I had been present the day before, when Mrs. Montagu, the literary lady, sat to Miss Reynolds for her picture; and that she said, 'she had bound up Mr. Gibbon's History without the last two offensive chapters; for that she thought the book so far good, as it gave, in an elegant manner, the substance of the bad writers, which the late Lord Lyttelton advised her to read.' *Johnson.* 'Sir, she has not read them: she shews none of this impetuosity to me: she does not know Greek, and, I fancy, knows little Latin. She is willing you should think she knows them; but she does not say she does.' *Boswell.* 'Mr. Harris, who was present, agreed with her.' *Johnson.* 'Harris was laughing at her, Sir. Harris is a sound sullen scholar; he does not like interlopers.'

Talking of drinking wine, he said, 'I did not leave off wine because I could not bear it; I have drunk three bottles of port without being the worse for it. University College has witnessed this.' *Boswell.* 'Why then, Sir, did you leave it off?' *Johnson.* 'Why, Sir, because it is so much better for a man to be sure that he is never to be intoxicated, never to lose the power over himself. I shall not begin to drink wine again, till I grow old, and want it.' *Boswell.* 'I think, Sir, you once said to me, that not to drink wine was a great deduction from life.' *Johnson.* 'It is a diminution of pleasure, to be sure; but I do not say a diminution of happiness. There is more happiness in being rational.' *Boswell.* 'But if we could have pleasure always, should not we be happy? The greatest part of men would compound for pleasure.' *Johnson*. 'Supposing we could have pleasure always, an intellectual man would not compound for it. The greatest part of men would compound, because the greatest part of men are gross.' *Boswell*. 'I allow there may be greater pleasure than from wine. I have had more pleasure from your conversation. I have indeed; I assure you I have.' *Johnson*. 'When we talk of pleasure, we mean sensual pleasure. When a man says, he had pleasure with a woman, he does not mean conversation, but something of a very different nature. Philosophers tell you, that pleasure is *contrary* to happiness. Gross men prefer animal pleasure. So there are men who have preferred living among savages. Now what a wretch must he be, who is content with such conversation as can be had among savages! You may remember an officer at Fort Augustus, who had served in America, told us of a woman whom they were obliged to *bind,* in order to get her back from savage life.' *Boswell*. 'She must have been an animal, a beast.' *Johnson*. 'Sir, she was a speaking cat.'

I mentioned to him that I had become very weary in a company where I heard not a single intellectual sentence, except that 'a man who had been settled ten years in Minorca was become a much inferiour man to what he was in London, because a man's mind grows narrow in a narrow place.' *Johnson*. 'A man's mind grows narrow in a narrow place, whose mind is enlarged only because he has lived in a large place: but what is got by books and thinking is preserved in a narrow place as well as in a large place. A man cannot know modes of life as well in Minorca as in London; but he may study mathematicks as well in Minorca.' *Boswell*. 'I don't know, Sir: if you had remained ten years in the Isle of Col, you would not have been the man that you now are.' *Johnson*. 'Yes, Sir, if I had been there from fifteen to twenty-five; but not if from twenty-five to thirty-five.'

Of Goldsmith he said, 'He was not an agreeable companion, for he talked always for fame. A man who does so never can be pleasing. The man who talks to unburthen his mind is the man to delight you. An eminent friend of ours is not so agreeable as the variety of his knowledge would otherwise make him, because he talks partly from ostentation.'

Soon after our arrival at Thrale's, I heard one of the maids calling eagerly on another, to go to Dr. Johnson. I wondered what this could mean. I afterwards learnt, that it was to give her a Bible, which he had brought from London as a present to her.

He was for a considerable time occupied in reading *Mémoires de Fontenelle,* leaning and swinging upon the low gate into the court, without his hat.

At dinner, Mrs. Thrale expressed a wish to go and see Scotland. *Johnson.* 'Seeing Scotland, Madam, is only seeing a worse England. It is seeing the flower gradually fade away to the naked stalk. Seeing the Hebrides, indeed, is seeing quite a different scene.'

On Thursday, April 9, I dined with him at Sir Joshua Reynolds's, with the Bishop of St. Asaph, (Dr. Shipley,) Mr. Allan Ramsay, Mr. Gibbon, Mr. Cambridge, and Mr. Langton. Mr. Ramsay had lately returned from Italy, and entertained us with his observations upon Horace's villa, which he had examined with great care. I relished this much, as it brought fresh into my mind what I had viewed with great pleasure thirteen years before. The Bishop, Dr. Johnson, and Mr. Cambridge, joined with Mr. Ramsay, in recollecting the various lines in Horace relating to the subject.

The Bishop said, it appeared from Horace's writings that he was a cheerful contented man. *Johnson.* 'We have no reason to believe that, my Lord. Are we to think Pope was happy, because he says so in his writings? We see in his writings what he wished the state of his mind to appear. Dr. Young, who pined for preferment, talks with contempt of it in his writings, and affects to despise every thing that he did not despise.' *Bishop of St. Asaph.* 'He was like other chaplains, looking for vacancies: but that is not peculiar to the clergy. I remember when I was with the army, after the battle of Lafeldt, the officers seriously grumbled that no general was killed.' *Boswell.* 'How hard is it that man can never be at rest.' *Ramsay.* 'It is not in his nature to be at rest. When he is at rest, he is in the worst state that he can be in; for he has nothing to agitate him. He is then like the man in the Irish song,

"There liv'd a young man in Ballinacrazy.
Who wanted a wife for to make him un*ai*sy."'

Goldsmith being mentioned, Johnson observed, that it was long before his merit came to be acknowledged. That he once complained to him, in ludicrous terms of distress, 'Whenever I write any thing, the publick *make a point* to know nothing about it:' but that his 'Traveller' brought him into high reputation. *Langton.* 'There is not one bad line in that poem; not one of Dryden's careless verses.' *Sir Joshua.* 'I was glad to hear Charles Fox say, it was one of the finest poems in the English language.' *Langton.* 'Why was you glad? You surely had no doubt of this before.' *Johnson.* 'Goldsmith had no settled notions upon any subject; so he talked always at random. It seemed to be his intention to blurt out whatever was in his mind, and see what would become of it. He was angry too, when catched in an absurdity; but it did not prevent him from falling into another the next minute. I remember Chamier, after talking with him for some time, said, "Well, I do believe he wrote this poem himself: and, let me tell you, that is believing a great deal." Chamier once asked him, what he meant by *slow*, the last word in the first line of "The Traveller,"

"Remote, unfriended, melancholy, slow."

Did he mean tardiness of locomotion? Goldsmith, who would say something without consideration, answered, "Yes." I was sitting by, and said, "No, Sir; you do not mean tardiness of locomotion; you mean, that sluggishness of mind which comes upon a man in solitude." Chamier believed then that I had written the line as much as if he had seen me write it. Goldsmith, however, was a man, who, whatever he wrote, did it better than any other man could do. He deserved a place in Westminster-Abbey, and every year he lived, would have deserved it better. He had, indeed, been at no pains to fill his mind with knowledge. He transplanted it from one place to another; and it did not settle in his mind; so he could not tell what was in his own books.'

We talked of living in the country. *Johnson.* 'No wise man will go to live in the country, unless he has something to do which can be better done in the country. For instance: if he is to shut himself up for a year to study a science, it is better to look out to the fields, than to an opposite wall. Then, if a man walks out in the country, there is nobody to keep him from walking in again: but if a man walks out in London, he is not sure when he shall walk in again. A great city is, to be sure, the school for studying life; and "The proper study of mankind is man," as Pope observes.' *Boswell.* 'I fancy London is the best place in the world for society; though I have heard that the very first society of Paris is still beyond any thing that we have here.' *Johnson.* 'Sir, I question if in Paris such a company as is sitting round this table could be got together in less than half a year. They talk in France of the felicity of men and women living together: the truth is, that there the men are not higher than the women, they know no more than the women do, and they are not held down in their conversation by the presence of women. In England, any man who wears a sword and a powdered wig is ashamed to be illiterate. I believe it is not so in France. Yet there is, probably, a great deal of learning in France, because they have such a number of religious estab-lishments; so many men who have nothing else to do but to study. I do not know this; but I take it upon the common prin-ciples of chance. Where there are many shooters, some will hit.'

We talked of old age. Johnson (now in his seventieth year,) said, 'It is a man's own fault, it is from want of use, if his mind grows torpid in old age.' The Bishop asked, if an old man does not lose faster than he gets. *Johnson.* 'I think not, my Lord, if he exerts himself.' One of the company rashly observed, that he thought it was happy for an old man that insensibility comes upon him. *Johnson:* (with a noble elevation and dis-dain,) 'No, Sir, I should never be happy by being less rational.'

This season there was a whimsical fashion in the newspapers of applying Shakspeare's words to describe living persons well known in the world; which was done under the title of '*Modern Characters from Shakspeare;*' many of which were admirably adapted. The fancy took so much, that they were afterwards collected into a pamphlet. Somebody said to John-son, across the table, that he had not been in those characters. 'Yes (said he) I have. I should have been sorry to be left out.' He then repeated what had been applied to him,

'I must borrow GARAGANTUA's mouth.'

Miss Reynolds not perceiving at once the meaning of this, he
was obliged to explain it to her, which had something of an
aukward and ludicrous effect. 'Why, Madam, it has a reference
to me, as using big words, which require the mouth of a giant
to pronounce them. Garagantua is the name of a giant in
Rabelais.'

On Friday, April 10, I found Johnson at home in the morning. He was much pleased with my paying so great attention
to his recommendation in 1763, the period when our acquaintance began, that I should keep a journal; and I could perceive
he was secretly pleased to find so much of the fruit of his mind
preserved; and as he had been used to imagine and say that he
always laboured when he said a good thing—it delighted him,
on a review, to find that his conversation teemed with point
and imagery.

We dined together with Mr. Scott (now Sir William Scott,
his Majesty's Advocate General,) at his chambers in the Temple, nobody else there. The company being small, Johnson was
not in such spirits as he had been the preceding day, and for a
considerable time little was said. At last he burst forth, 'Subordination is sadly broken down in this age. No man, now, has
the same authority which his father had,—except a gaoler. No
master has it over his servants: it is diminished in our colleges;
nay, in our grammar-schools.' *Boswell.* 'What is the cause of
this, Sir?' *Johnson.* 'Why the coming in of the Scotch,' (laughing sarcastically). *Boswell.* 'That is to say, things have been
turned topsy turvey.—But your serious cause?' *Johnson.* 'Why,
Sir, there are many causes, the chief of which is, I think, the
great increase of money. No man now depends upon the Lord
of a Manour, when he can send to another country, and fetch
provisions. The shoe-black at the entry of my court does not
depend on me. I can deprive him but of a penny a day, which
he hopes somebody else will bring him; and that penny I must
carry to another shoe-black, so the trade suffers nothing. But,
besides, there is a general relaxation of reverence. No son now
depends upon his father as in former times.'

I then slily introduced Mr. Garrick's fame, and his assuming
the airs of a great man. *Johnson.* 'Sir, it is wonderful how *little*

Garrick assumes. Consider, Sir: celebrated men, such as you have mentioned, have had their applause at a distance; but Garrick had it dashed in his face, sounded in his ears, and went home every night with the plaudits of a thousand in his *cranium*. Then, Sir, Garrick did not *find*, but *made* his way to the tables, the levees, and almost the bed-chambers of the great. Garrick has made a player a higher character.' *Scott.* 'And he is a very sprightly writer too.' *Johnson.* 'Yes, Sir; and all this supported by great wealth of his own acquisition. If all this had happened to me, I should have had a couple of fellows with long poles walking before me, to knock down every body that stood in the way. Yet Garrick speaks to *us*.' (smiling.) *Boswell.* 'And Garrick is a very good man, a charitable man.' *Johnson.* 'Sir, a liberal man. He has given away more money than any man in England. There may be a little vanity mixed; but he has shewn, that money is not his first object.' *Boswell.* 'Yet Foote used to say of him, that he walked out with an intention to do a generous action; but, turning the corner of a street, he met with the ghost of a halfpenny, which frightened him.' *Johnson.* 'Why, Sir, that is very true, too; for I never knew a man of whom it could be said with less certainty to-day, what he will do to-morrow, than Garrick; it depends so much on his humour at the time.' *Scott.* 'I am glad to hear of his liberality. He has been represented as very saving.' *Johnson.* 'With his domestick saving we have nothing to do. I remember drinking tea with him long ago, when Peg Woffington made it, and he grumbled at her for making it too strong. He had then begun to feel money in his purse, and did not know when he should have enough of it.'

We talked of war. *Johnson.* 'Every man thinks meanly of himself for not having been a soldier, or not having been at sea.' *Boswell.* 'Lord Mansfield does not.' *Johnson.* 'Sir, if Lord Mansfield were in a company of General Officers and Admirals who have been in service, he would shrink; he'd wish to creep under the table.' *Boswell.* 'No; he'd think he could *try* them all.' *Johnson.* 'Yes, if he could catch them: but they'd try him much sooner. No, Sir; were Socrates and Charles the Twelfth of Sweden both present in any company, and Socrates to say, "Follow me, and hear a lecture in philosophy;" and Charles, laying his hand on his sword, to say, "Follow me, and dethrone the Czar;" a man would be ashamed to follow Socrates. Sir, the impression is universal; yet it is strange. As to the sailor, when you look down from the quarter-deck to the space below, you see the utmost extremity of human misery: such crouding, such filth, such stench!' *Scott.* 'We find people fond of being sailors.' *Johnson.* 'I cannot account for that, any more than I can account for other strange perversions of imagination.'

His abhorrence of the profession of a sailor was uniformly violent; but in conversation he always exalted the profession of a soldier. And yet I have, in my large and various collection of his writings, a letter to an eminent friend, in which he expresses himself thus: 'My god-son called on me lately. He is weary, and rationally weary, of a military life. If you can place him in some other state, I think you may increase his happiness, and secure his virtue. A soldier's time is passed in distress and danger, or in idleness and corruption.' Such was his cool reflection in his study; but whenever he was warmed and animated by the presence of company, he, like other philosophers, whose minds are impregnated with poetical fancy, caught the common enthusiasm for splendid renown.

He sometimes could not bear being teazed with questions. I was once present when a gentleman asked so many, as, 'What did you do, Sir?' 'What did you say, Sir?' that he at last grew enraged, and said, 'I will not be put to the *question*. Don't you consider, Sir, that these are not the manners of a gentleman? I will not be baited with *what,* and *why*; what is this? what is that? why is a cow's tail long? why is a fox's tail bushy?' The gentleman, who was a good deal out of countenance, said, 'Why, Sir, you are so good, that I venture to trouble you.' *Johnson.* 'Sir, my being so *good* is no reason why you should be so *ill*.'

He talked with an uncommon animation of travelling into distant countries; that the mind was enlarged by it, and that an acquisition of dignity of character was derived from it. He expressed a particular enthusiasm with respect to visiting the wall of China. I catched it for the moment, and said I really believed I should go and see the wall of China had I not children, of whom it was my duty to take care. 'Sir, (said he,) by doing so, you would do what would be of importance in raising your children to eminence. There would be a lustre reflected upon them from your spirit and curiosity. They would be at all times regarded as the children of a man who had gone to view the wall of China. I am serious, Sir.'

When we had left Mr. Scott's, he said, 'Will you go home with me?' 'Sir, (said I,) it is late; but I'll go with you for three minutes.' *Johnson.* 'Or *four.*' We went to Mrs. Williams's room, where we found Mr. Allen the printer, who was the landlord of his house in Bolt-court, a worthy obliging man, and his very old acquaintance; and what was exceedingly amusing, though he was of a very diminutive size, he used, even in Johnson's presence, to imitate the stately periods and slow and solemn utterance of the great man.—I this evening boasted, that although I did not write what is called stenography, or short-hand, in appropriated characters devised for the purpose, I had a method of my own of writing half words, and leaving out some altogether, so as yet to keep the substance and language of any discourse which I had heard so much in view, that I could give it very completely soon after I had taken it down. He defied me, as he had once defied an actual short-hand writer; and he made the experiment by reading slowly and distinctly a part of Robertson's 'History of America,' while I endeavoured to write it in my way of taking notes. It was found that I had it very imperfectly; the conclusion from which was, that its excellence was principally owing to a studied arrangement of words, which could not be varied or abridged without an essential injury.

On Sunday, April 12, I found him at home before dinner; Dr. Dodd's poem entitled 'Thoughts in Prison,' was lying upon his table. This appearing to me an extraordinary effort by a man who was in Newgate for a capital crime, I was desirous to hear Johnson's opinion of it: to my surprize, he told me he had not read a line of it. I took up the book and read a passage to him. *Johnson.* 'Pretty well, if you are previously disposed to like them.' I read another passage, with which he was better pleased. He then took the book into his own hands, and having looked at the prayer at the end of it, he said, 'What *evidence* is there that this was composed the night before he suffered?

I do not believe it.' He then read aloud where he prays for the King, &c. and observed, 'Sir, do you think that a man the night before he is to be hanged cares for the succession of a royal family?—Though, he *may* have composed this prayer, then. A man who has been canting all his life, may cant to the last.—And yet a man who has been refused a pardon after so much petitioning, would hardly be praying thus fervently for the King.' He and I, and Mrs. Williams, went to dine with the Reverend Dr. Percy. And here I shall record a scene of too much heat between Dr. Johnson and Dr. Percy, which I should have suppressed, were it not that it gave occasion to display the truely tender and benevolent heart of Johnson, who, as soon as he found a friend was at all hurt by any thing which he had 'said in his wrath,' was not only prompt and desirous to be reconciled, but exerted himself to make ample reparation.

Books of Travels having been mentioned, Johnson praised Pennant very highly. Dr. Percy, knowing himself to be the heir male of the ancient Percies, and having the warmest and most dutiful attachment to the noble House of Northumberland, could not sit quietly and hear a man praised, who had spoken disrespectfully of Alnwick-Castle and the Duke's pleasure-grounds, especially as he thought meanly of his travels. He therefore opposed Johnson eagerly. *Johnson.* 'Pennant in what he said of Alnwick, has done what he intended; he has made you very angry.' *Percy.* 'He has said the garden is *trim*, which is representing it like a citizen's parterre, when the truth is, there is a very large extent of fine turf and gravel walks.' *Johnson.* 'According to your own account, Sir, Pennant is right. It *is* trim. Here is grass cut close, and gravel rolled smooth. Is not that trim? The extent is nothing against that; a mile may be as trim as a square yard. Your extent puts me in mind of the citizen's enlarged dinner, two pieces of roast-beef, and two puddings. There is no variety, no mind exerted in laying out the ground, no trees.' *Percy.* 'He pretends to give the natural history of Northumberland, and yet takes no notice of the immense number of trees planted there of late.' *Johnson.* 'That, Sir, has nothing to do with the *natural* history; that is *civil* history. A man who gives the natural history of the oak, is not to tell how many oaks have been planted in this place or that.

A man who gives the natural history of the cow, is not to tell how many cows are milked at Islington. The animal is the same, whether milked in the Park or at Islington.' *Percy*. 'Pennant does not describe well; a carrier who goes along the side of Lochlomond would describe it better.' *Johnson*. 'I think he describes very well.' *Percy*. 'I travelled after him.' *Johnson*. 'And *I* travelled after him.' *Percy*. 'But, my good friend, you are short-sighted, and do not see so well as I do.' I wondered at Dr. Percy's venturing thus. Dr. Johnson said nothing at the time; but inflammable particles were collecting for a cloud to burst. In a little while Dr. Percy said something more in disparagement of Pennant. *Johnson*. (pointedly) 'This is the resentment of a narrow mind, because he did not find every thing in Northumberland.' *Percy*. (feeling the stroke) 'Sir, you may be as rude as you please.' *Johnson*. 'Hold, Sir! Don't talk of rudeness; remember, Sir, you told me (puffing hard with passion struggling for a vent) I was short-sighted. We have done with civility. We are to be as rude as we please.' *Percy*. 'Upon my honour, Sir, I did not mean to be uncivil.' *Johnson*. 'I cannot say so, Sir; for I *did* mean to be uncivil, thinking *you* had been uncivil.' Dr. Percy rose, ran up to him, and taking him by the hand, assured him affectionately that his meaning had been misunderstood; upon which a reconciliation instantly took place. *Johnson*. 'My dear Sir, I am willing you shall *hang* Pennant.' *Percy*. (resuming the former subject) 'Pennant complains that the helmet is not hung out to invite to the hall of hospitality. Now I never heard that it was a custom to hang out a *helmet*.' *Johnson*. 'Hang him up, hang him up.' *Boswell*. (humouring the joke) 'Hang out his skull instead of a helmet, and you may drink ale out of it in your hall of Odin, as he is your enemy; that will be truly ancient.' *Johnson*. 'He's a *Whig*, Sir; a *sad dog* (smiling at his own violent expressions, merely for *political* difference of opinion). But he's the best traveller I ever read; he observes more things than any one else does.'

We had a calm after the storm, staid the evening and supped, and were pleasant and gay. But Dr. Percy told me he was very uneasy at what had passed; for there was a gentleman there who was acquainted with the Northumberland family, to whom he hoped to have appeared more respectable, by shewing how intimate he was with Dr. Johnson, and who might now on the contrary, go away with an opinion to his disadvantage He begged I would mention this to Dr. Johnson, which I afterwards did. His observation upon it was, 'This comes of *stratagem;* had he told me that he wished to appear to advantage before that gentleman, he should have been at the top of the house, all the time.' He spoke of Dr. Percy in the handsomest terms. 'Then, Sir, (said I,) may I be allowed to suggest a mode by which you may effectually counteract any unfavourable report of what passed. I will write a letter to you upon the subject of the unlucky contest of that day, and you will be kind enough to put in writing as an answer to that letter, what you have now said, and as Lord Percy is to dine with us at General Paoli's soon, I will take an opportunity to read the correspondence in his Lordship's presence.' This friendly scheme was accordingly carried into execution without Dr. Percy's knowledge. I breakfasted the day after with him, and informed him of my scheme, and its happy completion, for which he thanked me in the warmest terms, and was highly delighted with Dr. Johnson's letter in his praise, of which I gave him a copy. He said, 'I would rather have this than degrees from all the Universities in Europe. It will be for me, and my children and grand-children.'

'To JAMES BOSWELL, ESQ.

'SIR,

'THE debate between Dr. Percy and me is one of those foolish controversies, which begin upon a question of which neither party cares how it is decided, and which is, nevertheless, continued to acrimony, by the vanity with which every man resists confutation.

'If Percy is really offended, I am sorry; for he is a man whom I never knew to offend any one. He is a man very willing to learn, and very able to teach; a man, out of whose company I never go without having learned something. It is sure that he vexes me sometimes, but I am afraid it is by making me feel my own ignorance. So much extension of mind, and so much minute accuracy of enquiry, if you survey your whole circle of acquaintance, you will find so scarce, if you find it at all, that you will value Percy by comparison. Lord Hailes is somewhat like him: but Lord Hailes does not, perhaps, go beyond him in research; and I do not know that he equals him in elegance. Percy's attention to poetry has given grace and splendour to his studies of antiquity. A mere antiquarian is a rugged being.

'Upon the whole, you see that what I might say in sport or petulance to him, is very consistent with full conviction of his merit.

'I am, dear Sir,

'Your most, &c.

'SAM. JOHNSON.'

'April 23, 1778.'

On Monday, April 13, I dined with Johnson at Mr. Langton's, where were Dr. Porteus, then Bishop of Chester, now of London, and Dr. Stinton.

We talked of the styles of different painters, and how certainly a connoisseur could distinguish them. I asked, if there was as clear a difference of styles in language as in painting, or even as in hand-writing, so that the composition of every individual may be distinguished? *Johnson.* 'Yes. Those who have a style of eminent excellence, such as Dryden and Milton, can always be distinguished.' I had no doubt of this; but what I wanted to know was, whether there was really a peculiar style to every man whatever, as there is certainly a peculiar hand-writing, a peculiar countenance. The Bishop thought not. *Johnson.* 'Why, Sir, I think every man whatever has a peculiar style, which may be discovered by nice examination and comparison with others: but a man must write a great deal to make his style obviously discernible.'

Mr. Topham Beauclerk came in the evening, and he and Dr. Johnson and I staid to supper. It was mentioned that Dr. Dodd had once wished to be a member of *The Literary Club. Johnson.* 'I should be sorry if any of our Club were hanged. I will not say but some of them deserve it.' *Beauclerk;* (supposing this to be aimed at persons for whom he had at that time a wonderful fancy, which, however, did not last long,) was irritated, and eagerly said, 'You, Sir, have a friend (naming him) who deserves to be hanged; for he speaks behind their backs against those with whom he lives on the best terms, and attacks them in the news-papers. *He* certainly ought to be *kicked.*' *Johnson.* 'Sir, we all do this in some degree.' *Beauclerk.* 'He is very malignant.' *Johnson.* 'No, Sir; he is not malignant. He is mischievous, if you will. He would do no man an essential in jury; he may, indeed, love to make sport of people by vexing their vanity. I, however, once knew an old gentleman who was absolutely malignant. He really wished evil to others, and rejoiced at it.' *Boswell.* 'The gentleman, Mr. Beauclerk, against whom you are so violent, is, I know, a man of good principles. *Beauclerk.* 'Then he does not wear them out in practice.'

On Wednesday, April 15, I dined with Dr. Johnson at Mr. Dilly's, and was in high spirits, for I had been a good part of the morning with Mr. Orme, the able and eloquent historian of Hindostan, who expressed a great admiration of Johnson. 'I do not care (said he,) on what subject Johnson talks; but I love better to hear him talk than any body. He either gives you new thoughts, or a new colouring. It is a shame to the nation that he has not been more liberally rewarded. Had I been George the Third, and thought as he did about America, I would have given Johnson three hundred a year for his "Taxation no Tyranny" alone.' I repeated this, and Johnson was much pleased with such praise from such a man as Orme.

At Mr. Dilly's to-day were Mrs. Knowles, the ingenious Quaker lady, Miss Seward, the poetess of Lichfield, the Reverend Dr. Mayo, and the Rev. Mr. Beresford, Tutor to the Duke of Bedford. Before dinner Dr. Johnson seized upon Mr. Charles Sheridan's 'Account of the late Revolution in Sweden,' and seemed to read it ravenously, as if he devoured it, which was to all appearance his method of studying. 'He knows how to read better than any one (said Mrs. Knowles;) he gets at the substance of a book directly; he tears out the heart of it.' He kept it wrapt up in the tablecloth in his lap during the time of dinner, from an avidity to have one entertainment in readiness when he should have finished another; resembling (if I may use so coarse a simile) a dog who holds a bone in his paws in reserve, while he eats something else which has been thrown to him.

The subject of cookery having been very naturally introduced at a table where Johnson, who boasted of the niceness of his palate, owned that 'he always found a good dinner,' he said, 'I could write a better book of cookery than has ever yet been written; it should be a book upon philosophical principles.

Pharmacy is now made much more simple. Cookery may be made so too. A prescription which is now compounded of five ingredients, had formerly fifty in it. So in cookery, if the nature of the ingredients be well known, much fewer will do. Then as you cannot make bad meat good, I would tell what is the best butcher's meat, the best beef, the best pieces; how to choose young fowls; the proper season of different vegetables; and then how to roast and boil, and compound.' *Dilly.* 'Mrs. Glasse's "Cookery," which is the best, was written by Dr. Hill. Half the *trade* know this.' *Johnson.* 'Well, Sir. This shews how much better the subject of Cookery may be treated by a philosopher. I doubt if the book be written by Dr. Hill; for, in Mrs. Glasse's "Cookery," which I have looked into, salt-petre and sal-prunella are spoken of as different substances, whereas sal-prunella is only salt-petre burnt on charcoal; and Hill could not be ignorant of this. However, as the greatest part of such a book is made by transcription, this mistake may have been carelessly adopted. But you shall see what a Book of Cookery I shall make! I shall agree with Mr. Dilly for the copy-right.' *Miss Seward.* 'That would be Hercules with the distaff indeed.' *Johnson.* 'No, Madam. Women can spin very well; but they cannot make a good book of Cookery.'

Mrs. Knowles affected to complain that men had much more liberty allowed them than women. *Johnson.* 'Why, Madam, women have all the liberty they should wish to have. We have all the labour and the danger, and the women all the advantage. We go to sea, we build houses, we do every thing, in short, to pay our court to the women.' *Mrs. Knowles.* 'The Doctor reasons very wittily, but not convincingly. Now, take the instance of building; the mason's wife, if she is ever seen in liquor, is ruined; the mason may get himself drunk as often as he pleases, with little loss of character; nay, may let his wife and children starve.' *Johnson.* 'Madam, you must consider, if the mason does get himself drunk, and let his wife and children starve, the parish will oblige him to find security for their maintenance. We have different modes of restraining evil. Stocks for the men, a ducking-stool for women, and a pound for beasts. If we require more perfection from women than from ourselves, it is doing them honour. And women have not the same temptations that we have: they may always live in virtuous company; men must mix in the world indiscriminately. If a woman has no inclination to do what is wrong, being secured from it is no restraint to her. I am at liberty to walk into the Thames; but if I were to try it, my friends would restrain me in Bedlam, and I should be obliged to them.' *Mrs. Knowles.* 'Still, Doctor, I cannot help thinking it a hardship that more indulgence is allowed to men than to women. It gives a superiority to men, to which I do not see how they are entitled.' *Johnson.* 'It is plain, Madam, one or other must have the superiority. As Shakspeare says, "If two men ride on a horse, one must ride behind."' *Dilly.* 'I suppose, Sir, Mrs. Knowles would have them to ride in panniers, one on each side.' *Johnson.* 'Then, Sir, the horse would throw them both.' *Mrs. Knowles.* 'Well, I hope that in another world the sexes will be equal.' *Boswell.* 'That is being too ambitious, Madam. *We* might as well desire to be equal with the angels. We shall all, I hope, be happy in a future state, but we must not expect to be all happy in the same degree. It is enough if we be happy according to our several capacities. A worthy carman will get to heaven as well as Sir Isaac Newton. Yet, though equally good, they will not have the same degrees of happiness.' *Johnson.* 'Probably not.'

Dr. Mayo having asked Johnson's opinion of Soame Jenyns's 'View of the Internal Evidence of the Christian Religion;'— *Johnson.* 'I think it a pretty book; not very theological indeed; and there seems to be an affectation of ease and carelessness, as if it were not suitable to his character to be very serious about the matter.' *Boswell.* 'You should like his book, Mrs. Knowles, as it maintains, as you *friends* do, that courage is not a Christian virtue.' *Mrs. Knowles.* 'Yes, indeed, I like him there; but I cannot agree with him, that friendship is not a Christian virtue.' *Johnson.* 'Why, Madam, strictly speaking, he is right. All friendship is preferring the interest of a friend, to the neglect, or, perhaps, against the interest of others; so that an old Greek said, "He that has *friends* has *no friend*." Now Christianity recommends universal benevolence, to consider all men as our brethren, which is contrary to the virtue of friendship, as described by the ancient philosophers. Surely,

Madam, your sect must approve of this; for, you call all men
'riends.' *Mrs. Knowles.* 'We are commanded to do good to all
men, "but especially to them who are of the household of
Faith."' *Johnson.* 'Well, Madam. The household of Faith is
wide enough.' *Mrs. Knowles.* 'But, Doctor, our Saviour had
twelve Apostles, yet there was *one* whom he *loved*. John was
called "the disciple whom *Jesus* loved."' *Johnson.* (with eyes
sparkling benignantly) 'Very well, indeed, Madam. You have
said very well.' *Boswell.* 'A fine application. Pray, Sir, had you
ever thought of it?' *Johnson.* 'I had not, Sir.'

From this pleasing subject, he, I know not how or why,
made a sudden transition to one upon which he was a violent
aggressor; for he said, 'I am willing to love all mankind, *except
an American:*' and his inflammable corruption bursting into
horrid fire, he 'breathed out threatenings and slaughter;' calling
them, 'Rascals—Robbers—Pirates;' and exclaiming, he'd 'burn
and destroy them.' Miss Seward, looking to him with mild but
steady astonishment, said, 'Sir, this is an instance that we are
always most violent against those whom we have injured.'—
He was irritated still more by this delicate and keen reproach;
and roared out another tremendous volley, which one might
fancy could be heard across the Atlantick. During this tempest
I sat in great uneasiness, lamenting his heat of temper; till, by
degrees, I diverted his attention to other topicks.

Dr. Mayo. (to Dr. Johnson) 'Pray, Sir, have you read Edwards, of New England, on Grace?' *Johnson.* 'No, Sir.' *Boswell.*
'It puzzled me so much as to the freedom of the human will,
that the only relief I had was to forget it.' *Johnson.* 'All theory
is against the freedom of the will; all experience for it.'—I did
not push the subject any farther. I was glad to find him so mild
in discussing a question of the most abstract nature, involved
with theological tenets, which he generally would not suffer
to be in any degree opposed.

He as usual defended luxury; 'You cannot spend money in
luxury without doing good to the poor. Nay, you do more good
to them by spending it in luxury, than by giving it: for by
spending it in luxury, you make them exert industry, whereas
by giving it, you keep them idle. I own, indeed, there may be
more virtue in giving it immediately in charity, than in spend-

ing it in luxury; though there may be a pride in that too.' Miss Seward asked, if this was not Mandeville's doctrine of 'private vices publick benefits.' *Johnson.* 'The fallacy of that book is, that Mandeville defines neither vices nor benefits. He reckons among vices every thing that gives pleasure. He takes the narrowest system of morality, monastick morality, which holds pleasure itself to be a vice, such as eating salt with our fish, because it makes it taste better; and he reckons wealth as a publick benefit, which is by no means always true. Pleasure of itself is not a vice. Having a garden, which we all know to be perfectly innocent, is a great pleasure. At the same time, in this state of being there are many pleasures vices, which however are so immediately agreeable that we can hardly abstain from them. The happiness of Heaven will be, that pleasure and virtue will be perfectly consistent. Mandeville puts the case of a man who gets drunk in an alehouse; and says it is a publick benefit, because so much money is got by it to the publick. But it must be considered, that all the good gained by this, through the gradation of alehouse-keeper, brewer, maltster, and farmer, is overbalanced by the evil caused to the man and his family by his getting drunk. This is the way to try what is vicious, by ascertaining whether more evil than good is produced by it upon the whole, which is the case in all vice. It may happen that good is produced by vice; but not as vice; for instance, a robber may take money from its owner, and give it to one who will make a better use of it. Here is good produced; but not by the robbery as robbery, but as translation of property. I read Mandeville forty, or, I believe, fifty years ago. He did not puzzle me; he opened my views into real life very much. No, it is clear that the happiness of society depends on virtue. In Sparta, theft was allowed by general consent: theft, therefore, was *there* not a crime, but then there was no security; and what a life must they have had, when there was no security. Without truth there must be a dissolution of society. As it is, there is so little truth, that we are almost afraid to trust our ears; but how should we be, if falsehood were muliplied ten times? Society is held together by communication and information; and I remember this remark of Sir Thomas Browne's, "Do the devils lie? No; for then Hell could not subsist." '

Talking of Miss ――――, a literary lady, he said, 'I was obliged to speak to Miss Reynolds, to let her know that I desired she would not flatter me so much.' Somebody now observed, 'She flatters Garrick.' *Johnson.* 'She is in the right to flatter Garrick. She is in the right for two reasons; first, because she has the world with her, who have been praising Garrick these thirty years; and secondly, because she is rewarded for it by Garrick. Why should she flatter *me*? I can do nothing for her. Let her carry her praise to a better market (Then turning to Mrs. Knowles). You, Madam, have been flattering me all the evening; I wish you would give Boswell a little now. If you knew his merit as well as I do, you would say a great deal; he is the best travelling companion in the world.'

I expressed a horrour at the thought of death. *Mrs. Knowles.* 'Nay, thou should'st not have a horrour for what is the gate of life.' *Johnson.* (standing upon the hearth rolling about, with a serious, solemn, and somewhat gloomy air:) 'No rational man can die without uneasy apprehension.' *Boswell.* 'In prospect death is dreadful; but in fact we find that people die easy.' *Johnson.* 'Why, Sir, most people have not *thought* much of the matter, so cannot *say* much, and it is supposed they die easy. Few believe it certain they are then to die; and those who do, set themselves to behave with resolution, as a man does who is going to be hanged. He is not the less unwilling to be hanged.' *Miss Seward.* 'There is one mode of the fear of death, which is certainly absurd; and that is the dread of annihilation, which is only a pleasing sleep without a dream.' *Johnson.* 'It is neither pleasing, nor sleep; it is nothing. Now mere existence is so much better than nothing, that one would rather exist even in pain, than not exist.'

Of John Wesley he said, 'He can talk well on any subject.' *Boswell.* 'Pray, Sir, what has he made of his story of a ghost?' [1] *Johnson.* 'Why, Sir, he believes it; but not on sufficient author-

[1] John Wesley definitely believed in ghosts. The account of this one is recorded in his *Journal* under May 25, 1768. It appeared at Sunderland, not Newcastle, and told the girl to consult an attorney in order to recover a piece of property. She did as she was told and later the ghost reappeared to tell her that the attorney was not very active in her behalf. Wesley was impressed by the fact that the ghost was keeping an eye on the attorney.

ity. He did not take time enough to examine the girl. It wa
at Newcastle, where the ghost was said to have appeared to a
young woman several times, mentioning something about the
right to an old house, advising application to be made to an
attorney, which was done; and, at the same time, saying the
attorney would do nothing, which proved to be the fact. "This
(says John) is a proof that a ghost knows our thoughts." Now
(laughing) it is not necessary to know our thoughts, to tell
that an attorney will sometimes do nothing. Charles Wesley,
who is a more stationary man, does not believe the story. I am
sorry that John did not take more pains to inquire into the
evidence for it.' *Miss Seward,* (with an incredulous smile:)
What, Sir! about a ghost?' *Johnson,* (with solemn vehemence:)
Yes, Madam: this is a question which, after five thousand
years, is yet undecided; a question, whether in theology or
philosophy, one of the most important that can come before
the human understanding.'

Mrs. Knowles mentioned, as a proselyte to Quakerism, Miss
———, a young lady well known to Dr. Johnson, for whom he
had shewn much affection; while she ever had, and still retained, a great respect for him. Mrs. Knowles at the same time
took an opportunity of letting him know 'that the amiable
young creature was sorry at finding that he was offended at
her leaving the Church of England and embracing a simpler
faith;' and, in the gentlest and most persuasive manner, solicited
his kind indulgence for what was sincerely a matter of conscience. *Johnson,* (frowning very angrily,) 'Madam, she is
an odious wench. She could not have any proper conviction
that it was her duty to change her religion, which is the most
important of all subjects, and should be studied with all care,
and with all the helps we can get. She knew no more of the
Church which she left, and that which she embraced, than
she did of the difference between the Copernican and Ptole-
maick systems.' *Mrs. Knowles.* 'She had the New Testament
before her.' *Johnson.* 'Madam, she could not understand the
New Testament, the most difficult book in the world. for which
the study of a life is required.' *Mrs. Knowles.* 'It is clear as to
essentials.' *Johnson.* 'But not as to controversial points. The
heathens were easily converted, because they had nothing to

give up; but we ought not, without very strong conviction indeed, to desert the religion in which we have been educated. That is the religion given you, the religion in which it may be said Providence has placed you. If you live conscientiously in that religion, you may be safe. But errour is dangerous indeed, if you err when you choose a religion for yourself.' *Mrs. Knowles*. 'Must we then go by implicit faith?' *Johnson*. 'Why, Madam, the greatest part of our knowledge is implicit faith; and as to religion, have we heard all that a disciple of Confucius, all that a Mahometan, can say for himself?' He then rose again into passion, and attacked the young proselyte in the severest terms of reproach, so that both the ladies seemed to be much shocked.

We remained together till it was pretty late. Notwithstanding occasional explosions of violence, we were all delighted upon the whole with Johnson. I compared him at this time to a warm West-Indian climate, where you have a bright sun, quick vegetation, luxuriant foliage, luscious fruits; but where the same heat sometimes produces thunder, lightning, and earthquakes, in a terrible degree.

April 17, being Good-Friday, I waited on Johnson, as usual. I observed at breakfast that although it was a part of his abstemious discipline on this most solemn fast, to take no milk in his tea, yet when Mrs. Desmoulins inadvertently poured it in, he did not reject it. I talked of the strange indecision of mind, and imbecility in the common occurrences of life, which we may observe in some people. *Johnson*. 'Why, Sir, I am in the habit of getting others to do things for me.' *Boswell*. 'What, Sir! have you that weakness?' *Johnson*. 'Yes, Sir. But I always think afterwards I should have done better for myself.'

I told him that at a gentleman's house where there was thought to be such extravagance or bad management, that he was living much beyond his income, his lady had objected to the cutting of a pickled mango, and that I had taken an opportunity to ask the price of it, and found it was only two shillings; so here was a very poor saving. *Johnson*. 'Sir, that is the blundering œconomy of a narrow understanding. It is stopping one hole in a sieve.'

There was a very numerous congregation to-day at St.

Clement's church, which Dr. Johnson said he observed with
pleasure.

And now I am to give a pretty full account of one of the most
curious incidents in Johnson's life, of which he himself has
made the following minute on this day: 'In my return from
church, I was accosted by Edwards, an old fellow-collegian,
who had not seen me since 1729. He knew me, and asked if
I remembered one Edwards; I did not at first recollect the name,
but gradually as we walked along, recovered it, and told him
a conversation that had passed at an alehouse between us. My
purpose is to continue our acquaintance.'

It was in Butcher-row that this meeting happened. Mr. Edwards, who was a decent-looking elderly man in grey clothes,
and a wig of many curls, accosted Johnson with familiar confidence, knowing who he was, while Johnson returned his
salutation with a courteous formality, as to a stranger. But as
soon as Edwards had brought to his recollection their having
been at Pembroke-College together nine-and-forty years ago, he
seemed much pleased, asked where he lived, and said he should
be glad to see him in Bolt-court. *Edwards.* 'Ah, Sir! we are
old men now.' *Johnson,* (who never liked to think of being
old:) 'Don't let us discourage one another.' *Edwards.* 'Why,
Doctor, you look stout and hearty, I am happy to see you so;
for the newspapers told us you were very ill.' *Johnson.* 'Ay, Sir,
they are always telling lies of *us old fellows.*'

Wishing to be present at more of so singular a conversation
as that between two fellow-collegians, who had lived forty
years in London without ever having chanced to meet, I whispered to Mr. Edwards that Dr. Johnson was going home, and
that he had better accompany him now. So Edwards walked
along with us, I eagerly assisting to keep up the conversation.
Mr. Edwards informed Dr. Johnson that he had practised long
as a solicitor in Chancery, but that he now lived in the country
upon a little farm, about sixty acres, just by Stevenage in Hertfordshire, and that he came to London (to Barnard's Inn,
No. 6), generally twice a week. Johnson appearing to be in
a reverie, Mr. Edwards addressed himself to me, and expatiated
on the pleasure of living in the country. *Boswell.* 'I have no
notion of this, Sir. What you have to entertain you, is, I think,

xhausted in half an hour.' *Edwards*. 'What? don't you love to
ave hope realized? I see my grass, and my corn; and my trees
rowing. Now, for instance, I am curious to see if this frost
as not nipped my fruit-trees.' *Johnson,* (who we did not
magine was attending:) 'You find, Sir, you have fears as well
s hopes.'

When we got to Dr. Johnson's house, and were seated in his
ibrary, the dialogue went on admirably. *Edwards*. 'Sir, I re-
nember you would not let us say *prodigious* at College. For
ven then, Sir, (turning to me,) he was delicate in language,
nd we all feared him.' *Johnson,* (to Edwards:) 'From your
aving practised the law long, Sir, I presume you must be
ich.' *Edwards*. 'No, Sir; I got a good deal of money; but I had
a number of poor relations to whom I gave a great part of it.
ohnson. 'Sir, you have been rich in the most valuable sense
of the word.' *Edwards*. 'But I shall not die rich.' *Johnson*.
Nay, sure, Sir, it is better to live rich than to *die* rich.' *Edwards*. 'I wish I had continued at College.' *Johnson*. 'Why do
you wish that, Sir?' *Edwards*. 'Because I think I should have
had a much easier life than mine has been. I should have been
a parson, and had a good living, like Bloxam and several
others, and lived comfortably.' *Johnson*. 'Sir, the life of a
parson, of a conscientious clergyman, is not easy. I have always
considered a clergyman as the father of a larger family than
he is able to maintain. I would rather have Chancery suits
upon my hands than the cure of souls. No, Sir, I do not envy
a clergyman's life as an easy life, nor do I envy the clergyman
who makes it an easy life.'—Here taking himself up all of a
sudden, he exclaimed, 'O! Mr. Edwards! I'll convince you that
I recollect you. Do you remember our drinking together at an
alehouse near Pembroke gate.'

Edwards. 'You are a philosopher, Dr. Johnson. I have tried
too in my time to be a philosopher; but, I don't know how,
cheerfulness was always breaking in. I have been twice married, Doctor. You, I suppose, have never known what it was
to have a wife.' *Johnson*. 'Sir, I have known what it was to
have a wife, and (in a solemn tender faultering tone) I have
known what it was to *lose a wife*.—It had almost broke my
heart'

Edwards. 'How do you live, Sir? For my part, I must hav
my regular meals, and a glass of good wine. I find I requir
it.' *Johnson.* 'I now drink no wine, Sir. Early in life I dran
wine: for many years I drank none. I then for some years dran
a great deal.' *Edwards.* 'Some hogsheads, I warrant you.' *John
son.* 'I then had a severe illness, and left it off, and I have neve
begun it again. I never felt any difference upon myself from
eating one thing rather than another, nor from one kind o
weather rather than another. There are people, I believe, who
feel a difference; but I am not one of them. And as to regula
meals, I have fasted from the Sunday's dinner to the Tuesday':
dinner, without any inconvenience. I believe it is best to ea
just as one is hungry: but a man who is in business, or a man
who has a family, must have stated meals. I am a straggler. I
may leave this town and go to Grand Cairo, without being
missed here or observed there.' *Edwards.* 'Don't you eat supper, Sir?' *Johnson.* 'No, Sir.' *Edwards.* 'For my part, now, I
consider supper as a turnpike through which one must pass,
in order to get to bed.'

Johnson. 'You are a lawyer, Mr. Edwards. Lawyers know
life practically. A bookish man should always have them to
converse with. They have what he wants.' *Edwards.* 'I am
grown old: I am sixty-five.' *Johnson.* 'I shall be sixty-eight next
birth-day. Come, Sir, drink water, and put in for a hundred.'

Mr. Edwards mentioned a gentleman who had left his whole
fortune to Pembroke College. *Johnson.* 'Whether to leave one's
whole fortune to a College be right, must depend upon circumstances. I would leave the interest of the fortune I bequeathed to a College to my relations or my friends, for their
lives. It is the same thing to a College, which is a permanent
society, whether it gets the money now or twenty years hence;
and I would wish to make my relations or friends feel the
benefit of it.'

This interview confirmed my opinion of Johnson's most
humane and benevolent heart. His cordial and placid behaviour to an old fellow-collegian, a man so different from himself; and his telling him that he would go down to his farm
and visit him, shewed a kindliness of disposition very rare at
an advanced age. He observed, 'how wonderful it was that

hey had both been in London forty years, without having ever
nce met, and both walkers in the street too!' Mr. Edwards,
vhen going away, again recurred to his consciousness of senil-
ty, and looking full in Johnson's face, said to him, 'You'll find
n Dr. Young,

> "O my coevals! remnants of yourselves." '

ohnson did not relish this at all; but shook his head with
mpatience. Edwards walked off, seemingly highly pleased
vith the honour of having been thus noticed by Dr. Johnson.
When he was gone, I said to Johnson, I thought him but a
veak man. *Johnson.* 'Why, yes, Sir. Here is a man who has
passed through life without experience: yet I would rather
have him with me than a more sensible man who will not
talk readily.'

Johnson once observed to me, 'Tom Tyers described me the
best: "Sir (said he,) you are like a ghost: you never speak till
you are spoken to." '

Johnson had a noble ambition floating in his mind, and
had, undoubtedly, often speculated on the possibility of his
supereminent powers being rewarded in this great and liberal
country by the highest honours of the state. Sir William Scott
informs me, that upon the death of the late Lord Lichfield,
who was Chancellor of the University of Oxford, he said to
Johnson, 'What a pity it is, Sir, that you did not follow the
profession of the law. You might have been Lord Chancellor
of Great Britain, and attained to the dignity of the peerage:
and now that the title of Lichfield, your native city, is extinct,
you might have had it.' Johnson, upon this, seemed much
agitated; and, in an angry tone, exclaimed, 'Why will you vex
me by suggesting this, when it is too late?'

Yet no man had a higher notion of the dignity of literature
than Johnson, or was more determined in maintaining the respect which he justly considered as due to it. Of this, besides
the general tenor of his conduct in society, some characteristical instances may be mentioned.

He told Sir Joshua Reynolds, that once when he dined in
a numerous company of booksellers, where the room being
small, the head of the table, at which he sat, was almost close

to the fire, he persevered in suffering a great deal of inconvenience from the heat, rather than quit his place, and let one
of them sit above him.

Goldsmith, in his diverting simplicity, complained one day,
in a mixed company, of Lord Camden. 'I met him (said he) at
Lord Clare's house in the country, and he took no more notice
of me than if I had been an ordinary man.' The company
having laughed heartily, Johnson stood forth in defence of his
friend. 'Nay, Gentlemen, (said he,) Dr. Goldsmith is in the
right. A nobleman ought to have made up to such a man as
Goldsmith; and I think it is much against Lord Camden that
he neglected him.'

Nor could he patiently endure to hear that such respect
as he thought due only to higher intellectual qualities, should
be bestowed on men of slighter, though perhaps more amusing
talents. I told him, that one morning, when I went to breakfast
with Garrick, who was very vain of his intimacy with Lord
Camden, he accosted me thus:—'Pray now, did you—did you
meet a little lawyer turning the corner, eh?'—'No, Sir, (said I.)
Pray what do you mean by the question?'—'Why, (replied
Garrick, with an affected indifference, yet as if standing on
tip-toe,) Lord Camden has this moment left me. We have had
a long walk together.' *Johnson.* 'Well, Sir, Garrick talked very
properly. Lord Camden *was* a *little lawyer* to be associating
so familiarly with a player.'

Sir Joshua Reynolds observed, with great truth, that Johnson
considered Garrick to be as it were his *property*. He would
allow no man either to blame or to praise Garrick in his presence, without contradicting him.

Having fallen into a very serious frame of mind, in which
mutual expressions of kindness passed between us, such as
would be thought too vain in me to repeat, I talked with regret
of the sad inevitable certainty that one of us must survive the
other. *Johnson.* 'Yes, Sir, that is an affecting consideration. I
remember Swift, in one of his letters to Pope, says, "I intend
to come over, that we may meet once more; and when we
must part, it is what happens to all human beings."' *Boswell.*
'There is a strange unwillingness to part with life, independent
of serious fears as to futurity. A reverend friend of ours (nam-

ing him) tells me, that he feels an uneasiness at the thoughts of leaving his house, his study, his books.' *Johnson*. 'This is foolish. A man need not be uneasy on these grounds.' *Boswell*. I remember, many years ago, when my imagination was warm, and I happened to be in a melancholy mood, it distressed me to think of going into a state of being in which Shakspeare's poetry did not exist. A lady whom I then much admired, a very amiable woman, humoured my fancy, and relieved me by saying, "The first thing you will meet in the other world, will be an elegant copy of Shakspeare's works presented to you."' Dr. Johnson smiled benignantly at this, and did not appear to disapprove of the notion.

We went to St. Clement's church again in the afternoon, and then returned and drank tea and coffee in Mrs. Williams's room; Mrs. Desmoulins doing the honours of the tea-table. I observed that he would not even look at a proof-sheet of his 'Life of Waller' on Good-Friday.

On Saturday, April 14, I drank tea with him. The Gentleman who had dined with us at Dr. Percy's came in. Johnson attacked the Americans with intemperate vehemence of abuse. I said something in their favour; and added, that I was always sorry when he talked on that subject. This, it seems, exasperated him; though he said nothing at the time. The cloud was charged with sulphureous vapour, which was afterwards to burst in thunder.—We talked of a gentleman who was running out his fortune in London; and I said, 'We must get him out of it. All his friends must quarrel with him, and that will soon drive him away.' *Johnson*. 'Nay, Sir, we'll send *you* to him. If your company does not drive a man out of his house, nothing will.' This was a horrible shock, for which there was no visible cause. I afterwards asked him why he had said so harsh a thing. *Johnson*. 'Because, Sir, you made me angry about the Americans.' *Boswell*. 'But why did you not take your revenge directly?' *Johnson*. (smiling) 'Because, Sir, I had nothing ready. A man cannot strike till he has his weapons.' This was a candid and pleasant confession.

He shewed me to-night his drawing-room, very genteelly fitted up; and said, 'Mrs. Thrale sneered when I talked of my having asked you and your lady to live at my house. I was

obliged to tell her, that you would be in as respectable a situa
tion in my house as in hers. Sir, the insolence of wealth wil
creep out.' *Boswell*. 'She has a little both of the insolence o
wealth, and the conceit of parts.' *Johnson*. 'The insolence o
wealth is a wretched thing; but the conceit of parts has som
foundation. To be sure it should not be. But who is withou
it?' *Boswell*. 'Yourself, Sir.' *Johnson*. 'Why I play no tricks: ¡
lay no traps.' *Boswell*. 'No, Sir. You are six feet high, anc
you only do not stoop.'

On Saturday, April 25, I dined with him at Sir Joshua Reyn
olds's with the learned Dr. Musgrave, Counsellor Leland
of Ireland, son to the historian, Mrs. Cholmondeley, and some
more ladies.

Johnson. 'Demosthenes Taylor, as he was called, was the
most silent man that I have ever seen. I once dined in company
with him, and all he said during the whole time was no more
than *Richard*. How a man should say only Richard, it is not
easy to imagine. But it was thus: Dr. Douglas was talking of
Dr. Zachary Grey, and ascribing to him something that was
written by Dr. Richard Grey. So, to correct him, Taylor said,
(imitating his affected sententious emphasis and nod,)
"*Richard*." '

We talked of a lady's verses on Ireland. *Miss Reynolds*.
'Have you seen them, Sir?' *Johnson*. 'No, Madam. I have seen
a translation from Horace, by one of her daughters. She shewed
it me. I am vexed at being shewn verses in that manner.' *Miss
Reynolds*. 'But if they should be good, why not give them
hearty praise?' *Johnson*. 'Why, Madam, because I have not
then got the better of my bad humour from having been
shewn them. You must consider, Madam; before-hand they
may be bad, as well as good. Nobody has a right to put another under such a difficulty, that he must either hurt the
person by telling the truth, or hurt himself by telling what is
not true. A man, who is asked by an authour, what he thinks
of his work, is put to the torture, and is not obliged to speak
the truth; so that what he says is not to be considered as his
opinion; yet he has said it, and cannot retract it; and this
authour, when mankind are hunting him with a cannister
at his tail, can say, "I would not have published, had not John-

...on, or Reynolds, or Musgrave, or some other good judge commended the work." Yet I consider it as a very difficult question
in conscience, whether one should advise a man not to publish
a work, if profit be his object; for the man may say, "Had it
not been for you, I should have had the money." Now you
cannot be sure; for you have only your own opinion, and the
publick may think very differently.' *Sir Joshua Reynolds.* 'You
must upon such an occasion have two judgements; one as to
the real value of the work, the other as to what may please
the general taste at the time.' *Johnson.* 'But you can be *sure*
of neither; and therefore I should scruple much to give a sup-
pressive vote. Both Goldsmith's comedies were once refused;
his first by Garrick, his second by Colman, who was prevailed
on at last by much solicitation, nay, a kind of force, to bring
it on. His "Vicar of Wakefield" I myself did not think would
have had much success. It was written and sold to a bookseller
before his "Traveller;" but published after; so little expectation
had the bookseller from it. Had it been sold after "The Traveller," he might have had twice as much money for it, though
sixty guineas was no mean price. The bookseller had the advantage of Goldsmith's reputation from "The Traveller" in
the sale, though Goldsmith had it not in selling the copy.' *Sir
Joshua Reynolds.* '"The Beggar's Opera" affords a proof how
strangely people will differ in opinion about a literary performance. Burke thinks it has no merit.' *Johnson.* 'It was refused by one of the houses; but I should have thought it would
succeed, not from any great excellence in the writing, but
from the novelty, and the general spirit and gaiety of the piece,
which keeps the audience always attentive, and dismisses them
in good humour.'

His friend Edward Cave having been mentioned, he told
us, 'Cave used to sell ten thousand of "The Gentleman's
Magazine;" yet such was then his minute attention and anxiety
that the sale should not suffer the smallest decrease, that he
would name a particular person who he heard had talked of
leaving off the Magazine, and would say, "Let us have something good next month." '

On Tuesday, April 28, he was engaged to dine at General
Paoli's, where, as I have already observed, I was still enter-

tained in elegant hospitality, and with all the ease and comfort of a home. I called on him, and accompanied him in a hackney-coach. We stopped first at the bottom of Hedge-lane, into which he went to leave a letter, 'with good news for a poor man in distress,' as he told me. I did not question him particularly as to this. We stopped again at Wirgman's, the well-known *toy-shop*, in St. James's-Street, at the corner of St. James's-Place, to which he had been directed, but not clearly, for he searched about some time, and could not find it at first; and said, 'To direct one only to a corner shop is *toying* with one.' I suppose he meant this as a play upon the word *toy*: it was the first time that I knew him stoop to such sport. After he had been some time in the shop, he sent for me to come out of the coach, and help him to choose a pair of silver buckles, as those he had were too small. Probably this alteration in dress had been suggested by Mrs. Thrale, by associating with whom, his external appearance was much improved. He got better cloaths; and the dark colour, from which he never deviated, was enlivened by metal buttons. His wigs, too, were much better; and during their travels in France, he was furnished with a Paris-made wig, of handsome construction. This choosing of silver buckles was a negociation: 'Sir, (said he,) I will not have the ridiculous large ones now in fashion; and I will give no more than a guinea for a pair.' Such were the *principles* of the business; and, after some examination, he was fitted. As we drove along, I found him in a talking humour, of which I availed myself.

At General Paoli's were Sir Joshua Reynolds, Mr. Langton, Marchese Gherardi of Lombardy, and Mr. John Spottiswoode the younger, of Spottiswoode, the solicitor. At this time fears of an invasion were circulated; to obviate which, Mr. Spottiswoode observed, that Mr. Fraser the engineer, who had lately come from Dunkirk, said, that the French had the same fears of us. *Johnson.* 'It is thus that mutual cowardice keeps us in peace. Were one half of mankind brave, and one half cowards, the brave would be always beating the cowards. Were all brave, they would lead a very uneasy life; all would be continually fighting: but being all cowards, we go on very well.'

We talked of drinking wine. *Johnson.* 'I require wine, only when I am alone. I have then often wished for it, and often taken it.' *Spottiswoode.* 'What, by way of a companion, Sir?' *Johnson.* 'To get rid of myself, to send myself away. Wine gives great pleasure; and every pleasure is of itself a good. It is a good, unless counterbalanced by evil. A man may have a strong reason not to drink wine; and that may be greater than the pleasure. Wine makes a man better pleased with himself. I do not say that it makes him more pleasing to others. Sometimes it does. But the danger is, that while a man grows better pleased with himself, he may be growing less pleasing to others. Wine gives a man nothing. It neither gives him knowledge nor wit; it only animates a man, and enables him to bring out what a dread of the company has repressed. It only puts in motion what has been locked up in frost. But this may be good, or it may be bad.' *Spottiswoode.* 'So, Sir, wine is a key which opens a box; but this box may be either full or empty.' *Johnson.* 'Nay, Sir, conversation is the key: wine is a pick-lock, which forces open the box and injures it. A man should cultivate his mind so as to have that confidence and readiness without wine, which wine gives.' *Boswell.* 'The great difficulty of resisting wine is from benevolence. For instance, a good worthy man asks you to taste his wine, which he has had twenty years in his cellar.' *Johnson.* 'Sir, all this notion about benevolence arises from a man's imagining himself to be of more importance to others, than he really is. They don't care a farthing whether he drinks wine or not.' *Sir Joshua Reynolds.* 'Yes, they do for the time.' *Johnson.* 'For the time!— If they care this minute, they forget it the next. And as for the good worthy man; how do you know he is good and worthy? No good and worthy man will insist upon another man's drinking wine. As to the wine twenty years in the cellar,—of ten men, three say this, merely because they must say something; —three are telling a lie, when they say they have had the wine twenty years;—three would rather save the wine;—one, perhaps, cares. I allow it is something to please one's company; and people are always pleased with those who partake pleasure with them. But let us consider what a sad thing it would be, if we were obliged to drink or do any thing else that may happen to be agreeable to the company where we are.'

Langton. 'By the same rule you must join with a gang o
cut-purses.' *Johnson.* 'Yes, Sir: but yet we must do justice t
wine; we must allow it the power it possesses. To make a mar
pleased with himself, let me tell you, is doing a very grea
thing.'

Sir Joshua Reynolds. 'But to please one's company is a strong
motive.' *Johnson.* (who, from drinking only water, supposed
every body who drank wine to be elevated,) 'I won't argue any
more with you, Sir. You are too far gone.' *Sir Joshua.* 'I should
have thought so indeed, Sir, had I made such a speech as you
have now done.' *Johnson.* (drawing himself in, and, I really
thought blushing,) 'Nay, don't be angry. I did not mean to
offend you.' *Sir Joshua.* 'At first the taste of wine was disagreeable to me; but I brought myself to drink it, that I might be
like other people. The pleasure of drinking wine is so connected with pleasing your company, that altogether there is
something of social goodness in it.' *Johnson.* 'Sir, this is only
saying the same thing over again.' *Sir Joshua.* 'No, this is new.'
Johnson. 'You put it in new words, but it is an old thought.
This is one of the disadvantages of wine. It makes a man mistake words for thoughts.' *Boswell.* 'I think it is a new thought;
at least, it is in a new *attitude*.' *Johnson.* 'Nay, Sir, it is only
in a new coat; or an old coat with a new facing. (Then laughing heartily) It is the old dog in a new doublet.—An extraordinary instance however may occur where a man's patron will
do nothing for him, unless he will drink: *there* may be a good
reason for drinking.'

On Wednesday, April 29, I dined with him at Mr. Allan
Ramsay's, where were Lord Binning, Dr. Robertson the historian, Sir Joshua Reynolds, and the Honourable Mrs. Boscawen. Before Johnson came we talked a good deal of him;
Ramsay said he had always found him a very polite man, and
that he treated him with great respect, which he did very
sincerely. *Robertson.* 'He and I have been always very gracious;
the first time I met him was one evening at Strahan's, when he
had just had an unlucky altercation with Adam Smith, to
whom he had been so rough, that Strahan, after Smith was
gone, had remonstrated with him, and told him that I was
coming soon. and that he was uneasy to think that he might

behave in the same manner to me. "No, no, Sir, (said Johnson) I warrant you Robertson and I shall do very well." Accordingly he was gentle and good-humoured, and courteous with me the whole evening; and he has been so upon every occasion that we have met since. I have often said (laughing) that I have been in a great measure indebted to Smith for my good reception.' *Boswell.* 'His power of reasoning is very strong, and he has a peculiar art of drawing characters, which is as rare as good portrait painting.' *Sir Joshua Reynolds.* 'He is undoubtedly admirable in this; but, in order to mark the characters which he draws, he overcharges them, and gives people more than they really have, whether of good or bad.'

No sooner did he, of whom we had been thus talking so easily, arrive, than we were all as quiet as a school upon the entrance of the head-master; and were very soon set down to a table covered with such variety of good things, as contributed not a little to dispose him to be pleased.

Ramsay. 'I am old enough to have been a contemporary of Pope. His poetry was highly admired in his life-time, more a great deal than after his death.' *Johnson.* 'Sir, it has not been less admired since his death; no authours ever had so much fame in their own life-time as Pope and Voltaire; and Pope's poetry has been as much admired since his death as during his life; it has only not been as much talked of, but that is owing to its being now more distant, and people having other writings to talk of. Virgil is less talked of than Pope, and Homer is less talked of than Virgil; but they are not less admired. We must read what the world reads at the moment. It has been maintained that this superfœtation, this teeming of the press in modern times, is prejudicial to good literature, because it obliges us to read so much of what is of inferiour value, in order to be in the fashion; so that better works are neglected for want of time, because a man will have more gratification of his vanity in conversation, from having read modern books, than from having read the best works of antiquity. But it must be considered, that we have now more knowledge generally diffused; all our ladies read now, which is a great extension.'

Dr. Robertson expatiated on the character of a certain nobleman;[1] that he was one of the strongest-minded men that ever lived; that he would sit in company quite sluggish, while there was nothing to call forth his intellectual vigour; but the moment that any important subject was started, for instance, how this country is to be defended against a French invasion, he would rouse himself, and shew his extraordinary talents with the most powerful ability and animation. *Johnson*. 'Yet this man cut his own throat. The true strong and sound mind is the mind that can embrace equally great things and small. Now I am told the King of Prussia will say to a servant, "Bring me a bottle of such a wine, which came in such a year; it lies in such a corner of the cellars." I would have a man great in great things, and elegant in little things.' He said to me afterwards, when we were by ourselves, 'Robertson was in a mighty romantick humour, he talked of one whom he did not know; but I *downed* him with the King of Prussia.'—'Yes, Sir, (said I,) you threw a *bottle* at his head.'

An ingenious gentleman was mentioned, concerning whom both Robertson and Ramsay agreed that he had a constant firmness of mind; for after a laborious day, and amidst a multiplicity of cares and anxieties, he would sit down with his sisters and be quite cheerful and good-humoured. Such a disposition, it was observed, was a happy gift of nature. *Johnson*. 'I do not think so; a man has from nature a certain portion of mind; the use he makes of it depends upon his own free will. That a man has always the same firmness of mind I do not say; because every man feels his mind less firm at one time than at another; but I think a man's being in a good or bad humour depends upon his will.' I, however, could not help thinking that a man's humour is often uncontroulable by his will.

Johnson harangued against drinking wine. 'A man (said he) may choose whether he will have abstemiousness and knowledge, or claret and ignorance.' Dr. Robertson, (who is very companionable,) was beginning to dissent as to the proscription of claret. *Johnson:* (with a placid smile.) 'Nay, Sir, you shall not differ with me; as I have said that the man is most perfect who takes in the most things, I am for knowledge and

[1] Lord Clive (1725-1774), founder of the Empire of British India. He committed suicide.

claret.' *Robertson:* (holding a glass of generous claret in his hand.) 'Sir, I can only drink your health.' *Johnson.* 'Sir I should be sorry if *you* should be ever in such a state as to be able to do nothing more.'

Next day, Thursday, April 30, I found him at home by himself. *Johnson.* 'Well, Sir, Ramsay gave us a splendid dinner. I love Ramsay. You will not find a man in whose conversation there is more instruction, more information, and more elegance, than in Ramsay's.' *Boswell.* 'What I admire in Ramsay, is his continuing to be so young.' *Johnson.* 'Why, yes, Sir, it is to be admired. I value myself upon this, that there is nothing of the old man in my conversation. I am now sixty-eight, and I have no more of it than at twenty-eight.' *Boswell.* 'But, Sir, would not you wish to know old age? He who is never an old man, does not know the whole of human life; for old age is one of the divisions of it.' *Johnson.* 'Nay, Sir, what talk is this?' *Boswell.* 'I mean, Sir, the Sphinx's description of it;—morning, noon, and night. I would know night, as well as morning and noon.' *Johnson.* 'What, Sir, would you know what it is to feel the evils of old age? Would you have the gout? Would you have decrepitude?'—Seeing him heated, I would not argue any farther; but I was confident that I was in the right. *Johnson.* 'Mrs. Thrale's mother said of me what flattered me much. A clergyman was complaining of want of society in the country where he lived; and said, "They talk of *runts;*" (that is, young cows). "Sir, (said Mrs. Salusbury,) Mr. Johnson would learn to talk of runts:" meaning that I was a man who would make the most of my situation, whatever it was.' He added, 'I think myself a very polite man.'

On Saturday, May 2, I dined with him at Sir Joshua Reynolds's, where there was a very large company, and a great deal of conversation; but owing to some circumstance which I cannot now recollect, I have no record of any part of it, except that there were several people there by no means of the Johnsonian school; so that less attention was paid to him than usual, which put him out of humour; and upon some imaginary offence from me, he attacked me with such rudeness, that I was vexed and angry, because it gave those persons an opportunity of enlarging upon his supposed ferocity, and ill treatment of his best friends. I was so much hurt, and had my pride so much roused, that I kept away from him for a week, and, perhaps, might have kept away much longer, nay, gone to Scotland without seeing him again, had not we fortunately met and been reconciled. To such unhappy chances are human friendships liable.

On Friday, May 8, I dined with him at Mr. Langton's. I was reserved and silent, which I suppose he perceived, and might recollect the cause. After dinner, when Mr. Langton was called out of the room, and we were by ourselves, he drew his chair near to mine, and said, in a tone of conciliating courtesy, 'Well, how have you done?' *Boswell*. 'Sir, you have made me very uneasy by your behaviour to me when we were last at Sir Joshua Reynolds's. You know, my dear Sir, no man has a greater respect and affection for you, or would sooner go to the end of the world to serve you. Now to treat me so—.' He insisted that I had interrupted him, which I assured him was not the case; and proceeded—'But why treat me so before people who neither love you nor me?' *Johnson*. 'Well, I am sorry for it. I'll make it up to you twenty different ways, as you please.' *Boswell*. 'I said to-day to Sir Joshua, when he observed that you *tossed* me sometimes—I don't care how often, or how high he tosses me, when only friends are present, for then I fall upon soft ground: but I do not like falling on stones, which is the case when enemies are present.—I think this is a pretty good image, Sir.' *Johnson*. 'Sir, it is one of the happiest I have ever heard.'

When Mr. Langton returned to us, the 'flow of talk' went on. Johnson called the East-Indians barbarians. *Boswell*. 'You will except the Chinese, Sir?' *Johnson*. 'No, Sir.' *Boswell*. 'Have they not arts?' *Johnson*. 'They have pottery.' *Boswell*. 'What do you say to the written characters of their language?' *Johnson*. 'Sir, they have not an alphabet. They have not been able to form what all other nations have formed.' *Boswell*. 'There is more learning in their language than in any other, from the immense number of their characters.' *Johnson*. 'It is only more difficult from its rudeness; as there is more labour in hewing down a tree with a stone than with an axe.'

On Saturday, May 9, we fulfilled our purpose of dining by ourselves at the Mitre, according to old custom. There was, on these occasions, a little circumstance of kind attention to Mrs. Williams, which must not be omitted. Before coming out, and leaving her to dine alone, he gave her her choice of a chicken, a sweetbread, or any other little nice thing, which was carefully sent to her from the tavern, ready-drest.

Our conversation to-day, I know not how, turned, (I think for the only time at any length, during our long acquaintance,) upon the sensual intercourse between the sexes, the delight of which he ascribed chiefly to imagination. 'Were it not for imagination, Sir, (said he,) a man would be as happy in the arms of a chambermaid as of a Duchess. But such is the adventitious charm of fancy, that we find men who have violated the best principles of society, and ruined their fame and their fortune, that they might possess a woman of rank.' It would not be proper to record the particulars of such a conversation in moments of unreserved frankness, when nobody was present on whom it could have any hurtful effect. That subject, when philosophically treated, may surely employ the mind in as curious discussion, and as innocently, as anatomy; provided that those who do treat it keep clear of inflammatory incentives.

'From grave to gay, from lively to severe,'—we were soon engaged in very different speculation; humbly and reverently considering and wondering at the universal mystery of all things, as our imperfect faculties can now judge of them. 'There are (said he) innumerable questions to which the inquisitive mind can in this state receive no answer: Why do you and I exist? Why was this world created? Since it was to be created, why was it not created sooner?'

On Sunday, May 10, I supped with him at Mr. Hoole's, with Sir Joshua Reynolds. I have neglected the memorial of this evening, so as to remember no more of it than two particulars; one, that he strenuously opposed an argument by Sir Joshua, that virtue was preferable to vice, considering this life only; and that a man would be virtuous were it only to preserve his character: and that he expressed much wonder at the curious formation of the bat, a mouse with wings; saying, that 'it was almost as strange a thing in physiology, as if the fabulous dragon could be seen.'

On Tuesday, May 12, I waited on the Earl of Marchmont, to know if his Lordship would favour Dr. Johnson with information concerning Pope, whose Life he was about to write. Johnson had not flattered himself with the hopes of receiving any civility from this nobleman; for he said to me, when I mentioned Lord Marchmont as one who could tell him a great deal about Pope, 'Sir, he will tell *me* nothing.' I had the honour of being known to his Lordship, and applied to him of myself, without being commissioned by Johnson. His Lordship behaved in the most polite and obliging manner, promised to tell all he recollected about Pope, and was so very courteous as to say, 'Tell Dr. Johnson I have a great respect for him, and am ready to shew it in any way I can. I am to be in the city to-morrow, and will call at his house as I return.' His Lordship however asked, 'Will he write the Lives of the Poets impartially? He was the first that brought Whig and Tory into a Dictionary. And what do you think of his definition of Excise? Do you know the history of his aversion to the word *transpire?*' Then taking down the folio Dictionary, he shewed it with this censure on its secondary sense: 'To escape from secrecy to notice; a sense lately innovated from France, without necessity.' The truth was, Lord Bolingbroke, who left the Jacobites, first used it; therefore, it was to be condemned. He should have shewn what word would do for it, if it was unnecessary.' I afterwards put the question to Johnson: 'Why, Sir, (said he,) *get abroad.' Boswell.* 'That, Sir, is using two words.' *Johnson.* 'Sir, there is no end of this. You may as well insist to have a word for old age.' *Boswell.* 'Well, Sir, *Senectus.' Johnson.* 'Nay, Sir, to insist always that there should be one word to express a thing in English, because there is one in another language, is to change the language.'

I proposed to Lord Marchmont that he should revise Johnson's Life of Pope: 'So (said his Lordship) you would put me in a dangerous situation. You know he knocked down Osborne the bookseller.'

Elated with the success of my spontaneous exertion to pro-

cure material and respectable aid to Johnson for his very
favourite work, 'The Lives of the Poets,' I hastened down to
Mr. Thrale's at Streatham, where he now was, that I might
insure his being at home next day; and after dinner, when I
thought he would receive the good news in the best humour,
I announced it eagerly: 'I have been at work for you to-day,
Sir. I have been with Lord Marchmont. He bade me tell you
he has a great respect for you, and will call on you to-morrow
at one o'clock, and communicate all he knows about Pope.'—
Here I paused, in full expectation that he would be pleased
with this intelligence, would praise my active merit, and
would be alert to embrace such an offer from a nobleman.
But whether I had shewn an over-exultation, which provoked
his spleen; or whether he was seized with a suspicion that
I had obtruded him on Lord Marchmont, and had humbled
him too much; or whether there was any thing more than an
unlucky fit of ill-humour, I know not; but, to my surprize, the
result was,—*Johnson.* 'I shall not be in town to-morrow. I don't
care to know about Pope.' *Mrs. Thrale:* (surprized as I was,
and a little angry.) 'I suppose, Sir, Mr. Boswell thought, that
as you are to write Pope's Life, you would wish to know about
him.' *Johnson.* 'Wish! why yes. If it rained knowledge I'd hold
out my hand; but I would not give myself the trouble to go in
quest of it.' There was no arguing with him at the moment. Some time afterwards he said. 'Lord Marchmont will call
on me, and then I shall call on Lord Marchmont.' Mr. Thrale
was uneasy at his unaccountable caprice; and told me, that if
I did not take care to bring about a meeting between Lord
Marchmont and him, it would never take place, which would
be a great pity. I sent a card to his Lordship, to be left at Johnson's house, acquainting him, that Dr. Johnson could not be
in town next day, but would do himself the honour of waiting
on him at another time.—I give this account fairly, as a specimen of that unhappy temper with which this great and good
man had occasionally to struggle, from something morbid in
his constitution. But it must not be erroneously supposed that
he was, in the smallest degree, careless concerning any work
which he undertook, or that he was generally thus peevish. It
will be seen, that in the following year he had a very agreeable

interview with Lord Marchmont, at his Lordship's house; and this very afternoon he soon forgot any fretfulness, and fell into conversation as usual.

Mrs. Thrale mentioned Dryden. *Johnson.* 'He puzzled himself about predestination.—How foolish was it in Pope to give all his friendship to Lords, who thought they honoured him by being with him; and to choose such Lords as Burling-ton, and Cobham, and Bolingbroke! Bathurst was negative, a pleasing man; and I have heard no ill of Marchmont; and then always saying, "I do not value you for being a Lord;" which was a sure proof that he did. I never say, I do not value Boswell more for being born to an estate, because I do not care.' *Boswell.* 'Nor for being a Scotchman?' *Johnson.* 'Nay, Sir, I do value you more for being a Scotchman. You are a Scotchman without the faults of Scotchmen. You would not have been so valuable as you are, had you not been a Scotch-man.'

Amongst the numerous prints pasted on the walls of the dining-room at Streatham, was Hogarth's 'Modern Midnight Conversation.' I asked him what he knew of Parson Ford, who makes a conspicuous figure in the riotous groupe. *Johnson.* 'Sir, he was my acquaintance and relation, my mother's nephew. He had purchased a living in the country, but not simoniacally. I never saw him but in the country. I have been told he was a man of great parts; very profligate, but I never heard he was impious.' *Boswell.* 'Was there not a story of his ghost having appeared?' *Johnson.* 'Sir, it was believed. A waiter at the Hum-mums, in which house Ford died, had been absent for some time, and returned, not knowing that Ford was dead. Going down to the cellar, according to the story, he met him; going down again he met him a second time. When he came up, he asked some of the people of the house what Ford could be doing there. They told him Ford was dead. The waiter took a fever, in which he lay for some time. When he recovered, he said he had a message to deliver to some women from Ford; but he was not to tell what, or to whom. He walked out; he was followed; but somewhere about St. Paul's they lost him. He came back, and said he had delivered the message, and the women exclaimed, "Then we are all undone!" Dr.

Pellet, who was not a credulous man, inquired into the truth of this story, and he said, the evidence was irresistible. My wife went to the Hummums; (it is a place where people get themselves cupped.) I believe she went with intention to hear about this story of Ford. At first they were unwilling to tell her; but, after they had talked to her, she came away satisfied that it was true. To be sure the man had a fever; and this vision may have been the beginning of it. But if the message to the women, and their behaviour upon it, were true as related, there was something supernatural. That rests upon his word; and there it remains.'

After Mrs. Thrale was gone to bed, Johnson and I sat up late. We resumed Sir Joshua Reynolds's argument on the preceding Sunday, that a man would be virtuous though he had no other motive than to preserve his character. *Johnson.* 'Sir, it is not true: for as to this world vice does not hurt a man's character.' *Boswell.* 'Yes, Sir, debauching a friend's wife will.' *Johnson.* 'No, Sir. A man is chosen Knight of the shire, not the less for having debauched ladies.' *Boswell.* 'What, Sir, if he debauched the ladies of gentlemen in the county, will not there be a general resentment against him?' *Johnson.* 'No, Sir. He will lose those particular gentlemen; but the rest will not trouble their heads about it.' (warmly.) *Boswell.* 'Well, Sir, I cannot think so.' *Johnson.* 'Nay, Sir, there is no talking with a man who will dispute what every body knows, (angrily.) Don't you know this?' *Boswell.* 'No, Sir; and I wish to think better of your country than you represent it.'

Next morning I stated to Mrs. Thrale at breakfast, before he came down, the dispute of last night as to the influence of character upon success in life. She said he was certainly wrong. But she would not encounter Johnson upon the subject.

I staid all this day with him at Streatham. He talked a great deal, in very good humour.

Looking at Messrs. Dilly's splendid edition of Lord Chesterfield's miscellaneous works, he laughed, and said, 'Here now are two speeches ascribed to him, both of which were written by me: and the best of it is, they have found out that one is like Demosthenes, and the other like Cicero.'

He censured Lord Kames's 'Sketches of the History of Man,'

for misrepresenting Clarendon's account of the appearance of Sir George Villier's ghost, as if Clarendon were weakly credulous; when the truth is, that Clarendon only says, that the story was upon a better foundation of credit, than usually such discourses are founded upon; nay, speaks thus of the person who was reported to have seen the vision, 'the poor man, *if he had been at all waking;*' which Lord Kames has omitted. He added, 'in this book it is maintained that virtue is natural to man, and that if we would but consult our own hearts we should be virtuous. Now after consulting our own hearts all we can, and with all the helps we have, we find how few of us are virtuous. This is saying a thing which all mankind know not to be true.' *Boswell.* 'Is not modesty natural?' *Johnson.* 'I cannot say, Sir, as we find no people quite in a state of nature; but I think the more they are taught, the more modest they are. The French are a gross, ill-bred, untaught people; a lady there will spit on the floor and rub it with her foot. What I gained by being in France was, learning to be better satisfied with my own country. Time may be employed to more advantage from nineteen to twenty-four almost in any way than in travelling; when you set travelling against mere negation, against doing nothing, it is better to be sure; but how much more would a young man improve were he to study during those years. Indeed, if a young man is wild, and must run after women and bad company, it is better this should be done abroad, as, on his return, he can break off such connections, and begin at home a new man, with a character to form, and acquaintances to make. How little does travelling supply to the conversation of any man who has travelled? how little to Beauclerk?'

I talked of a country life.—*Johnson.* 'Were I to live in the country, I would not devote myself to the acquisition of popularity; I would live in a much better way, much more happily; I would have my time at my own command.' *Boswell.* 'But, Sir, is it not a sad thing to be at a distance from all our literary friends?' *Johnson.* 'Sir, you will by and by have enough of this conversation, which now delights you so much.'

As he was a zealous friend of subordination, he was at all

times watchful to repress the vulgar cant against the manners of the great; 'High people, Sir, (said he,) are the best; take a hundred ladies of quality, you'll find them better wives, better mothers, more willing to sacrifice their own pleasure to their children, than a hundred other women. Tradeswomen (I mean the wives of tradesmen) in the city, who are worth from ten to fifteen thousand pounds, are the worst creatures upon the earth, grossly ignorant, and thinking viciousness fashionable. Farmers, I think, are often worthless fellows. Few lords will cheat; and, if they do, they'll be ashamed of it: farmers cheat and are not ashamed of it: they have all the sensual vices too of the nobility, with cheating into the bargain. There is as much fornication and adultery amongst farmers as amongst noblemen.' *Boswell.* 'The notion of the world, Sir, however is, that the morals of women of quality are worse than those in lower stations.' *Johnson.* 'Yes, Sir, the licentiousness of one woman of quality makes more noise than that of a number of women in lower stations; then, Sir, you are to consider the malignity of women in the city against women of quality, which will make them believe any thing of them, such as that they call their coachmen to bed. No, Sir, so far as I have observed, the higher in rank, the richer ladies are, they are the better instructed and the more virtuous.'

Mr. Langton has been pleased, at my request, to favour me with some particulars of Dr. Johnson's visit to Warley-camp, where this gentleman was at the time stationed as a Captain in the Lincolnshire militia. I shall give them in his own words in a letter to me.

'It was in the summer of the year 1778, that he complied with my invitation to come down to the Camp at Warley, and he staid with me about a week; the scene appeared, notwithstanding a great degree of ill health that he seemed to labour under, to interest and amuse him, as agreeing with the disposition that I believe you know he constantly manifested towards enquiring into subjects of the military kind. He sate, with a patient degree of attention, to observe the proceedings of a regimental court-martial, that happened to be called in the time of his stay with us; and one night, as late as at eleven o'clock, he accompanied the Major of the regiment in going what are styled, the *Rounds,* where he might observe the forms of visiting the guards, for the seeing that they and their sentries are ready in their duty on their several posts.

'In walking among the tents, and observing the difference between those of the officers and private men, he said that the superiority of accommodation of the better conditions of life, to that of the inferiour ones, was never exhibited to him in so distinct a view. The civilities paid to him in the camp were, from the gentlemen of the Lincolnshire regiment, one of the officers of which accommodated him with a tent in which he slept; and from General Hall, who very courteously invited him to dine with him, where he appeared to be very well pleased with his entertainment, and the civilities he received on the part of the General; the attention likewise, of the General's aid-de-camp, Captain Smith, seemed to be very welcome to him, as appeared by their engaging in a great deal of discourse together.'

'To JAMES BOSWELL, ESQ.

'DEAR SIR,

'I HAVE received two letters from you, of which the second complains of the neglect shown to the first. You must not tye your friends to such punctual correspondence. You have all possible assurances of my affection and esteem; and there ought to be no need of reiterated professions. When it may happen that I can give you either counsel or comfort, I hope it will never happen to me that I should neglect you; but you must not think me criminal or cold if I say nothing, when I have nothing to say.

'I wish you would a little correct or restrain your imagination, and imagine that happiness, such as life admits, may be had at other places as well as London. Without asserting Stoicism, it may be said, that it is our business to exempt ourselves as much as we can from the power of external things. There is but one solid basis of happiness; and that is, the reasonable hope of a happy futurity. This may be had every where.

'I do not blame your preference of London to other places, for it is really to be preferred, if the choice is free; but few have the choice of their place, or their manner of life; and mere pleasure ought not to be the prime motive of action.

'Mrs. Thrale, poor thing, has a daughter. Mr. Thrale dislikes the times, like the rest of us. Mrs. Williams is sick; Mrs. Desmoulins is poor. I have miserable nights. Nobody is well but Mr. Levett.

'I am, dear Sir, Your most, &c.

'SAM. JOHNSON.'

'London, July 3, 1778.'

We surely cannot but admire the benevolent exertions of his great and good man, especially when we consider how grievously he was afflicted with bad health, and how uncomfortable his home was made by the perpetual jarring of those whom he charitably accommodated under his roof. He has sometimes suffered me to talk jocularly of his group of females, and call them his *Seraglio*. He thus mentions them, together with honest Levett, in one of his letters to Mrs. Thrale: 'Williams hates every body; Levett hates Desmoulins, and does not love Williams; Desmoulins hates them both; Poll loves none of them.'

1779: ÆTAT. 70.]—In 1779, Johnson gave the world a luminous proof that the vigour of his mind in all its faculties, whether memory, judgement, or imagination, was not in the least abated; for this year came out the first four volumes of his 'Prefaces, biographical and critical, to the most eminent of the English Poets,' published by the booksellers of London. The remaining volumes came out in the year 1780. The Poets were selected by the several booksellers who had the honorary copy right, which is still preserved among them by mutual compact, notwithstanding the decision of the House of Lords against the perpetuity of Literary Property. We have his own authority, that by his recommendation the poems of Blackmore, Watts, Pomfret, and Yalden, were added to the collection. Of this work I shall speak more particularly hereafter.

On the 22d of January, I wrote to him on several topicks, and mentioned that as he had been so good as to permit me to have the proof sheets of his 'Lives of the Poets,' I had written to his servant, Francis, to take care of them for me.

'MR. BOSWELL TO DR. JOHNSON.

'Edinburgh, Feb. 2, 1779.

'MY DEAR SIR,

'GARRICK's death is a striking event; not that we should be surprised with the death of any man, who has lived sixty-two years; but because there was a *vivacity* in our late celebrated friend, which drove away the thoughts of *death* from any association with *him*. I am sure you will be tenderly affected with his departure; and I would wish to hear from you upon the subject. I was obliged to him in my days of effervescence in London, and since that time I received many civilities from him. Do you remember how pleasing it was, when I received a letter from him at Inverary, upon our first return to civilized living after our Hebridean journey? I shall always remember him with affection as well as admiration.

'On Saturday last, being the 30th of January, I drank coffee and old port, and had solemn conversation with the Reverend Mr. Falconer, a nonjuring bishop, a very learned and worthy man. He gave two toasts, which you will believe I drank with cordiality, Dr Samuel Johnson, and Flora Macdonald. I sat about four hours with him, and it was really as if I had been living in the last century. This venerable gentleman did me the honour to dine with me yesterday, and he laid his hands upon the heads of my little ones. We had a good deal of curious literary conversation, particularly about Mr. Thomas Ruddiman, with whom he lived in great friendship.

'Any fresh instance of the uncertainty of life makes one embrace more closely a valuable friend. My dear and much respected Sir, may GOD preserve you long in this world while I am in it.

　　　　　'I am ever,
　　　　　　　　'Your much obliged,
　　　　　　　　　　'And affectionate humble servant,
　　　　　　　　　　　　　'JAMES BOSWELL.'

On the 23d of February I wrote to him again, complaining of his silence, as I had heard he was ill, and had written to Mr. Thrale, for information concerning him; and I announced my intention of soon being again in London.

　　　　　'To JAMES BOSWELL, ESQ.
'DEAR SIR,
　　'WHY should you take such delight to make a bustle, to write to Mr. Thrale that I am negligent, and to Francis to do what is so very unnecessary. Thrale, you may be sure, cared not about it; and I shall spare Francis the trouble, by ordering a set both of the Lives and Poets to dear Mrs. Boswell, in acknowledgement of her marmalade. Persuade her to accept them, and accept them kindly. If I thought she would receive them scornfully, I would send them to Miss Boswell, who, I hope, has yet none of her mamma's ill-will to me.

'Mrs. Thrale waits in the coach.
　　　　　　　　'I am, dear Sir, &c.
　　　　　　　　　　　'SAM. JOHNSON.'

'March 13, 1779.'

This letter crossed me on the road to London, where I arrived on Monday, March 15, and next morning at a late hour, found Dr. Johnson sitting over his tea, attended by Mrs. Desmoulins, Mr. Levett, and a clergyman, who had come to submit some poetical pieces to his revision. It is wonderful what a number and variety of writers, some of them even unknown to him, prevailed on his good-nature to look over their works, and suggest corrections and improvements. I found that the subject under immediate consideration was a translation of Horace. When Johnson had done reading, the authour asked him bluntly, 'If upon the whole it was a good translation?' Johnson, whose regard for truth was uncommonly strict, seemed to be puzzled for a moment, what answer to make, as he certainly could not honestly commend the performance: with exquisite address he evaded the question thus, 'Sir, I do not say that it may not be made a very good translation.' Here nothing whatever in favour of the performance was affirmed, and yet the writer was not shocked. A printed 'Ode to the Warlike Genius of Britain,' came next in review; the bard was a lank bony figure, with short black hair; he was writhing himself in agitation, while Johnson read, and shewing his teeth in a grin of earnestness, exclaimed in broken sentences, and in a keen sharp tone, 'Is that poetry, Sir?' *Johnson.* 'Why, Sir, there is here a great deal of what is called poetry.'

Although I was several times with him in the course of the following days, such it seems were my occupations, such my negligence, that I have preserved no memorial of his conversation till Friday, March 26, when I visited him. He said he expected to be attacked on account of his 'Lives of the Poets.' 'However (said he) I would rather be attacked than unnoticed. For the worst thing you can do to an authour is to be silent as to his works. An assault upon a town is a bad thing; but starving it is still worse; an assault may be unsuccessful; you may have more men killed than you kill; but if you starve the town, you are sure of victory.'

Talking of a friend of ours associating with persons of very discordant principles and characters; I said he was a very universal man, quite a man of the world. *Johnson.* 'Yes, Sir;

but one may be so much a man of the world as to be nothing in the world. I remember a passage in Goldsmith's "Vicar of Wakefield," which he was afterwards fool enough to expunge: "I do not love a man who is zealous for nothing."' *Boswell.* 'That was a fine passage.' *Johnson.* 'Yes, Sir: there was another fine passage too, which he struck out: "When I was a young man, being anxious to distinguish myself, I was perpetually starting new propositions. But I soon gave this over; for, I found that generally what was new was false."'

During my stay in London this spring, I find I was unaccountably negligent in preserving Johnson's sayings, more so than at any time when I was happy enough to have an opportunity of hearing his wisdom and wit. There is no help for it now. I must content myself with presenting such scraps as I have. But I am nevertheless ashamed and vexed to think how much has been lost. It is not that there was a bad crop this year; but that I was not sufficiently careful in gathering it in. I, therefore, in some instances can only exhibit a few detached fragments.

On Wednesday, March 31, when I visited him, and confessed an excess of which I had very seldom been guilty; that I had spent a whole night in playing at cards, and that I could not look back on it with satisfaction; instead of a harsh animadversion, he mildly said, 'Alas, Sir, on how few things can we look back with satisfaction.'

On Thursday, April 1, he commended one of the Dukes of Devonshire for 'a dogged veracity.' He said too, 'London is nothing to some people; but to a man whose pleasure is intellectual, London is the place. And there is no place where œconomy can be so well practised as in London. More can be had here for the money, even by ladies, than any where else. You cannot play tricks with your fortune in a small place; you must make an uniform appearance. Here a lady may have well-furnished apartments, and elegant dress, without any meat in her kitchen.'

I was amused by considering with how much ease and coolness he could write or talk to a friend, exhorting him not to suppose that happiness was not to be found as well in other places as in London; when he himself was at all times sensible of its being, comparatively speaking, a heaven upon earth. The truth is, that by those who from sagacity, attention, and experience, have learnt the full advantage of London, its pre-eminence over every other place, not only for variety of enjoyment, but for comfort, will be felt with a philosophical exultation. The freedom from remark and petty censure, with which life may be passed there, is a circumstance which a man who knows the teazing restraint of a narrow circle must relish highly. Mr. Burke, whose orderly and amiable domestick habits might make the eye of observation less irksome to him than to most men, said once very pleasantly, in my hearing, 'Though I have the honour to represent Bristol, I should not like to live there; I should be obliged to be so much *upon my good behaviour*.' In London, a man may live in splendid society at one time, and in frugal retirement at another, without animadversion. There, and there alone, a man's own house is truly his *castle*, in which he can be in perfect safety from intrusion whenever he pleases. I never shall forget how well this was expressed to me one day by Mr. Meynell: 'The chief advantage of London (said he) is, that a man is always *so near his burrow*.'

On Friday, April 2, being Good-Friday, I visited him in the morning as usual; we insensibly fell into a train of ridicule upon the foibles of one of our friends, a very worthy man. It happened also remarkably enough, that the subject of the sermon preached to us to-day by Dr. Burrows, the rector of St. Clement Danes, was the certainty that at the last day we must give an account of 'the deeds done in the body;' and, amongst various acts of culpability he mentioned evil-speaking. As we were moving slowly along in the croud from church, Johnson jogged my elbow, and said, 'Did you attend to the sermon?'—'Yes, Sir, (said I,) it was very applicable to *us*.' He, however, stood upon the defensive. 'Why, Sir, the sense of ridicule is given us, and may be lawfully used.'

On Saturday, April 3, I visited him at night, and found him sitting in Mrs. Williams's room, with her, and one who he afterwards told me was a natural son of the second Lord Southwell. The table had a singular appearance, being covered with a heterogeneous assemblage of oysters and porter for his company, and tea for himself. I mentioned my having heard an eminent physician, who was himself a Christian, argue in favour of universal toleration, and maintain, that no man could be hurt by another man's differing from him in opinion. *Johnson.* 'Sir, you are to a certain degree hurt by knowing that even one man does not believe.'

On Easter-day, after solemn service at St. Paul's, I dined with him: Mr. Allen the printer was also his guest. He was uncommonly silent; and I have not written down any thing except a single curious fact, which, having the sanction of his inflexible veracity, may be received as a striking instance of human insensibility and inconsideration. As he was passing by a fishmonger who was skinning an eel alive, he heard him 'curse it, because it would not lye still.'

On Wednesday, April 7, I dined with him at Sir Joshua Reynolds's. I have not marked what company was there. Johnson harangued upon the qualities of different liquors; and spoke with great contempt of claret, as so weak, that 'a man would be drowned by it before it made him drunk.' He was persuaded to drink one glass of it, that he might judge, not from recollection, which might be dim, but from immediate sensation. He shook his head, and said, 'Poor stuff! No, Sir, claret is the liquor for boys; port, for men; but he who aspires to be a hero (smiling) must drink brandy. In the first place, the flavour of brandy is most grateful to the palate; and then brandy will do soonest for a man what drinking *can* do for him. There are, indeed, few who are able to drink brandy. That is a power rather to be wished for than attained. And yet, (proceeded he) as in all pleasure hope is a considerable part, I know not but fruition comes too quick by brandy.' I reminded him how heartily he and I used to drink wine together, when we were first acquainted; and how I used to have a head-ache after sitting up with him. He did not like to have this recalled, or, perhaps, thinking that I boasted improperly, resolved to have a witty stroke at me: 'Nay, Sir, it was not the *wine* that made your head ache, but the *sense* that I put into it.' *Boswell.* 'What, Sir! Will sense make the head ache?' *Johnson.* 'Yes, Sir, (with a smile) when it is not used to it.'

On Thursday, April 8, I dined with him at Mr. Allan Ramay's, with Lord Graham and some other company. We talked of Shakspeare's witches. *Johnson.* 'They are beings of his own creation; they are a compound of malignity and meanness, without any abilities; and are quite different from the Italian magician. King James says, in his "Dæmonology," 'Magicians command the devils; witches are their servants." The Italian magicians are elegant beings.' *Ramsay.* 'Opera witches, not Drury-lane witches.' Johnson observed, that abilities might be employed in a narrow sphere, as in getting money, which he said he believed no man could do, without vigorous parts, though concentrated to a point.

Lord Graham commended Dr. Drummond at Naples, as a man of extraordinary talents; and added, that he had a great love of liberty. *Johnson.* 'He is *young*, my Lord; (looking to his Lordship with an arch smile) all *boys* love liberty, till experience convinces them they are not so fit to govern themselves as they imagined. We are all agreed as to our own liberty; we would have as much of it as we can get; but we are not agreed as to the liberty of others: for in proportion as we take, others must lose. I believe we hardly wish that the mob should have liberty to govern us.' *Ramsay.* 'The result is, that order is better than confusion.' *Johnson.* 'The result is, that order cannot be had but by subordination.'

On Friday, April 16, I had been present at the trial of the unfortunate Mr. Hackman,[1] who, in a fit of frantick jealous love, had shot Miss Ray, the favourite of a nobleman. Johnson, in whose company I dined to-day, with some other friends, was much interested by my account of what passed, and particularly with his prayer for the mercy of heaven. He said, in a solemn fervid tone, 'I hope he *shall* find mercy.'

This day a violent altercation arose between Johnson and Beauclerk, which having made much noise at the time, I think it proper, in order to prevent any future misrepresentation, to give a minute account of it.

[1] James Hackman (1752-1779), a clergyman who had formerly been in the army. The unfortunate woman was Martha Ray who was the mother of nine children by the Earl of Sandwich, First Lord of the Admiralty.

In talking of Hackman, Johnson argued, as Judge Black
stone had done, that his being furnished with two pistols wa
a proof that he meant to shoot two persons. Mr. Beauclerk
said, 'No; for that every wise man who intended to shoot him
self, took two pistols, that he might be sure of doing it at once
Lord ——— ———'s[1] cook shot himself with one pistol, and
lived ten days in great agony. Mr. ———,[2] who loved buttered
muffins, but durst not eat them because they disagreed with
his stomach, resolved to shoot himself; and then he eat three
buttered muffins for breakfast, before shooting himself, know
ing that he should not be troubled with indigestion: *he* had
two charged pistols; one was found lying charged upon the
table by him, after he had shot himself with the other.' 'Well
(said Johnson, with an air of triumph,) you see here one pistol
was sufficient.' Beauclerk replied smartly, 'Because it happened
to kill him.' And either then, or a very little afterwards, being
piqued at Johnson's triumphant remark, added, 'This is what
you don't know, and I do.' There was then a cessation of the
dispute; and some minutes intervened, during which, dinner
and the glass went on cheerfully; when Johnson suddenly and
abruptly exclaimed, 'Mr. Beauclerk, how came you to talk so
petulantly to me, as "This is what you don't know, but what I
know"? One thing I know, which *you* don't seem to know,
that you are very uncivil.' *Beauclerk.* 'Because *you* began by
being uncivil, (which you always are.)' The words in paren-
thesis were, I believe, not heard by Dr. Johnson. Here again
there was a cessation of arms. Johnson told me, that the reason
why he waited at first some time without taking any notice of
what Mr. Beauclerk said, was because he was thinking whether
he should resent it. But when he considered that there were
present a young Lord and an eminent traveller, two men of
the world with whom he had never dined before, he was apprehensive that they might think they had a right to take such
liberties with him as Beauclerk did, and therefore resolved he
would not let it pass; adding, that 'he would not appear a

[1] Lord Charles Spencer's
[2] Mr. Delmis—who was probably the original of the gentleman in
Pickwick who "killed himself on principle" after eating three-shillings'
worth of crumpets.

:oward.' A little while after this, the conversation turned on he violence of Hackman's temper. Johnson then said, 'It was his business to *command* his temper, as my friend, Mr. Beau-:lerk, should have done some time ago.' *Beauclerk.* 'I should learn of *you,* Sir.' *Johnson.* 'Sir, you have given *me* opportuni-:ies enough of learning, when I have been in *your* company. No man loves to be treated with contempt.' *Beauclerk.* (with a polite inclination towards Johnson) 'Sir, you have known me twenty years, and however I may have treated others, you may be sure I could never treat you with contempt.' *Johnson.* 'Sir, you have said more than was necessary.' Thus it ended; and Beauclerk's coach not having come for him till very late, Dr. Johnson and another gentleman sat with him a long time after the rest of the company were gone; and he and I dined at Beauclerk's on the Saturday se'nnight following.

After this tempest had subsided. I recollect the following particulars of his conversation:

'I am always for getting a boy forward in his learning; for that is a sure good. I would let him at first read *any* English book which happens to engage his attention; because you have done a great deal when you have brought him to have enter-tainment from a book. He'll get better books afterwards.'

'To be contradicted, in order to force you to talk, is mighty unpleasing. You *shine,* indeed; but it is by being *ground.*'

On Saturday, April 24, I dined with him at Mr. Beauclerk's, with Sir Joshua Reynolds, Mr. Jones, (afterwards Sir William,) Mr. Langton, Mr. Steevens, Mr. Paradise, and Dr. Higgins. I mentioned that Mr. Wilkes had attacked Garrick to me, as a man who had no friend. *Johnson.* 'I believe he is right, Sir. He had friends, but no friend. Garrick was so dif-fused, he had no man to whom he wished to unbosom himself. He found people always ready to applaud him, and that al-ways for the same thing: so he saw life with great uniformity.' One of the company mentioned Lord Chesterfield, as a man who had no friend. *Johnson.* 'There were more materials to make friendship in Garrick, had he not been so diffused.' *Boswell.* 'Garrick was pure gold, but beat out to thin leaf. Lord Chesterfield was tinsel.' *Johnson.* 'Garrick was a very good man, the cheerfullest man of his age; a decent liver in a profession which is supposed to give indulgence to licentiousness; and a man who gave away, freely, money acquired by himself. He began the world with a great hunger for money; the son of a half-pay officer, bred in a family, whose study was to make four-pence do as much as others made four-pence halfpenny do. But, when he had got money, he was very liberal.' I presumed to animadvert on his eulogy on Garrick, in his 'Lives of the Poets.' 'You say, Sir, his death eclipsed the gaiety of nations.' *Johnson.* 'I could not have said more nor less. It is the truth; *eclipsed,* not *extinguished;* and his death *did* eclipse; it was like a storm.' *Boswell.* 'But why nations? Did his gaiety extend farther than his own nation?' *Johnson.* 'Why, Sir, some exaggeration must be allowed. Besides, nations may be said— if we allow the Scotch to be a nation, and to have gaiety,— which they have not. *You* are an exception, though. Come, gentlemen, let us candidly admit that there is one Scotchman who is cheerful.' *Beauclerk.* 'But he is a very unnatural Scotchman.' I, however, continued to think the compliment to Garrick hyperbolically untrue. His acting had ceased some time before his death; at any rate he had acted in Ireland but a short time, at an early period of his life, and never in Scotland. I objected also to what appears an anticlimax of praise, when contrasted with the preceding panegyrick,—'and diminished the publick stock of harmless pleasure!'—'Is not *harmless pleasure* very tame?' *Johnson.* 'Nay, Sir, harmless pleasure is the highest praise. Pleasure is a word of dubious import; pleasure is in general dangerous, and pernicious to virtue; to be able therefore to furnish pleasure that is harmless, pleasure pure and unalloyed, is as great a power as man can possess.' This was, perhaps, as ingenious a defence as could be made; still, however, I was not satisfied.

Talking of the effects of drinking, he said, 'Drinking may be practised with great prudence; a man who exposes himself when he is intoxicated, has not the art of getting drunk; a sober man who happens occasionally to get drunk, readily enough goes into a new company, which a man who has been drinking should never do. Such a man will undertake any thing; he is without skill in inebriation. I used to slink home, when I had drunk too much. A man accustomed to self-examination will be conscious when he is drunk, though an habitual drunkard will not be conscious of it. I knew a physician who for twenty years was not sober; yet in a pamphlet, which he wrote upon fevers, he appealed to Garrick and me for his vindication from a charge of drunkenness. A bookseller (naming him) who got a large fortune by trade, was so habitually and equably drunk, that his most intimate friends never perceived that he was more sober at one time than another.'

Johnson and I passed the evening at Miss Reynolds's, Sir Joshua's sister. I mentioned that an eminent friend of ours, talking of the common remark, that affection descends, said, that 'this was wisely contrived for the preservation of mankind; for which it was not so necessary that there should be affection from children to parents, as from parents to children; nay, there would be no harm in that view though children should at a certain age eat their parents.' *Johnson.* 'But, Sir, if this were known generally to be the case, parents would not have affection for children.' *Boswell.* 'True, Sir; for it is in expectation of a return that parents are so attentive to their children; and I know a very pretty instance of a little girl of whom her father was very fond, who once when he was in a melancholy fit, and had gone to bed, persuaded him to rise in good humour by saying, "My dear papa, please to get up, and let me help you on with your clothes, that I may learn to do it when you are an old man." '

Soon after this time a little incident occurred, which I will not suppress, because I am desirous that my work should be, as much as is consistent with the strictest truth, an antidote to the false and injurious notions of his character, which have been given by others, and therefore I infuse every drop of genuine sweetness into my biographical cup.

'TO DR. JOHNSON.

'MY DEAR SIR,

'I AM in great pain with an inflamed foot, and obliged to keep my bed, so am prevented from having the pleasure to dine at Mr. Ramsay's to-day, which is very hard; and my spirits are sadly sunk

Will you be so friendly as to come and sit an hour with me in the evening.

> 'I am ever
> 'Your most faithful,
> 'And affectionate humble servant,
> 'JAMES BOSWELL.'

'South Audley-street,
    Monday, April 26.'

He came to me in the evening, and brought Sir Joshua Reynolds. I need scarcely say, that their conversation, while they sate by my bedside, was the most pleasing opiate to pain that could have been administered.

Johnson being now better disposed to obtain information concerning Pope than he was last year, sent by me to my Lord Marchmont a present of those volumes of his 'Lives of the Poets,' which were at this time published, with a request to have permission to wait on him; and his Lordship, who had called on him twice, obligingly appointed Saturday, the first of May, for receiving us.

On that morning Johnson came to me from Streatham, and after drinking chocolate, at General Paoli's, in South-Audley-street, we proceeded to Lord Marchmont's, in Curzon-street. His Lordship met us at the door of his library, and with great politeness said to Johnson, 'I am not going to make an encomium upon *myself,* by telling you the high respect I have for *you,* Sir.' Johnson was exceedingly courteous; and the interview, which lasted about two hours, during which the Earl communicated his anecdotes of Pope, was as agreeable as I could have wished. When we came out, I said to Johnson, that considering his Lordship's civility, I should have been vexed if he had again failed to come. 'Sir, (said he,) I would rather have given twenty pounds than not have come.' I accompanied him to Streatham, where we dined, and returned to town in the evening.

He had, before I left London, resumed the conversation concerning the appearance of a ghost at Newcastle upon Tyne, which Mr. John Wesley believed, but to which Johnson did not give credit. I was, however, desirous to examine the question closely, and at the same time wished to be made acquainted with Mr. John Wesley; for though I differed from him in some points, I admired his various talents, and loved his pious zeal. At my request, therefore, Dr. Johnson gave me a letter of introduction to him.

'To the Reverend Mr. John Wesley.

'Sir,

'Mr. Boswell, a gentleman who has been long known to me, is desirous of being known to you, and has asked this recom-mendation, which I give him with great willingness, because I think it very much to be wished that worthy and religious men should be acquainted with each other.

'I am, Sir,

'Your most humble servant,

'Sam. Johnson.'

'May 3, 1779.'

Mr. Wesley being in the course of his ministry at Edin-burgh, I presented this letter to him, and was very politely received. I begged to have it returned to me, which was ac-cordingly done. His state of the evidence as to the ghost did not satisfy me.

I did not write to Johnson, as usual, upon my return to my family; but tried how he would be affected by my silence.

'To James Boswell, Esq.

'Dear Sir,

'What can possibly have happened, that keeps us two such strangers to each other? I expected to have heard from you when you came home; I expected afterwards. I went into the country and returned; and yet there is no letter from Mr. Boswell. No ill I hope has happened; and if ill should happen, why should it be concealed from him who loves you? Is it a fit of humour, that has disposed you to try who can hold out longest without writing? If it be, you have the victory. But I am afraid of something bad; set me free from my suspicions.

'My thoughts are at present employed in guessing the reason of your silence: you must not expect that I should tell you any thing, if I had any thing to tell. Write, pray write to me, and let me know what is, or what has been the cause of this long interruption.

'I am, dear Sir,

'Your most affectionate humble servant,

'Sam. Johnson.'

'July 13, 1779.'

'To Dr. Samuel Johnson.

'Edinburgh, July 17, 1779.

'My dear Sir,

'What may be justly denominated a supine indolence of mind has been my state of existence since I last returned to Scotland. In a livelier state I had often suffered severely from long intervals of silence on your part; and I had even been chid by you for expressing my uneasiness. I was willing to take advantage of my insensibility, and while I could bear the experiment to try whether your affection for me, would, after an unusual silence on my part, make you write first. This afternoon I have had very high satisfaction by receiving your kind letter of inquiry, for which I most gratefully thank you. I am doubtful if it was right to make the experiment; though I have gained by it. I was beginning to grow tender, and to upbraid myself, especially after having dreamt two nights ago that I was with you. I and my wife, and my four children, are all well. I would not delay one post to answer your letter; but as it is late, I have not time to do more. You shall soon hear from me, upon many and various particulars; and I shall never again put you to any test. I ever am, with veneration, my dear Sir,

'Your much obliged,

'And faithful humble servant,

'James Boswell.'

On the 22d of July, I wrote to him again; and gave him an account of my last interview with my worthy friend, Mr. Edward Dilly, at his brother's house at Southill, in Bedfordshire, where he died soon after I parted from him, leaving me a very kind remembrance of his regard.

My letter was a pretty long one, and contained a variety of particulars; but he, it should seem, had not attended to it; for his next to me was as follows:

'To James Boswell, Esq.

'My dear Sir,

'Are you playing the same trick again, and trying who can keep silence longest? Remember that all tricks are either knavish or childish; and that it is as foolish to make experiments upon the constancy of a friend, as upon the chastity of a wife.

'What can be the cause of this second fit of silence, I cannot conjecture; but after one trick, I will not be cheated by another, nor will harrass my thoughts with conjectures about the motives of a man who, probably, acts only by caprice. I therefore suppose you are well, and that Mrs. Boswell is well too; and that the fine summer has restored Lord Auchinleck. I am much better than you left me; I think I am better than when I was in Scotland.

'I forgot whether I informed you that poor Thrale has been in great danger. Mrs. Thrale likewise has miscarried, and been much indisposed. Every body else is well.

'Mr. Thrale goes to Brighthelmston, about Michaelmas, to be jolly and ride a hunting. I shall go to town, or perhaps to Oxford. Exercise and gaiety, or rather carelessness, will, I hope, dissipate all remains of his malady; and I likewise hope by the change of place, to find some opportunities of growing yet better myself. I am, dear Sir,

                                   'Your humble servant,
                                          'SAM. JOHNSON.'

'Streatham, Sept. 9, 1779.'

My readers will not be displeased at being told every slight circumstance of the manner in which Dr. Johnson contrived to amuse his solitary hours. He sometimes employed himself in chymistry, sometimes in watering and pruning a vine, and sometimes in small experiments, at which those who may smile, should recollect that there are moments which admit of being soothed only by trifles.

My friend Colonel James Stuart, second son of the Earl of Bute, who had distinguished himself as a good officer of the Bedfordshire militia, had taken a publick-spirited resolution to serve his country in its difficulties, by raising a regular regiment, and taking the command of it himself. Having been in Scotland recruiting, he obligingly asked me to accompany him to Leeds, then the head-quarters of his corps; from thence to London for a short time, and afterwards to other places to which the regiment might be ordered. Such an offer, at a time of the year when I had full leisure, was very pleasing; especially as I was to accompany a man of sterling good sense, information, discernment, and conviviality; and was to have a second crop, in one year, of London and Johnson. Of this I informed my illustrious friend, in characteristical warm terms, in a letter dated the 30th of September, from Leeds.

On Monday, October 4, I called at his house before he was up. He sent for me to his bedside, and expressed his satisfaction at this incidental meeting, with as much vivacity as if he had been in the gaiety of youth. He called briskly, 'Frank, go and get coffee, and let us breakfast *in splendour.*'

On Sunday, October 10, we dined together at Mr. Strahan's. The conversation having turned on the prevailing practice of going to the East-Indies in quest of wealth;—*Johnson.* 'A man had better have ten thousand pounds at the end of ten years passed in England, than twenty thousand pounds at the end of ten years passed in India, because you must compute what you *give* for money; and a man who has lived ten years in India, has given up ten years of social comfort and all those advantages which arise from living in England. The ingenious Mr. Brown, distinguished by the name of *Capability Brown,* told me, that he was once at the seat of Lord Clive, who had returned from India with great wealth; and that he shewed him at the door of his bed-chamber a large chest, which he said he had once had full of gold; upon which Brown observed, "I am glad you can bear it so near your bed-chamber."'

We talked of the state of the poor in London.—*Johnson.* 'Saunders Welch, the Justice, who was once High-Constable of Holborn, and had the best opportunities of knowing the state of the poor, told me, that I under-rated the number, when I computed that twenty a week, that is, above a thousand a year, died of hunger; not absolutely of immediate hunger; but of the wasting and other diseases which are the consequences of hunger. This happens only in so large a place as London, where people are not known. What we are told about the great sums got by begging is not true: the trade is over-stocked. And, you may depend upon it, there are many who cannot get work. A particular kind of manufacture fails: those who have been used to work at it, can, for some time, work at nothing else. You meet a man begging; you charge him with idleness: he says, "I am willing to labour. Will you give me work?"—"I cannot."—"Why, then you have no right to charge me with idleness."'

We left Mr. Strahan's at seven, as Johnson had said he intended to go to evening prayers. As we walked along, he complained of a little gout in his toe, and said, 'I shan't go to prayers to-night; I shall go to-morrow. Whenever I miss church on a Sunday, I resolve to go another day. But I do not always do it.' This was a fair exhibition of that vibration between pious resolutions and indolence, which many of us have too often experienced.

I went home with him, and we had a long quiet conversation.

He said, 'Dodsley first mentioned to me the scheme of an English Dictionary; but I had long thought of it.' *Boswell.* 'You did not know what you were undertaking.' *Johnson.* 'Yes, Sir, I knew very well what I was undertaking,—and very well how to do it,—and have done it very well.' *Boswell.* 'An excellent climax! and it *has* availed you. In your Preface you say, "What would it avail me in this gloom of solitude?" You have been agreeably mistaken.'

He, I know not why, shewed upon all occasions an aversion to go to Ireland, where I proposed to him that we should make a tour. *Johnson.* 'It is the last place where I should wish to travel.' *Boswell.* 'Should you not like to see Dublin, Sir?' *Johnson.* 'No, Sir; Dublin is only a worse capital.' *Boswell.* 'Is not the Giant's-Causeway worth seeing?' *Johnson.* 'Worth seeing, yes; but not worth going to see.'

1780: ÆTAT. 71.]—In 1780, the world was kept in impatience for the completion of his 'Lives of the Poets,' upon which he was employed so far as his indolence allowed him to labour.

His friend Dr. Lawrence having now suffered the greatest affliction to which a man is liable, and which Johnson himself had felt in the most severe manner; Johnson wrote to him in an admirable strain of sympathy and pious consolation.

'To DR. LAWRENCE.

'DEAR SIR,
        'AT a time when all your friends ought to shew their kindness, and with a character which ought to make all that know you your friends, you may wonder that you have yet heard nothing from me.
    'I have been hindered by a vexatious and incessant cough, for which within these ten days I have been bled once, fasted four or five times, taken physick five times, and opiates, I think, six. This day it seems to remit.
    'The loss, dear Sir, which you have lately suffered, I felt many

years ago, and know therefore how much has been taken from you, and how little help can be had from consolation. He that outlives a wife whom he has long loved, sees himself disjoined from the only mind that has the same hopes, and fears, and interest; from the only companion with whom he has shared much good or evil; and with whom he could set his mind at liberty to retrace the past, or anticipate the future. The continuity of being is lacerated; the settled course of sentiment and action is stopped; and life stands suspended and motionless, till it is driven by external causes into a new channel. But the time of suspense is dreadful.

'Our first recourse in this distressful solitude, is, perhaps for want of habitual piety, to a gloomy acquiescence in necessity. Of two mortal beings, one must lose the other; but surely there is a higher and better comfort to be drawn from the consideration of that Providence which watches over all, and a belief that the living and the dead are equally in the hands of GOD, who will reunite those whom he has separated, or who sees that it is best not to reunite them.

'I am, dear Sir,
'Your most affectionate,
'And most humble servant,
'SAM. JOHNSON.'

'January 20, 1780.'

'To JAMES BOSWELL, ESQ.

'DEAR SIR,

'FOR the difficulties which you mention in your affairs I am sorry; but difficulty is now very general: it is not therefore less grievous, for there is less hope of help. I pretend not to give you advice, not knowing the state of your affairs; and general counsels about prudence and frugality would do you little good. You are, however, in the right not to increase your own perplexity by a journey hither; and I hope that by staying at home you will please your father.

'Poor dear Beauclerk. His wit and his folly, his acuteness and maliciousness, his merriment and reasoning, are now over. Such another will not often be found among mankind. He directed himself to be buried by the side of his mother, an instance of tenderness which I hardly expected. He has left his children to the care of Lady Di, and if she dies, of Mr. Langton, and of Mr. Leicester, his relation, and a man of good character. His library has been offered to sale to the Russian ambassador.

'Poor Mr. Thrale has been in extreme danger from an apoplectical disorder, and recovered, beyond the expectation of his physicians; he is now at Bath, that his mind may be quiet, and Mrs. Thrale and Miss are with him.

'Having told you what has happened to your friends, let me say something to you of yourself. You are always complaining of melancholy, and I conclude from those complaints that you are fond of it. No man talks of that which he is desirous to conceal, and every man desires to conceal that of which he is ashamed. Do not pretend to deny it; make it an invariable and obligatory law to yourself, never to mention your own mental diseases; if you are never to speak of them, you will think on them but little, and if you think little of them, they will molest you rarely. When you talk of them, it is plain that you want either praise or pity; for praise there is no room, and pity will do you no good; therefore, from this hour speak no more, think no more, about them.

'Please to make my compliments to your lady, and to the young ladies. I should like to see them, pretty loves.

'I am, dear Sir,
'Yours affectionately,
'SAM. JOHNSON.'

'April 8, 1780.'

Mrs. Thrale being now at Bath with her husband, the correspondence between Johnson and her was carried on briskly. I shall present my readers with one of her original letters to him at this time, which will amuse them probably more than those well-written but studied epistles which she has inserted in her collection, because it exhibits the easy vivacity of their literary intercourse.

'MRS. THRALE TO DR. JOHNSON.

'YESTERDAY'S evening was passed at Mrs. Montagu's: there was Mr. Melmoth; I do not like him *though*, nor he me; it was expected we should have pleased each other; he is, however, just Tory enough to hate the Bishop of Peterborough for Whiggism, and Whig enough to abhor you for Toryism.

'Mrs. Montagu flattered him finely; so he had a good afternoon on't. This evening we spend at a concert. Poor Queeney's[1] sore eyes have just released her; she had a long confinement, and could neither read nor write, so my master treated her very good-naturedly with the visits of a young woman in this town, a taylor's daughter, who professes musick, and teaches so as to give six lessons a day

---

[1] Queeney was the nickname of Mrs. Thrale's eldest daughter, Hester.

to ladies, at five and threepence a lesson. Miss Burney says she is a great performer; and I respect the wench for getting her living so prettily; she is very modest and pretty-mannered, and not seventeen years old.

'You live in a fine whirl indeed; if I did not write regularly you would half forget me, and that would be very wrong, for I *felt* my regard for you in my *face* last night, when the criticisms were going on.

'This morning it was all connoisseurship; we went to see some pictures painted by a gentleman-artist, Mr. Taylor, of this place; my master makes one, every where, and has got a good dawling companion to ride with him now. He looks well enough, but I have no notion of health for a man whose mouth cannot be sewed up. Burney and I and Queeney teize him every meal he eats, and Mrs. Montagu is quite serious with him; but what *can* one do? He will eat, I think, and if he does eat I know he will not live; it makes me very unhappy, but I must bear it. Let me always have your friendship. I am, most sincerely, dear Sir,

'Your faithful servant,

'H. L. T.'

'Bath, Friday, April 28.'

From Mr. Langton I received soon after this time a letter, of which I extract a passage, relative both to Mr. Beauclerk and Dr. Johnson.

'The melancholy information you have received concerning Mr. Beauclerk's death is true. Had his talents been directed to any sufficient degree as they ought, I have always been strongly of opinion that they were calculated to make an illustrious figure; and that opinion, as it had been in part formed upon Dr. Johnson's judgment, receives more and more confirmation by hearing what, since his death, Dr. Johnson has said concerning them; a few evenings ago, he was at Mr. Vesey's, where Lord Althorpe, who was one of a numerous company there, addressed Dr. Johnson on the subject of Mr. Beauclerk's death, saying, "Our CLUB has had a great loss since we met last." He replied, "A loss, that perhaps the whole nation could not repair!" The Doctor then went on to speak of his endowments, and particularly extolled the wonderful ease with which he uttered what was highly excellent. He said, that "no man ever was so free when he was going to say a good thing, from a *look* that expressed that it was coming; or, when he had said it, from a look that expressed that it *had* come." At Mr. Thrale's, some days before, when we were talking on the same subject, he said, referring to the same idea of his wonderful facility, "That Beau-clerk's talents were those which he had felt himself more disposed to envy, than those of any whom he had known."

'On the evening I have spoken of above, at Mr. Vesey's, you would have been much gratified, as it exhibited an instance of the high importance in which Dr. Johnson's character is held, I think even beyond any I ever before was witness to. The company con-sisted chiefly of ladies, among whom were the Duchess Dowager of Portland, the Duchess of Beaufort, whom I suppose from her rank, I must name before her mother Mrs. Boscawen, and her elder sister Mrs. Lewson, who was likewise there; Lady Lucan, Lady Clermont, and others of note both for their station and understandings. Among the gentlemen were Lord Althorpe, whom I have before named, Lord Macartney, Sir Joshua Reynolds, Lord Lucan, Mr. Wraxal, a very agreeable ingenious man; Dr. Warren, Mr. Pepys, the Master in Chancery, whom I believe you know, and Dr. Barnard, the Provost of Eton. As soon as Dr. Johnson was come in and had taken a chair, the company began to collect round him, till they became not less than four, if not five, deep; those behind standing, and listening over the heads of those that were sitting near him. The conversation for some time was chiefly between Dr. Johnson and the Provost of Eton, while the others contributed occasionally their remarks. Without attempting to detail the particulars of the conversation, which perhaps if I did, I should spin my account out to a tedious length, I thought, my dear Sir, this general account of the respect with which our valued friend was attended to, might be acceptable.'

'To JAMES BOSWELL, ESQ.
'DEAR SIR,

'I FIND you have taken one of your fits of taciturnity, and have resolved not to write till you are written to; it is but a peevish humour, but you shall have your way.

'I have sat at home in Bolt-court, all the summer, thinking to write the Lives, and a great part of the time only thinking. Several of them, however, are done, and I still think to do the rest.

'Mr. Thrale and his family have, since his illness, passed their time first at Bath, and then at Brighthelmston; but I have been at neither place. I would have gone to Lichfield, if I could have had time, and I might have had time, if I had been active; but I have missed much, and done little.

'I know not whether I shall get a ramble this autumn; it is now about the time when we were travelling. I have, however, better health than I had then, and hope you and I may yet shew ourselves cn some part of Europe, Asia, or Africa. In the mean time let us play no trick, but keep each other's kindness by all means in our power.

'I suppose your little ladies are grown tall; and your son is become a learned young man. I love them all, and I love your naughty lady, whom I never shall persuade to love me. When the Lives are done, I shall send them to complete her collection, but must send them in paper, as for want of a pattern, I cannot bind them to fit the rest.

'I am, Sir,

'Yours most affectionately,

'SAM. JOHNSON.'

'London, Aug. 21, 1780.'

On his birth-day, Johnson has this note,

'I am now beginning the seventy-second year of my life, with more strength of body, and greater vigour of mind, than I think is common at that age.'

But still he complains of sleepless nights and idle days, and forgetfulness, or neglect of resolutions. He thus pathetically expresses himself,

'Surely I shall not spend my whole life with my own total disapprobation.'

'To JAMES BOSWELL, ESQ.

'DEAR SIR,

'I AM sorry to write you a letter that will not please you, and yet it is at last what I resolve to do. This year must pass without an interview; the summer has been foolishly lost, like many other of my summers and winters. I hardly saw a green field, but staid in town to work, without working much.

'Mr. Thrale is now going to Brighthelmston, and expects me to go with him; and how long I shall stay, I cannot tell. I do not much like the place, but yet I shall go, and stay while my stay is desired. We must, therefore, content ourselves with knowing what we know as well as man can know the mind of man, that we love one another, and that we wish each other's happiness, and that the lapse of a year cannot lessen our mutual kindness.

'I was pleased to be told that I accused Mrs. Boswell unjustly, in supposing that she bears me ill-will. I love you so much, that I would be glad to love all that love you, and that you love; and I have love very ready for Mrs. Boswell, if she thinks it worthy of acceptance. I hope all the young ladies and gentlemen are well.

'You lately told me of your health: I can tell you in return, that my health has been for more than a year past, better than it has been for many years before. Perhaps it may please GOD to give us some time together before we are parted.

'I am, dear Sir,
'Yours, most affectionately,
'SAM. JOHNSON.'

'October 17, 1780.'

Being disappointed in my hopes of meeting Johnson this year, so that I could hear none of his admirable sayings, I shall compensate for this want by inserting a collection of them, for which I am indebted to my worthy friend Mr. Langton, whose kind communications have been separately interwoven in many parts of this work.

'When in good humour he would talk of his own writings with a wonderful frankness and candour, and would even criticise them with the closest severity. One day, having read over one of his Ramblers, Mr. Langton asked him, how he liked that paper; he shook his head, and answered, "too wordy." At another time, when one was reading his tragedy of "Irene," to a company at a house in the country, he left the room; and somebody having asked him the reason of this, he replied, "Sir, I thought it had been better." '

'It is well known that there was formerly a rude custom for those who were sailing upon the Thames, to accost each other as they passed, in the most abusive language they could invent, generally, however, with as much satirical humour as they were capable of producing. Addison gives a specimen of this ribaldry, in Number 383 of "The Spectator." Johnson was once eminently successful in this species of contest; a fellow having attacked him with some coarse raillery, Johnson answered him thus, "Sir, your wife, *under pretence of keeping a bawdy-house,* is a receiver of stolen goods." '

'As Johnson always allowed the extraordinary talents of Mr. Burke, so Mr. Burke was fully sensible of the wonderful powers of Johnson. Mr. Langton recollects having passed an evening with both of them, when Mr. Burke repeatedly entered upon topicks which it was evident he would have illustrated with extensive knowledge and richness of expression; but Johnson always seized upon the conversation, in which, however, he acquitted himself in a most masterly manner. As Mr. Burke and Mr. Langton were walking home, Mr. Burke observed that Johnson had been very great that night; Mr. Langton joined in this, but added, he could have wished to hear more from another person; (plainly intimating that he meant Mr. Burke). "O, no (said Mr. Burke) it is enough for me to have rung the bell to him." '

'Beauclerk having observed to him of one of their friends, that he was aukward at counting money, "Why, Sir, said Johnson, I am likewise aukward at counting money. But then, Sir, the reason is plain; I have had very little money to count." '

'He had an abhorrence of affectation. Talking of old Mr. Langton, of whom he said, "Sir, you will seldom see such a gentleman, such are his stores of literature, such his knowledge in divinity, and such his exemplary life;" he added, "and Sir, he has no grimace, no gesticulation, no bursts of admiration on trivial occasions; he never embraces you with an overacted cordiality." '

'Being in company with a gentleman who thought fit to maintain Dr. Berkeley's ingenious philosophy, that nothing exists but as perceived by some mind; when the gentleman was going away, Johnson said to him, "Pray, Sir, don't leave us; for we may perhaps forget to think of you, and then you will cease to exist." '

'Many a man is mad in certain instances, and goes through life without having it perceived:—for example, a madness has seized a person of supposing himself obliged literally to pray continually—had the madness turned the opposite way and the person thought it a crime ever to pray, it might not improbably have continued unobserved.'

'He observed once, at Sir Joshua Reynolds's, that a beggar in the street will more readily ask alms from a *man*, though there should be no marks of wealth in his appearance, than from even a well-dressed *woman*; which he accounted for from the greater degree of carefulness as to money that is to be found in women; saying farther upon it, that, the opportunities in general that they possess of improving their condition are much fewer than men have; and adding, as he looked round the company, which consisted of men only,—there is not one of us who does not think he might be richer if he would use his endeavour.'

'An observation of Bathurst's may be mentioned, which Johnson repeated, appearing to acknowledge it to be well founded, namely, it was somewhat remarkable how seldom, on occasion of coming into the company of any new person, one felt any wish or inclination to see him again.'

1781: ÆTAT. 72.]—In 1781 Johnson at last completed his 'Lives of the Poets,' of which he gives this account: 'Some time in March I finished the "Lives of the Poets," which I wrote in my usual way, dilatorily and hastily, unwilling to work, and working with vigour and haste.' In a memorandum previous to this, he says of them: 'Written, I hope, in such a manner as may tend to the promotion of piety.'

This is the work which of all Dr. Johnson's writings will perhaps be read most generally, and with most pleasure. Philology and biography were his favourite pursuits, and those who lived most in intimacy with him, heard him upon all occasions, when there was a proper opportunity, take delight in expatiating upon the various merits of the English Poets: upon the niceties of their characters, and the events of their progress through the world which they contributed to illuminate. His mind was so full of that kind of information, and it was so well arranged in his memory, that in performing what he had undertaken in this way, he had little more to do than to put his thoughts upon paper, exhibiting first each Poet's life, and then subjoining a critical examination of his genius and works. But when he began to write, the subject swelled in such a manner, that instead of prefaces to each poet, of no more than a few pages, as he had originally intended, he produced an ample, rich, and most entertaining view of them in every respect. The booksellers, justly sensible of the great additional value of the copy-right, presented him with another hundred pounds, over and above two hundred, for which his agreement was to furnish such prefaces as he thought fit.

This was, however, but a small recompence for such a collection of biography. As he was so good as to make me a present of the greatest part of the original, and indeed only manuscript of this admirable work, I have an opportunity of observing with wonder the correctness with which he rapidly struck off such glowing composition.

That he, however, had a good deal of trouble, and some anxiety in carrying on the work, we see from a series of letters to Mr. Nichols the printer, whose variety of literary inquiry and obliging disposition, rendered him very useful to Johnson. Mr. Steevens appears, from the papers in my possession, to have supplied him with some anecdotes and quotations; and I observe the fair hand of Mrs. Thrale as one of his copyists of select passages. But he was principally indebted to my steady friend Mr. Isaac Reed, of Staple-inn, whose extensive and accurate knowledge of English literary History I do not express with exaggeration, when I say it is wonderful; and all who have the pleasure of his acquaintance can bear testimony to the frankness of his communications in private society.

It is not my intention to dwell upon each of Johnson's 'Lives of the Poets,' or attempt an analysis of their merits, which, were I able to do it, would take up too much room in this work; yet I shall make a few observations upon some of them.

The Life of *Cowley* he himself considered as the best of the whole, on account of the dissertation which it contains on the *Metaphysical Poets*. Johnson has exhibited them at large, with such happy illustration from their writings, and in so luminous a manner, that indeed he may be allowed the full merit of novelty, and to have discovered to us, as it were, a new planet in the poetical hemisphere.

So easy is his style in these Lives, that I do not recollect more than three uncommon or learned words; one, when giving an account of the approach of Waller's mortal disease, he says, 'he found his legs grow *tumid;*' by using the expression his legs *swelled,* he would have avoided this; and there would have been no impropriety in its being followed by the interesting question to his physician, 'What that *swelling* meant?'

Another, when he mentions that Pope had *emitted* proposals; when *published* or *issued* would have been more readily understood; and a third, when he calls Orrery and Dr. Delany, writers both undoubtedly *veracious*; when *true, honest,* or *faithful,* might have been used. Yet, it must be owned, that none of these are *hard* or *too big* words; that custom would make them seem as easy as any others; and that a language is richer and capable of more beauty of expression, by having a greater variety of synonimes.

His dissertation upon the unfitness of poetry for the aweful subjects of our holy religion, though I do not entirely agree with him, has all the merit of originality, with uncommon force and reasoning.

Against his Life of *Milton,* the hounds of Whiggism have opened in full cry. But of Milton's great excellence as a poet, where shall we find such a blazon as by the hand of Johnson? I shall select only the following passage concerning '*Paradise Lost:*'

'Fancy can hardly forbear to conjecture with what temper Milton surveyed the silent progress of his work, and marked his reputation stealing its way in a kind of subterraneous current, through fear and silence. I cannot but conceive him calm and confident, little disappointed, not at all dejected, relying on his own merit with steady consciousness, and waiting without impatience, the vicissitudes of opinion, and the impartiality of a future generation.'

Indeed even Dr. Towers, who may be considered as one of the warmest zealots of *The Revolution Society* itself, allows, that 'Johnson has spoken in the highest terms of the abilities of that great poet, and has bestowed on his principal poetical compositions the most honourable encomiums.'

That a man, who venerated the Church and Monarchy as Johnson did, should speak with a just abhorrence of Milton as a politician, or rather as a daring foe to good polity, was surely to be expected; and to those who censure him, I would recommend his commentary on Milton's celebrated complaint of his situation, when by the lenity of Charles the Second, 'a lenity of which (as Johnson well observes) the world has had perhaps no other example; he, who had written in justification of the murder of his Sovereign, was safe under an *Act of Oblivion*.'

'No sooner is he safe than he finds himself in danger, *fallen on evil days and evil tongues, and with darkness and with danger compassed round*. This darkness, had his eyes been better employed, had undoubtedly deserved compassion; but to add the mention of danger was ungrateful and unjust. He was fallen, indeed, on *evil days*; the time was come in which regicides could no longer boast their wickedness. But of *evil tongues* for Milton to complain, required impudence at least equal to his other powers; Milton, whose warmest advocates must allow, that he never spared any asperity of reproach, or brutality of insolence.'

I have, indeed, often wondered how Milton, 'an acrimonious and surly Republican,'—a man 'who in his domestick relations was so severe and arbitrary,' and whose head was filled with the hardest and most dismal tenets of Calvinism, should have been such a poet; should not only have written with sublimity, but with beauty, and even gaiety; should have exquisitely painted the sweetest sensations of which our nature is capable; imaged the delicate raptures of connubial love; nay, seemed to be animated with all the spirit of revelry. It is a proof that in the human mind the departments of judgement and imagination, perception and temper, may sometimes be divided by strong partitions; and that the light and shade in the same character may be kept so distinct as never to be blended.

In the Life of *Milton,* Johnson took occasion to maintain his own and the general opinion of the excellence of rhyme over blank verse, in English poetry; and quotes this apposite illustration of it by 'an ingenious critick,' that *it seems to be verse only to the eye.* The gentleman whom he thus characterises, is (as he told Mr. Seward) Mr. Lock, of Norbury Park, in Surrey, whose knowledge and taste in the fine arts is universally celebrated; with whose elegance of manners the writer of the present work has felt himself much impressed, and to whose virtues a common friend, who has known him long, and is not much addicted to flattery, gives the highest testimony.

I could, with pleasure, expatiate upon the masterly execution of the Life of *Dryden,* which we have seen was one of

Johnson's literary projects at an early period, and which it is
remarkable, that after desisting from it, from a supposed scantiness of materials, he should, at an advanced age, have exhibited so amply.

His defence of that great poet against the illiberal attacks
upon him, as if his embracing the Roman Catholick communion had been a time-serving measure, is a piece of reasoning at once able and candid. In drawing Dryden's character,
Johnson has given, though I suppose unintentionally, some
touches of his own. Thus: 'The power that predominated in
his intellectual operations was rather strong reason than quick
sensibility. Upon all occasions that were presented, he studied
rather than felt; and produced sentiments not such as Nature
enforces, but meditation supplies. With the simple and ele-
mental passions as they spring separate in the mind, he seems
not much acquainted. He is, therefore, with all his variety
of excellence, not often pathetick; and had so little sensibility
of the power of effusions purely natural, that he did not esteem
them in others.'—It may indeed be observed, that in all the
numerous writings of Johnson, whether in prose or verse, and
even in his Tragedy, of which the subject is the distress of an
unfortunate Princess, there is not a single passage that ever
drew a tear.

The Life of *Pope* was written by Johnson *con amore,* both
from the early possession which that writer had taken of his
mind, and from the pleasure which he must have felt, in for
ever silencing all attempts to lessen his poetical fame, by dem-
onstrating his excellence, and pronouncing the following triumphant eulogium:—'After all this, it is surely superfluous to
answer the question that has once been asked, Whether Pope
was a poet? otherwise than by asking in return, If Pope be not
a poet, where is poetry to be found? To circumscribe poetry
by a definition, will only shew the narrowness of the definer;
though a definition which shall exclude Pope will not easily
be made. Let us look round upon the present time, and back
upon the past; let us enquire to whom the voice of mankind
has decreed the wreath of poetry; let their productions be
examined, and their claims stated, and the pretensions of Pope
will be no more disputed.'

I remember once to have heard Johnson say, 'Sir, a thousand years may elapse before there shall appear another man with a power of versification equal to that of Pope.' That power must undoubtedly be allowed its due share in enhancing the value of his captivating composition.

Speaking of Pope's not having been known to excel in conversation, Johnson observes, that 'traditional memory retains no sallies of raillery, or sentences of observation; nothing either pointed or solid, wise or merry; and that one apophthegm only is recorded.' In this respect, Pope differed widely from Johnson, whose conversation was, perhaps, more admirable than even his writings, however excellent. Mr. Wilkes has, however, favoured me with one repartee of Pope, of which Johnson was not informed. Johnson, after justly censuring him for having 'nursed in his mind a foolish dis-esteem of Kings,' tells us, 'yet a little regard shewn him by the Prince of Wales melted his obduracy; and he had not much to say when he was asked by his Royal Highness, *how he could love a Prince, while he disliked Kings?*' The answer which Pope made, was, 'The young lion is harmless, and even playful; but when his claws are full grown he becomes cruel, dreadful, and mischievous.'

But although we have no collection of Pope's sayings, it is not therefore to be concluded, that he was not agreeable in social intercourse; for Johnson has been heard to say, that 'the happiest conversation is that of which nothing is distinctly remembered but a general effect of pleasing impression.' The late Lord Somerville, who saw much both of great and brilliant life, told me, that he had dined in company with Pope, and that after dinner the *little man*, as he called him, drank his bottle of Burgundy, and was exceedingly gay and entertaining.

In the Life of *Swift*, it appears to me that Johnson had a certain degree of prejudice against that extraordinary man. Mr. Thomas Sheridan imputed it to a supposed apprehension in Johnson, that Swift had not been sufficiently active in obtaining for him an Irish degree when it was solicited, but of this there was not sufficient evidence; and let me not presume to charge Johnson with injustice, because he did not think so highly of the writings of this authour, as I have done from my youth upwards. Yet that he had an unfavourable bias is evident, were it only from that passage in which he speaks of Swift's practice of saving, as, 'first ridiculous and at last detestable;' and yet after some examination of circumstances, finds himself obliged to own, that 'it will perhaps appear that he only liked one mode of expence better than another, and saved merely that he might have something to give.'

One observation which Johnson makes in Swift's life should be often inculcated:

'It may be justly supposed, that there was in his conversation what appears so frequently in his letters, an affectation of familiarity with the great, an ambition of momentary equality, sought and enjoyed by the neglect of those ceremonies which custom has established as the barriers between one order of society and another. This transgression of regularity was by himself and his admirers termed greatness of soul; but a great mind disdains to hold any thing by courtesy, and therefore never usurps what a lawful claimant may take away. He that encroaches on another's dignity puts himself in his power; he is either repelled with helpless indignity, or endured by clemency and condescension.'

While the world in general was filled with admiration of Johnson's 'Lives of the Poets,' there were narrow circles in which prejudice and resentment were fostered, and from which attacks of different sorts issued against him. By some violent Whigs he was arraigned of injustice to Milton; by some Cambridge men of depreciating Gray; and his expressing with a dignified freedom what he really thought of George, Lord Lyttelton, gave offence to some of the friends of that nobleman, and particularly produced a declaration of war against him from Mrs. Montagu, the ingenious Essayist on Shakspeare, between whom and his Lordship a commerce of reciprocal compliments had long been carried on. These minute inconveniencies gave not the least disturbance to Johnson. He nobly said, when I talked to him of the feeble, though shrill outcry which had been raised, 'Sir, I considered myself as entrusted with a certain portion of truth. I have given my opinion sincerely; let them shew where they think me wrong.'

I wrote to him in February, complaining of having been troubled by a recurrence of the perplexing question of Liberty and Necessity;—and mentioning that I hoped soon to meet him again in London.

'To James Boswell, Esq.

'Dear Sir,

'I hoped you had got rid of all this hypocrisy of misery. What have you to do with Liberty and Necessity? Or what more than to hold your tongue about it? Do not doubt but I shall be most heartily glad to see you here again, for I love every part about you but your affectation of distress.

'I have at last finished my Lives, and have laid up for you a load of copy, all out of order, so that it will amuse you a long time to set it right. Come to me, my dear Bozzy, and let us be as happy as we can. We will go again to the Mitre, and talk old times over.

'I am, dear Sir,

'Yours affectionately,

'Sam. Johnson.'

'March 14, 1781.'

On Monday, March 19, I arrived in London, and on Tuesday, the 20th, met him in Fleet-street, walking, or rather indeed moving along; for his peculiar march is thus described in a very just and picturesque manner, in a short Life of him published very soon after his death:—'When he walked the streets, what with the constant roll of his head, and the concomitant motion of his body, he appeared to make his way by that motion, independent of his feet.' That he was often much stared at while he advanced in this manner, may easily be believed; but it was not safe to make sport of one so robust as he was. Mr. Langton saw him one day, in a fit of absence, by a sudden start, drive the load off a porter's back, and walk forward briskly, without being conscious of what he had done. The porter was very angry, but stood still, and eyed the huge figure with much earnestness, till he was satisfied that his wisest course was to be quiet, and take up his burthen again.

Our accidental meeting in the street after a long separation was a pleasing surprize to us both. He stepped aside with me into Falcon-court, and made kind inquiries about my family, and as we were in a hurry going different ways, I promised to call on him next day; he said he was engaged to go out in the morning. 'Early, Sir?' said I. *Johnson:* 'Why, Sir, a London morning does not go with the sun.'

I waited on him next evening, and he gave me a great portion of his original manuscript of his 'Lives of the Poets,' which he had preserved for me.

I found on visiting his friend, Mr. Thrale, that he was now very ill, and had removed, I suppose by the solicitation of Mrs. Thrale, to a house in Grosvenor-square. I was sorry to see him sadly changed in his appearance.

He told me I might now have the pleasure to see Dr. Johnson drink wine again, for he had lately returned to it. When I mentioned this to Johnson, he said, 'I drink it now sometimes, but not socially.' The first evening that I was with him at Thrale's, I observed he poured a quantity of it into a large glass, and swallowed it greedily. Every thing about his character and manners was forcible and violent; there never was any moderation; many a day did he fast, many a year did he refrain from wine; but when he did eat, it was voraciously; when he did drink wine, it was copiously. He could practise abstinence, but not temperance.

Mrs. Thrale and I had a dispute, whether Shakspeare or Milton had drawn the most admirable picture of a man. I was for Shakspeare; Mrs. Thrale for Milton; and after a fair hearing, Johnson decided for my opinion.

He said, 'Mrs. Montagu has dropt me. Now, Sir, there are people whom one should like very well to drop, but would not wish to be dropped by.' He certainly was vain of the society of ladies, and could make himself very agreeable to them, when he chose it; Sir Joshua Reynolds agreed with me that he could. Mr. Gibbon, with his usual sneer, controverted it, perhaps in resentment of Johnson's having talked with some disgust of his ugliness, which one would think a *philosopher* would not mind. Dean Marlay wittily observed, 'A lady may be vain when she can turn a wolf-dog into a lap-dog.'

On Sunday, April 1, I dined with him at Mr. Thrale's, with Sir Philip Jennings Clerk and Mr. Perkins, who had the superintendence of Mr. Thrale's brewery, with a salary of five hundred pounds a year. Sir Philip had the appearance of a gentleman of ancient family, well advanced in life. He wore his own white hair in a bag of goodly size, a black velvet coat, with an embroidered waistcoat, and very rich laced ruffles; which Mrs. Thrale said were old fashioned, but which, for that reason, I thought the more respectable, more like a Tory; yet Sir Philip was then in Opposition in Parliament. 'Ah, Sir, (said Johnson,) ancient ruffles and modern principles do not agree.' Sir Philip defended the opposition to the American war ably and with temper, and I joined him. He said, the majority of the nation was against the ministry. *Johnson.* 'As to the American war, the *sense* of the nation is *with* the ministry. The majority of those who can *understand* is with it; the majority of those who can only *hear* is against it; and as those who can only hear are more numerous than those who can understand, and Opposition is always loudest, a majority of the rabble will be for Opposition.'

This boisterous vivacity entertained us; but the truth in my opinion was, that those who could understand the best were against the American war, as almost every man now is, when the question has been coolly considered.

Mrs. Thrale gave high praise to Mr. Dudley Long, (now North). *Johnson.* 'Nay, my dear lady, don't talk so. Mr. Long's character is very *short*. It is nothing. He fills a chair. He is a man of genteel appearance, and that is all. I know nobody who blasts by praise as you do: for whenever there is exaggerated praise, every body is set against a character. They are provoked to attack it. Now there is Pepys; you praised that man with such disproportion, that I was incited to lessen him, perhaps more than he deserves. His blood is upon your head. By the same principle, your malice defeats itself; for your censure is too violent. And yet (looking to her with a leering smile) she is the first woman in the world, could she but restrain that wicked tongue of hers;—she would be the only woman, could she but command that little whirligig.'

Upon the subject of exaggerated praise I took the liberty to say, that I thought there might be very high praise given to a known character which deserved it, and therefore it would not be exaggerated. Thus, one might say of Mr. Edmund Burke, He is a very wonderful man. *Johnson.* 'No, Sir, you would not be safe if another man had a mind perversely to contradict. He might answer, "Where is all the wonder? Burke is, to be sure, a man of uncommon abilities, with a great quantity of matter in his mind, and a great fluency of language in his mouth. But we are not to be stunned and astonished by him." So you see, Sir, even Burke would suffer, not from any fault of his own, but from your folly.'

One of the gentlemen said, he had seen three folio volumes of Dr. Johnson's sayings collected by me. 'I must put you right, Sir, (said I;) for I am very exact in authenticity. You could not see folio volumes, for I have none: you might have seen some in quarto and octavo. This is inattention which one should guard against.' *Johnson.* 'Sir, it is a want of concern about veracity. He does not know that he saw *any* volumes. If he had seen them he could have remembered their size.'

Mr. Thrale appeared very lethargick to-day. I saw him again on Monday evening, at which time he was not thought to be in immediate danger; but early in the morning of Wednesday the 4th, he expired. Johnson was in the house, and thus mentions the event: 'I felt almost the last flutter of his pulse, and looked for the last time upon the face that for fifteen years had never been turned upon me but with respect and benignity.' Upon that day there was a *Call* of the *Literary Club;* but Johnson apologised for his absence by the following note:

'MR. JOHNSON knows that Sir Joshua Reynolds and the other gentlemen will excuse his incompliance with the Call, when they are told that Mr. Thrale died this morning.'

Mr. Thrale's death was a very essential loss to Johnson, who, although he did not foresee all that afterwards happened, was sufficiently convinced that the comforts which Mr. Thrale's family afforded him, would now in a great measure cease. He, however, continued to shew a kind attention to his widow and children as long as it was acceptable; and he took upon him, with a very earnest concern, the office of one of his executors, the importance of which seemed greater than usual to him, from his circumstances having been always such, that he had scarcely any share in the real business of life. His friends of the *Club* were in hopes that Mr. Thrale might have

made a liberal provision for him for his life, which, as Mr
Thrale left no son, and a very large fortune, it would have
been highly to his honour to have done; and, considering Dr.
Johnson's age, could not have been of long duration; but he
bequeathed him only two hundred pounds, which was the
legacy given to each of his executors. I could not but be somewhat diverted by hearing Johnson talk in a pompous manner
of his new office, and particularly of the concerns of the brewery, which it was at last resolved should be sold. Lord Lucan
tells a very good story, which, if not precisely exact, is certainly characteristical: that when the sale of Thrale's brewery
was going forward, Johnson appeared bustling about, with
an ink-horn and pen in his button-hole, like an excise-man;
and on being asked what he really considered to be the value
of the property which was to be disposed of, answered, 'We
are not here to sell a parcel of boilers and vats, but the poten-
tiality of growing rich, beyond the dreams of avarice.'

On Saturday, April 7, I dined with him at Mr. Hoole's, with
Governour Bouchier and Captain Orme, both of whom had
been long in the East-Indies; and being men of good sense
and observation, were very entertaining. Johnson defended the
oriental regulation of different *casts* of men, which was objected to as totally destructive of the hopes of rising in society
by personal merit. He shewed that there was a *principle* in it
sufficiently plausible by analogy. 'We see (said he) in metals
that there are different species; and so likewise in animals,
though one species may not differ very widely from another,
as in the species of dogs,—the cur, the spaniel, the mastiff. The
Bramins are the mastiffs of mankind.'

On Thursday, April 12, I dined with him at a Bishop's,
where were Sir Joshua Reynolds, Mr. Berenger, and some
more company. He had dined the day before at another Bishop's. I have unfortunately recorded none of his conversation
at the Bishop's where we dined together: but I have preserved
his ingenious defence of his dining twice abroad in
Passion-week; a laxity, in which I am convinced he would not
have indulged himself at the time when he wrote his solemn
paper in 'The Rambler,' upon that aweful season. It appeared
to me, that by being much more in company, and enjoying

more luxurious living, he had contracted a keener relish of pleasure, and was consequently less rigorous in his religious rites. This he would not acknowledge; but he reasoned, with admirable sophistry, as follows: 'Why, Sir, a Bishop's calling company together in this week, is, to use the vulgar phrase, not *the thing*. But you must consider laxity is a bad thing; but preciseness is also a bad thing; and your general character may be more hurt by preciseness than by dining with a Bishop in Passion-week. There might be a handle for reflection. It might be said, "He refused to dine with a Bishop in Passion-week, but was three Sundays absent from church."' *Boswell.* 'Very true, Sir. But suppose a man to be uniformly of good conduct, would it not be better that he should refuse to dine with a Bishop in this week, and so not encourage a bad practice by his example?' *Johnson.* 'Why, Sir, you are to consider whether you might not do more harm by lessening the influence of a Bishop's character by your disapprobation in refusing him, than by going to him.'

On Friday, April 13, being Good-Friday, I went to St. Clement's church with him, as usual. There I saw again his old fellow-collegian, Edwards, to whom I said, 'I think, Sir, Dr. Johnson and you meet only at Church.'—'Sir, (said he,) it is the best place we can meet in, except Heaven, and I hope we shall meet there too.' Dr. Johnson told me, that there was very little communication between Edwards and him, after their unexpected renewal of acquaintance. 'But (said he, smiling) he met me once, and said, "I am told you have written a very pretty book called *The Rambler*." I was unwilling that he should leave the world in total darkness, and sent him a set.'

Mr. Berenger visited him to-day, and was very pleasing. We talked of an evening society for conversation at a house in town, of which we were all members, but of which Johnson said, 'It will never do, Sir. There is nothing served about there, neither tea, nor coffee, nor lemonade, nor any thing whatever; and depend upon it, Sir, a man does not love to go to a place from whence he comes out exactly as he went in.' I endeavoured for argument's sake, to maintain that men of learning and talents might have very good intellectual society, without the aid of any little gratifications of the senses. Berenger joined with Johnson, and said, that without these any meeting would be dull and insipid. He would therefore have all the slight refreshments; nay, it would not be amiss to have some cold meat, and a bottle of wine upon a side-board. 'Sir, (said Johnson to me, with an air of triumph,) Mr. Berenger knows the world. Every body loves to have good things furnished to them without any trouble.'

On Sunday, April 15, being Easter-day, after solemn worship in St. Paul's church, I found him alone; Dr. Scott, of the Commons, came in. He talked of its having been said, that Addison wrote some of his best papers in 'The Spectator,' when warm with wine. Dr. Johnson did not seem willing to admit this. Dr. Scott, as a confirmation of it, related, that Blackstone, a sober man, composed his 'Commentaries' with a bottle of port before him; and found his mind invigorated and supported in the fatigue of his great Work, by a temperate use of it.

Dr. Scott left us, and soon afterwards we went to dinner. Our company consisted of Mrs. Williams, Mrs. Desmoulins, Mr. Levett, Mr. Allen, the printer, and Mrs. Hall, sister of the Reverend Mr. John Wesley, and resembling him, as I thought, both in figure and manner. Johnson produced now, for the first time, some handsome silver salvers, which he told me he had bought fourteen years ago; so it was a great day.

He mentioned a thing as not unfrequent, of which I had never heard before,—being *called,* that is, hearing one's name pronounced by the voice of a known person at a great distance, far beyond the possibility of being reached by any sound uttered by human organs. Macbean asserted that this inexplicable *calling* was a thing very well known. Dr. Johnson said, that one day at Oxford, as he was turning the key of his chamber, he heard his mother distinctly call *Sam.* She was then at Lichfield; but nothing ensued. The phænomenon is, I think, as wonderful as any other mysterious fact, which many people are very slow to believe, or rather, indeed, reject with an obstinate contempt.

Some time after this, upon his making a remark which escaped my attention, Mrs. Williams and Mrs. Hall were both together striving to answer him. He grew angry, and called out loudly, 'Nay, when you both speak at once, it is intolerable.' But checking himself, and softening, he said, 'This one may say, though you *are* ladies.' Then he brightened into gay humour, and addressed them in the words of one of the songs in 'The Beggar's Opera,'

'But two at a time there's no mortal can bear.'

On Friday, April 20, I spent with him one of the happiest days that I remember to have enjoyed in the whole course of my life. Mrs. Garrick, whose grief for the loss of her husband was, I believe, as sincere as wounded affection and admiration could produce, had this day, for the first time since his death, a select party of his friends to dine with her. The company was Miss Hannah More, who lived with her, and whom she called her Chaplain; Mrs. Boscawen, Mrs. Elizabeth Carter, Sir Joshua Reynolds, Dr. Burney, Dr. Johnson, and myself. We found ourselves very elegantly entertained at her house in the Adelphi, where I have passed many a pleasing hour with him 'who gladdened life.' She looked very well, talked of her husband with complacency, and while she cast her eyes on his portrait, which hung over the chimney-piece, said, that 'death was now the most agreeable object to her.' The very semblance of David Garrick was cheering.

We were all in fine spirits; and I whispered to Mrs. Boscawen, 'I believe this is as much as can be made of life.' In addition to a splendid entertainment, we were regaled with Lichfield ale, which had a peculiar appropriated value. Sir Joshua, and Dr. Burney, and I, drank cordially of it to Dr. Johnson's health; and though he would not join us, he as cordially answered, 'Gentlemen, I wish you all as well as you do me.'

The general effect of this day dwells upon my mind in fond remembrance; but I do not find much conversation recorded. What I have preserved shall be faithfully given.

One of the company mentioned Mr. Thomas Hollis, the strenuous Whig, who used to send over Europe presents of democratical books, with their boards stamped with daggers and caps of liberty. Mrs. Carter having said of the same person, 'I doubt he was an Atheist.' *Johnson.* 'I don't know that. He might perhaps have become one, if he had had time to ripen, (smiling.) He might have *exuberated* into an Atheist.'

In the evening we had a large company in the drawing-room, several ladies, the Bishop of Killaloe, Dr. Percy, Mr. Chamberlayne, of the Treasury, &c. &c.

Talking of a very respectable authour, he told us a curious circumstance in his life, which was, that he had married a printer's devil. *Reynolds.* 'A printer's devil, Sir! Why, I thought a printer's devil was a creature with a black face and in rags.' *Johnson.* 'Yes, Sir. But I suppose, he had her face washed, and put clean clothes on her. (Then looking very serious, and very earnest.) And she did not disgrace him;—the woman had a bottom of good sense.' The word *bottom* thus introduced, was so ludicrous when contrasted with his gravity, that most of us could not forbear tittering and laughing; though I recollect that the Bishop of Killaloe kept his countenance with perfect steadiness, while Miss Hannah More slyly hid her face behind a lady's back who sat on the same settee with her. His pride could not bear that any expression of his should excite ridicule, when he did not intend it; he therefore resolved to assume and exercise despotick power, glanced sternly around, and called out in a strong tone, 'Where's the merriment?' Then collecting himself, and looking aweful, to make us feel how he could impose restraint, and as it were searching his mind for a still more ludicrous word, he slowly pronounced, 'I say the *woman* was *fundamentally* sensible;' as if he had said, hear this now, and laugh if you dare. We all sat composed as at a funeral.

He and I walked away together; we stopped a little while by the rails of the Adelphi, looking on the Thames, and I said to him with some emotion that I was now thinking of two friends we had lost, who once lived in the buildings behind us, Beauclerk and Garrick. 'Ay, Sir, (said he, tenderly) and two such friends as cannot be supplied.'

For some time after this day I did not see him very often, and of the conversation which I did enjoy, I am sorry to find I have preserved but little. I was at this time engaged in a variety of other matters, which required exertion and assiduity, and necessarily occupied almost all my time.

His disorderly habits, when 'making provision for the day that was passing over him,' appear from the following anecdote, communicated to me by Mr. John Nichols:—'In the year 1763, a young bookseller, who was an apprentice to Mr. Whiston, waited on him with a subscription to his 'Shakspeare:' and observing that the Doctor made no entry in any book of the subscriber's name, ventured diffidently to ask, whether he would please to have the gentleman's address, that it might be properly inserted in the printed list of subscribers.—*I shall print no List of Subscribers;*' said Johnson, with great abruptness: but almost immediately recollecting himself, added, very complacently, 'Sir, I have two very cogent reasons for not printing any list of subscribers;—one, that I have lost all the names, —the other, that I have spent all the money.'

Johnson could not brook appearing to be worsted in argument, even when he had taken the wrong side, to shew the force and dexterity of his talents. When, therefore, he perceived that his opponent gained ground, he had recourse to some sudden mode of robust sophistry. Once when I was pressing upon him with visible advantage, he stopped me thus:—'My dear Boswell, let's have no more of this; you'll make nothing of it. I'd rather have you whistle a Scotch tune.'

Care, however, must be taken to distinguish between Johnson when he 'talked for victory,' and Johnson when he had no desire but to inform and illustrate.—'One of Johnson's principal talents (says an eminent friend of his) was shewn in maintaining the wrong side of an argument, and in a splendid perversion of the truth.—If you could contrive to have his fair opinion on a subject, and without any bias from personal prejudice, or from a wish to be victorious in argument, it was wisdom itself, not only convincing, but overpowering.'

I asked him if he was not dissatisfied with having so small a share of wealth, and none of those distinctions in the state which are the objects of ambition. He had only a pension of three hundred a year. Why was he not in such circumstances as to keep his coach? Why had he not some considerable office? *Johnson.* 'Sir, I have never complained of the world; nor do I think that I have reason to complain. It is rather to be wondered at that I have so much. My pension is more out of the usual course of things than any instance that I have known. Here, Sir, was a man avowedly no friend to Government at the time, who got a pension without asking for it. I never courted the great; they sent for me; but I think they now give me up. They are satisfied; they have seen enough of me.' Upon my observing that I could not believe this, for they must certainly be highly pleased by his conversation; conscious of his own superiority, he answered, 'No, Sir; great Lords and great Ladies don't love to have their mouths stopped.' This was very expressive of the effect which the force of his understanding and brilliancy of his fancy could not but produce; and, to be sure, they must have found themselves strangely diminished in his company. When I warmly declared how happy I was at all times to hear him;—'Yes, Sir, (said he); but if you were Lord Chancellor, it would not be so: you would then consider your own dignity.'

In one of his little memorandum-books is the following minute:

'August 9, 3 P.M ætat. 72, in the summer-house at Streatham. 'After innumerable resolutions formed and neglected, I have retired hither, to plan a life of greater diligence, in hope that I may yet be useful, and be daily better prepared to appear before my Creator and my Judge, from whose infinite mercy I humbly call for assistance and support.

'My purpose is,

'To pass eight hours every day in some serious employment.

'Having prayed, I purpose to employ the next six weeks upon the Italian language, for my settled study.'

In autumn he went to Oxford, Birmingham, Lichfield, and Ashbourne, for which very good reasons might be given in the conjectural yet positive manner of writers, who are proud to account for every event which they relate. He himself, however, says,

'The motives of my journey I hardly know; I omitted it last year, and am not willing to miss it again.'

But some good considerations arise, amongst which is the kindly recollection of Mr. Hector, surgeon, at Birmingham.

'Hector is likewise an old friend, the only companion of my childhood that passed through the school with me. We have always loved one another; perhaps we may be made better by some serious conversation, of which however I have no distinct hope.'

1782: ÆTAT. 73.]—In 1782, his complaints increased, and the
history of his life this year, is little more than a mournful recital of the variations of his illness, in the midst of which,
however, the powers of his mind were in no degree impaired.

At a time when he was less able than he had once been to
sustain a shock, he was suddenly deprived of Mr. Levett, which
event he thus communicated to Dr. Lawrence:

'SIR,

'OUR old friend, Mr. Levett, who was last night eminently
cheerful, died this morning. The man who lay in the same room,
hearing an uncommon noise, got up and tried to make him speak,
but without effect. He then called Mr. Holder, the apothecary,
who, though when he came he thought him dead, opened a vein,
but could draw no blood. So has ended the long life of a very useful
and very blameless man.

'I am, Sir,
'Your most humble servant,
'SAM. JOHNSON.'

'Jan. 17, 1782.'

Such was Johnson's affectionate regard for Levett, that he
honoured his memory with the following pathetick verses:

'Condemn'd to Hope's delusive mine,
    As on we toil from day to day,
By sudden blast or slow decline
    Our social comforts drop away.

Well try'd through many a varying year,
    See *Levett* to the grave descend;
Officious, innocent, sincere,
    Of every friendless name the friend.

Yet still he fills Affection's eye,
    Obscurely wise, and coarsely kind;
Nor, letter'd arrogance, deny
    Thy praise to merit unrefin'd.

When fainting Nature call'd for aid,
    And hov'ring Death prepar'd the blow,
His vigorous remedy display'd
    The power of art without the show.

In Misery's darkest caverns known,
　　His ready help was ever nigh,
Where hopeless Anguish pour'd his groan,
　　And lonely Want retir'd to die.

No summons mock'd by chill delay,
　　No petty gains disdain'd by pride;
The modest wants of every day
　　The toil of every day supply'd.

His virtues walk'd their narrow round,
　　Nor made a pause, nor left a void;
And sure th' Eternal Master found
　　His single talent well employ'd.

The busy day, the peaceful night,
　　Unfelt, uncounted, glided by;
His frame was firm, his powers were bright,
　　Though now his eightieth year was nigh.

Then, with no throbs of fiery pain,
　　No cold gradations of decay,
Death broke at once the vital chain,
　　And freed his soul the nearest way.'

'TO MR. HECTOR, IN BIRMINGHAM.

'DEAR SIR,

'I HOPE I do not very grossly flatter myself to imagine that you and dear Mrs. Careless will be glad to hear some account of me. I performed the journey to London with very little inconvenience, and came safe to my habitation, where I found nothing but ill health, and, of consequence, very little cheerfulness. I then went to visit a little way into the country, where I got a complaint by a cold which has hung eight weeks upon me, and from which I am, at the expence of fifty ounces of blood, not yet free. I am afraid I must once more owe my recovery to warm weather, which seems to make no advances towards us.

'Such is my health, which will, I hope, soon grow better. In other respects I have no reason to complain. I know not that I have written any thing more generally commended than the Lives of the Poets; and have found the world willing enough to caress me, if my health had invited me to be in much company; but this season I have been almost wholly employed in nursing myself.

'When summer comes I hope to see you again, and will not put tt my visit to the end of the year. I have lived so long in London, hat I did not remember the difference of seasons.

'Your health, when I saw you, was much improved. You will be prudent enough not to put it in danger. I hope, when we meet again, we shall all congratulate each other upon fair prospects of onger life; though what are the pleasures of the longest life, when placed in comparison with a happy death?

'I am, dear Sir,
'Yours most affectionately,
'SAM. JOHNSON.'
'London, March 21, 1782.'

On the 30th of August, I informed him that my honoured father had died that morning; a complaint under which he had long laboured having suddenly come to a crisis.

In answer to my next letter, I received one from him, dissuading me from hastening to him as I had proposed. My wife was now so much convinced of his sincere friendship for me, and regard for her, that, without any suggestion on my part, she wrote him a very polite and grateful letter:

'DR. JOHNSON TO MRS. BOSWELL.
'DEAR LADY,
'I HAVE not often received so much pleasure as from your invitation to Auchinleck. The journey thither and back is, indeed, too great for the latter part of the year; but if my health were fully recovered, I would suffer no little heat and cold, nor a wet or a rough road to keep me from you. I am, indeed, not without hope of seeing Auchinleck again; but to make it a pleasant place I must see its lady well, and brisk, and airy. For my sake, therefore, among many greater reasons, take care, dear Madam, of your health, spare no expence, and want no attendance that can procure ease, or preserve it. Be very careful to keep your mind quiet; and do not think it too much to give an account of your recovery to Madam,

'Your, &c.
'SAM. JOHNSON.'
'London, Sept. 7, 1782.'

'TO JAMES BOSWELL, ESQ.
'DEAR SIR,
'HAVING passed almost this whole year in a succession of disorders, I went in October to Brighthelmston, whither I came in a state of so much weakness, that I rested four times in walking be-

tween the inn and the lodging. By physick and abstinence I grew
better, and am now reasonably easy, though at a great distance from
health. I am afraid, however, that health begins, after seventy, and
often long before, to have a meaning different from that which it
had at thirty. But it is culpable to murmur at the established order
of the creation, as it is vain to oppose it. He that lives, must grow
old; and he that would rather grow old than die, has GOD to thank
for the infirmities of old age.

'Mrs. Thrale and the three Misses are now for the winter, in
Argyll-street. Sir Joshua Reynolds has been out of order, but is well
again; and I am, dear Sir,

                              'Your affectionate humble servant,
                                                 'SAM. JOHNSON.'
'London, Dec. 7, 1782.'

The death of Mr. Thrale had made a very material alteration
with respect to Johnson's reception in that family. The manly
authority of the husband no longer curbed the lively exuber-
ance of the lady; and as her vanity had been fully gratified, by
having the Colossus of Literature attached to her for many
years, she gradually became less assiduous to please him.
Whether her attachment to him was already divided by another
object, I am unable to ascertain; but it is plain that Johnson's
penetration was alive to her neglect or forced attention; for on
the 6th of October this year, we find him making a 'parting
use of the library' at Streatham, and pronouncing a prayer,
which he composed 'On leaving Mr. Thrale's family.'

'Almighty GOD, Father of all mercy, help me by thy grace, that I
may, with humble and sincere thankfulness, remember the comforts
and conveniencies which I have enjoyed at this place; and that I
may resign them with holy submission, equally trusting in thy protection when Thou givest, and when Thou takest away. Have
mercy upon me, O LORD, have mercy upon me.

'To thy fatherly protection, O LORD, I commend this family.
Bless, guide, and defend them, that they may so pass through this
world, as finally to enjoy in thy presence everlasting happiness, for
JESUS CHRIST'S sake. Amen.'

One cannot read this prayer, without some emotions not very
favourable to the lady whose conduct occasioned it.

1783: ÆTAT. 74.]—In 1783, he was more severely afflicted

han ever but still the same ardour for literature, the same con-
tant piety, the same kindness for his friends, and the same
ivacity, both in conversation and writing, distinguished him.

On Friday, March 21, having arrived in London the night
before, I was glad to find him at Mrs. Thrale's house, in Argyll-
treet, appearances of friendship between them being still kept
ip. I was shewn into his room, and after the first salutation he
aid, 'I am glad you are come. I am very ill.' He looked pale,
and was distressed with a difficulty of breathing; but after the
common inquiries he assumed his usual strong animated style
of conversation.

He sent a message to acquaint Mrs. Thrale that I was
arrived. I had not seen her since her husband's death. She soon
appeared, and favoured me with an invitation to stay to dinner,
which I accepted. There was no other company but herself
and three of her daughters, Dr. Johnson, and I. She too said,
she was very glad I was come, for she was going to Bath, and
should have been sorry to leave Dr. Johnson before I came.
This seemed to be attentive and kind; and I who had not been
informed of any change, imagined all to be as well as formerly.
He was little inclined to talk at dinner, and went to sleep after
it; but when he joined us in the drawing-room, he seemed re
vived, and was again himself.

After musing for some time, he said, 'I wonder how I should
have any enemies; for I do harm to nobody.' *Boswell*. 'In the
first place, Sir, you will be pleased to recollect, that you set out
with attacking the Scotch; so you got a whole nation for your
enemies.' *Johnson*. 'Why, I own, that by my definition of *oats*
I meant to vex them.'

Next day, Saturday, March 22, I found him still at Mrs.
Thrale's, but he told me that he was to go to his own house in
the afternoon. He was better, but I perceived he was but an
unruly patient, for Sir Lucas Pepys, who visited him, while I
was with him said, 'If you were *tractable*, Sir, I should prescribe
for you.'

I had paid a visit to General Oglethorpe in the morning, and
was told by him that Dr. Johnson saw company on Saturday
evenings, and he would meet me at Johnson's, that night.
When I mentioned this to Johnson, not doubting that it would

please him, as he had a great value for Oglethorpe, the fretful
ness of his disease unexpectedly shewed itself; his anger sud
denly kindled, and he said, with vehemence, 'Did not you tel
him not to come? Am I to be *hunted* in this manner?' I satisfied
him that I could not divine that the visit would not be con
venient, and that I certainly could not take it upon me of my
own accord to forbid the General.

I found Dr. Johnson in the evening in Mrs. Williams'
room, at tea and coffee with her and Mrs. Desmoulins, who
were also both ill; it was a sad scene, and he was not in a very
good humour. He said of a performance that had lately come
out, 'Sir, if you should search all the mad-houses in England
you would not find ten men who would write so, and think i'
sense.' I was glad when General Oglethorpe's arrival was an
nounced, and we left the ladies. Dr. Johnson attended him in
the parlour, and was as courteous as ever.

On Sunday, March 23, I breakfasted with Dr. Johnson, who
seemed much relieved, having taken opium the night before
Mrs. Desmoulins made tea; and she and I talked before him
upon a topick which he had once borne patiently from me
when we were by ourselves,—his not complaining of the world
because he was not called to some great office, nor had attained
to great wealth. He flew into a violent passion, I confess with
some justice, and commanded us to have done. 'Nobody, (said
he) has a right to talk in this manner, to bring before a man
his own character, and the events of his life, when he does no
choose it should be done. I never have sought the world; the
world was not to seek me. It is rather wonderful that so much
has been done for me.'

On the subject of the right employment of wealth, Johnson
observed, 'A man cannot make a bad use of his money, so far
as regards Society, if he does not hoard it; for if he either
spends it or lends it out, Society has the benefit. It is in general
better to spend money than to give it away; for industry is more
promoted by spending money than by giving it away. A man
who spends his money is sure he is doing good with it: he is
not so sure when he gives it away. A man who spends ten
thousand a year will do more good than a man who spends two
thousand and gives away eight.'

In the evening I came to him again. He was somewhat fretful from his illness. A gentleman asked him, whether he had been abroad to-day. 'Don't talk so childishly, (said he.) You may as well ask if I hanged myself to-day.' I mentioned politicks. *Johnson.* 'Sir, I'd as soon have a man to break my bones as talk to me of publick affairs, internal or external. I have lived to see things all as bad as they can be.'

Having mentioned his friend the second Lord Southwell, he said, 'Lord Southwell was the highest-bred man without insolence that I ever was in company with; the most *qualitied* I ever saw. Lord Orrery was not dignified: Lord Chesterfield was, but he was insolent.'

On Sunday, March 30, I found him at home in the evening, and had the pleasure to meet with Dr. Brocklesby, whose reading, and knowledge of life, and good spirits, supply him with a never-failing source of conversation. He mentioned a respectable gentleman, who became extremely penurious near the close of his life. Johnson said there must have been a degree of madness about him. 'Not at all, Sir, (said Dr. Brocklesby,) his judgement was entire.' Unluckily, however, he mentioned that although he had a fortune of twenty-seven thousand pounds, he denied himself many comforts, from an apprehension that he could not afford them. 'Nay, Sir, (cried Johnson,) when the judgement is so disturbed that a man cannot count, that is pretty well.'

I shall here insert a few of Johnson's sayings, without the formality of dates, as they have no reference to any particular time or place.

Sir Joshua once observed to him, that he had talked above the capacity of some people with whom they had been in company together. 'No matter, Sir, (said Johnson); they consider it as a compliment to be talked to, as if they were wiser than they are. So true is this, Sir, that Baxter made it a rule in every sermon that he preached, to say something that was above the capacity of his audience.'

He said to Sir William Scott, 'The age is running mad after innovation; all the business of the world is to be done in a new way; men are to be hanged in a new way; Tyburn itself is not safe from the fury of innovation.' It having been argued that this was an improvement,—'No, Sir, (said he, eagerly,) it is *not* an improvement: they object that the old method drew together a number of spectators. Sir, executions are intended to draw spectators. If they do not draw spectators, they don't answer their purpose. The old method was most satisfactory to all parties; the publick was gratified by a procession; the criminal was supported by it. Why is all this to be swept away?'

Johnson's attention to precision and clearness in expression was very remarkable. He disapproved of parentheses; and I believe in all his voluminous writings, not half a dozen of them will be found. He never used the phrases *the former* and *the latter,* having observed, that they often occasioned obscurity; he therefore contrived to construct his sentences so as not to have occasion for them, and would even rather repeat the same words, in order to avoid them.

Such was the heat and irritability of his blood, that not only did he pare his nails to the quick; but scraped the joints of his fingers with a pen-knife, till they seemed quite red and raw.

The heterogeneous composition of human nature was remarkably exemplified in Johnson. His liberality in giving his money to persons in distress was extraordinary. Yet there lurked about him a propensity to paltry saving. One day I owned to him that 'I was occasionally troubled with a fit of *narrowness.*' 'Why, Sir, (said he,) so am I. *But I do not tell it.*' He has now and then borrowed a shilling of me; and when I asked for it again, seemed to be rather out of humour. A droll little circumstance once occurred: As if he meant to reprimand my minute exactness as a creditor, he thus addressed me;—'Boswell, *lend* me sixpence—*not to be repaid.*'

Johnson, for sport perhaps, or from the spirit of contradiction, eagerly maintained that Derrick had merit as a writer. Mr. Morgann argued with him directly, in vain. At length he had recourse to this device. 'Pray, Sir, (said he,) whether do you reckon Derrick or Smart the best poet?' Johnson at once felt himself rouzed; and answered, 'Sir, there is no settling the point of precedency between a louse and a flea.'

He would not allow Mr. David Hume any credit for his political principles, though similar to his own; saying of him, 'Sir, he was a Tory by chance.'

I never shall forget the indulgence with which he treated Hodge, his cat: for whom he himself used to go out and buy oysters, lest the servants having that trouble should take a dislike to the poor creature. I am, unluckily, one of those who have an antipathy to a cat, so that I am uneasy when in the room with one; and I own, I frequently suffered a good deal from the presence of this same Hodge. I recollect him one day scrambling up Dr. Johnson's breast, apparently with much satisfaction, while my friend smiling and half-whistling, rubbed down his back, and pulled him by the tail; and when I observed he was a fine cat, saying, 'why yes, Sir, but I have had cats whom I liked better than this;' and then as if perceiving Hodge to be out of countenance, adding, 'but he is a very fine cat, a very fine cat indeed.'

This reminds me of the ludicrous account which he gave Mr. Langton, of the despicable state of a young Gentleman of good family. 'Sir, when I heard of him last, he was running about town shooting cats.' And then in a sort of kindly reverie, he bethought himself of his own favourite cat, and said, 'But Hodge shan't be shot; no, no, Hodge shall not be shot.'

On Thursday, April 10, I introduced to him, at his house in Bolt-court, the Honourable and Reverend William Stuart, son of the Earl of Bute; a gentleman truly worthy of being known to Johnson; being, with all the advantages of high birth, learning, travel, and elegant manners, an exemplary parish priest in every respect.

After some compliments on both sides, the tour which Johnson and I had made to the Hebrides was mentioned.—*Johnson.* 'I got an acquisition of more ideas by it than by any thing that I remember. I saw quite a different system of life.' *Boswell.* 'You would not like to make the same journey again?' *Johnson.* 'Why no, Sir; not the same: it is a tale told. Gravina, an Italian critick, observes, that every man desires to see that of which he has read; but no man desires to read an account of what he has seen: so much does description fall short of reality. Description only excites curiosity: seeing satisfies it. Other people may go and see the Hebrides.' *Boswell.* 'I should wish to go and see some country totally different from what I have been used to; such as Turkey, where religion and every thing else are differ-

ent.' *Johnson.* 'Yes, Sir; there are two objects of curiosity,—the
Christian world, and the Mahometan world. All the rest may
be considered as barbarous.'

Mr. Lowe, the painter, was very much distressed that a large
picture which he had painted was refused to be received into
the Exhibition of the Royal Academy. Mrs. Thrale knew Johnson's character so superficially, as to represent him as unwilling
to do small acts of benevolence; and mentions, in particular,
that he would hardly take the trouble to write a letter in favour
of his friends. The truth, however, is, that he was remarkable,
in an extraordinary degree, for what she denies to him; and,
above all, for this very sort of kindness, writing letters for those
to whom his solicitations might be of service. He now gave Mr.
Lowe the following, of which I was diligent enough, with his
permission, to take copies at the next coffee-house, while Mr.
Windham was so good as to stay by me.

'To Sir Joshua Reynolds.

'Sir,
    'Mr. Lowe considers himself as cut off from all credit and all
hope, by the rejection of his picture from the Exhibition. Upon
this work he has exhausted all his powers, and suspended all his
expectations: and, certainly, to be refused an opportunity of taking
the opinion of the publick, is in itself a very great hardship. It is
to be condemned without a trial.

'If you could procure the revocation of this incapacitating edict,
you would deliver an unhappy man from great affliction. The
Council has sometimes reversed its own determination; and I hope,
that by your interposition this luckless picture may be got admitted.
I am, &c.

                                               'Sam. Johnson.'
'April 12, 1783.'

'To Mr. Barry.
'Sir,
    'Mr. Lowe's exclusion from the Exhibition gives him more
trouble than you and the other gentlemen of the Council could
imagine or intend. He considers disgrace and ruin as the inevitable
consequence of your determination.

'He says, that some pictures have been received after rejection;
and if there be any such precedent, I earnestly intreat that you will
use your interest in his favour. Of his work I can say nothing; I

pretend not to judge of painting; and this picture I never saw: but I conceive it extremely hard to shut out any man from the possibility of success; and therefore I repeat my request that you will propose the re-consideration of Mr. Lowe's case; and if there be any among the Council with whom my name can have any weight, be pleased to communicate to them the desire of, Sir,

'Your most humble servant,

'SAM. JOHNSON.'

'April 12, 1783.'

Such intercession was too powerful to be resisted; and Mr. Lowe's performance was admitted at Somerset Place. The subject, as I recollect, was the Deluge, at that point of time when the water was verging to the top of the last uncovered mountain. Near to the spot was seen the last of the antediluvian race, exclusive of those who were saved in the ark of Noah. This was one of those giants, then the inhabitants of the earth, who had still strength to swim, and with one of his hands held aloft his infant child. Upon the small remaining dry spot appeared a famished lion, ready to spring at the child and devour it. Mr. Lowe told me that Johnson said to him, 'Sir, your picture is noble and probable.'—'A compliment, indeed, (said Mr. Lowe,) from a man who cannot lie, and cannot be mistaken.'

On April 18, (being Good-Friday,) I found him at breakfast, in his usual manner upon that day, drinking tea without milk, and eating a cross-bun to prevent faintness; we went to St. Clement's church, as formerly. When we came home from church, he placed himself on one of the stone-seats at his garden-door, and I took the other, and thus in the open air and in a placid frame of mind, he talked away very easily. *Johnson.* 'Were I a country gentleman, I should not be very hospitable, I should not have crowds in my house.' *Boswell.* 'Sir Alexander Dick tells me, that he remembers having a thousand people in a year to dine at his house: that is, reckoning each person as one, each time that he dined there.' *Johnson.* 'That, Sir, is about three a day.' *Boswell.* 'How your statement lessens the idea.' *Johnson.* 'That, Sir, is the good of counting. It brings every thing to a certainty, which before floated in the mind indefinitely.'

Mr. Walker, the celebrated master of elocution, came in, and then we went up stairs into the study. I asked him if he had taught many clergymen. *Johnson.* 'I hope not.' *Walker.* 'I have taught only one, and he is the best reader I ever heard, not by my teaching, but by his own natural talents.' *Johnson.* 'Were he the best reader in the world, I would not have it told that he was taught.'

Mrs. Burney, wife of his friend Dr. Burney, came in, and he seemed to be entertained with her conversation.

Garrick's funeral was talked of as extravagantly expensive. Johnson, from his dislike to exaggeration, would not allow that it was distinguished by any extraordinary pomp. 'Were there not six horses to each coach?' said Mrs. Burney. *Johnson.* 'Madam, there were no more six horses than six phœnixes.'

Mrs. Burney wondered that some very beautiful new buildings should be erected in Moorfields, in so shocking a situation as between Bedlam and St. Luke's Hospital; and said she could not live there. *Johnson.* 'Nay, Madam, you see nothing there to hurt you. You no more think of madness by having windows that look to Bedlam, than you think of death by having windows that look to a church-yard.' *Mrs. Burney.* 'We may look to a church-yard, Sir; for it is right that we should be kept in mind of death.' *Johnson.* 'Nay, Madam, if you go to that, it is right that we should be kept in mind of madness, which is occasioned by too much indulgence of imagination. I think a very moral use may be made of these new buildings: I would have those who have heated imaginations live there, and take warning.' *Mrs. Burney.* 'But, Sir, many of the poor people that are mad, have become so from disease, or from distressing events. It is, therefore, not their fault, but their misfortune; and, therefore, to think of them, is a melancholy consideration.'

On Sunday, April 20, being Easter-day, after attending solemn service at St. Paul's, I came to Dr. Johnson, and found Mr. Lowe, the painter, sitting with him. Mr. Lowe mentioned the great number of new buildings of late in London, yet that Dr. Johnson had observed, that the number of inhabitants was not increased. *Johnson.* 'Why, Sir, the bills of mortality prove that no more people die now than formerly; so it is plain no more live. The register of births proves nothing, for not one tenth of the people of London are born there.' *Boswell.* 'I be-

ieve, Sir, a great many of the children born in London die
arly.' Johnson. 'Why, yes, Sir.' Boswell. 'But those who do
ive, are as stout and strong people as any: Dr. Price says, they
must be naturally stronger to get through.' Johnson. 'That is
system, Sir. A great traveller observes, that it is said there are
no weak or deformed people among the Indians; but he with
much sagacity assigns the reason of this, which is, that the
hardship of their life as hunters and fishers, does not allow
weak or diseased children to grow up. Now had I been an
Indian, I must have died early; my eyes would not have served
me to get food. I indeed now could fish, give me English tackle;
but had I been an Indian I must have starved, or they would
have knocked me on the head, when they saw I could do noth
ing.' Boswell. 'Perhaps they would have taken care of you: we
are told they are fond of oratory, you would have talked to
them.' Johnson. 'Nay, Sir, I should not have lived long enough
to be fit to talk; I should have been dead before I was ten years
old. Depend upon it, Sir, a savage, when he is hungry, will
not carry about with him a looby of nine years old, who cannot help himself. They have no affection, Sir.' Boswell. 'But
some of the Indians have affection.' Johnson. 'Sir, that they
help some of their children is plain; for some of them live,
which they could not do without being helped.'

Having next day gone to Mr. Burke's seat in the country,
from whence I was recalled by an express, that a near relation
of mine had killed his antagonist in a duel, and was himself
dangerously wounded, I saw little of Dr. Johnson till Monday,
April 28, when I spent a considerable part of the day with him,
and introduced the subject, which then chiefly occupied my
mind. Johnson. 'I do not see, Sir, that fighting is absolutely
forbidden in Scripture; I see revenge forbidden, but not self-
defence.' Boswell. 'The Quakers say it is; "Unto him that
smiteth thee on one cheek, offer also the other."' Johnson.
'But stay, Sir; the text is meant only to have the effect of moder-
ating passion; it is plain that we are not to take it in a literal
sense. So in 1745, my friend, Tom Cumming, the Quaker,
said, he would not fight, but he would drive an ammunition
cart; and we know that the Quakers have sent flannel waistcoats to our soldiers, to enable them to fight better.'

Talking of a man who was grown very fat, so as to be incommoded with corpulency; he said, 'He eats too much, Sir.' *Boswell.* 'I don't know, Sir, you will see one man fat who eats moderately, and another lean who eats a great deal.' *Johnson.* 'Nay, Sir, whatever may be the quantity that a man eats, it is plain that if he is too fat, he has eaten more than he should have done. One man may have a digestion that consumes food better than common; but it is certain that solidity is encreased by putting something to it.'

I have no minute of any interview with Johnson till Thursday, May 15, when I find what follows:—*Boswell.* 'I wish much to be in Parliament, Sir.' *Johnson.* 'Why, Sir, unless you come resolved to support any administration, you would be the worse for being in Parliament, because you would be obliged to live more expensively.' *Boswell.* 'Perhaps, Sir, I should be the less happy for being in Parliament. I never would sell my vote, and I should be vexed if things went wrong.' *Johnson.* 'That's cant, Sir. It would not vex you more in the house, than in the gallery: publick affairs vex no man.' *Boswell.* 'Have not they vexed yourself a little, Sir? Have not you been vexed by all the turbulence of this reign?' *Johnson.* 'Sir, I have never slept an hour less, nor eat an ounce less meat. I would have knocked the factious dogs on the head, to be sure; but I was not *vexed.*' *Boswell.* 'I declare, Sir, upon my honour, I did imagine I was vexed, and took a pride in it; but it *was,* perhaps, cant; for I own I neither ate less, nor slept less.' *Johnson.* 'My dear friend, clear your *mind* of cant. You may *talk* as other people do: you may say to a man, "Sir, I am your most humble servant." You are *not* his most humble servant. You may say, "These are sad times; it is a melancholy thing to be reserved to such times." You don't mind the times. You tell a man, "I am sorry you had such bad weather the last day of your journey, and were so much wet." You don't care six-pence whether he was wet or dry. You may *talk* in this manner; it is a mode of talking in Society: but don't *think* foolishly.'

On Monday, May 26, I found him at tea, and the celebrated Miss Burney, the authour of 'Evelina' and 'Cecilia,' with him. I mentioned 'Cecilia.' *Johnson.* (with an air of animated satisfaction) 'Sir, if you talk of "Cecilia," talk on.'

I asked whether a man naturally virtuous, or one who has overcome wicked inclinations is the best. *Johnson.* 'Sir, to *you*, the man who has overcome wicked inclinations is not the best. He has more merit to *himself*. I would rather trust my money to a man who has no hands, and so a physical impossibility to steal, than to a man of the most honest principles. There is a witty satirical story of Foote. He had a small bust of Garrick placed upon his bureau. "You may be surprized (said he) that I allow him to be so near my gold;—but you will observe he has no hands." '

On Friday, May 29, being to set out for Scotland next morning, I passed a part of the day with him in more than usual earnestness; as his health was in a more precarious state than at any time when I had parted from him. He, however, was quick and lively, and critical as usual. I mentioned one who was a very learned man. *Johnson.* 'Yes, Sir, he has a great deal of learning; but it never lies straight. There is never one idea by the side of another; 'tis all entangled: and then he drives it so aukwardly upon conversation.'

I stated to him an anxious thought, by which a sincere Christian might be disturbed. Suppose a man who has led a good life for seven years, commits an act of wickedness, and instantly dies; will his former good life have any effect in his favour? *Johnson.* 'Sir, if a man has led a good life for seven years, and then is hurried by passion to do what is wrong, and is suddenly carried off, depend upon it he will have the reward of his seven years' good life; GOD will not take a catch of him. Upon this principle Richard Baxter believes that a Suicide may be saved. "If, (says he) it should be objected that what I maintain may encourage suicide, I answer, I am not to tell a lie to prevent it." '

I assured him, that in the extensive and various range of his acquaintance there never had been any one who had a more sincere respect and affection for him than I had. He said, 'I believe it, Sir. Were I in distress, there is no man to whom I should sooner come than to you. I should like to come and have a cottage in your park, toddle about, live mostly on milk, and be taken care of by Mrs. Boswell. She and I are good friends now; are we not?'

He embraced me, and gave me his blessing, as usual when I was leaving him for any length of time. I walked from his door to-day, with a fearful apprehension of what might happen before I returned.

My anxious apprehensions at parting with him this year proved to be but too well founded; for not long afterwards he had a dreadful stroke of the palsy, of which there are very full and accurate accounts in letters written by himself, which shew with what composure of mind, and resignation to the Divine Will, his steady piety enabled him to behave.

'To Mr. Edmund Allen.

'Dear Sir,

'It has pleased God, this morning, to deprive me of the powers of speech; and as I do not know but that it may be his further good pleasure to deprive me soon of my senses, I request you will on the receipt of this note, come to me, and act for me, as the exigencies of my case may require.

'I am,

'Sincerely yours,

'Sam. Johnson.'

'June 17, 1783.'

'To the Reverend Dr. John Taylor.

'Dear Sir,

'It has pleased God, by a paralytick stroke in the night, to deprive me of speech.

'I am very desirous of Dr. Heberden's assistance, as I think my case is not past remedy. Let me see you as soon as it is possible. Bring Dr. Heberden with you, if you can; but come yourself at all events. I am glad you are so well, when I am so dreadfully attacked.

'I think that by a speedy application of stimulants much may be done. I question if a vomit, vigorous and rough, would not rouse the organs of speech to action. As it is too early to send, I will try to recollect what I can, that can be suspected to have brought on this dreadful distress.

'I have been accustomed to bleed frequently for an asthmatick complaint; but have forborne for some time by Dr. Pepys's persuasion, who perceived my legs beginning to swell. I sometimes alleviate a painful, or more properly an oppressive, constriction of my chest, by opiates; and have lately taken opium frequently, but the last, or two last times, in smaller quantities. My largest dose is three grains, and last night I took but two. You will suggest these things (and they are all that I can call to mind) to Dr. Heberden.

'I am, &c.

'SAM. JOHNSON.'

'June 17, 1783.'

Two days after he wrote thus to Mrs. Thrale:

'On Monday, the 16th, I sat for my picture, and walked a considerable way with little inconvenience. In the afternoon and evening I felt myself light and easy, and began to plan schemes of life. Thus I went to bed, and in a short time waked and sat up, as has been long my custom, when I felt a confusion and indistinctness in my head, which lasted, I suppose, about half a minute. I was alarmed, and prayed GOD, that however he might afflict my body, he would spare my understanding. This prayer, that I might try the integrity of my faculties, I made in Latin verse. The lines were not very good, but I knew them not to be very good: I made them easily, and concluded myself to be unimpaired in my faculties.

'Soon after I perceived that I had suffered a paralytick stroke, and that my speech was taken from me. I had no pain, and so little dejection in this dreadful state, that I wondered at my own apathy, and considered that perhaps death itself, when it should come, would excite less horrour than seems now to attend it.

'In order to rouse the vocal organs, I took two drams. Wine has been celebrated for the production of eloquence. I put myself into violent motion, and I think repeated it; but all was vain. I then went to bed, and, strange as it may seem, I think, slept. When I saw light, it was time to contrive what I should do. Though GOD stopped my speech, he left me my hand; I enjoyed a mercy which was not granted to my dear friend Lawrence, who now perhaps overlooks me as I am writing, and rejoices that I have what he wanted. My first note was necessarily to my servant, who came in talking, and could not immediately comprehend why he should read what I put into his hands.

'I then wrote a card to Mr. Allen, that I might have a discreet friend at hand, to act as occasion should require. In penning this note, I had some difficulty; my hand, I knew not how nor why, made wrong letters. I then wrote to Dr. Taylor to come to me, and bring Dr. Heberden; and I sent to Dr. Brocklesby, who is my neighbour. My physicians are very friendly, and give me great hopes; but you may imagine my situation. I have so far recovered my vocal powers, as to repeat the Lord's Prayer with no very imperfect articulation. My memory, I hope, yet remains as it was; but such an attack produces solicitude for the safety of every faculty.'

'To Mr. Thomas Davies.

'Dear Sir,

'I have had, indeed, a very heavy blow; but God, who yet spares my life, I humbly hope will spare my understanding, and restore my speech. As I am not at all helpless, I want no particular assistance, but am strongly affected by Mrs. Davies's tenderness; and when I think she can do me good, shall be very glad to call upon her. I had ordered friends to be shut out; but one or two have found the way in; and if you come you shall be admitted: for I know not whom I can see, that will bring more amusement on his tongue, or more kindness in his heart. I am, &c.

'Sam. Johnson.'

'June 18, 1783.'

It gives me great pleasure to preserve such a memorial of Johnson's regard for Mr. Davies, to whom I was indebted for my introduction to him. He indeed loved Davies cordially, of which I shall give the following little evidence. One day, when he had treated him with too much asperity, Tom, who was not without pride and spirit, went off in a passion; but he had hardly reached home, when Frank, who had been sent after him, delivered this note:—'Come, come, dear Davies, I am always sorry when we quarrel; send me word that we are friends.'

'To James Boswell, Esq.

'Dear Sir,

'Your anxiety about my health is very friendly, and very agreeable with your general kindness. I have, indeed, had a very frightful blow. On the 17th of last month, about three in the morning, as near as I can guess, I perceived myself almost totally deprived of speech. I had no pain. My organs were so obstructed, that I could say *no*, but could scarcely say *yes*. I wrote the necessary directions, for it pleased God to spare my hand, and sent for Dr. Heberden and Dr. Brocklesby. Between the time in which I discovered my own disorder, and that in which I sent for the doctors, I had, I believe, in spite of my surprize and solicitude, a little sleep, and Nature began to renew its operations. They came, and gave the directions which the disease required, and from that time I have been continually improving in articulation. I can now speak, but the nerves are weak, and I cannot continue discourse long; but strength, I hope, will return. The physicians consider me as cured. I was last Sunday at church. On Tuesday I took an airing to Hampstead, and dined with THE CLUB, where Lord Palmerston was proposed, and, against my opinion, was rejected. I design to go next week with Mr. Langton to Rochester, where I purpose to stay about ten days, and then try some other air. I have many kind invitations. Most of my friends have, indeed, been very attentive. Thank dear Lord Hailes for his present.

'I hope you found at your return every thing gay and prosperous, and your lady, in particular, quite recovered and confirmed. Pay her my respects.

> 'I am, dear Sir,
> 'Your most humble servant,
> 'SAM. JOHNSON.'

'London, July 3, 1783.'

Such was the general vigour of his constitution, that he recovered from this alarming and severe attack with wonderful quickness; so that in July he was able to make a visit to Mr. Langton at Rochester, where he passed about a fortnight, and made little excursions as easily as at any time of his life. In August he went as far as the neighbourhood of Salisbury, to Heale, the seat of William Bowles, Esq. In his diary I find a short but honourable mention of this visit:—'August 28, I came to Heale without fatigue. 30. I am entertained quite to my mind.'

'TO DR. BROCKLESBY.

'Heale, near Salisbury, Aug. 29, 1783

'DEAR SIR,

'WITHOUT appearing to want a just sense of your kind attention, I cannot omit to give an account of the day which seemed to appear in some sort perilous. I rose at five and went out at six, and having reached Salisbury about nine, went forward a few miles in my friend's chariot. I was no more wearied with the journey, though it was a high-hung, rough coach, than I should have been forty years ago. We shall now see what air will do. The country is all a plain; and the house in which I am, so far as I can judge from my window, for I write before I have left my chamber, is sufficiently pleasant.

'Be so kind as to continue your attention to Mrs. Williams; it is great consolation to the well, and still greater to the sick, that they find themselves not neglected; and I know that you will be desirous of giving comfort even where you have no great hope of giving help.

'Since I wrote the former part of the letter, I find that by the course of the post I cannot send it before the thirty-first.

'I am, &c.

'SAM. JOHNSON.'

While he was here he had a letter from Dr. Brocklesby, acquainting him of the death of Mrs. Williams, which affected him a good deal. Though for several years her temper had not been complacent, she had valuable qualities, and her departure left a blank in his house. Upon this occasion he, according to his habitual course of piety, composed a prayer.

I shall here insert a few particulars concerning him, with which I have been favoured by one of his friends.

'A friend was one day, about two years before his death, struck with some instance of Dr. Johnson's great candour. "Well, Sir, (said he,) I will always say that you are a very candid man."— "Will you, (replied the Doctor,) I doubt then you will be very singular. But, indeed, Sir, (continued he,) I look upon myself to be a man very much misunderstood. I am not an uncandid, nor am I a severe man. I sometimes say more than I mean, in jest; and people are apt to believe me serious: however, I am more candid than I was when I was younger. As I know more of mankind I expect less of them, and am ready now to call a man *a good man,* upon easier terms than I was formerly." '

His fortitude and patience met with severe trials during this year. The stroke of the palsy has been related circumstantially; but he was also afflicted with the gout, and was besides troubled with a complaint which not only was attended with immediate inconvenience, but threatened him with a painful chirurgical operation, from which most men would shrink. The complaint was a *sarcocele,* which Johnson bore with uncommon firmness, and was not at all frightened while he looked forward to amputation. He was attended by Mr. Pott and Mr. Cruikshank. I have before me a letter of the 30th of July this year, to Mr. Cruikshank, in which he says, 'I am going to put myself into your hands;' and another, accompanying a set of

his 'Lives of the Poets,' in which he says, 'I beg your acceptance of these volumes, as an acknowledgement of the great
favours which you have bestowed on, Sir, your most obliged
and most humble servant.' I have in my possession several more
letters from him to Mr. Cruikshank, and also to Dr. Mudge at
Plymouth, which it would be improper to insert, as they are
filled with unpleasing technical details. I shall, however,
extract from his letters to Dr. Mudge such passages as shew
either a felicity of expression, or the undaunted state of his
mind.

'My conviction of your skill, and my belief of your friendship,
determine me to intreat your opinion and advice.'—'In this state I
with great earnestness desire you to tell me what is to be done.
Excision is doubtless necessary to the cure, and I know not any
means of palliation. The operation is doubtless painful; but is it
dangerous? The pain I hope to endure with decency; but I am
loth to put life into much hazard.'—'By representing the gout as an
antagonist to the palsy, you have said enough to make it welcome.
This is not strictly the first fit, but I hope it is as good as the first; for
it is the second that ever confined me; and the first was ten years
ago, much less fierce and fiery than this.'—'Write, dear Sir, what
you can, to inform or encourage me. The operation is not delayed
by any fears or objections of mine.'

'To BENNET LANGTON, ESQ.

'DEAR SIR,

'You may very reasonably charge me with insensibility of your
kindness, and that of Lady Rothes, since I have suffered so much
time to pass without paying any acknowledgement. I now, at last,
return my thanks; and why I did it not sooner I ought to tell you.
I went into Wiltshire as soon as I well could, and was there much
employed in palliating my own malady. Disease produces much self-
ishness. A man in pain is looking after ease; and lets most other
things go as chance shall dispose of them. In the mean time I have
lost a companion, to whom I have had recourse for domestick
amusement for thirty years, and whose variety of knowledge never
was exhausted; and now return to a habitation vacant and desolate.
I carry about a very troublesome and dangerous complaint, which
admits no cure but by the chirurgical knife. Let me have your prayers. I am, &c.

                                                    'SAM. JOHNSON.'

'London, Sept. 29, 1783.'

Happily the complaint abated without his being put to the torture of amputation. But we must surely admire the manly resolution which he discovered while it hung over him.

In a letter to the same gentleman he writes, 'The gout has within these four days come upon me with a violence which I never experienced before. It made me helpless as an infant.' And in another, having mentioned Mrs. Williams, he says,—'whose death following that of Levett, has now made my house a solitude. She left her little substance to a charity-school. She is, I hope, where there is neither darkness, nor want, nor sorrow.'

He this autumn received a visit from the celebrated Mrs. Siddons. Mr. Kemble has favoured me with the following minute of what passed at this visit.

'When Mrs. Siddons came into the room, there happened to be no chair ready for her, which he observing, said with a smile, "Madam, you who so often occasion a want of seats to other people, will the more easily excuse the want of one yourself."

'Having placed himself by her, he with great good humour entered upon a consideration of the English drama; and, among other inquiries, particularly asked her which of Shakspeare's characters she was most pleased with. Upon her answering that she thought the character of Queen Catherine, in Henry the Eighth, the most natural:—"I think so too, Madam, (said he;) and whenever you perform it, I will once more hobble out to the theatre myself." Mrs. Siddons promised she would do herself the honour of acting his favourite part for him; but many circumstances happened to prevent the representation of King Henry the Eighth during the Doctor's life.

'In the course of the evening he thus gave his opinion upon the merits of some of the principal performers whom he remembered to have seen upon the stage. "Mrs. Porter, in the vehemence of rage, and Mrs. Clive in the sprightliness of humour, I have never seen equalled. What Clive did best, she did better than Garrick; but could not do half so many things well; she was a better romp than any I ever saw in nature. Pritchard, in common life, was a vulgar ideot; she would talk of her *gownd:* but, when she appeared upon the stage, seemed to be inspired by gentility and understanding. I once talked with Colley Cibber, and thought him ignorant of the principles of his art. Garrick, Madam, was no declaimer; there was not one of his own scene-shifters who could not have spoken *To be, or not to be,* better than he did; yet he was the only actor I ever saw whom I could call a master both in tragedy and comedy; though I liked him best in comedy. A true conception of character, and natural expression of it, were his distinguishing excellencies." Having expatiated, with his usual force and eloquence, on Mr. Garrick's extraordinary eminence as an actor, he concluded with this compliment to his social talents: "And after all, Madam, I thought him less to be envied on the stage than at the head of a table." '

Johnson, indeed, had thought more upon the subject of acting than might be generally supposed. Talking of it one day to Mr. Kemble, he said, 'Are you, Sir, one of those enthusiasts who believe yourself transformed into the very character you represent?' Upon Mr. Kemble's answering that he had never felt so strong a persuasion himself; 'To be sure not, Sir, (said Johnson;) the thing is impossible. And if Garrick really believed himself to be that monster, Richard the Third, he deserved to be hanged every time he performed it.'

A pleasing instance of the generous attention of one of his friends has been discovered by the publication of Mrs. Thrale's collection of Letters. In a letter to one of the Miss Thrales, he writes,

'A friend, whose name I will tell when your mamma has tried to guess it, sent to my physician to enquire whether this long train of illness had brought me into difficulties for want of money, with an invitation to send to him for what occasion required. I shall write this night to thank him, having no need to borrow.'

And afterwards, in a letter to Mrs. Thrale,

'Since you cannot guess, I will tell you, that the generous man was Gerard Hamilton. I returned him a very thankful and respectful letter.'

I applied to Mr. Hamilton, by a common friend, and he has been so obliging as to let me have Johnson's letter to him upon this occasion, to adorn my collection.

'To the Right Honourable William Gerard Hamilton.

'Dear Sir,

'Your kind enquiries after my affairs, and your generous offers have been communicated to me by Dr. Brocklesby. I return thanks

with great sincerity, having lived long enough to know what gratitude is due to such friendship; and entreat that my refusal may not
be imputed to sullenness or pride. I am, indeed, in no want. Sickness is, by the generosity of my physicians, of little expence to me.
But if any unexpected exigence should press me, you shall see, dear
Sir, how cheerfully I can be obliged to so much liberality.

'I am, Sir,

'Your most obedient

'And most humble servant,

'SAM. JOHNSON.'

'November 19, 1783.'

I consulted him on two questions of a very different nature:
one, whether the unconstitutional influence exercised by the
Peers of Scotland in the election of the representatives of the
Commons, by means of fictitious qualifications, ought not to be
resisted;—the other, What, in propriety and humanity, should
be done with old horses unable to labour. I gave him some
account of my life at Auchinleck; and expressed my satisfaction that the gentlemen of the county had, at two publick
meetings, elected me their Chairman.

'TO JAMES BOSWELL, ESQ.

'DEAR SIR,

'LIKE all other men who have great friends, you begin to feel
the pangs of neglected merit; and all the comfort that I can give you
is, by telling you that you have probably more pangs to feel, and
more neglect to suffer. You have, indeed, begun to complain too
soon; and I hope I am the only confidant of your discontent. Your
friends have not yet had leisure to gratify personal kindness; they
have hitherto been busy in strengthening their ministerial interest.
If a vacancy happens in Scotland, give them early intelligence; and
as you can serve Government as powerfully as any of your probable
competitors, you may make in some sort a warrantable claim.

'Of the exaltations and depressions of your mind you delight to
talk, and I hate to hear. Drive all such fancies from you.

'On the day when I received your letter, I think, the foregoing
page was written; to which, one disease or another has hindered me
from making any additions. I am now a little better. But sickness
and solitude press me very heavily. I could bear sickness better, if
I were relieved from solitude.

'Your question about the horses gives me more perplexity. I

know not well what advice to give you. I can only recommend a rule which you do not want;—give as little pain as you can. I suppose that we have a right to their service while their strength lasts; what we can do with them afterwards I cannot so easily determine. But let us consider. Nobody denies that man has a right first to milk the cow, and to sheer the sheep, and then to kill them for his table. May he not, by parity of reason, first work a horse, and then kill him the easiest way, that he may have the means of another horse, or food for cows and sheep? Man is influenced in both cases by different motives of self-interest. He that rejects the one must reject the other.

'I am, &c.
'SAM. JOHNSON.'

'London, Dec. 24, 1783.'

'A happy and pious Christmas; and many happy years to you, your lady, and children.'

Notwithstanding the complication of disorders under which Johnson now laboured, he did not resign himself to despondency and discontent, but with wisdom and spirit endeavoured to console and amuse his mind with as many innocent enjoyments as he could procure. Sir John Hawkins has mentioned the cordiality with which he insisted that such of the members of the old club in Ivy-lane as survived, should meet again and dine together, which they did, twice at a tavern, and once at his house: and in order to insure himself society in the evening for three days in the week, he instituted a club at the Essex Head, in Essex-street, then kept by Samuel Greaves, an old servant of Mr. Thrale's.

'To SIR JOSHUA REYNOLDS.

'DEAR SIR,

'IT is inconvenient to me to come out, I should else have waited on you with an account of a little evening Club which we are establishing in Essex-street, in the Strand, and of which you are desired to be one. It will be held at the Essex Head, now kept by an old servant of Thrale's. The company is numerous, and, as you will see by the list, miscellaneous. The terms are lax, and the expences light. Mr. Barry was adopted by Dr. Brocklesby, who joined with me in forming the plan. We meet thrice a week, and he who misses forfeits two-pence.

'If you are willing to become a member, draw a line under your name. Return the list. We meet for the first time on Monday at eight.

'I am, &c.

'SAM. JOHNSON.'

'Dec. 4, 1783.'

It did not suit Sir Joshua to be one of this Club. But when I mention only Mr. Daines Barrington, Dr. Brocklesby, Mr. Murphy, Mr. John Nichols, Mr. Cooke, Mr. Joddrel, Mr. Paradise, Dr. Horsley, Mr. Windham, I shall sufficiently obviate the misrepresentation of it by Sir John Hawkins, as if it had been a low ale-house association, by which Johnson was degraded. Johnson himself, like his name-sake Old Ben, composed the Rules of his Club.

In the end of this year he was seized with a spasmodick asthma of such violence, that he was confined to the house in great pain, being sometimes obliged to sit all night in his chair, a recumbent posture being so hurtful to his respiration, that he could not endure lying in bed; and there came upon him at the same time that oppressive and fatal disease, a dropsy. It was a very severe winter, which probably aggravated his complaints; and the solitude in which Mr. Levett and Mrs. Williams had left him, rendered his life very gloomy. Mrs. Desmoulins, who still lived, was herself so very ill, that she could contribute very little to his relief. He, however, had none of that unsocial shyness which we commonly see in people afflicted with sickness. He did not hide his head from the world, in solitary abstraction; he did not deny himself to the visits of his friends and acquaintances; but at all times, when he was not overcome by sleep, was ready for conversation as in his best days.

1784: ÆTAT. 75.]—And now I am arrived at the last year of the life of *Samuel Johnson,* a year in which, although passed in severe indisposition, he nevertheless gave many evidences of the continuance of those wondrous powers of mind, which raised him so high in the intellectual world. His conversation and his letters of this year were in no respect inferiour to those of former years.

The following is a remarkable proof of his being alive to the most minute curiosities of literature.

'To Mr. Dilly, Bookseller, in the Poultry.

'Sir,

'There is in the world a set of books which used to be sold by
the booksellers on the bridge, and which I must entreat you to
procure me. They are called, *Burton's Books;* the title of one is
Admirable Curiosities, Rarities, and Wonders in England. I believe there are about five or six of them; they seem very proper to
allure backward readers; be so kind as to get them for me, and send
me them with the best printed edition of "Baxter's Call to the
Unconverted."

'I am, &c.

'Sam. Johnson.'

'Jan. 6, 1784.'

'To James Boswell, Esq.

'Dear Sir,

'I hear of many enquiries which your kindness has disposed
you to make after me. I have long intended you a long letter,
which perhaps the imagination of its length hindered me from beginning. I will, therefore, content myself with a shorter.

'Having promoted the institution of a new Club in the neighbourhood, at the house of an old servant of Thrale's, I went thither
to meet the company, and was seized with a spasmodick asthma so
violent, that with difficulty I got to my own house, in which I
have been confined eight or nine weeks, and from which I know
not when I shall be able to go even to church. The asthma, however, is not the worst. A dropsy gains ground upon me; my legs
and thighs are very much swollen with water, which I should be
content if I could keep there, but I am afraid that it will soon be
higher. My nights are very sleepless and very tedious. And yet I
am extremely afraid of dying.

'My physicians try to make me hope, that much of my malady is
the effect of cold, and that some degree at least of recovery is to be
expected from vernal breezes and summer suns. If my life is pro-
longed to autumn, I should be glad to try a warmer climate; though
how to travel with a diseased body, without a companion to conduct me, and with very little money, I do not well see. Ramsay has
recovered his limbs in Italy; and Fielding was sent to Lisbon,
where, indeed, he died; but he was, I believe, past hope when he
went. Think for me what I can do.

'I received your pamphlet, and when I write again may perhaps
tell you some opinion about it; but you will forgive a man struggling with disease his neglect of disputes, politicks, and pamphlets.

Let me have your prayers. My compliments to your lady, and young ones. Ask your physicians about my case: and desire Sir Alexander Dick to write me his opinion.

'I am, dear Sir, &c.

'SAM. JOHNSON.'

'Feb. 11, 1784.'

In consequence of Johnson's request that I should ask our physicians about his case, and desire Sir Alexander Dick to send his opinion, I transmitted him a letter from that very amiable Baronet, then in his eighty-first year, with his faculties as entire as ever; and mentioned his expressions to me in the note accompanying it: 'With my most affectionate wishes for Dr. Johnson's recovery, in which his friends, his country, and all mankind have so deep a stake:' and at the same time a full opinion upon his case by Dr. Gillespie, who, like Dr. Cullen, had the advantage of having passed through the gradations of surgery and pharmacy, and by study and practice had attained to such skill, that my father settled on him two hundred pounds a year for five years, and fifty pounds a year during his life, as an *honorarium* to secure his particular attendance. The opinion was conveyed in a letter to me, beginning, 'I am sincerely sorry for the bad state of health your very learned and illustrious friend, Dr. Johnson, labours under at present.'

'To JAMES BOSWELL, ESQ.

'DEAR SIR,

'PRESENTLY after I had sent away my last letter, I received your kind medical packet. I am very much obliged both to you and your physicians for your kind attention to my disease. Dr. Gillespie has sent me an excellent *consilium medicum,* all solid practical experimental knowledge. I am at present, in the opinion of my physicians, (Dr. Heberden and Dr. Brocklesby,) as well as my own, going on very hopefully. I have just begun to take vinegar of squills.[1] The powder hurt my stomach so much, that it could not be continued.

'Return Sir Alexander Dick my sincere thanks for his kind let-

---

[1] A solution in vinegar of the active ingredient of the bulbous root of *Urginea Scilla*. It is a cardiac stimulant, a powerful expectorant and a diuretic.

ter; and bring with you the rhubarb which he so tenderly offers me.

'I hope dear Mrs. Boswell is now quite well, and that no evil, either real or imaginary, now disturbs you.

                                            'I am, &c.
                                            'SAM. JOHNSON.'
'London, March 2, 1784.'

I also applied to three of the eminent physicians who had chairs in our celebrated school of medicine at Edinburgh, Doctors Cullen, Hope, and Monro, to each of whom I sent the following letter:

'DEAR SIR,

'DR. JOHNSON has been very ill for some time; and in a letter of anxious apprehension he writes to me, "Ask your physicians about my case."

'This, you see, is not authority for a regular consultation: but I have no doubt of your readiness to give your advice to a man so eminent, and who, in his Life of Garth, has paid your profession a just and elegant compliment: "I believe every man has found in physicians great liberality and dignity of sentiment, very prompt effusions of beneficence, and willingness to exert a lucrative art, where there is no hope of lucre."

'Dr. Johnson is aged seventy-four. Last summer he had a stroke of the palsy, from which he recovered almost entirely. He had, before that, been troubled with a catarrhous cough. This winter he was seized with a spasmodick asthma, by which he has been confined to his house for about three months. Dr. Brocklesby writes to me, that upon the least admission of cold, there is such a constriction upon his breast, that he cannot lie down in his bed, but is obliged to sit up all night, and gets rest and sometimes sleep, only by means of laudanum and syrup of poppies; and that there are œdematous tumours on his legs and thighs. Dr. Brocklesby trusts a good deal to the return of mild weather. Dr. Johnson says, that a dropsy gains ground upon him; and he seems to think that a warmer climate would do him good. I understand he is now rather better, and is using vinegar of squills. I am, with great esteem, dear Sir,

                        'Your most obedient humble servant,
                                            'JAMES BOSWELL.'
'March 7, 1784.'

All of them paid the most polite attention to my letter, and its venerable object. Dr. Cullen's words concerning him were,

'It would give me the greatest pleasure to be of any service to a man whom the publick properly esteem, and whom I esteem and respect as much as I do Dr. Johnson.' Dr. Hope's, 'Few people have à better claim on me than your friend, as hardly a day passes that I do not ask his opinion about this or that word.' Dr. Monro's, 'I most sincerely join you in sympathizing with that very worthy and ingenious character, from whom his country has derived much instruction and entertainment.'

Dr. Hope corresponded with his friend Dr. Brocklesby. Doctors Cullen and Monro wrote their opinions and prescriptions to me, which I afterwards carried with me to London, and, so far as they were encouraging, communicated to Johnson.

I wrote to him, March 28, from York, informing him that I was thus far on my way to him, but that news of the dissolution of Parliament having arrived, I was to hasten back to my own county, where I had carried an Address to his Majesty by a great majority, and had some intention of being a candidate to represent the county in Parliament.

'To JAMES BOSWELL, Esq.

'DEAR SIR,

'You could do nothing so proper as to haste back when you found the Parliament dissolved. With the influence which your Address must have gained you, it may reasonably be expected that your presence will be of importance, and your activity of effect.

'Your solicitude for me gives me that pleasure which every man feels from the kindness of such a friend; and it is with delight I relieve it by telling, that Dr. Brocklesby's account is true, and that I am, by the blessing of GOD, wonderfully relieved.

'You are entering upon a transaction which requires much prudence. You must endeavour to oppose without exasperating; to practise temporary hostility, without producing enemies for life. This is, perhaps, hard to be done; yet it has been done by many, and seems most likely to be effected by opposing merely upon general principles, without descending to personal or particular censures or objections. One thing I must enjoin you, which is seldom observed in the conduct of elections;—I must entreat you to be scrupulous in the use of strong liquors. One night's drunkenness may defeat the labours of forty days well employed. Be firm, but not clamorous; be active, but not malicious; and you may form such an interest, as may not only exalt yourself, but dignify your family.

'Let me hear, from time to time, how you are employed, and what progress you make.

'Make dear Mrs. Boswell, and all the young Boswells, the sincere compliments of, Sir, your affectionate humble servant,

'SAM. JOHNSON.'

'London, March 30, 1784.'

To Mr. Langton he wrote with that cordiality which was suitable to the long friendship which had subsisted between him and that gentleman.

March 27. 'Since you left me, I have continued in my own opinion, and in Dr. Brocklesby's, to grow better with respect to all my formidable and dangerous distempers; though to a body battered and shaken as mine has lately been, it is to be feared that weak attacks may be sometimes mischievous. I have, indeed, by standing carelessly at an open window, got a very troublesome cough, which it has been necessary to appease by opium, in larger quantities than I like to take, and I have not found it give way so readily as I expected; its obstinacy, however, seems at last disposed to submit to the remedy, and I know not whether I should then have a right to complain of any morbid sensation. My asthma is, I am afraid, constitutional and incurable; but it is only occasional, and unless it be excited by labour or by cold, gives me no molestation, nor does it lay very close siege to life; for Sir John Floyer, whom the physical race consider as authour of one of the best books upon it, panted on to ninety, as was supposed; and why were we content with supposing a fact so interesting, of a man so conspicuous, because he corrupted, at perhaps seventy or eighty, the register, that he might pass for younger than he was? He was not much less than eighty, when to a man of rank who modestly asked him his age, he answered, "Go look;" though he was in general a man of civility and elegance.

'The ladies, I find, are at your house all well, except Miss Langton, who will probably soon recover her health by light suppers. Let her eat at dinner as she will, but not take a full stomach to bed. Pay my sincere respects to the two principal ladies in your house; and when you write to dear Miss Langton in Lincolnshire, let her know that I mean not to break our league of friendship, and that I have a set of Lives for her, when I have the means of sending it.'

'To the Reverend Dr. Taylor, Ashbourne, Derbyshire.

'Dear Sir,

'What can be the reason that I hear nothing from you? I hope nothing disables you from writing. What I have seen, and what I have felt, gives me reason to fear every thing. Do not omit giving me the comfort of knowing, that after all my losses I have yet a friend left.

'I want every comfort. My life is very solitary and very cheerless. Though it has pleased God wonderfully to deliver me from the dropsy, I am yet very weak, and have not passed the door since the 13th of December. I hope for some help from warm weather, which will surely come in time.

'I could not have the consent of the physicians to go to church yesterday; I therefore received the holy Sacrament at home, in the room where I communicated with dear Mrs. Williams, a little before her death. O! my friend, the approach of death is very dreadful. I am afraid to think on that which I know I cannot avoid. It is vain to look round and round for that help which cannot be had. Yet we hope and hope, and fancy that he who has lived to-day may live to-morrow. But let us learn to derive our hope only from God.

'In the mean time, let us be kind to one another. I have no friend now living but you and Mr. Hector, that was the friend of my youth. Do not neglect, dear Sir,

'Yours affectionately,

'Sam. Johnson.'

'London, Easter-Monday,
    April 12, 1784.'

What follows is a beautiful specimen of his gentleness and complacency to a young lady his god-child, one of the daughters of his friend Mr. Langton, then I think in her seventh year. He took the trouble to write it in a large round hand, nearly resembling printed characters, that she might have the satisfaction of reading it herself. The original lies before me, but shall be faithfully restored to her; and I dare say will be preserved by her as a jewel as long as she lives.

'To Miss Jane Langton, in Rochester, Kent.

'My Dearest Miss Jenny,

'I am sorry that your pretty letter has been so long without being answered; but, when I am not pretty well, I do not always write plain enough for young ladies. I am glad, my dear, to see that you write so well, and hope that you mind your pen, your book, and your needle, for they are all necessary. Your books will give you knowledge, and make you respected; and your needle will find you useful employment when you do not care to read. When you are a little older, I hope you will be very diligent in learning arithmetick; and, above all, that through your whole life you will carefully say your prayers, and read your Bible.

'I am, my dear,

'Your most humble servant,

'SAM. JOHNSON.'

'May 10, 1784.'

On Wednesday, May 5, I arrived in London, and next morning had the pleasure to find Dr. Johnson greatly recovered. I but just saw him; for a coach was waiting to carry him to Islington, to the house of his friend the Reverend Mr. Strahan, where he went sometimes for the benefit of good air, which, notwithstanding his having formerly laughed at the general opinion upon the subject, he now acknowledged was conducive to health.

One morning afterwards, when I found him alone, he communicated to me, with solemn earnestness, a very remarkable circumstance which had happened in the course of his illness, when he was much distressed by the dropsy. He had shut himself up, and employed a day in particular exercises of religion, —fasting, humiliation, and prayer. On a sudden he obtained extraordinary relief, for which he looked up to Heaven with grateful devotion. He made no direct inference from this fact; but from his manner of telling it, I could perceive that it appeared to him as something more than an incident in the common course of events.

On Sunday, May 9, I found Colonel Vallancy, the celebrated antiquarian and engineer of Ireland, with him. On Monday, the 10th, I dined with him at Mr. Paradise's, where was a large company; Mr. Bryant, Mr. Joddrel, Mr. Hawkins Browne, &c. On Thursday, the 13th, I dined with him at Mr. Joddrel's, with another large company; the Bishop of Exeter, Lord Monboddo, Mr. Murphy, &c.

On Saturday, May 15, I dined with him at Dr. Brocklesby's, where were Colonel Vallancy, Mr. Murphy, and that ever-

cheerful companion Mr. Devaynes, apothecary to his Majesty.
Of these days, and others on which I saw him, I have no
memorials, except the general recollection of his being able
and animated in conversation, and appearing to relish society
as much as the youngest man. I find only these three small
particulars:—One, when a person was mentioned, who said,
'I have lived fifty-one years in this world without having had
ten minutes of uneasiness;' he exclaimed, 'The man who says
so, lies: he attempts to impose on human credulity.' The
Bishop of Exeter in vain observed, that men were very different. His Lordship's manner was not impressive, and I learnt
afterwards that Johnson did not find out that the person who
talked to him was a Prelate; if he had, I doubt not that he
would have treated him with more respect; for once talking of
George Psalmanazar, whom he reverenced for his piety, he
said, 'I should as soon think of contradicting a *Bishop*.' One
of the company provoked him greatly by doing what he could
least of all bear, which was quoting something of his own writing, against what he then maintained. 'What, Sir, (cried the
gentleman,) do you say to

> "The busy day, the peaceful night,
>   Unfelt, uncounted, glided by?" '

Johnson finding himself thus presented as giving an instance
of a man who had lived without uneasiness, was much
offended, for he looked upon such quotation as unfair. His
anger burst out in an unjustifiable retort, insinuating that the
gentleman's remark was a sally of ebriety; 'Sir, there is one passion I would advise you to command: when you have drunk
out that glass, don't drink another.' Here was exemplified
what Goldsmith said of him, with the aid of a very witty image
from one of Cibber's Comedies: 'There is no arguing with
Johnson; for if his pistol misses fire, he knocks you down with
the butt end of it.'—Another was this: when a gentleman of
eminence in the literary world was violently censured for attacking people by anonymous paragraphs in newspapers; he,
from the spirit of contradiction as I thought, took up his defence, and said, 'Come, come, this is not so terrible a crime; he
means only to vex them a little. I do not say that I should do it;

but there is a great difference between him and me.' Another, when I told him that a young and handsome Countess had said to me, 'I should think that to be praised by Dr. Johnson would make one a fool all one's life;' and that I answered, 'Madam, I shall make him a fool to-day, by repeating this to him,' he said, 'I am too old to be made a fool; but if you say I am made a fool, I shall not deny it. I am much pleased with a compliment, especially from a pretty woman.'

On the evening of Saturday, May 15, he was in fine spirits, at our Essex-Head Club. He told us, 'I dined yesterday at Mrs. Garrick's, with Mrs. Carter, Miss Hannah More, and Miss Fanny Burney. Three such women are not to be found: I know not where I could find a fourth, except Mrs. Lennox, who is superiour to them all.' *Boswell.* 'What! had you them all to yourself, Sir?' *Johnson.* 'I had them all as much as they were had; but it might have been better had there been more company there.' *Boswell.* 'Might not Mrs. Montagu have been a fourth?' *Johnson.* 'Sir, Mrs. Montagu does not make a trade of her wit; but Mrs. Montagu is a very extraordinary woman; she has a constant stream of conversation, and it is always impregnated; it has always meaning.' *Boswell.* 'Mr. Burke has a constant stream of conversation.' *Johnson.* 'Yes, Sir; if a man were to go by chance at the same time with Burke under a shed, to shun a shower, he would say—"this is an extraordinary man." If Burke should go into a stable to see his horse drest, the ostler would say—we have had an extraordinary man here. When Burke does not descend to be merry, his conversation is very superiour indeed. There is no proportion between the powers which he shews in serious talk and in jocularity. When he lets himself down to that, he is in the kennel.' Mr. Windham now said low to me, that he differed from our great friend in this observation; for that Mr. Burke was often very happy in his merriment. It would not have been right for either of us to have contradicted Johnson at this time, in a Society all of whom did not know and value Mr. Burke as much as we did. It might have occasioned something more rough, and at any rate would probably have checked the flow of Johnson's good-humour. He called to us with a sudden air of exultation, as the thought started into his mind, 'O! Gentlemen, I must tell you a very great thing. The Empress of Russia has ordered the "Rambler" to be translated into the Russian language: so I shall be read on the banks of the Wolga. Horace boasts that his fame would extend as far as the banks of the Rhone; now the Wolga is farther from me than the Rhone was from Horace.' *Boswell.* 'You must certainly be pleased with this, Sir.' *Johnson.* 'I am pleased, Sir, to be sure. A man is pleased to find he has succeeded in that which he has endeavoured to do.'

One of the company mentioned his having seen a noble person driving in his carriage, and looking exceedingly well, notwithstanding his great age. *Johnson.* 'Ah, Sir; that is nothing. Bacon observes, that a stout healthy old man is like a tower undermined.'

On Sunday, May 16, I found him alone; he talked of Mrs. Thrale with much concern, saying, 'Sir, she has done every thing wrong, since Thrale's bridle was off her neck;' and was proceeding to mention some circumstances which have since been the subject of publick discussion, when he was interrupted by the arrival of Dr. Douglas, now Bishop of Salisbury.

Johnson, talking of the fear of death, said, 'Some people are not afraid, because they look upon salvation as the effect of an absolute decree, and think they feel in themselves the marks of sanctification. Others, and those the most rational in my opinion, look upon salvation as conditional; and as they never can be sure that they have complied with the conditions, they are afraid.'

On Wednesday, May 19, I sat a part of the evening with him, by ourselves. I observed, that the death of our friends might be a consolation against the fear of our own dissolution, because we might have more friends in the other world than in this. He perhaps felt this as a reflection upon his apprehension as to death; and said, with heat, 'How can a man know *where* his departed friends are, or whether they will be his friends in the other world? How many friendships have you known formed upon principles of virtue? Most friendships are formed by caprice or by chance, mere confederacies in vice or leagues in folly.'

He charged Mr. Langton with what he thought want of judgement upon an interesting occasion. 'When I was ill, (said

ie) I desired he would tell me sincerely in what he thought
my life was faulty. Sir, he brought me a sheet of paper, on
which he had written down several texts of Scripture, recommending christian charity. And when I questioned him what
occasion I had given for such an animadversion, all that he
could say amounted to this,—that I sometimes contradicted
people in conversation. Now what harm does it do to any man
to be contradicted?' *Boswell.* 'I suppose he meant the *manner*
of doing it; roughly,—and harshly.' *Johnson.* 'And who is the
worse for that?' *Boswell.* 'It hurts people of weak nerves.' *Johnson.* 'I know no such weak-nerved people.' Mr. Burke, to whom
I related this conference, said, 'It is well, if when a man comes
to die, he has nothing heavier upon his conscience than having
been a little rough in conversation.'

Johnson, at the time when the paper was presented to him,
though at first pleased with the attention of his friend, whom
he thanked in an earnest manner, soon exclaimed, in a loud
and angry tone, 'What is your drift, Sir?' Sir Joshua Reynolds
pleasantly observed, that it was a scene for a comedy, to see a
penitent get into a violent passion and belabour his confessor.

He had now a great desire to go to Oxford, as his first
jaunt after his illness; we talked of it for some days, and I had
promised to accompany him. He was impatient and fretful
tonight, because I did not at once agree to go with him on
Thursday. When I considered how ill he had been, and what
allowance should be made for the influence of sickness upon
his temper, I resolved to indulge him, though with some inconvenience to myself, as I wished to attend the musical meeting in honour of Handel, in Westminster-Abbey, on the following Saturday.

On Thursday, June 3, the Oxford post-coach took us up in
the morning at Bolt-court. The other two passengers were Mrs
Beresford and her daughter, two very agreeable ladies from
America; they were going to Worcestershire, where they then
resided. Frank had been sent by his master the day before to
take places for us; and I found from the way-bill, that Dr.
Johnson had made our names be put down. Mrs. Beresford,
who had read it, whispered me, 'Is this the great Dr. Johnson?'
I told her it was; so she was then prepared to listen. As she

soon happened to mention in a voice so low that Johnson did not hear it, that her husband had been a member of the American Congress, I cautioned her to beware of introducing that subject, as she must know how very violent Johnson was against the people of that country. He talked a great deal, but I am sorry I have preserved little of the conversation. Miss Beresford was so much charmed, that she said to me aside, 'How he does talk! Every sentence is an essay.' She amused herself in the coach with knotting; he would scarcely allow this species of employment any merit. 'Next to mere idleness (said he) I think knotting is to be reckoned in the scale of insignificance; though I once attempted to learn knotting. Dempster's sister (looking to me) endeavoured to teach me it; but I made no progress.'

I was surprised at his talking without reserve in the publick post-coach of the state of his affairs; 'I have (said he) about the world I think above a thousand pounds, which I intend shall afford Frank an annuity of seventy pounds a year.' Indeed his openness with people at a first interview was remarkable. He said once to Mr. Langton, 'I think I am like Squire Richard in "The Journey to London," "*I'm never strange in a strange place.*"' He was truly *social*. He strongly censured what is much too common in England among persons of condition, —maintaining an absolute silence, when unknown to each other; as for instance, when occasionally brought together in a room before the master or mistress of the house has appeared. 'Sir, that is being so uncivilised as not to understand the common rights of humanity.'

At the inn where we stopped he was exceedingly dissatisfied with some roast mutton which we had for dinner. The ladies I saw wondered to see the great philosopher, whose wisdom and wit they had been admiring all the way, get into ill-humour from such a cause. He scolded the waiter, saying, 'It is as bad as bad can be: it is ill-fed, ill-killed, ill-kept, and ill-drest.'

He bore the journey very well, and seemed to feel himself elevated as he approached Oxford, that magnificent and venerable seat of Learning, Orthodoxy, and Toryism. Frank came in the heavy coach, in readiness to attend him; and we were received with the most polite hospitality at the house of his old friend Dr. Adams, Master of Pembroke College, who had given us a kind invitation. Before we were set down, I communicated to Johnson my having engaged to return to London directly, for the reason I have mentioned, but that I would hasten back to him again. He was pleased that I had made this journey merely to keep him company.

I fulfilled my intention by going to London, and returned to Oxford on Wednesday the 9th of June, when I was happy to find myself again in the same agreeable circle at Pembroke College, with the comfortable prospect of making some stay. Johnson welcomed my return with more than ordinary glee.

After dinner, when one of us talked of there being a great enmity between Whig and Tory;—*Johnson.* 'Why not so much, I think, unless when they come into competition with each other. There is none when they are only common acquaintance, none when they are of different sexes. A Tory will marry into a Whig family, and a Whig into a Tory family, without any reluctance. But indeed, in a matter of much more concern than political tenets, and that is religion, men and women do not concern themselves much about difference of opinion; and ladies set no value on the moral character of men who pay their addresses to them; the greatest profligate will be as well received as the man of the greatest virtue, and this by a very good woman, by a woman who says her prayers three times a day.' Our ladies endeavoured to defend their sex from this charge; but he roared them down! 'No, no; a lady will take Jonathan Wild as readily as St. Austin, if he has threepence more; and, what is worse, her parents will give her to him. Women have a perpetual envy of our vices; they are less vicious than we, not from choice, but because we restrict them; they are the slaves of order and fashion; their virtue is of more consequence to us than our own, so far as concerns this world.'

Miss Adams mentioned a gentleman of licentious character, and said, 'Suppose I had a mind to marry that gentleman, would my parents consent?' *Johnson.* 'Yes, they'd consent, and you'd go. You'd go though they did not consent.' *Miss Adams.* 'Perhaps their opposing might make me go.' *Johnson.* 'O, very well; you'd take one whom you think a bad man, to have the pleasure of vexing your parents. You put me in mind of Dr Barrowby, the physician, who was very fond of swine's flesh One day, when he was eating it, he said, 'I wish I was a Jew.'— 'Why so? (said somebody); the Jews are not allowed to eat you favourite meat.'—'Because, (said he,) I should then have the gust of eating it, with the pleasure of sinning.'—Johnson then proceeded in his declamation.

Dr. Wall, physician at Oxford, drank tea with us. Johnson had in general a peculiar pleasure in the company of physicians, which was certainly not abated by the conversation of this learned, ingenious, and pleasing gentleman. Johnson said, 'It is wonderful how little good Radcliffe's travelling fellowships have done. I know nothing that has been imported by them; yet many additions to our medical knowledge might be got in foreign countries. Inoculation, for instance, has saved more lives than war destroys: and the cures performed by the Peruvian-bark[1] are innumerable. But it is in vain to send our travelling physicians to France, and Italy, and Germany, for all that is known there is known here; I'd send them out of Christendom; I'd send them among barbarous nations.'

On Friday, June 11, we talked at breakfast, of forms of prayer. *Johnson.* 'I know of no good prayers but those in the "Book of Common Prayer."' *Dr. Adams*, (in a very earnest manner): 'I wish, Sir, you would compose some family prayers.' We all now gathered about him, and two or three of us at a time joined in pressing him to execute this plan. He seemed to be a little displeased at the manner of our importunity, and in great agitation called out, 'Do not talk thus of what is so aweful. I know not what time GOD will allow me in this world. There are many things which I wish to do.' Some of us persisted, and Dr. Adams said, 'I never was more serious about any thing in my life.' *Johnson.* 'Let me alone, let me alone; I am overpowered.' And then he put his hands before his face, and reclined for some time upon the table.

Dr. Johnson and I went in Dr. Adams's coach to dine with Dr. Nowell, Principal of St. Mary Hall, at his beautiful villa at Iffley, on the banks of the Isis, about two miles from Oxford. While we were upon the road, I had the resolution to ask

[1] Cinchona bark, whence quinine is now derived.

Johnson whether he thought that the roughness of his manner had been an advantage or not, and if he would not have done more good if he had been more gentle. I proceeded to answer myself thus: 'Perhaps it has been of advantage, as it has given weight to what you said: you could not, perhaps, have talked with such authority without it.' *Johnson.* 'No, Sir; I have done more good as I am. Obscenity and Impiety have always been repressed in my company.' *Boswell.* 'True, Sir; and that is more than can be said of every Bishop. Greater liberties have been taken in the presence of a Bishop, though a very good man, from his being milder, and therefore not commanding such awe. Yet, Sir, many people who might have been benefited by your conversation, have been frightened away. A worthy friend of ours has told me, that he has often been afraid to talk to you.' *Johnson.* 'Sir, he need not have been afraid, if he had any thing rational to say. If he had not, it was better he did not talk.'

We talked of a certain clergyman of extraordinary character, who by exerting his talents in writing on temporary topicks, and displaying uncommon intrepidity, had raised himself to affluence. I maintained that we ought not to be indignant at his success; for merit of every sort was entitled to reward. *Johnson.* 'Sir, I will not allow this man to have merit. No, Sir; what he has is rather the contrary; I will, indeed, allow him courage, and on this account we so far give him credit. We have more respect for a man who robs boldly on the highway, than for a fellow who jumps out of a ditch, and knocks you down behind your back. Courage is a quality so necessary for maintaining virtue, that it is always respected, even when it is associated with vice.'

I censured the coarse invectives which were become fashionable in the House of Commons, and said that if members of parliament must attack each other personally in the heat of debate, it should be done more genteelly. *Johnson.* 'No, Sir; that would be much worse. Abuse is not so dangerous when there is no vehicle of wit or delicacy, no subtle conveyance. The difference between coarse and refined abuse is as the difference between being bruised by a club, and wounded by a poisoned arrow.'

On Saturday, June 12, there drank tea with us at Dr. Adams's, Mr. John Henderson, student of Pembroke-College, celebrated for his wonderful acquirements in Alchymy, Judicial Astrology, and other abstruse and curious learning; and the Reverend Herbert Croft, who, I am afraid, was somewhat mortified by Dr. Johnson's not being highly pleased with some 'Family Discourses,' which he had printed; they were in too familiar a style to be approved of by so manly a mind. I have no note of this evening's conversation, except a single fragment. When I mentioned Thomas Lord Lyttelton's vision, the prediction of the time of his death, and its exact fulfilment:— *Johnson.* 'It is the most extraordinary thing that has happened in my day. I heard it with my own ears, from his uncle, Lord Westcote. I am so glad to have every evidence of the spiritual world, that I am willing to believe it.' *Dr. Adams.* 'You have evidence enough; good evidence, which needs not such support.' *Johnson.* 'I like to have more.'

Mr. Henderson, with whom I had sauntered in the venerable walks of Merton-College, and found him a very learned and pious man, supped with us. Dr. Johnson surprised him not a little, by acknowledging with a look of horrour, that he was much oppressed by the fear of death. The amiable Dr. Adams suggested that GOD was infinitely good. *Johnson.* 'That he is infinitely good, as far as the perfection of his nature will allow, I certainly believe; but it is necessary for good upon the whole, that individuals should be punished. As to an *individual*, therefore, he is not infinitely good; and as I cannot be *sure* that I have fulfilled the conditions on which salvation is granted, I am afraid I may be one of those who shall be damned.' (looking dismally.) *Dr. Adams.* 'What do you mean by damned?' *Johnson.* (passionately and loudly) 'Sent to Hell, Sir, and punished everlastingly.' *Dr. Adams.* 'I don't believe that doctrine.' *Johnson.* 'Hold, Sir; do you believe that some will be punished at all?' *Dr. Adams.* 'Being excluded from Heaven will be a punishment; yet there may be no great positive suffering.' *Johnson.* 'Well, Sir; but, if you admit any degree of punishment, there is an end of your argument for infinite goodness simply considered; for, infinite goodness would inflict no punishment whatever. There is not infinite goodness physically considered; morally there is.' *Boswell.* 'But may not a man attain to such a degree of hope as not to be uneasy from the fear of death?' *Johnson.* 'A man may have such a degree of hope as to keep him quiet. You see I am not quiet, from the vehemence with which I talk; but I do not despair.' *Mrs. Adams.* 'You seem, Sir, to forget the merits of our Redeemer.' *Johnson.* 'Madam, I do not forget the merits of my Redeemer; but my Redeemer has said that he will set some on his right hand and some on his left.'—He was in gloomy agitation, and said, 'I'll have no more on't.'

From the subject of death we passed to discourse of life, whether it was upon the whole more happy or miserable. Johnson was decidedly for the balance of misery.

It was observed to Dr. Johnson, that it seemed strange that he, who has so often delighted his company by his lively and brilliant conversation, should say he was miserable. *Johnson.* 'Alas! it is all outside; I may be cracking my joke, and cursing the sun. *Sun, how I hate thy beams!*' I knew not well what to think of this declaration; whether to hold it as a genuine picture of his mind, or as the effect of his persuading himself contrary to fact, that the position which he had assumed as to human unhappiness, was true.

On Sunday, June 13, our philosopher was calm at breakfast. There was something exceedingly pleasing in our leading a College life, without restraint, and with superiour elegance, in consequence of our living in the Master's house, and having the company of ladies. Mrs. Kennicot related, in his presence, a lively saying of Dr. Johnson to Miss Hannah More, who had expressed a wonder that the poet who had written 'Paradise Lost,' should write such poor Sonnets:—'Milton, Madam, was a genius that could cut a Colossus from a rock; but could not carve heads upon cherry-stones.'

We talked of the casuistical question, Whether it was allowable at any time to depart from *Truth? Johnson.* 'The general rule is, that Truth should never be violated, because it is of the utmost importance to the comfort of life, that we should have a full security by mutual faith; and occasional inconveniencies should be willingly suffered that we may preserve it. There must, however, be some exceptions. If, for instance, a murderer should ask you which way a man is gone, you may tell him what is not true, because you are under a previous obligation not to betray a man to a murderer.' *Boswell.* 'Supposing the person who wrote *Junius* were asked whether he was the authour, might he deny it?' *Johnson.* 'I don't know what to say to this. If you were *sure* that he wrote *Junius,* would you, if he denied it, think as well of him afterwards? Yet it may be urged, that what a man has no right to ask, you may refuse to communicate; and there is no other effectual mode of preserving a secret, and an important secret, the discovery of which may be very hurtful to you, but a flat denial; for if you are silent, or hesitate, or evade, it will be held equivalent to a confession. But stay, Sir; here is another case. Supposing the authour had told me confidentially that he had written *Junius,* and I were asked if he had, I should hold myself at liberty to deny it, as being under a previous promise, express or implied, to conceal it. Now what I ought to do for the authour, may I not do for myself? But I deny the lawfulness of telling a lie to a sick man for fear of alarming him. You have no business with consequences; you are to tell the truth. Besides, you are not sure what effect your telling him that he is in danger may have. It may bring his distemper to a crisis, and that may cure him. Of all lying, I have the greatest abhorrence of this, because I believe it has been frequently practised on myself.'

I cannot help thinking that there is much weight in the opinion of those who have held, that Truth, as an eternal and immutable principle, ought, upon no account whatever, to be violated, from supposed previous or superiour obligations, of which every man being to judge for himself, there is great danger that we may too often, from partial motives, persuade ourselves that they exist; and probably whatever extraordinary instances may sometimes occur, where some evil may be prevented by violating this noble principle, it would be found that human happiness would, upon the whole, be more perfect were Truth universally preserved.

In the morning of Tuesday, June 15, while we sat at Dr. Adams's, we talked of a printed letter from the Reverend Herbert Croft, to a young gentleman who had been his pupil, in which he advised him to read to the end of whatever books

he should begin to read. *Johnson.* 'This is surely a strange
advice; you may as well resolve that whatever men you happen
to get acquainted with, you are to keep to them for life. A
book may be good for nothing; or there may be only one thing
in it worth knowing; are we to read it all through? These
Voyages, (pointing to the three large volumes of "Voyages
to the South Sea," which were just come out) *who* will read
them through? A man had better work his way before the
mast, than read them through; they will be eaten by rats and
mice, before they are read through. There can be little entertainment in such books; one set of Savages is like another.'
Boswell. 'I do not think the people of Otaheité can be reckoned
Savages.' *Johnson.* 'Don't cant in defence of Savages.' *Boswell.*
'They have the art of navigation.' *Johnson.* 'A dog or a cat can
swim.' *Boswell.* 'They carve very ingeniously.' *Johnson.* 'A cat
can scratch, and a child with a nail can scratch.'

Upon his mentioning that when he came to College he
wrote his first exercise twice over; but never did so afterwards;
Miss Adams. 'I suppose, Sir, you could not make them better?' *Johnson.* 'Yes, Madam, to be sure, I could make them
better. Thought is better than no thought.' *Miss Adams.* 'Do
you think, Sir, you could make your Ramblers better?' *Johnson.*
'Certainly I could.' *Boswell.* 'I'll lay a bet, Sir, you cannot.'
Johnson. 'But I will, Sir, if I choose. I shall make the best of
them you shall pick out, better.' *Boswell.* 'But you may add to
them. I will not allow of that.' *Johnson.* 'Nay, Sir, there are
three ways of making them better;—putting out,—adding,-
or correcting.'

On Wednesday, June 19, Dr. Johnson and I returned to
London; he was not well to-day, and said very little, employing
himself chiefly in reading Euripides. He expressed some displeasure at me, for not observing sufficiently the various objects
upon the road. 'If I had your eyes, Sir, (said he) I should count
the passengers.' [1] It was wonderful how accurate his observation
of visual objects was, notwithstanding his imperfect eyesight,
owing to a habit of attention. That he was much satisfied with
the respect paid to him at Dr. Adams's, is thus attested by himself: 'I returned last night from Oxford, after a fortnight's

[1] i.e., those who passed by.

abode with Dr. Adams, who treated me as well as I could expect or wish; and he that contents a sick man, a man whom it is impossible to please, has surely done his part well.'

After his return to London from this excursion, I saw him frequently, but have few memorandums: I shall therefore here insert some particulars which I collected at various times.

Johnson was present when a tragedy was read, in which there occurred this line:

'Who rules o'er freemen should himself be free.'

The company having admired it much, 'I cannot agree with you (said Johnson:) It might as well be said,

"Who drives fat oxen should himself be fat."

Johnson having argued for some time with a pertinacious gentleman; his opponent, who had talked in a very puzzling manner, happened to say, 'I don't understand you, Sir:' upon which Johnson observed, 'Sir, I have found you an argument; but I am not obliged to find you an understanding.'

Talking to me of Horry Walpole, (as Horace late Earl of Orford was often called,) Johnson allowed that he got together a great many curious little things, and told them in an elegant manner. Mr. Walpole thought Johnson a more amiable character after reading his Letters to Mrs. Thrale: but never was one of the true admirers of that great man. We may suppose a prejudice conceived, if he ever heard Johnson's account that when he made the speeches in parliament for the Gentleman's Magazine, 'he always took care to put Sir Robert Walpole in the wrong, and to say every thing he could against the electorate of Hanover.'

It may be observed, that his frequent use of the expression, *No, Sir,* was not always to intimate contradiction; for he would say so, when he was about to enforce an affirmative proposition which had not been denied. I used to consider it as a kind of flag of defiance; as if he had said, 'Any argument you may offer against this, is not just. No, Sir, it is not.' It was like Falstaff's 'I deny your Major.'

Sir Joshua Reynolds having said that he took the altitude of a man's taste by his stories and his wit, and of his understanding by the remarks which he repeated; being always sure that he must be a weak man who quotes common things with an emphasis as if they were oracles;—Johnson agreed with him; and Sir Joshua having also observed that the real character of a man was found out by his amusements,—Johnson added, 'Yes, Sir; no man is a hypocrite in his pleasures.'

It may be worth remarking, among the *minutiæ* of my collection, that Johnson was once drawn to serve in the militia, the Trained Bands of the City of London, and that Mr. Rackstrow, of the Museum in Fleet-street, was his Colonel. It may be believed he did not serve in person; but the idea, with all its circumstances, is certainly laughable. He upon that occasion provided himself with a musket, and with a sword and belt, which I have seen hanging in his closet.

He was very constant to those whom he once employed, if they gave him no reason to be displeased. When somebody talked of being imposed on in the purchase of tea and sugar, and such articles: 'That will not be the case, (said he,) if you go to a *stately shop*, as I always do. In such a shop it is not worth their while to take a petty advantage.'

The difference, he observed, between a well-bred and an ill-bred man is this: 'One immediately attracts your liking, the other your aversion. You love the one till you find reason to hate him; you hate the other till you find reason to love him.'

He seemed to take a pleasure in speaking in his own style; for when he had carelessly missed it, he would repeat the thought translated into it. Talking of the Comedy of 'The Rehearsal,' he said, 'It has not wit enough to keep it sweet.' This was easy;—he therefore caught himself, and pronounced a more rounded sentence; 'It has not vitality enough to preserve it from putrefaction.'

Though he had no taste for painting, he admired much the manner in which Sir Joshua Reynolds treated of his art, in his 'Discourses to the Royal Academy.' He observed one day of a passage in them, 'I think I might as well have said this myself:' and once when Mr. Langton was sitting by him, he read one of them very eagerly, and expressed himself thus: 'Very well, Master Reynolds; very well, indeed. But it will not be understood.'

His generous humanity to the miserable was almost beyond example. The following instance is well attested: Coming home late one night, he found a poor woman lying in the street so much exhausted that she could not walk; he took her upon his back, and carried her to his house, where he discovered that she was one of those wretched females who had fallen into the lowest state of vice, poverty, and disease. Instead of harshly upbraiding her, he had her taken care of with all tenderness for a long time, at considerable expence, till she was restored to health, and endeavoured to put her into a virtuous way of living.

He once in his life was known to have uttered what is called a *bull*: Sir Joshua Reynolds, when they were riding together in Devonshire, complained that he had a very bad horse, for that even when going down hill he moved slowly step by step. 'Ay (said Johnson,) and when he *goes* up hill, he *stands still*.'

He had a great aversion to gesticulating in company. He called once to a gentleman who offended him in that point, 'Don't *attitudenise*.' And when another gentleman thought he was giving additional force to what he uttered, by expressive movements of his hands, Johnson fairly seized them, and held them down.

On Tuesday, June 22, I dined with him at *The Literary Club*, the last time of his being in that respectable society. The other members present were the Bishop of St. Asaph, Lord Eliot, Lord Palmerston, Dr. Fordyce, and Mr. Malone. He looked ill; but had such a manly fortitude, that he did not trouble the company with melancholy complaints. They all shewed evident marks of kind concern about him, with which he was much pleased, and he exerted himself to be as entertaining as his indisposition allowed him.

The anxiety of his friends to preserve so estimable a life, as long as human means might be supposed to have influence, made them plan for him a retreat from the severity of a British winter, to the mild climate of Italy. This scheme was at last brought to a serious resolution at General Paoli's, where I had often talked of it. One essential matter, however, I understood was necessary to be previously settled, which was obtaining such an addition to his income, as would be sufficient to

enable him to defray the expence in a manner becoming the
first literary character of a great nation, and, independent of
all his other merits, the Authour of *The Dictionary of the
English Language.* The person to whom I above all others
thought I should apply to negociate this buisness, was the Lord
Chancellor, because I knew that he highly valued Johnson,
and that Johnson highly valued his Lordship; so that it was
no degradation of my illustrious friend to solicit for him the
favour of such a man.

I first consulted with Sir Joshua Reynolds, who perfectly
coincided in opinion with me; and I therefore, though personally very little known to his Lordship, wrote to him, stating
the case, and requesting his good offices for Dr. Johnson. I
mentioned that I was obliged to set out for Scotland early in
the following week, so that if his Lordship should have any
commands for me as to this pious negociation, he would be
pleased to send them before that time; otherwise Sir Joshua
Reynolds would give all attention to it.

This application was made not only without any suggestion
on the part of Johnson himself, but was utterly unknown to
him, nor had he the smallest suspicion of it. Any insinuations,
therefore, which since his death have been thrown out, as if
he had stooped to ask what was superfluous, are without any
foundation. But, had he asked it, it would not have been superfluous; for though the money he had saved proved to be more
than his friends imagined, or than I believe he himself, in his
carelessness concerning worldly matters, knew it to be, had
he travelled upon the Continent, an augmentation of his income would by no means have been unnecessary.

On Wednesday, June 23, I visited him in the morning, after
having been present at the shocking sight of fifteen men executed before Newgate. I said to him, I was sure that human
life was not machinery, that is to say, a chain of fatality planned
and directed by the Supreme Being, as it had in it so much
wickedness and misery, so many instances of both, as that by
which my mind was now clouded. Were it machinery it would
be better than it is in these respects, though less noble, as not
being a system of moral government. He agreed with me now,
as he always did, upon the great question of the liberty of the

human will, which has been in all ages perplexed with so much sophistry. 'But, Sir, as to the doctrine of Necessity, no man believes it. If a man should give me arguments that I do not see, though I could not answer them, should I believe that I do not see?' It will be observed, that Johnson at all times made the just distinction between doctrines *contrary* to reason, and doctrines *above* reason.

On Thursday, June 24, I dined with him at Mr. Dilly's. I recollect nothing that passed this day, except Johnson's quickness, who, when Dr. Beattie observed, as something remarkable which had happened to him, that he had chanced to see both No. 1, and No. 1000, of the hackney-coaches, the first and the last; 'Why, Sir, (said Johnson,) there is an equal chance for one's seeing those two numbers as any other two.'

On Friday, June 25, I dined with him at General Paoli's, where, he says in one of his letters to Mrs. Thrale, 'I love to dine.' There was a variety of dishes much to his taste, of all which he seemed to me to eat so much, that I was afraid he might be hurt by it; and I whispered to the General my fear, and begged he might not press him. 'Alas! (said the General,) see how very ill he looks; he can live but a very short time. Would you refuse any slight gratifications to a man under sentence of death? There is a humane custom in Italy, by which persons in that melancholy situation are indulged with having whatever they like best to eat and drink, even with expensive delicacies.'

On Sunday, June 27, I found him rather better. I mentioned to him a young man who was going to Jamaica with his wife and children, in expectation of being provided for by two of her brothers settled in that island, one a clergyman, and the other a physician. *Johnson.* 'It is a wild scheme, Sir, unless he has a positive and deliberate invitation. There was a poor girl, who used to come about me, who had a cousin in Barbadoes, that, in a letter to her, expressed a wish she should come out to that Island, and expatiated on the comforts and happiness of her situation. The poor girl went out: her cousin was much surprised, and asked her how she could think of coming. "Because (said she), you invited me."—"Not I," answered the cousin. The letter was then produced. "I see it is true, (said she,) that I did invite you: but I did not think you would come." They lodged her in an out-house, where she passed her time miserably; and as soon as she had an opportunity she returned to England. Always tell this, when you hear of people going abroad to relations, upon a notion of being well received. In the case which you mention, it is probable the clergyman spends all he gets, and the physician does not know how much he is to get.'

We this day dined at Sir Joshua Reynolds's, with General Paoli, Lord Eliot, (formerly Mr. Eliot, of Port Eliot,) Dr. Beattie, and some other company. Talking of Lord Chesterfield;—*Johnson.* 'His manner was exquisitely elegant, and he had more knowledge than I expected.' *Boswell.* 'Did you find, Sir, his conversation to be of a superiour style?' *Johnson.* 'Sir, in the conversation which I had with him I had the best right to superiority, for it was upon philology and literature.' Lord Eliot, who had travelled at the same time with Mr. Stanhope, Lord Chesterfield's natural son, justly observed, that it was strange that a man who shewed he had so much affection for his son as Lord Chesterfield did, by writing so many long and anxious letters to him, almost all of them when he was Secretary of State, which certainly was a proof of great goodness of disposition, should endeavour to make his son a rascal. His Lordship told us, that Foote had intended to bring on the stage a father who had thus tutored his son, and to shew the son an honest man to every one else, but practising his father's maxims upon him, and cheating him. *Johnson.* 'I am much pleased with this design; but I think there was no occasion to make the son honest at all. No; he should be a consummate rogue: the contrast between honesty and knavery would be the stronger. It should be contrived so that the father should be the only sufferer by the son's villainy, and thus there would be poetical justice.'

An addition to our company came after we went up to the drawing-room; Dr. Johnson seemed to rise in spirits as his audience increased. He entered upon a curious discussion of the difference between intuition and sagacity; one being immediate in its effect, the other requiring a circuitous process; one he observed was the *eye* of the mind, the other the *nose* of the mind.

A young gentleman present took up the argument against him, and maintained that no man ever thinks of the *nose of the mind,* not adverting that though that figurative sense seems strange to us, as very unusual, it is truly not more forced than Hamlet's 'In my *mind's eye,* Horatio.' He persisted much too long, and appeared to Johnson as putting himself forward as his antagonist with too much presumption; upon which he called to him in a loud tone, 'What is it you are contending for, if you *be* contending?'—And afterwards imagining that the gentleman retorted upon him with a kind of smart drollery, he said, 'Mr. *****, it does not become you to talk so to me. Besides, ridicule is not your talent; you have *there* neither intuition nor sagacity.'—The gentleman protested that he had intended no improper freedom, but had the greatest respect for Dr. Johnson. After a short pause, during which we were somewhat uneasy,—*Johnson.* 'Give me your hand, Sir. You were too tedious, and I was too short.' *Mr. *****.* 'Sir, I am honoured by your attention in any way.' *Johnson.* 'Come, Sir, let's have no more of it. We offended one another by our con tention; let us not offend the company by our compliments.'

He now said, 'He wished much to go to Italy, and that he dreaded passing the winter in England.' I said nothing; but enjoyed a secret satisfaction in thinking that I had taken the most effectual measures to make such a scheme practicable.

On Monday, June 28, I had the honour to receive from the Lord Chancellor the following letter:

'TO JAMES BOSWELL, ESQ.

'SIR,

'I SHOULD have answered your letter immediately; if, (being much engaged when I received it) I had not put it in my pocket, and forgot to open it till this morning.

'I am much obliged to you for the suggestion; and I will adopt and press it as far as I can. The best argument, I am sure, and I hope it is not likely to fail, is Dr. Johnson's merit.—But it will be necessary, if I should be so unfortunate as to miss seeing you, to converse with Sir Joshua on the sum it will be proper to ask,—in short, upon the means of setting him out. It would be a reflection on us all, if such a man should perish for want of the means to take care of his health.

'Yours, &c.

'THURLOW.'

This letter gave me a very high satisfaction; I next day went and shewed it to Sir Joshua Reynolds, who was exceedingly pleased with it. He thought that I should now communicate the negociation to Dr. Johnson, who might afterwards complain if the attention with which he had been honoured, should be too long concealed from him. I intended to set out for Scotland next morning; but Sir Joshua cordially insisted that I should stay another day, that Johnson and I might dine with him, that we three might talk of his Italian Tour; and, as Sir Joshua expressed himself, 'have it all out.' I hastened to Johnson, and was told by him that he was rather better to-day. *Boswell.* 'I am very anxious about you, Sir, and particularly that you should go to Italy for the winter, which I believe is your own wish.' *Johnson.* 'It is, Sir.' *Boswell.* 'You have no objection, I presume, but the money it would require.' *Johnson.* 'Why, no, Sir.' Upon which I gave him a particular account of what had been done, and read to him the Lord Chancellor's letter.—He listened with much attention; then warmly said, 'This is taking prodigious pains about a man.'— 'O! Sir, (said I, with most sincere affection,) your friends would do every thing for you.' He paused,—grew more and more agitated,—till tears started into his eyes, and he exclaimed with fervent emotion, 'GOD bless you all.' I was so affected that I also shed tears.—After a short silence, he renewed and extended his grateful benediction, 'GOD bless you all, for JESUS CHRIST's sake.' We both remained for some time unable to speak.—He rose suddenly and quitted the room, quite melted in tenderness. He staid but a short time, till he had recovered his firmness; soon after he returned I left him, having first engaged him to dine at Sir Joshua Reynolds's, next day.—I never was again under that roof which I had so long reverenced.

On Wednesday, June 30, the friendly confidential dinner with Sir Joshua Reynolds took place, no other company being present. Had I known that this was the last time that I should enjoy in this world, the conversation of a friend whom I so much respected, and from whom I derived so much instruction and entertainment, I should have been deeply affected. When I now look back to it, I am vexed that a single word should have been forgotten.

Both Sir Joshua and I were so sanguine in our expectations, that we expatiated with confidence on the liberal provision which we were sure would be made for him, conjecturing whether munificence would be displayed in one large donation, or in an ample increase of his pension. He himself catched so much of our enthusiasm, as to allow himself to suppose it not impossible that our hopes might in one way or other be realised. He said that he would rather have his pension doubled than a grant of a thousand pounds; 'For, (said he,) though probably I may not live to receive as much as a thousand pounds, a man would have the consciousness that he should pass the remainder of his life in splendour, how long soever it might be.' Considering what a moderate proportion an income of six hundred pounds a year bears to innumerable fortunes in this country, it is worthy of remark, that a man so truly great should think it splendour.

As an instance of extraordinary liberality of friendship, he told us, that Dr. Brocklesby had upon this occasion, offered him a hundred a year for his life. A grateful tear started into his eye, as he spoke this in a faultering tone.

Sir Joshua and I endeavoured to flatter his imagination with agreeable prospects of happiness in Italy. 'Nay, (said he,) I must not expect much of that; when a man goes to Italy merely to feel how he breathes the air, he can enjoy very little.'

Our conversation turned upon living in the country, which Johnson, whose melancholy mind required the dissipation of quick successive variety, had habituated himself to consider as a kind of mental imprisonment. 'Yet, Sir, (said I,) there are many people who are content to live in the country.' *Johnson*. 'Sir, it is in the intellectual world as in the physical world; we are told by natural philosophers that a body is at rest in the place that is fit for it; they who are content to live in the country, are *fit* for the country.'

Talking of various enjoyments, I argued that a refinement

of taste was a disadvantage, as they who have attained to it must be seldomer pleased than those who have no nice discrimination, and are therefore satisfied with every thing that comes in their way. *Johnson.* 'Nay, Sir; that is a paltry notion. Endeavour to be as perfect as you can in every respect.'

I accompanied him in Sir Joshua Reynolds's coach, to the entry of Bolt-court. He asked me whether I would not go with him to his house; I declined it, from an apprehension that my spirits would sink. We bade adieu to each other affectionately in the carriage. When he had got down upon the foot-pavement, he called out, 'Fare you well;' and without looking back, sprung away with a kind of pathetick briskness, if I may use that expression, which seemed to indicate a struggle to conceal uneasiness, and impressed me with a foreboding of our long, long separation.

I remained one day more in town, to have the chance of talking over my negociation with the Lord Chancellor; but the multiplicity of his Lordship's important engagements did not allow of it; so I left the management of the business in the hands of Sir Joshua Reynolds.

Soon after this time Dr. Johnson had the mortification of being informed by Mrs. Thrale, that 'what she supposed he never believed,' was true; namely, that she was actually going to marry Signor Piozzi, an Italian musick-master.[1] He endeavoured to prevent it; but in vain. If she would publish the whole of the correspondence that passed between Dr. Johnson and her on the subject, we should have a full view of his real sentiments. As it is, our judgement must be biassed by that characteristick specimen which Sir John Hawkins has given us: 'Poor Thrale! I thought that either her virtue or her vice would have restrained her from such a marriage. She is now become a subject for her enemies to exult over; and for her friends, if she has any left, to forget, or pity.'

It must be admitted that Johnson derived a considerable portion of happiness from the comforts and elegancies which

[1] Gabriel Piozzi (1740-1809). National chauvinism, social snobbery and Protestant narrowness combined to produce a violent condemnation of this marriage. It turned out, however, to be a far happier union than her marriage to Thrale.

he enjoyed in Mr. Thrale's family; but Mrs. Thrale assures us he was indebted for these to her husband alone, who certainly respected him sincerely. Her words are,

> '*Veneration for his virtue, reverence for his talents,* delight *in his conversation, and* habitual endurance of a yoke my husband first put upon me, *and of which he contentedly bore his share for sixteen or seventeen years, made me go on so long with* Mr. Johnson; *but the perpetual confinement I will own to have been* terrifying *in the first years of our friendship, and* irksome *in the last; nor could I pretend to* support *it without help, when my coadjutor was no more.*'

Alas! how different is this from the declarations which I have heard Mrs. Thrale make in his life-time, without a single murmur against any peculiarities, or against any one circumstance which attended their intimacy.

As a sincere friend of the great man whose Life I am writing, I think it necessary to guard my readers against the mistaken notion of Dr. Johnson's character, which this lady's 'Anecdotes' of him suggest; for from the very nature and form of her book, it 'lends deception lighter wings to fly.'

'Let it be remembered, (says an eminent critick,) that she has comprised in a small volume all that she could recollect of Dr. Johnson in *twenty years,* during which period, doubtless, some severe things were said by him; and they who read the book in *two hours,* naturally enough suppose that his whole conversation was of this complexion. But the fact is, I have been often in his company, and never *once* heard him say a severe thing to any one; and many others can attest the same. When he did say a severe thing, it was generally extorted by ignorance pretending to knowledge, or by extreme vanity or affectation.

'Two instances of inaccuracy, (adds he,) are peculiarly worthy of notice:

'It is said, "*That natural roughness of his manner so often mentioned, would, notwithstanding the regularity of his notions, burst through them all from time to time; and he once bade a very celebrated lady, who praised him with too much zeal perhaps, or perhaps too strong an emphasis, (which always offended him,) consider what her flattery was worth, before she choaked him with it.*"

'Now let the genuine anecdote be contrasted with this.—The person thus represented as being harshly treated, though a very celebrated lady, was *then* just come to London from an obscure situation in the country. At Sir Joshua Reynolds's one evening, she met Dr. Johnson. She very soon began to pay her court to him in the most fulsome strain. "Spare me, I beseech you, dear Madam," was his reply. She still *laid it on.* "Pray, Madam, let us have no more of this;" he rejoined. Not paying any attention to these warnings, she continued still her eulogy. At length, provoked by this indelicate and *vain* obtrusion of compliment, he exclaimed, "Dearest lady, consider with yourself what your flattery is worth, before you bestow it so freely."

'How different does this story appear, when accompanied with all these circumstances which really belong to it, but which Mrs. Thrale either did not know, or has suppressed.

I have had occasion several times, in the course of this work, to point out the incorrectness of Mrs. Thrale, as to particulars which consisted with my own knowledge. But indeed she has, in flippant terms enough, expressed her disapprobation of that anxious desire of authenticity which prompts a person who is to record conversations, to write them down *at the moment.* Unquestionably, if they are to be recorded at all, the sooner it is done the better. This lady herself says,

'To recollect, however, and to repeat the sayings of Dr. Johnson, is almost all that can be done by the writers of his Life; as his life, at least since my acquaintance with him, consisted in little else than talking, when he was not employed in some serious piece of work.'

She boasts of her having kept a common-place book; and we find she noted, at one time or other, in a very lively manner, specimens of the conversation of Dr. Johnson, and of those who talked with him; but had she done it recently, they probably would have been less erroneous; and we should have been relieved from those disagreeable doubts of their authenticity, with which we must now peruse them.

She says of him,

'He was the most charitable of mortals, without being what we call an active friend. Admirable at giving counsel; no man saw his way so clearly; but he would not stir a finger for the assistance of those to whom he was willing enough to give advice.' And again on the same page, 'If you wanted a slight favour, you must apply to people of other dispositions; for not a step would Johnson move to

*obtain a man a vote in a society, to repay a compliment which might
be useful or pleasing, to write a letter of request, &c. or to obtain a
hundred pounds a year more for a friend who perhaps had already
two or three. No force could urge him to diligence, no importunity
could conquer his resolution to stand still.'*

It is amazing that one who had such opportunities of knowing Dr. Johnson, should appear so little acquainted with his
real character. I am certain that a *more active friend* has rarely
been found in any age. This work, which I fondly hope will
rescue his memory from obloquy, contains a thousand instances of his benevolent exertions in almost every way that
can be conceived; and particularly in employing his pen with
a generous readiness for those to whom its aid could be useful.
Indeed his obliging activity in doing little offices of kindness,
both by letters and personal application, was one of the most
remarkable features in his character.

I certainly, then, do not claim too much in behalf of my
illustrious friend in saying, that however smart and entertaining Mrs. Thrale's 'Anecdotes' are, they must not be held as
good evidence against him; for wherever an instance of harshness and severity is told, I beg leave to doubt its perfect authenticity; for though there may have been *some* foundation
for it, yet, like that of his reproof to the 'very celebrated lady,'
it may be so exhibited in the narration as to be very unlike
the real fact.

The evident tendency of the following anecdote is to represent Dr. Johnson as extremely deficient in affection, tenderness,
or even common civility.

*When I one day lamented the loss of a first cousin killed in
America,—"Prithee, my dear, (said he,) have done with canting;
how would the world be the worse for it, I may ask, if all your
relations were at once spitted like larks, and roasted for Presto's
supper?"—Presto was the dog that lay under the table while we
talked.'*

I suspect this too of exaggeration and distortion. I allow that
he made her an angry speech; but let the circumstances fairly
appear, as told by Mr. Baretti, who was present:

'Mrs. Thrale, while supping very heartily upon larks, laid down her knife and fork, and abruptly exclaimed, "O, my dear Mr. Johnson, do you know what has happened? The last letters from abroad have brought us an account that our poor cousin's head was taken off by a cannonball." Johnson, who was shocked both at the fact, and her light unfeeling manner of mentioning it, replied, "Madam, it would give *you* very little concern if all your relations were spitted like those larks, and drest for Presto's supper."'

It is with concern that I find myself obliged to animadvert on the inaccuracies of Mrs. Piozzi's 'Anecdotes,' and perhaps I may be thought to have dwelt too long upon her little collec tion. But as from Johnson's long residence under Mr. Thrale's roof, and his intimacy with her, the account which she has given of him may have made an unfavourable and unjust impression, my duty, as a faithful biographer, has obliged me reluctantly to perform this unpleasing task.

Having left the *pious negociation,* as I called it, in the best hands, I shall here insert what relates to it. Johnson wrote to Sir Joshua Reynolds on July 6, as follows:

'I am going, I hope, in a few days, to try the air of Derbyshire, but hope to see you before I go. Let me, howevei, mention to you what I have much at heart.—If the Chancellor should continue his attention to Mr. Boswell's request, and confer with you on the means of relieving my languid state, I am very desirous to avoid the appearance of asking money upon false pretences. I desire you to represent to his Lordship, what, as soon as it is suggested, he will perceive to be reasonable,—That, if I grow much worse, I shall be afraid to leave my physicians, to suffer the inconveniencies of travel, and pine in the solitude of a foreign country;—That, if I grow much better, of which indeed there is now little appearance, I shall not wish to leave my friends and my domestick comforts; for I do not travel for pleasure or curiosity; yet if I should recover, curiosity would revive.—In my present state, I am desirous to make a struggle for a little longer life, and hope to obtain some help from a softer climate. Do for me what you can.'

He wrote to me July 26:

'I wish your affairs could have permitted a longer and continued exertion of your zeal and kindness. They that have your kindness may want your ardour. In the mean time I am very feeble, and very dejected.'

By a letter from Sir Joshua Reynolds I was informed, that the Lord Chancellor had called on him, and acquainted him that the application had not been successful; but that his Lordship, after speaking highly in praise of Johnson, as a man who was an honour to his country, desired Sir Joshua to let him know, that on granting a mortgage of his pension, he should draw on his Lordship to the amount of five or six hundred pounds; and that his Lordship explained the meaning of the mortgage to be, that he wished the business to be conducted in such a manner, that Dr. Johnson should appear to be under the least possible obligation. Sir Joshua mentioned, that he had by the same post communicated all this to Dr. Johnson.

How Johnson was affected upon the occasion will appear from what he wrote to Sir Joshua Reynolds:

'Ashbourne, Sept. 9. Many words I hope are not necessary between you and me, to convince you what gratitude is excited in my heart by the Chancellor's liberality, and your kind offices.

'I have enclosed a letter to the Chancellor, which, when you have read it, you will be pleased to seal with a head, or any other general seal, and convey it to him: had I sent it directly to him, I should have seemed to overlook the favour of your intervention.'

'To the Lord High Chancellor.

'My Lord,
'After a long and not inattentive observation of mankind, the generosity of your Lordship's offer raises in me not less wonder than gratitude. Bounty, so liberally bestowed, I should gladly receive, if my condition made it necessary; for, to such a mind, who would not be proud to own his obligations? But it has pleased God to restore me to so great a measure of health, that if I should now appropriate so much of a fortune destined to do good, I could not escape from myself the charge of advancing a false claim. My journey to the continent, though I once thought it necessary, was never much encouraged by my physicians; and I was very desirous that your Lordship should be told of it by Sir Joshua Reynolds, as an event very uncertain; for if I grew much better, I should not be willing, if much worse, not able, to migrate.—Your Lordship was first solicited without my knowledge; but, when I was told, that you were pleased to honour me with your patronage, I did not expect to

hear of a refusal; yet, as I have had no long time to brood hope, and have not rioted in imaginary opulence, this cold reception has been scarce a disappointment; and, from your Lordship's kindness, I have received a benefit, which only men like you are able to bestow. I shall now live *mihi carior*, with a higher opinion of my own merit.

> 'I am, my Lord,
> > 'Your Lordship's most obliged,
> > 'Most grateful, and
> > > 'Most humble servant,
> > > > 'SAM. JOHNSON.'

'Sept. 1784.'

Upon this unexpected failure I abstain from presuming to make any remarks, or to offer any conjectures.

Let us now contemplate Johnson thirty years after the death of his wife, still retaining for her all the tenderness of affection.

> 'To the Reverend Mr. Bagshaw, at Bromley.
> 'Sir,
>
> 'Perhaps you may remember, that in the year 1753, you committed to the ground my dear wife. I now entreat your permission to lay a stone upon her; and have sent the inscription, that, if you find it proper, you may signify your allowance.
>
> 'You will do me a great favour by shewing the place where she lies, that the stone may protect her remains.
>
> 'Mr. Ryland will wait on you for the inscription, and procure it to be engraved. You will easily believe that I shrink from this mournful office. When it is done, if I have strength remaining, I will visit Bromley once again, and pay you part of the respect to which you have a right from, Reverend Sir,
> > 'Your most humble servant,
> > > 'SAM. JOHNSON.'

'July 12, 1784.'

Next day he set out on a jaunt to Staffordshire and Derbyshire, flattering himself that he might be in some degree relieved.

During his absence from London he kept up a correspondence with several of his friends, from which I shall select what appears to me proper for publication, without attending nicely to chronological order.

To Dr. Brocklesby, he writes, Ashbourne, July 20.

'The kind attention which you have so long shewn to my health and happiness, makes it as much a debt of gratitude as a call of interest, to give you an account of what befals me, when accident recovers me from your immediate care.—The journey of the first day was performed with very little sense of fatigue; the second day brought me to Lichfield, without much lassitude; but I am afraid that I could not have borne such violent agitation for many days together. I staid five days at Lichfield, but, being unable to walk, had no great pleasure, and yesterday (19th) I came hither, where I am to try what air and attention can perform. The asthma has no abatement. Opiates stop the fit, so as that I can sit and some-times lie easy, but they do not now procure me the power of mo-tion; and I am afraid that my general strength of body does not encrease. The weather indeed is not benign; but how low is he sunk whose strength depends upon the weather!—I am now looking into Floyer, who lived with his asthma to almost his ninetieth year. His book by want of order is obscure, and his asthma, I think, not of the same kind with mine. Something however I may perhaps learn. --My appetite still continues keen enough; and what I consider as a symptom of radical health, I have a voracious delight in raw sum-mer fruit, of which I was less eager a few years ago.—You will be pleased to communicate this account to Dr. Heberden, and if any thing is to be done, let me have your joint opinion.'

August 19. 'The relaxation of the asthma still continues, yet I do not trust it wholly to itself, but soothe it now and then with an opiate. I not only perform the perpetual act of respiration with less labour, but I can walk with fewer intervals of rest, and with greater freedom of motion.—I never thought well of Dr. James's com-pounded medicines; his ingredients appeared to me sometimes in-efficacious and trifling, and sometimes heterogeneous and destruc-tive of each other. This prescription exhibits a composition of about three hundred and thirty grains, in which there are four grains of emetick tartar, and six drops [of] thebaick tincture. He that writes thus, surely writes for shew. The basis of his medicine is the gum ammoniacum, which dear Dr. Lawrence used to give, but of which I never saw any effect. We will, if you please, let this medicine alone. The squills have every suffrage, and in the squills we will rest for the present.'

August 26. 'I suffered you to escape last post without a letter, but you are not to expect such indulgence very often; for I write not so much because I have any thing to say, as because I hope for an answer; and the vacancy of my life here makes a letter of great value.—I have here little company and little amusement, and thus

abandoned to the contemplation of my own miseries, I am sometimes gloomy and depressed; this too I resist as I can, and find opium,
I think, useful, but I seldom take more than one grain.—Is not this
strange weather? Winter absorbed the spring, and now autumn is
come before we have had summer. But let not our kindness for
each other imitate the inconstancy of the seasons.'

Lichfield, Sept. 29. 'On one day I had three letters about the
air-balloon:[1] yours was far the best, and has enabled me to impart
to my friends in the country an idea of this species of amusement.
In amusement, mere amusement, I am afraid it must end, for I
do not find that its course can be directed so as that it should serve
any purposes of communication; and it can give no new intelligence of the state of the air at different heights, till they have
ascended above the height of mountains, which they seem never
likely to do.—I came hither on the 27th. How long I shall stay, I
have not determined. My dropsy is gone, and my asthma much remitted, but I have felt myself a little declining these two days, or
at least to-day; but such vicissitudes must be expected. One day
may be worse than another; but this last month is far better than
the former; if the next should be as much better than this, I shall
run about the town on my own legs.'

October 6. 'The fate of the balloon[2] I do not much lament: to
make new balloons, is to repeat the jest again. We now know a
method of mounting into the air, and, I think, are not likely to
know more. The first experiment, however, was bold, and deserved
applause and reward. But since it has been performed, and its
event is known, I had rather now find a medicine that can ease an
asthma.'

October 25. 'You write to me with a zeal that animates, and a
tenderness that melts me. I am not afraid either of a journey to
London, or a residence in it. I came down with little fatigue, and
am now not weaker. In the smoky atmosphere I was delivered from
the dropsy, which I consider as the original and radical disease. The
town is my element; there are my friends, there are my books, to
which I have not yet bidden farewell, and there are my amusements. Sir Joshua told me long ago, that my vocation was to
publick life, and I hope still to keep my station, till God shall bid
me *Go in peace.'*

[1] On September 15, 1784, Vincent Lunardi, secretary to the Neapoli-
tan ambassador, had made a successful balloon ascent from London.
The event occasioned immense excitement.

[2] This was another balloon which had been destroyed on the
ground on September 29th.

To Dr. Burney.

August 2. 'The weather, you know, has not been balmy; I am
now reduced to think, and am at last content to talk of the weather.
Pride must have a fall.—I have lost dear Mr. Allen, and wherever
I turn, the dead or the dying meet my notice, and force my attention upon misery and mortality. Mrs. Burney's escape from so much
danger, and her ease after so much pain, throws, however, some
radiance of hope upon the gloomy prospect. May her recovery be
perfect, and her continuance long.—I struggle hard for life. I take
physick, and take air; my friend's chariot is always ready.'

To Mr. Windham.

August. 'The tenderness with which you have been pleased to
treat me, through my long illness, neither health nor sickness can, I
hope, make me forget; and you are not to suppose, that after we
parted you were no longer in my mind. But what can a sick man
say, but that he is sick? His thoughts are necessarily concentered in
himself; he neither receives nor can give delight; his enquiries are
after alleviations of pain, and his efforts are to catch some momentary comfort.—Though I am now in the neighbourhood of the
Peak, you must expect no account of its wonders, of its hills, its
waters, its caverns, or its mines; but I will tell you, dear Sir, what I
hope you will not hear with less satisfaction, that, for about a week
past, my asthma has been less afflictive.'

Lichfield. October 2. 'Whither or when I shall make my next re-
move, I cannot tell; but I entreat you, dear Sir, to let me know, from
time to time, where you may be found, for your residence is a very
powerful attractive to, Sir, your most humble servant.'

To the Right Hon. William Gerard Hamilton.

'Dear Sir,
        'Considering what reason you gave me in the spring to con-
clude that you took part in whatever good or evil might befal me,
I ought not to have omitted so long the account which I am now
about to give you.—My diseases are an asthma and a dropsy, and,
what is less curable, seventy-five. Of the dropsy, in the beginning
of the summer, or in the spring, I recovered to a degree which
struck with wonder both me and my physicians: the asthma now
is likewise, for a time, very much relieved. I went to Oxford, where
the asthma was very tyrannical, and the dropsy began again to
threaten me; but seasonable physick stopped the inundation: I
then returned to London, and in July took a resolution to visit

Staffordshire and Derbyshire, where I am yet struggling with my diseases. The dropsy made another attack, and was not easily ejected, but at last gave way. The asthma suddenly remitted in bed, on the 13th of August, and, though now very oppressive, is, I think, still something gentler than it was before the remission. My limbs are miserably debilitated, and my nights are sleepless and tedious.— When you read this, dear Sir, you are not sorry that I wrote no sooner. I will not prolong my complaints. I hope still to see you *in a happier hour,* to talk over what we have often talked, and perhaps to find new topicks of merriment, or new incitements to curiosity.

'I am, dear Sir, &c.

'SAM. JOHNSON.'

'Lichfield, Oct. 20, 1784.'

To SIR JOSHUA REYNOLDS.

Sept. 9. 'I could not answer your letter before this day, because I went on the sixth to Chatsworth, and did not come back till the post was gone.—Many words, I hope, are not necessary between you and me, to convince you what gratitude is excited in my heart, by the Chancellor's liberality and your kind offices. I did not indeed expect that what was asked by the Chancellor would have been refused, but since it has, we will not tell that any thing has been asked.—I have enclosed a letter to the Chancellor, which, when you have read it, you will be pleased to seal with a head, or other general seal, and convey it to him; had I sent it directly to him, I should have seemed to overlook the favour of your intervention.— My last letter told you of my advance in health, which, I think, in the whole still continues. I do not despair of supporting an English winter.—At Chatsworth, I met young Mr. Burke, who led me very commodiously into conversation with the Duke and Duchess. We had a very good morning. The dinner was publick.'

Sept. 18. 'I flattered myself that this week would have given me a letter from you, but none has come. Write to me now and then, but direct your next to Lichfield.—I think, and I hope, am sure, that I still grow better; I have sometimes good nights; but am still in my legs weak, but so much mended, that I go to Lichfield in hope of being able to pay my visits on foot, for there are no coaches. —I have three letters this day, all about the balloon, I could have been content with one. Do not write about the balloon, whatever else you may think proper to say.'

October 2. 'I am always proud of your approbation, and therefore was much pleased that you liked my letter. When you copied it, you invaded the Chancellor's right rather than mine.—The re-

fusal I did not expect, but I had never thought much about it, for I
doubted whether the Chancellor had so much tenderness for me
as to ask. He, being keeper of the King's conscience, ought not to
be supposed capable of an improper petition.—All is not gold that
glitters, as we have often been told; and the adage is verified in
your place and my favour; but if what happens does not make us
richer, we must bid it welcome, if it makes us wiser.—I do not at
present grow better, nor much worse; my hopes, however, are somewhat abated, and a very great loss is the loss of hope, but I struggle
on as I can.'

This various mass of correspondence, which I have thus
brought together, is valuable, both as an addition to the store
which the publick already has of Johnson's writings, and as
exhibiting a genuine and noble specimen of vigour and vivacity of mind, which neither age nor sickness could impair or
diminish.

We now behold Johnson for the last time, in his native city.
While here, he felt a revival of all the tenderness of filial affection, an instance of which appeared in his ordering the grave-
stone and inscription over Elizabeth Blaney[1] to be substan-
tially and carefully renewed.

To Mr. Henry White, a young clergyman, with whom he
now formed an intimacy, so as to talk to him with great freedom, he mentioned that he could not in general accuse himself of having been an undutiful son. 'Once, indeed, (said he,)
I was disobedient; I refused to attend my father to Uttoxeter-
market. Pride was the source of that refusal, and the remembrance of it was painful. A few years ago, I desired to atone
for this fault; I went to Uttoxeter in very bad weather, and
stood for a considerable time bareheaded in the rain, on the
spot where my father's stall used to stand. In contrition I stood,
and I hope the penance was expiatory.'

'I told him (says Miss Seward) in one of my latest visits to
him, of a wonderful learned pig, which I had seen at Notting-
ham; and which did all that we have observed exhibited by
dogs and horses. The subject amused him. "Then, (said he,)

---

[1] This was a young woman, a servant girl in Lichfield, whom Boswell
believed to have died from a violent and unrequited love for Johnson's
father. The story, which Boswell took from Hawkins' *Life of Johnson,*
has not stood up under investigation.

the pigs are a race unjustly calumniated. *Pig* has, it seems, not been wanting to *man*, but *man* to *pig*. We do not allow *time* for his education, we kill him at a year old." Mr. Henry White, who was present, observed that if this instance had happened in or before Pope's time, he would not have been justified in instancing the swine as the lowest degree of groveling instinct. Dr. Johnson seemed pleased with the observation, while the person who made it proceeded to remark, that great torture must have been employed, ere the indocility of the animal could have been subdued.—"Certainly, (said the Doctor;) but, (turning to me,) how old is your pig?" I told him, three years old. "Then, (said he,) the pig has no cause to complain; he would have been killed the first year if he had not been *educated,* and protracted existence is a good recompence for very considerable degrees of torture." '

As Johnson had now very faint hopes of recovery, and as Mrs. Thrale was no longer devoted to him, it might have been supposed that he would naturally have chosen to remain in the comfortable house of his beloved wife's daughter, and end his life where he began it. Such was his intellectual ardour even at this time, that he said to one friend, 'Sir, I look upon every day to be lost, in which I do not make a new acquaintance;' and to another, when talking of his illness, 'I will be conquered; I will not capitulate.' And such was his love of London, so high a relish had he of its magnificent extent, and variety of intellectual entertainment, that he languished when absent from it, his mind having become quite luxurious from the long habit of enjoying the metropolis; and, therefore, although at Lichfield, surrounded with friends, who loved and revered him, and for whom he had a very sincere affection, he still found that such conversation as London affords, could be found no where else. These feelings, joined, probably, to some flattering hopes of aid from the eminent physicians and surgeons in London, who kindly and generously attended him without accepting of fees, made him resolve to return to the capital.

From Lichfield he came to Birmingham, where he passed a few days with his worthy old schoolfellow, Mr. Hector, who thus writes to me:

'He was very solicitous with me to recollect some of our most early transactions, and transmit them to him, for I perceived nothing gave him greater pleasure than calling to mind those days of our innocence. I complied with his request, and he only received them a few days before his death. I have transcribed for your inspection, exactly the minutes I wrote to him.'

This paper having been found in his repositories after his death, Sir John Hawkins has inserted it entire, and I have made occasional use of it, and other communications from Mr. Hector, in the course of this Work. I have both visited and corresponded with him since Dr. Johnson's death, and by my inquiries concerning a great variety of particulars have obtained additional information. I followed the same mode with the Reverend Dr. Taylor, in whose presence I wrote down a good deal of what he could tell; and he, at my request, signed his name, to give it authenticity. It is very rare to find any person who is able to give a distinct account of the life even of one whom he has known intimately, without questions being put to them. My friend, Dr. Kippis, has told me, that on this account it is a practice with him to draw out a biographical catechism.

Johnson then proceeded to Oxford, where he was again kindly received by Dr. Adams, who was pleased to give me the following account in one of his letters, (Feb. 17th, 1785):

'His last visit was, I believe, to my house, which he left after a stay of four or five days. We had much serious talk together, for which I ought to be the better as long as I live. You will remember some discourse which we had in the summer upon the subject of prayer, and the difficulty of this sort of composition. He reminded me of this, and of my having wished him to try his hand, and to give us a specimen of the style and manner that he approved. He added, that he was now in a right frame of mind, and as he could not possibly employ his time better, he would in earnest set about it. But I find upon enquiry, that no papers of this sort were left behind him, except a few short ejaculatory forms suitable to his present situation.'

Dr. Adams had not then received accurate information on this subject; for it has since appeared that various prayers had been composed by him at different periods, which, inter

ningled with pious resolutions, and some short notes of his
life, were entitled by him 'Prayers and Meditations,' and have,
in pursuance of his earnest requisition, in the hopes of doing
good, been published, with a judicious well-written Preface,
by the Reverend Mr. Strahan, to whom he delivered them.

Soon after Johnson's return to the metropolis, both the
asthma and dropsy became more violent and distressful. He
had for some time kept a journal in Latin of the state of his
illness, and the remedies which he used, under the title of
Ægri Ephemeris,[1] which he began on the 6th of July, but continued it no longer than the 8th of November; finding, I suppose, that it was a mournful and unavailing register. It is in
my possession; and is written with great care and accuracy.

Still his love of literature did not fail. A very few days before
his death he transmitted to his friend Mr. John Nichols, a list
of the authours of the Universal History, mentioning their
several shares in that work. It has, according to his direction,
been deposited in the British Museum, and is printed in the
Gentleman's Magazine for December, 1784.

During his sleepless nights he amused himself by translating into Latin verse, from the Greek, many of the epigrams
in the *Anthologia*. These translations, with some other poems
by him in Latin, he gave to his friend Mr. Langton, who,
having added a few notes, sold them to the booksellers for a
small sum, to be given to some of Johnson's relations, which
was accordingly done; and they are printed in the collection
of his works.

I shall now fulfil my promise of exhibiting specimens of
various sorts of imitation of Johnson's style.

In the 'Transactions of the Royal Irish Academy, 1787,' there
is an 'Essay on the Style of Dr. Samuel Johnson,' by the Reverend Robert Burrowes, whose respect for the great object
of his criticism is thus evinced in the concluding paragraph:

'I have singled him out from the whole body of English writers,
because his universally-acknowledged beauties would be most apt
to induce imitation; and I have treated rather on his faults than
his perfections, because an essay might comprize all the observa-

[1] A Diary of Sickness.

tions I could make upon his faults, while volumes would not be sufficient for a treatise on his perfections.'

Mr. Burrowes has analysed the composition of Johnson, and pointed out its peculiarities with much acuteness; and I would recommend a careful perusal of his Essay to those, who being captivated by the union of perspicuity and splendour which the writings of Johnson contain, without having a sufficient portion of his vigour of mind, may be in danger of becoming bad copyists of his manner. I, however, cannot but observe, and I observe it to his credit, that this learned gentleman has himself caught no mean degree of the expansion and harmony, which, independent of all other circumstances, characterise the sentences of Johnson.

The ludicrous imitators of Johnson's style are innumerable. Their general method is to accumulate hard words, without considering, that, although he was fond of introducing them occasionally, there is not a single sentence in all his writings where they are crowded together, as in the first verse of the following imaginary Ode by him to Mrs. Thrale, which appeared in the newspapers:

'*Cervisial coctor's viduate* dame
Opin'st thou this gigantick frame,
　Procumbing at thy shrine:
Shall, *catenated* by thy charms,
A captive in thy *ambient* arms,
　Perennially be thine?'

This, and a thousand other such attempts, are totally unlike the original, which the writers imagined they were turning into ridicule. There is not similarity enough for burlesque, or even for caricature.

Mr. Colman, in his 'Prose on several Occasions,' has 'A Letter from *Lexiphanes;* containing Proposals for a *Glossary* or *Vocabulary* of the *Vulgar Tongue:* intended as a Supplement to a larger *Dictionary.*' It is evidently meant as a sportive sally of ridicule on Johnson, whose style is thus imitated, without being grossly overcharged.

'It is easy to foresee, that the idle and illiterate will complain that I have increased their labours by endeavouring to diminish them;

and that I have explained what is more easy by what is more difficult. I expect, on the other hand, the liberal acknowledgements of the learned. He who is buried in scholastick retirement, secluded from the assemblies of the gay, and remote from the circles of the polite, will at once comprehend the definitions, and be grateful for such a seasonable and necessary elucidation of his mother tongue. Annexed to this letter is a short specimen of the work, thrown together in a vague and desultory manner, not even adhering to alphabetical concatenation.'

The serious imitators of Johnson's style, whether intentionally or by the imperceptible effect of its strength and animation, are, as I have had already occasion to observe, so many, that I might introduce quotations from a numerous body of writers in our language, since he appeared in the literary world. I shall point out only the following:

EDWARD GIBBON, ESQ.

'Of all our passions and appetites, the love of power is of the most imperious and unsociable nature, since the pride of one man requires the submission of the multitude. In the tumult of civil discord the laws of society lose their force, and their place is seldom supplied by those of humanity. The ardour of contention, the pride of victory, the despair of success, the memory of past injuries, and the fear of future dangers, all contribute to inflame the mind, and to silence the voice of pity.'

MISS BURNEY.

'My family, mistaking ambition for honour, and rank for dignity, have long planned a splendid connection for me, to which, though my invariable repugnance has stopped any advances, their wishes and their views immovably adhere. I am but too certain they will now listen to no other. I dread, therefore, to make a trial where I despair of success; I know not how to risk a prayer with those who may silence me by a command.'

The Reverend *Dr. Knox,* master of Tunbridge school, appears to have Johnson's style perpetually in his mind; and to his assiduous, though not servile, study of it, we may partly ascribe the extensive popularity of his writings.

In his 'Essays, Moral and Literary,' No. 3, we find the following passage:—

'The polish of external grace may indeed be deferred till the approach of manhood. When solidity is obtained by pursuing the modes prescribed by our forefathers, then may the file be used. The firm substance will bear attrition, and the lustre then acquired will be durable.'

There is, however, one in No. 11, which is blown up into such tumidity, as to be truly ludicrous. The writer means to tell us, that Members of Parliament, who have run in debt by extravagance, will sell their votes to avoid an arrest, which he thus expresses:—

'They who build houses and collect costly pictures and furniture, with the money of an honest artisan or mechanick, will be very glad of emancipation from the hands of a bailiff, by a sale of their senatorial suffrage.'

Yet whatever merit there may be in any imitations of Johnson's style, every good judge must see that they are obviously different from the original; for all of them are either deficient in its force, or overloaded with its peculiarities; and the powerful sentiment to which it is suited is not to be found.

Johnson's affection for his departed relations seemed to grow warmer as he approached nearer to the time when he might hope to see them again. It probably appeared to him that he should upbraid himself with unkind inattention, were he to leave the world without having paid a tribute of respect to their memory.

'To Mr. Green, Apothecary, at Lichfield.

'Dear Sir,

'I have enclosed the Epitaph for my Father, Mother, and Brother, to be all engraved on the large size, and laid in the middle aisle in St. Michael's church, which I request the clergyman and church-wardens to permit.

'The first care must be to find the exact place of interment, that the stone may protect the bodies. Then let the stone be deep, massy, and hard; and do not let the difference of ten pounds, or more, defeat our purpose.

'I have enclosed ten pounds, and Mrs. Porter will pay you ten more, which I gave her for the same purpose. What more is wanted shall be sent; and I beg that all possible haste may be made, for I wish to have it done while I am yet alive. Let me know, dear Sir, that you receive this.

> 'I am, Sir,
>> 'Your most humble servant,
>>> 'Sam. Johnson.'

'Dec. 2, 1784.'

'To Mrs. Lucy Porter, in Lichfield.

'Dear Madam,

'I am very ill, and desire your prayers. I have sent Mr. Green the Epitaph, and a power to call on you for ten pounds.

'I laid this summer a stone over Tetty, in the chapel of Bromley, in Kent. The inscription is in Latin, of which this is the English. [Here a translation.]

'That this is done, I thought it fit that you should know. What care will be taken of us, who can tell? May God pardon and bless us, for Jesus Christ's sake.

> 'I am, &c.
>> 'Sam. Johnson.'

'Dec. 2, 1784.'

My readers are now, at last, to behold *Samuel Johnson* preparing himself for that doom, from which the most exalted powers afford no exemption to man. Death had always been to him an object of terrour; so that, though by no means happy, he still clung to life with an eagerness at which many have wondered. At any time when he was ill, he was very much pleased to be told that he looked better. An ingenious member of the *Eumelian Club* informs me, that upon one occasion when he said to him that he saw health returning to his cheek, Johnson seized him by the hand and exclaimed, 'Sir, you are one of the kindest friends I ever had.'

His own state of his views of futurity will appear truly rational; and may, perhaps, impress the unthinking with seriousness.

'You know, (says he,) I never thought confidence with respect to futurity any part of the character of a brave, a wise, or a good man. Bravery has no place where it can avail nothing; wisdom impresses strongly the consciousness of those faults, of which it is, perhaps, itself an aggravation; and goodness, always wishing to be better, and imputing every deficience to criminal negligence, and every fault to voluntary corruption, never dares to suppose the condition of forgiveness fulfilled, nor what is wanting in the crime supplied by penitence.

'This is the state of the best; but what must be the condition of him whose heart will not suffer him to rank himself among the best, or among the good? Such must be his dread of the approaching trial, as will leave him little attention to the opinion of those whom he is leaving for ever; and the serenity that is not felt, it can be no virtue to feign.'

His great fear of death, and the strange dark manner in which Sir John Hawkins imparts the uneasiness which he expressed on account of offences with which he charged himself, may give occasion to injurious suspicions, as if there had been something of more than ordinary criminality weighing upon his conscience.[1] On that account, therefore, as well as from the regard to truth which he inculcated, I am to mention, (with all possible respect and delicacy, however,) that his conduct, after he came to London, and had associated with Savage and others, was not so strictly virtuous, in one respect, as when he was a younger man. It was well known, that his amorous inclinations were uncommonly strong and impetuous. He owned to many of his friends, that he used to take women of the town to taverns, and hear them relate their history.— In short, it must not be concealed, that, like many other good and pious men, among whom we may place the Apostle Paul upon his own authority, Johnson was not free from propensities which were ever 'warring against the law of his mind,'— and that in his combats with them, he was sometimes overcome.

Here let the profane and licentious pause; let them not thoughtlessly say that Johnson was an *hypocrite,* or that his *principles* were not firm, because his *practice* was not uniformly conformable to what he professed.

Let the question be considered independent of moral and religious association; and no man will deny that thousands, in many instances, act against conviction. Is a prodigal, for

[1] Johnson's mental disturbances were of an order and scope beyond Boswell's comprehension. His lifelong fear of insanity was not groundless.

example, an *hypocrite*, when he owns he is satisfied that his
extravagance will bring him to ruin and misery? We are *sure*
he *believes* it; but immediate inclination, strengthened by
indulgence, prevails over that belief in influencing his conduct. Why then shall credit be refused to the *sincerity* of those
who acknowledge their persuasion of moral and religious duty,
yet sometimes fail of living as it requires? I heard Dr. Johnson
once observe, 'There is something noble in publishing truth,
though it condemns one's self.' And one who said in his presence, 'he had no notion of people being in earnest in their
good professions, whose practice was not suitable to them,'
was thus reprimanded by him:—'Sir, are you so grossly ignorant
of human nature as not to know that a man may be very sincere
in good principles, without having good practice?'

But let no man encourage or soothe himself in 'presumptuous sin,' from knowing that Johnson was sometimes hurried
into indulgences which he thought criminal. I have exhibited
this circumstance as a shade in so great a character, both from
my sacred love of truth, and to shew that he was not so weakly
scrupulous as he has been represented by those who imagine
that the sins, of which a deep sense was upon his mind, were
merely such little venial trifles as pouring milk into his tea on
Good-Friday. His understanding will be defended by my statement, if his consistency of conduct be in some degree impaired.
But what wise man would, for momentary gratifications, deliberately subject himself to suffer such uneasiness as we find
was experienced by Johnson in reviewing his conduct as compared with his notion of the ethicks of the gospel? Let the following passages be kept in remembrance:

'O, GOD, giver and preserver of all life, by whose power I was
created, and by whose providence I am sustained, look down upon
me with tenderness and mercy; grant that I may not have been
created to be finally destroyed; that I may not be preserved to add
wickedness to wickedness.'—'O, LORD, let me not sink into total depravity; look down upon me, and rescue me at last from the captivity of sin.'—'Almighty and most merciful Father, who hast continued my life from year to year, grant that by longer life I may
become less desirous of sinful pleasures, and more careful of eternal
happiness.'—'Let not my years be multiplied to increase my guilt;

but as my age advances, let me become more pure in my thoughts, more regular in my desires, and more obedient to thy laws.'—'Forgive, O merciful LORD, whatever I have done contrary to thy laws. Give me such a sense of my wickedness as may produce true contrition and effectual repentance; so that when I shall be called into another state, I may be received among the sinners to whom sorrow and reformation have obtained pardon, for JESUS CHRIST's sake. Amen.'

Such was the distress of mind, such the penitence of Johnson, in his hours of privacy, and in his devout approaches to his Maker. His *sincerity,* therefore, must appear to every candid mind unquestionable.

It is of essential consequence to keep in view, that there was in this excellent man's conduct no false principle of *commutation,* no *deliberate* indulgence in sin, in consideration of a counter-balance of duty. His offending, and his repenting, were distinct and separate: and when we consider his almost unexampled attention to truth, his inflexible integrity, his constant piety, who will dare to 'cast a stone' at him? Besides, let it never be forgotten, that he cannot be charged with any offence indicating badness of *heart,* any thing dishonest, base, or malignant; but that, on the contrary, he was charitable in an extraordinary degree: so that even in one of his own rigid judgements of himself, (Easter-eve, 1781,) while he says, 'I have corrected no external habits;' he is obliged to own, 'I hope that since my last communion I have advanced, by pious reflections, in my submission to GOD, and my benevolence to man.'

I am conscious that this is the most difficult and dangerous part of my biographical work, and I cannot but be very anxious concerning it. I trust that I have got through it, preserving at once my regard to truth,—to my friend,—and to the interests of virtue and religion. Nor can I apprehend that more harm can ensue from the knowledge of the irregularity of Johnson, guarded as I have stated it, than from knowing that Addison and Parnell were intemperate in the use of wine; which he himself, in his Lives of those celebrated writers and pious men, has not forborne to record.

It is not my intention to give a very minute detail of the

particulars of Johnson's remaining days, of whom it was now evident, that the crisis was fast approaching, when he must *die like men, and fall like one of the Princes.*[1] Yet it will be instructive, as well as gratifying to the curiosity of my readers, to record a few circumstances, on the authenticity of which they may perfectly rely, as I have been at the utmost pains to obtain an accurate account of his last illness, from the best authority.

Dr. Heberden, Dr. Brocklesby, Dr. Warren, and Dr. Butter, physicians, generously attended him, without accepting of any fees, as did Mr. Cruikshank, surgeon; and all that could be done from professional skill and ability, was tried, to prolong a life so truly valuable. He himself, indeed, having, on account of his very bad constitution, been perpetually applying himself to medical inquiries, united his own efforts with those of the gentlemen who attended him; and imagining that the dropsical collection of water which oppressed him might be drawn off by making incisions in his body, he, with his usual resolute defiance of pain, cut deep, when he thought that his surgeon had done it too tenderly.

About eight or ten days before his death, when Dr. Brocklesby paid him his morning visit, he seemed very low and desponding, and said, 'I have been as a dying man all night.' He then emphatically broke out in the words of Shakespeare,

> 'Can'st thou not minister to a mind diseas'd;
> Pluck from the memory a rooted sorrow;
> Raze out the written troubles of the brain;
> And, with some sweet oblivious antidote,
> Cleanse the stuff'd bosom of that perilous stuff,
> Which weighs upon the heart?'

To which Dr. Brocklesby readily answered, from the same great poet:

> '————————therein the patient
> Must minister to himself.'[2]

Having no near relations, it had been for some time Johnson's intention to make a liberal provision for his faithful

[1] *Psalm* lxxxii, 7.
[2] *Macbeth*, Act V., sc. 3.

servant, Mr. Francis Barber, whom he looked upon as particularly under his protection, and whom he had all along treated truly as an humble friend. Having asked Dr. Brocklesby what would be a proper annuity to bequeath to a favourite servant, and being answered that it must depend on the circumstances of the master; and, that in the case of a nobleman, fifty pounds a year was considered as an adequate reward for many years' faithful service;—'Then, (said Johnson,) shall I be *nobilissimus*, for I mean to leave Frank seventy pounds a year, and I desire you to tell him so.' It is strange, however, to think, that Johnson was not free from that general weakness of being averse to execute a will, so that he delayed it from time to time; and had it not been for Sir John Hawkins's repeatedly urging it, I think it is probable that his kind resolution would not have been fulfilled.

The consideration of the numerous papers of which he was possessed, seems to have struck Johnson's mind with a sudden anxiety, and as they were in great confusion, it is much to be lamented that he had not entrusted some faithful and discreet person with the care and selection of them; instead of which, he, in a precipitate manner, burnt large masses of them, with little regard, as I apprehend, to discrimination. Not that I suppose we have thus been deprived of any compositions which he had ever intended for the publick eye; but, from what escaped the flames, I judge that many curious circumstances relating both to himself and other literary characters have perished.

Two very valuable articles, I am sure, we have lost, which were two quarto volumes, containing a full, fair, and most particular account of his own life, from his earliest recollection. I owned to him, that having accidentally seen them, I had read a great deal in them; and apologizing for the liberty I had taken, asked him if I could help it. He placidly answered, 'Why, Sir, I do not think you could have helped it.' I said that I had, for once in my life, felt half an inclination to commit theft. It had come into my mind to carry off those two volumes, and never see him more. Upon my inquiring how this would have affected him, 'Sir, (said he,) I believe I should have gone mad.'

During his last illness, Johnson experienced the steady and kind attachment of his numerous friends. Mr. Hoole has drawn up a narrative of what passed in the visits which he paid him during that time, from the 10th of November to the 13th of December, the day of his death, inclusive, and has favoured me with a perusal of it, with permission to make extracts, which I have done. And I think it highly to the honour of Mr. Windham, that his important occupations as an active statesman did not prevent him from paying assiduous respect to the dying Sage, whom he revered. Mr. Langton informs me, that, 'one day he found Mr. Burke and four or five more friends sitting with Johnson. Mr. Burke said to him, "I am afraid, Sir, such a number of us may be oppressive to you."—"No, Sir, (said Johnson,) it is not so; and I must be in a wretched state, indeed, when your company would not be a delight to me." Mr. Burke, in a tremulous voice, expressive of being very tenderly affected, replied, "My dear Sir, you have always been too good to me." Immediately afterwards he went away. This was the last circumstance in the acquaintance of these two eminent men.'

The following particulars of his conversation, within a few days of his death, I give on the authority of Mr. John Nichols:

'He said, that the Parliamentary Debates were the only part of his writings which then gave him any compunction: but that at the time he wrote them, he had no conception he was imposing upon the world, though they were frequently written from very slender materials, and often from none at all,—the mere coinage of his own imagination. He never wrote any part of his works with equal velocity. Three columns of the Magazine, in an hour, was no uncommon effort, which was faster than most persons could have transcribed that quantity.

'Of his friend Cave, he always spoke with great affection. "Yet (said he,) Cave, (who never looked out of his window, but with a view to the Gentleman's Magazine,) was a penurious pay-master; he would contract for lines by the hundred, and expect the long hundred; but he was a good man, and always delighted to have his friends at his table."

'When talking of a regular edition of his own works, he said, "that he had power, [from the booksellers,] to print such an edition, if his health admitted it; but had no power to assign over any edition, unless he could add notes, and so alter them as to make them new works; which his state of health forbade him to think of. I may possibly live, (said he,) or rather breath, three days, or perhaps three weeks; but find myself daily and gradually weaker."

'He said at another time, three or four days only before his death, speaking of the little fear he had of undergoing a chirurgical operation, "I would give one of these legs for a year more of life, I mean of comfortable life, not such as that which I now suffer;"—and lamented much his inability to read during his hours of restlessness. "I used formerly, (he added,) when sleepless in bed, *to read like a Turk.*"

'Whilst confined by his last illness, it was his regular practice to have the church-service read to him, by some attentive and friendly Divine. The Rev. Mr. Hoole performed this kind office in my presence for the last time, when, by his own desire, no more than the Litany was read; in which his responses were in the deep and sonorous voice which Mr. Boswell has occasionally noticed, and with the most profound devotion that can be imagined. His hearing not being quite perfect, he more than once interrupted Mr. Hoole, with "Louder, my dear Sir, louder, I entreat you, or you pray in vain!"—and, when the service was ended, he, with great earnestness, turned round to an excellent lady who was present, saying, "I thank you, Madam, very heartily, for your kindness in joining me in this solemn exercise. Live well, I conjure you; and you will not feel the compunction at the last, which I now feel." So truly humble were the thoughts which this great and good man entertained of his own approaches to religious perfection.'

It is to the mutual credit of Johnson and Divines of different communions, that although he was a steady Church-of-England man, there was, nevertheless, much agreeable intercourse between him and them. Let me particularly name the late Mr. La Trobe, and Mr. Hutton, of the Moravian profession. His intimacy with the English Benedictines, at Paris, has been mentioned; and as an additional proof of the charity in which he lived with good men of the Romish Church, I am happy in this opportunity of recording his friendship with the Reverend Thomas Hussey, D.D. His Catholick Majesty's Chaplain of Embassy at the Court of London, that very respectable man, eminent not only for his powerful eloquence as a preacher, but for his various abilities and acquisitions.—Nay, though Johnson loved a Presbyterian the least of all, this did not prevent his having a long and uninterrupted social connection with the Reverend Dr. James Fordyce, who, since his death, hath gratefully celebrated him in a warm strain of devotional composition.

Amidst the melancholy clouds which hung over the dying Johnson, his characteristical manner shewed itself on different occasions.

When Dr. Warren, in the usual style, hoped that he was better; his answer was, 'No, Sir; you cannot conceive with what acceleration I advance towards death.'

A man whom he had never seen before was employed one night to sit up with him. Being asked next morning how he liked his attendant, his answer was, 'Not at all, Sir: the fellow's an ideot; he is as aukward as a turn-spit when first put into the wheel, and as sleepy as a dormouse.'

Mr. Windham having placed a pillow conveniently to support him, he thanked him for his kindness, and said, 'That will do,—all that a pillow can do.'

As he opened a note which his servant brought to him, he said, 'An odd thought strikes me:—we shall receive no letters in the grave.'

He requested three things of Sir Joshua Reynolds:—To forgive him thirty pounds which he had borrowed of him;—to read the Bible;—and never to use his pencil on a Sunday. Sir Joshua readily acquiesced.

Indeed he shewed the greatest anxiety for the religious improvement of his friends, to whom he discoursed of its infinite consequence. He begged of Mr. Hoole to think of what he had said, and to commit it to writing: and, upon being afterwards assured that this was done, pressed his hands, and in an earnest tone thanked him. Dr. Brocklesby having attended him with the utmost assiduity and kindness as his physician and friend, he was peculiarly desirous that this gentleman should not entertain any loose speculative notions, but be confirmed in the truths of Christianity, and insisted on his writing down in his presence, as nearly as he could collect it, the import of what passed on the subject: and Dr. Brocklesby having complied with the request, he made him sign the paper, and urged him to keep it in his own custody as long as he lived.

Johnson, with that native fortitude, which, amidst all his bodily distress and mental sufferings, never forsook him, asked Dr. Brocklesby, as a man in whom he had confidence, to tell him plainly whether he could recover. 'Give me (said he) a direct answer.' The Doctor having first asked him if he could bear the whole truth, which way soever it might lead, and being answered that he could, declared that, in his opinion, he could not recover without a miracle. 'Then, (said Johnson,) I will take no more physick, not even my opiates; for I have prayed that I may render up my soul to GOD unclouded.' In this resolution he persevered, and, at the same time, used only the weakest kinds of sustenance. Being pressed by Mr. Windham to take somewhat more generous nourishment, lest too low a diet should have the very effect which he dreaded, by debilitating his mind, he said, 'I will take any thing but inebriating sustenance.'

The Reverend Mr. Strahan, who was the son of his friend, and had been always one of his great favourites, had, during his last illness, the satisfaction of contributing to soothe and comfort him. That gentleman's house, at Islington, of which he is Vicar, afforded Johnson, occasionally and easily, an agreeable change of place and fresh air; and he attended also upon him in town in the discharge of the sacred offices of his profession.

Mr. Strahan has given me the agreeable assurance, that, after being in much agitation, Johnson became quite composed, and continued so till his death.

Having, as has been already mentioned, made his will on the 8th and 9th of December, and settled all his worldly affairs, he languished till Monday, the 13th of that month, when he expired, about seven o'clock in the evening, with so little apparent pain that his attendants hardly perceived when his dissolution took place.

About two days after his death, the following very agreeable account was communicated to Mr. Malone, in a letter by the Honourable John Byng, to whom I am much obliged for granting me permission to introduce it in my work.

'DEAR SIR,

'SINCE I saw you, I have had a long conversation with Caw-
ston, who sat up with Dr. Johnson, from nine o'clock, on Sunday
evening, till ten o'clock, on Monday morning. And, from what I
can gather from him, it should seem, that Dr. Johnson was perfectly composed, steady in hope, and resigned to death. At the interval of each hour, they assisted him to sit up in his bed, and
move his legs, which were in much pain; when he regularly addressed himself to fervent prayer; and though, sometimes, his voice
failed him, his senses never did, during that time. The only sustenance he received, was cyder and water. He said his mind was
prepared, and the time to his dissolution seemed long. At six in the
morning, he enquired the hour, and, on being informed, said that
all went on regularly, and he felt he had but a few hours to live.

'This account has given us the satisfaction of thinking that that
great man died as he lived, full of resignation, strengthened in faith,
and joyful in hope.'

A few days before his death, he had asked Sir John Hawkins,
as one of his executors, where he should be buried; and on
being answered, 'Doubtless, in Westminster Abbey,' seemed
to feel a satisfaction, very natural to a Poet; and indeed, in my
opinion, very natural to every man of any imagination, who
has no family sepulchre in which he can be laid with his fathers. Accordingly, upon Monday, December 20, his remains
were deposited in that noble and renowned edifice; and over
his grave was placed a large blue flag-stone, with this inscription:

'SAMUEL JOHNSON, LL.D.
Obiit XIII *die Decembris,*
Anno Domini
M. DCC. LXXXIV.
Ætatis suæ LXXV.'

His funeral was attended by a respectable number of his
friends, particularly such of the members of *The Literary
Club* as were then in town; and was also honoured with the
presence of several of the Reverend Chapter of Westminster.
Mr. Burke, Sir Joseph Banks, Mr. Windham, Mr. Langton,
Sir Charles Bunbury, and Mr. Colman, bore his pall. His

schoolfellow, Dr. Taylor, performed the mournful office of reading the burial service.

I trust, I shall not be accused of affectation, when I declare, that I find myself unable to express all that I felt upon the loss of such a 'Guide, Philosopher, and Friend.' I shall, therefore, not say one word of my own, but adopt those of an eminent friend, which he uttered with an abrupt felicity, superior to all studied compositions:—'He has made a chasm, which not only nothing can fill up, but which nothing has a tendency to fill up.—Johnson is dead.—Let us go to the next best:—there is nobody;—no man can be said to put you in mind of Johnson.'

As Johnson had abundant homage paid to him during his life, so no writer in this nation ever had such an accumulation of literary honours after his death. A sermon upon that event was preached in St. Mary's church, Oxford, before the University, by the Reverend Mr. Agutter, of Magdalen College. The Lives, the Memoirs, the Essays, both in prose and verse, which have been published concerning him, would make many volumes. The numerous attacks too upon him, I consider as part of his consequence, upon the principle which he himself so well knew and asserted. Many who trembled at his presence, were forward in assault, when they no longer apprehended danger. When one of his little pragmatical foes was invidiously snarling at his fame, at Sir Joshua Reynolds's table, the Reverend Dr. Parr exclaimed, with his usual bold animation, 'Ay, now that the old lion is dead, every ass thinks he may kick at him.'

A monument for him, in Westminster-Abbey, was resolved upon soon after his death, and was supported by a most respectable contribution; but the Dean and Chapter of St. Paul's having come to a resolution of admitting monuments there, upon a liberal and magnificent plan, that Cathedral was afterwards fixed on, as the place in which a cenotaph should be erected to his memory: and in the cathedral of his native city of Lichfield, a smaller one is to be erected. To compose his epitaph, could not but excite the warmest competition of genius. I should not forgive myself were I to omit the following sepulchral verses on the authour of *The English Dictionary*, written by the Right Honourable Henry Flood:

> 'No need of Latin or of Greek to grace
>   Our JOHNSON's memory, or inscribe his grave;
> His native language claims this mournful space,
>   To pay the Immortality he gave.'

The character of *Samuel Johnson* has, I trust, been so developed in the course of this work, that they who have honoured it with a perusal, may be considered as well acquainted with him. As, however, it may be expected that I should collect into one view the capital and distinguishing features of this extraordinary man, I shall endeavour to acquit myself of that part of my biographical undertaking, however difficult it may be to do that which many of my readers will do better for themselves.

His figure was large and well formed, and his countenance of the cast of an ancient statue; yet his appearance was rendered strange and somewhat uncouth, by convulsive cramps, by the scars of that distemper which it was once imagined the royal touch could cure, and by a slovenly mode of dress. He had the use only of one eye; yet so much does mind govern and even supply the deficiency of organs, that his visual perceptions, as far as they extended, were uncommonly quick and accurate. So morbid was his temperament, that he never knew the natural joy of a free and vigorous use of his limbs: when he walked, it was like the struggling gait of one in fetters; when he rode, he had no command or direction of his horse, but was carried as if in a balloon. That with his constitution and habits of life he should have lived seventy-five years, is a proof that an inherent *vivida vis* is a powerful preservative of the human frame.

Man is, in general, made up of contradictory qualities; and these will ever shew themselves in strange succession, where a consistency in appearance at least, if not in reality, has not been attained by long habits of philosophical discipline. In proportion to the native vigour of the mind, the contradictory qualities will be the more prominent, and more difficult to be adjusted; and, therefore, we are not to wonder, that Johnson exhibited an eminent example of this remark which I have made upon human nature. At different times, he seemed a different man, in some respects; not, however, in any great or essential article, upon which he had fully employed his mind, and settled certain principles of duty, but only in his manners, and in the display of argument and fancy in his talk. He was prone to superstition, but not to credulity. Though his imagination might incline him to a belief of the marvellous and the mysterious, his vigorous reason examined the evidence with jealousy. He was a sincere and zealous Christian, of high Church-of-England and monarchical principles, which he would not tamely suffer to be questioned; and had, perhaps, at an early period, narrowed his mind somewhat too much, both as to religion and politicks. His being impressed with the danger of extreme latitude in either, though he was of a very independent spirit, occasioned his appearing somewhat unfavourable to the prevalence of that noble freedom of sentiment which is the best possession of man. Nor can it be denied, that he had many prejudices; which, however, frequently suggested many of his pointed sayings, that rather shew a playfulness of fancy than any settled malignity. He was steady and inflexible in maintaining the obligations of religion and morality; both from a regard for the order of society, and from a veneration for the GREAT SOURCE of all order; correct, nay stern in his taste; hard to please, and easily offended; impetuous and irritable in his temper, but of a most humane and benevolent heart, which shewed itself not only in a most liberal charity, as far as his circumstances would allow, but in a thousand instances of active benevolence. He was afflicted with a bodily disease, which made him often restless and fretful; and with a constitutional melancholy, the clouds of which darkened the brightness of his fancy, and gave a gloomy cast to his whole course of thinking: we, therefore, ought not to wonder at his sallies of impatience and passion at any time; especially when provoked by obtrusive ignorance, or presuming petulance; and allowance must be made for his uttering hasty and satirical sallies, even against his best friends. And, surely, when it is considered, that, 'amidst sickness and

sorrow,' he exerted his faculties in so many works for the benefit of mankind, and particularly that he atchieved the great
and admirable *Dictionary* of our language, we must be astonished at his resolution. The solemn text, 'of him to whom
much is given, much will be required,' seems to have been
ever present to his mind, in a rigorous sense, and to have made
him dissatisfied with his labours and acts of goodness, however
comparatively great; so that the unavoidable consciousness
of his superiority was, in that respect, a cause of disquiet. He
suffered so much from this, and from the gloom which perpetually haunted him, and made solitude frightful, that it may
be said of him, 'If in this life only he had hope, he was of all
men most miserable.' He loved praise, when it was brought
to him; but was too proud to seek for it. He was somewhat
susceptible of flattery. As he was general and unconfined in
his studies, he cannot be considered as master of any one particular science; but he had accumulated a vast and various
collection of learning and knowledge, which was so arranged
in his mind, as to be ever in readiness to be brought forth.
But his superiority over other learned men consisted chiefly
in what may be called the art of thinking, the art of using his
mind; a certain continual power of seizing the useful substance of all that he knew, and exhibiting it in a clear and
forcible manner; so that knowledge, which we often see to be
no better than lumber in men of dull understanding, was,
in him, true, evident, and actual wisdom. His moral precepts
are practical; for they are drawn from an intimate acquaintance
with human nature. His maxims carry conviction; for they are
founded on the basis of common sense, and a very attentive and
minute survey of real life. His mind was so full of imagery,
that he might have been perpetually a poet; yet it is remarkable,
that, however rich his prose is in this respect, his poetical
pieces, in general, have not much of that splendour, but are
rather distinguished by strong sentiment, and acute observation, conveyed in harmonious and energetick verse, particularly in heroick couplets. Though usually grave, and even
aweful, in his deportment, he possessed uncommon and peculiar powers of wit and humour; he frequently indulged himself
in colloquial pleasantry; and the heartiest merriment was often

enjoyed in his company; with this great advantage, that as it was entirely free from any poisonous tincture of vice or impiety, it was salutary to those who shared in it. He had accustomed himself to such accuracy in his common conversation, that he at all times expressed his thoughts with great force, and an elegant choice of language, the effect of which was aided by his having a loud voice, and a slow deliberate utterance. In him were united a most logical head with a most fertile imagination, which gave him an extraordinary advantage in arguing: for he could reason close or wide, as he saw best for the moment. Exulting in his intellectual strength and dexterity, he could, when he pleased, be the greatest sophist that ever contended in the lists of declamation; and, from a spirit of contradiction, and a delight in shewing his powers, he would often maintain the wrong side with equal warmth and ingenuity; so that, when there was an audience, his real opinions could seldom be gathered from his talk; though when he was in company with a single friend, he would discuss a subject with genuine fairness: but he was too conscientious to make errour permanent and pernicious, by deliberately writing it; and, in all his numerous works, he earnestly inculcated what appeared to him to be the truth; his piety being constant, and the ruling principle of all his conduct.

Such was *Samuel Johnson*, a man whose talents, acquirements, and virtues, were so extraordinary, that the more his character is considered, the more he will be regarded by the present age, and by posterity, with admiration and reverence.

INDEX